Study and Solutions Guide for

ALGEBRA AND TRIGONOMETRY:
A GRAPHING APPROACH
SECOND EDITION

Larson/Hostetler/Edwards

Bruce H. Edwards
University of Florida
Gainesville, Florida

Dianna L. Zook
Indiana University
Purdue University at Fort Wayne, Indiana

HOUGHTON MIFFLIN COMPANY   Boston   New York

Sponsoring Editor: Christine B. Hoag
Senior Associate Editor: Maureen Brooks
Managing Editor: Catherine B. Cantin
Assistant Editor: Carolyn Johnson
Supervising Editor: Karen Carter
Associate Project Editor: Rachel D'Angelo Wimberly
Editorial Assistant: Caroline Lipscomb
Production Supervisor: Lisa Merrill
Art Supervisor: Gary Crespo
Marketing Associate: Ros Kane
Marketing Assistant: Kate Burden Thomas

Printed in the United States of America.

International Standard Book Number: 0–669–41725–4

23456789–VG 01 00 99 98 97

TO THE STUDENT

The *Study and Solutions Guide for Algebra and Trigonometry: A Graphing Approach,* Second Edition, is a supplement to the text by Roland E. Larson, Robert P. Hostetler, and Bruce H. Edwards.

As mathematics instructors, we often have students come to us with questions about the assigned homework. When we ask to see their work, the reply often is "I didn't know where to start." The purpose of the *Study Guide* is to provide brief summaries of the topics covered in the textbook and enough detailed solutions to problems so that you will be able to work the remaining exercises.

This *Study Guide* is the result of the efforts of Larson Texts, Inc.

If you have any corrections or suggestions for improving this *Study Guide,* we would appreciate hearing from you. Good luck with your study of algebra and trigonometry.

Bruce H. Edwards
358 Little Hall
University of Florida
Gainesville, Florida 32611
(be@math.ufl.edu)

Dianna L. Zook
Indiana University,
Purdue University
at Fort Wayne, Indiana 46805

CONTENTS

STUDY STRATEGIES

■ Attend all classes and come prepared. Have your homework completed. Bring the text, paper, pen or pencil, and a calculator (scientific or graphing) to each class.

■ Read the section in the text that is to be covered before class. Make notes about any questions that you have and, if they are not answered during the lecture, ask them at the appropriate time.

■ Participate in class. As mentioned above, ask questions. Also, do not be afraid to answer questions.

■ Take notes on all definitions, concepts, rules, formulas and examples. After class, read your notes and fill in any gaps, or make notations of any questions that you have.

■ DO THE HOMEWORK!!! You learn mathematics by doing it yourself. Allow at least two hours outside of each class for homework. Do not fall behind.

■ Seek help when needed. Visit your instructor during office hours and come prepared with specific questions; check with your school's tutoring service; find a study partner in class; check additional books in the library for more examples—just do something before the problem becomes insurmountable.

■ Do not cram for exams. Each chapter in the text contains a chapter review and this study guide contains a practice test at the end of each chapter. (The answers are at the back of the study guide.) Work these problems a few days before the exam and review any areas of weakness.

CHAPTER P
Prerequisites

CHAPTER P
Prerequisites

Section P.1   Real Numbers

■ You should know the following sets.

(a) The set of real numbers includes the rational numbers and the irrational numbers.

(b) The set of rational numbers includes all real numbers that can be written as the ratio p/q of two integers, where $q \neq 0$.

(c) The set of irrational numbers includes all real numbers which are not rational.

(d) The set of integers: $\{\ldots, -3, -2, -1, 0, 1, 2, 3, \ldots\}$

(e) The set of whole numbers: $\{0, 1, 2, 3, 4, \ldots\}$

(f) the set of natural numbers: $\{1, 2, 3, 4, \ldots\}$

■ The real number line is used to represent the real numbers.

■ Know the inequality symbols.

(a) $a < b$ means a is less than b.

(b) $a \leq b$ means a is less than or equal to b.

(c) $a > b$ means a is greater than b.

(d) $a \geq b$ means a is greater than or equal to b.

■ You should know that
$$|a| = \begin{cases} a, & \text{if } a \geq 0 \\ -a, & \text{if } a < 0. \end{cases}$$

■ Know the properties of absolute value.

(a) $|a| \geq 0$　　　(b) $|-a| = |a|$　　　(c) $|ab| = |a|\,|b|$　　　(d) $\left|\dfrac{a}{b}\right| = \dfrac{|a|}{|b|}$

■ The distance between a and b on the real line is $|b - a| = |a - b|$.

■ You should be able to identify the terms in an algebraic expression.

■ You should know and be able to use the basic rules of algebra.

■ Commutative Property

(a) Addition: $a + b = b + a$　　　　　(b) Multiplication: $a \cdot b = b \cdot a$

■ Associative Property

(a) Addition: $(a + b) + c = a + (b + c)$　　　　(b) Multiplication: $(ab)c = a(bc)$

■ Identity Property

(a) Addition: 0 is the identity; $a + 0 = 0 + a = a$

(b) Multiplication: 1 is the identity; $a \cdot 1 = 1 \cdot a = a$

■ Inverse Property

(a) Addition: $-a$ is the inverse of a; $a + (-a) = -a + a = 0$

(b) Multiplication: $1/a$ is the inverse of a, $a \neq 0$; $a(1/a) = (1/a)a = 1$

■ Distributive Property

(a) Left: $a(b + c) = ab + ac$　　　　(b) Right: $(a + b)c = ac + bc$

continued

■ Properties of Negatives

(a) $(-1)a = -a$

(b) $-(-a) = a$

(c) $(-a)b = a(-b) = -ab$

(d) $(-a)(-b) = ab$

(e) $-(a + b) = (-a) + (-b) = -a - b$

■ Properties of Zero

(a) $a \pm 0 = a$

(b) $a \cdot 0 = 0$

(c) $0 \div a = 0/a = 0, a \neq 0$

(d) If $ab = 0$, then $a = 0$ or $b = 0$.

(e) $a/0$ is undefined.

■ Properties of Fractions ($b \neq 0, d \neq 0$)

(a) Equivalent Fractions: $a/b = c/d$ if and only if $ad = bc$.

(b) Rule of Signs: $-a/b = a/-b = -(a/b)$ and $-a/-b = a/b$

(c) Equivalent Fractions: $a/b = ac/bc, c \neq 0$

(d) Addition and Subtraction

1. Like Denominators: $(a/b) \pm (c/b) = (a \pm c)/b$

2. Unlike Denominators: $(a/b) \pm (c/d) = (ad \pm bc)/bd$

(e) Multiplication: $(a/b) \cdot (c/d) = ac/bd$

(f) Division: $(a/b) \div (c/d) = (a/b) \cdot (d/c) = ad/bc$ if $c \neq 0$.

■ Properties of Equality

(a) If $a = b$, then $a + c = b + c$.

(b) If $a = b$, then $ac = bc$.

(c) If $a + c = b + c$, then $a = b$.

(d) If $ac = bc$ and $c \neq 0$, then $a = b$.

Solutions to Odd-Numbered Exercises

1. $-9, -\frac{7}{2}, 5, \frac{2}{3}, \sqrt{2}, 0, 1$

(a) Natural numbers: 5, 1

(b) Integers: $-9, 5, 0, 1$

(c) Rational numbers: $-9, -\frac{7}{2}, 5, \frac{2}{3}, 0, 1$

(d) Irrational numbers: $\sqrt{2}$

3. $2.01, 0.666\ldots, -13, 0.010110111\ldots$

(a) Natural numbers: none

(b) Integers: -13

(c) Rational numbers: $2.01, 0.666\ldots, -13$

(d) Irrational numbers: $0.010110111\ldots$

5. $-\pi, -\frac{1}{3}, \frac{6}{3}, \frac{1}{2}\sqrt{2}, -7.5$

(a) Natural numbers: $\frac{6}{3}$ (since it equals 2)

(b) Integers: $\frac{6}{3}$

(c) Rational numbers: $-\frac{1}{3}, \frac{6}{3}, -7.5$

(d) Irrational numbers: $-\pi, \frac{1}{2}\sqrt{2}$

7. $\frac{5}{8} = 0.625$

9. $\frac{41}{333} = 0.\overline{123}$

11. $-1 < 2.5$

13. $\frac{3}{2} < 7$

15. $-4 > -8$

17. $\frac{5}{6} > \frac{2}{3}$

19. The inequality $x \leq 5$ is the set of all real numbers less than or equal to 5. The interval is unbounded.

21. The inequality $x < 0$ is the set of all negative real numbers. The interval is unbounded.

23. The inequality $x \geq 4$ is the set of all real numbers greater than or equal to 4. The interval is unbounded.

25. The inequality $-2 < x < 2$ is the set of all real numbers greater than -2 and less than 2. The interval is bounded.

27. The inequality $-1 \leq x < 0$ is the set of all negative real numbers greater than or equal to -1. The interval is bounded.

29. $\frac{127}{90} \approx 1.41111, \frac{584}{413} \approx 1.41404, \frac{7071}{5000} \approx 1.41420, \sqrt{2} \approx 1.41421, \frac{47}{33} \approx 1.42424$

31. $x < 0$ **33.** $y \geq 0$ **35.** $A \geq 30$

37. $|-10| = -(-10) = 10$ **39.** $|3 - \pi| = -(3 - \pi) = \pi - 3 \approx 0.1416$

41. $\dfrac{-5}{|-5|} = \dfrac{-5}{-(-5)} = \dfrac{-5}{5} = -1$ **43.** $-3|-3| = -3[-(-3)] = -9$

45. $-|16.25| + 20 = -16.25 + 20 = 3.75$ **47.** $|-3| > -|-3|$ since $3 > -3$.

49. $-5 = -|5|$ since $-5 = -5$.   **51.** $-|-2| = -|2|$ since $-2 = -2$.

53. $d(-1, 3) = |3 - (-1)| = |3 + 1| = 4$ **55.** $d\left(-\frac{5}{2}, 0\right) = \left|0 - \left(-\frac{5}{2}\right)\right| = \frac{5}{2}$

57. $d(126, 75) = |75 - 126| = 51$ **59.** $d\left(\frac{16}{5}, \frac{112}{75}\right) = \left|\frac{112}{75} - \frac{16}{5}\right| = \frac{128}{75}$

61. $d(x, 5) = |x - 5|$ and $d(x, 5) \leq 3$, thus $|x - 5| \leq 3$.

63. $d(7, 18) = |7 - 18| = 11$ miles

65. $d(y, 0) = |y - 0| = |y|$ and $d(y, 0) \geq 6$, thus $|y| \geq 6$.

67.

Budgeted Expense, b	Actual Expense, a	$|a - b|$	$0.05b$
$112,700	$113,356	$656	$5635

The actual expense difference is greater than $500 (but less than 5% of the budget) so it does not pass the test.

69.

Budgeted Expense, b	Actual Expense, a	$|a - b|$	$0.05b$
$37,640	$37,335	$305	$1882

Since $305 < $500 and $305 < $1882, it passes the "budget variance test."

71. $|77.8 - 92.2| = 14.4 billion deficit for 1960

73. $|1031.3 - 1252.7| = \$221.4$ billion deficit for 1990

75. (a) $|u + v| \neq |u| + |v|$ if u is positive and v is negative or vice versa.

(b) $|u + v| \leq |u| + |v|$

They are equal when u and v have the same sign. If they differ in sign, $|u + v|$ is less than $|u| + |v|$.

77. $7x + 4$
Terms: $7x, 4$

79. $4x^3 + x - 5$
Terms: $4x^3, x, -5$

81. $4x - 6$
(a) $4(-1) - 6 = -4 - 6 = -10$
(b) $4(0) - 6 = 0 - 6 = -6$

83. $x^2 - 3x + 4$
(a) $(-2)^2 - 3(-2) + 4 = 4 + 6 + 4 = 14$
(b) $(2)^2 - 3(2) + 4 = 4 - 6 + 4 = 2$

85. $\dfrac{x + 1}{x - 1}$

(a) $\dfrac{1 + 1}{1 - 1} = \dfrac{2}{0}$ is undefined.

You cannot divide by zero.

(b) $\dfrac{-1 + 1}{-1 - 1} = \dfrac{0}{-2} = 0$

87. $x + 9 = 9 + x$
Commutative (addition)

89. $\dfrac{1}{(h + 6)}(h + 6) = 1, h \neq -6$
Inverse (multiplication)

91. $2(x + 3) = 2x + 6$
Distributive Property

93. $1 \cdot (1 + x) = 1 + x$
Identity (multiplication)

95. $x(3y) = (x \cdot 3)y$ Associative (multiplication)
$= (3x)y$ Commutative (multiplication)

97. $\dfrac{81 - (90 - 9)}{5} = \dfrac{81 - 81}{5} = \dfrac{0}{5} = 0$

99. $\dfrac{8 - 8}{-9 + (6 + 3)} = \dfrac{0}{-9 + 9} = \dfrac{0}{0}$ which is undefined.

101. $(4 - 7)(-2) = (-3)(-2) = 6$

103. $\frac{3}{16} + \frac{5}{16} = \frac{8}{16} = \frac{1}{2}$

105. $\frac{5}{8} - \frac{5}{12} + \frac{1}{6} = \frac{15}{24} - \frac{10}{24} + \frac{4}{24} = \frac{9}{24} = \frac{3}{8}$

107. $\frac{4}{5} \cdot \frac{1}{2} \cdot \frac{3}{4} = \frac{3}{10}$

109. $12 \div \frac{1}{4} = 12 \cdot \frac{4}{1} = 12 \cdot 4 = 48$

111. $-3 + \frac{3}{7} \approx -2.57$

113. $\dfrac{11.46 - 5.37}{3.91} \approx 1.56$

115.

n	1	0.5	0.01	0.0001	0.000001
$5/n$	5	10	500	50,000	5,000,000

117.

n	1	10	100	10,000	100,000
$5/n$	5	0.5	0.05	0.0005	0.00005

Section P.2   Exponents and Radicals

■ You should know the properties of exponents.

(a) $a^1 = a$

(b) $a^0 = 1, a \neq 0$

(c) $a^m a^n = a^{m+n}$

(d) $a^m/a^n = a^{m-n}, a \neq 0$

(e) $a^{-n} = 1/a^n, a \neq 0$

(f) $(a^m)^n = a^{mn}$

(g) $(ab)^n = a^n b^n$

(h) $(a/b)^n = a^n/b^n, b \neq 0$

(i) $(a/b)^{-n} = (b/a)^n, a \neq 0, b \neq 0$

(j) $|a^2| = |a|^2 = a^2$

■ You should be able to write numbers in scientific notation, $\pm c \times 10^n$, where $1 \leq c < 10$ and n is an integer.

■ You should be able to use your calculator to evaluate expressions involving exponents.

■ You should know the properties of radicals.

(a) $\sqrt[n]{a^m} = \left(\sqrt[n]{a}\right)^m$

(b) $\sqrt[n]{a} \cdot \sqrt[n]{b} = \sqrt[n]{ab}$

(c) $\dfrac{\sqrt[n]{a}}{\sqrt[n]{b}} = \sqrt[n]{\dfrac{a}{b}}$

(d) $\sqrt[m]{\sqrt[n]{a}} = \sqrt[mn]{a}$

(e) $\left(\sqrt[n]{a}\right)^n = a$

(f) For n even, $\sqrt[n]{a^n} = |a|$.

For n odd, $\sqrt[n]{a^n} = a$.

(g) $a^{1/n} = \sqrt[n]{a}$

(h) $a^{m/n} = \left(\sqrt[n]{a}\right)^m = \sqrt[n]{a^m}$

■ You should be able to simplify radicals.

(a) All possible factors have been removed from the radical sign.

(b) All fractions have radical-free denominators.

(c) The index for the radical has been reduced as far as possible

■ You should be able to use your calculator to evaluate radicals.

Solutions to Odd-Numbered Exercises

1. (a) $4^2 \cdot 3 = 16 \cdot 3 = 48$

(b) $3 \cdot 3^3 = 3^4 = 81$

3. (a) $(3^3)^2 = 3^6 = 729$

(b) $-3^2 = -9$

5. (a) $\dfrac{3}{3^{-4}} = 3^{1+4} = 3^5 = 243$

   (b) $24(-2)^{-5} = \dfrac{24}{(-2)^5} = \dfrac{24}{-32} = -\dfrac{3}{4}$

7. $(-4)^3(5^2) = (-64)(25) = -1600$

9. $\dfrac{3^6}{7^3} = \dfrac{729}{343} \approx 2.125$

11. When $x = 2,\ -3x^3 = -3(2)^3 = -24.$

13. When $x = 10,\ 6x^0 - (6x)^0 = 6(10)^0 - (60)^0 = 6(1) - 1 = 5.$

15. (a) $(-5z)^3 = (-5)^3 z^3 = -125z^3$

   (b) $5x^4(x^2) = 5x^{4+2} = 5x^6$

17. (a) $\dfrac{7x^2}{x^3} = 7x^{2-3} = 7x^{-1} = \dfrac{7}{x}$

   (b) $\dfrac{12(x+y)^3}{9(x+y)} = \dfrac{4}{3}(x+y)^{3-1} = \dfrac{4}{3}(x+y)^2$

19. (a) $(x+5)^0 = 1,\ x \neq -5$

   (b) $(2x^2)^{-2} = \dfrac{1}{(2x^2)^2} = \dfrac{1}{4x^4}$

21. (a) $\left(\dfrac{x}{10}\right)^{-1} = \dfrac{10}{x}$

   (b) $\left(\dfrac{x^{-3}y^4}{5}\right)^{-3} = \left(\dfrac{y^4}{5x^3}\right)^{-3} = \left(\dfrac{5x^3}{y^4}\right)^3 = \dfrac{5^3 x^9}{y^{12}} = \dfrac{125x^9}{y^{12}}$

23. (a) $3^n \cdot 3^{2n} = 3^{n+2n} = 3^{3n}$

   (b) $\left(\dfrac{a^{-2}}{b^{-2}}\right)\left(\dfrac{b}{a}\right)^3 = \left(\dfrac{b^2}{a^2}\right)\left(\dfrac{b^3}{a^3}\right) = \dfrac{b^5}{a^5}$

Radical Form	*Rational Exponent Form*
25. $\sqrt{9} = 3$ Given	$9^{1/2} = 3$ Answer
27. $\sqrt[5]{32} = 2$ Answer	$32^{1/5} = 2$ Given
29. $\sqrt{196} = 14$ Answer	$196^{1/2} = 14$ Given
31. $\sqrt[3]{-216} = -6$ Given	$(-216)^{1/3} = -6$ Answer
33. $\sqrt[4]{81^3} = 27$ Given	$81^{3/4} = 27$ Answer

35. $\sqrt{9} = 3$

37. $-\sqrt[3]{-27} = -(-3) = 3$

39. $\left(\sqrt[3]{-125}\right)^3 = -125$

41. $32^{-3/5} = \dfrac{1}{32^{3/5}} = \dfrac{1}{(\sqrt[5]{32})^3} = \dfrac{1}{(2)^3} = \dfrac{1}{8}$

43. $\left(-\dfrac{1}{64}\right)^{-1/3} = (-64)^{1/3} = \sqrt[3]{-64} = -4$

45. $\sqrt[5]{-27^3} = (-27)^{3/5} \approx -7.225$

47. $(1.2^{-2})\sqrt{75} + 3\sqrt{8} \approx 14.499$

49. (a) $\sqrt{8} = \sqrt{4 \cdot 2} = \sqrt{4}\sqrt{2} = 2\sqrt{2}$

   (b) $\sqrt[3]{24} = \sqrt[3]{8 \cdot 3} = \sqrt[3]{8}\sqrt[3]{3} = 2\sqrt[3]{3}$

51. (a) $\sqrt{72x^3} = \sqrt{36x^2 \cdot 2x} = 6x\sqrt{2x}$

   (b) $\sqrt{\dfrac{18^2}{z^3}} = \dfrac{\sqrt{18^2}}{\sqrt{z^2 \cdot z}} = \dfrac{18}{z\sqrt{z}}$

53. (a) $\sqrt[3]{16x^5} = \sqrt[3]{8x^3 \cdot 2x^2} = 2x\sqrt[3]{2x^2}$

   (b) $\sqrt{75x^2y^{-4}} = \sqrt{\dfrac{75x^2}{y^4}} = \dfrac{\sqrt{25x^2 \cdot 3}}{\sqrt{y^4}} = \dfrac{5|x|\sqrt{3}}{y^2}$

55. $5^{4/3} \cdot 5^{8/3} = 5^{12/3} = 5^4 = 625$

57. $\dfrac{(2x^2)^{3/2}}{2^{1/2}x^4} = \dfrac{2^{3/2}(x^2)^{3/2}}{2^{1/2}x^4} = \dfrac{2^{3/2}x^3}{2^{1/2}x^4} = 2^{3/2 - 1/2}x^{3-4} = 2^1 x^{-1} = \dfrac{2}{x}$

59. $\dfrac{x^{-3} \cdot x^{1/2}}{x^{3/2} \cdot x^{-1}} = \dfrac{x^{1/2} \cdot x^1}{x^{3/2} \cdot x^3} = x^{1/2 + 1 - 3/2 - 3} = x^{-3} = \dfrac{1}{x^3}, x > 0$

61. (a) $\dfrac{1}{\sqrt{3}} = \dfrac{1}{\sqrt{3}} \cdot \dfrac{\sqrt{3}}{\sqrt{3}} = \dfrac{\sqrt{3}}{3}$

   (b) $\dfrac{8}{\sqrt[3]{2}} = \dfrac{8}{\sqrt[3]{2}} \cdot \dfrac{\sqrt[3]{4}}{\sqrt[3]{4}} = \dfrac{8\sqrt[3]{4}}{2} = 4\sqrt[3]{4}$

63. (a) $\dfrac{2x}{5 - \sqrt{3}} = \dfrac{2x}{5 - \sqrt{3}} \cdot \dfrac{5 + \sqrt{3}}{5 + \sqrt{3}}$

$$= \dfrac{2x(5 + \sqrt{3})}{25 - 3} = \dfrac{x(5 + \sqrt{3})}{11}$$

   (b) $\dfrac{3}{\sqrt{5} + \sqrt{6}} \cdot \dfrac{\sqrt{5} - \sqrt{6}}{\sqrt{5} - \sqrt{6}} = \dfrac{3(\sqrt{5} - \sqrt{6})}{5 - 6}$

$$= -3(\sqrt{5} - \sqrt{6})$$

$$= 3(\sqrt{6} - \sqrt{5})$$

65. $\dfrac{\sqrt{8}}{2} = \dfrac{\sqrt{4 \cdot 2}}{2} = \dfrac{2\sqrt{2}}{2} = \dfrac{\sqrt{2}}{1} \cdot \dfrac{\sqrt{2}}{\sqrt{2}} = \dfrac{2}{\sqrt{2}}$

67. $\dfrac{\sqrt{5} + \sqrt{3}}{3} = \dfrac{\sqrt{5} + \sqrt{3}}{3} \cdot \dfrac{\sqrt{5} - \sqrt{3}}{\sqrt{5} - \sqrt{3}} = \dfrac{5 - 3}{3(\sqrt{5} - \sqrt{3})}$

$$= \dfrac{2}{3(\sqrt{5} - \sqrt{3})}$$

69. (a) $\sqrt[4]{3^2} = 3^{2/4} = 3^{1/2} = \sqrt{3}$

   (b) $\sqrt[6]{(x + 1)^4} = (x + 1)^{4/6} = (x + 1)^{2/3} = \sqrt[3]{(x + 1)^2}$

71. (a) $\sqrt{\sqrt{32}} = (32^{1/2})^{1/2} = 32^{1/4} = \sqrt[4]{32} = \sqrt[4]{16 \cdot 2} = 2\sqrt[4]{2}$

   (b) $\sqrt{\sqrt[4]{2x}} = ((2x)^{1/4})^{1/2} = (2x)^{1/8} = \sqrt[8]{2x}$

73. (a) $2\sqrt{50} + 12\sqrt{8} = 2\sqrt{25 \cdot 2} + 12\sqrt{4 \cdot 2}$

$$= 2(5\sqrt{2}) + 12(2\sqrt{2}) = 10\sqrt{2} + 24\sqrt{2} = 34\sqrt{2}$$

   (b) $10\sqrt{32} - 6\sqrt{18} = 10\sqrt{16 \cdot 2} - 6\sqrt{9 \cdot 2}$

$$= 10(4\sqrt{2}) - 6(3\sqrt{2}) = 40\sqrt{2} - 18\sqrt{2} = 22\sqrt{2}$$

75. (a) $5\sqrt{x} - 3\sqrt{x} = 2\sqrt{x}$

   (b) $-2\sqrt{9y} + 10\sqrt{y} = -2(3\sqrt{y}) + 10\sqrt{y} = -6\sqrt{y} + 10\sqrt{y} = 4\sqrt{y}$

77. $\sqrt{5} + \sqrt{3} \approx 3.968.$ and $\sqrt{5 + 3} = \sqrt{8} \approx 2.828$
Thus, $\sqrt{5} + \sqrt{3} > \sqrt{5 + 3}.$

79. $\sqrt{3^2 + 2^2} = \sqrt{9 + 4} = \sqrt{13} \approx 3.606$

Thus, $5 > \sqrt{3^2 + 2^2}.$

81. $57,500,000 = 5.75 \times 10^7$ square miles

83. $0.0000899 = 8.99 \times 10^{-5}$ gram per cm^3

85. $5.24 \times 10^8 = 524,000,000$ servings

87. $4.8 \times 10^{-10} = 0.00000000048$ electrostatic units

89. (a) $750\left(1 + \dfrac{0.11}{365}\right)^{800} \approx 954.448$

   (b) $\dfrac{67,000,000 + 93,000,000}{0.0052} = 30,769,230,769.2 \approx 3.077 \times 10^{10}$

91. (a) $\sqrt{4.5 \times 10^9} \approx 67,082.039$

   (b) $\sqrt[3]{6.3 \times 10^4} \approx 39.791$

93. When any positive integer is squared, the units digit is 0, 1, 4, 5, 6, or 9.
Therefore, $\sqrt{5233}$ is not an integer.

95. $T = 2\pi\sqrt{\dfrac{2}{32}} = 2\pi\sqrt{\dfrac{1}{16}} = 2\pi\left(\dfrac{1}{4}\right) = \dfrac{\pi}{2} \approx 1.57$ sec

97. $r = 1 - \left(\dfrac{3225}{12,000}\right)^{1/4} \approx 0.280$ or 28%

99. Time $= \dfrac{\text{Distance}}{\text{Rate}} = \dfrac{93,000,000 \text{ miles}}{11,160,000 \text{ miles per minute}} = \dfrac{25}{3}$ minutes

Section P.3 Polynomials and Factoring

- Given a polynomial in x, $a_n x^n + a_{n-1}x^{n-1} + \cdots + a_1 x + a_0$, where $a_n \neq 0$, and n is a nonnegative integer, you should be able to identify the following:

    (a) Degree: n

    (b) Terms: $a_n x^n, a_{n-1}x^{n-1}, \ldots, a_1 x, a_0$

    (c) Coefficients: $a_n, a_{n-1}, \ldots, a_1, a_0$

    (d) Leading coefficient: a_n

    (e) Constant term: a_0

- You should be able to add and subtract polynomials.

- You should be able to multiply polynomials by either

    (a) The Distributive Properties

    (b) The Vertical Method

- You should know the special binomial products.

    (a) $(ax + b)(cx + d) = acx^2 + adx + bcx + bd$ FOIL
    $$= acx^2 + (ad + bc)x + bd$$

    (b) $(u \pm v)^2 = u^2 \pm 2uv + v^2$

    (c) $(u + v)(u - v) = u^2 - v^2$

    (d) $(u \pm v)^3 = u^3 \pm 3u^2v + 3uv^2 \pm v^3$

- You should be able to factor out all common factors, the first step in factoring.

- You should be able to factor the following special polynomial forms.

    (a) $u^2 - v^2 = (u + v)(u - v)$

    (b) $u^2 \pm 2uv + v^2 = (u \pm v)^2$

    (c) $mx^2 + nx + r = (ax + b)(cx + d)$, where $m = ac, r = bd, n = ad + bc$

    Note: Not all trinomials can be factored (using real coefficients).

    (d) $u^3 \pm v^3 = (u \pm v)(u^2 \mp uv + v^2)$

- You should be able to factor by grouping.

Solutions to Odd-Numbered Exercises

1. $(6x + 5) - (8x + 15) = 6x + 5 - 8x - 15$
$$= (6x - 8x) + (5 - 15) = -2x - 10$$

3. $-(x^3 - 2) + (4x^3 - 2x) = -x^3 + 2 + 4x^3 - 2x$
$$= (4x^3 - x^3) - 2x + 2 = 3x^3 - 2x + 2$$

5. $(15x^2 - 6) - (-8x^3 - 14x^2 - 17) = 15x^2 - 6 + 8x^3 + 14x^2 + 17$
$$= 8x^3 + (15x^2 + 14x^2) + (-6 + 17) = 8x^3 + 29x^2 + 11$$

7. $3x(x^2 - 2x + 1) = 3x(x^2) + 3x(-2x) + 3x(1) = 3x^3 - 6x^2 + 3x$

9. $-5z(3z - 1) = -5z(3z) + (-5z)(-1) = -15z^2 + 5z$

11. $(1 - x^3)(4x) = 1(4x) - x^3(4x) = 4x - 4x^4 = -4x^4 + 4x$

13. $(x + 3)(x + 4) = x^2 + 4x + 3x + 12$ FOIL
$$= x^2 + 7x + 12$$

15. $(3x - 5)(2x + 1) = 6x^2 + 3x - 10x - 5$ FOIL
$$= 6x^2 - 7x - 5$$

17. $(2x - 5y)^2 = 4x^2 - 2(5y)(2x) + 25y^2$
$$= 4x^2 - 20xy + 25y^2$$

19. $[(x - 3) + y]^2 = (x - 3)^2 + 2y(x - 3) + y^2$
$$= x^2 - 6x + 9 + 2xy - 6y + y^2$$
$$= x^2 + 2xy + y^2 - 6x - 6y + 9$$

21. $(x + 10)(x - 10) = x^2 - 100$

23. $(x + 2y)(x - 2y) = x^2 - (2y)^2 = x^2 - 4y^2$

25. $[(m - 3) + n][(m - 3) - n] = (m - 3)^2 - n^2$
$$= m^2 - 6m + 9 - n^2$$
$$= m^2 - n^2 - 6m + 9$$

27. $(2r^2 - 5)(2r^2 + 5) = (2r^2)^2 - 5^2 = 4r^4 - 25$

29. $(x + 1)^3 = x^3 + 3x^2(1) + 3x(1^2) + 1^3$
$$= x^3 + 3x^2 + 3x + 1$$

31. $(2x - y)^3 = (2x)^3 - 3(2x)^2y + 3(2x)y^2 - y^3$
$$= 8x^3 - 12x^2y + 6xy^2 - y^3$$

33. $5x(x + 1) - 3x(x + 1) = 2x(x + 1)$
$$= 2x^2 + 2x$$

35. $(u + 2)(u - 2)(u^2 + 4) = (u^2 - 4)(u^2 + 4)$
$$= u^4 - 16$$

37. No. $(x^2 + 1) + (-x^2 + 3) = 4$ which is not a second degree polynomial.

39. (a) $500(1 + r)^2 = 500(r + 1)^2 = 500(r^2 + 2r + 1)$
$$= 500r^2 + 1000r + 500$$

(b)

r	$5\frac{1}{2}\%$	7%	8%	$8\frac{1}{2}\%$	9%
$500(1 + r)^2$	\$556.51	\$572.45	\$583.20	\$588.61	\$594.05

Remember to write the interest rate in decimal form: $5\frac{1}{2}\% = 0.055$.

(c) As r increases, the amount increases.

41. Volume = (length)(width)(height)
$$= (15 - 2x)\left(\frac{45 - 3x}{2}\right)(x)$$
$$= \frac{3}{2}x(x - 15)(2x - 15)$$

If $x = 3$, volume = 486.
If $x = 5$, volume = 375.
If $x = 7$, volume = 84.

43. (a) $T = R + B = 1.1x + (0.14x^2 - 4.43x + 58.40)$
$$= 0.14x^2 - 3.33x + 58.40$$

(b)

x mi/hr	30	40	55
T feet	84.50	149.20	298.75

(c) As the speed increases, the total stopping distance increases.

45. $(x + 1)(x + 4) = x(x + 4) + 1(x + 4)$
$$= x^2 + 4x + x + 4$$

This illustrates the Distributive Property.

47. $3x + 6 = 3(x + 2)$

49. $2x^3 - 6x = 2x(x^2 - 3)$

51. $x^2 - 36 = x^2 - 6^2 = (x + 6)(x - 6)$

53. $16y^2 - 9 = (4y + 3)(4y - 3)$

55. $(x - 1)^2 - 4 = [(x - 1) + 2][(x - 1) - 2]$
$$= (x + 1)(x - 3)$$

57. $x^2 - 4x + 4 = x^2 - 2(2)x + 2^2 = (x - 2)^2$

59. $4t^2 + 4t + 1 = (2t)^2 + 2(2t)(1) + 1^2$
$$= (2t + 1)^2$$

61. $x^2 + x - 2 = (x + 2)(x - 1)$

63. $s^2 - 5s + 6 = (s - 3)(s - 2)$

65. $20 - y - y^2 = (5 + y)(4 - y)$
$$\text{or} -(y + 5)(y - 4)$$

67. $3x^2 - 5x + 2 = (3x - 2)(x - 1)$

69. $5x^2 + 26x + 5 = (5x + 1)(x + 5)$

71. $x^3 - 8 = x^3 - 2^3 = (x - 2)(x^2 + 2x + 4)$

73. $y^3 + 64 = y^3 + 4^3 = (y + 4)(y^2 - 4y + 16)$

75. $x^3 - x^2 + 2x - 2 = x^2(x - 1) + 2(x - 1)$
$$= (x - 1)(x^2 + 2)$$

77. $2x^3 - x^2 - 6x + 3 = x^2(2x - 1) - 3(2x - 1)$
$$= (2x - 1)(x^2 - 3)$$

79. $x^3 - 9x = x(x^2 - 9) = x(x + 3)(x - 3)$

81. $x^3 - 4x^2 = x^2(x - 4)$

83. $x^2 - 2x + 1 = (x - 1)^2$

85. $1 - 4x + 4x^2 = (1 - 2x)^2$

87. $2x^2 + 4x - 2x^3 = -2x(-x - 2 + x^2)$
$$= -2x(x^2 - x - 2)$$
$$= -2x(x + 1)(x - 2)$$

89. $9x^2 + 10x + 1 = (9x + 1)(x + 1)$

91. $3x^3 + x^2 + 15x + 5 = x^2(3x + 1) + 5(3x + 1)$
$$= (3x + 1)(x^2 + 5)$$

93. $x^4 - 4x^3 + x^2 - 4x = x(x^3 - 4x^2 + x - 4)$
$$= x[x^2(x - 4) + (x - 4)]$$
$$= x(x - 4)(x^2 + 1)$$

95. $25 - (z + 5)^2 = [5 + (z + 5)][5 - (z + 5)]$
$$= -z(z + 10)$$

97. $(x^2 + 1)^2 - 4x^2 = [(x^2 + 1) + 2x][(x^2 + 1) - 2x]$
$$= (x^2 + 2x + 1)(x^2 - 2x + 1)$$
$$= (x + 1)^2(x - 1)^2$$

99. $2t^3 - 16 = 2(t^3 - 8) = 2(t - 2)(t^2 + 2t + 4)$

101. $4x(2x - 1) + (2x - 1)^2 = (2x - 1)[4x + (2x - 1)]$
$$= (2x - 1)(6x - 1)$$

103. $2(x + 1)(x - 3)^2 - 3(x + 1)^2(x - 3) = (x + 1)(x - 3)[2(x - 3) - 3(x + 1)]$
$$= (x + 1)(x - 3)[2x - 6 - 3x - 3]$$
$$= (x + 1)(x - 3)(-x - 9)$$
$$= -(x + 1)(x - 3)(x + 9)$$

105. $7x(2)(x^2 + 1)(2x) - (x^2 + 1)^2(7) = 7(x^2 + 1)[4x^2 - (x^2 + 1)]$
$$= 7(x^2 + 1)(3x^2 - 1)$$

107. $2x(x - 5)^4 - x^2(4)(x - 5)^3 = 2x(x - 5)^3[(x - 5) - 2x]$
$$= 2x(x - 5)^3(-x - 5)$$
$$= -2x(x - 5)^3(x + 5)$$

109. $\dfrac{x^2}{2}(x^2 + 1)^4 - (x^2 + 1)^5 = (x^2 + 1)^4\left[\dfrac{x^2}{2} - (x^2 + 1)\right]$

$$= (x^2 + 1)^4\left(-\dfrac{x^2}{2} - 1\right)$$

$$= -(x^2 + 1)^4\left(\dfrac{x^2}{2} + 1\right)$$

111. $a^2 - b^2 = (a + b)(a - b)$

Matches model (b).

113. $a^2 + 2a + 1 = (a + 1)^2$

Matches model (a).

115. $3x^2 + 7x + 2 = (3x + 1)(x + 2)$

117. $2x^2 + 7x + 3 = (2x + 1)(x + 3)$

119. $A = \pi(r + 2)^2 - \pi r^2$
$$= \pi[(r + 2)^2 - r^2]$$
$$= \pi[r^2 + 4r + 4 - r^2]$$
$$= \pi(4r + 4)$$
$$= 4\pi(r + 1)$$

121. $A = 8(18) - 4x^2$
$$= 4(36 - x^2)$$
$$= 4(6 - x)(6 + x)$$

123. For $x^2 + bx - 15$ to be factorable, b must equal $m + n$ where $mn = -15$.

Factors of -15	Sum of factors
$(15)(-1)$	$15 + (-1) = 14$
$(-15)(1)$	$-15 + 1 = -14$
$(3)(-5)$	$3 + (-5) = -2$
$(-3)(5)$	$-3 + 5 = 2$

The possible b values are $14, -14, -2,$ or 2.

125. For $2x^2 + 5x + c$ to be factorable, the factors of $2c$ must add up to 5.

Possible c values	$2c$	Factors of $2c$ that add up to 5
2	4	$(1)(4) = 4$ and $1 + 4 = 5$
3	6	$(2)(3) = 6$ and $2 + 3 = 5$
-3	-6	$(6)(-1) = -6$ and $6 + (-1) = 5$
-7	-14	$(7)(-2) = -14$ and $7 + (-2) = 5$
-12	-24	$(8)(-3) = -24$ and $8 + (-3) = 5$

These are a few possible c values. There are *many* correct answers.

If $c = 2$: $2x^2 + 5x + 2 = (2x + 1)(x + 1)$
If $c = 3$: $2x^2 + 5x + 3 = (2x + 3)(x + 1)$
If $c = -3$: $2x^2 + 5x - 3 = (2x - 1)(x + 3)$
If $c = -7$: $2x^2 + 5x - 7 = (2x + 7)(x - 1)$
If $c = -12$: $2x^2 + 5x - 12 = (2x - 3)(x + 4)$

127. $9x^2 - 9x - 54 = 9(x^2 - x - 6) = 9(x + 2)(x - 3)$

The error in the problem in the book was that 3 was factored out of the first binomial but not out of the second binomial.

$$(3x + 6)(3x - 9) = 3(x + 2)(3)(x - 3) = 9(x + 2)(x - 3).$$

129. (a) $V = \pi R^2 h - \pi r^2 h$ (b) The average radius is $\dfrac{R + r}{2}$.

$ = \pi h(R^2 - r^2)$ The thickness of the shell is $R - r$.

$ = \pi h(R - r)(R + r)$ $V = \pi h(R - r)(R + r) = 2\pi\left(\dfrac{R + r}{2}\right)(R - r)h$

Section P.4   Fractional Expressions

- ■   You should be able to find the domain of a fractional expression.
- ■   You should know that a rational expression is the quotient of two polynomials.
- ■   You should be able to simplify rational expressions by reducing them to lowest terms. This may involve factoring both the numerator and the denominator.
- ■   You should be able to add, subtract, multiply, and divide rational expressions.
- ■   You should be able to simplify compound fractions.

Solutions to Odd-Numbered Exercises

1. The domain of the polynomial $3x^2 - 4x + 7$ is the set of all real numbers.

3. The domain of the polynomial $4x^3 + 3, x \geq 0$ is the set of non-negative real numbers, since the polynomial is restricted to that set.

5. The domain of $\dfrac{1}{x - 2}$ is the set of all real numbers x such that $x \neq 2$.

7. The domain of $\dfrac{x - 1}{x(x - 4)}$ is the set of all real numbers x such that $x \neq 0$ and $x \neq 4$.

9. The domain of $\sqrt{x + 1}$ is the set of all real numbers x such that $x \geq -1$.

11. $\dfrac{5}{2x} = \dfrac{5(3x)}{(2x)(3x)} = \dfrac{5(3x)}{6x^2}, x \neq 0$

   The missing factor is $3x, x \neq 0$

13. $\dfrac{15x^2}{10x} = \dfrac{5x(3x)}{5x(2)} = \dfrac{3x}{2}, x \neq 0$

15. $\dfrac{3xy}{xy + x} = \dfrac{x(3y)}{x(y + 1)} = \dfrac{3y}{y + 1}, x \neq 0$

17. $\dfrac{x - 5}{10 - 2x} = \dfrac{x - 5}{-2(x - 5)} = -\dfrac{1}{2}, x \neq 5$

19. $\dfrac{x^3 + 5x^2 + 6x}{x^2 - 4} = \dfrac{x(x + 2)(x + 3)}{(x + 2)(x - 2)} = \dfrac{x(x + 3)}{x - 2}, x \neq -2$

21. $\dfrac{y^2 - 7y + 12}{y^2 + 3y - 18} = \dfrac{(y - 3)(y - 4)}{(y + 6)(y - 3)} = \dfrac{y - 4}{y + 6}, y \neq 3$

23. $\dfrac{2 - x + 2x^2 - x^3}{x - 2} = \dfrac{(2 - x) + x^2(2 - x)}{-(2 - x)} = \dfrac{(2 - x)(1 + x^2)}{-(2 - x)} = -(1 + x^2), x \neq 2$

25. $\dfrac{z^3 - 8}{z^2 + 2z + 4} = \dfrac{(z - 2)(z^2 + 2z + 4)}{z^2 + 2z + 4} = z - 2$

27.

x	0	1	2	3	4	5	6
$\dfrac{x^2 - 2x - 3}{x - 3}$	1	2	3	undef.	5	6	7
$x + 1$	1	2	3	4	5	6	7

The expressions are equivalent except at $x = 3$.

29. $\dfrac{5x^3}{2x^3 + 4} = \dfrac{5x^3}{2(x^3 + 2)}$. There are no common factors so this expression is in

reduced form. In this case factors of terms were incorrectly cancelled.

31. $\dfrac{\pi r^2}{(2r)^2} = \dfrac{\pi r^2}{4r^2} = \dfrac{\pi}{4}$

33. $\dfrac{5}{x - 1} \cdot \dfrac{x - 1}{25(x - 2)} = \dfrac{1}{5(x - 2)}, x \neq 1$

35. $\dfrac{r}{r - 1} \cdot \dfrac{r^2 - 1}{r^2} = \dfrac{r(r + 1)(r - 1)}{r^2(r - 1)} = \dfrac{r + 1}{r}, r \neq 1$

37. $\dfrac{t^2 - t - 6}{t^2 + 6t + 9} \cdot \dfrac{t + 3}{t^2 - 4} = \dfrac{(t - 3)(t + 2)(t + 3)}{(t + 3)^2(t + 2)(t - 2)} = \dfrac{t - 3}{(t + 3)(t - 2)}, t \neq -2$

39. $\dfrac{3(x + y)}{4} \div \dfrac{x + y}{2} = \dfrac{3(x + y)}{4} \cdot \dfrac{2}{x + y} = \dfrac{3}{2}, x \neq -y$

41. $\dfrac{\left[\dfrac{x^2}{(x + 1)^2}\right]}{\left[\dfrac{x}{(x + 1)^3}\right]} = \dfrac{x^2}{(x + 1)^2} \cdot \dfrac{(x + 1)^3}{x} = x(x + 1), x \neq -1, 0$

43. $\dfrac{5}{x - 1} + \dfrac{x}{x - 1} = \dfrac{5 + x}{x - 1} = \dfrac{x + 5}{x - 1}$

45. $6 - \dfrac{5}{x + 3} = \dfrac{6(x + 3)}{(x + 3)} - \dfrac{5}{x + 3} = \dfrac{6(x + 3) - 5}{x + 3} = \dfrac{6x + 13}{x + 3}$

47. $\dfrac{3}{x - 2} + \dfrac{5}{2 - x} = \dfrac{3}{x - 2} - \dfrac{5}{x - 2} = -\dfrac{2}{x - 2}$

49. $\dfrac{1}{x^2 - x - 2} - \dfrac{x}{x^2 - 5x + 6} = \dfrac{1}{(x - 2)(x + 1)} - \dfrac{x}{(x - 2)(x - 3)}$

$$= \dfrac{(x - 3) - x(x + 1)}{(x + 1)(x - 2)(x - 3)}$$

$$= \dfrac{-x^2 - 3}{(x + 1)(x - 2)(x - 3)} = -\dfrac{x^2 + 3}{(x + 1)(x - 2)(x - 3)}$$

51. $-\dfrac{1}{x} + \dfrac{2}{x^2 + 1} + \dfrac{1}{x^3 + x} = \dfrac{-(x^2 + 1)}{x(x^2 + 1)} + \dfrac{2x}{x(x^2 + 1)} + \dfrac{1}{x(x^2 + 1)}$

$$= \dfrac{-x^2 - 1 + 2x + 1}{x(x^2 + 1)} = \dfrac{-x^2 + 2x}{x(x^2 + 1)} = \dfrac{-x(x - 2)}{x(x^2 + 1)}$$

$$= -\dfrac{x - 2}{x^2 + 1} = \dfrac{2 - x}{x^2 + 1}, x \neq 0$$

53. $x^2(x^2 + 1)^{-5} - (x^2 + 1)^{-4} = (x^2 + 1)^{-5}[x^2 - (x^2 + 1)]$

$$= -\dfrac{1}{(x^2 + 1)^5}$$

55. $\dfrac{\left(\dfrac{x}{2}-1\right)}{(x-2)} = \dfrac{\left(\dfrac{x}{2}-\dfrac{2}{2}\right)}{\left(\dfrac{x-2}{1}\right)} = \dfrac{x-2}{2}\cdot\dfrac{1}{x-2} = \dfrac{1}{2},\ x\neq 2$

57. $\dfrac{\left[\dfrac{1}{(x+h)^2}-\dfrac{1}{x^2}\right]}{h} = \dfrac{\left[\dfrac{1}{(x+h)^2}-\dfrac{1}{x^2}\right]}{h}\cdot\dfrac{x^2(x+h)^2}{x^2(x+h)^2}$

$$= \dfrac{x^2-(x+h)^2}{hx^2(x+h)^2}$$

$$= \dfrac{x^2-(x^2+2xh+h^2)}{hx^2(x+h)^2}$$

$$= \dfrac{-h(2x+h)}{hx^2(x+h)^2}$$

$$= -\dfrac{2x+h}{x^2(x+h)^2},\ h\neq 0$$

59. $\dfrac{\left(\sqrt{x}-\dfrac{1}{2\sqrt{x}}\right)}{\sqrt{x}} = \dfrac{\left(\sqrt{x}-\dfrac{1}{2\sqrt{x}}\right)}{\sqrt{x}}\cdot\dfrac{2\sqrt{x}}{2\sqrt{x}} = \dfrac{2x-1}{2x},\ x>0$

61. $\dfrac{\dfrac{t^2}{\sqrt{t^2+1}}-\sqrt{t^2+1}}{t^2} = \dfrac{\left[\dfrac{t^2}{\sqrt{t^2+1}}-\sqrt{t^2+1}\right]}{t^2}\cdot\dfrac{\sqrt{t^2+1}}{\sqrt{t^2+1}}$

$$= \dfrac{t^2-(t^2+1)}{t^2\sqrt{t^2+1}} = -\dfrac{1}{t^2\sqrt{t^2+1}}$$

63. $\dfrac{\sqrt{x+2}-\sqrt{x}}{2} = \dfrac{\sqrt{x+2}-\sqrt{x}}{2}\cdot\dfrac{\sqrt{x+2}+\sqrt{x}}{\sqrt{x+2}+\sqrt{x}}$

$$= \dfrac{(x+2)-x}{2(\sqrt{x+2}+\sqrt{x})} = \dfrac{2}{2(\sqrt{x+2}+\sqrt{x})}$$

$$= \dfrac{1}{\sqrt{x+2}+\sqrt{x}}$$

65. (a) $\dfrac{1}{16}$ minute to copy one page

(b) $x\dfrac{1}{16} = \dfrac{x}{16}$ minutes to copy x pages

(c) $\dfrac{60}{16} = \dfrac{15}{4}$ minutes to copy 60 pages

67. Average $= \dfrac{\left(\dfrac{x}{3}+\dfrac{2x}{5}\right)}{2} = \dfrac{\left(\dfrac{x}{3}+\dfrac{2x}{5}\right)}{2}\cdot\dfrac{15}{15}$

$$= \dfrac{5x+6x}{30} = \dfrac{11x}{30}$$

69. (a) $r = \dfrac{\left(\dfrac{24[48(400) - 15,000]}{48}\right)}{\left[15,000 + \dfrac{48(400)}{12}\right]} \approx 0.1265 = 12.65\%$

(b) $r = \dfrac{\left[\dfrac{24(NM - P)}{N}\right]}{\left(P + \dfrac{NM}{12}\right)} = \dfrac{24(NM - P)}{N} \cdot \dfrac{12}{12P + NM} = \dfrac{288(NM - P)}{N(12P + NM)}$

$r = \dfrac{288[48(400) - 15,000]}{48[12(15,000) + 48(400)]} \approx 0.1265 = 12.65\%$

71. $T = 10\left(\dfrac{4t^2 + 16t + 75}{t^2 + 4t + 10}\right)$

(a)

t	0	1	2	3	4	5
T	75°	63.3°	55.9°	51.3°	48.3°	46.4°

(b)

73. $\dfrac{x\left(\dfrac{x}{2}\right)}{x(2x + 1)} = \dfrac{\dfrac{x}{2}}{2x + 1} \cdot \dfrac{2}{2} = \dfrac{x}{2(2x + 1)}$

Section P.5   The Cartesian Plane

- ■ You should be able to plot points.
- ■ You should know that the distance between (x_1, y_1) and (x_2, y_2) in the plane is

    $$d = \sqrt{(x_2 - x_1)^2 + (y_2 - y_1)^2}.$$

- ■ You should know that the midpoint of the line segment joining (x_1, y_1) and (x_2, y_2) is

    $$\left(\dfrac{x_1 + x_2}{2}, \dfrac{y_1 + y_2}{2}\right).$$

- ■ You should know the equation of a circle: $(x - h)^2 + (y - k)^2 = r^2$.

Solutions to Odd-Numbered Exercises

1.

3.

5. A: $(2, 6)$, B: $(-6, -2)$, C: $(4, -4)$, D: $(-3, 2)$

7. A:$(0, 5)$, B:$(-3, -6)$, C:$(1, -4.5)$, D:$(-4, 2)$

9. $(-3, 4)$ **11.** $(-5, -5)$ **13.** On the x-axis, $y = 0$.

  On the y-axis, $x = 0$.

15. $x > 0$ $\implies$ x lies in Quadrant I or in Quadrant IV.

  $y < 0$ $\implies$ y lies in Quadrant III or in Quadrant IV.

  $x > 0$ and $y < 0$ $\implies$ (x, y) lies in Quadrant IV.

17. $x = -4$ $\implies$ x is negative $\implies$ x lies in Quadrant II or Quadrant III.

  $y > 0$ $\implies$ y lies in Quadrant I or Quadrant II.

  $x = -4$ and $y > 0$ $\implies$ (x, y) lies in Quadrant II.

19. $y < -5$ $\implies$ y is negative $\implies$ y lies in either Quadrant III or Quadrant IV.

21. Since $(x, -y)$ is in Quadrant II, we know that $x < 0$ and $-y > 0$. If $-y > 0$, then $y < 0$.

  $x < 0$ $\implies$ x lies in Quadrant II or in Quadrant III.

  $y < 0$ $\implies$ y lies in Quadrant III or in Quadrant IV.

  $x < 0$ and $y < 0$ $\implies$ (x, y) lies in Quadrant III.

23. If $xy > 0$, then either x and y are both positive, or both negative. Hence, (x, y) lies in either Quadrant I or Quadrant III.

25.

27. The x-coordinates are increased by 2, and the y-coordinates are increased by 5:

  $(0, 1)$, $(4, 2)$, $(1, 4)$.

29. $y = 2 - \frac{1}{2}x$

x	-2	-1	$-\frac{1}{2}$	0	$\frac{1}{2}$	1	2
y	3	$\frac{5}{2}$	$\frac{9}{4}$	2	$\frac{7}{4}$	$\frac{3}{2}$	1

31. $\left(\dfrac{1200 - 60}{60}\right)(100) = 1900\%$

33. The highest price of milk is approximately $13.70 per 100 lb. This occurred in 1990.

35. The minimum wage increased most rapidly in the 1970s.

37. The point (65, 83) represents an entrance exam score of 65.

39. (a) The distance between (0, 2) and (4, 2) is 4.
The distance between (4, 2) and (4, 5) is 3.
The distance between (0, 2) and (4, 5) is
$$\sqrt{(4 - 0)^2 + (5 - 2)^2} = \sqrt{16 + 9} = \sqrt{25} = 5.$$

  (b) $4^2 + 3^2 = 16 + 9 = 25 = 5^2$

41. (a) The distance between $(-1, 1)$ and $(9, 1)$ is 10.
The distance between $(9, 1)$ and $(9, 4)$ is 3.
The distance between $(-1, 1)$ and $(9, 4)$ is
$$\sqrt{(9 - (-1))^2 + (4 - 1)^2} = \sqrt{100 + 9} = \sqrt{109}.$$

  (b) $10^2 + 3^2 = 109 = \left(\sqrt{109}\right)^2$

43. $d = |5 - (-3)| = 8$

45. $d = |2 - (-3)| = 5$

47. (a)

  (b) $d = \sqrt{(9 - 1)^2 + (7 - 1)^2}$
  $= \sqrt{64 + 36} = 10$

  (c) $\left(\dfrac{9 + 1}{2}, \dfrac{7 + 1}{2}\right) = (5, 4)$

49. (a)

  (b) $d = \sqrt{(4 + 4)^2 + (-5 - 10)^2}$
  $= \sqrt{64 + 225} = 17$

  (c) $\left(\dfrac{4 - 4}{2}, \dfrac{-5 + 10}{2}\right) = \left(0, \dfrac{5}{2}\right)$

51. (a)

(b) $d = \sqrt{(5 + 1)^2 + (4 - 2)^2}$

$\qquad = \sqrt{36 + 4} = 2\sqrt{10}$

(c) $\left(\dfrac{-1 + 5}{2}, \dfrac{2 + 4}{2}\right) = (2, 3)$

53. (a)

(b) $d = \sqrt{\left(\dfrac{1}{2} + \dfrac{5}{2}\right)^2 + \left(1 - \dfrac{4}{3}\right)^2}$

$\qquad d = \sqrt{9 + \dfrac{1}{9}} = \dfrac{\sqrt{82}}{3}$

(c) $\left(\dfrac{-\frac{5}{2} + \frac{1}{2}}{2}, \dfrac{\frac{4}{3} + 1}{2}\right) = \left(-1, \dfrac{7}{6}\right)$

55. (a)

(b) $d = \sqrt{(6.2 + 3.7)^2 + (5.4 - 1.8)^2}$

$\qquad = \sqrt{98.01 + 12.96}$

$\qquad = \sqrt{110.97}$

(c) $\left(\dfrac{6.2 - 3.7}{2}, \dfrac{5.4 + 1.8}{2}\right) = (1.25, 3.6)$

57. (a)

(b) $d = \sqrt{(48 + 36)^2 + (-72 + 18)^2}$

$\qquad = \sqrt{7056 + 2916}$

$\qquad = \sqrt{9972} = 6\sqrt{277}$

(c) $\left(\dfrac{-36 + 48}{2}, \dfrac{-18 - 72}{2}\right) = (6, -45)$

59. $\left(\dfrac{1991 + 1995}{2}, \dfrac{\$520{,}000 + \$740{,}000}{2}\right) = (1993, \$630{,}000)$

61. $d_1 = \sqrt{(4 - 2)^2 + (0 - 1)^2} = \sqrt{5}$

$\quad d_2 = \sqrt{(4 + 1)^2 + (0 + 5)^2} = \sqrt{50}$

$\quad d_3 = \sqrt{(2 + 1)^2 + (1 + 5)^2} = \sqrt{45}$

$\quad \left(\sqrt{5}\right)^2 + \left(\sqrt{45}\right)^2 = \left(\sqrt{50}\right)^2$

63. $d_1 = \sqrt{(0 - 1)^2 + (0 - 2)^2} = \sqrt{5}$

$\quad d_2 = \sqrt{(0 - 2)^2 + (0 - 1)^2} = \sqrt{5}$

$\quad d_3 = \sqrt{(3 - 1)^2 + (3 - 2)^2} = \sqrt{5}$

$\quad d_4 = \sqrt{(3 - 2)^2 + (3 - 1)^2} = \sqrt{5}$

$\quad d_1 = d_2 = d_3 = d_4$

65. $d_1 = \sqrt{(0-2)^2 + (9-5)^2} = \sqrt{4+16} = \sqrt{20} = 2\sqrt{5}$

$d_2 = \sqrt{(-2-0)^2 + (0-9)^2} = \sqrt{4+81} = \sqrt{85}$

$d_3 = \sqrt{(0-(-2))^2 + (-4-0)^2} = \sqrt{4+16} = \sqrt{20} = 2\sqrt{5}$

$d_4 = \sqrt{(0-2)^2 + (-4-5)^2} = \sqrt{4+81} = \sqrt{85}$

Opposite sides have equal lengths of $2\sqrt{5}$ and $\sqrt{85}$.

67. $(x-0)^2 + (y-0)^2 = 3^2$

$\qquad x^2 + y^2 = 9$

69. $(x-2)^2 + (y+1)^2 = 4^2$

$\qquad (x-2)^2 + (y+1)^2 = 16$

71. $(x+1)^2 + (y-2)^2 = r^2$

$(0+1)^2 + (0-2)^2 = r^2 \implies r^2 = 5$

$(x+1)^2 + (y-2)^2 = 5$

73. $r = \dfrac{1}{2}\sqrt{(6-0)^2 + (8-0)^2} = \dfrac{1}{2}\sqrt{100} = 5$

Center $= \left(\dfrac{0+6}{2}, \dfrac{0+8}{2}\right) = (3, 4)$

$(x-3)^2 + (y-4)^2 = 25$

75. Center: $(0, 0)$

Radius $= 2$

77. Center: $(1, -3)$

Radius $= 2$

79. Center: $\left(\frac{1}{2}, \frac{1}{2}\right)$

Radius $= \frac{3}{2}$

81. Since $x_m = \dfrac{x_1 + x_2}{2}$ and $y_m = \dfrac{y_1 + y_2}{2}$ we have:

$\qquad 2x_m = x_1 + x_2 \qquad\qquad 2y_m = y_1 + y_2$

$2x_m - x_1 = x_2 \qquad\qquad 2y_m - y_1 = y_2$

Thus, $(x_2, y_2) = (2x_m - x_1, 2y_m - y_1)$.

83. The midpoint of the given line segment is $\left(\dfrac{x_1 + x_2}{2}, \dfrac{y_1 + y_2}{2}\right)$.

The midpoint between (x_1, y_1) and $\left(\dfrac{x_1 + x_2}{2}, \dfrac{y_1 + y_2}{2}\right)$ is

$$\left(\dfrac{x_1 + \dfrac{x_1 + x_2}{2}}{2}, \dfrac{y_1 + \dfrac{y_1 + y_2}{2}}{2}\right) = \left(\dfrac{3x_1 + x_2}{4}, \dfrac{3y_1 + y_2}{4}\right).$$

The midpoint between $\left(\dfrac{x_1 + x_2}{2}, \dfrac{y_1 + y_2}{2}\right)$ and (x_2, y_2) is

$$\left(\dfrac{\dfrac{x_1 + x_2}{2} + x_2}{2}, \dfrac{\dfrac{y_1 + y_2}{2} + y_2}{2}\right) = \left(\dfrac{x_1 + 3x_2}{4}, \dfrac{y_1 + 3y_2}{4}\right).$$

Thus, the three points are

$$\left(\dfrac{3x_1 + x_2}{4}, \dfrac{3y_1 + y_2}{4}\right), \left(\dfrac{x_1 + x_2}{2}, \dfrac{y_1 + y_2}{2}\right), \text{ and } \left(\dfrac{x_1 + 3x_2}{4}, \dfrac{y_1 + 3y_2}{4}\right).$$

85. $d = \sqrt{(45 - 10)^2 + (40 - 15)^2} = \sqrt{35^2 + 25^2} = \sqrt{1850}$

$$= 5\sqrt{74} \approx 43 \text{ yards}$$

87.

The points are reflected through the y-axis.

89. (a) It appears that the number of artists elected alternates between 7 and 8 per year in the 1990s. If this pattern continues, 7 or 8 would be elected in 1996.

(b) Since 1986 and 1987 were the first two years that artists were elected, there was a larger number of artists chosen.

Section P.6   Exploring Data: Representing Data Graphically

- You should know how to construct line plots.
- You should know how to construct stem and leaf plots.
- You should be able to draw and interpret histograms and frequency distributions.
- You should be able to construct a line graph.

Solutions to Odd-Numbered Exercises

1. (a) The price 1.109 occurred with the greatest frequency (6).

   (b) The prices range from 0.999 to 1.189.

3. By scanning the data, we see that the largest number is 24 and the smallest number is 10. We construct the line plot on the interval [10, 24] as follows.

   The score of 15 occurred with the greatest frequency (5).

5. By scanning the data, we see that the largest number is 100 and the smallest number is 70. We construct the line plot on the interval [70, 100] as follows.

   The scores of 81 and 85 occurred with the greatest frequency (4).

7. Since the scores range from 70 to 100, the stems are 7, 8, 9 and 10.

Stems	Leaves
7	0 5 5 5 7 7 8 8 8
8	1 1 1 1 2 3 4 5 5 5 5 7 8 9 9 9
9	0 2 8
10	0 0

9. Since the expenditures range from 663 to 1800, the stems are 6, 7, . . . ,17, 18.

Stems	Leaves
6	63 76 92
7	62 64
8	04 18 34 34 41 48 50 63 64 65 85 98
9	03 13 15 16 19 19 32 40 43 64 64 74 74
10	03 24 24 29 45 49 56 61 96 98
11	23 24 31 38 55 97
12	52 65
13	36 51
14	
15	
16	
17	
18	00

11. The projected loss of 500 million in 1995 is 500% of the loss in 1991.

13.

15.

17. (a) The savings decreased from 9% to 4%. The decrease is 55.6%.

(b) No. The trend of low savings limits the amount of funds available for capital improvements and research in industries.

19.

21.

You can conclude that the receipts are increasing in a steady rate.

❑ Review Exercises for Chapter P

Solutions to Odd-Numbered Exercises

1. $\{11, -14, -\frac{8}{9}, \frac{5}{2}, \sqrt{6}, 0.4\}$

    (a) Natural numbers: 11

    (b) Integers: 11, −14

    (c) Rational numbers: $11, -14, -\frac{8}{9}, \frac{5}{2}, 0.4$

    (d) Irrational numbers: $\sqrt{6}$

3. (a) $\frac{5}{6} = 0.8\overline{3}$

    (b) $\frac{7}{8} = 0.875$

5. $x \leq 7$,   The set consists of all real numbers less than or equal to 7.

7. $d(x, 7) = |x - 7|$ and $d(x, 7) \geq 4$, thus $|x - 7| \geq 4$.

9. $d(y, -30) = |y - (-30)| = |y + 30|$ and $d(y, -30) < 5$, thus $|y + 30| < 5$.

11. $|-3| + 4(-2) - 6 = 3 - 8 - 6 = -11$

13. $2x + (3x - 10) = (2x + 3x) - 10$

    Associative Property of Addition

15. $(t + 4)(2t) = (2t)(t + 4)$

    Commutative Property of Multiplication

17. (a) $(-2z)^3 = (-2)^3 z^3 = -8z^3$

    (b) $(a^2 b^4)(3ab^{-2}) = 3a^{2+1}b^{4-2} = 3a^3 b^2$

19. (a) $\dfrac{6^2 u^3 v^{-3}}{12u^{-2}v} = \dfrac{36u^{3-(-2)}v^{-3-1}}{12} = 3u^5 v^{-4} = \dfrac{3u^5}{v^4}$

    (b) $\dfrac{3^{-4}m^{-1}n^{-3}}{9^{-2}mn^{-3}} = \dfrac{9^2 n^3}{3^4 mmn^3} = \dfrac{81}{81m^2} = \dfrac{1}{m^2} = m^{-2}$

21. $30{,}296{,}000{,}000 = 3.0296 \times 10^{10}$

23. $4.833 \times 10^8 = 483{,}300{,}000$

25. (a) $1800(1 + 0.08)^{24} \approx 11{,}414.125$

    (b) $0.0024\,(7{,}658{,}400) = 18{,}380.160$

27. Radical form: $\sqrt{16} = 4$

    Rational exponent form: $16^{1/2} = 4$

29. $\sqrt{4x^4} = 2x^2$

31. $\dfrac{1}{2 - \sqrt{3}} = \dfrac{1}{2 - \sqrt{3}} \cdot \dfrac{2 + \sqrt{3}}{2 + \sqrt{3}} = \dfrac{2 + \sqrt{3}}{4 - 3}$

    $= \dfrac{2 + \sqrt{3}}{1} = 2 + \sqrt{3}$

33. $\sqrt{50} - \sqrt{18} = \sqrt{25 \cdot 2} - \sqrt{9 \cdot 2} = 5\sqrt{2} - 3\sqrt{2} = 2\sqrt{2}$

35. $A = wh = 8\sqrt{3}\,\sqrt{24^2 - (8\sqrt{3})^2} = 8\sqrt{3}\,\sqrt{384}$

    $= 8\sqrt{3}(8\sqrt{6}) = 64\sqrt{18} = 64(3\sqrt{2}) = 192\sqrt{2}$

37. $\dfrac{x - 1}{1 - x} = \dfrac{x - 1}{-(x - 1)} = -1,\ x \neq 1$

    The error is an improper cancellation.

39. $(2x)^4 = 2^4 x^4 = 16x^4$

    The exponent is to be applied to the whole quantity inside the parentheses.

41. $\sqrt{3^2 + 4^2} = \sqrt{9 + 16} = \sqrt{25} = 5$

The square root of a sum is NOT the sum of the square roots.

43. $-(3x^2 + 2x) + (1 - 5x) = -3x^2 - 2x + 1 - 5x = -3x^2 - 7x + 1$

45. $(2x - 3)^2 = (2x)^2 - 2(2x)(3) + 9 = 4x^2 - 12x + 9$

47. $(x^2 - 2x + 1)(x^3 - 1) = (x^2 - 2x + 1)x^3 - (x^2 - 2x + 1)$
$$= x^5 - 2x^4 + x^3 - x^2 + 2x - 1$$

49. $(y^2 - y)(y^2 + 1)(y^2 + y + 1) = (y^4 - y^3 + y^2 - y)(y^2 + y + 1)$
$$= (y^4 - y^3 + y^2 - y)y^2 + (y^4 - y^3 + y^2 - y)y + (y^4 - y^3 + y^2 - y)$$
$$= y^6 - y^5 + y^4 - y^3 + y^5 - y^4 + y^3 - y^2 + y^4 - y^3 + y^2 - y$$
$$= y^6 + y^4 - y^3 - y.$$

51. $(x + 3)(x + 5) = x(x + 5) + 3(x + 5)$

Distributive Property

53. $x^3 - x = x(x^2 - 1) = x(x + 1)(x - 1)$

55. $2x^2 + 21x + 10 = (2x + 1)(x + 10)$

57. $x^3 - x^2 + 2x - 2 = x^2(x - 1) + 2(x - 1)$
$$= (x - 1)(x^2 + 2)$$

59. (a)

The surface is the sum of the area of the side, $2\pi rh$, and the areas of the top and bottom which are each πr^2.

$$S = 2\pi rh + \pi r^2 + \pi r^2 = 2\pi rh + 2\pi r^2.$$

(b) $S = 2\pi rh + 2\pi r^2 = 2\pi r(r + h)$

61. $\dfrac{x^2 - 4}{x^4 - 2x^2 - 8} \cdot \dfrac{x^2 + 2}{x^2} = \dfrac{(x - 2)(x + 2)}{(x^2 - 4)(x^2 + 2)} \cdot \dfrac{x^2 + 2}{x^2}$

$$= \dfrac{(x - 2)(x + 2)}{(x - 2)(x + 2)} \cdot \dfrac{1}{x^2} = \dfrac{1}{x^2}, \quad x \neq \pm 2$$

63. $\dfrac{x^2(5x - 6)}{2x + 3} \div \dfrac{5x}{2x + 3} = \dfrac{x^2(5x - 6)}{2x + 3} \cdot \dfrac{2x + 3}{5x} = \dfrac{x(5x - 6)}{5}, \quad x \neq 0, \ -\dfrac{3}{2}$

65. $x - 1 + \dfrac{1}{x + 2} + \dfrac{1}{x - 1} = \dfrac{(x - 1)^2(x + 2) + (x - 1) + (x + 2)}{(x + 2)(x - 1)}$

$$= \dfrac{(x^2 - 2x + 1)(x + 2) + 2x + 1}{(x + 2)(x - 1)}$$

$$= \dfrac{x^3 - 2x^2 + x + 2x^2 - 4x + 2 + (2x + 1)}{(x + 2)(x - 1)}$$

$$= \dfrac{x^3 - x + 3}{(x + 2)(x - 1)}$$

67. $\dfrac{1}{x} - \dfrac{x-1}{x^2+1} = \dfrac{1(x^2+1) - x(x-1)}{x(x^2+1)}$

$$= \dfrac{x^2 + 1 - x^2 + x}{x(x^2+1)}$$

$$= \dfrac{x+1}{x(x^2+1)}$$

69. $\dfrac{\dfrac{1}{x} - \dfrac{1}{y}}{(x^2 - y^2)} = \dfrac{y-x}{xy} \cdot \dfrac{1}{(x-y)(x+y)}$

$$= \dfrac{-1}{xy(x+y)}, \; x \neq y$$

71. $d_1 = \sqrt{(22-3)^2 + (5-2)^2} = \sqrt{19^2 + 3^2} = \sqrt{370}$

$d_2 = \sqrt{(22-11)^2 + (5-13)^2} = \sqrt{11^2 + 8^2} = \sqrt{185}$

$d_3 = \sqrt{(11-3)^2 + (13-2)^2} = \sqrt{64 + 121} = \sqrt{185}$

$d_2^2 + d_3^2 = d_1^2 = 370$

73. $x > 0$ means (x, y) is in Quadrant I or IV.

$y > -2$ means (x, y) is in Quadrant III or IV.

Combining (x, y) is in Quadrant IV.

75. $(-3, 8), \; (1, 5)$

(a)

(b) $d = \sqrt{(1 - (-3))^2 + (5-8)^2}$

$$= \sqrt{4^2 + 3^2} = \sqrt{25} = 5$$

(c) $\left(\dfrac{-3+1}{2}, \dfrac{8+5}{2}\right) = \left(-1, \dfrac{13}{2}\right)$

77.

❑ Chapter Test for Chapter P

1. $-\frac{10}{3} \approx -3.3$ and $-|-4| = -4$, hence $-\frac{10}{3} > -|-4|$.

2. $d\left(-5.4, 3\frac{3}{4}\right) = \left|3\frac{3}{4} - (-5.4)\right| = |3.75 + 5.4| = 9.15$

3. (a) $27\left(-\frac{2}{3}\right) = -27\left(\frac{2}{3}\right) = -18$

    (b) $\dfrac{5}{18} \div \dfrac{15}{8} = \dfrac{5}{18} \cdot \dfrac{8}{15} = \dfrac{5 \cdot 2 \cdot 4}{2 \cdot 9 \cdot 3 \cdot 5} = \dfrac{4}{27}$

4. (a) $\left(\dfrac{-3}{5}\right)^3 = \dfrac{-27}{125}$

    (b) $\left(\dfrac{3^2}{2}\right)^{-3} = \left(\dfrac{2}{3^2}\right)^3 = \dfrac{2^3}{3^6} = \dfrac{8}{729}$

5. (a) $\sqrt{5} \cdot \sqrt{125} = \sqrt{5} \cdot 5\sqrt{5} = 25$

    (b) $\dfrac{\sqrt{72}}{\sqrt{2}} = \dfrac{6\sqrt{2}}{\sqrt{2}} = 6$

6. (a) $\dfrac{5.4 \times 10^8}{3 \times 10^3} = 1.8 \times 10^{8-3} = 1.8 \times 10^5$

    (b) $(3 \times 10^4)^3 = 3^3 \times 10^{12} = 27 \times 10^{12} = 2.7 \times 10^{13}$

7. (a) $3z^2(2z^3)^2 = 3z^2 4 \cdot z^6 = 12z^8$

    (b) $(u - 2)^{-4}(u - 2)^{-3} = (u - 2)^{-7} = \dfrac{1}{(u - 2)^7}$

8. (a) $\left(\dfrac{x^{-2}y^2}{3}\right)^{-1} = \dfrac{3}{x^{-2}y^2} = \dfrac{3x^2}{y^2}$

    (b) $\sqrt[3]{\dfrac{16}{v^5}} = \sqrt[3]{\dfrac{2^3 \cdot 2}{v^3 v^2}} = \dfrac{2}{v}\sqrt[3]{\dfrac{2}{v^2}}$

9. (a) $9z\sqrt{8z} - 3\sqrt{2z^3} = 9z \cdot 2\sqrt{2z} - 3z\sqrt{2z} = 15z\sqrt{2z}$

    (b) $-5\sqrt{16y} + 10\sqrt{y} = -5 \cdot 4\sqrt{y} + 10\sqrt{y} = -10\sqrt{y}$

10. $(x^2 + 3) - [3x + (8 - x^2)] = x^2 + 3 - 3x - 8 + x^2 = 2x^2 - 3x - 5$

11. $\left(x + \sqrt{5}\right)\left(x - \sqrt{5}\right) = x^2 - 5$

12. $\dfrac{8x}{x - 3} + \dfrac{24}{3 - x} = \dfrac{8x}{x - 3} - \dfrac{24}{x - 3} = \dfrac{8x - 24}{x - 3} = \dfrac{8(x - 3)}{x - 3} = 8, \ x \neq 3$

13. $\left(\dfrac{2}{x} - \dfrac{2}{x + 1}\right) \div \dfrac{4}{x^2 - 1} = \dfrac{2(x + 1) - 2x}{x(x + 1)} \cdot \dfrac{(x - 1)(x + 1)}{4} = \dfrac{2}{x} \cdot \dfrac{x - 1}{4} = \dfrac{x - 1}{2x}, \ x \neq \pm 1$

14. (a) $2x^4 - 3x^3 - 2x^2 = x^2(2x^2 - 3x - 2) = x^2(2x + 1)(x - 2)$

    (b) $x^3 + 2x^2 - 4x - 8 = x^2(x + 2) - 4(x + 2) = (x + 2)(x^2 - 4)$

$$= (x + 2)(x + 2)(x - 2)$$
$$= (x + 2)^2(x - 2)$$

15. (a) $\dfrac{16}{\sqrt[3]{16}} = \dfrac{16}{\sqrt[3]{8 \cdot 2}} = \dfrac{16}{2} \dfrac{1}{2^{1/3}} \cdot \dfrac{2^{2/3}}{2^{2/3}} = 4 \cdot 2^{2/3} = 4\sqrt[3]{4}$

    (b) $\dfrac{6}{1 - \sqrt{3}} = \dfrac{6}{1 - \sqrt{3}} \cdot \dfrac{1 + \sqrt{3}}{1 + \sqrt{3}} = \dfrac{6(1 + \sqrt{3})}{1 - 3} = -3(1 + \sqrt{3})$

16. Midpoint $= \left(\dfrac{-2 + 6}{2}, \dfrac{5 + 0}{2}\right) = \left(2, \dfrac{5}{2}\right)$

Distance $= \sqrt{(-2 - 6)^2 + (5 - 0)^2}$

$$= \sqrt{64 + 25} = \sqrt{89} \approx 9.43$$

17.

C H A P T E R 1
Functions and Their Graphs

C H A P T E R   1
Functions and Their Graphs

Section 1.1   Graphs and Graphing Utilities

■ You should be able to use the point-plotting method of graphing.

■ You should be able to find x- and y-intercepts.

   (a) To find the x-intercepts, let $y = 0$ and solve for x.

   (b) To find the y-intercepts, let $x = 0$ and solve for y.

■ You should know how to graph an equation with a graphing utility. You should be able to determine an appropriate viewing rectangle.

■ You should be able to use the zoom and trace features of a graphing utility.

Solutions to Odd-Numbered Exercises

1. $y = \sqrt{x + 4}$

   (a) $(0, 2)$: $2 \stackrel{?}{=} \sqrt{0 + 4}$

           $2 = 2$ ✓

   Yes, the point *is* on the graph.

   (b) $(5, 3)$: $3 \stackrel{?}{=} \sqrt{5 + 4}$

           $3 = \sqrt{9}$ ✓

   Yes, the point *is* on the graph.

3. $y = 4 - |x - 2|$

   (a) $(1, 5)$: $5 \stackrel{?}{=} 4 - |1 - 2|$

           $5 \neq 4 - 1$

   No, the point *is not* on the graph.

   (b) $(6, 0)$: $0 \stackrel{?}{=} 4 - |6 - 2|$

           $0 = 4 - 4$ ✓

   Yes, the point *is* on the graph.

5. $2x - y - 3 = 0$

   (a) $(1, 2)$: $2(1) - (2) - 3 \stackrel{?}{=} 0$

              $-3 \neq 0$

   No, the point *is not* on the graph.

   (b) $(1, -1)$: $2(1) - (-1) - 3 \stackrel{?}{=} 0$

              $2 + 1 - 3 = 0$ ✓

   Yes, the point *is* on the graph.

7. $x^2 y - x^2 + 4y = 0$

   (a) $\left(1, \frac{1}{5}\right)$: $(1)^2\left(\frac{1}{5}\right) - (1)^2 + 4\left(\frac{1}{5}\right) \stackrel{?}{=} 0$

               $\frac{1}{5} - 1 + \frac{4}{5} = 0$ ✓

   Yes, the point *is* on the graph.

   (b) $\left(2, \frac{1}{2}\right)$: $(2)^2\left(\frac{1}{2}\right) - (2)^2 + 4\left(\frac{1}{2}\right) \stackrel{?}{=} 0$

               $2 - 4 + 2 = 0$ ✓

   Yes, the point *is* on the graph.

9. $y = -2x + 3$

x	-1	0	1	$\frac{3}{2}$	2
y	5	3	1	0	-1

11. $y = x^2 - 2x$

x	-1	0	1	2	3
y	3	0	-1	0	3

13. $y = \frac{1}{4}x - 3$

x	-2	-1	0	1	2
y	$-\frac{7}{2}$	$-\frac{13}{4}$	-3	$-\frac{11}{4}$	$-\frac{5}{2}$

15. $y = \sqrt{x - 1}$

x	1	2	5	10	17
y	0	1	2	3	4

17. $y = -\frac{1}{4}x - 3$

x	-2	-1	0	1	2
y	$-\frac{5}{2}$	$-\frac{11}{4}$	-3	$-\frac{13}{4}$	$-\frac{7}{2}$

19.

$y = x - 5$

Intercepts: $(5, 0)$, $(0, -5)$

21.

$y = x^2 + x - 2$

Intercepts: $(1, 0)$, $(-2, 0)$, $(0, -2)$

23.

$y = x\sqrt{x + 6}$

Intercepts: $(0, 0)$, $(-6, 0)$

25.

$$y = \frac{2x}{x - 1}$$

Intercept: $(0, 0)$

27. $y = 1 - x$ has intercepts $(1, 0)$ and $(0, 1)$.

Matches graph (d).

29. $y = \sqrt{9 - x^2}$ has intercepts $(\pm 3, 0)$ and $(0, 3)$. Matches graph (f).

31. $y = x^3 - x + 1$ has a y-intercept of $(0, 1)$ and the points $(1, 1)$ and $(-2, -5)$ are on the graph. Matches (a).

33. $y = -3x + 2$

35. $y = 1 - x^2$

37. $y = x^2 - 3x$

39. $y = x^3 + 2$

41. $y = \sqrt{x - 3}$

43. $y = |x - 2|$

45. $x = y^2 - 1$

47. $y = 3 - \frac{1}{2}x$

Intercepts: (6,0), (0, 3)

49. $y = x^2 - 4x + 3$

Intercepts: (3, 0), (1, 0), (0, 3)

51. $y = x(x - 2)^2$

Intercepts: (0, 0), (2, 0)

53. $y = \sqrt[3]{x}$

Intercepts: (0, 0)

55. $y = \frac{5}{2}x + 5$

Both settings show
the line and its intercept.
The first setting is better.

57. $-x^2 + 10x - 5$

Both settings show
the line and its
intercept. The second
setting is better.

59. $y = 4x^2 - 25$

Range/Window

Xmin=-5
Xmax=5
Xscl=1
Ymin=-30
Ymax=10
Yscl=5

61. $y = |x| + |x - 10|$

Range/Window

Xmin=-30
Xmax=30
Xscl=5
Ymin=-10
Ymax=50
Yscl=5

63. $y = 0.25x - 50$

The first graph shows a sharper increase.

65. $x^2 + y^2 = 64$

$$y^2 = 64 - x^2$$
$$y = \pm\sqrt{64 - x^2}$$

Use: $y_1 = \sqrt{64 - x^2}$
$$y_2 = -\sqrt{64 - x^2}$$

67. $x^2 + y^2 = 49$

$$y^2 = 49 - x^2$$
$$y = \pm\sqrt{49 - x^2}$$

Use: $y_1 = \sqrt{49 - x^2}$
$$y_2 = -\sqrt{49 - x^2}$$

69. $y_1 = \frac{1}{4}(x^2 - 8)$

$$y_2 = \frac{1}{4}x^2 - 2$$

The graphs are identical.
The Distributive Property is illustrated.

71. $y_1 = \frac{1}{5}[10(x^2 - 1)]$

$$y_2 = 2(x^2 - 1)$$

The graphs are identical.
The Associative Property of Multiplication is illustrated.

73. $y = 225{,}000 - 20{,}000t, \ 0 \le t \le 8$

(a) Range/Window

Xmin=-1
Xmax=9
Xscl=1
Ymin=-60000
Ymax=230000
Yscl=10000

(b)

75. Most likely you would need to change the viewing window. For example, let $y_1 = x^2 + 12$. This graph would not show up on the standard window. Change the range/window to the following setting and try again.

```
Xmin=-5
Xmax=5
Xscl=1
Ymin=-5
Ymax=40
Yscl=5
```

77. (a)

Year	1920	1930	1940	1950	1960	1970	1980	1990
Life Expectancy	54.1	59.7	62.9	68.2	69.7	70.8	73.7	75.4
Model	52.8	58.7	63.3	66.9	69.9	72.4	74.6	76.4

(b) When $t = 48$, $y \approx 77.7$ years.

(c) When $t = 50$, $y \approx 78.0$ years.

79. (a) $y = 0.086t + 0.872, \ 0 \le t \le 4$

Year	1990	1991	1992	1993	1994
t	0	1	2	3	4
y	0.872	0.958	1.044	1.130	1.216

81. $y = \sqrt{5 - x}$

(a) $(2, y) \approx (2, 1.73)$

(b) $(x, 3) = (-4, 3)$

83. $y = x^5 - 5x$

(a) $(-0.5, y) \approx (-0.5, 2.47)$

(b) $(x, -4) = (1, -4)$ or $(x, -4) \approx (-1.65, -4)$

85. $9x^5 + 4x^3 - 7$

Terms: $9x^5, 4x^3, -7$

87. False. $(3 + 4)^2 = 7^2 = 49$

$3^2 + 4^2 = 9 + 16 = 25$

Section 1.2   Lines in the Plane

You should know the following important facts about lines.

■   The graph of $y = mx + b$ is a straight line. It is called a linear equation.

■   The slope of the line through (x_1, y_1) and (x_2, y_2) is

$$m = \frac{y_2 - y_1}{x_2 - x_1}.$$

■   (a) If $m > 0$, the line rises from left to right.

   (b) If $m = 0$, the line is horizontal.

   (c) If $m < 0$, the line falls from left to right.

   (d) If m is undefined, the line is vertical.

■   Equations of Lines

   (a) Slope-Intercept: $y = mx + b$

   (b) Point-Slope: $y - y_1 = m(x - x_1)$

   (c) Two-Point: $y - y_1 = \dfrac{y_2 - y_1}{x_2 - x_1}(x - x_1)$

   (d) General: $Ax + By + C = 0$

   (e) Vertical: $x = a$

   (f) Horizontal: $y = b$

■   Given two distinct nonvertical lines

$$L_1: y = m_1 x + b_1 \quad \text{and} \quad L_2: y = m_2 x + b_2$$

   (a) L_1 is parallel to L_2 if and only if $m_1 = m_2$ and $b_1 \neq b_2$.

   (b) L_1 is perpendicular to L_2 if and only if $m_1 = -1/m_2$.

Solutions to Odd-Numbered Exercises

1. (a) $m = \frac{2}{3}$. Since the slope is positive, the line rises. Matches L_2.

   (b) m is undefined. The line is vertical. Matches L_3.

   (c) $m = -2$. The line falls. Matches L_1.

3. Slope $= \dfrac{\text{rise}}{\text{run}} = \dfrac{8}{5}$

5. Slope $= \dfrac{\text{rise}}{\text{run}} = \dfrac{0}{1} = 0$

7. Slope $= \dfrac{\text{rise}}{\text{run}} = \dfrac{-8}{2} = -4$

9.

11.

$$\text{Slope} = \frac{6+2}{1+3} = 2$$

13.

Slope is undefined.

15.

$$\text{Slope} = \frac{2+2}{1+2} = \frac{4}{3}$$

17. Since $m = 0$, y does not change. Three points are $(0, 1)$, $(3, 1)$, and $(-1, 1)$.

19. Since $m = 1$, y increases by 1 for every one unit increase in x. Three points are $(6, -5)$, $(7, -4)$, and $(8, -3)$.

21. Since m is undefined, x does not change. Three points are $(-8, 0)$, $(-8, 2)$, and $(-8, 3)$.

23. $m_{L_1} = \dfrac{9+1}{5-0} = 2$

$m_{L_2} = \dfrac{1-3}{4-0} = -\dfrac{1}{2} = -\dfrac{1}{m_{L_1}}$

L_1 and L_2 are perpendicular.

25. $m_{L_1} = \dfrac{0-6}{-6-3} = \dfrac{2}{3}$

$m_{L_2} = \dfrac{\frac{7}{3}+1}{5-0} = \dfrac{2}{3} = m_{L_1}$

L_1 and L_2 are parallel.

27. Yes, any pair of points on a line can be used to calculate the slope of the line. The rate of change remains the same on a line.

29. (a) $m = 135$. The sales are increasing 135 units per year.

(b) $m = 0$. There is no change in sales.

(c) $m = -40$. The sales are decreasing 40 units per year.

31. (a)

(b) Decreased most rapidly in 1989
  Increased most rapidly in 1988.·

33. $y = 0.5x - 3$

The second setting shows the x and y intercepts more clearly.

35. $5x - y + 3 = 0$

$\qquad y = 5x + 3$

Slope: $m = 5$

y-intercept: $(0, 3)$

37. $5x - 2 = 0$

$x = \frac{2}{5}$

Slope: undefined

No y-intercept

39. $7x + 6y - 30 = 0$

$y = -\frac{7}{6}x + 5$

Slope: $m = -\frac{7}{6}$

y-intercept: $(0, 5)$

41. $y + 1 = \dfrac{5 + 1}{-5 - 5}(x - 5)$

$y = -\dfrac{3}{5}(x - 5) - 1$

$y = -\dfrac{3}{5}x + 2 \implies 3x + 5y - 10 = 0$

43. $y - \dfrac{1}{2} = \dfrac{\frac{5}{4} - \frac{1}{2}}{\frac{1}{2} - 2}(x - 2)$

$y = -\dfrac{1}{2}(x - 2) + \dfrac{1}{2}$

$y = -\dfrac{1}{2}x + \dfrac{3}{2} \implies x + 2y - 3 = 0$

45. Since both points have $x = -8$, the slope is undefined.

$x = -8 \implies x + 8 = 0$

47. $y - 0.6 = \dfrac{-0.6 - 0.6}{-2 - 1}(x - 1)$

$y = 0.4(x - 1) + 0.6$

$y = 0.4x + 0.2 \implies 2x - 5y + 1 = 0$

49. Slope $= \dfrac{\text{rise}}{\text{run}}$

$-\dfrac{12}{100} = -\dfrac{2000}{y}$

$-12y = -200,000$

$y = 16,666\frac{2}{3}$ feet ≈ 3.16 miles

51. $y + 2 = 3(x - 0)$

$\quad y = 3x - 2 \implies 3x - y - 2 = 0$

53. $y - 6 = -2(x + 3)$

$\quad y = -2x \implies 2x + y = 0$

55. $y - 0 = -\frac{1}{3}(x - 4)$

$\quad y = -\frac{1}{3}x + \frac{4}{3} \implies x + 3y - 4 = 0$

57. $\quad x = 6$

$x - 6 = 0$

59. $y - \dfrac{5}{2} = \dfrac{4}{3}(x - 4) \implies 8x - 6y - 17 = 0$

61. $\quad \dfrac{x}{5} + \dfrac{y}{-3} = 1$

$-3x + 5y + 15 = 0$

$a = 5$ and $b = -3$ are the x- and y-intercepts.

63. $\quad \dfrac{x}{2} + \dfrac{y}{3} = 1$

$3x + 2y - 6 = 0$

65. $4x - 2y = 3$

$\quad\quad y = 2x - \dfrac{3}{2}$

Slope: $m = 2$

(a) $y - 1 = 2(x - 2)$

$\quad\quad y = 2x - 3 \implies 2x - y - 3 = 0$

(b) $y - 1 = -\dfrac{1}{2}(x - 2)$

$\quad\quad y = -\dfrac{1}{2}x + 2 \implies x + 2y - 4 = 0$

67. $y = -3$

slope: $m = 0$

(a) $y = 0$

(b) $x = -1 \implies x + 1 = 0$

69. $L_1: y = 2x \qquad L_2: y = -2x \qquad L_3: y = \frac{1}{2}x$

L_2 and L_3 are perpendicular.

71. $L_1: y = -\frac{1}{2}x$

$L_2: y = -\frac{1}{2}x + 3$

$L_3: y = 2x - 4$

L_1 and L_2 are parallel.

L_3 is perpendicular to L_1 and L_2.

73. $(6, 2540)$, $m = 125$

$V - 2540 = 125(t - 6)$

$V - 2540 = 125t - 750$

$V = 125t + 1790$

75. $(6, 20400)$, $m = -2000$

$V - 20400 = -2000(t - 6)$

$V - 20400 = -2000t + 12000$

$V = -2000t + 32400$

77. The slope is $m = -10$. This represents the decrease in the amount of the loan each week. Matches graph (b).

79. The slope is $m = 0.25$. This represents the increase in travel cost for each mile driven. Matches graph (a).

81. Set the distance between $(4, -1)$ and (x, y) equal to the distance between $(-2, 3)$ and (x, y).

$$\sqrt{(x - 4)^2 + [y - (-1)]^2} = \sqrt{[x - (-2)]^2 + (y - 3)^2}$$

$$(x - 4)^2 + (y + 1)^2 = (x + 2)^2 + (y - 3)^2$$

$$x^2 - 8x + 16 + y^2 + 2y + 1 = x^2 + 4x + 4 + y^2 - 6y + 9$$

$$-8x + 2y + 17 = 4x - 6y + 13$$

$$0 = 12x - 8y - 4$$

$$0 = 4(3x - 2y - 1)$$

$$0 = 3x - 2y - 1$$

This line is the perpendicular bisector of the line segment connecting $(4, -1)$ and $(-2, 3)$.

83. Using the points $(0, 32)$ and $(100, 212)$, we have

$$m = \frac{212 - 32}{100 - 0} = \frac{180}{100} = \frac{9}{5}$$

$$F - 32 = \frac{9}{5}(C - 0)$$

$$F = \frac{9}{5}C + 32.$$

85. Using the points (1994, 28,500) and (1996, 32,900), we have:

$$m = \frac{32900 - 28500}{1996 - 1994} = \frac{4400}{2} = 2200$$

$$S - 28500 = 2200(t - 1994)$$

$$S = 2200t - 4,385,300$$

When $t = 2000$ we have $S = 2200(2000) - 4,360,500$ or $41,700.

87. (a) Using the points (0, 875) and (5, 0), where the first coordinate represents the year t and the second coordinate represents the value V, we have

$$m = \frac{0 - 875}{5 - 0} = -175$$

$$V = -175t + 875, \ 0 \le t \le 5.$$

(b)

(c)

t	0	1	2	3	4	5
V	875	700	525	350	175	0

89. Sale price = List price − 15% of the list price

$$S = L - 0.15L$$

$$S = 0.85L$$

91. (a) $C = 36,500 + 5.25t + 11.50t$

$\qquad = 16.75t + 36,500$

(b) $R = 27t$

(c) $P = R - C$

$\qquad = 27t - (16.75t + 36,500)$

$\qquad = 10.25t - 36,500$

(d) $\quad 0 = 10.25t - 36,500$

$\quad 36,500 = 10.25t$

$\qquad\quad t \approx 3561$ hours

93. (a) Using the regression capabilities of a graphing utility, you obtain $y = 71.08t - 10.29$.

(c) For $t = 20$ (year 2000), $y \approx 1,411,000$.

(b)

(d) The slope is the average increase per year.

95. (a) $x = 50 - \dfrac{p - 580}{15}$. Note that when $p = 580$, $x = 50$ and when $p = 625$, $x = 47$.

(b)

(c) If $p = 595$, $x = 49$.

If $p = 655$, $x = 45$.

Section 1.3   Functions

■ Given a set or an equation, you should be able to determine if it represents a function.

■ Given a function, you should be able to do the following.

(a) Find the domain.

(b) Evaluate it at specific values.

Solutions to Odd-Numbered Exercises

1. Yes, it does represent a function. Each domain value is matched with only one range value.

3. No, it does not represent a function. The domain values are each matched with three range values.

5. Yes, it does represent a function. Each input value is matched with only one output value.

7. No, it does not represent a function. The input values of 10 and 7 are each matched with two output values.

9. (a) Each element of A is matched with exactly one element of B, so it does represent a function.

(b) The element 1 in A is matched with two elements, -2 and 1 of B, so it does not represent a function.

(c) Each element of A is matched with exactly one element of B, so it does represent a function.

11. Each are functions. For each year there corresponds one and only one circulation.

13. $x^2 + y^2 = 4 \implies y = \pm\sqrt{4 - x^2}$

Thus, y *is not* a function of x. For instance, the values $y = 2$ and -2 both correspond to $x = 0$.

15. $x^2 + y = 4 \implies y = 4 - x^2$

Thus, y *is* a function of x.

17. $2x + 3y = 4 \implies y = \frac{1}{3}(4 - 2x)$

Thus, y *is* a function of x.

19. $y^2 = x^2 - 1 \implies y = \pm\sqrt{x^2 - 1}$

Thus, y *is not* a function of x. For instance, the values $y = \sqrt{3}$ and $-\sqrt{3}$ both correspond to $x = 2$.

21. $y = |4 - x|$

This is a function of x.

23. $f(s) = \dfrac{1}{s + 1}$

   (a) $f(4) = \dfrac{1}{(4) + 1} = \dfrac{1}{5}$

   (b) $f(0) = \dfrac{1}{(0) + 1} = 1$

   (c) $f(4x) = \dfrac{1}{(4x) + 1} = \dfrac{1}{4x + 1}$

   (d) $f(x + c) = \dfrac{1}{(x + c) + 1} = \dfrac{1}{x + c + 1}$

25. $f(x) = 2x - 3$

   (a) $f(1) = 2(1) - 3 = -1$

   (b) $f(-3) = 2(-3) - 3 = -9$

   (c) $f(x - 1) = 2(x - 1) - 3 = 2x - 5$

27. $h(t) = t^2 - 2t$

   (a) $h(2) = 2^2 - 2(2) = 0$

   (b) $h(1.5) = (1.5)^2 - 2(1.5) = -0.75$

   (c) $h(x + 2) = (x + 2)^2 - 2(x + 2) = x^2 + 2x$

29. $f(y) = 3 - \sqrt{y}$

   (a) $f(4) = 3 - \sqrt{4} = 1$

   (b) $f(0.25) = 3 - \sqrt{0.25} = 2.5$

   (c) $f(4x^2) = 3 - \sqrt{4x^2} = 3 - 2|x|$

31. $q(x) = \dfrac{1}{x^2 - 9}$

   (a) $q(0) = \dfrac{1}{0^2 - 9} = -\dfrac{1}{9}$

   (b) $q(3) = \dfrac{1}{3^2 - 9}$ is undefined.

   (c) $q(y + 3) = \dfrac{1}{(y + 3)^2 - 9} = \dfrac{1}{y^2 + 6y}$

33. $f(x) = \dfrac{|x|}{x}$

   (a) $f(2) = \dfrac{|2|}{2} = 1$

   (b) $f(-2) = \dfrac{|-2|}{-2} = -1$

   (c) $f(x - 1) = \dfrac{|x - 1|}{x - 1}$

35. $f(x) = \begin{cases} 2x + 1, & x < 0 \\ 2x + 2, & x \geq 0 \end{cases}$

   (a) $f(-1) = 2(-1) + 1 = -1$

   (b) $f(0) = 2(0) + 2 = 2$

   (c) $f(2) = 2(2) + 2 = 6$

37. $f(x) = x^2 - 3$

x	-2	-1	0	1	2
$f(x)$	1	-2	-3	-2	1

39. $h(t) = \frac{1}{2}|t + 3|$

t	-5	-4	-3	-2	-1
$h(t)$	1	$\frac{1}{2}$	0	$\frac{1}{2}$	1

41. $f(x) = \begin{cases} -\frac{1}{2}x + 4, & x \leq 0 \\ (x - 2)^2, & x > 0 \end{cases}$

x	-2	-1	0	1	2
$f(x)$	5	$\frac{9}{2}$	4	1	0

43. $15 - 3x = 0$

   $3x = 15$

   $x = 5$

45. $x^2 - 9 = 0$

   $x^2 = 9$

   $x = \pm 3$

47.
$$f(x) = g(x)$$
$$x^2 = x + 2$$
$$x^2 - x - 2 = 0$$
$$(x + 1)(x - 2) = 0$$
$$x = -1 \ \text{ or } \ x = 2$$

49.
$$f(x) = g(x)$$
$$\sqrt{3x} + 1 = x + 1$$
$$\sqrt{3x} = x$$
$$3x = x^2$$
$$0 = x^2 - 3x$$
$$0 = x(x - 3)$$
$$x = 0 \ \text{ or } \ x = 3$$

51. $f(x) = 5x^2 + 2x - 1$

Since $f(x)$ is a polynomial, the domain is all real numbers x.

53. $h(t) = \dfrac{4}{t}$

Domain: All real numbers except $t = 0$

55. $g(y) = \sqrt{y - 10}$

Domain: $y - 10 \geq 0$
$$y \geq 10$$

57. $f(x) = \sqrt[4]{1 - x^2}$

Domain: $1 - x^2 \geq 0$
$$-x^2 \geq -1$$
$$x^2 \leq 1$$
$$x^2 - 1 \leq 0$$
$$-1 \leq x \leq 1$$

59. $g(x) = \dfrac{1}{x} - \dfrac{1}{x + 2}$

Domain: All real numbers except
$x = 0, \ x = -2$.

61. $f(x) = x^2$

$$\{(-2, 4), (-1, 1), (0, 0), (1, 1), (2, 4)\}$$

63. $f(x) = \sqrt{x + 2}$

$$\{(-2, 0), (-1, 1), \left(0, \sqrt{2}\right), \left(1, \sqrt{3}\right), (2, 2)\}$$

65. The domain is the set of inputs of the function and the range is the set of corresponding outputs.

67. By plotting the points, we have a parabola, so $g(x) = cx^2$. Since $(-4, -32)$ is on the graph, we have $-32 = c(-4)^2 \implies c = -2$. Thus, $g(x) = -2x^2$.

69. Since the function is undefined at 0, we have $r(x) = \dfrac{c}{x}$. Since $(-8, -4)$ is on the graph, we have

$$-4 = \dfrac{c}{-8} \implies c = 32. \text{ Thus, } r(x) = \dfrac{32}{x}.$$

71.
$$f(x) = x^2 - x + 1$$
$$f(2 + h) = (2 + h)^2 - (2 + h) + 1$$
$$= 4 + 4h + h^2 - 2 - h + 1$$
$$= h^2 + 3h + 3$$
$$f(2) = (2)^2 - 2 + 1 = 3$$
$$f(2 + h) - f(2) = h^2 + 3h$$
$$\frac{f(2 + h) - f(2)}{h} = h + 3, \ h \neq 0$$

73. $f(x) = x^3$
$$f(x + c) = (x + c)^3 = x^3 + 3x^2 c + 3xc^2 + c^3$$
$$\frac{f(x + c) - f(x)}{c} = \frac{(x^3 + 3x^2 c + 3xc^2 + c^3) - x^3}{c}$$
$$= \frac{c(3x^2 + 3xc + c^2)}{c}$$
$$= 3x^2 + 3xc + c^2, \ c \neq 0$$

75. $g(x) = 3x - 1$
$$\frac{g(x) - g(3)}{x - 3} = \frac{(3x - 1) - 8}{x - 3} = \frac{3x - 9}{x - 3} = \frac{3(x - 3)}{x - 3} = 3, \ x \neq 3$$

77. $A = \pi r^2, \ C = 2\pi r$
$$r = \frac{C}{2\pi}$$
$$A = \pi \left(\frac{C}{2\pi}\right)^2 = \frac{C^2}{4\pi}$$

79. (a)

Height, x	Width	Volume, V
1	$24 - 2(1)$	$1[24 - 2(1)]^2 = 484$
2	$24 - 2(2)$	$2[24 - 2(2)]^2 = 800$
3	$24 - 2(3)$	$3[24 - 2(3)]^2 = 972$
4	$24 - 2(4)$	$4[24 - 2(4)]^2 = 1024$
5	$24 - 2(5)$	$5[24 - 2(5)]^2 = 980$
6	$24 - 2(6)$	$6[24 - 2(6)]^2 = 864$

The volume is maximum when $x = 4$.

(b)

$$V = x(24 - 2x)^2$$

Domain: $0 < x < 12$

V is a function of x.

81. $A = \dfrac{1}{2}bh = \dfrac{1}{2}xy$

Since $(0, y)$, $(1, 2)$, and $(x, 0)$ all lie on the same line, the slopes between any pair are equal.

$$\frac{1 - y}{2 - 0} = \frac{0 - 1}{x - 2}$$

$$1 - y = -\frac{2}{x - 2}$$

$$y = \frac{2}{x - 2} + 1$$

$$y = \frac{x}{x - 2}$$

Therefore,

$$A = \frac{1}{2}x\left(\frac{x}{x - 2}\right) = \frac{x^2}{2(x - 2)}.$$

The domain of A includes x-values such that $2x^2/[2(x - 2)] > 0$. Solving this inequality we find that the domain is $x > 2$.

83. $V = l \cdot w \cdot h = x \cdot y \cdot x = x^2y$ where $4x + y = 108$.

Thus, $y = 108 - 4x$ and $V = x^2(108 - 4x) = 108x^2 - 4x^3$ where $0 < x < 27$.

85.   (a) Cost = variable costs + fixed costs

$C = 12.30x + 98,000$

(b) Revenue = price per unit × number of units

$R = 17.98x$

(c) Profit = Revenue − Cost

$P = 17.98x - (12.30x + 98,000)$

$P = 5.68x - 98,000$

87.   (a) $f(1992) = 28$

(b) $\dfrac{f(1994) - f(1991)}{1994 - 1991} = \dfrac{9 - 60}{3} = \dfrac{-51}{3} = -17$

This is the average decrease per year in the population.

(c)

t	1988	1989	1990	1991	1992	1993	1994	1995
N	9.0	19.8	43.9	53.6	30.9	16.7	10.2	6.9
actual number	10	16	50	60	28	15	9	8

Section 1.4   Graphs of Functions

- You should be able to determine the domain and range of a function from its graph.
- You should be able to use the vertical line test for functions.
- You should be able to determine when a function is constant, increasing, or decreasing.
- You should be able to find relative maximum and minimum values of a function.
- You should know that f is
  - (a) Odd if $f(-x) = -f(x)$.
  - (b) Even if $f(-x) = f(x)$.

Solutions to Odd-Numbered Exercises

1. $f(x) = \sqrt{x^2 - 1}$

Domain: $(-\infty, -1] \cup [1, \infty)$

Range: $[0, \infty)$

3. $h(x) = \sqrt{16 - x^2}$

Domain: $[-4, 4]$

Range: $[0, 4]$

5. $g(x) = 1 - x^2$

Domain: All real numbers

Range: $(-\infty, 1]$

7. $f(x) = |x + 3|$

Domain: All real numbers

Range: $[0, \infty)$

9. $y = \frac{1}{2}x^2$

A vertical line intersects the graph just once, so y is a function of x.

11. $x - y^2 = 1 \implies y = \pm\sqrt{x - 1}$

y is not a function of x. Graph $y_1 = \sqrt{x - 1}$ and $y_2 = -\sqrt{x - 1}$.

13. $x^2 = 2xy - 1$

A vertical line intersects the graph just once, so y is a function of x. Solve for y and graph

$$y = \frac{x^2 + 1}{2x}.$$

15. $f(x) = -0.2x^2 + 3x + 32$

The second setting shows the most complete graph.

17. $f(x) = 4x^3 - x^4$

The first setting shows the most complete graph.

19. $f(x) = \frac{3}{2}x$

   (a) f is increasing on $(-\infty, \infty)$.

   (b) Since $f(-x) = -f(x)$, f is odd.

21. $f(x) = x^3 - 3x^2 + 2$

   (a) f is increasing on $(-\infty, 0)$ and $(2, \infty)$.

     f is decreasing on $(0, 2)$.

   (b) $f(-x) \neq -f(x)$

       $f(-x) \neq f(x)$

     f is neither odd nor even.

23. Yes, for every value of y there corresponds exactly one value of x.

25. $f(x) = 3x^4 - 6x^2$

   (a)

   (b) Increasing on $(-1, 0)$ and $(1, \infty)$

     Decreasing on $(-\infty, -1)$ and $(0, 1)$

   (c) Since $f(-x) = f(x)$, f is even.

27. $f(x) = x\sqrt{x + 3}$

   (a)

   (b) Increasing on $(-2, \infty)$

     Decreasing on $(-3, -2)$

   (c) $f(-x) \neq -f(x)$

       $f(-x) \neq f(x)$

     f is neither odd nor even.

29. $f(-x) = (-x)^6 - 2(-x)^2 + 3$

          $= x^6 - 2x^2 + 3$

          $= f(x)$

   f is even.

31. $g(-x) = (-x)^3 - 5(-x)$

          $= -x^3 + 5x$

          $= -g(x)$

   g is odd.

33. $f(-t) = (-t)^2 + 2(-t) - 3$

          $= t^2 - 2t - 3$

          $\neq f(t) \neq -f(t)$

   f is neither even nor odd.

35. $\left(-\frac{3}{2}, 4\right)$

   (a) If f is even, another point is $\left(\frac{3}{2}, 4\right)$.

   (b) If f is odd, another point is $\left(\frac{3}{2}, -4\right)$.

37. $f(x) = 3$, even

39. $f(x) = 5 - 3x$, neither even nor odd

41. $f(x) = \sqrt{1 - x}$, neither even nor odd

43. $g(t) = \sqrt[3]{t - 1}$, neither even nor odd

45. $f(x) = \begin{cases} x + 3, & x \leq 0 \\ 3, & 0 < x \leq 2, \\ 2x - 1, & x > 2 \end{cases}$

Neither even nor odd

47. $f(x) = \begin{cases} 2x + 3, & x < 0 \\ 3 - x, & x \geq 0 \end{cases}$

49. $f(x) = \begin{cases} x^2 + 5, & x \leq 1 \\ -x^2 + 4x + 3, & x > 1 \end{cases}$

51. $f(x) = x^2 - 6x$

Relative minimum: $(3, -9)$

53. $y = 2x^3 + 3x^2 - 12x$

Relative minimum: $(1, -7)$

Relative maximum: $(-2, 20)$

55. $h(x) = (x - 1)\sqrt{x}$

Relative minimum: $(0.33, -0.38)$

((0, 0) is not a relative maximum because it occurs at the endpoint of the domain $[0, \infty)$.)

57. (a) Let x and y be the length and width
  of the rectangle. The $100 = 2x + 2y$ or
  $y = 50 - x$. Thus, the area is

  $A = xy = x(50 - x)$.

(c) The maximum area is 625 m² when
  $x = y = 25$ cm. That is, the rectangle
  is a square.

(b)

59. $s(x) = 2\left(\frac{1}{4}x - \left[\!\left[\frac{1}{4}x\right]\!\right]\right)$

Domain: $(-\infty, \infty)$

Range: $[0, 2)$

Sawtooth pattern

61. (a) $C_2(t) = 0.65 - 0.4\left[\!\left[-(t - 1)\right]\!\right]$ is the appropriate model since the cost does not increase until after the next
  minute of conversation has started.

(b)

The cost of an 18-minute 45 second call is

$C = 0.65 - 0.4[[-(18 - 1)]] = 0.65 + 0.4(18)$

$= \$7.85.$

63. $f(x) = 4 - x \ge 0$

  $4 \ge x$

$(-\infty, 4]$

65. $f(x) = x^2 - 9 \ge 0$

  $x^2 \ge 9$

  $x \ge 3$ or $x \le -3$

  $[3, \infty)$ or $(-\infty, -3]$

67. $f(x) = 1 - x^4 \geq 0$

$\qquad\qquad 1 \geq x^4$

$\qquad\qquad -1 \leq x \leq 1$

$[-1, 1]$

69. $f(x) = x^2 + 1 \geq 0$

All x

$(-\infty, \infty)$

71. $h = $ top $-$ bottom

$\quad = (-x^2 + 4x - 1) - 2$

$\quad = -x^2 + 4x - 3$

73. $h = $ top $-$ bottom

$\quad = (4x - x^2) - 2x$

$\quad = 2x - x^2$

75. $L = $ right $-$ left

$\quad = \frac{1}{2}y^2 - 0$

$\quad = \frac{1}{2}y^2$

77. $y = -87.49 + 16.28t - 4.82t^2 - 1.17t^3$

(a) Domain: $-4 \leq t \leq 3$

(b)

(c) Most accurate in 1992

Least accurate in 1990

(d) The balance would continue to decrease.

79. $f(x) = a_{2n+1}x^{2n+1} + a_{2n-1}x^{2n-1} + \cdots + a_3x^3 + a_1x$

$f(-x) = a_{2n+1}(-x)^{2n+1} + a_{2n-1}(-x)^{2n-1} + \cdots + a_3(-x)^3 + a_1(-x)$

$\qquad = -a_{2n+1}x^{2n+1} - a_{2n-1}x^{2n-1} - \cdots - a_3x^3 - a_1x = -f(x)$

Therefore, $f(x)$ is odd.

Section 1.5   Shifting, Reflecting, and Stretching Graphs

■ You should know the graphs of the most commonly used functions in algebra, and be able to reproduce them on your graphing utility.

(a) Constant function: $f(x) = c$ ⌐

(b) Identity function: $f(x) = x$ ╱

(c) Absolute value function: $f(x) = |x|$ ⋁

(d) Square root function: $f(x) = \sqrt{x}$

(e) Squaring function: $f(x) = x^2$ ⋃

(f) Cubing function: $f(x) = x^3$

■ You should know how the graph of a function is changed by vertical and horizontal shifts.

■ You should know how the graph of a function is changed by reflection.

■ You should know how the graph of a function is changed by nonrigid transformations, like stretches and shrinks.

■ You should know how the graph of a function is changed by a sequence of transformations.

Solutions to Odd-Numbered Exercises

1.

3.

5.

7.

9.

11. (a) $y = f(x) + 2$ (b) $y = -f(x)$ (c) $y = f(x - 2)$

(d) $y = f(x + 3)$ (e) $y = f(2x)$ (f) $y = f(-x)$

13. Horizontal shift two units to the right of $y = x^3$

$$y = (x - 2)^3$$

15. Reflection in the x-axis of $y = x^2$

$$y = -x^2$$

17. Reflection in the x-axis and a vertical shift one unit upward of $y = \sqrt{x}$

19. Vertical shift one unit downward of $y = x^2$
$$y = x^2 - 1$$

21. Reflection in the x-axis and a vertical shift one unit upward

$$y = 1 - x^3$$

23. Vertical shift three units upward of $y = x$

25. $y = \sqrt{x} + 2$ is $f(x)$ shifted up two units.

27. $y = \sqrt{x - 2}$ is $f(x)$ shifted right two units.

29. $y = \sqrt{2x}$ is a vertical stretch of $f(x)$ by $\sqrt{2}$.

31. $y = |x + 2|$ is $f(x)$ shifted left two units.

33. $y = -|x|$ is $f(x)$ reflected in the x-axis.

35. $y = \frac{1}{3}|x|$ is a vertical shrink of $f(x)$.

37. $f(x) = x^3 - 3x^2$

$g(x) = f(x + 2) = (x + 2)^3 - 3(x + 2)^2$ horizontal shift 2 units to the left

$h(x) = f\left(\frac{1}{2}x\right) = f\left(\frac{1}{2}x\right)^3 - 3\left(\frac{1}{2}x\right)^2$ stretch horizontally by factor of 2

39. $f(x) = x^3 - 3x^2$

$g(x) = -\frac{1}{3}f(x) = -\frac{1}{3}(x^3 - 3x^2)$ reflection in the x-axis and vertical shrink

$h(x) = f(-x) = (-x)^3 - 3(-x)^2$ reflection in the y-axis

41. $g(x) = 4 - x^3$ is obtained from $f(x)$ by a reflection in the x-axis followed by a vertical shift upward of four units.

43. $h(x) = \frac{1}{4}(x + 2)^3$ is obtained from $f(x)$ by a left shift of two units and a vertical shrink by a factor of $\frac{1}{4}$.

45. $p(x) = \left(\frac{1}{3}x\right)^3 + 2$ is obtained from $f(x)$ by a horizontal stretch, followed by a vertical shift of two units upward.

47. The graph of g is obtained from that of f by first negating f, and then shifting vertically one unit upward:
$g(x) = -x^3 + 3x^2 + 1$.

49. (a) $P(x) = 80 + 20x - 0.5x^2, 0 \le x \le 20$

(b) $P(x)$ is shifted downward by a vertical shift of -2500.

$P(x) = -2420 + 20x - 0.5x^2, 0 \le x \le 20$

(c) $P(x)$ is changed by a *horizontal stretch.*

$$P(x) = 80 + 20\left(\frac{x}{100}\right) - 0.5\left(\frac{x}{100}\right)^2$$

$$= 80 + 0.2x - 0.00005x^2 \text{ or } 80 + \frac{1}{5}x - \frac{x^2}{20{,}000}$$

51. (a)

(b)

(c)

(d)

(e)

(f)

All the graphs pass through the origin. The graphs of the odd powers of x are symmetric to the origin and the graphs of the even powers are symmetric to the y-axis. As the powers increase, the graphs become flatter in the interval $-1 < x < 1$.

53.

The graph of $y = (x - 3)^3$ is a horizontal shift of $f(x) = x^3$.

55. $f(x) = x^2(x - 6)^2$

57. $f(x) = x^2(x - 6)^3$

59. (a) For each time t there corresponds one and only one temperature T.

(b) $T(4) \approx 60°, \ T(15) \approx 72°$

(c) All the temperature changes would be one hour later.

(d) The temperature would be decreased by one degree.

61. $f(x - 4)$

63. $f(x + 4)$

65. $2f(x)$

Section 1.6   Combinations of Functions

■ Given two functions, f and g, you should be able to form the following functions (if defined):

1. Sum: $(f + g)(x) = f(x) + g(x)$

2. Difference: $(f - g)(x) = f(x) - g(x)$

3. Product: $(fg)(x) = f(x)g(x)$

4. Quotient: $(f/g)(x) = f(x)/g(x), \ g(x) \neq 0$

5. Composition of f with g: $(f \circ g)(x) = f(g(x))$

6. Composition of g with f: $(g \circ f)(x) = g(f(x))$

Solutions to Odd-Numbered Exercises

1.

3.

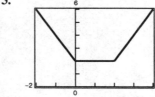

5. $f(x) = x + 1, g(x) = x - 1$

$(f + g)(x) = f(x) + g(x) = (x + 1) + (x - 1) = 2x$

$(f - g)(x) = f(x) - g(x) = (x + 1) - (x - 1) = 2$

$(fg)(x) = f(x) \cdot g(x) = (x + 1)(x - 1) = x^2 - 1$

$\left(\dfrac{f}{g}\right)(x) = \dfrac{f(x)}{g(x)} = \dfrac{x + 1}{x - 1}, \ x \neq 1$

7. $f(x) = x^2, g(x) = 1 - x$

$(f + g)(x) = f(x) + g(x) = x^2 + (1 - x) = x^2 - x + 1$

$(f - g)(x) = f(x) - g(x) = x^2 - (1 - x) = x^2 + x - 1$

$(fg)(x) = f(x) \cdot g(x) = x^2(1 - x) = x^2 - x^3$

$\left(\dfrac{f}{g}\right)(x) = \dfrac{f(x)}{g(x)} = \dfrac{x^2}{1 - x}, x \neq 1$

9. $f(x) = x^2 + 5, g(x) = \sqrt{1 - x}$

$(f + g)(x) = f(x) + g(x) = (x^2 + 5) + \sqrt{1 - x}$

$(f - g)(x) = f(x) - g(x) = (x^2 + 5) - \sqrt{1 - x}$

$(fg)(x) = f(x) \cdot g(x) = (x^2 + 5)\sqrt{1 - x}$

$\left(\dfrac{f}{g}\right)(x) = \dfrac{f(x)}{g(x)} = \dfrac{x^2 + 5}{\sqrt{1 - x}}, \ x < 1$

11. $f(x) = \dfrac{1}{x}, g(x) = \dfrac{1}{x^2}$

$(f + g)(x) = f(x) + g(x) = \dfrac{1}{x} + \dfrac{1}{x^2} = \dfrac{x + 1}{x^2}$

$(f - g)(x) = f(x) - g(x) = \dfrac{1}{x} - \dfrac{1}{x^2} = \dfrac{x - 1}{x^2}$

$(fg)(x) = f(x) \cdot g(x) = \dfrac{1}{x}\left(\dfrac{1}{x^2}\right) = \dfrac{1}{x^3}$

$\left(\dfrac{f}{g}\right)(x) = \dfrac{f(x)}{g(x)} = \dfrac{1/x}{1/x^2} = \dfrac{x^2}{x} = x, \ x \neq 0$

13. $(f + g)(3) = f(3) + g(3) = (3^2 + 1) + (3 - 4) = 9$

15. $(f - g)(0) = f(0) - g(0) = [0^2 + 1] - (0 - 4) = 5$

17. $(f - g)(2t) = f(2t) - g(2t) = [(2t)^2 + 1] - (2t - 4) = 4t^2 - 2t + 5$

19. $(fg)(4) = f(4)g(4) = (4^2 + 1)(4 - 4) = 0$

21. $\left(\dfrac{f}{g}\right)(5) = \dfrac{f(5)}{g(5)} = \dfrac{5^2 + 1}{5 - 4} = 26$

23. $\left(\dfrac{f}{g}\right)(-1) - g(3) = \dfrac{f(-1)}{g(-1)} - g(3)$

$$= \dfrac{(-1)^2 + 1}{-1 - 4} - (3 - 4)$$

$$= -\dfrac{2}{5} + 1 = \dfrac{3}{5}$$

25. $f(x) = \frac{1}{2}x, g(x) = x - 1, (f + g)(x) = \frac{3}{2}x - 1$

27. $f(x) = x^2, g(x) = -2x, (f + g)(x) = x^2 - 2x$

29. $f(x) = 3x, g(x) = -\dfrac{x^3}{10}, (f + g)(x) = 3x - \dfrac{x^3}{10}$

For $0 \le x \le 2, f(x)$ contributes most to the magnitude.
For $x > 6, g(x)$ contributes most to the magnitude.

31. (a) $T(x) = R(x) + B(x) = \frac{3}{4}x + \frac{1}{15}x^2$

(b)

(c) $B(x)$ contributes more to $T(x)$ at higher speeds.

33.

35. $f(x) = x^2, g(x) = x - 1$

(a) $(f \circ g)(x) = f(g(x)) = f(x - 1) = (x - 1)^2$

(b) $(g \circ f)(x) = g(f(x)) = g(x^2) = x^2 - 1$

(c) $(f \circ f)(x) = f(f(x)) = f(x^2) = (x^2)^2 = x^4$

37. $f(x) = 3x + 5, g(x) = 5 - x$

(a) $(f \circ g)(x) = f(g(x)) = f(5 - x) = 3(5 - x) + 5 = 20 - 3x$

(b) $(g \circ f)(x) = g(f(x)) = g(3x + 5) = 5 - (3x + 5) = -3x$

(c) $(f \circ f)(x) = f(f(x)) = f(3x + 5) = 3(3x + 5) + 5 = 9x + 20$

39. (a) $(f \circ g)(x) = f(g(x)) = f(x^2) = \sqrt{x^2 + 4}$

$(g \circ f)(x) = g(f(x)) = g(\sqrt{x + 4}) = (\sqrt{x + 4})^2$

$= x + 4, \; x \geq -4$

(b)

They are not equal.

41. (a) $(f \circ g)(x) = f(g(x)) = f(3x + 1)$

$= \frac{1}{3}(3x + 1) - 3 = x - \frac{8}{3}$

(b) $(g \circ f)(x) = g(f(x)) = g(\frac{1}{3}x - 3)$

$= 3(\frac{1}{3}x - 3) + 1 = x - 8$

(b)

They are not equal.

43. (a) $(f \circ g)(x) = f(g(x)) = f(x^6) = (x^6)^{2/3} = x^4$

$(g \circ f)(x) = g(f(x)) = g(x^{2/3}) = (x^{2/3})^6 = x^4$

(b)

They are equal.

45. (a) $(f + g)(3) = f(3) + g(3) = 2 + 1 = 3$

(b) $\left(\dfrac{f}{g}\right)(2) = \dfrac{f(2)}{g(2)} = \dfrac{0}{2} = 0$

47. (a) $(f \circ g)(2) = f(g(2)) = f(2) = 0$

(b) $(g \circ f)(2) = g(f(2)) = g(0) = 4$

49. Let $f(x) = x^2$ and $g(x) = 2x + 1$, then $(f \circ g)(x) = h(x)$. This is not a unique solution. For example, if $f(x) = (x + 1)^2$ and $g(x) = 2x$, then $(f \circ g)(x) = h(x)$ as well.

51. Let $f(x) = \sqrt[3]{x}$ and $g(x) = x^2 - 4$, then $(f \circ g)(x) = h(x)$. This answer is not unique. Other possibilities may be:

$f(x) = \sqrt[3]{x - 4}$ and $g(x) = x^2$ or

$f(x) = \sqrt[3]{-x}$ and $g(x) = 4 - x^2$ or

$f(x) = \sqrt[9]{x}$ and $g(x) = (4 - x^2)^3$

$f \circ g = \sqrt[3]{x^2 - 4}$

53. Let $f(x) = 1/x$ and $g(x) = x + 2$, then $(f \circ g)(x) = h(x)$. Again, this is not a unique solution. Other possibilities may be:

$f(x) = \dfrac{1}{x + 2}$ and $g(x) = x$ or

$f(x) = \dfrac{1}{x + 1}$ and $g(x) = x + 1$ or

$f(x) = \dfrac{1}{x^2 + 2}$ and $g(x) = \sqrt{x}$

55. Let $f(x) = x^2 + 2x$ and $g(x) = x + 4$. Then $(f \circ g)(x) = h(x)$. (Answer is not unique.)

57. (a) The domain of $f(x) = \sqrt{x}$ is $x \geq 0$.

(b) The domain of $g(x) = x^2 + 1$ is all real numbers.

(c) $(f \circ g)(x) = f(g(x)) = f(x^2 + 1) = \sqrt{x^2 + 1}$

The domain of $f \circ g$ is all real numbers.

59. (a) The domain of $f(x) = 3/(x^2 - 1)$ is all real numbers except $x = \pm 1$.

(b) The domain of $g(x) = x + 1$ is all real numbers.

(c) $f \circ g = f(g(x)) = f(x + 1) = \dfrac{3}{(x + 1)^2 - 1} = \dfrac{3}{x^2 + 2x} = \dfrac{3}{x(x + 2)}$

This domain of $f \circ g$ is all real numbers except $x = 0$ and $x = -2$.

61. $f(x) = 3x - 4$

$$\frac{f(x + h) - f(x)}{h} = \frac{[3(x + h) - 4] - (3x - 4)}{h}$$

$$= \frac{3x + 3h - 4 - 3x + 4}{h}$$

$$= \frac{3h}{h}$$

$$= 3, \ h \neq 0$$

63. $f(x) = \dfrac{4}{x}$

$$\frac{f(x + h) - f(x)}{h} = \frac{\dfrac{4}{x + h} - \dfrac{4}{x}}{h} = \frac{\dfrac{4x - 4(x + h)}{x(x + h)}}{\dfrac{h}{1}}$$

$$= \frac{4x - 4x - 4h}{x(x + h)} \cdot \frac{1}{h}$$

$$= \frac{-4h}{x(x + h)} \cdot \frac{1}{h}$$

$$= \frac{-4}{x(x + h)}, \ h \neq 0$$

65. (a) $(A \circ r)(t)$ gives the area of the circle as a function of time.

$(A \circ r)(t) = A(r(t))$

$= A(0.6t)$

$= \pi(0.6t)^2 = 0.36\pi t^2$

67. $(C \circ x)(t) = C(x(t))$

$= 60(50t) + 750$

$= 3000t + 750$

$C \circ x$ represents the cost after t production hours.

69. $g(f(x)) = g(x - 500,000) = 0.03(x - 500,000)$

represents 3 percent of the amount over $500,000.

(b)

The cost increases to $15,000 when $t = 4.75$ hours.

71. Let $f(x)$ and $g(x)$ be odd functions, and define $h(x) = f(x)g(x)$. Then,

$$h(-x) = f(-x)g(-x)$$
$$= [-f(x)][-g(x)] \quad \text{since } f \text{ and } g \text{ are both odd}$$
$$= f(x)g(x) = h(x).$$

Thus, h is even.

Let $f(x)$ and $g(x)$ be even functions, and define $h(x) = f(x)g(x)$. Then,

$$h(-x) = f(-x)g(-x)$$
$$= f(x)g(x) \quad \text{since } f \text{ and } g \text{ are both even}$$
$$= h(x).$$

Thus, h is even.

73. $g(-x) = \frac{1}{2}[f(-x) + f(-(-x))] = \frac{1}{2}[f(-x) + f(x)] = g(x),$

which shows that g is even.

$$h(-x) = \frac{1}{2}[f(-x) - f(-(-x))] = \frac{1}{2}[f(-x) - f(x)]$$
$$= -\frac{1}{2}[f(x) - f(-x)] = -h(x),$$

which shows that h is odd.

75. (a) $f(x) = g(x) + h(x)$

$$= \frac{1}{2}[f(x) + f(-x)] + \frac{1}{2}[f(x) - f(-x)]$$

$$= \frac{1}{2}[(x^2 - 2x + 1) + (x^2 + 2x + 1)] + \frac{1}{2}[(x^2 - 2x + 1) - (x^2 + 2x + 1)]$$

$$= (x^2 + 1) + (-2x)$$

(b) $f(x) = g(x) + h(x)$

$$= \frac{1}{2}[f(x) + f(-x)] + \frac{1}{2}[f(x) - f(-x)]$$

$$= \frac{1}{2}\left[\left(\frac{1}{x + 1} + \frac{1}{-x + 1}\right)\right] + \frac{1}{2}\left[\left(\frac{1}{x + 1} - \frac{1}{-x + 1}\right)\right] = \frac{1}{1 - x^2} + \frac{-x}{1 - x^2}$$

$$= \frac{-1}{x^2 - 1} + \frac{x}{x^2 - 1}$$

77.

79.

81. $xy > 0$ means $x > 0$ and $y > 0$, or $x < 0$ and $y < 0$. Thus, it lies in Quadrant I or III.

Section 1.7   Inverse Functions

■ Two functions f and g are inverses of each other if $f(g(x)) = x$ for every x in the domain of g and $g(f(x)) = x$ for every x in the domain of f.

■ Be able to find the inverse of a function, if it exists.

1. Replace $f(x)$ with y.

2. Interchange x and y.

3. Solve for y. If this equation represents y as a function of x, then you have found $f^{-1}(x)$. If this equation does not represent y as a function of x, then f does not have an inverse function.

■ A function f has an inverse function if and only if no **horizontal** line crosses the graph of f at more than one point.

■ A function f has an inverse function if and only if f is one-to-one.

Solutions to Odd-Numbered Exercises

1. The inverse is a line through $(-1, 0)$.
Matches graph (c).

3. The inverse is half a parabola starting at $(1, 0)$.
Matches graph (a).

5. $f^{-1}(x) = \dfrac{x}{8} = \dfrac{1}{8}x$

$f(f^{-1}(x)) = f\left(\dfrac{x}{8}\right) = 8\left(\dfrac{x}{8}\right) = x$

$f^{-1}(f(x)) = f^{-1}(8x) = \dfrac{8x}{8} = x$

7. $f^{-1}(x) = x - 10$

$f(f^{-1}(x)) = f(x - 10) = (x - 10) + 10 = x$

$f^{-1}(f(x)) = f^{-1}(x + 10) = (x + 10) - 10 = x$

9. $f^{-1}(x) = x^3$

$f(f^{-1}(x)) = f(x^3) = \sqrt[3]{x^3} = x$

$f^{-1}(f(x)) = f^{-1}(\sqrt[3]{x}) = (\sqrt[3]{x})^3 = x$

11. (a) $f(g(x)) = f\left(\dfrac{x}{2}\right) = 2\left(\dfrac{x}{2}\right) = x$

$g(f(x)) = g(2x) = \dfrac{2x}{2} = x$

13. (a) $f(g(x)) = f\left(\dfrac{x - 1}{5}\right) = 5\left(\dfrac{x - 1}{5}\right) + 1 = x$

$g(f(x)) = g(5x + 1) = \dfrac{(5x + 1) - 1}{5} = x$

(b)

(b)

15. (a) $f(g(x)) = f\left(\sqrt[3]{x}\right) = \left(\sqrt[3]{x}\right)^3 = x$

$g(f(x)) = g(x^3) = \sqrt[3]{x^3} = x$

(b)

Reflections in the line $y = x$

17. (a) $f(g(x)) = f(x^2 + 4),\ x \geq 0$

$= \sqrt{(x^2 + 4) - 4} = x$

$g(f(x)) = g\left(\sqrt{x - 4}\right)$

$= \left(\sqrt{x - 4}\right)^2 + 4 = x$

(b)

Reflections in
the line $y = x$

19. (a) $f(g(x)) = f\left(\sqrt[3]{1 - x}\right) = 1 - \left(\sqrt[3]{1 - x}\right)^3 = 1 - (1 - x) = x$

$g(f(x)) = g(1 - x^3) = \sqrt[3]{1 - (1 - x^3)} = \sqrt[3]{x^3} = x$

(b)

Reflections in the line $y = x$

21. Since no horizontal line crosses the graph of f at more than one point, f **has** an inverse.

23. Since some horizontal lines cross the graph of f twice, f does **not** have an inverse.

25. $g(x) = \dfrac{4 - x}{6}$

g passes the horizontal line test, so g **has** an inverse.

27. $h(x) = |x + 4| - |x - 4|$

h does not pass the horizontal line test, so h does **not** have an inverse.

29. $f(x) = -2x\sqrt{16 - x^2}$

f does not pass the horizontal line test, so f does **not** have an inverse.

31. $f(x) = 2x - 3$

$y = 2x - 3$

$x = 2y - 3$

$y = \dfrac{x + 3}{2}$

$f^{-1}(x) = \dfrac{x + 3}{2}$

Reflections in the line $y = x$

33. $f(x) = x^5$

$y = x^5$

$x = y^5$

$y = \sqrt[5]{x}$

$f^{-1}(x) = \sqrt[5]{x}$

Reflections in the line $y = x$

35. $f(x) = \sqrt{x}$

$y = \sqrt{x}$

$x = \sqrt{y}$

$y = x^2$

$f^{-1}(x) = x^2, \ x \geq 0$

Reflections in the line $y = x$

37. $f(x) = \sqrt{4 - x^2}, \ 0 \leq x \leq 2$

$y = \sqrt{4 - x^2}$

$x = \sqrt{4 - y^2}$

$f^{-1}(x) = \sqrt{4 - x^2}, \ 0 \leq x \leq 2$

Reflections in the line $y = x$

39. $f(x) = \sqrt[3]{x - 1}$

$y = \sqrt[3]{x - 1}$

$x = \sqrt[3]{y - 1}$

$x^3 = y - 1$

$y = x^3 + 1$

$f^{-1}(x) = x^3 + 1$

Reflections in the line $y = x$

41. $f(x) = x^4$

$y = x^4$

$x = y^4$

$y = \pm \sqrt[4]{x}$

This does not represent y as a function of x.
f does not have an inverse.

43. $g(x) = \dfrac{x}{8}$

$y = \dfrac{x}{8}$

$x = \dfrac{y}{8}$

$y = 8x$

This is a function of x, so g has an inverse.
$g^{-1}(x) = 8x$

45. $p(x) = -4$

$y = -4$

Since $y = -4$ for all x, the graph is a horizontal
line and fails the horizontal line test. p does not have
an inverse.

47. $f(x) = (x + 3)^2, \ x \geq -3 \implies y \geq 0$

$y = (x + 3)^2, \ x \geq -3, \ y \geq 0$

$x = (y + 3)^2, \ y \geq -3, \ x \geq 0$

$\sqrt{x} = y + 3 \quad, \ y \geq -3, \ x \geq 0$

$y = \sqrt{x} - 3, \ x \geq 0, \ y \geq -3$

This is a function of x, so f has an inverse.

$f^{-1}(x) = \sqrt{x} - 3, \ x \geq 0$

49. $h(x) = \dfrac{4}{x^2}$ is not one-to-one, and does not have an inverse. For example, $h(1) = g(-1) = 4$.

51. $f(x) = \sqrt{2x + 3} \implies x \geq -\dfrac{3}{2}, \ y \geq 0$

$y = \sqrt{2x + 3}, \ x \geq -\dfrac{3}{2}, \ y \geq 0$

$x = \sqrt{2y + 3}, \ y \geq -\dfrac{3}{2}, \ x \geq 0$

$x^2 = 2y + 3, \ x \geq 0, \ y \geq -\dfrac{3}{2}$

$y = \dfrac{x^2 - 3}{2}, \ x \geq 0, \ y \geq -\dfrac{3}{2}$

This is a function of x, so f has an inverse.

$f^{-1}(x) = \dfrac{x^2 - 3}{2}, \ x \geq 0$

53. $g(x) = x^2 - x^4$

The graph fails the horizontal line test, so g does not have an inverse.

55. $f(x) = 25 - x^2, \ x \leq 0 \implies y \leq 25$

$y = 25 - x^2, \ x \leq 0, \ y \leq 25$

$x = 25 - y^2, \ y \leq 0, \ x \leq 25$

$y^2 = 25 - x, \ x \leq 25, \ y \leq 0$

$y = -\sqrt{25 - x}, \ x \leq 25, \ y \leq 0$

This is a function of x, so f has an inverse.

$f^{-1}(x) = -\sqrt{25 - x}, \ x \leq 25$

57. If we let $f(x) = (x - 2)^2, \ x \geq 2$, then f has an inverse. [Note: we could also let $x \leq 2$.]

$$f(x) = (x - 2)^2, \ x \geq 2 \implies y \geq 0$$

$$y = (x - 2)^2, \ x \geq 2, \ y \geq 0$$

$$x = (y - 2)^2, \ x \geq 0, \ y \geq 2$$

$$\sqrt{x} = y - 2, \quad x \geq 0, \ y \geq 2$$

$$\sqrt{x} + 2 = y, \quad\quad x \geq 0, \ y \geq 2$$

Thus, $f^{-1}(x) = \sqrt{x} + 2, \ x \geq 0$.

59. If we let $f(x) = |x + 2|, \ x \geq -2$, then f has an inverse. [Note: we could also let $x \leq -2$.]

$$f(x) = |x + 2|, \ x \geq -2$$

$$f(x) = x + 2 \ \text{ when } \ x \geq -2$$

$$y = x + 2, \ x \geq -2, \ y \geq 0$$

$$x = y + 2, \ x \geq 0, \ y \geq -2$$

$$x - 2 = y, \quad\quad x \geq 0, \ y \geq -2$$

Thus, $f^{-1}(x) = x - 2, \ x \geq 0$.

61.

x	$f(x)$
-2	-4
-1	-2
1	2
3	3

x	$f^{-1}(x)$
-4	-2
-2	-1
2	1
3	3

63. $f(x) = x^3 + x + 1$

The graph of the inverse relation is an inverse function since it satisfies the vertical line test.

65. $g(x) = \dfrac{3x^2}{x^2 + 1}$

The graph of the inverse relation is not an inverse function since it does not satisfy the vertical line test.

67. False, $f(x) = x^2$ is even and does not have an inverse.

69. True

In Exercises 71, 73, and 75, $f(x) = \frac{1}{8}x - 3$, $f^{-1}(x) = 8(x + 3)$, $g(x) = x^3$, $g^{-1}(x) = \sqrt[3]{x}$.

71. $(f^{-1} \circ g^{-1})(1) = f^{-1}(g^{-1}(1)) = f^{-1}(\sqrt[3]{1}) = 8(\sqrt[3]{1} + 3) = 32$

73. $(f^{-1} \circ f^{-1})(6) = f^{-1}(f^{-1}(6)) = f^{-1}(8[6 + 3]) = f^{-1}(72) = 8(72 + 3) = 600$

75. $(f \circ g)(x) = f(g(x)) = f(x^3) = \frac{1}{8}x^3 - 3$

$$y = \tfrac{1}{8}x^3 - 3$$
$$x = \tfrac{1}{8}y^3 - 3$$
$$x + 3 = \tfrac{1}{8}y^3$$
$$8(x + 3) = y^3$$
$$\sqrt[3]{8(x + 3)} = y$$
$$(f \circ g)^{-1}(x) = 2\sqrt[3]{x + 3}$$

In Exercises 77 and 79, $f(x) = x + 4$, $f^{-1}(x) = x - 4$, $g(x) = 2x - 5$, $g^{-1}(x) = \dfrac{x + 5}{2}$.

77. $(g^{-1} \circ f^{-1})(x) = g^{-1}(f^{-1}(x)) = g^{-1}(x - 4) = \dfrac{(x - 4) + 5}{2} = \dfrac{x + 1}{2}$

79. $(f \circ g)(x) = f(g(x)) = f(2x - 5) = (2x - 5) + 4 = 2x - 1$

$$(f \circ g)^{-1}(x) = \dfrac{x + 1}{2}$$

Note that $(f \circ g)^{-1}(x) = (g^{-1} \circ f^{-1})(x)$.

81. Let $(f \circ g)^{-1}(x) = y$ which implies that $(f \circ g)(y) = x$. Hence, $f(g(y)) = x$ or $f^{-1}(x) = g(y)$ and
$g^{-1}(f^{-1}(x)) = (g^{-1} \circ f^{-1}) = y$. Thus, $(f \circ g)^{-1}(x) = (g^{-1} \circ f^{-1})(x)$.

83. (a)
$$y = 8 + 0.75x$$
$$x = 8 + 0.75y$$
$$x - 8 = 0.75y$$
$$\frac{x - 8}{0.75} = y$$
$$f^{-1}(x) = \frac{x - 8}{0.75}$$

x = hourly wage
y = number of units produced

(b)

(c) If 10 units are produced, then $y = 8 + 0.75(10) = \$15.50$.

(d) If the hourly wage is $22.25, then
$$y = \frac{22.25 - 8}{0.75} = 19 \text{ units}.$$

85. (a)
$$y = 0.03x^2 + 254.50, \ 0 < x < 100$$
$$x = 0.03y^2 + 254.50$$
$$x - 254.50 = 0.03y^2$$
$$\frac{x - 254.50}{0.03} = y^2$$
$$\sqrt{\frac{x - 254.50}{0.03}} = y, \ x > 254.50$$
$$f^{-1}(x) = \sqrt{\frac{x - 254.50}{0.03}}$$

x = temperature in degrees Fahrenheit
y = percent load for a diesel engine

(b)

(c)
$$0.03x^2 + 254.50 < 500$$
$$0.03x^2 < 245.5$$
$$x^2 < 8183\tfrac{1}{3}$$
$$x < 90.46$$

Thus, $0 < x < 90.46$.

❏ Review Exercises for Chapter 1

Solutions to Odd-Numbered Exercises

1. $y = -\frac{1}{2}x + 2$

x	-2	0	2	3	4
y	3	2	1	$\frac{1}{2}$	0

3. $y - 2x - 3 = 0$

$y = 2x + 3$

Line with x-intercept $\left(-\frac{3}{2}, 0\right)$ and y-intercept $(0, 3)$

5. $x - 5 = 0$

$x = 5$ is a vertical line through $(5, 0)$.

7. $y = \sqrt{5 - x}$

Domain: $(-\infty, 5]$

x	5	4	1	-4
y	0	1	2	3

9. $y + 2x^2 = 0$

$y = -2x^2$ is a parabola.

x	0	± 1	± 2
y	0	-2	-8

11. $y = \sqrt{25 - x^2}$

Domain: $-5 \leq x \leq 5$

x	0	± 3	± 4	± 5
y	5	4	3	0

Semicircle

13. $y = \frac{1}{4}(x + 1)^3$

Intercepts: $(-1, 0), \left(0, \frac{1}{4}\right)$

15. $y = \frac{1}{4}x^4 - 2x^2$

Intercepts: $(0, 0), \left(\pm 2\sqrt{2}, 0\right) \approx (\pm 2.83, 0)$

17. $y = x\sqrt{9 - x^2}$

Intercepts: $(0, 0), (\pm 3, 0)$

19. $y = |x - 4| - 4$

Intercepts: $(0, 0), (8, 0)$

21. The setting is:

Xmin=-20
Xmax=50
Xscl=10
Ymin=-2
Ymax=1
Yscl=0.5

23. (a)

(b) $y = 31.7t + 306.2$

(c)

(d) $t = 8 \implies y = 559.8$

$t = 10 \implies y = 623.2$

25. $(-4.5, 6), (2.1, 3)$

$$m = \frac{3 - 6}{2.1 - (-4.5)} = \frac{-3}{6.6} = -\frac{30}{66} = -\frac{5}{11}$$

27. $m = \dfrac{5/2 - 1}{5 - 3/2} = \dfrac{3/2}{7/2} = \dfrac{3}{7}$

29. $(-2, 5), (0, t), (1, 1)$ are collinear.

$$\frac{t - 5}{0 - (-2)} = \frac{1 - 5}{1 - (-2)}$$

$$\frac{t - 5}{2} = \frac{-4}{3}$$

$$3(t - 5) = -8$$

$$3t - 15 = -8$$

$$3t = 7$$

$$t = \frac{7}{3}$$

31. The line through $(1, -4)$ and $(5, 10)$ is:

$$y + 4 = \frac{10 + 4}{5 - 1}(x - 1)$$

$$y + 4 = \frac{7}{2}(x - 1)$$

$$2y + 8 = 7(x - 1)$$

$$2y + 8 = 7x - 7$$

$$7x - 2y = 15$$

For $(t, 3)$ to be on this line also, it must satisfy the equation $7x - 2y = 15$.

$$7(t) - 2(3) = 15$$

$$7t = 21$$

Thus, $t = 3$.

33. $(2 + 4, -1 + 1) = (6, 0)$

$\quad (6 + 4, 0 + 1) = (10, 1)$

$\quad (2 - 4, -1 - 1) = (-2, -2)$

35. $(-6 + 1, -5 - 2) = (-5, -7)$

$\quad (-6 + 2, -5 - 4) = (-4, -9)$

$\quad (-6 + 3, -5 - 6) = (-3, -11)$

37. $(0, 0), (0, 10)$

$$m = \frac{10 - 0}{0 - 0} = \frac{10}{0} \text{ undefined.}$$

The line is vertical.

$x = 0$

39. $y - 1 = \dfrac{6 - 1}{14 - 2}(x - 2) = \dfrac{5}{12}(x - 2) \implies y = \dfrac{5}{12}x + \dfrac{1}{6}$ or $5x - 12y + 2 = 0$

41. $y - 0 = \dfrac{2 - 0}{6 + 1}(x + 1) = \dfrac{2}{7}(x + 1) \implies y = \dfrac{2}{7}x + \dfrac{2}{7}$ or $2x - 7y + 2 = 0$

43. $y - (-5) = \frac{3}{2}(x - 0)$

$\qquad y + 5 = \frac{3}{2}x$

$\qquad\qquad y = \frac{3}{2}x - 5$ or $0 = 3x - 2y - 10$

45. $\qquad y - 0 = -\frac{2}{3}(x - 3)$

$\qquad\qquad 3y = -2(x - 3)$

$\qquad\qquad 3y = -2x + 6$

$\qquad 2x + 3y - 6 = 0$

47. $5x - 4y = 8 \implies y = \frac{5}{4}x - 2$ and $m = \frac{5}{4}$

(a) Parallel slope: $m = \frac{5}{4}$

$\qquad y - (-2) = \frac{5}{4}(x - 3)$

$\qquad 4y + 8 = 5x - 15$

$\qquad 0 = 5x - 4y - 23$

(b) Perpendicular slope: $m = -\frac{4}{5}$

$\qquad y - (-2) = -\frac{4}{5}(x - 3)$

$\qquad 5y + 10 = -4x + 12$

$\qquad 4x + 5y - 2 = 0$

49. $(6, 12{,}500), \quad m = 850$

$\qquad y - 12{,}500 = 850(t - 6)$

$\qquad\qquad y = 850t - 5100 + 12{,}500$

$\qquad\qquad y = 850t + 7400$

51. The distance between $(-2, -5)$ and (x, y) equals the distance between $(6, 3)$ and (x, y).

$$\sqrt{(x + 2)^2 + (y + 5)^2} = \sqrt{(x - 6)^2 + (y - 3)^2}$$

$$(x + 2)^2 + (y + 5)^2 = (x - 6)^2 + (y - 3)^2$$

$$x^2 + 4x + 4 + y^2 + 10y + 25 = x^2 - 12x + 36 + y^2 - 6y + 9$$

$$4x + 10y + 29 = -12x - 6y + 45$$

$$16x + 16y - 16 = 0$$

$$x + y - 1 = 0$$

This line is the perpendicular bisector of the line segment joining the two points.

53. $(2, \ 160{,}000), \ (3, \ 185{,}000)$

$$m = \frac{185{,}000 - 160{,}000}{3 - 2} = 25{,}000$$

$S - 160{,}000 = 25{,}000(t - 2)$

$\qquad S = 25{,}000t + 110{,}000$

For the fourth quarter let $t = 4$. Then we have

$\qquad S = 25{,}000(4) + 110{,}000 = \$210{,}000.$

55. $\qquad 16x - y^4 = 0$

$\qquad\qquad y^4 = 16x$

$\qquad\qquad y = \pm 2\sqrt[4]{x}$

y is **not** a function of x. Some x-values correspond to two y-values.

57. $y = \sqrt{1 - x}$

Each x value, $x \leq 1$, corresponds to only one y value so y **is** a function of x.

59. $f(x) = x^2 + 1$

(a) $f(2) = 2^2 + 1 = 5$

(b) $f(t^2) = (t^2)^2 + 1 = t^4 + 1$

(c) $-f(x) = -(x^2 + 1) = -x^2 - 1$

61. $f(x) = \sqrt{25 - x^2}$

Domain: $25 - x^2 \geq 0$

                    $(5 + x)(5 - x) \geq 0$

Critical numbers: $x = \pm 5$

Test intervals: $(-\infty, -5), (-5, 5), (5, \infty)$

Solution set: $[-5, 5]$

63. $g(s) = \dfrac{5}{3s - 9} = \dfrac{5}{3(s - 3)}$

Domain: All real numbers except $s = 3$

65. $f(x) = \dfrac{3x}{2(3 - x)}$

The second setting shows the most complete graph.

67. (a) Increasing on $(-2, 0)$ and $(2, \infty)$

Decreasing on $(-\infty, -2)$ and $(0, 2)$

(b) Relative maximum at $(0, 16)$

Relative minimum at $(\pm 2, 0)$

(c) Since $f(x) = f(-x)$ (the graph is symmetric about the y-axis), the function is even.

69. (a) $f(x) = \tfrac{1}{2}x - 3$

                $y = \tfrac{1}{2}x - 3$

                $x = \tfrac{1}{2}y - 3$

            $x + 3 = \tfrac{1}{2}y$

        $2(x + 3) = y$

            $f^{-1}(x) = 2x + 6$

(b)

(c) $f^{-1}(f(x)) = f^{-1}\left(\tfrac{1}{2}x - 3\right)$

$\qquad\qquad = 2\left(\tfrac{1}{2}x - 3\right) + 6$

$\qquad\qquad = x - 6 + 6$

$\qquad\qquad = x$

$f(f^{-1}(x)) = f(2x + 6)$

$\qquad\qquad = \tfrac{1}{2}(2x + 6) - 3$

$\qquad\qquad = x + 3 - 3$

$\qquad\qquad = x$

71. (a) $f(x) = \sqrt{x+1}$

$y = \sqrt{x+1}$

$x = \sqrt{y+1}$

$x^2 = y + 1$

$x^2 - 1 = y$

$f^{-1}(x) = x^2 - 1, \ x \geq 0$

Note: The inverse must have a restricted domain.

(b)

(c) $f^{-1}(f(x)) = f^{-1}\left(\sqrt{x+1}\right)$

$= \left(\sqrt{x+1}\right)^2 - 1$

$= x + 1 - 1$

$= x$

$f(f^{-1}(x)) = f(x^2 - 1)$

$= \sqrt{(x^2 - 1) + 1}$

$= \sqrt{x^2} = x \ \text{ for } \ x \geq 0$

73. $f(x) = 2(x-4)^2$ is increasing on $[4, \infty)$.

Let $f(x) = 2(x-4)^2, \ x \geq 4$ and $y \geq 0$.

$y = 2(x-4)^2$

$x = 2(y-4)^2, \ x \geq 0, \ y \geq 4$

$\dfrac{x}{2} = (y-4)^2$

$\sqrt{\dfrac{x}{2}} = y - 4$

$\sqrt{\dfrac{x}{2}} + 4 = y$

$f^{-1}(x) = \sqrt{\dfrac{x}{2}} + 4, \ x \geq 0$

75. $(f - g)(4) = f(4) - g(4)$

$= [3 - 2(4)] - \sqrt{4}$

$= -5 - 2$

$= -7$

77. $(fh)(1) = f(1)h(1) = (3 - 2(1))(3(1)^2 + 2)$

$= (1)(5) = 5$

79. $(h \circ g)(7) = h(g(7))$

$= h\left(\sqrt{7}\right)$

$= 3\left(\sqrt{7}\right)^2 + 2$

$= 23$

81. $g^{-1}(3) = 9$ because $g(9) = 3$.

83.

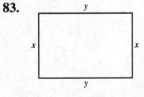

(a) $2x + 2y = 24$

$y = 12 - x$

$A = xy = x(12 - x)$

(b) Since x and y cannot be negative, we have $0 \leq x \leq 12$. The domain is $[0, 12]$.

(c) The maximum area of 36 occurs when $x = 6$ and the rectangle is a 6×6 square.

❑ Chapter Test for Chapter 1

1. $y = 4 - \frac{3}{4}|x|$

$x = 0 \implies y = 4 \quad (0, 4)$

$y = 0 \implies 4 = \frac{3}{4}|x| \implies |x| = \frac{16}{3} \implies x = \pm\frac{16}{3}$

Intercepts: $(0, 4)$, $\left(\frac{16}{3}, 0\right)$, $\left(-\frac{16}{3}, 0\right)$

2. $y = 4 - (x - 2)^2$

$x = 0 \implies y = 4 - 4 = 0 \quad (0, 0)$

$y = 0 \implies 0 = 4 - (x - 2)^2 \implies (x - 2) = \pm 2$

$x = 0, 4$

Intercepts: $(0, 0)$, $(4, 0)$

3. $y = x - x^3$

$x = 0 \implies y = 0 \quad (0, 0)$

$y = 0 \implies 0 = x(1 - x)(1 + x)$

Intercepts: $(0, 0)$, $(1, 0)$, $(-1, 0)$

4. $y = \sqrt{3 - x}$

$x = 0 \implies y = \sqrt{3}$

$y = 0 \implies 0 = \sqrt{3 - x} \implies x = 3$

Intercepts: $\left(0, \sqrt{3}\right)$, $(3, 0)$

5. $y - (-1) = \frac{3}{2}(x - 3) = \frac{3}{2}x - \frac{9}{2}$

$\qquad y = \frac{3}{2}x - \frac{11}{2}$

Additional points: $(1, -4)$, $\left(4, \frac{1}{2}\right)$, $(5, 2)$

6. $3x - 2y - 9 = 0$

$x = 0 \implies -2y = 9 \implies y = -\frac{9}{2}$

$y = 0 \implies 3x = 9 \implies x = 3$

Intercepts: $\left(0, -\frac{9}{2}\right)$, $(3, 0)$

7. $5x + 2y = 3$

$\qquad 2y = 3 - 5x$

$\qquad y = \frac{3}{2} - \frac{5}{2}x$

Slope of the perpendicular line is $\frac{2}{5}$.

$\qquad y - 4 = \frac{2}{5}(x - 0)$

$\qquad 5y - 20 = 2x$

$2x - 5y + 20 = 0$

8. No, for some x there corresponds more than one value of y. For instance, if $x = 1$, $y = \pm 1/\sqrt{3}$.

9. $f(-6) = 10 - \sqrt{3 - (-6)} = 10 - 3 = 7$

10. $f(t - 3) = 10 - \sqrt{3 - (t - 3)} = 10 - \sqrt{6 - t}$

11. $\dfrac{f(x) - f(2)}{x - 2} = \dfrac{10 - \sqrt{3 - x} - 9}{x - 2} = \dfrac{\sqrt{3 - x} - 1}{2 - x}$

12. $3 - x \geq 0 \implies$ domain is all $x \leq 3$.

13. $C = 5.60x + 24{,}000$

$$P = R - C = 9.20x - (5.60x + 24{,}000)$$
$$= 3.60x - 24{,}000$$

14. (a)   (b)

15. $h(x) = \frac{1}{4}x^4 - 2x^2 = \frac{1}{4}x^2(x^2 - 8)$

By graphing h, you see that the graph is increasing on $(-2, 0)$ and $(2, \infty)$, and decreasing on $(-\infty, -2)$ and $(0, 2)$.

16. $g(t) = |t + 2| - |t - 2|$.

By graphing g, you see that the graph is increasing on $(-2, 2)$, and constant on $(-\infty, -2)$ and $(2, \infty)$.

17. (a) $(f - g)(x) = x^2 - \sqrt{2 - x}$, Domain: $x \leq 2$

(b) $\left(\dfrac{f}{g}\right)(x) = \dfrac{x^2}{\sqrt{2 - x}}$, Domain: $x < 2$

(c) $(f \circ g)(x) = f(\sqrt{2 - x}) = 2 - x$, Domain $x \leq 2$

(d) $y = \sqrt{2 - x}$

$x = \sqrt{2 - y}$ Interchange x and y

$x^2 = 2 - y$

$y = g^{-1}(x) = 2 - x^2,\quad x \geq 0$

18. Its graph must satisfy the Horizontal Line Test. The function must be one-to-one. The graphs of a function and its inverse are reflections in the line $y = x$.

❑ Practice Test for Chapter 1

1. Use a graphing utility to graph the equation $y = 4/x^2 - 5$. Approximate any x-intercepts of the graph.

2. Use a graphing utility to graph the equation $y = |x - 3| + 2$. Approximate any x-intercepts of the graph.

3. Graph $3x - 5y = 15$ by hand.

4. Graph $y = \sqrt{9 - x}$ by hand.

5. Solve $5x + 4 = 7x - 8$.

6. Solve $\dfrac{x}{3} - 5 = \dfrac{x}{5} + 1$.

7. Solve $\dfrac{3x + 1}{6x - 7} = \dfrac{2}{5}$ graphically and analytically.

8. Solve $(x - 3)^2 + 4 = (x + 1)^2$ graphically and analytically.

9. Find an equation for the line passing through the points $(3, -2)$ and $(4, -5)$. Use a graphing utility to sketch a graph of the line.

10. Find an equation of the line that passes through the point $(-1, 5)$ and has slope -3. Use a graphing utility to sketch a graph of the line.

11. Does the equation $x^4 + y^4 = 16$ represent y as a function of x?

12. Evaluate the function $f(x) = |x - 2|/(x - 2)$ at the points $x = 0$, $x = 2$, and $x = 4$.

13. Find the domain of the function $f(x) = 5/(x^2 - 16)$.

14. Find the domain of the function $g(t) = \sqrt{4 - t}$.

15. Use a graphing utility to sketch the graph of the function $f(x) = 3 - x^6$ and determine if the function is even, odd, or neither.

16. Use a graphing utility to approximate any relative minimum or maximum values of the function $y = 4 - x + x^3$.

17. Compare the graph of $f(x) = x^3 - 3$ with the graph of $y = x^3$.

18. Compare the graph of $f(x) = \sqrt{x - 6}$ with the graph of $y = \sqrt{x}$.

19. Find $g \circ f$ if $f(x) = \sqrt{x}$ and $g(x) = x^2 - 2$. What is the domain of $g \circ f$?

20. Find f/g if $f(x) = 3x^2$ and $g(x) = 16 - x^4$. What is the domain of f/g?

21. Show that $f(x) = 3x + 1$ and $g(x) = \dfrac{x - 1}{3}$ are inverse functions algebraically and graphically.

22. Find the inverse of $f(x) = \sqrt{9 - x^2}$, $0 \le x \le 3$. Graph f and f^{-1} in the same viewing rectangle.

C H A P T E R 2
Intercepts, Zeros, and Solutions

CHAPTER 2
Intercepts, Zeros, and Solutions

Section 2.1   Linear Equations and Modeling

■ You should know how to solve linear equations: $ax + b = 0$.

■ An identity is an equation whose solution consists of every real number in its domain.

■ To solve an equation you can:

(a) Add or subtract the same quantity from both sides.

(b) Multiply or divide both sides by the same nonzero quantity.

■ To solve an equation that can be simplified to a linear equation:

(a) Remove all symbols of grouping and all fractions.

(b) Combine like terms.

(c) Solve by algebra.

(d) Check the answer.

■ A "solution" that does not satisfy the original equation is called an extraneous solution.

■ You should be able to set up mathematical models to solve problems.

■ You should be able to translate key words and phrases.

(a) Equality:

Equals, Equal to, is, are, was, will be, represents

(b) Addition:

Sum, plus, greater, increased by, more than, exceeds, total of

(c) Subtraction:

Difference, minus, less than, decreased by, subtracted from, reduced by, the remainder

(d) Multiplication:

Product, multiplied by, twice, times, percent of

(e) Division:

Quotient, divided by, ratio, per

(f) Consecutive:

Next, subsequent

■ You should know the following formulas:

(a) Perimeter:

1. Square: $P = 4s$

2. Rectangle: $P = 2L + 2W$

3. Circle: $C = 2\pi r$

(b) Area:

1. Square: $A = s^2$

2. Rectangle: $A = LW$

3. Circle: $A = \pi r^2$

4. Triangle: $A = \left(\dfrac{1}{2}\right)bh$

(c) Volume

1. Cube: $V = s^3$

2. Rectangular solid: $V = LWH$

3. Cylinder: $V = \pi r^2 h$

4. Sphere: $V = \left(\dfrac{4}{3}\right)\pi r^3$

(d) Simple Interest: $I = Prt$

(e) Compound Interest: $A = P\left(1 + \dfrac{r}{n}\right)^{nt}$

(f) Distance: $D = r \cdot t$

(g) Temperature: $F = \dfrac{9}{5}C + 32$

■ You should be able to solve word problems. Study the examples in the text carefully.

Solutions to Odd-Numbered Exercises

1. $5x - 3 = 3x + 5$

(a) $5(0) - 3 \stackrel{?}{=} 3(0) + 5$

$-3 \neq 5$

$x = 0$ *is not* a solution.

(b) $5(-5) - 3 \stackrel{?}{=} 3(-5) + 5$

$-28 \neq -10$

$x = -5$ *is not* a solution.

(c) $5(4) - 3 \stackrel{?}{=} 3(4) + 5$

$17 = 17$

$x = 4$ *is* a solution.

(d) $5(10) - 3 \stackrel{?}{=} 3(10) + 5$

$47 \neq 35$

$x = 10$ *is not* a solution.

3. $\dfrac{5}{2x} - \dfrac{4}{x} = 3$

(a) $\dfrac{5}{2(-1/2)} - \dfrac{5}{(-1/2)} \stackrel{?}{=} 3$

$3 = 3$

$x = -\frac{1}{2}$ *is* a solution.

(b) $\dfrac{5}{2(4)} - \dfrac{4}{4} \stackrel{?}{=} 3$

$-\dfrac{3}{8} \neq 3$

$x = 4$ *is not* a solution.

(c) $\dfrac{5}{2(0)} - \dfrac{4}{0}$ is undefined.

$x = 0$ *is not* a solution.

(d) $\dfrac{5}{2(1/4)} - \dfrac{4}{1/4} \stackrel{?}{=} 3$

$-6 \neq 3$

$x = \frac{1}{4}$ *is not* a solution.

5. $(x + 5)(x - 3) = 20$

(a) $(3 + 5)(3 - 3) \stackrel{?}{=} 20$

$0 \neq 20$

$x = 3$ *is not* a solution.

(b) $(-2 + 5)(-2 - 3) \stackrel{?}{=} 20$

$-15 \neq 20$

$x = -2$ *is not* a solution.

(c) $(0 + 5)(0 - 3) \stackrel{?}{=} 20$

$-15 \neq 20$

$x = 0$ *is not* a solution.

(d) $(-7 + 5)(-7 - 3) \stackrel{?}{=} 20$

$20 = 20$

$x = -7$ *is* a solution.

7. $2(x - 1) = 2x - 2$ is an *identity* by the Distributive Property. It is true for all real values of x.

9. $-6(x - 3) + 5 = -2x + 10$ is *conditional*. There are real values of x for which the equation is not true.

11. $x^2 - 8x + 5 = (x - 4)^2 - 11$ is an *identity* since $(x - 4)^2 - 11 = x^2 - 8x + 16 - 11 = x^2 - 8x + 5$.

13. $3 + \dfrac{1}{x + 1} = \dfrac{4x}{x + 1}$ is *conditional*. There are real values of x for which the equation is not true.

15. Equivalent equations are derived from the substitution principle and simplification techniques. They have the same solution(s).

$2x + 3 = 8$ and $2x = 5$ are equivalent equations.

17.

$$4x + 32 = 83 \qquad \text{Original Equation (Given equation)}$$

$$4x + 32 - 32 = 83 - 32 \qquad \text{Subtract 32 from both sides (Additional Property of Equality)}$$

$$4x = 51 \qquad \text{Simplify (Additive Inverse Property)}$$

$$\frac{4x}{4} = \frac{51}{4} \qquad \text{Divide both sides by 4 (Multiplication Property of Equality)}$$

$$x = \frac{51}{4} \qquad \text{Simplify (Multiplicative Inverse Property)}$$

19. $3x = 15$

$\quad x = 5$

21. $s + 12 = 18$

$\quad s = 6$

23. $3(x - 1) = 4 \qquad \text{or} \qquad 3(x - 1) = 4$

$\quad x - 1 = \frac{4}{3} \qquad\qquad\qquad 3x - 3 = 4$

$\quad x = \frac{4}{3} + 1 \qquad\qquad\qquad 3x = 7$

$\quad x = \frac{7}{3} \qquad\qquad\qquad\quad x = \frac{7}{3}$

The second way is easier since you are not working with fractions until the end of the solution.

25.

$$8x - 5 = 3x + 10$$

$$8x - 3x - 5 + 5 = 3x - 3x + 10 + 5$$

$$5x = 15$$

$$x = 3$$

27.

$$2(x + 5) - 7 = 3(x - 2)$$

$$2x + 10 - 7 = 3x - 6$$

$$2x + 3 = 3x - 6$$

$$-x = -9$$

$$x = 9$$

29. $6[x - (2x + 3)] = 8 - 5x$

$\quad 6[-x - 3] = 8 - 5x$

$\quad -6x - 18 = 8 - 5x$

$\quad -x = 26$

$\quad x = -26$

31.

$$\frac{5x}{4} + \frac{1}{2} = x - \frac{1}{2}$$

$$4\left(\frac{5x}{4}\right) + 4\left(\frac{1}{2}\right) = 4(x) - 4\left(\frac{1}{2}\right)$$

$$5x + 2 = 4x - 2$$

$$x = -4$$

33. $\frac{3}{2}(z + 5) - \frac{1}{4}(z + 24) = 0$

$\quad 4\left(\frac{3}{2}\right)(z + 5) - 4\left(\frac{1}{4}\right)(z + 24) = 4(0)$

$\quad 6(z + 5) - (z + 24) = 0$

$\quad 6z + 30 - z - 24 = 0$

$\quad 5z = -6$

$\quad z = -\frac{6}{5}$

35.

$$0.25x + 0.75(10 - x) = 3$$

$$4(0.25x) + 4(0.75)(10 - x) = 4(3)$$

$$x + 3(10 - x) = 12$$

$$x + 30 - 3x = 12$$

$$-2x = -18$$

$$x = 9$$

37.
$$\frac{100 - 4u}{3} = \frac{5u + 6}{4} + 6$$

$$12\left(\frac{100 - 4u}{3}\right) = 12\left(\frac{5u + 6}{4}\right) + 12(6)$$

$$4(100 - 4u) = 3(5u + 6) + 72$$

$$400 - 16u = 15u + 18 + 72$$

$$-31u = -310$$

$$u = 10$$

39.
$$\frac{5x - 4}{5x + 4} = \frac{2}{3}$$

$$3(5x - 4) = 2(5x + 4)$$

$$15x - 12 = 10x + 8$$

$$5x = 20$$

$$x = 4$$

41.
$$\frac{1}{x - 3} + \frac{1}{x + 3} = \frac{10}{x^2 - 9}$$

$$\frac{(x + 3) + (x - 3)}{x^2 - 9} = \frac{10}{x^2 - 9}$$

$$2x = 10$$

$$x = 5$$

43.
$$\frac{x}{x + 4} + \frac{4}{x + 4} + 2 = 0$$

$$\frac{x + 4}{x + 4} + 2 = 0$$

$$1 + 2 = 0$$

$$3 = 0$$

Contradiction : no solution

45.
$$\frac{7}{2x + 1} - \frac{8x}{2x - 1} = -4$$

$$7(2x - 1) - 8x(2x + 1) = -4(2x + 1)(2x - 1)$$

$$14x - 7 - 16x^2 - 8x = -16x^2 + 4$$

$$6x = 11$$

$$x = \frac{11}{6}$$

47.
$$\frac{1}{x} + \frac{2}{x - 5} = 0$$

$$1(x - 5) + 2x = 0$$

$$3x - 5 = 0$$

$$3x = 5$$

$$x = \frac{5}{3}$$

49. $\dfrac{3}{x(x - 3)} + \dfrac{4}{x} = \dfrac{1}{x - 3}$

$$3 + 4(x - 3) = x$$

$$3 + 4x - 12 = x$$

$$3x = 9$$

$$x = 3$$

A check reveals that $x = 3$ is an extraneous solution, so there is no solution.

51.
$$(x + 2)^2 + 5 = (x + 3)^2$$

$$x^2 + 4x + 4 + 5 = x^2 + 6x + 9$$

$$4x + 9 = 6x + 9$$

$$-2x = 0$$

$$x = 0$$

53.
$$(x + 2)^2 - x^2 = 4(x + 1)$$

$$x^2 + 4x + 4 - x^2 = 4x + 4$$

$$4 = 4$$

The equation is an identity; every real number is a solution.

55. You need $a(-3) + b = c(-3)$ or $b = (c - a)(-3) = 3(a - c)$. One answer is $a = 2$, $c = 1$ and $b = 3$ $(2x + 3 = x)$ and another is $a = 6$, $c = 1$, and $b = 15$ $(6x + 15 = x)$.

57.
$$16 = 0.432x - 10.44$$
$$26.44 = 0.432x$$
$$\frac{26.44}{0.432} = x \approx 61.2 \text{ inches}$$

59.
$$248 = 2(24) + 2(4x) + 2(6x)$$
$$248 = 48 + 8x + 12x$$
$$200 = 20x$$
$$x = 10 \text{ cm}$$

61. *Model:* (1980 weekly earnings) = (percentage increase)(1980 weekly earnings) + (1980 weekly earnings)

Labels: 1992 weekly earnings = \$688, percentage increases = p, 1980 weekly earnings = \$400

Equation: $688 = 400p + 400$

$$\frac{288}{400} = p$$
$$p = 0.72 = 72\%$$

Answer: percentage increase = p = 72%

63. *Model:* (1992 price of gold) = (percentage decrease)(1980 price of gold) + (1980 price of gold)

Labels: 1992 price of gold = \$350, percentage decrease = p, 1980 price of gold = \$613

Equation:
$$350 = 613 - 613p$$
$$-263 = -613p$$
$$\frac{-263}{-613} = p$$
$$p \approx 0.43 = 43\%$$

Answer: percentage decrease = 43%

65. Rate $= \dfrac{\text{Distance}}{\text{Time}} = \dfrac{50 \text{ kilometers}}{\frac{1}{2} \text{ hours}} = 100$ kilometers/hours

Total time $= \dfrac{\text{Total distance}}{\text{Rate}} = \dfrac{300 \text{ kilometers}}{100 \text{ kilometers/hours}} = 3$ hours

67. (a) Time for the first family: $t_1 = \dfrac{d}{r_1} = \dfrac{160}{42} \approx 3.8$ hr

Time for the other family: $t_2 = \dfrac{d}{r_2} = \dfrac{160}{50} = 3.2$ hr

(b) $t = \dfrac{d}{r} = \dfrac{100}{42 + 50} = \dfrac{100}{92} \approx 1.1$ hr

(c) $d = rt = 42\left(\dfrac{160}{42} - \dfrac{160}{50}\right) = 25.6$ mi

69. Let x = wind speed, then the rate to the city = $600 + x$,
the rate from the city = $600 - x$,
the distance to the city = 1500 kilometers,
the distance traveled so far in the return trip = $1500 - 300 = 1200$ kilometers.

$$\text{Time} = \frac{\text{Distance}}{\text{Rate}}$$

$$\frac{1500}{600 + x} = \frac{1200}{600 - x}$$

$$1500(600 - x) = 1200(600 + x)$$

$$900,000 - 1500x = 720,000 + 1200x$$

$$180,000 = 2700x$$

$$66\tfrac{2}{3} = x$$

Wind speed: $66\tfrac{2}{3}$ km/hr

71. $\text{Time} = \dfrac{\text{Distance}}{\text{Rate}}$

$$t = \frac{3.86 \times 10^8 \text{ meters}}{3.0 \times 10^8 \text{ meters per second}}$$

$$t \approx 1.29 \text{ seconds}$$

73. Let h = height of the building in feet

(a)

(b) $\dfrac{h \text{ feet}}{80 \text{ feet}} = \dfrac{4 \text{ feet}}{3.5 \text{ feet}}$

$$\frac{h}{80} = \frac{4}{3.5}$$

$$3.5h = 320$$

$$h \approx 91.4 \text{ feet}$$

75. Let x = amount in the $7\frac{1}{2}\%$ fund. Then
$12{,}000 - x$ = amount in the 10% fund.

$$1000 = 0.075x + 0.10(12{,}000 - x)$$

$$1000 = 0.075x + 1200 - 0.10x$$

$$0.025x = 200$$

$$x = \$8000$$

You must invest
$12{,}000 - x = 12{,}000 - 8000 = \$4000$
in the 10% fund.

77. Let r be the simple interest rate of the variable-rate fund. Then

$$2054.40 = r(8000) + .095(12{,}000)$$

$$2054.40 = 8000r + 1140$$

$$914.40 = 8000r$$

$$r = 0.1143 \text{ or } 11.43\%.$$

79. Let x = number of pounds of \$2.49 nuts. Then
$100 - x$ = number of pounds of \$3.89 nuts.

$$2.49x + 3.89(100 - x) = 3.19(100)$$

$$2.49x - 3.89 - 3.89x = 319$$

$$-1.40x = -70$$

$$x = \frac{-70}{-1.40}$$

$$x = 50 \text{ lbs of } \$2.49 \text{ nuts}$$

$$100 - x = 50 \text{ lbs of } \$3.89 \text{ nuts}$$

Use 50 pounds of each kind.

81. $W_1 x = W_2(L - x)$

$$50x = 75(10 - x)$$

$$50x = 750 - 75x$$

$$125x = 750$$

$$x = 6 \text{ feet from the 50-pound child.}$$

83. $A = \dfrac{1}{2}bh$

$$2A = bh$$

$$\frac{2A}{b} = h$$

85. $A = \dfrac{1}{2}(a + b)h$

$$\frac{2A}{b} = h$$

$$\frac{2A - ah}{h} = b$$

Section 2.2 Solving Equations Graphically

■ You should be able to find the intercepts of the graph of an equation.

■ You should be able to find the zeros of a function $y = f(x)$ by solving the equation $f(x) = 0$.

■ You should be able to find the solutions of an equation graphically using a graphing utility.

■ You should be able to use the zoom and trace features to find solutions to any desired accuracy.

■ You should be able to find the points of intersection of two graphs.

Solutions to Odd-Numbered Exercises

1. $y = x - 5$

Let $y = 0$: $0 = x - 5$ $\Rightarrow$ $x = 5$ $\Rightarrow$ $(5, 0)$ x-intercept

Let $x = 0$: $y = 0 - 5$ $\Rightarrow$ $y = -5$ $\Rightarrow$ $(0, -5)$ y-intercept

3. $y = x^2 + x - 2$

Let $y = 0$: $(x^2 + x - 2) = (x + 2)(x - 1) = 0$ $\Rightarrow$ $x = -2, 1$ $\Rightarrow$ $(-2, 0), (1, 0)$ x-intercepts

Let $x = 0$: $y = 0^2 + 0 - 2 = -2$ $\Rightarrow$ $(0, -2)$ y-intercept

5. $y = x\sqrt{x + 2}$

Let $y = 0$: $0 = x\sqrt{x + 2}$ $\Rightarrow$ $x = 0, -2$ $\Rightarrow$ $(0, 0), (-2, 0)$ x-intercepts

Let $x = 0$: $y = 0\sqrt{0 + 2} = 0$ $\Rightarrow$ $(0, 0)$ y-intercept

7. $y = |x - 2| - 3$

Let $y = 0$: $|x - 2| - 3 = 0$ $\Rightarrow$ $|x - 2| = 3$ $\Rightarrow$ $x = -1, 5$ $\Rightarrow$ $(-1, 0), (5, 0)$ x-intercepts

Let $x = 0$: $|0 - 2| - 3 = |-2| - 3 = 2 - 3 = -1 = y$ $\Rightarrow$ $(0, -1)$ y-intercept

9. $xy - 2y - x + 1 = 0$

Let $y = 0$: $-x + 1 = 0$ $\Rightarrow$ $x = 1$ $\Rightarrow$ $(1, 0)$ x-intercept

Let $x = 0$: $-2y + 1 = 0$ $\Rightarrow$ $y = \frac{1}{2}$ $\Rightarrow$ $\left(0, \frac{1}{2}\right)$ y-intercept

11. $f(x) = 12 - 4x$

13. $f(x) = x^2 - 2.5x - 6$

15. $f(x) = \dfrac{x + 2}{3} - \dfrac{x - 1}{5} - 1$

17.

$(3, 0)$

$y = 0 = 2(x - 1) - 4 = 2x - 2 - 4 = 2x - 6$ $\Rightarrow$ $2x = 6$ $\Rightarrow$ $x = 3$

19.

$(10, 0)$

$y = 0 = 20 - (3x - 10) = 20 - 3x + 10 = 30 - 3x$ $\Rightarrow$ $3x = 30$ $\Rightarrow$ $x = 10$

21. $25(x - 3) = 12(x + 2) - 10$

$25x - 75 = 12x + 24 - 10$

$13x - 89 = 0$

23. $\dfrac{2x}{3} = 10 - \dfrac{1}{x}$

$\dfrac{2x}{3} + \dfrac{1}{x} - 10 = 0$

25. $\dfrac{3}{x + 2} - \dfrac{4}{x - 2} = 5$

$\dfrac{3}{x + 2} - \dfrac{4}{x - 2} - 5 = 0$

27. $27 - 4x = 12$

$-4x = -15$

$x = \dfrac{15}{4}$

$27 - 4x - 12 = 0$

$f(x) = 15 - 4x = 0$

$x = 3.75 = \dfrac{15}{4}$

29. $\dfrac{3x}{2} + \dfrac{1}{4}(x - 2) = 10$

$\dfrac{6x}{4} + \dfrac{x}{4} = 10 + \dfrac{1}{2}$

$\dfrac{7x}{4} = \dfrac{21}{2}$

$x = 6$

$f(x) = \dfrac{3x}{2} + \dfrac{1}{4}(x - 2) - 10 = 0$

$x = 6.0$

31. $3(x + 3) = 5(1 - x) - 1$

$3x + 9 = 5 - 5x - 1$

$8x = -5$

$x = -\dfrac{5}{8}$

$f(x) = 3(x + 3) - 5(1 - x) + 1 = 0$

$x = -0.625$

33. $\dfrac{1}{4}(x^2 - 10x + 17) = 0$

$x = 2.172,\ 7.828$

35. $x^3 + x + 4 = 0$

$x = -1.379$

37. $2x^3 - x^2 - 18x + 9 = 0$

$x = -3.0,\ 0.5,\ 3.0$

39.
$$x^4 = 2x^3 + 1$$
$$x^4 - 2x^3 - 1 = 0$$
$$x = -0.717, \ 2.107$$

41.
$$\frac{2}{x + 2} = 3$$
$$\frac{2}{x + 2} - 3 = 0$$
$$x = -1.333$$

43.
$$|x - 3| = 4$$
$$|x - 3| - 4 = 0$$
$$x = -1, 7$$

45. (a)

x	-1	0	1	2	3	4
$3.2x - 5.8$	-9	-5.8	-2.6	0.6	3.8	7.0

(b) $1 < x < 2$ because of the sign change.

(c)

x	1.5	1.6	1.7	1.8	1.9	2
$3.2x - 5.8$	-1	-0.68	-0.36	-0.04	0.28	0.6

(d) $1.8 < x < 1.9$. To improve accuracy, evaluate the expression in this interval and determine where the sign changes.

(e) $x = 1.8125$

47. $y = 2 - x$
$y = 2x - 1$
$(x, y) = (1, 1)$

49. $2x + y = 6 \implies y = -2x + 6$
$-x + y = 0 \implies y = x$
$(2, 2)$

51. $x - y = -4 \implies y = x + 4$
$x^2 - y = -2 \implies y = x^2 + 2$
$(-1, 3), (2, 6)$

53. $y = 9 - 2x$
$y = x - 3$
$(4, 1)$

55. $y = 4 - x^2$
$y = 2x - 1$
$(x, y) = (1.449, 1.898), \ (-3.449, -7.899)$

57. $y = 8$
$y = 3x^2 + 2x$
$(x, y) = (-2, 8), \ (1.333, 8)$

59. $y = 2x^2$

$y = x^4 - 2x^2$

$(x, y) = (0, 0), (2, 8), (-2, 8)$

61. (a) $\dfrac{1 + 0.73205}{1 - 0.73205} = \dfrac{1.73205}{0.26795}$

$$= 6.464079 = 6.46$$

(b) $\dfrac{1 + 0.73205}{1 - 0.73205} = \dfrac{1.73205}{0.26795}$

$$= \dfrac{1.73}{0.27}$$

$$= 6.407407 = 6.41$$

The second method decreases the accuracy.

63. (a) $T = \dfrac{x}{63} + \dfrac{(280 - x)}{54}$

(b) Domain: $0 \le x \le 280$

(c) If the time was 4 hours and 45 minutes, then $T = 4\frac{3}{4}$ and $x \approx 164.5$ miles.

65. (a) $C = x + 0.33(55 - x)$

(b) Domain: $0 \le x \le 55$

(c) If the final mixture is 60% concentrate, then $C = 0.6(55) = 33$ and $x = 22.2$.

67. (a) Area $= A(x) = 4x + 8x = 12x$

(b)

(c) $A(x) = 12x = 200 \implies x \approx 16.67$

69. (a) The graph indicates that there are 5 zeros.

(b) If $k = 25$, then there is one zero (≈ -4.25). If $k = 15$, then there are three zeros.

(c) No, the range of this function is $(-\infty, \infty)$ and hence, the graph must cross the x-axis at least once.

71. $T = I + S = x + 10,000 - \frac{1}{2}x = 10,000 + \frac{1}{2}x$

73. If $T = 13,800 = 10,000 + \frac{1}{2}x$

$$3800 = \tfrac{1}{2}x$$

$$x = \$7600$$

75. The number reached 31 million in 1990. To answer the questions algebraically, solve the equation $0.43t + 30.86 = 31$. To answer the question graphically, draw the horizontal line $y = 31$ and note where it intersects the histogram.

Section 2.3   Complex Numbers

- You should know how to work with complex numbers.
- Operations on complex numbers
  - (a) Addition: $(a + bi) + (c + di) = (a + c) + (b + d)i$
  - (b) Subtraction: $(a + bi) - (c + di) = (a - c) + (b - d)i$
  - (c) Multiplication: $(a + bi)(c + di) = (ac - bd) + (ad + bc)i$
  - (c) Division: $\dfrac{a + bi}{c + di} = \dfrac{a + bi}{c + di} \cdot \dfrac{c - di}{c - di} = \dfrac{ac + bd}{c^2 + d^2} + \dfrac{bc - ad}{c^2 + d^2}i$
- The complex conjugate of $a + bi$ is $a - bi$:
  $$(a + bi)(a - bi) = a^2 + b^2$$
- The additive inverse of $a + bi$ is $-a - bi$.
- The multiplicative inverse of $a + bi$ is
  $$\dfrac{a - bi}{a^2 + b^2}.$$
- $\sqrt{-a} = \sqrt{a}\,i$ for $a > 0$.

Solutions to Odd-Numbered Exercises

1. $a + bi = -10 + 6i$

   $a = -10$

   $b = 6$

3. $(a - 1) + (b + 3)i = 5 + 8i$

   $a - 1 = 5 \quad \Rightarrow \quad a = 6$

   $b + 3 = 8 \quad \Rightarrow \quad b = 5$

5. $4 + \sqrt{-9} = 4 + 3i$

7. $2 - \sqrt{-27} = 2 - \sqrt{27}\,i = 2 - 3\sqrt{3}\,i$

9. $\sqrt{-75} = \sqrt{75}\,i = 5\sqrt{3}\,i$

11. $-6i + i^2 = -6i - 1 = -1 - 6i$

13. $8 = 8 + 0i = 8$

15. $\sqrt{-0.09} = \sqrt{0.09}\,i = 0.3i$

17. $(5 + i) + (6 - 2i) = 11 - i$

19. $(8 - i) - (4 - i) = 8 - i - 4 + i = 4$

21. $\left(-2 + \sqrt{-8}\right) + \left(5 - \sqrt{-50}\right) = -2 + 2\sqrt{2}\,i + 5 - 5\sqrt{2}\,i$
$$= 3 - 3\sqrt{2}\,i$$

23. $13i - (14 - 7i) = 13i - 14 + 7i = -14 + 20i$

25. $-\left(\frac{3}{2} + \frac{5}{2}i\right) + \left(\frac{5}{3} + \frac{11}{3}i\right) = -\frac{3}{2} - \frac{5}{2}i + \frac{5}{3} + \frac{11}{3}i$
$$= -\frac{9}{6} - \frac{15}{6}i + \frac{10}{6} + \frac{22}{6}i$$
$$= \frac{1}{6} + \frac{7}{6}i$$

27. $\sqrt{-6} \cdot \sqrt{-2} = \left(\sqrt{6}\,i\right)\left(\sqrt{2}\,i\right) = \sqrt{12}\,i^2 = \left(2\sqrt{3}\right)(-1) = -2\sqrt{3}$

29. $\left(\sqrt{-10}\right)^2 = \left(\sqrt{10}\,i\right)^2 = 10i^2 = -10$

31. $(1 + i)(3 - 2i) = 3 - 2i + 3i - 2i^2$
$$= 3 + i + 2$$
$$= 5 + i$$

33. $6i(5 - 2i) = 30i - 12i^2 = 30i + 12 = 12 + 30i$

35. $\left(\sqrt{14} + \sqrt{10}\,i\right)\left(\sqrt{14} - \sqrt{10}\,i\right) = 14 - 10i^2 = 14 + 10 = 24$

37. $(4 + 5i)^2 = 16 + 40i + 25i^2 = 16 + 40i - 25$
$$= -9 + 40i$$

39. $(2 + 3i)^2 + (2 - 3i)^2 = 4 + 12i + 9i^2 + 4 - 12i + 9i^2$
$$= 4 + 12i - 9 + 4 - 12i - 9$$
$$= -10$$

41. $\sqrt{-6}\sqrt{-6} = \sqrt{6}i\,\sqrt{6}i = 6i^2 = -6 \quad \left(\sqrt{-6}\,\sqrt{-6} \neq \sqrt{(-6)(-6)}\right)$

43. The complex conjugate of $5 + 3i$ is $5 - 3i$.
$(5 + 3i)(5 - 3i) = 25 - 9i^2 = 25 + 9 = 34$

45. The complex conjugate of $-2 - \sqrt{5}i$ is $-2 + \sqrt{5}i$.
$\left(-2 - \sqrt{5}i\right)\left(-2 + \sqrt{5}i\right) = 4 - 5i^2 = 4 + 5 = 9$

47. The complex conjugate of $20i$ is $-20i$.
$(20i)(-20i) = -400i^2 = 400$

49. The complex conjugate of $\sqrt{8}$ is $\sqrt{8}$.
$\left(\sqrt{8}\right)\left(\sqrt{8}\right) = 8$

51. $\dfrac{6}{i} = \dfrac{6}{i} \cdot \dfrac{-i}{-i} = \dfrac{-6i}{-i^2} = \dfrac{-6i}{1} = -6i$

53. $\dfrac{4}{4 - 5i} = \dfrac{4}{4 - 5i} \cdot \dfrac{4 + 5i}{4 + 5i} = \dfrac{4(4 + 5i)}{16 + 25} = \dfrac{16 + 20i}{41} = \dfrac{16}{41} + \dfrac{20}{41}i$

55. $\dfrac{2 + i}{2 - i} = \dfrac{2 + i}{2 - i} \cdot \dfrac{2 + i}{2 + i} = \dfrac{4 + 4i + i^2}{4 + 1} = \dfrac{3 + 4i}{5} = \dfrac{3}{5} + \dfrac{4}{5}i$

57. $\dfrac{6 - 7i}{i} = \dfrac{6 - 7i}{i} \cdot \dfrac{-i}{-i} = \dfrac{-6i - 7}{1} = -7 - 6i$

59. $\dfrac{1}{(4 - 5i)^2} = \dfrac{1}{16 - 40i + 25i^2} = \dfrac{1}{-9 - 40i} \cdot \dfrac{-9 + 40i}{-9 + 40i}$
$$= \dfrac{-9 + 40i}{81 + 1600} = \dfrac{-9 + 40i}{1681} = -\dfrac{9}{1681} + \dfrac{40}{1681}i$$

61. $\dfrac{2}{1+i} - \dfrac{3}{1-i} = \dfrac{2(1-i) - 3(1+i)}{(1+i)(1-i)}$

$$= \dfrac{2 - 2i - 3 - 3i}{1+1}$$

$$= \dfrac{-1 - 5i}{2}$$

$$= -\dfrac{1}{2} - \dfrac{5}{2}i$$

63. $\dfrac{i}{3-2i} + \dfrac{2i}{3+8i} = \dfrac{i(3+8i) + 2i(3-2i)}{(3-2i)(3+8i)}$

$$= \dfrac{3i + 8i^2 + 6i - 4i^2}{9 + 24i - 6i - 16i^2}$$

$$= \dfrac{4i^2 + 9i}{9 + 18i + 16}$$

$$= \dfrac{-4 + 9i}{25 + 18i} \cdot \dfrac{25 - 18i}{25 - 18i}$$

$$= \dfrac{-100 + 72i + 225i - 162i^2}{625 + 324}$$

$$= \dfrac{-100 + 297i + 162}{949}$$

$$= \dfrac{62 + 297i}{949}$$

$$= \dfrac{62}{949} + \dfrac{297}{949}i$$

65.

$i = i$	$i^5 = i$	$i^9 = i$	$i^{13} = i$
$i^2 = -1$	$i^6 = -1$	$i^{10} = -1$	$i^{14} = -1$
$i^3 = -i$	$i^7 = -i$	$i^{11} = -i$	$i^{15} = -i$
$i^4 = 1$	$i^8 = 1$	$i^{12} = 1$	$i^{16} = 1$

The numbers exhibit a periodic pattern: $i, -1, -i, 1$, etc.

67. $-6i^3 + i^2 = -6i^2i + i^2$

$$= -6(-1)i + (-1)$$

$$= 6i - 1$$

$$= -1 + 6i$$

69. $-5i^5 = -5i^2i^2i$

$$= -5(-1)(-1)i$$

$$= -5i$$

71. $\left(\sqrt{-75}\right)^3 = \left(5\sqrt{3}i\right)^3 = 5^3\left(\sqrt{3}\right)^3 i^3$

$$= 125\left(3\sqrt{3}\right)(-i)$$

$$= -375\sqrt{3}i$$

73. $\dfrac{1}{i^3} = \dfrac{1}{-i} = \dfrac{1}{-i} \cdot \dfrac{i}{i} = \dfrac{1}{-i^2} = \dfrac{i}{1} = i$

75. $4 + 3i$

77. $0 + 6i = 6i$

79.

81.

83. The complex number 0 is in the Mandelbrot Set since for $c = 0$, the corresponding Mandelbrot sequence is 0, 0, 0, 0, 0, 0, . . . which is bounded.

85. The complex number $\frac{1}{2}i$, is in the Mandelbrot Set since for $c = \frac{1}{2}i$, the corresponding Mandelbrot sequence is

$\frac{1}{2}i, -\frac{1}{4} + \frac{1}{2}i, -\frac{3}{16} + \frac{1}{4}i, -\frac{7}{256} + \frac{13}{32}i, \frac{-10,767}{65,536} + \frac{1957}{4096}i, -\frac{864,513,055}{4,294,967,296} + \frac{46,037,845}{134,217,728}i$

which is bounded. Or in decimal form

$0.5i, -0.25 + 0.5i, -0.1875 + 0.25i, -0.02734 + 0.40625i,$

$-0.164291 + 0.477783i, -0.201285 + 0.343009i.$

87. The complex number 1 is not in the Mandelbrot Set since for $c = 1$, the corresponding Mandelbrot sequence is 1, 2, 5, 26, 677, 458,330 which is unbounded.

89. $(2)^3 = 8$

$\left(-1 + \sqrt{3}i\right)^3 = (-1)^3 + 3(-1)^2\left(\sqrt{3}i\right) + 3(-1)\left(\sqrt{3}i\right)^2 + \left(\sqrt{3}i\right)$

$\qquad = -1 + 3\sqrt{3}i - 9i^2 + 3\sqrt{3}i^3$

$\qquad = -1 + 3\sqrt{3}i + 9 - 3\sqrt{3}i$

$\qquad = 8$

$\left(-1 - \sqrt{3}i\right)^3 = (-1)^3 + 3(-1)^2\left(-\sqrt{3}i\right) + 3(-1)\left(-\sqrt{3}i\right)^2\left(\sqrt{3}i\right)^3$

$\qquad = -1 - 3\sqrt{3}i - 9i^2 - 3\sqrt{3}i^3$

$\qquad = -1 - 3\sqrt{3}i + 9 + 3\sqrt{3}i$

$\qquad = 8$

The three numbers are cube roots of 8.

91. $(a + bi) + (a - bi) = 2a$ which is a real number.
$(a + bi) - (a - bi) = 2bi$ is an imaginary number.

93. $\overline{(a_1 + b_1i)(a_2 + b_2i)} = \overline{(a_1a_2 - b_1b_2) + (a_1b_2 + b_1a_2)i}$

$\qquad = (a_1a_2 - b_1b_2) - (a_1b_2 + b_1a_2)i$

$\overline{(a_1 + b_1i)}\ \overline{(a_2 + b_2i)} = (a_1 - b_1i)(a_2 - b_2i)$

$\qquad = (a_1a_2 - b_1b_2i) - (a_1b_2 + b_1a_2)i,$

which are equal.

95. $(x^3 - 3x^2) - (6 - 2x - 4x^2) = x^3 - 3x^2 - 6 + 2x + 4x^2 = x^3 + x^2 + 2x - 6$

97. $\left(3x - \frac{1}{2}\right)(x + 4) = 3x^2 - \frac{1}{2}x + 12x - \frac{1}{2}(4) = 3x^2 + \frac{23}{2}x - 2$

99. $[(x + y) + 3]^2 = (x + y)^2 + 6(x + y) + 9 = x^2 + 2xy + y^2 + 6x + 6y + 9$

101.
$$F = \alpha \frac{m_1 m_2}{r^2}$$
$$Fr^2 = \alpha\, m_1 m_2$$
$$r^2 = \frac{\alpha\, m_1 m_2}{F}$$
$$r = \sqrt{\frac{\alpha\, m_1 m_2}{F}} \quad (r > 0 \text{ is distance})$$

103. $\text{Time} = \dfrac{\text{Distance}}{\text{Speed}} = \dfrac{200}{100} + \dfrac{200}{80} = \dfrac{1600 + 2000}{800} = \dfrac{9}{2}\,\text{hrs}$

$\text{Average speed} = \dfrac{\text{Distance}}{\text{Time}} = \dfrac{400}{9/2} = \dfrac{800}{9} \approx 88.9\,\text{km/hr}$

Section 2.4   Solving Equations Algebraically

- ■ You should be able to solve a quadratic equation by factoring, if possible.
- ■ You should be able to solve a quadratic equation of the form $u^2 = d$ by extracting square roots.
- ■ You should be able to solve a quadratic equation by completing the square.
- ■ You should know and be able to use the Quadratic Formula: For $ax^2 + bx + c = 0, a \neq 0$,

$$x = \frac{-b \pm \sqrt{b^2 - 4ac}}{2a}.$$

- ■ You should be able to determine the types of solutions of a quadratic equation by checking the discriminant $b^2 - 4ac$.
  - (a) If $b^2 - 4ac > 0$, there are two distinct real solutions.
  - (b) If $b^2 - 4ac = 0$, there is one repeated real solution.
  - (c) If $b^2 - 4ac < 0$, there is no real solution.
- ■ You should be able to solve certain types of nonlinear or nonquadratic equations.
- ■ For equations involving radicals or fractional powers, raise both sides to the same power.
- ■ For equations that are of the quadratic type, $au^2 + bu + c = 0, a \neq 0$, use either factoring or the quadratic equation.
- ■ For equations with fractions, multiply both sides by the least common denominator to clear the fractions.
- ■ For equations involving absolute value, remember that the expression inside the absolute value can be positive or negative.
- ■ Always check for extraneous solutions.

Solutions to Odd-Numbered Exercises

1. $2x^2 = 3 - 5x$

Standard form: $2x^2 + 5x - 3 = 0$

3. $\frac{1}{5}(3x^2 - 10) = 12x$

$3x^2 - 10 = 60x$

Standard form: $3x^2 - 60x - 10 = 0$

5. $6x^2 + 3x = 0$

$3x(2x + 1) = 0$

$3x = 0$ or $2x + 1 = 0$

$x = 0$ or $x = -\frac{1}{2}$

7. $x^2 - 2x - 8 = 0$

$(x - 4)(x + 2) = 0$

$x - 4 = 0$ or $x + 2 = 0$

$x = 4$ or $x = -2$

9. $3 + 5x - 2x^2 = 0$

$(3 - x)(1 + 2x) = 0$

$3 - x = 0$ or $1 + 2x = 0$

$x = 3$ or $x = -\frac{1}{2}$

11. $x^2 + 4x = 12$

$x^2 + 4x - 12 = 0$

$(x + 6)(x - 2) = 0$

$x + 6 = 0$ or $x - 2 = 0$

$x = -6$ or $x = 2$

13. $x^2 = 7$

$x = \pm\sqrt{7}$

$\approx \pm 2.65$

15. $(x - 12)^2 = 18$

$x - 12 = \pm 3\sqrt{2}$

$x = 12 \pm 3\sqrt{2}$

$x \approx 16.24$ or ≈ 7.76

17. $x^2 + 6x + 2 = 0$

$x^2 + 6x = -2$

$x^2 + 6x + 3^2 = -2 + 3^2$

$(x + 3)^2 = 7$

$x + 3 = \pm\sqrt{7}$

$x = -3 \pm\sqrt{7}$

19. $9x^2 - 18x + 3 = 0$

$x^2 - 2x + \frac{1}{3} = 0$

$x^2 - 2x = -\frac{1}{3}$

$x^2 - 2x + 1^2 = -\frac{1}{3} + 1^2$

$(x - 1)^2 = \frac{2}{3}$

$x - 1 = \pm\sqrt{\frac{2}{3}}$

$x = 1 \pm\sqrt{\frac{2}{3}}$

$x = 1 \pm \frac{\sqrt{6}}{3}$

21. $y = (x + 3)^2 - 4$

$0 = (x + 3)^2 - 4$

$4 = (x + 3)^2$

$\pm\sqrt{4} = x + 3$

$-3 \pm 2 = x$

$x = -1$ or $x = -5$

The x-intercepts are $(-1, 0)$ and $(-5, 0)$. The x-intercepts of the graph are solutions to the equation $0 = (x + 3)^2 - 4$.

23. $y = -4x^2 + 4x + 3$

The x-intercepts are $\left(-\frac{1}{2}, 0\right)$ and $\left(\frac{3}{2}, 0\right)$.

$$0 = -4x^2 + 4x + 3$$
$$4x^2 - 4x = 3$$
$$4(x^2 - x) = 3$$
$$x^2 - x = \frac{3}{4}$$
$$x^2 - x + \left(\frac{1}{2}\right)^2 = \frac{3}{4} + \left(\frac{1}{2}\right)^2$$
$$\left(x - \frac{1}{2}\right)^2 = 1$$
$$x - \frac{1}{2} = \pm\sqrt{1}$$
$$x = \frac{1}{2} \pm 1$$
$$x = \frac{3}{2} \text{ or } x = -\frac{1}{2}$$

25. $y = \frac{1}{4}(4x^2 - 20x + 25)$

The x- intercept is $\left(\frac{5}{2}, 0\right)$.

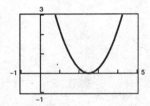

$$\frac{1}{4}(4x^2 - 20x + 25) = 0$$
$$4x^2 - 20x + 25 = 0$$
$$(2x - 5)^2 = 0$$
$$2x - 5 = 0$$
$$x = \frac{5}{2}$$

27. $y = -(x^2 - 4x + 5)$

$$-(x^2 - 4x + 5) = 0$$
$$x^2 - 4x + 5 = 0$$

The discriminant $b^2 - 4ac = (-4)^2 - 4(1)(5) = -4$ is negative and hence there are no real solutions (and no x-intercepts). By the Quadratic Formula,

$$x = \frac{4 \pm \sqrt{-4}}{2} = 2 \pm i.$$

29. The graph does not have any x-intercepts and thus the equation has no real solution.

$$y = 2x^2 - 5x + 5$$

31. The graph has two x-intercepts and hence the equation has two real solutions.

$$y = \frac{1}{5}x^2 + \frac{6}{5}x - 8$$

33. $-x^2 + 2x + 2 = 0$

$$x = \frac{-b \pm \sqrt{b^2 - 4ac}}{2a}$$
$$= \frac{-2 \pm \sqrt{2^2 - 4(-1)(2)}}{2(-1)}$$
$$= \frac{-2 \pm 2\sqrt{3}}{-2} = 1 \pm \sqrt{3}$$

35. $x^2 + 8x - 4 = 0$

$$x = \frac{-b \pm \sqrt{b^2 - 4ac}}{2a}$$
$$= \frac{-8 \pm \sqrt{8^2 - 4(1)(-4)}}{2(1)}$$
$$= \frac{-8 \pm 4\sqrt{5}}{2} = -4 \pm 2\sqrt{5}$$

37. $$28x - 49x^2 = 4$$

$$-49x^2 + 28x - 4 = 0$$

$$x = \frac{-b \pm \sqrt{b^2 - 4ac}}{2a}$$

$$= \frac{-28 \pm \sqrt{28^2 - 4(-49)(-4)}}{2(-49)}$$

$$= \frac{-28 \pm 0}{-98} = \frac{2}{7}$$

41. $4x^2 + 16x + 15 = 0$

$$x = \frac{-b \pm \sqrt{b^2 - 4ac}}{2a}$$

$$= \frac{-16 \pm \sqrt{16^2 - 4(4)(15)}}{2(4)}$$

$$= \frac{-16 + \sqrt{16}}{8}$$

$$= -2 \pm \frac{1}{2} = -\frac{3}{2}, \ -\frac{5}{2}.$$

45. $(x + 3)^3 = 81$

$$x + 3 = \pm 9$$

$$x + 3 = 9 \quad \text{or} \quad x + 3 = -9$$

$$x = 6 \quad \text{or} \qquad x = -12$$

49. $(x - (-4))(x - 6) = 0$

$$(x + 4)(x - 6) = 0$$

$$x^2 - 2x - 24 = 0$$

51. (a) $4x + 3y = 100$ (amount of fence)

$$y = \tfrac{1}{3}(100 - 4x)$$

$$\text{Area} = A(x) = (2x)y = (2x)\tfrac{1}{3}(100 - 4x)$$

$$= \tfrac{8}{3}x(25 - x).$$

(c)

$$x = 12.5, \ y = 16.67 \ \text{or} \ 25 \times \tfrac{50}{3}$$

—CONTINUED—

39. $x^2 - 2x + 2 = 0$

$$x = \frac{-b \pm \sqrt{b^2 - 4ac}}{2a}$$

$$= \frac{2 \pm \sqrt{(-2)^2 - 4(1)(2)}}{2(1)}$$

$$= \frac{2 \pm \sqrt{-4}}{2} = 1 \pm i$$

43. $x^2 - 2x - 1 = 0$

$$x^2 - 2x = 1$$

$$x^2 - 2x + 1^2 = 1 + 1^2$$

$$(x - 1)^2 = 2$$

$$x - 1 = \pm\sqrt{2}$$

$$x = 1 \pm \sqrt{2}$$

47. False. The product must equal zero to use the the Zero-Factor Property.

(b)

x	y	Area
2	$\frac{92}{3}$	$\frac{368}{3}$
4	28	224
6	$\frac{76}{3}$	304
8	$\frac{68}{3}$	$\frac{1088}{3}$
10	20	400
12	$\frac{52}{3}$	416
14	$\frac{44}{3}$	$\frac{1232}{3}$

Approximate dimension for maximum area:

$$x = 12, \ y = \tfrac{52}{3} \ \text{or} \ 24 \times \tfrac{52}{3}.$$

51. **–CONTINUED–**

(d) The graphs $y_1 = \frac{8}{3}x(25 - x)$ and $y_2 = 350$ intersect at $x = 7.5$ and $x = 17.5$. The dimensions are therefore $15 \times 23\frac{1}{3}$ or 35×10.

(e)
$$\frac{8}{3}x(25 - x) = 350$$
$$-8x^2 + 100x = 1050$$
$$4x^2 - 50x - 525 = 0$$
$$(2x - 35)(2x - 15) = 0$$
$$x = \frac{35}{2} = 17.5 \text{ or } x = \frac{15}{2} = 7.5$$

The dimensions are therefore $15 \times 23\frac{1}{3}$ or 35×10.

53. $4x^4 - 18x^2 = 0$
$$2x^2(2x^2 - 9) = 0$$
$$2x^2 = 0 \implies x = 0$$
$$2x^2 - 9 = 0 \implies x = \pm\frac{3\sqrt{2}}{2}$$

55. $x^4 - 81 = 0$
$$(x^2 + 9)(x + 3)(x - 3) = 0$$
$$x^2 + 9 = 0 \implies x = \pm 3i$$
$$x + 3 = 0 \implies x = -3$$
$$x - 3 = 0 \implies x = 3$$

57. $5x^3 + 30x^2 + 45x = 0$
$$5x(x^2 + 6x + 9) = 0$$
$$5x(x + 3)^2 = 0$$
$$5x = 0 \implies x = 0$$
$$x + 3 = 0 \implies x = -3$$

59. $x^3 - 3x^2 - x + 3 = 0$
$$x^2(x - 3) - (x - 3) = 0$$
$$(x - 3)(x^2 - 1) = 0$$
$$(x - 3)(x + 1)(x - 1) = 0$$
$$x - 3 = 0 \implies x = 3$$
$$x + 1 = 0 \implies x = -1$$
$$x - 1 = 0 \implies x = 1$$

61. $x^4 - x^3 + x - 1 = 0$
$$x^3(x - 1) + (x - 1) = 0$$
$$(x - 1)(x^3 + 1) = 0$$
$$(x - 1)(x + 1)(x^2 - x + 1) = 0$$
$$x - 1 = 0 \implies x = 1$$
$$x + 1 = 0 \implies x = -1$$
$$x^2 - x + 1 = 0 \implies x = \frac{1}{2} \pm \frac{\sqrt{3}}{2}i \qquad \text{(By the Quadratic Formula)}$$

63.
$$x^4 - 4x^2 + 3 = 0$$
$$(x^2 - 3)(x^2 - 1) = 0$$
$$(x + \sqrt{3})(x - \sqrt{3})(x + 1)(x - 1) = 0$$
$$x + \sqrt{3} = 0 \implies x = -\sqrt{3}$$
$$x - \sqrt{3} = 0 \implies x = \sqrt{3}$$
$$x + 1 = 0 \implies x = -1$$
$$x - 1 = 0 \implies x = 1$$

65.
$$4x^4 - 65x^2 + 16 = 0$$
$$(4x^2 - 1)(x^2 - 16) = 0$$
$$(2x + 1)(2x - 1)(x + 4)(x - 4) = 0$$
$$2x + 1 = 0 \implies x = -\tfrac{1}{2}$$
$$2x - 1 = 0 \implies x = \tfrac{1}{2}$$
$$x + 4 = 0 \implies x = -4$$
$$x - 4 = 0 \implies x = 4$$

67.
$$\frac{1}{t^2} + \frac{8}{t} + 15 = 0$$
$$1 + 8t + 15t^2 = 0$$
$$(1 + 3t)(1 + 5t) = 0$$
$$1 + 3t = 0 \implies t = -\frac{1}{3}$$
$$1 + 5t = 0 \implies t = -\frac{1}{5}$$

69. $2x + 9\sqrt{x} - 5 = 0$
$$(2\sqrt{x} - 1)(\sqrt{x} + 5) = 0$$
$$\sqrt{x} = \tfrac{1}{2} \implies x = \tfrac{1}{4}$$

$(\sqrt{x} = -5$ is not a solution.)

You can see graphically that there is only one solution.

71. $y = x^3 - 2x^2 - 3x$

$$0 = x^3 - 2x^2 - 3x$$
$$0 = x(x + 1)(x - 3)$$
$$x = 0$$
$$x + 1 = 0 \implies x = -1$$
$$x - 3 = 0 \implies x = 3$$

x-intercepts: $(-1, 0), (0, 0), (3, 0)$

73. $y = x^4 - 10x^2 + 9$

$$0 = x^4 - 10x^2 + 9$$
$$0 = (x^2 - 1)(x^2 - 9)$$
$$0 = (x + 1)(x - 1)(x + 3)(x - 3)$$
$$x + 1 = 0 \implies x = -1$$
$$x - 1 = 0 \implies x = 1$$
$$x + 3 = 0 \implies x = -3$$
$$x - 3 = 0 \implies x = 3$$

x-intercepts: $(\pm 1, 0), (\pm 3, 0)$

75. $\sqrt{x - 10} - 4 = 0$

$\sqrt{x - 10} = 4$

$x - 10 = 16$

$x = 26$

77. $\sqrt[3]{2x + 5} + 3 = 0$

$\sqrt[3]{2x + 5} = -3$

$2x + 5 = -27$

$2x = -32$

$x = -16$

79. $\sqrt{x + 1} - 3x = 1$

$\sqrt{x + 1} = 3x + 1$

$x + 1 = 9x^2 + 6x + 1$

$0 = 9x^2 + 5x$

$0 = x(9x + 5)$

$x = 0$

$9x + 5 = 0 \implies x = -\frac{5}{9}, \text{extraneous}$

81. $\sqrt{x} - \sqrt{x - 5} = 1$

$\sqrt{x} = 1 + \sqrt{x - 5}$

$\left(\sqrt{x}\right)^2 = \left(1 + \sqrt{x - 5}\right)^2$

$x = 1 + 2\sqrt{x - 5} + x - 5$

$4 = 2\sqrt{x - 5}$

$2 = \sqrt{x - 5}$

$4 = x - 5$

$9 = x$

83. $(x - 5)^{2/3} = 16$

$x - 5 = \pm 16^{3/2}$

$x - 5 = \pm 64$

$x = 69, -59$

85. $3x(x - 1)^{1/2} + 2(x - 1)^{3/2} = 0$

$(x - 1)^{1/2}[3x + 2(x - 1)] = 0$

$(x - 1)^{1/2}(5x - 2) = 0$

$(x - 1)^{1/2} = 0 \implies x - 1 = 0 \implies x = 1$

$5x - 2 = 0 \implies x = \frac{2}{5} \text{ which is extraneous.}$

87. $y = \sqrt{11x - 30} - x$

x-intercepts: $(5, 0), (6, 0)$

$0 = \sqrt{11x - 30} - x$

$x = \sqrt{11x - 30}$

$x^2 = 11x - 30$

$x^2 - 11x + 30 = 0$

$(x - 5)(x - 6) = 0$

$x - 5 = 0 \implies x = 5$

$x - 6 = 0 \implies x = 6$

89. $y = \sqrt{7x + 36} - \sqrt{5x + 16} - 2$

    x-intercepts: $(0, 0)$, $(4, 0)$

$$0 = \sqrt{7x + 36} - \sqrt{5x + 16} - 2$$
$$\sqrt{7x + 36} = 2 + \sqrt{5x + 16}$$
$$\left(\sqrt{7x + 36}\right)^2 = \left(2 + \sqrt{5x + 16}\right)^2$$
$$7x + 36 = 4 + 4\sqrt{5x + 16} + 5x + 16$$
$$7x + 36 = 5x + 20 + 4\sqrt{5x + 16}$$
$$2x + 16 = 4\sqrt{5x + 16}$$
$$x + 8 = 2\sqrt{5x + 16}$$
$$x^2 + 16x + 64 = 4(5x + 16)$$
$$x^2 + 16x + 64 = 20x + 64$$
$$x^2 - 4x = 0$$
$$x(x - 4) = 0$$
$$x = 0$$
$$x - 4 = 0 \implies x = 4$$

91. $\dfrac{20 - x}{x} = x$

$$20 - x = x^2$$
$$0 = x^2 + x - 20$$
$$0 = (x + 5)(x - 4)$$
$$x + 5 = 0 \implies x = -5$$
$$x - 4 = 0 \implies x = 4$$

93.
$$\frac{1}{x} - \frac{1}{x + 1} = 3$$
$$x(x + 1)\frac{1}{x} - x(x + 1)\frac{1}{x + 1} = x(x + 1)(3)$$
$$x + 1 - x = 3x(x + 1)$$
$$1 = 3x^2 + 3x$$
$$0 = 3x^2 + 3x - 1; \quad a = 3, \quad b = 3, \quad c = -1$$
$$x = \frac{-3 \pm \sqrt{(3)^2 - 4(3)(-1)}}{2(3)} = \frac{-3 \pm \sqrt{21}}{6}$$

95.
$$x = \frac{3}{x} + \frac{1}{2}$$
$$(2x)(x) = (2x)\left(\frac{3}{x}\right) + (2x)\left(\frac{1}{2}\right)$$
$$2x^2 = 6 + x$$
$$2x^2 - x - 6 = 0$$
$$(2x + 3)(x - 2) = 0$$
$$2x + 3 = 0 \implies x = -\frac{3}{2}$$
$$x - 2 = 0 \implies x = 2$$

97.
$$\frac{4}{x + 1} - \frac{3}{x + 2} = 1$$
$$4(x + 2) - 3(x + 1) = (x + 1)(x + 2), x \neq -2, -1$$
$$4x + 8 - 3x - 3 = x^2 + 3x + 2$$
$$x^2 + 2x - 3 = 0$$
$$(x - 1)(x + 3) = 0$$
$$x - 1 = 0 \implies x = 1$$
$$x + 3 = 0 \implies x = -3$$

99. $|2x - 1| = 5$

$2x - 1 = 5 \implies x = 3$

$-(2x - 1) = 5 \implies x = -2$

101. $|x| = x^2 + x - 3$

$x = x^2 + x - 3$ OR $-x = x^2 + x - 3$

$x^2 - 3 = 0$ $x^2 + 2x - 3 = 0$

$x = \pm\sqrt{3}$ $(x - 1)(x + 3) = 0$

$x - 1 = 0 \implies x = 1$

$x + 3 = 0 \implies x = -3$

Only $x = \sqrt{3}$, and $x = -3$ are solutions to the original equation. $x = -\sqrt{3}$ and $x = 1$ are extraneous. Note that the graph of $y = x^2 + x - 3 - |x|$ has two x-intercepts.

103. $y = \dfrac{1}{x} - \dfrac{4}{x - 1} - 1$

$0 = \dfrac{1}{x} - \dfrac{4}{x - 1} - 1$

$0 = (x - 1) - 4x - x(x - 1)$

$0 = x - 1 - 4x - x^2 + x$

$0 = -x^2 - 2x - 1$

$0 = x^2 + 2x + 1$

$0 = (x + 1)^2$

x-intercept: $(-1, 0)$

$x + 1 = 0 \implies x = -1$

105. $y = |x + 1| - 2$

$0 = |x + 1| - 2$

$2 = |x + 1|$

$x + 1 = 2 \quad$ or $\quad -(x + 1) = 2$

$x = 1 \quad$ or $\quad -x - 1 = 2$

$-x = 3$

$x = -3$

x-intercept: $(1, 0), (-3, 0)$

107. $\left(x - \sqrt{2}\right)\left(x + \sqrt{2}\right)(x - 4) = 0$

$(x^2 - 2)(x - 4) = 0$

$x^3 - 4x^2 - 2x + 8 = 0$

109. Number of students $= x$

Cost per student $= f$

$$fx = 1700 \implies f = \frac{1700}{x}$$

$$(f - 7.50)(x + 6) = 1700$$

$$\left(\frac{1700}{x} - 7.5\right)(x + 6) = 1700$$

$$(3400 - 15x)(x + 6) = 3400x$$

$$-15x^2 - 90x + 20{,}400 = 0$$

$$x = \frac{90 \pm \sqrt{(-90)^2 - 4(-15)(20{,}400)}}{2(-15)} = \frac{90 \pm 1110}{-30}$$

Using the positive value for x we conclude that the original number was $x = 34$ students. You could solve this problem graphically by graphing

$$y = \left(\frac{1700}{x} - 7.5\right)(x + 6) - 1700$$

and finding the point where the graph crossed the x-axis ($x = 34$).

111. The distance between $(1, 2)$ and $(x, -10)$ is 13.

$$\sqrt{(x - 1)^2 + (-10 - 2)^2} = 13$$

$$(x - 1)^2 + (12)^2 = 13^2$$

$$x^2 - 2x + 1 + 144 = 169$$

$$x^2 - 2x - 24 = 0$$

$$(x + 4)(x - 6) = 0$$

$$x + 4 = 0 \implies x = -4$$

$$x - 6 = 0 \implies x = 6$$

$$x \approx 0.382 \text{ mile}$$

113. (a) $C = 0.45x^2 - 1.65x + 50.75, \quad 10 \leq x \leq 25$

(b) If $C = 150$, then $x = 16.797$ degrees.

(c) If the temperature is increased 10° to 20°, then C increases from 79.25 to 197.75, a factor of 2.5.

115. (a) $D = -0.024s^2 + 1.455s + 431.5, \ 0 < s \le 75$

(b) The greatest distance is $D = 453.552$ corresponding to $s = 30.313$. The trip will take $D/s = 453.552/30.313 = 14.962$ hours.

(c) The distance traveled in 8 hours is $8s$. The point of intersection of D with $y_2 = 8s$ is $s = 54.883$ mph, corresponding to a distance of 439.063 miles

117.
$$S = \pi r \sqrt{r^2 + h^2}$$
$$S^2 = \pi^2 r^2 (r^2 + h^2)$$
$$S^2 = \pi^2 r^4 + \pi^2 r^2 h^2$$
$$\frac{S^2 - \pi^2 r^4}{\pi^2 r^2} = h^2$$
$$h = \frac{\sqrt{S^2 - \pi^2 r^4}}{\pi r}$$

119.
$$20 + \sqrt{20 - a} = b$$
$$\sqrt{20 - a} = b - 20$$
$$20 - a = b^2 - 40b + 400$$
$$-a = b^2 - 40b + 380$$
$$a = -b^2 + 40b - 380$$

This formula gives the relationship between a and b. From the original equation we know that $a \le 20$ and $b \ge 20$. Choose a b value, where $b \ge 20$ and then solve for a, keeping in mind that $a \le 20$. Some possibilities are:

$b = 20, \quad a = 20$

$b = 21, \quad a = 19$

$b = 22, \quad a = 16$

$b = 23, \quad a = 11$

$b = 24, \quad a = \ \ 4 \quad \longleftarrow \left(\begin{array}{l} \text{This is the one given} \\ \text{in your textbook.} \end{array} \right)$

$b = 25, \quad a = -5$

Section 2.5   Solving Inequalities Algebraically and Graphically

■ You should know the properties of inequalities.

(a) Transitive: $a < b$ and $b < c$ implies $a < c$.

(b) Addition: $a < b$ and $c < d$ implies $a + c < b + d$.

(c) Adding or Subtracting a Constant: $a \pm c < b \pm c$ if $a < b$.

(d) Multiplying or Dividing by a Constant: For $a < b$,

   1. If $c > 0$, then $ac < bc$ and $\dfrac{a}{c} < \dfrac{b}{c}$.

   2. If $c < 0$, then $ac > bc$ and $\dfrac{a}{c} > \dfrac{b}{c}$.

■ You should know that

$$|x| = \begin{cases} x & \text{if } x \ge 0 \\ -x & \text{if } x < 0 \end{cases}.$$

■ You should be able to solve absolute value inequalities.

(a) $|x| < a$ if and only if $-a < x < a$.

(b) $|x| > a$ if and only if $x < -a$ or $x > a$.

■ You should be able to solve polynomial inequalities.

(a) Find the critical numbers.

   1. Values that make the expression zero

   2. Values that make the expression undefined

(b) Test one value in each interval on the real number line resulting from the critical numbers.

(c) Determine the solution intervals.

■ You should be able to solve rational and other types of inequalities.

Solutions to Odd-Numbered Problems

1. $x < 3$

Matches (d).

3. $-3 < x \le 4$

Matches (c).

5. (a) $x = 3$

$5(3) - 12 \overset{?}{>} 0$

$3 > 0$

Yes, $x = 3$ is a solution.

(b) $x = -3$

$5(-3) - 12 \overset{?}{>} 0$

$-27 \not> 0$

No, $x = -3$ is not a solution.

(c) $x = \frac{5}{2}$

$5\left(\frac{5}{2}\right) - 12 \overset{?}{>} 0$

$\frac{1}{2} > 0$

Yes, $x = \frac{5}{2}$ is a solution.

(d) $x = \frac{3}{2}$

$5\left(\frac{3}{2}\right) - 12 \overset{?}{>} 0$

$-\frac{9}{2} \not> 0$

No, $x = \frac{3}{2}$ is not a solution.

7. (a) $x = 13$

$|13 - 10| \overset{?}{\geq} 3$

$3 \overset{?}{\geq} 3$

Yes, $x = 13$ is a solution.

(b) $x = -1$

$|-1 - 10| \overset{?}{\geq} 3$

$11 \geq 3$

Yes, $x = -1$ is a solution.

(c) $x = 14$

$|14 - 10| \overset{?}{\geq} 3$

$4 \geq 3$

Yes, $x = 14$ is a solution.

(d) $x = 9$

$|9 - 10| \overset{?}{\geq} 3$

$1 \not\geq 3$

No, $x = 9$ is not a solution.

9. $-10x < 40$

$-\frac{1}{10}(-10) > -\frac{1}{10}(40)$

$x > -4$

11. $4(x + 1) < 2x + 3$

$4x + 4 < 2x + 3$

$2x < -1$

$x < -\frac{1}{2}$

13. $1 < 2x + 3 < 9$

$-2 < 2x < 6$

$-1 < x < 3$

15. $-4 < \dfrac{2x - 3}{3} < 4$

$-12 < 2x - 3 < 12$

$-9 < 2x < 15$

$-\dfrac{9}{2} < x < \dfrac{15}{2}$

17. $-1 < -\dfrac{x}{3} < 1$

$-1(-3) > x > (-3)$

$3 > x > -3$

or $-3 < x < 3$

19. $6x > 12$

$x > 2$

21. $5 - 2x \geq 1$

$-2x \geq -4$

$x \leq 2$

23. $0 \leq 2(x + 4) < 20$

$0 \leq x + 4 < 10$

$-4 \leq x < 6$

25. $y = 2x - 3$

(a) $y \geq 1$

$2x - 3 \geq 1$

$2x \geq 4$

$x \geq 2$

(b) $y \leq 0$

$2x - 3 \leq 0$

$2x \leq 3$

$x \leq \dfrac{3}{2}$

27. $y = -\frac{1}{2}x + 2$

(a) $0 \leq y \leq 3$

$0 \leq -\frac{1}{2}x + 2 \leq 3$

$-2 \leq -\frac{1}{2}x \leq 1$

$4 \geq x \geq -2$

(b) $y \geq 0$

$-\frac{1}{2}x + 2 \geq 0$

$-\frac{1}{2}x \geq -2$

$x \leq 4$

29. $x - 5 \geq 0$

$\qquad x \geq 5$

$\qquad [5, \infty)$

31. $\left|\dfrac{x}{2}\right| > 3$

$\qquad \dfrac{x}{2} < -3$ or $\dfrac{x}{2} > 3$

$\qquad x < -6 \qquad x > 6$

33. $|x - 20| \leq 4$

$\qquad -4 \leq x - 20 \leq 4$

$\qquad 16 \leq x \leq 24$

35. $|x - 20| \geq 4$

$\qquad x - 20 \leq -4$ or $x - 20 \geq 4$

$\qquad x \leq 16 \qquad x \geq 24$

37. $\left|\dfrac{x - 3}{2}\right| \geq 5$

$\qquad \dfrac{x - 3}{2} \leq -5$ or $\dfrac{x - 3}{2} \geq 5$

$\qquad x - 3 \leq -10 \qquad x - 3 \geq 10$

$\qquad x \leq -7 \qquad x \geq 13$

39. $|x - 5| < 0$

No solution. The absolute value of a number can never be less than zero.

41. $y = |x - 3|$

(a) $\qquad y \leq 2$

$\qquad |x - 3| \leq 2$

$\qquad -2 \leq x - 3 \leq 2$

$\qquad 1 \leq x \leq 5$

(b) $\qquad y \geq 4$

$\qquad |x - 3| \geq 4$

$\qquad x - 3 \leq -4$ or $x - 3 \geq 4$

$\qquad x \leq -1 \qquad x \geq 7$

43. The midpoint of the interval $[-3, 3]$ is 0. The interval represents all real numbers x no more than 3 units from 0.

$\qquad |x - 0| \leq 3$

$\qquad |x| \leq 3$

45. The graph shows all real numbers at least 3 units from 7.

$\qquad |x - 7| \geq 3$

47. All real numbers within 10 units of 12

$\qquad |x - 12| \leq 10$

49. (a) and (b) $y = 0.067x - 5.638$

The plot looks linear.

(c) $\quad\quad 3 \geq 0.067x - 5.638$

$\quad\quad 8.638 \geq 0.067x$

$\quad\quad\quad\quad x \geq 129$

(d) IQ scores are not a good predictor of GPAs. Other factors include study habits, class attendance, and attitude.

51. $\quad\quad (x + 2)^2 < 25$

$\quad\quad x^2 + 4x + 4 < 25$

$\quad\quad x^2 + 4x - 21 < 0$

$\quad\quad (x + 7)(x - 3) < 0$

Critical numbers: $x = -7, x = 3$

Test intervals: $(-\infty, -7), (-7, 3), (3, \infty)$

Test: Is $(x + 7)(x - 3) < 0$?

Solution set: $(-7, 3)$

53. $\quad\quad x^2 + 4x + 4 \geq 9$

$\quad\quad x^2 + 4x - 5 \geq 0$

$\quad\quad (x + 5)(x - 1) \geq 0$

Critical numbers: $x = -5, x = 1$

Test intervals: $(-\infty, -5), (-5, 1), (1, \infty)$

Test: Is $(x + 5)(x - 1) \geq 0$?

Solution set: $(-\infty, -5] \cup [1, \infty)$

55. $\quad\quad x^2 + x < 6$

$\quad\quad x^2 + x - 6 < 0$

$\quad\quad (x + 3)(x - 2) < 0$

Critical numbers: $x = -3, x = 2$

Test intervals: $(-\infty, -3), (-3, 2), (2, \infty)$

Test: Is $(x + 3)(x - 2) < 0$?

Solution set: $(-3, 2)$

57. $\quad\quad x^3 - 4x \geq 0$

$\quad\quad x(x + 2)(x - 2) \geq 0$

Critical number: $x = 0, x = \pm 2$

Test intervals: $(-\infty, -2), (-2, 0), (0, 2), (2, \infty)$

Test: Is $x(x + 2)(x - 2) \geq 0$?

Solution set: $[-2, 0] \cup [2, \infty)$

59. $y = -x^2 + 2x + 3$

(a) $y \leq 0$ when $x \leq -1$ or $x \geq 3$.

(b) $y \geq 3$ when $0 \leq x \leq 2$.

61. $y = \frac{1}{8}x^3 - \frac{1}{2}x$

(a) $y \geq 0$ when $-2 \leq x \leq 0, 2 \leq x < \infty$.

(b) $y \leq 6$ when $x \leq 4$.

63. $\dfrac{1}{x} - x > 0$

$\dfrac{1 - x^2}{x} > 0$

Critical numbers: $x = 0, x = \pm 1$

Test intervals: $(-\infty - 1), (-1, 0), (0, 1), (1, \infty)$

Test: Is $\dfrac{1 - x^2}{x} > 0$?

Solution set: $(-\infty, -1) \cup (0, 1)$

65. $\dfrac{x + 6}{x + 1} - 2 < 0$

$\dfrac{x + 6 - 2(x + 1)}{x + 1} < 0$

$\dfrac{4 - x}{x + 1} < 0$

Critical numbers: $x = -1, x = 4$

Test intervals: $(-\infty, -1), (-1, 4), (4, \infty)$

Test: Is $\dfrac{4 - x}{x + 1} < 0$?

Solution set: $(-\infty, -1) \cup (4, \infty)$

67. $y = \dfrac{3x}{x - 2}$

(a) $y \le 0$ when $0 \le x < 2$.

(b) $y \ge 6$ when $2 < x \le 4$.

69. $y = \dfrac{2x^2}{x^2 + 4}$

(a) $y \ge 1$ when $x \le -2$ or $x \ge 2$.

This can also be expressed as $|x| \ge 2$.

(b) $y \le 2$ for all real numbers x.

This can also be expressed as $-\infty < x < \infty$.

71. $4 - x^2 \ge 0$

$(2 + x)(2 - x) \ge 0$

Critical numbers: $x = \pm 2$

Test intervals: $(-\infty, -2), (-2, 2), (2, \infty)$

Test: Is $4 - x^2 \ge 0$?

Domain: $[-2, 2]$

73. $P = 5.9556 + 1.492t + 0.0056t^2, \ 0 \le t \le 40$

(a)

(b) $5.9556 + 1.492t + 0.0056t^2 \ge 25$

$0.0056t^2 + 1.492t - 19.0444 \ge 0$

By the Quadratic Formula, the critical numbers are $t \approx -278.63$ and $t \approx 12.21$. Only $t \approx 12.21$ makes sense, and this corresponds to the year 1962.

75. According to the graph, if the frequency is 600 vibrations per second, then the thickness is approximately 3.6 mm.

77. According to the graph, if the thickness is less than 3 mm, then the frequency is less than 500: $0 < v < 500$.

Section 2.6   Exploring Data: Linear Models and Scatter Plots

■ You should know how to construct a scatter plot.

■ You should know how to fit a line to data by

(a) Visually determining the line.

(b) Finding the least squares regression line.

Solutions to Odd-Numbered Exercises

1. Negative correlation—y decreases as x increases.

3. No correlation.

5. (a)

(b) Yes. The cancer mortality increases linearly with increased exposure to the carcinogenic substance.

7. (a) $y = 0.42x + 1.50$

(b)

(c) Yes, the model appears valid.

9. (a) $y = 0.95x + 0.92$

(b)

(c) Yes, the model appears valid.

11. (a) $d = 0.066F$ or $F = 15.15d$

(b)

The model fits well.

(c) If $F = 55$, then $d \approx 0.066(55) = 3.63$ cm.

13. (a) $R = 1.21t + 4.73$

(b)

(c) The slope is the average increase in the monthly basic rate per year.

(d) For the year 2000, $t = 20$, and $R \approx \$28.84$.

15. (a) $y = 47.77x + 103.77$

(b)

(c) The slope is the average increase in sales for increases in advertising expenditures.

(d) If $x = \$1500$, then $y \approx \$175,000$.

17. (a) $y = -0.64x + 1321.56$

(b)

(c) The negative slope indicates that the amount of mortgage debt held by commercial banks is increasing as the amount held by savings institutions decreases.

❑ Review Exercises for Chapter 2

Solutions to Odd-Numbered Exercises

1.
$$6 - (x - 2)^2 = 2 + 4x - x^2$$
$$6 - (x^2 - 4x + 4) = 2 + 4x - x^2$$
$$2 + 4x - x^2 = 2 + 4x - x^2$$
$$0 = 0 \qquad \text{Identity}$$

All real numbers are solutions.

3. $2x^2 + 7x - 4 = 0$

(a) $x = 0$

$2(0)^2 + 7(0) - 4 \stackrel{?}{=} 0$

No, $x = 0$ is not a solution.

(b) $x = -4$

$2(-4)^2 + 7(-4) - 4 \stackrel{?}{=} 0$

$32 - 88 - 4 \stackrel{?}{=} 0$

$0 = 0$

Yes, $x = -4$ is a solution.

(c) $x = \frac{1}{2}$

$2\left(\frac{1}{2}\right)^2 + 7\left(\frac{1}{2}\right) - 4 \stackrel{?}{=} 0$

$\frac{1}{2} + \frac{7}{2} - 4 \stackrel{?}{=} 0$

$0 = 0$

Yes, $x = \frac{1}{2}$ is a solution.

(d) $x = -1$

$2(-1)^2 + 7(-1) - 4 \stackrel{?}{=} 0$

$2 - 7 - 4 \stackrel{?}{=} 0$

No, $x = -1$ is not a solution.

5. $3x - 2(x + 5) = 10$
$$3x - 2x - 10 = 10$$
$$x = 20$$

7. $4(x + 3) - 3 = 2(4 - 3x) - 4$
$$4x + 12 - 3 = 8 - 6x - 4$$
$$4x + 9 = -6x + 4$$
$$10x = -5$$
$$x = -\frac{1}{2}$$

9. $3\left(1 - \dfrac{1}{5t}\right) = 0$
$$1 - \frac{1}{5t} = 0$$
$$1 = \frac{1}{5t}$$
$$5t = 1$$
$$t = \frac{1}{5}$$

11. $6x = 3x^2$
$$0 = 3x^2 - 6x$$
$$0 = 3x(x - 2)$$
$$3x = 0 \implies x = 0$$
$$x - 2 = 0 \implies x = 2$$

13. $(x + 4)^2 = 18$
$$x + 4 = \pm\sqrt{18}$$
$$x = -4 \pm 3\sqrt{2}$$

15. $x^2 - 12x + 30 = 0$

$$x^2 - 12x = -30$$

$$x^2 - 12x + 36 = -30 + 36$$

$$(x - 6)^2 = 6$$

$$x - 6 = \pm\sqrt{6}$$

$$x = 6 \pm \sqrt{6}$$

17. $5x^4 - 12x^3 = 0$

$$x^3(5x - 12) = 0$$

$$x^3 = 0 \quad \text{or} \quad 5x - 12 = 0$$

$$x = 0 \quad \text{or} \qquad x = \tfrac{12}{5}$$

19. $\dfrac{4}{(x - 4)^2} = 1$

$$4 = (x - 4)^2$$

$$\pm 2 = x - 4$$

$$4 \pm 2 = x$$

$$x = 6 \quad \text{or} \quad x = 2$$

21. $\sqrt{x + 4} = 3$

$$\left(\sqrt{x + 4}\right)^2 = (3)^2$$

$$x + 4 = 9$$

$$x = 5$$

23. $\qquad 2\sqrt{x} - 5 = 0$

$$2\sqrt{x} = 5$$

$$4x = 25$$

$$x = \tfrac{25}{4}$$

25. $\sqrt{2x + 3} + \sqrt{x - 2} = 2$

$$\left(\sqrt{2x + 3}\right)^2 = \left(2 - \sqrt{x - 2}\right)^2$$

$$2x + 3 = 4 - 4\sqrt{x - 2} + x - 2$$

$$x + 1 = -4\sqrt{x - 2}$$

$$(x + 1)^2 = \left(-4\sqrt{x - 2}\right)^2$$

$$x^2 + 2x + 1 = 16(x - 2)$$

$$x^2 - 14x + 33 = 0$$

$$(x - 3)(x - 11) = 0$$

$x = 3$, extraneous or $x = 11$, extraneous

No solution.

(You can verify that the graph of
$y = \sqrt{2x + 3} + \sqrt{x - 2} - 2$ lies above the
x-axis.)

27. $(x - 1)^{2/3} - 25 = 0$

$$(x - 1)^{2/3} = 25$$

$$(x - 1)^2 = 25^3$$

$$x - 1 = \pm\sqrt{25^3}$$

$$x = 1 \pm 125$$

$$x = 126 \quad \text{or} \quad x = -124$$

29. $(x + 4)^{1/2} + 5x(x + 4)^{3/2} = 0$

$(x + 4)^{1/2}[1 + 5x(x + 4)] = 0$

$(x + 4)^{1/2}(5x^2 + 20x + 1) = 0$

$$(x + 4)^{1/2} = 0 \quad \text{OR} \quad 5x^2 + 20x + 1 = 0$$

$$x = -4$$

$$x = \frac{-20 \pm \sqrt{400 - 20}}{10}$$

$$x = \frac{-20 \pm 2\sqrt{95}}{10}$$

$$x = -2 \pm \frac{\sqrt{95}}{5}$$

31. $|x - 5| = 10$

$x - 5 = -10 \quad \text{or} \quad x - 5 = 10$

$x = -5 \qquad\qquad x = 15$

33. $|x^2 - 3| = 2x$

$$x^2 - 3 = 2x \quad \text{OR} \qquad x^2 - 3 = -2x$$

$$x^2 - 2x - 3 = 0 \qquad x^2 + 2x - 3 = 0$$

$$(x - 3)(x + 1) = 0 \qquad (x + 3)(x - 1) = 0$$

$$x = 3 \quad \text{or} \quad x = -1 \qquad x = -3 \quad \text{or} \quad x = 1$$

The only solutions to the original equation are $x = 3$ or $x = 1$. ($x = -3$ and $x = -1$ are extraneous.)

35. $y = 4x^3 - 12x^2 + 8x$

$0 = 4x^3 - 12x^2 + 8x$

$0 = 4x(x^2 - 3x + 2)$

$0 = 4x(x - 1)(x - 2)$

$x = 0, \; x = 1, \; \text{or} \; x = 2$

x-intercepts: $(0, 0), (1, 0), (2, 0)$

37. $y = \dfrac{1}{x} + \dfrac{1}{x + 1} - 2$

$0 = \dfrac{1}{x} + \dfrac{1}{x + 1} - 2$

$2 = \dfrac{1}{x} + \dfrac{1}{x + 1}$

$2x(x + 1) = (x + 1) + x$

$2x^2 + 2x = 2x + 1$

$2x^2 = 1$

x-intercepts: $\left(\pm\dfrac{\sqrt{2}}{2}, 0 \right)$

$x^2 = \dfrac{1}{2}$

$$x = \pm\sqrt{\dfrac{1}{2}} = \pm\dfrac{\sqrt{2}}{2}$$

39.

$$\sqrt{x^2 + 1} + x - 9 = 0$$
$$\left(\sqrt{x^2 + 1}\right)^2 = (9 - x)^2$$
$$x^2 + 1 = 81 - 18x + x^2$$
$$18x = 80$$
$$x = \frac{40}{9}$$

Intercept $\left(\frac{40}{9}, 0\right) \approx (4.44, 0)$

41.
$$V = \frac{1}{3}\pi r^2 h$$
$$3V = \pi r^2 h$$
$$\frac{3V}{\pi h} = r^2$$
$$r = \sqrt{\frac{3V}{\pi h}}$$

Since r represents the radius of a cone, r is positive only.

43.
$$L = \frac{k}{3\pi r^2 p}$$
$$3\pi r^2 p L = k$$
$$p = \frac{k}{3\pi r^2 L}$$

45. $y = C\sqrt{x + 1}$
$8 = C\sqrt{3 + 1}$
$8 = C\sqrt{3 + 1}$
$8 = C(2)$
$4 = C$

47. $(7 + 5i) + (-4 + 2i) = (7 - 4) + (5i + 2i)$
$$= 3 + 7i$$

49. $5i(13 - 8i) = 65i - 40i^2 = 40 + 65i$

51. $(10 - 8i)(2 - 3i) = 20 - 30i - 16i + 24i^2$
$$= -4 - 46i$$

53. $\dfrac{6 + i}{i} = \dfrac{6 + i}{i} \cdot \dfrac{-i}{-i} = \dfrac{-6i - i^2}{-i^2}$

$$= \dfrac{-6i + 1}{1} = 1 - 6i$$

55. $\dfrac{4}{-3i} = \dfrac{4}{-3i} \cdot \dfrac{3i}{3i} = \dfrac{12i}{9} = \dfrac{4i}{3} = \dfrac{4}{3}i$

57.

$y = 3x^2 + 1$ has no x-intercepts, and hence has no real zeros.

$$3x^2 + 1 = 0$$
$$3x^2 = -1$$
$$x^2 = -\frac{1}{3}$$
$$x = \pm\sqrt{-\frac{1}{3}} = \sqrt{\frac{1}{3}}i \text{ (2 complex zeros)}$$

59.

$y = x^3 - 4x^2 + 5x$ has one x-intercept, $(0, 0)$. Hence, there is one real zero.

$$x^3 - 4x^2 + 5x = 0$$
$$x(x^2 - 4x + 5) = 0$$
$$x = 0 \quad \text{or} \quad x = \frac{4 \pm \sqrt{(-4)^2 - 4(1)(5)}}{2}$$
$$= \frac{4 \pm \sqrt{-4}}{2}$$
$$= 2 \pm i$$

61. $\frac{1}{2}(3 - x) > \frac{1}{3}(2 - 3x)$

$3(3 - x) > 2(2 - 3x)$

$9 - 3x > 4 - 6x$

$3x > -5$

$x > -\frac{5}{3}, \left(-\frac{5}{3}, \infty\right)$

63. $\frac{x - 5}{3 - x} < 0$

Critical numbers: $x = 5, x = 3$

Test intervals: $(-\infty, 3), (3, 5), (5, \infty)$

Test: Is $\frac{x - 5}{3 - x} < 0$?

Solution set: $(-\infty, 3) \cup (5, \infty)$

65. $|x - 2| < 1$

$-1 < x - 2 < 1$

$1 < x < 3$

which can be written as $(1, 3)$.

67. $\left|x - \frac{3}{2}\right| \geq \frac{3}{2}$

$x - \frac{3}{2} \leq -\frac{3}{2}$ or $x - \frac{3}{2} \geq \frac{3}{2}$

$x \leq 0$ or $x \geq 3$

which can be written as $(-\infty, 0] \cup [3, \infty)$.

69.

The graphs of $y_1 = \frac{x}{5} - 6$ and $y_2 = -\frac{x}{2} + 6$ cross

at $x = \frac{120}{7}$. Hence, $\frac{x}{5} - 6 \leq -\frac{x}{2} + 6$ for $x \leq \frac{120}{7}$.

71. The graph of $y = (x - 4)|x|$ is above the x-axis for $x > 4$. Hence, $(x - 4)|x| > 0$ for $x > 4$.

73. $2x - 10 \geq 0$

$2x \geq 10$

$x \geq 5$

Domain: $[5, \infty)$

75. September's profit + October's profit = 689,000

Let x = September's profit.

$1 < x < 3$

Then $x + 0.12x$ = October's profit

$x + (x + 0.12x) = 689,000$

$2.12x = 689,000$

$x = 325,000$

$x + 0.12x = 364,000$

September: $325,000

October: $364,000

77. Let x = the number of quarts of pure antifreeze.

30% of $(10 - x)$ + 100% of x = 50% of 10

$0.30(10 - x) + 1.00x = 0.50(10)$

$3 - 0.30x + 1.00x = 5$

$0.70x = 2$

$x = \frac{2}{0.70} = \frac{20}{7} = 2\frac{6}{7}$ quarts

79. Let x = the number of farmers in the group.

$$\text{Cost per farmer} = \frac{48,000}{x}$$

If two more farmers join the group, the cost per farmer will be $\dfrac{48,000}{x + 2}$.

Since this new cost is \$4000 less than the original cost:

$$\frac{48,000}{x} - 4000 = \frac{48,000}{x + 2}$$

$$48,000(x + 2) - 4000x(x + 2) = 48,000x$$

$$12(x + 2) - x(x + 2) = 12x \qquad \text{Divide both sides by 4000.}$$

$$12x + 24 - x^2 - 2x = 12x$$

$$0 = x^2 + 2x - 24$$

$$0 = (x + 6)(x - 4)$$

$$x = -6, \text{extraneous} \quad \text{or} \quad x = 4$$

$$x = 4 \text{ farmers}$$

81.

	Rate	Time	Distance
To work	r	$\dfrac{56}{r}$	56
From work	$r + 8$	$\dfrac{56}{r + 8}$	56

$$\text{Time} = \frac{\text{Distance}}{\text{Rate}}$$

Time to work = Time from work + 10 minutes

$$\frac{56}{r} = \frac{56}{r + 8} + \frac{1}{6} \quad \text{Convert minutes to portion of an hour.}$$

$$6(r + 8)(56) = 6r(56) + r(r + 8)$$

$$336r + 2688 = 336r + r^2 + 8r$$

$$0 = r^2 + 8r - 2688$$

$$0 = (r - 48)(r + 56)$$

Using the positive value for r, we have $r = 48$ mph. The average speed on the trip home was $r + 8 = 56$ mph.

83. c, b, d, a

85. (a) $y = -1.20x + 64.27$

(b)

(c) The point (27, 44) seems out of place. By eliminating it, the revised model is $y = -1.43x + 66.44$.

❑ **Cumulative Test for Chapters P–2**

1. $\dfrac{8x^2y^{-3}}{30x^{-1}y^2} = \dfrac{8x^3}{30y^5} = \dfrac{4x^3}{15y^5}$

2. $\sqrt{24x^4y^3} = \sqrt{2^2 \cdot 6(x^2)^2y(y^2)} = 2x^2y\sqrt{6y}$

3. $4x - [2x + 3(2 - x)] = 4x - 2x - 6 + 3x = 5x - 6$

4. $(x - 2)(x^2 + x - 3) = x^3 + x^2 - 3x - 2x^2 - 2x + 6$
$$= x^3 - x^2 - 5x + 6$$

5. $\dfrac{2}{s + 3} - \dfrac{1}{s + 1} = \dfrac{2s + 2 - s - 3}{(s + 1)(s + 3)} = \dfrac{s - 1}{(s + 1)(s + 3)}$

6. $25 - (x - 2)^2 = [5 - (x - 2)][5 + (x - 2)] = (7 - x)(3 + x)$

7. $x - 5x^2 - 6x^3 = -x(6x^2 + 5x - 1) = -x(6x - 1)(x + 1)$
$$= x(x + 1)(1 - 6x)$$

8. $54 - 16x^3 = 2(27 - 8x^3) = 2(3 - 2x)(9 + 6x + 4x^2)$

9. $x - 3y + 12 = 0$
$$-3y = -x - 12$$
$$y = \dfrac{x}{3} + 4$$

10. $y = x^2 - 9$

11. $y = \sqrt{4 - x}$

12. Slope $= \dfrac{8 - 1}{3 - (-1/2)} = \dfrac{7}{7/2} = 2$
$$y - 8 = 2(x - 3)$$
$$y = 2x + 2$$

13. No, for some x there corresponds two values of y.

14. $f(6) = \dfrac{6}{6 - 2} = \dfrac{3}{2}$

$f(2)$ is undefined (division by zero).

$f(s + 2) = \dfrac{s + 2}{(s + 2) - 2} = \dfrac{s + 2}{s}$

15. (a) $r(x) = \frac{1}{2}\sqrt[3]{x}$ is a vertical shrink of $y = \sqrt[3]{x}$.

(b) $h(x) = \sqrt[3]{x} + 2$ is a vertical shift 2 units upward.

(c) $g(x) = \sqrt[3]{x + 2}$ is a horizontal shift 2 units to the left.

16. $h(x) = 5x - 2$ Is one-to-one, since it is a nonvertical line.

$$y = 5x - 2$$

$$x = 5y - 2 \qquad \text{Interchange } x \text{ and } y.$$

$$h^{-1}(x) = y = \tfrac{1}{5}(x + 2) \qquad \text{Solve for } y.$$

17. $2x - 3(x - 4) = 5$

$$2x - 3x + 12 = 5$$

$$-x = -7$$

$$x = 7$$

18. $\dfrac{2}{t - 3} + \dfrac{2}{t - 2} = \dfrac{10}{t^2 + 5t + 6} = \dfrac{10}{(t - 3)(t - 2)}$

$$2(t - 2) + 2(t - 3) = 10$$

$$4t - 10 = 10$$

$$t = 5$$

19. $3y^2 + 6y + 2 = 0$

$$y = \frac{-6 \pm \sqrt{6^2 - 4(3)(2)}}{2(3)}$$

$$= \frac{-6 \pm \sqrt{12}}{6}$$

$$= -1 \pm \frac{1}{3}\sqrt{3}$$

20. $\sqrt{x + 10} = x - 2$

$$x + 10 = (x - 2)^2 = x^2 - 4x + 4$$

$$x^2 - 5x - 6 = 0$$

$$(x - 6)(x + 1) = 0$$

$$x = 6 \qquad (x = -1 \text{ is extraneous.})$$

21. Using your graphing utility, you obtain $y = 0.0568x - 1.5808$. For $x = 88$, $y \approx 3.4$.

❏ Practice Test for Chapter 2

1. Solve the equation $\frac{1}{2}x - \frac{1}{3}(x - 1) = 10$. Verify your answer with a graphing utility.

2. Solve the equation $(x + 1)^2 - 6 = x^2 + 3x$ and verify your answer with a graphing utility.

3. Solve $A = \frac{1}{2}(a + b)h$ for a.

4. 301 is what percent of 4300?

5. Cindy has \$6.05 in quarters and nickels. How many of each coin does she have if there are 53 coins in all?

6. Ed has \$15,000 invested in two funds paying $9\frac{1}{2}\%$ and 11% simple interest, respectively. How much is invested in each if the yearly interest is \$1582.50?

7. Use a graphing utility to approximate any points of intersection of $y = 3x^2 - 4$ and $y = 2 - x$.

8. Use a graphing utility to approximate any points of intersection of $y = 2x^2 + 3$ and $y = 5 + \sqrt{x}$.

9. Write $\dfrac{2}{1 + i}$ in standard form.

10. Write $\dfrac{3 + i}{2} - \dfrac{i + 1}{4}$ in standard form.

11. Solve $28 + 5x - 3x^2 = 0$ by factoring.

12. Solve $(x - 2)^2 = 24$ by taking the square root of both sides.

13. Solve $x^2 - 4x - 9 = 0$ by completing the square.

14. Solve $x^2 + 5x - 1 = 0$ by the Quadratic Formula.

15. Solve $3x^2 - 2x + 4 = 0$ by the Quadratic Formula.

16. The perimeter of a rectangle is 1100 feet. Find the dimension so that the enclosed area will be 60,000 square feet.

17. Find two consecutive even positive integers whose product is 624.

18. Solve $x^3 - 10x^2 + 24x = 0$ by factoring.

19. Solve $\sqrt[3]{6 - x} = 4$.

20. Solve $(x^2 - 8)^{2/5} = 4$.

21. Solve $x^4 - x^2 - 12 = 0$.

22. Solve $4 - 3x > 16$.

23. Solve $\left|\dfrac{x - 3}{2}\right| < 5$.

24. Solve $\dfrac{x + 1}{x - 3} < 2$.

25. Solve $|3x - 4| \geq 9$.

26. Use a graphing utility to find the least squares regression line for the points $(-1, 0)$, $(0, 1)$, $(3, 3)$ and $(4, 5)$. Graph the points and the line.

CHAPTER 3
Polynomial and Rational Functions

CHAPTER 3
Polynomial and Rational Functions

Section 3.1 Quadratic Functions

You should know the following facts about parabolas.

- $f(x) = ax^2 + bx + c$, $a \neq 0$, is a quadratic function, and its graph is a parabola.

- If $a > 0$, the parabola opens upward and the vertex is the minimum point. If $a < 0$, the parabola opens downward and the vertex is the maximum point.

- The vertex is $(-b/2a, f(-b/2a))$.

- To find the x-intercepts (if any), solve

    $ax^2 + bx + c = 0$.

- The standard form of the equation of a parabola is

    $f(x) = a(x - h)^2 + k$

    where $a \neq 0$.

    (a) The vertex is (h, k).

    (b) The axis is the vertical line $x = h$.

Solutions to Odd-Numbered Exercises

1. $f(x) = (x - 2)^2$ opens upward and has vertex $(2, 0)$. Matches graph (g).

3. $f(x) = x^2 - 2$ opens upward and has vertex $(0, -2)$. Matches graph (b).

5. $f(x) = 4 - (x - 2)^2 = -(x - 2)^2 + 4$ opens downward and has vertex $(2, 4)$. Matches graph (f).

7. $f(x) = x^2 + 3$ opens upward and has vertex $(0, 3)$. Matches graph (e).

9. (a) $y = \frac{1}{2}x^2$

Vertical shrink

(b) $y = -\frac{1}{8}x^2$

Vertical shrink and reflection in the x-axis

(c) $y = \frac{3}{2}x^2$

Vertical stretch

(d) $y = -3x^2$

Vertical stretch and reflection in the x-axis

120

11. (a) $y = (x - 1)^2$

Horizontal translation one unit to the right

(b) $y = (x + 1)^2$

Horizontal translation one unit to the left

(c) $y = (x - 3)^2$

Horizontal translation three units to the right

(d) $y = (x + 3)^2$

Horizontal translation three units to the left

13. $f(x) = 16 - x^2$
Vertex: $(0, 16)$
Intercepts: $(-4, 0)$, $(0, 16)$, $(4, 0)$

15. $h(x) = x^2 - 8x + 16 = (x - 4)^2$
Vertex: $(4, 0)$
Intercepts: $(0, 16)$, $(4, 0)$

17. $f(x) = x^2 - x + \frac{5}{4} = \left(x - \frac{1}{2}\right)^2 + 1$
Vertex: $\left(\frac{1}{2}, 1\right)$
Intercepts: $\left(0, \frac{5}{4}\right)$

19. $f(x) = -x^2 + 2x + 5 = -(x - 1)^2 + 6$
Vertex: $(1, 6)$
Intercepts: $\left(1 - \sqrt{6}, 0\right)$, $(0, 5)$, $\left(1 + \sqrt{6}, 0\right)$

21. $h(x) = 4x^2 - 4x + 21 = 4\left(x - \frac{1}{2}\right)^2 + 20$

Vertex: $\left(\frac{1}{2}, 20\right)$

Intercept: $(0, 21)$

23. $f(x) = -(x^2 + 2x - 3) = -(x + 1)^2 + 4$

Vertex: $(-1, 4)$

Intercepts: $(-3, 0), (0, 3), (1, 0)$

25. $f(x) = 2x^2 - 16x + 31$

$\quad\quad = 2(x - 4)^2 - 1$

Vertex: $(4, -1)$

Intercepts: $\left(4 \pm \frac{1}{2}\sqrt{2}, 0\right), (0, 31)$

27. $(1, 0)$ is the vertex.

$f(x) = a(x - 1)^2 + 0 = a(x - 1)^2$

Since the graph passes through the point $(0, 1)$ we have:

$\quad 1 = a(0 - 1)^2$

$\quad 1 = a$

$\quad f(x) = 1(x - 1)^2 = (x - 1)^2$

29. $(-2, 2)$ is the vertex.

$f(x) = a(x + 2)^2 + 2$

Since the graph passes through the point $(-1, 0)$, we have:

$\quad 0 = a(-1 + 2)^2 + 2$

$\quad -2 = a$

$\quad f(x) = -2(x + 2)^2 + 2$

31. $(-2, 5)$ is the vertex.

$f(x) = a(x + 2)^2 + 5$

Since the graph passes through the point $(0, 9)$, we have:

$\quad 9 = a(0 + 2)^2 + 5$

$\quad 4 = 4a$

$\quad 1 = a$

$\quad f(x) = 1(x + 2)^2 + 5 = (x + 2)^2 + 5$

33. $(3, 4)$ is the vertex.

$f(x) = a(x - 3)^2 + 4$

Since the graph passes through the point $(1, 2)$, we have:

$\quad 2 = a(1 - 3)^2 + 4$

$\quad -2 = 4a$

$\quad -\frac{1}{2} = a$

$\quad f(x) = -\frac{1}{2}(x - 3)^2 + 4$

35. $(5, 12)$ is the vertex.

$f(x) = a(x - 5)^2 + 12$

Since the graph passes through the point $(7, 15)$, we have:

$\quad 15 = a(7 - 5)^2 + 12$

$\quad 3 = 4a \quad \Rightarrow \quad a = \frac{3}{4}$

$\quad f(x) = \frac{3}{4}(x - 5)^2 + 12$

37. $y = x^2 - 16$ $0 = x^2 - 16$

x-intercepts: $(\pm 4, 0)$ $x^2 = 16$

$x = \pm 4$

39. $y = x^2 - 4x - 5$ $0 = x^2 - 4x - 5$

x-intercepts: $(5, 0), (-1, 0)$ $0 = (x - 5)(x + 1)$

$x = 5$ or $x = -1$

41. $y = x^2 - 4x$

$0 = x^2 - 4x$

$0 = x(x - 4)$

$x = 0$ or $x = 4$

x-intercepts: $(0, 0),\ (4, 0)$

43. $y = 2x^2 - 7x - 30$

$0 = 2x^2 - 7x - 30$

$0 = (2x + 5)(x - 6)$

$x = -\frac{5}{2}$ or $x = 6$

x-intercepts: $\left(-\frac{5}{2}, 0\right),\ (6, 0)$

45. $f(x) = [x - (-1)](x - 3)$ opens upward

$\quad = (x + 1)(x - 3)$

$\quad = x^2 - 2x - 3$

$f(x) = -[x - (-1)](x - 3)$

$\quad = -(x + 1)(x - 3)$ opens

$\quad = -(x^2 - 2x - 3)$ downward

$\quad = -x^2 + 2x + 3$

Note: $f(x) = a(x + 1)(x - 3)$ has x-intercepts $(-1, 0)$ and $(3, 0)$ for all real numbers $a \neq 0$.

47. $f(x) = [x - (-3)]\left[x - \left(-\frac{1}{2}\right)\right](2)$ opens upward

$\quad = (x + 3)\left(x + \frac{1}{2}\right)(2)$

$\quad = (x + 3)(2x + 1)$

$\quad = 2x^2 + 7x + 3$

$f(x) = -(2x^2 + 7x + 3)$ opens downward

$\quad = -2x^2 - 7x - 3$

Note: $f(x) = a(x + 3)(2x + 1)$ has x-intercepts $(-3, 0)$ and $\left(-\frac{1}{2}, 0\right)$ for all real numbers $a \neq 0$.

49. Let $x =$ the first number and $y =$ the second number. Then the sum is

$x + y = 110 \quad \Rightarrow \quad y = 110 - x.$

The product is $P(x) = xy = x(110 - x) = 110x - x^2.$

$P(x) = -x^2 + 110x$

$\quad = -(x^2 - 110x + 3025 - 3025)$

$\quad = -[(x - 55)^2 - 3025]$

$\quad = -(x - 55)^2 + 3025$

The maximum value of the product occurs at the vertex of $P(x)$ and is 3025. This happens when $x = y = 55$.

51.

$2x + 2y = 100$

$y = 50 - x$

(a) $A(x) = xy = x(50 - x)$

Domain: $0 < x < 50$

—CONTINUED—

51. —CONTINUED—

(b)

(c) The area is maximum (625 square feet) when $x = y = 25$. The rectangle has dimensions 25 ft $\times$ 25 ft. Algebraically, you have:

$$A(x) = -(x^2 - 50x)$$
$$= -(x^2 - 50x + 625) + 625$$
$$= -(x - 25)^2 + 625$$

53. $R = 900x - 0.1x^2 = -0.1x^2 + 900x$

The vertex occurs at

$$x = -\frac{b}{2a} = -\frac{900}{2(-0.1)} = 4500.$$

The revenue is maximum when $x = 4500$ units.

55. (a) $4x + 3y = 200 \implies y = \frac{1}{3}(200 - 4x)$ (b)

x	y	Area
2	$\frac{1}{3}[200 - 4(2)]$	$2xy = 256$
4	$\frac{1}{3}[200 - 4(4)]$	$2xy \approx 490$
6	$\frac{1}{3}[200 - 4(6)]$	$2xy = 704$
8	$\frac{1}{3}[200 - 4(8)]$	$2xy = 896$
10	$\frac{1}{3}[200 - 4(10)]$	$2xy \approx 1067$
12	$\frac{1}{3}[200 - 4(12)]$	$2xy = 1216$

x	y	Area
20	$\frac{1}{3}[200 - 4(20)]$	$2xy = 1600$
22	$\frac{1}{3}[200 - 4(22)]$	$2xy \approx 1643$
24	$\frac{1}{3}[200 - 4(24)]$	$2xy = 1664$
26	$\frac{1}{3}[200 - 4(26)]$	$2xy = 1664$
28	$\frac{1}{3}[200 - 4(28)]$	$2xy \approx 1643$
30	$\frac{1}{3}[200 - 4(30)]$	$2xy = 1600$

(c) $A = 2xy = 2x\left(\dfrac{200 - 4x}{3}\right) = \dfrac{2x(4)(50 - x)}{3}$

$\qquad = \dfrac{8x(50 - x)}{3}$

(d)

This area is maximum when $x = 25$ feet and $y = \frac{100}{3} = 33\frac{1}{3}$ feet.

(e) $A = \dfrac{8}{3}x(50 - x)$

$\qquad = -\dfrac{8}{3}(x^2 - 50x)$

$\qquad = -\dfrac{8}{3}(x^2 - 50x + 625 - 625)$

$\qquad = -\dfrac{8}{3}[(x - 25)^2 - 625]$

$\qquad = -\dfrac{8}{3}(x - 25)^2 + \dfrac{5000}{3}$

The maximum area occurs at the vertex and is 5000/3 square feet. This happens when $x = 25$ feet and $y = (200 - 4(25))/3 = 100/3$ feet. The dimensions are $2x = 50$ feet by $33\frac{1}{3}$ feet.

57. $y = -\dfrac{1}{12}x^2 + 2x + 4$

(a)

(b) When $x = 0$, $y = 4$ feet.

(c) The vertex occurs at

$$x = -\frac{b}{2a} = -\frac{2}{2(-1/12)} = 12.$$

The maximum height is

$$y = -\frac{1}{12}(12)^2 + 2(12) + 4$$

$$= 16 \text{ feet.}$$

(d) You can solve this part graphically by finding the x-intercept of the graph:

$$x \approx 25.856.$$

When the ball strikes the ground, $y = 0$.

$$0 = -\frac{1}{12}x^2 + 2x + 4$$

$$0 = x^2 - 24x - 48 \quad \text{Multiply both sides by } -12.$$

$$x = \frac{-(-24) \pm \sqrt{(-24)^2 - 4(1)(-48)}}{2(1)}$$

$$= \frac{24 \pm \sqrt{768}}{2} = \frac{24 \pm 16\sqrt{3}}{2} = 12 \pm 8\sqrt{3}$$

Using the positive value for x, we have $x = 12 + 8\sqrt{3} \approx 25.86$ feet.

59. $V = 0.77x^2 - 1.32x - 9.31$, $5 \le x \le 40$

(a)

(b) $V(16) = 166.69$ board feet

(c) $500 = 0.77x^2 - 1.32x - 9.31$

$$0 = 0.77x^2 - 1.32x - 509.31$$

Using the Quadratic Formula and selecting the positive value for x, we have $x \approx 26.6$ inches in diameter. Or, use a graphing utility.

61. $C = 4024.5 + 51.4t - 3.1t^2$, $-10 \le t \le 30$

(a)

(b) $-\dfrac{b}{2a} = \dfrac{-51.4}{2(-3.1)} \approx 8.29$

The vertex occurs when $x \approx 8.29$ which corresponds to 1968. The warnings may not have had an immediate effect, but over time they and other findings about the health risks of cigarettes have had an effect.

(c) $C(0) = 4024.5$ annually; $\dfrac{4024.5}{366} \approx 11$ daily

63. (a) If $f(x) = ax^2 + bx + c$ has two real zeros, then by the Quadratic Formula they are

$$x = \frac{-b \pm \sqrt{b^2 - 4ac}}{2a}.$$

The average of the zeros of f is

$$\frac{\dfrac{-b - \sqrt{b^2 - 4ac}}{2a} + \dfrac{-b + \sqrt{b^2 - 4ac}}{2a}}{2} = \frac{\dfrac{-2b}{2a}}{2} = -\frac{b}{2a}.$$

This is the x-coordinate of the vertex of the graph.

(b) The zeros of $f(x) = \frac{1}{2}(x - 3)^2 - 2$

$$= \frac{1}{2}(x^2 - 6x + 5)$$

$$= \frac{1}{2}(x - 15)(x - 1) \text{ are } x = 1, 5.$$

The x-coordinate of the vertex is 3, the average of 1 and 5.

Section 3.2 Polynomial Functions of Higher Degree

- You should know the following basic principles about polynomials.
- $f(x) = a_n x^n + a_{n-1}x^{n-1} + \cdots + a_2 x^2 + a_1 x + a_0$ is a polynomial function of degree n.
- If f is of odd degree and
  - (a) $a_n > 0$, then
    - 1. $f(x) \to \infty$ as $x \to \infty$.
    - 2. $f(x) \to -\infty$ as $x \to -\infty$.
  - (b) $a_n < 0$, then
    - 1. $f(x) \to -\infty$ as $x \to \infty$.
    - 2. $f(x) \to \infty$ as $x \to -\infty$.
- If f is of even degree and
  - (a) $a_n > 0$, then
    - 1. $f(x) \to \infty$ as $x \to \infty$.
    - 2. $f(x) \to \infty$ as $x \to -\infty$.
  - (b) $a_n < 0$, then
    - 1. $f(x) \to -\infty$ as $x \to \infty$.
    - 2. $f(x) \to -\infty$ as $x \to -\infty$.
- The following are equivalent for a polynomial function.
  - (a) $x = a$ is a zero of a function.
  - (b) $x = a$ is a solution of the polynomial equation $f(x) = 0$.
  - (c) $(x - a)$ is a factor of the polynomial.
  - (d) $(a, 0)$ is an x-intercept of the graph of f.
- A polynomial of degree n has at most n distinct zeros.
- If f is a polynomial function such that $a < b$ and $f(a) \neq f(b)$, then f takes on every value between $f(a)$ and $f(b)$ in the interval $[a, b]$.
- If you can find a value where a polynomial is positive and another value where it is negative, then there is at least one real zero between the values.

Solutions to Odd-Numbered Exercises

1. $f(x) = -2x + 3$ is a line with y-intercept $(0, 3)$. Matches graph (f).

3. $f(x) = -2x^2 - 5x$ is a parabola with x-intercepts $(0, 0)$ and $\left(-\frac{5}{2}, 0\right)$ and opens downward. Matches graph (c).

5. $f(x) = -\frac{1}{4}x^4 + 3x^2$ has intercepts $(0, 0)$ and $\left(\pm 2\sqrt{3}, 0\right)$. Matches graph (e).

7. $f(x) = x^4 + 2x^3$ has intercepts $(0, 0)$ and $(-2, 0)$. Matches graph (g).

9. $y = x^3$

   (a) $f(x) = (x - 2)^3$

        Horizontal shift two units to the right

   (b) $f(x) = x^3 - 2$

        Vertical shift two units downward

   (c) $f(x) = -\frac{1}{2}x^3$

        Reflection in the x-axis and a vertical shrink

   (d) $f(x) = (x - 2)^3 - 2$

        Horizontal shift two units to the right and a vertical shift two units downward

11. $y = x^4$

   (a) $f(x) = (x + 3)^4$

        Horizontal shift three units to the left

   (b) $f(x) = x^4 - 3$

        Vertical shift three units downward

—CONTINUED—

11. **—CONTINUED—**

(c) $f(x) = 4 - x^4$

Reflection in the x-axis and then a vertical shift four units upward

(d) $f(x) = \frac{1}{2}(x - 1)^4$

Horizontal shift one unit to the right and a vertical shrink

13. $f(x) = 3x^3 - 9x + 1$; $g(x) = 3x^3$

15. $f(x) = -(x^4 - 4x^3 + 16x)$; $g(x) = -x^4$

17. $f(x) = 2x^2 - 3x + 1$

Degree: 2

Leading coefficient: 2

The degree is even and the leading coefficient is positive. The graph rises to the left and right.

19. $g(x) = 5 - \frac{7}{2}x - 3x^2$

Degree: 2

Leading coefficient: -3

The degree is even and the leading coefficient is negative. The graph falls to the left and right.

21. $f(x) = 2x^5 - 5x^3 + 7.5$

Degree: 5

Leading coefficient: 2

The degree is odd and the leading coefficient is positive. The graph falls to the left and rises to the right.

23. $f(x) = 6 - 2x + 4x^2 - 5x^3$

Degree: 3

Leading coefficient: -5

The degree is odd and the leading coefficient is negative. The graph rises to the left and falls to the right.

25. $h(t) = -\frac{2}{3}(t^2 - 5t + 3)$

Degree: 2

Leading coefficient: $-\frac{2}{3}$

The degree is even and the leading coefficient is negative. The graph falls to the left and right.

27. $f(x) = x^2 - 25$

$\qquad = (x + 5)(x - 5)$

$\quad x = \pm 5$

29. $h(t) = t^2 - 6t + 9$

$\qquad = (t - 3)^2$

$\quad t = 3$

31. $f(x) = x^2 + x - 2$

$\qquad = (x + 2)(x - 1)$

$\quad x = -2, 1$

33. $f(t) = t^3 - 4t^2 + 4t$

$\qquad = t(t - 2)^2$

$\quad t = 0, 2$

35. $f(x) = 3x^2 - 12x + 3$

$= 3(x^2 - 4x + 1)$

$x = \dfrac{4 \pm \sqrt{16 - 4}}{2} = 2 \pm \sqrt{3}$

37. $g(t) = \dfrac{1}{2}t^4 - \dfrac{1}{2}$

$= \dfrac{1}{2}(t + 1)(t - 1)(t^2 + 1)$

$t = \pm 1$

39. $f(x) = 2x^4 - 2x^2 - 40$

$= 2(x^2 + 4)(x + \sqrt{5})(x - \sqrt{5})$

$x = \pm\sqrt{5}$

41. $f(x) = 5x^4 + 15x^2 + 10$

$= 5(x^4 + 3x^2 + 2)$

$= 5(x^2 + 2)(x^2 + 1)$

No real zeros

43. $y = 4x^3 - 20x^2 + 25x$

$0 = 4x^3 - 20x^2 + 25x$

$0 = x(2x - 5)^2$

$x = 0 \text{ or } x = \dfrac{5}{2}$

x-intercepts: $(0, 0), \left(\dfrac{5}{2}, 0\right)$

45. $y = x^5 - 5x^3 + 4x$

$0 = x^5 - 5x^3 + 4x$

$0 = x(x^2 - 1)(x^2 - 4)$

$0 = x(x + 1)(x - 1)(x + 2)(x - 2)$

$x = 0, \pm 1, \pm 2$

47. $f(x) = (x - 0)(x - 10)$

$f(x) = x^2 - 10x$

Note: $f(x) = a(x - 0)(x - 10) = ax(x - 10)$ has zeros 0 and 10 for all real numbers *a*.

49. $f(x) = (x - 2)(x - (-6))$

$= (x - 2)(x + 6)$

$= x^2 + 4x - 12$

Note: $f(x) = a(x - 2)(x + 6)$ has zeros 2 and -6 for all real numbers *a*.

51. $f(x) = (x - 0)(x - (-2))(x - (-3))$
$= x(x + 2)(x + 3)$
$= x^3 + 5x^2 + 6x$

Note: $f(x) = ax(x + 2)(x + 3)$ has zeros
$0, -2, -3$ for all real numbers a.

53. $f(x) = (x - 4)(x + 3)(x - 3)(x - 0)$
$= (x - 4)(x^2 - 9)x$
$= x^4 - 4x^3 - 9x^2 + 36x$

Note: $f(x) = a(x^4 - 4x^3 - 9x^2 + 36x)$ has these
zeros for all real numbers a.

55. $f(x) = \left[x - \left(1 + \sqrt{3}\right)\right]\left[x - \left(1 - \sqrt{3}\right)\right]$
$= \left[(x - 1) - \sqrt{3}\right]\left[(x - 1) + \sqrt{3}\right]$
$= (x - 1)^2 - \left(\sqrt{3}\right)^2$
$= x^2 - 2x + 1 - 3$
$= x^2 - 2x - 2$

Note: $f(x) = a(x^2 - 2x - 2)$ has these zeros for all real numbers a.

57. $f(x) = x^3 - 3x^2 + 3$

(a)

The functions has three zeros. They are
in the intervals $(-1, 0)$, $(1, 2)$ and $(2, 3)$.

(b) $-0.879, \ 1.347, \ 2.532$

59. $g(x) = 3x^4 + 4x^3 - 3$

(a)

The function has two zeros. They are in the
intervals $(-2, -1)$ and $(0, 1)$.

(b) $-1.585, 0.779$

61. $f(x) = -\frac{3}{2}$

Horizontal line

Xmin=-4
Xmax=4
Xscl=1
Ymin=-3
Ymax=1
Yscl=1

63. $f(t) = \frac{1}{4}(t^2 - 2t + 15)$
$= \frac{1}{4}(t - 1)^2 + \frac{7}{2}$

Parabola; opens upward
Vertex: $\left(1, \frac{7}{2}\right)$

Xmin=-10
Xmax=10
Xscl=1
Ymin=-2
Ymax=28
Yscl=2

65. $f(x) = x^2(x - 4)$

Two x-intercepts

67. $g(t) = -\frac{1}{4}(t - 2)^2(t + 2)^2$

Two x-intercepts
y-axis symmetry

69. $f(x) = x^3 - 4x = x(x + 2)(x - 2)$

Symmetric to origin
Three x-intercepts

71. $g(x) = \frac{1}{5}(x + 1)^2(x - 3)(2x - 9)$

Three x-intercepts
No symmetry

73. $f(x) = x^4$; $f(x)$ is even.

(a) $g(x) = f(x) + 2$

Vertical shift two units upward

$g(-x) = f(-x) + 2$

$\qquad = f(x) + 2$

$\qquad = g(x)$

Even

(b) $g(x) = f(x + 2)$

Horizontal shift two units to the left

Neither odd nor even

(c) $g(x) = f(-x) = (-x)^4 = x^4$

Reflection in the y-axis
The graph looks the same.
Even

(d) $g(x) = -f(x) = -x^4$

Reflection in the x-axis
Even

(e) $g(x) = f(\frac{1}{2}x) = \frac{1}{16}x^4$

Horizontal shrink
Even

(f) $g(x) = \frac{1}{2}f(x) = \frac{1}{2}x^4$

Vertical shrink
Even

(g) $g(x) = f(x^{3/4}) = (x^{3/4}) = x^3$

Odd

(h) $g(x) = (f \circ f)(x) = f(f(x)) = f(x^4) = (x^4)^4 = x^{16}$

Even

75. (a) $V(x)$ = length × width × height

$\qquad = (24 - 2x)(24 - 4x)x$

$\qquad = 8x(6 - x)(12 - x)$

(b) Domain $0 < x < 6$

(c)

Maximum occurs at $x \approx 2.54$.

77. The point of diminishing returns (where the graph changes from curving upward to curving downward) occurs when $x = 200$. The point is (200, 160) which corresponds to spending $2,000,000 on advertising to obtain a revenue of $160 million.

79. (a) $y_1 = -0.158t^3 + 2.850t^2 - 3.814t + 74.703$

(b) $y_2 = -0.007t^3 + 0.196t^2 + 2.533t + 60.844$

(c)

The median price of homes in the South is less than in the Northeast.

Section 3.3 Real Zeros of Polynomial Functions

You should know the following basic techniques and principles of polynomial division.

■ The Division Algorithm (Long Division of Polynomials)

■ Synthetic Division

■ $f(k)$ is equal to the remainder of $f(x)$ divided by $(x - k)$.

■ $f(k) = 0$ if and only if $(x - k)$ is a factor of $f(x)$.

■ The Rational Zero Test

■ The Upper and Lower Bound Rule

Solutions to Odd-Numbered Exercises

1. $y_2 = 4 + \dfrac{4}{x - 1}$

$= \dfrac{4(x - 1) + 4}{x - 1}$

$= \dfrac{4x - 4 + 4}{x - 1}$

$= \dfrac{4x}{x - 1}$

$= y_1$

3. $y_2 = x - 2 + \dfrac{4}{x + 2}$

$= \dfrac{(x - 2)(x + 2) + 4}{x + 2}$

$= \dfrac{x^2 - 4 + 4}{x + 2}$

$= \dfrac{x^2}{x + 2}$

$= y_1$

5. $y_2 = x^3 - 4x + \dfrac{4x}{x^2 + 1}$

$= \dfrac{(x^3 - 4x)(x^2 + 1) + 4x}{x^2 + 1}$

$= \dfrac{x^5 + x^3 - 4x^3 - 4x + 4x}{x^2 + 1}$

$= \dfrac{x^5 - 3x^3}{x^2 + 1} = y_1$

7.
$$
\begin{array}{r}
2x + 4 \\
x + 3 \overline{)\ 2x^2 + 10x + 12} \\
-(2x^2 + 6x) \\
\hline
4x + 12 \\
-(4x + 12) \\
\hline
0
\end{array}
$$

$\dfrac{2x^2 + 10x + 12}{x + 3} = 2x + 4$

9.
$$
\begin{array}{r}
x^2 - 3x + 1 \\
4x + 5 \overline{)\ 4x^3 - 7x^2 - 11x + 5} \\
-(4x^3 + 5x^2) \\
\hline
-12x^2 - 11x \\
-(-12x^2 - 15x) \\
\hline
4x + 5 \\
-(4x + 5) \\
\hline
0
\end{array}
$$

$\dfrac{4x^3 - 7x^2 - 11x + 5}{4x + 5} = x^2 - 3x + 1$

11.
$$
\begin{array}{r}
x^3 + 3x^2 \qquad\ - 1 \\
x + 2 \overline{)\ x^4 + 5x^3 + 6x^2\ -x - 2} \\
\underline{-\ (x^4 + 2x^3)} \\
3x^3 + 6x^2 \\
\underline{-\ (3x^3\ + 6x^2)} \\
-x - 2 \\
\underline{-(-x - 2)} \\
0
\end{array}
$$

$$
\frac{x^4 + 5x^3 + 6x^2 - x - 2}{x + 2} = x^3 + 3x^2 - 1
$$

13.
$$
\begin{array}{r}
7 \\
x + 2 \overline{)\ 7x + 3} \\
\underline{-\ (7x + 14)} \\
-11
\end{array}
$$

$$
\frac{7x + 3}{x + 2} = 7 - \frac{11}{x + 2}
$$

15.
$$
\begin{array}{r}
3x\ + 5 \\
2x^2 + 0x + 1 \overline{)\ 6x^3 + 10x^2 +\ x\ + 8} \\
\underline{-\ (6x^3 +\ 0x^2 + 3x)} \\
10x^2 - 2x\ + 8 \\
\underline{-\ (10x^2 + 0x\ + 5)} \\
-\ 2x\ + 3
\end{array}
$$

$$
\frac{6x^3 + 10x^2 + x + 8}{2x^2 + 1} = 3x + 5 - \frac{2x - 3}{2x^2 + 1}
$$

17.
$$
\begin{array}{r}
x^2 + 2x\ + 4 \\
x^2 - 2x + 3 \overline{)\ x^4 + 0x^3 + 3x^2 + 0x\ + 1} \\
\underline{-\ (x^4 - 2x^3 + 3x^2)} \\
2x^3 + 0x^2\ + 0x \\
\underline{-\ (2x^3 - 4x^2\ + 6x)} \\
4x^2\ - 6x\ +\ 1 \\
\underline{-\ (4x^2\ - 8x\ + 12)} \\
2x\ - 11
\end{array}
$$

$$
\Rightarrow \quad \frac{x^4 + 3x^2 + 1}{x^2 - 2x + 3} = x^2 + 2x + 4 + \frac{2x - 11}{x^2 - 2x + 3}
$$

19.
$$
\begin{array}{r}
2x \\
x^2 - 2x + 1 \overline{)\ 2x^3 - 4x^2 - 15x\ + 5} \\
\underline{-(2x^3 - 4x^2 +\ 2x)} \\
-\ 17x\ + 5
\end{array}
$$

$$
\frac{2x^3 - 4x^2 - 15x + 5}{(x - 1)^2} = 2x - \frac{17x - 5}{(x - 1)^2}
$$

21.
$$
\begin{array}{r}
x^{2n}\ +\ 6x^n\ +\ 9 \\
x^n + 3 \overline{)\ x^{3n} + 9x^{2n} + 27x^n + 27} \\
\underline{-\ (x^{3n} + 3x^{2n})} \\
6x^{2n}\ + 27x^n \\
\underline{-\ (6x^{2n}\ + 18x^n)} \\
9x^n\ + 27 \\
\underline{-\ (9x^n\ + 27)} \\
0
\end{array}
$$

$$
\frac{x^{3n} + 9x^{2n} + 27x^n + 27}{x^n + 3} = x^{2n} + 6x^n + 9
$$

23.

$$
\begin{array}{r|rrrr}
-2 & 4 & 8 & -9 & -18 \\
 & & -8 & 0 & 18 \\
\hline
 & 4 & 0 & -9 & 0
\end{array}
$$

$$\frac{4x^3 + 8x^2 - 9x - 18}{x + 2} = 4x^2 - 9$$

25.

$$
\begin{array}{r|rrrr}
4 & 5 & -6 & 0 & 8 \\
 & & 20 & 56 & 224 \\
\hline
 & 5 & 14 & 56 & 232
\end{array}
$$

$$\frac{5x^3 - 6x^2 + 8}{x - 4} = 5x^2 + 14x + 56 + \frac{232}{x - 4}$$

27.

$$
\begin{array}{r|rrrr}
-8 & 1 & 0 & 0 & 512 \\
 & & -8 & 64 & -512 \\
\hline
 & 1 & -8 & 64 & 0
\end{array}
$$

$$\frac{x^3 + 512}{x + 8} = x^2 - 8x + 64$$

29.

$$
\begin{array}{r|rrrrr}
2 & -3 & 0 & 0 & 0 & 0 \\
 & & -6 & -12 & -24 & -48 \\
\hline
 & -3 & -6 & -12 & -24 & -48
\end{array}
$$

$$\frac{-3x^4}{x - 2} = -3x^3 - 6x^2 - 12x - 24 - \frac{48}{x - 2}$$

31.

$$
\begin{array}{r|rrrr}
-\frac{1}{2} & 4 & 16 & -23 & -15 \\
 & & -2 & -7 & 15 \\
\hline
 & 4 & 14 & -30 & 0
\end{array}
$$

$$\frac{4x^3 + 16x^2 - 23x - 15}{x + \frac{1}{2}} = 4x^2 + 14x - 30$$

33. A divisor divides evenly into the dividend if the remainder is zero.

35. $f(x) = x^3 - x^2 - 14x + 11,\ k = 4$

$$
\begin{array}{r|rrrr}
4 & 1 & -1 & -14 & 11 \\
 & & 4 & 12 & -8 \\
\hline
 & 1 & 3 & -2 & 3
\end{array}
$$

$$f(x) = (x - 4)(x^2 + 3x - 2) + 3/(x - 4)$$
$$f(4) = (0)(26) + 3 = 3$$

37. $f(x) = x^3 + 3x^2 - 2x - 14,\ k = \sqrt{2}$

$$
\begin{array}{r|rrrr}
\sqrt{2} & 1 & 3 & -2 & -14 \\
 & & \sqrt{2} & 2 + 3\sqrt{2} & 6 \\
\hline
 & 1 & 3 + \sqrt{2} & 3\sqrt{2} & -8
\end{array}
$$

$$f(x) = \left(x - \sqrt{2}\right)\left[x^2 + \left(3 + \sqrt{2}\right)x + 3\sqrt{2}\right] - 8/(\sqrt{2})$$
$$f(\sqrt{2}) = (0)(4 + 6\sqrt{2}) - 8 = -8$$

39. $f(x) = 4x^3 - 13x + 10$

(a)
$$
\begin{array}{r|rrrr}
1 & 4 & 0 & -13 & 10 \\
 & & 4 & 4 & -9 \\
\hline
 & 4 & 4 & -9 & \underline{1} = f(1)
\end{array}
$$

(b)
$$
\begin{array}{r|rrrr}
-2 & 4 & 0 & -13 & 10 \\
 & & -8 & 16 & -6 \\
\hline
 & 4 & -8 & 3 & \underline{4} = f(-2)
\end{array}
$$

(c)
$$
\begin{array}{r|rrrr}
\frac{1}{2} & 4 & 0 & -13 & 10 \\
 & & 2 & 1 & -6 \\
\hline
 & 4 & 2 & -12 & \underline{4} = f(\tfrac{1}{2})
\end{array}
$$

(d)
$$
\begin{array}{r|rrrr}
8 & 4 & 0 & -13 & 10 \\
 & & 32 & 256 & 1944 \\
\hline
 & 4 & 32 & 243 & \underline{1954} = f(8)
\end{array}
$$

41.

$$
2\ \big|\begin{array}{cccc} 1 & 0 & -7 & 6 \\ & 2 & 4 & -6 \\ \hline 1 & 2 & -3 & 0 \end{array}
$$

$$x^3 - 7x + 6 = (x - 2)(x^2 + 2x - 3)$$
$$= (x - 2)(x + 3)(x - 1)$$

Zeros: $2, -3, 1$

43.

$$
\tfrac{1}{2}\ \big|\begin{array}{cccc} 2 & -15 & 27 & -10 \\ & 1 & -7 & 10 \\ \hline 2 & -14 & 20 & 0 \end{array}
$$

$$2x^3 - 15x^2 + 27x - 10$$
$$= \left(x - \tfrac{1}{2}\right)(2x^2 - 14x + 20)$$
$$= (2x - 1)(x - 2)(x - 5)$$

Zeros: $\tfrac{1}{2}, 2, 5$

45.

$$
\sqrt{3}\ \big|\begin{array}{cccc} 1 & 2 & -3 & -6 \\ & \sqrt{3} & 3 + 2\sqrt{3} & 6 \\ \hline 1 & 2 + \sqrt{3} & 2\sqrt{3} & 0 \end{array}
$$

$$
-\sqrt{3}\ \big|\begin{array}{ccc} 1 & 2 + \sqrt{3} & 2\sqrt{3} \\ & -\sqrt{3} & -2\sqrt{3} \\ \hline 1 & 2 & 0 \end{array}
$$

$$x^3 + 2x^2 - 3x - 6 = \left(x - \sqrt{3}\right)\left(x + \sqrt{3}\right)(x + 2)$$

Zeros: $\pm\sqrt{3}, -2$

47.

$$
1 + \sqrt{3}\ \big|\begin{array}{cccc} 1 & -3 & 0 & 2 \\ & 1 + \sqrt{3} & 1 - \sqrt{3} & -2 \\ \hline 1 & -2 + \sqrt{3} & 1 - \sqrt{3} & 0 \end{array}
$$

$$
1 - \sqrt{3}\ \big|\begin{array}{ccc} 1 & -2 + \sqrt{3} & 1 - \sqrt{3} \\ & 1 - \sqrt{3} & -1 + \sqrt{3} \\ \hline 1 & -1 & 0 \end{array}
$$

$$x^3 - 3x^2 + 2 = \left[x - \left(1 + \sqrt{3}\right)\right]\left[x - \left(1 - \sqrt{3}\right)\right](x - 1)$$
$$= (x - 1)\left(x - 1 - \sqrt{3}\right)\left(x - 1 + \sqrt{3}\right)$$

Zeros: $1, 1 \pm \sqrt{3}$

49. (a) $R = 16.823 + 1.415t - 0.115t^2 - 0.023t^3$

(b)

(c)

t	-5	-4	-3	-2	-1	0	1	2	3
R	9.75	10.80	12.16	13.72	15.32	16.82	18.10	19.01	19.41

—CONTINUED—

49. —CONTINUED—

(d)
$$
\begin{array}{r|rrrr}
6 & -0.023 & -0.115 & 1.415 & 16.823 \\
  &   & -0.138 & -1.518 & -0.618 \\
\hline
  & -0.023 & -0.253 & -0.103 & 16.205
\end{array}
$$

$R(6) \approx 16.205$. Since the cubic falls to the right, it is not accurate for values past 1996.

51. $f(x) = x^3 + 3x^2 - x - 3$

Possible rational zeros: $\pm 1,\ \pm 3$

Zeros shown on graph: $-3,\ -1,\ 1$

53. $f(x) = 2x^4 - 17x^3 + 35x^2 + 9x - 45$

Possible rational zeros: $\pm 1, \pm 3, \pm 5, \pm 9, \pm 15, \pm 45,$
$\pm \frac{1}{2}, \pm \frac{3}{2}, \pm \frac{5}{2}, \pm \frac{9}{2}, \pm \frac{15}{2}, \pm \frac{45}{2}$

Zeros shown of graph: $-1,\ \frac{3}{2},\ 3,\ 5$

55. $f(x) = x^3 + x^2 - 4x - 4$

(a) Possible rational zeros: $\pm 1,\ \pm 2,\ \pm 4$

(b)

(c) $-2, -1, 2$ on graph

57. $f(x) = -4x^3 + 15x^2 - 8x - 3$

(a) Possible rational zeros: $\pm \frac{1}{4},\ \pm \frac{1}{2},\ \pm \frac{3}{4},\ \pm 1,\ \pm \frac{3}{2},\ \pm 3$

(b)

(c) $-\frac{1}{4},\ 1, 3$ on graph

59. $f(x) = -2x^4 + 13x^3 - 21x^2 + 2x + 8$

(a) Possible rational zeros:
$\pm \frac{1}{2},\ \pm 1,\ \pm 2,\ \pm 4,\ \pm 8$

(b)

(c) $-\frac{1}{2},\ 1,\ 2,\ 4$ on graph

61. $f(x) = 32x^3 - 52x^2 + 17x + 3$

(a) Possible rational zeros: $\pm 1,\ \pm 3,\ \pm \frac{1}{2},\ \pm \frac{3}{2}, \pm \frac{1}{4}, \pm \frac{3}{4},$
$\pm \frac{1}{8}, \pm \frac{3}{8}, \pm \frac{1}{16},\ \pm \frac{3}{16},\ \pm \frac{1}{32},\ \pm \frac{3}{32}$

(b)

(c) $-\frac{1}{8},\ \frac{3}{4},\ 1$ on graph

63. (a) $f(x) = 4x^3 + 7x^2 - 11x - 18$

Possible rational zeros: $\pm 1, \pm 2, \pm 3, \pm 6, \pm 9,$
$\pm 18, \pm \frac{1}{2}, \pm \frac{3}{2}, \pm \frac{9}{2}, \pm \frac{1}{4}, \pm \frac{3}{4}, \pm \frac{9}{4}$

(b)

$$
\begin{array}{r|rrrr}
-2 & 4 & 7 & -11 & -18 \\
   &   & -8 & 2 & 18 \\
\hline
   & 4 & -1 & -9 & 0
\end{array}
$$

The zeros of $4x^2 - x - 9$ are $x = -2$ and
$x = \dfrac{1 \pm \sqrt{1 + 4(4)(9)}}{8} = \dfrac{1}{8} \pm \dfrac{\sqrt{145}}{8}.$

65. $z^4 - z^3 - 2z - 4 = 0$

Possible rational zeros: $\pm 1, \pm 2, \pm 4$

$$
\begin{array}{r|rrrrr}
-1 & 1 & -1 & 0 & -2 & -4 \\
   &   & -1 & 2 & -2 & 4 \\
\hline
   & 1 & -2 & 2 & -4 & 0
\end{array}
$$

$$
\begin{array}{r|rrrr}
2 & 1 & -2 & 2 & -4 \\
  &   & 2 & 0 & 4 \\
\hline
  & 1 & 0 & 2 & 0
\end{array}
$$

$z^4 - z^3 - 2z - 4 = (x + 1)(x - 2)(x^2 + 2) = 0$

The only real zeros are -1 and 2. You can verify this by graphing the function $f(z) = z^4 - z^3 - 2z - 4$.

67. $x^4 - 13x^2 - 12x = 0$

$x(x^3 - 13x - 12) = 0$

$\qquad\qquad x = 0$ is a solution.

Possible rational zeros of $x^3 - 13x - 12 = 0$ are $\pm 1, \pm 2, \pm 3, \pm 4, \pm 6$ and ± 12. Using a graphing utility or synthetic division, you find that the zeros are $0, -1, -3, 4$.

69. $2x^4 - 11x^3 - 6x^2 + 64x + 32 = 0$

Using a graphing utility, you can see that there are three zeros. Using synthetic division, you can verify that these zeros are $-2, -\frac{1}{2}, 4$.

71. $f(x) = x^4 - 3x^2 + 2$

(a) From the calculator we have
$x = \pm 1$ and $x \approx \pm 1.414$.

(b)
$$
\begin{array}{r|rrrrr}
1 & 1 & 0 & -3 & 0 & 2 \\
  &   & 1 & 1 & -2 & -2 \\
\hline
  & 1 & 1 & -2 & -2 & 0
\end{array}
$$

$$
\begin{array}{r|rrrr}
-1 & 1 & 1 & -2 & -2 \\
   &   & -1 & 0 & 2 \\
\hline
   & 1 & 0 & -2 & 0
\end{array}
$$

$f(x) = (x - 1)(x + 1)(x^2 - 2)$

$\qquad = (x - 1)(x + 1)(x - \sqrt{2})(x + \sqrt{2})$

The exact roots are $x = \pm 1, \pm \sqrt{2}$.

73. $h(x) = x^5 - 7x^4 + 10x^3 + 14x^2 - 24x$

(a) $h(x) = x(x^4 - 7x^3 + 10x^2 + 14x - 24)$
From the calculator we have $x = 0, 3, 4$ and $x \approx \pm 1.414$.

(b)
$$
\begin{array}{r|rrrrr}
3 & 1 & -7 & 10 & 14 & -24 \\
  &   & 3 & -12 & -6 & 24 \\
\hline
  & 1 & -4 & -2 & 8 & 0
\end{array}
$$

$$
\begin{array}{r|rrrr}
4 & 1 & -4 & -2 & 8 \\
  &   & 4 & 0 & -8 \\
\hline
  & 1 & 0 & -2 & 0
\end{array}
$$

$f(x) = x(x - 3)(x - 4)(x^2 - 2)$

$\qquad = x(x - 3)(x - 4)(x - \sqrt{2})(x + \sqrt{2})$

The exact roots are $x = 0, 3, 4, \pm \sqrt{2}$.

75. $f(x) = x^4 - 4x^3 + 15$

(a)
4	1	-4	0	0	15
		4	0	0	0
	1	0	0	0	15

4 is an upper bound.

(b)
-1	1	-4	0	0	15
		-1	5	-5	5
	1	-5	5	-5	20

-1 is a lower bound.

77. $f(x) = x^4 - 4x^3 + 16x - 16$

(a)
5	1	-4	0	16	-16
		5	5	25	205
	1	1	5	41	189

5 is an upper bound.

(b)
-3	1	-4	0	16	-16
		-3	21	-63	141
	1	-7	21	-47	125

-3 is a lower bound.

79. $P(x) = x^4 - \frac{25}{4}x^2 + 9$

$\qquad = \frac{1}{4}(4x^4 - 25x^2 + 36)$

$\qquad = \frac{1}{4}(4x^2 - 9)(x^2 - 4)$

$\qquad = \frac{1}{4}(2x + 3)(2x - 3)(x + 2)(x - 2)$

The zeros are $\pm\frac{3}{2}$ and ±2.

81. $f(x) = x^3 - \frac{1}{4}x^2 - x + \frac{1}{4}$

$\qquad = \frac{1}{4}(4x^3 - x^2 - 4x + 1)$

$\qquad = \frac{1}{4}[x^2(4x - 1) - 1(4x - 1)]$

$\qquad = \frac{1}{4}(4x - 1)(x^2 - 1)$

$\qquad = \frac{1}{4}(4x - 1)(x + 1)(x - 1)$

The zeros are $\frac{1}{4}$ and ± 1.

83. $f(x) = x^3 - 1 = (x - 1)(x^2 + x + 1)$
Rational zeros: 1 $(x = 1)$
Irrational zeros: 0
Matches (d).

85. $f(x) = x^3 - x = x(x + 1)(x - 1)$
Rational zeros: 3 $(x = 0, \pm1)$
Irrational zeros: 0
Matches (b).

87. $g(x) = -f(x)$. This function would have the same zeros as $f(x)$ so r_1, r_2, and r_3 are also zeros of $g(x)$.

89. $g(x) = f(x - 5)$. The graph of $g(x)$ is a horizontal shift of the graph of $f(x)$ five units to the right so the zeros of $g(x)$ are $5 + r_1$, $5 + r_2$, and $5 + r_3$.

91. $g(x) = 3 + f(x)$. Since $g(x)$ is a vertical shift of the graph of $f(x)$, the zeros of $g(x)$ cannot be determined.

93. (a)

(b) $V = l \cdot w \cdot h = (15 - 2x)(9 - 2x)x$

$\qquad = x(9 - 2x)(15 - 2x)$

Since length, width, and height cannot be negative, we have $0 < x < \frac{9}{2}$ for the domain.

(c)

Volume of box (y-axis: 25, 50, 75, 100, 125)
Length of sides of squares removed (x-axis: 1 2 3 4 5)

The volume is maximum when $x \approx 1.82$.
The dimensions are: length $= 15 - 2(1.82) = 11.36$
$\qquad\qquad\qquad\quad$ width $= 9 - 2(1.82) = 5.36$
$\qquad\qquad\qquad\quad$ height $= x = 1.82$
1.82 cm $\times$ 5.36 cm $\times$ 11.36 cm

(d) $56 = x(9 - 2x)(15 - 2x)$

$56 = 135x - 48x^2 + 4x^3$

$0 = 4x^3 - 48x^2 + 135x - 56$

The zeros of this polynomial are $\frac{1}{2}, \frac{7}{2}$, and 8.
x cannot equal 8 since it is not in the domain of V.
[The length cannot equal -1 and the width cannot equal -7. The product of $(8)(-1)(-7) = 56$ so it showed up as an extraneous solution.]

95. $y = -5.05x^3 + 3857x - 38,411.25,\ 13 \le x \le 18$

(a)

(b) The second air-fuel ration of 16.89 can be obtained by finding the second point where the curves y and $y_1 = 2400$ intersect.

(c) Solve $-5.05x^3 + 3857x - 38,411.25 = 2400$ or $-5.05x^3 + 3857x - 40,811.25 = 0$ by synthetic division.

$$
\begin{array}{r|rrrr}
15 & -5.05 & 0 & 3857 & -40811.25 \\
& & -75.75 & -1136.25 & 40811.25 \\
\hline
& -5.05 & -75.75 & 2720.75 & 0
\end{array}
$$

(d) The positive zero of the quadratic $-5.05x^2 - 75.75x + 2720.75$ can be found by the Quadratic Formula.

$$x \approx \frac{75.75 - \sqrt{(75.75)^2 - 4(-5.05)(2720.75)}}{2(-5.05)} \approx 16.89$$

97. (a)

(b) By graphing I together with $y_2 = 525$, you see that the curves intersect at $x \approx 1.51$, or 1991.

(c) Yes, the curve is increasing to the right.

Section 3.4   The Fundamental Theorem of Algebra

- You should know that if f is a polynomial of degree $n > 0$, then f has at least one zero in the complex number system. (Fundamental Theorem of Algebra)

- You should know that if $a + bi$ is a complex zero of a polynomial f, with real coefficients, then $a - bi$ is also a complex zero of f.

- You should know the difference between a factor that is irreducible over the rationals (such as $x^2 - 7$) and a factor that is irreducible over the reals (such as $x^2 + 9$).

Solutions to Odd-Numbered Exercises

1. $f(x) = x(x - 6)^2 = x(x - 6)(x - 6)$
The three zeros are $x = 0$, $x = 6$, and $x = 6$.

3. $h(t) = (t - 3)(t - 2)(t - 3i)(t + 3i)$
The four zeros are $t = 3$, $t = 2$, $t = 3i$, and $t = -3i$.

5. $f(x) = x^3 - 4x^2 + x - 4 = x^2(x - 4) + 1(x - 4)$
$\quad = (x - 4)(x^2 + 1)$
The only real zero of $f(x)$ is $x = 4$. This corresponds to the x-intercept of $(4, 0)$ on the graph.

7. $f(x) = x^4 + 4x^2 + 4 = (x^2 + 2)^2$

$f(x)$ has no real zeros and the graph of $f(x)$ has no x-intercepts.

9. $f(x) = x^2 + 25 = (x + 5i)(x - 5i)$
The zeros of $f(x)$ are $x = \pm 5i$.

11. $h(x) = x^2 - 4x + 1$

h has no rational zeros. By the Quadratic Formula, the zeros are $x = \dfrac{4 \pm \sqrt{16 - 4}}{2} = 2 \pm \sqrt{3}$.

$h(x) = \left[x - (2 + \sqrt{3})\right]\left[x - (2 - \sqrt{3})\right] = (x - 2 - \sqrt{3})(x - 2 + \sqrt{3})$

13. $f(x) = x^4 - 81$

$\qquad = (x^2 - 9)(x^2 + 9)$

$\qquad = (x + 3)(x - 3)(x + 3i)(x - 3i)$

The zeros of $f(x)$ are $x = \pm 3$ and $x = \pm 3i$.

15. $f(z) = z^2 - 2z + 2$

f has no rational zeros. By the Quadratic Formula, the zeros are $z = \dfrac{2 \pm \sqrt{4 - 8}}{2} = 1 \pm i$.

$f(z) = [z - (1 + i)][z - (1 - i)] = (z - 1 - i)(x - 1 + i)$

17. $f(t) = t^3 - 3t^2 - 15t + 125$

Possible rational zeros: $\pm 1, \pm 5, \pm 25, \pm 125$

$$
\begin{array}{r|rrrr}
-5 & 1 & -3 & -15 & 125 \\
   &   & -5 & 40 & -125 \\
\hline
   & 1 & -8 & 25 & 0
\end{array}
$$

By the Quadratic Formula, the zeros of $t^2 - 8t + 25$ are $t = \dfrac{8 \pm \sqrt{64 - 100}}{2} = 4 \pm 3i$.

The zeros of $f(t)$ are $t = -5$ and $t = 4 \pm 3i$.

$f(t) = [t - (-5)][t - (4 + 3i)][t - (4 - 3i)]$

$\qquad = (t + 5)(t - 4 - 3i)(t - 4 + 3i)$

19. $f(x) = 16x^3 - 20x^2 - 4x + 15$

The graph reveals one zero at $x = -\dfrac{3}{4}$.

$$
\begin{array}{r|rrrr}
-\dfrac{3}{4} & 16 & -20 & -4 & 15 \\
   &   & -12 & 24 & -15 \\
\hline
   & 16 & -32 & 20 & 0
\end{array}
$$

By the Quadratic Formula, the zeros of $16x^2 - 32x + 20 = 4(4x^2 - 8x + 5)$ are $x = \dfrac{8 \pm \sqrt{64 - 80}}{8} = 1 \pm \dfrac{1}{2}i$.

The zeros of $f(x)$ are $x = -\dfrac{3}{4}$ and $x = 1 \pm \dfrac{1}{2}i$.

$(4x + 3)\left(x - 1 + \dfrac{1}{2}i\right)\left(x - 1 - \dfrac{1}{2}i\right)$

21. $f(x) = 5x^3 - 9x^2 + 28x + 6$

Possible rational zeros: $\pm 1,\ \pm 2,\ \pm 3,\ \pm 6, \pm\dfrac{1}{5}, \pm\dfrac{2}{5}, \pm\dfrac{3}{5}, \pm\dfrac{6}{5}$

$$-\frac{1}{5} \quad\begin{array}{|rrrr} 5 & -9 & 28 & 6 \\ & -1 & 2 & -6 \\ \hline 5 & -10 & 30 & 0 \end{array}$$

By the Quadratic Formula, the zeros of $5x^2 - 10x + 30 = 5(x^2 - 2x + 6)$ are $x = \dfrac{2 \pm \sqrt{4 - 24}}{2} = 1 \pm \sqrt{5}i$.

The zeros of $f(x)$ are $x = -\frac{1}{5}$ and $x = 1 \pm \sqrt{5}i$.

$$f(x) = \left[x - \left(-\frac{1}{5}\right)\right](5)\left[x - \left(1 + \sqrt{5}i\right)\right]\left[x - \left(1 - \sqrt{5}i\right)\right]$$
$$= (5x + 1)\left(x - 1 - \sqrt{5}i\right)\left(x - 1 + \sqrt{5}i\right)$$

23. $f(x) = x^4 + 10x^2 + 9$

$\quad = (x^2 + 1)(x^2 + 9)$

$\quad = (x + i)(x - i)(x + 3i)(x - 3i)$

The zeros of $f(x)$ are $x = \pm i$ and $x = \pm 3i$.

25. $g(x) = x^4 - 4x^3 + 8x^2 - 16x + 16$

Possible rational zeros: $\pm 1,\ \pm 2,\ \pm 4,\ \pm 8,\ \pm 16$

$$\begin{array}{r|rrrrr} 2 & 1 & -4 & 8 & -16 & 16 \\ & & 2 & -4 & 8 & -16 \\ \hline 2 & 1 & -2 & 4 & -8 & 0 \\ & & 2 & 0 & 8 & \\ \hline & 1 & 0 & 4 & 0 & \end{array}$$

$g(x) = (x - 2)(x - 2)(x^2 + 4)$

$\quad = (x - 2)^2(x + 2i)(x - 2i)$

The zeros of g are 2 and $\pm 2i$.

27. $f(x) = 2x^4 + 5x^3 + 4x^2 + 5x + 2$

The graph reveals one zero at $x = -2$ and $x = -\frac{1}{2}$.

$$\begin{array}{r|rrrrr} -2 & 2 & 5 & 4 & 5 & 2 \\ & & -4 & -2 & -4 & -2 \\ \hline & 2 & 1 & 2 & 1 & 0 \end{array}$$

$$\begin{array}{r|rrrr} -\frac{1}{2} & 2 & 1 & 2 & 1 \\ & & -1 & 0 & -1 \\ \hline & 2 & 0 & 2 & 0 \end{array}$$

The zeros of $2x^2 + 2 = 2(x^2 + 1)$ are $x = \pm i$.

The zeros of $f(x)$ are $(x + 2)(2x + 1)(x - i)(x + i)$.

29. $f(x) = (x - 1)(x - 5i)(x + 5i)$

$\quad = (x - 1)(x^2 + 25)$

$\quad = x^3 - x^2 + 25x - 25$

Note: $f(x) = a(x^3 - x^2 + 25x - 25)$, where a is any real number, has the zero 1 and $\pm 5i$.

31. $f(x) = (x - 2)(x - 4 - i)(x - 4 + i)$

$\qquad = (x - 2)(x^2 - 8x + 17)$

$\qquad = x^3 - 10x^2 + 33x - 34$

33. $f(x) = (x - i)(x + i)(x - 6i)(x + 6i)$

$\qquad = (x^2 + 1)(x^2 + 36)$

$\qquad = x^4 + 37x^2 + 36$

Note: $f(x) = a(x^4 + 37x^2 + 36)$, where a is any real number, has the zeros $\pm i$ and $\pm 6i$.

35. If $1 + \sqrt{3}i$ is a zero, so is its conjugate $1 - \sqrt{3}i$.

$f(x) = (x + 5)^2(x - 1 + \sqrt{3}i)(x - 1 - \sqrt{3}i)$

$\qquad = (x^2 + 10x + 25)(x^2 - 2x + 4)$

$\qquad = x^4 + 8x^3 + 9x^2 - 10x + 100$

37. $f(x) = x^4 + 6x^2 - 27$

(a) $f(x) = (x^2 + 9)(x^2 - 3)$

(b) $f(x) = (x^2 + 9)(x + \sqrt{3})(x - \sqrt{3})$

(c) $f(x) = (x + 3i)(x - 3i)(x + \sqrt{3})(x - \sqrt{3})$

39.

$$
\begin{array}{r}
x^2 - 2x + 3 \\
x^2 - 2x - 2\overline{)x^4 - 4x^3 + 5x^2 - 2x - 6} \\
\underline{x^4 - 2x^3 - 2x^2} \\
-2x^3 + 7x^2 - 2x \\
\underline{-2x^3 + 4x^2 + 4x} \\
3x^2 - 6x - 6 \\
\underline{3x^2 - 6x - 6} \\
0
\end{array}
$$

$f(x) = (x^2 - 2x + 3)(x^2 - 2x - 2)$

(a) $f(x) = (x^2 - 2x - 2)(x^2 - 2x + 3)$

(b) $f(x) = (x - 1 + \sqrt{3})(x - 1 - \sqrt{3})(x^2 - 2x + 3)$

(c) $f(x) = (x - 1 + \sqrt{3})(x - 1 - \sqrt{3})(x - 1 + \sqrt{2}i)(x - 1 - \sqrt{2}i)$

Note: Use the Quadratic Formula for (b) and (c).

41. $f(x) = 2x^3 + 3x^2 + 50x + 75$

Since $5i$ is a zero, so is $-5i$.

$$
\begin{array}{r|rrrr}
5i & 2 & 3 & 50 & 75 \\
& & 10i & -50 + 15i & -75 \\
\hline
& 2 & 3 + 10i & 15i & 0
\end{array}
$$

$$
\begin{array}{r|rrr}
-5i & 2 & 3 + 10i & 15i \\
& & -10i & -15i \\
\hline
& 2 & 3 & 0
\end{array}
$$

The zero of $2x + 3$ is $x = -\frac{3}{2}$. The zeros of f are $x = -\frac{3}{2}$ and $x = \pm 5i$.

Alternate Solution

Since $x = \pm 5i$ are zeros of $f(x)$, $(x + 5i)(x - 5i) = x^2 + 25$ is a factor of $f(x)$. By long division we have:

$$
\begin{array}{r}
2x + 3 \\
x^2 + 0x + 25\overline{)2x^3 + 3x^2 + 50x + 75} \\
\underline{2x^3 + 0x^2 + 50x} \\
3x^2 + 0x + 75 \\
\underline{3x^2 + 0x + 75} \\
0
\end{array}
$$

Thus, $f(x) = (x^2 + 25)(2x + 3)$ and the zeros of f are $x = \pm 5i$ and $x = -\frac{3}{2}$.

43. $f(x) = 2x^4 - x^3 + 7x^2 - 4x - 4$

Since $2i$ is a zero, so is $-2i$.

$2i$	2	-1	7	-4	-4
		$4i$	$-8 - 2i$	$4 - 2i$	4
	2	$-1 + 4i$	$-1 - 2i$	-2	0

$-2i$	2	$-1 + 4i$	$-1 - 2i$	$-2i$
		$-4i$	$2i$	$2i$
	2	-1	-1	0

The zeros of $2x^2 - x - 1 = (2x + 1)(x - 1)$ are $x = -\frac{1}{2}$ and $x = 1$. The zeros of f are $x = \pm 2i$, $x = -\frac{1}{2}$, and $x = 1$.

Alternate Solution

Since $x = \pm 2i$ are zeros of $f(x)$, $(x + 2i)(x - 2i) = x^2 + 4$ is a factor of $f(x)$. By long division we have:

$$
\begin{array}{r}
2x^2 - x - 1 \\
x^2 + 0x + 4 \overline{\smash{\big)}\, 2x^4 - x^3 + 7x^2 - 4x - 4} \\
\underline{2x^4 + 0x^3 + 8x^2} \\
-x^3 - x^2 - 4x \\
\underline{-x^3 + 0x^2 - 4x} \\
-x^2 + 0x - 4 \\
\underline{-x^2 + 0x - 4} \\
0
\end{array}
$$

Thus, $f(x) = (x^2 + 4)(2x^2 - x - 1)$

$\qquad = (x + 2i)(x - 2i)(2x + 1)(x - 1)$

and the zeros of f are $x = \pm 2i$, $x = -\frac{1}{2}$, and $x = 1$.

45. $g(x) = 4x^3 + 23x^2 + 34x - 10$

Since $-3 + i$ is a zero, so is $-3 - i$.

$-3 + i$	4	23	34	-10
		$-12 + 4i$	$-37 - i$	10
	4	$11 + 4i$	$-3 - i$	0

$-3 - i$	4	$11 + 4i$	$-3 - i$
		$-12 - 4i$	$3 + i$
	4	-1	0

The zeros of $4x - 1$ is $x = \frac{1}{4}$. The zeros of $g(x)$ are $x = -3 \pm i$ and $x = \frac{1}{4}$.

—CONTINUED—

45. —CONTINUED—

Alternate Solution

Since $-3 \pm i$ are zeros of $g(x)$,

$$[x - (-3 + i)][x - (-3 - i)] = [(x - 3) - i][(x + 3) + i]$$
$$= (x + 3)^2 - i^2 = x^2 + 6x + 10$$

is a factor of $g(x)$. By long division we have:

$$
\begin{array}{r}
4x - 1 \\
x^2 + 6x + 10\overline{\smash{)}4x^3 + 23x^2 + 34x - 10} \\
\underline{4x^3 + 24x^2 + 40x} \\
-x^2 - 6x - 10 \\
\underline{-x^2 - 6x - 10} \\
0
\end{array}
$$

Thus, $g(x) = (x^2 + 6x + 10)(4x - 1)$ and the zeros of g are $x = -3 \pm i$ and $x = \frac{1}{4}$.

47. (a) The root feature yields the real roots 1 and 2, and the complex roots $-3 \pm 1.414i$.

(b) By synthetic division,

$$
\begin{array}{r|rrrrr}
1 & 1 & 3 & -5 & -21 & 22 \\
  &   & 1 & 4 & -1 & -22 \\
\hline
  & 1 & 4 & -1 & -22 & 0
\end{array}
$$

$$
\begin{array}{r|rrrr}
2 & 1 & 4 & -1 & -22 \\
  &   & 2 & 12 & 22 \\
\hline
  & 1 & 6 & 11 & 0
\end{array}
$$

The complex roots of $x^2 + 6x + 11$ are

$$x = \frac{-6 \pm \sqrt{6^2 - 4(11)}}{2} = -3 \pm \sqrt{2}i.$$

49. (a) The root feature yields the real root 0.75, and the complex roots $0.5 \pm 1.118i$.

(b) By synthetic division,

$$
\begin{array}{r|rrrr}
\frac{3}{4} & 8 & -14 & 18 & -9 \\
  &   & 6 & -6 & 9 \\
\hline
  & 8 & -8 & 12 & 0
\end{array}
$$

The complex roots of $8x^2 - 8x + 12$ are

$$x = \frac{8 \pm \sqrt{64 - 4(8)(12)}}{2(8)} = \frac{1}{2} \pm \frac{\sqrt{5}}{2}i.$$

51. $f(x) = x^3 + ix^2 + ix - 1$

(a)
$$
\begin{array}{r|rrrr}
i & 1 & i & i & -1 \\
  &   & i & -2 & -1 - 2i \\
\hline
  & 1 & 2i & -2 + i & -2 - 2i
\end{array}
$$

Since the remainder is not zero, $x = i$ is not a zero of f.

(b) The theorem that states that complex zeros occur in conjugate pairs has the condition that the coefficients of f must be real numbers. This polynomial has complex coefficients for x^2 and x.

53. (a) No, the answers will not change if the graph is shifted to the right 2 units.

(b) No, the answer will not change.

55. No. Setting $P = R - C = xp - C = x(140 - 0.0001x) - (80x + 150,000) = 9,000,000$ yields a quadratic with no real roots:

$$-0.0001x^2 + 60x - 9,150,000 = 0$$

57. $f(x) = [x - (a + bi)][x - (a - bi)]$

$= [(x - a) - bi][(x - a) + bi]$

$= (x - a)^2 - (bi)^2$

$= x^2 - 2ax + a^2 + b^2$

59.

Section 3.5   Rational Functions and Asymptotes

■ You should know the following basic facts about rational functions.

   (a) A function of the form $f(x) = P(x)/Q(x)$, $Q(x) \neq 0$, where $P(x)$ and $Q(x)$ are polynomials, is called a rational function.

   (b) The domain of a rational function is the set of all real numbers except those which make the denominator zero.

   (c) If $f(x) = P(x)/Q(x)$ is in reduced form, and a is a value such that $Q(a) = 0$, then the line $x = a$ is a vertical asymptote of the graph of f. $f(x) \to \infty$ or $f(x) \to -\infty$ as $x \to a$.

   (d) The line $y = b$ is a horizontal asymptote of the graph of f if $f(x) \to b$ as $x \to \infty$ or $x \to -\infty$.

   (e) Let $f(x) = \dfrac{P(x)}{Q(x)} = \dfrac{a_n x^n + a_{n-1}x^{n-1} + \cdots + a_1 x + a_0}{b_m x^m + b_{m-1}x^{m-1} + \cdots + b_1 x + b_0}$ where $P(x)$ and $Q(x)$ have no common factors.

   1. If $n < m$, then the x-axis ($y = 0$) is a horizontal asymptote.

   2. If $n = m$, then $y = \dfrac{a_n}{b_m}$ is a horizontal asymptote.

   3. If $n > m$, then there are no horizontal asymptotes.

Solutions to Odd-Numbered Exercises

1. $f(x) = \dfrac{1}{x - 1}$

(a)

x	$f(x)$	x	$f(x)$	x	$f(x)$
0.5	-2	1.5	2	5	0.25
0.9	-10	1.1	10	10	$0.\overline{1}$
0.99	-100	1.01	100	100	$0.\overline{01}$
0.999	-1000	1.001	1000	1000	$0.\overline{001}$

(b) The zero of the denominator is $x = 1$, so $x = 1$ is a vertical asymptote. The degree of the numerator is less than the degree of the denominator so the x-axis, or $y = 0$ is a horizontal asymptote.

(c) The domain is all real numbers except $x = 1$.

3. $f(x) = \dfrac{3x}{|x - 1|}$

(a)

x	$f(x)$
0.5	3
0.9	27
0.99	297
0.999	2997

x	$f(x)$
1.5	9
1.1	33
1.01	303
1.001	3003

x	$f(x)$
5	3.75
10	$3.\overline{33}$
100	$3.\overline{03}$
1000	$3.\overline{003}$

(b) The zero of the denominator is $x = 1$, so $x = 1$ is a vertical asymptote. Since $f(x) \to 3$ as $x \to \infty$ and $f(x) \to -3$ as $x \to -\infty$, both $y = 3$ and $y = -3$ are horizontal asymptotes.

(c) The domain is all real numbers except $x = 1$.

5. $f(x) = \dfrac{3x^2}{x^2 - 1}$

(a)

x	$f(x)$
0.5	-1
0.9	-12.79
0.99	-147.8
0.999	-1498

x	$f(x)$
1.5	5.4
1.1	17.29
1.01	152.3
1.001	1502.3

x	$f(x)$
5	3.125
10	$3.\overline{03}$
100	$3.\overline{0003}$
1000	3

(b) The zeros of the denominator are $x = \pm 1$ so both $x = 1$ and $x = -1$ are vertical asymptotes.

Since the degree of the numerator equals the degree of the denominator, $y = \frac{3}{1} = 3$ is a horizontal asymptote.

(c) The domain is all real numbers except $x = \pm 1$.

7. $f(x) = \dfrac{2}{x + 2}$

Vertical asymptote: $y = -2$
Horizontal asymptote: $y = 0$
Matches graph (a).

9. $f(x) = \dfrac{4x + 1}{x}$

Vertical asymptote: $x = 0$
Horizontal asymptote: $y = 4$
Matches graph (c).

11. $f(x) = \dfrac{x - 2}{x - 4}$

Vertical asymptote: $x = 4$
Horizontal asymptote: $y = 1$
Matches graph (b).

13. $f(x) = \dfrac{1}{x^2}$

Domain: all real numbers except $x = 0$
Vertical asymptote: $x = 0$
Horizontal asymptote: $y = 0$
[Degree of $p(x) <$ degree of $q(x)$]

15. $f(x) = \dfrac{2 + x}{2 - x} = \dfrac{x + 2}{-x + 2}$

Domain: all real numbers except $x = 2$
Vertical asymptote: $x = 2$
Horizontal asymptote: $y = -1$
[Degree of $p(x) =$ degree of $q(x)$]

17. $f(x) = \dfrac{x^3}{x^2 - 1}$

Domain: all real numbers except $x = \pm 1$
Vertical asymptote: $x = \pm 1$
Horizontal asymptotes: None
[Degree of $p(x) >$ degree of $q(x)$]

19. $f(x) = \dfrac{3x^2 + 1}{x^2 + x + 9}$

Domain: All real numbers. The denominator has no real zeros. [Try the Quadratic Formula on the denominator.]

Vertical asymptote: None

Horizontal asymptote: $y = 3$

[Degree of $p(x)$ = degree of $q(x)$]

21. $f(x) = \dfrac{x^2 - 4}{x + 2}$, $g(x) = x - 2$

(a) Domain of f: all real numbers except -2
Domain of g: all real numbers

(b) Since $x + 2$ is a common factor of both the numerator and the denominator of $f(x)$, $x = -2$ is not a vertical asymptote of f. f has no vertical asymptotes.

(c)

x	-4	-3	-2.5	-2	-1.5	-1	0
$f(x)$	-6	-5	-4.5	undef.	-3.5	-3	-2
$g(x)$	-6	-5	-4.5	-4	-3.5	-3	-2

(d) f and g differ only where f is undefined.

23. $f(x) = \dfrac{x - 3}{x^2 - 3x}$, $g(x) = \dfrac{1}{x}$

(a) Domain of f: all real number except 0 and 3
Domain of g: all real numbers except 0

(b) Since $x - 3$ is a common factor of both the numerator and the denominator of f, $x = 3$ is not a vertical asymptote of f. The only vertical asymptote is $x = 0$.

(c)

x	-1	-0.5	0	0.5	2	3	4
$f(x)$	-1	-2	undef.	2	$\frac{1}{2}$	undef.	$\frac{1}{4}$
$g(x)$	-1	-2	undef	2	$\frac{1}{2}$	$\frac{1}{3}$	$\frac{1}{4}$

(d) They differ only at $x = 3$, where f is undefined and g is defined.

25. $f(x) = \dfrac{1}{(x + 2)(x - 1)} = \dfrac{1}{x^2 + x - 2}$

27. $f(x) = \dfrac{2x^2}{x^2 + 1}$

29. $f(x) = 4 - \dfrac{1}{x}$

(a) As $x \to \pm\infty$, $f(x) \to 4$.

(b) As $x \to \infty$, $f(x) \to 4$ but is less than 4.

(c) As $x \to -\infty$, $f(x) \to 4$ but is greater than 4.

31. $f(x) = \dfrac{2x - 1}{x - 3}$

(a) As $x \to \pm\infty$, $f(x) \to 2$.

(b) As $x \to \infty$, $f(x) \to 2$ but is greater than 2.

(c) As $x \to -\infty$, $f(x) \to 2$ but is less than 2.

33. $f(x) = \dfrac{x^2 - 4}{x + 1} = \dfrac{(x + 2)(x - 2)}{x + 1}$

The zeros of f correspond to the zeros of the numerator and are $x = \pm2$.

35. $f(x) = 1 - \dfrac{2}{x - 3} = \dfrac{x - 5}{x - 3}$

The zero of f corresponds to the zero of the numerator and is $x = 5$.

37. $C = \dfrac{255p}{100 - p}, \ 0 \leq p < 100$

   (a) $C(10) = \dfrac{255(10)}{100 - 10} \approx 28.33$ million dollars

   (b) $C(40) = \dfrac{255(40)}{100 - 40} = 170$ million dollars

   (c) $C(75) = \dfrac{255(75)}{100 - 75} = 765$ million dollars

   (d) $C \rightarrow \infty$ as $x \rightarrow 100$. No, it would not be possible to remove 100% of the pollutants.

39. (a)

M	200	400	600	800	1000	1200	1400	1600	1800	2000
t	0.472	0.596	0.710	0.817	0.916	1.009	1.096	1.178	1.255	1.328

   The greater the mass, the more time required per oscillation. The model is a good fit to the actual data.

   (b) You can find M corresponding to $t = 1.056$ by finding the point of intersection of

   $$t = \dfrac{38M + 16{,}965}{10(M + 500)} \quad \text{and} \quad t = 1.056.$$

   If you do this, you obtain $M \approx 1306$ grams.

41. $N = \dfrac{20(5 + 3t)}{1 + 0.04t}, \ 0 \leq t$

   (a) $N(5) \approx 333$ deer

   $N(10) = 500$ deer

   $N(25) = 800$ deer

   (b) The herd is limited by the horizontal asymptote: $N = \dfrac{60}{0.04} = 1500$ deer

43. $P = \dfrac{0.5 + 0.9(n - 1)}{1 + 0.9(n - 1)}, \ 0 < n$

   (a)

n	1	2	3	4	5	6	7	8	9	10
P	0.50	0.74	0.82	0.86	0.89	0.91	0.92	0.93	0.94	0.95

   P approaches 1 as n increases.

   (b) $P = \dfrac{0.9n - 0.4}{0.9n + 0.1}$

   The percentage of correct responses is limited by a horizontal asymptote:

   $$P = \dfrac{0.9}{0.9} = 1 = 100\%$$

45. $225 - 50x = 0$

   $-50x = -225$

   $x = \dfrac{-225}{(-50)} = \dfrac{9}{2}$

47. $2z^2 - 3z - 35 = 0$

   $(2z + 7)(z - 5) = 0$

   $z = -\dfrac{7}{2}, \ 5$

Section 3.6   Graphs of Rational Functions

■ You should be able to graph $f(x) = \dfrac{p(x)}{q(x)}$.

(a) Find the x- and y-intercepts.

(b) Find any vertical or horizontal asymptotes.

(c) Plot additional points.

(d) If the degree of the numerator is one more than the degree of the denominator, use long division to find the slant asymptote.

Solutions to Odd-Numbered Exercises

1. $g(x) = \dfrac{2}{x} + 1$

Vertical shift one unit upward

3. $g(x) = -\dfrac{2}{x}$

Reflection in the x-axis

5. $g(x) = \dfrac{2}{x^2} - 2$

Vertical shift two units downward

7. $g(x) = \dfrac{2}{(x-2)^2}$

Horizontal shift two units to the right

9. $g(x) = \dfrac{4}{(x+2)^3}$

Horizontal shift two units to the left

11. $g(x) = -\dfrac{4}{x^3}$

Reflection in the x-axis the left

13. $f(x) = \dfrac{1}{x + 2}$

y-intercept: $\left(0, \dfrac{1}{2}\right)$

Vertical asymptote: $x = -2$

Horizontal asymptote: $y = 0$

x	-4	-3	-1	0	1
y	$-\dfrac{1}{2}$	-1	1	$\dfrac{1}{2}$	$\dfrac{1}{3}$

15. $h(x) = -\dfrac{1}{x + 2}$

y-intercept: $\left(0, -\dfrac{1}{2}\right)$

Vertical asymptote: $x = -2$

Horizontal asymptote: $y = 0$

x	-4	-3	-1	0
y	$\dfrac{1}{2}$	1	-1	$-\dfrac{1}{2}$

Note: This is the graph of $f(x) = \dfrac{1}{x + 2}$

(Exercise 13) reflected about the *x*-axis.

17. $C(x) = \dfrac{5 + 2x}{1 + x} = \dfrac{2x + 5}{x + 1}$

x-intercept: $\left(-\dfrac{5}{2}, 0\right)$

y-intercept: $(0, 5)$

Vertical asymptote: $x = -1$

Horizontal asymptote: $y = 2$

x	-4	-3	-2	0	1	2
$C(x)$	1	$\dfrac{1}{2}$	-1	5	$\dfrac{7}{2}$	3

19. $g(x) = \dfrac{1}{x + 2} + 2 = \dfrac{2x + 5}{x + 2}$

Intercepts: $\left(-\dfrac{5}{2}, 0\right), \left(0, \dfrac{5}{2}\right)$

Vertical asymptote: $x = -2$

Horizontal asymptote: $y = 2$

x	-4	-3	-1	0	1
y	$\dfrac{3}{2}$	1	3	$\dfrac{5}{2}$	$\dfrac{7}{3}$

Note: This is the graph of $f(x) = \dfrac{1}{x + 2}$

(Exercise 13) shifted upward two units.

21. $f(x) = \dfrac{x^2}{x^2 + 9}$

Intercept: $(0, 0)$

Horizontal asymptote: $y = 1$

y-axis symmetry

x	± 1	± 2	± 3
y	$\dfrac{1}{10}$	$\dfrac{4}{13}$	$\dfrac{1}{2}$

23. $h(x) = \dfrac{x^2}{x^2 - 9}$

Intercept: $(0, 0)$

Vertical asymptotes: $x = \pm 3$
Horizontal asymptote: $y = 1$
y-axis symmetry

x	± 5	± 4	± 2	± 1	0
y	$\frac{25}{16}$	$\frac{16}{7}$	$-\frac{4}{5}$	$-\frac{1}{8}$	0

25. $g(s) = \dfrac{s}{s^2 + 1}$

Intercept: $(0, 0)$

Horizontal asymptote: $y = 0$
Origin symmetry

s	-2	-1	0	0	1
$g(s)$	$-\frac{2}{5}$	$-\frac{1}{2}$	0	$\frac{1}{2}$	$\frac{2}{5}$

27. $g(x) = \dfrac{4(x + 1)}{x(x - 4)}$

Intercept: $(-1, 0)$

Vertical asymptotes: $x = 0$ and $x = 4$

Horizontal asymptote: $y = 0$

x	-2	-1	1	2	3	5	6
y	$-\frac{1}{3}$	0	$-\frac{8}{3}$	-3	$-\frac{16}{3}$	$\frac{24}{5}$	$\frac{7}{3}$

29. $f(x) = \dfrac{3x}{x^2 - x - 2} = \dfrac{3x}{(x + 1)(x - 2)}$

Intercept: $(0, 0)$

Vertical asymptotes: $x = -1, 2$

Horizontal asymptote: $y = 0$

x	-3	0	1	3	4
y	$-\frac{9}{10}$	0	$-\frac{3}{2}$	$\frac{9}{4}$	$\frac{6}{5}$

31. $f(x) = \dfrac{2 + x}{1 - x} = -\dfrac{x + 2}{x - 1}$

x-intercept: $(-2, 0)$

y-intercept: $(0, 2)$

Vertical asymptote: $x = 1$

Horizontal asymptote: $y = -1$

Domain: $x \neq 1$ or $(-\infty, 1) \cup (1, \infty)$

33. $f(t) = \dfrac{3t + 1}{t}$

t-intercept: $\left(-\dfrac{1}{3}, 0\right)$

Vertical asymptote: $t = 0$

Horizontal asymptote: $y = 3$

Domain: $t \neq 0$ or $(-\infty, 0) \cup (0, \infty)$

35. $h(t) = \dfrac{4}{t^2 + 1}$

Domain: all real numbers OR $(-\infty, \infty)$

Horizontal asymptote: $y = 0$

37. $f(t) = \dfrac{2t^2}{t^2 - 4}$

Domain: all real numbers except ± 2,
   OR $(-\infty, -2) \cup (-2, 2) \cup (2, \infty)$

Vertical asymptote: $x = \pm 2$
Horizontal asymptote: $y = 2$

39. $f(x) = \dfrac{20x}{x^2 + 1} - \dfrac{1}{x} = \dfrac{19x^2 - 1}{x(x^2 + 1)}$

Domain: all real numbers except 0,
   OR $(-\infty, 0) \cup (0, \infty)$

Vertical asymptote: $x = 0$
Horizontal asymptote: $y = 0$
Origin Symmetry

41. $h(x) = \dfrac{6x}{\sqrt{x^2 + 1}}$

There are two horizontal asymptotes: $y = \pm 6$

43. $f(x) = \dfrac{4(x - 1)^2}{x^2 - 4x + 5}$

The graph crosses its horizontal asymptote: $y = 4$

45. $h(x) = \dfrac{6 - 2x}{3 - x} = \dfrac{2(3 - x)}{3 - x}$

Since $h(x)$ is not reduced and $(3 - x)$ is a factor of both the numerator and the denominator, $x = 3$ is not a horizontal asymptote. There is a hole in the graph at $x = 3$.

47. False. The graph would have two distinct branches that are separated by the vertical asymptote.

49. $f(x) = \dfrac{2x^2 + 1}{x} = 2x + \dfrac{1}{x}$

Vertical asymptote: $x = 0$
Slant asymptote: $y = 2x$
Origin symmetry

51. $g(x) = \dfrac{x^2 + 1}{x} = x + \dfrac{1}{x}$

Vertical asymptote: $x = 0$
Slant asymptote: $y = x$
Origin symmetry

53. $f(x) = \dfrac{x^3}{x^2 - 1} = x + \dfrac{x}{x^2 - 1}$

Intercept: $(0, 0)$
Vertical asymptotes: $x = \pm 1$
Slant asymptote: $y = x$
Origin symmetry

55. $f(x) = \dfrac{x^2 - x + 1}{x - 1} = x + \dfrac{1}{x - 1}$

y-intercept: $(0, -1)$
Vertical asymptote: $x = 1$
Slant asymptote: $y = x$

57. (a) x-intercept: $(-1, 0)$

(b) $0 = \dfrac{x + 1}{x - 3}$

$0 = x + 1$

$-1 = x$

59. (a) x-intercepts: $(\pm 1, 0)$

(b) $0 = \dfrac{1}{x} - x$

$x = \dfrac{1}{x}$

$x^2 = 1$

$x = \pm 1$

61. $y = \dfrac{2x^2 + x}{x + 1} = 2x - 1 + \dfrac{1}{x + 1}$

Domain: all real numbers except $x = -1$
Vertical asymptote: $x = -1$
Slant asymptote: $y = 2x - 1$

63. $g(x) = \dfrac{1 + 3x^2 - x^3}{x^2} = \dfrac{1}{x^2} + 3 - x = -x + 3 + \dfrac{1}{x^2}$

Domain: all real numbers except 0
OR $(-\infty, 0) \cup (0, \infty)$
Vertical asymptote: $x = 0$
Slant asymptote: $y = -x + 3$

65. $y = \dfrac{1}{x+5} + \dfrac{4}{x}$

(a)

x-intercept: $(-4, 0)$

(b)
$$0 = \frac{1}{x+5} + \frac{4}{x}$$

$$-\frac{4}{x} = \frac{1}{x+5}$$

$$-4(x+5) = x$$

$$-4x - 20 = x$$

$$-5x = 20$$

$$x = -4$$

67. $y = x - \dfrac{6}{x-1}$

(a)

x-intercept: $(-2, 0), (3, 0)$

(b)
$$0 = x - \frac{6}{x-1}$$

$$\frac{6}{x-1} = x$$

$$6 = x(x-1)$$

$$0 = x^2 - x - 6$$

$$0 = (x+2)(x-3)$$

$$x = -2, \quad x = 3$$

69. (a) $0.25(50) + 0.75(x) = C(50 + x)$

$$C = \frac{12.50 + 0.75x}{50 + x} \cdot \frac{4}{4}$$

$$C = \frac{50 + 3x}{4(50 + x)}$$

$$= \frac{3x + 50}{4(x + 50)}$$

(b) Domain: $x > 0$ and $x \le 1000 - 50$
Thus, $0 \le x \le 950$ OR $[0, 950]$.

(c)

As the tank is filled, the rate that the concentration is increasing slows down. It approaches the horizontal asymptote of $C = \frac{3}{4} = 0.75$.

71. $f(x) = \dfrac{3(x+1)}{x^2 + x + 1}$

Minimum: $(-2, -1)$
Maximum: $(0, 3)$

73. (a) $A = xy$ and

$$(x - 2)(y - 4) = 30$$

$$y - 4 = \frac{30}{x - 2}$$

$$y = 4 + \frac{30}{x - 2} = \frac{4x + 22}{x - 2}$$

Thus, $A = xy = x\left(\frac{4x + 22}{x - 2}\right) = \frac{2x(x + 11)}{x - 2}$.

(b) Domain: Since the margins on the left and right are each 1 inch, $x > 2$, OR $(2, \infty)$.

(c)

The area is minimum when $x \approx 5.87$ in. and $y \approx 11.75$ in.

75. $C = 100\left(\frac{200}{x^2} + \frac{x}{x + 30}\right)$, $1 \le x$

The minimum occurs when $x \approx 40.4 \approx 40$.

77. $C = \frac{3t^2 + t}{t^3 + 50}$, $0 \le t$

(a) The horizontal asymptote is the t-axis, or $C = 0$. This indicates that the chemical eventually dissipates.

(b)

The maximum occurs when $t \approx 4.5$.

79. (a)

(b)

$$y = 2.81t + 68.77$$

(c)

$$y = -0.18t^2 + 5.52t + 60.12$$

(d) The quadratic and rational models fit the data better than the line. The rational model may be a better predictor since the parabola is near its maximum.

81. $y = x + 1 + \dfrac{a}{x - 2}$

This has a slant asymptote of $x + 1$ and a vertical asymptote of $x = 2$.

$$0 = -2 + 1 + \frac{a}{-2 - 2}$$

Since $x = -2$ is a zero, $(-2, 0)$ is on the graph. Use this point to solve for a.

$$1 = \frac{a}{-4}$$

$$-4 = a$$

Hence, $y = x + 1 + \dfrac{-4}{x - 2} = \dfrac{x^2 - x - 6}{x - 2}$.

❑ Review Exercises for Chapter 3

Solutions to Odd-Numbered Exercises

1. $f(x) = \left(x + \frac{3}{2}\right)^2 + 1$

Vertex: $\left(-\frac{3}{2}, 1\right)$

y-intercept: $\left(0, \frac{13}{4}\right)$

No x-intercepts

3. $f(x) = \frac{1}{3}(x^2 + 5x - 4)$

$= \frac{1}{3}\left(x^2 + 5x + \frac{25}{4} - \frac{25}{4} - 4\right)$

$= \frac{1}{3}\left[\left(x - \frac{5}{2}\right)^2 - \frac{41}{4}\right]$

$= \frac{1}{3}\left(x - \frac{5}{2}\right)^2 - \frac{41}{12}$

Vertex: $\left(\frac{5}{2}, -\frac{41}{12}\right)$

y-intercept: $\left(0, -\frac{4}{3}\right)$

x-intercepts: $0 = \frac{1}{3}(x^2 + 5x - 4)$

$0 = x^2 + 5x - 4$

$x = \frac{-5 \pm \sqrt{41}}{2}$ Use the Quadratic Formula.

$\left(\frac{-5 \pm \sqrt{41}}{2}, 0\right)$

5. Vertex: $(1, -4)$ $\implies$ $f(x) = a(x - 1)^2 - 4$

Point: $(2, -3)$ $\implies$ $-3 = a(2 - 1)^2 - 4$

$1 = a$

Thus, $f(x) = (x - 1)^2 - 4$.

7. (a) $y = 2x^2$
Vertical stretch

(b) $y = -2x^2$
Vertical stretch and a reflection in the x-axis

(c) $y = x^2 + 2$
Vertical shift two units upward

(d) $y = (x + 2)^2$
Horizontal shift two units to the left

9. $g(x) = x^2 - 2x$

$= x^2 - 2x + 1 - 1$

$= (x - 1)^2 - 1$

The minimum occurs at the vertex $(1, -1)$.

11. $f(x) = 6x - x^2$

$= -(x^2 - 6x + 9 - 9)$

$= -(x - 3)^2 + 9$

The maximum occurs at the vertex $(3, 9)$.

13. $f(t) = -2t^2 + 4t + 1$

$\qquad = -2(t^2 - 2t + 1 - 1) + 1$

$\qquad = -2[(t - 1)^2 - 1] + 1$

$\qquad = -2(t - 1)^2 + 3$

The maximum occurs at the vertex $(1, 3)$.

15. $h(x) = x^2 + 5x - 4$

$\qquad = x^2 + 5x + \frac{25}{4} - \frac{25}{4} - 4$

$\qquad = \left(x + \frac{5}{2}\right)^2 - \frac{25}{4} - \frac{16}{4}$

$\qquad = \left(x + \frac{5}{2}\right)^2 - \frac{41}{4}$

The minimum occurs at the vertex $\left(-\frac{5}{2}, -\frac{41}{4}\right)$.

17. (a)

x	y	Area
1	$4 - \frac{1}{2}(1)$	$(1)[4 - \frac{1}{2}(1)] = \frac{7}{2}$
2	$4 - \frac{1}{2}(2)$	$(2)[4 - \frac{1}{2}(2)] = 6$
3	$4 - \frac{1}{2}(3)$	$(3)[4 - \frac{1}{2}(3)] = \frac{15}{2}$
4	$4 - \frac{1}{2}(4)$	$(4)[4 - \frac{1}{2}(4)] = 8$
5	$4 - \frac{1}{2}(5)$	$(5)[4 - \frac{1}{2}(5)] = \frac{15}{2}$
6	$4 - \frac{1}{2}(6)$	$(6)[4 - \frac{1}{2}(6)] = 6$

(b) The dimensions that will produce a maximum area are $x = 4$ and $y = 2$.

(c) $A = xy = x\left(\dfrac{8 - x}{2}\right)$ since $x + 2y - 8 = 0 \implies y = \dfrac{8 - x}{2}$.

Since the figure is in the first quadrant and x and y must be positive, the domain of $A = x\left(\dfrac{8 - x}{2}\right)$ is $0 < x < 8$.

(d)

The maximum area of 8 occurs at the vertex when $x = 4$ and $y = \dfrac{8 - 4}{2} = 2$.

(e) $A = x\left(\dfrac{8 - x}{2}\right)$

$\qquad = \dfrac{1}{2}(8x - x^2)$

$\qquad = -\dfrac{1}{2}(x^2 - 8x) \quad$ or $\quad -\dfrac{1}{2}x^2 + 4x$

$\qquad = -\dfrac{1}{2}(x^2 - 8x + 16 - 16)$

$\qquad = -\dfrac{1}{2}[(x - 4)^2 - 16]$

$\qquad = -\dfrac{1}{2}(x - 4)^2 + 8$

The maximum area of 8 occurs when $x = 4$ and $y = \dfrac{8 - 4}{2} = 2$.

19. $f(x) = -x^2 + 6x + 9$

The degree is even and the leading coefficient is negative. The graph falls to the left and right.

21. $f(x) = \frac{3}{4}(x^4 + 3x^2 + 2)$

The degree is even and the leading coefficient is positive. The graph rises to the left and right.

23. $f(x) = \frac{1}{2}x^3 - 2x + 1$; $g(x) = \frac{1}{2}x^3$

25. $g(x) = x^4 - x^3 - 2x^2$

27. $f(t) = t^3 - 3t = t(t^2 - 3)$

Intercepts: $(0, 0)\ \left(\pm\sqrt{3}, 0\right)$

The graph rises to th right and falls to the left.

29. $f(x) = x(x + 3)^2$

31. (a) The combined length and girth is

$$y + 4x = 216$$

$$y = 216 - 4x.$$

The volume is

$$V = x^2y = x^2(216 - 4x).$$

(b)

The volume is maximum when $x = 36$ centimeters and $y = 216 - 4(36) = 72$ centimeters.

33. $y_1 = \dfrac{x^2}{x - 2}$

$$y_2 = x + 2 + \frac{4}{x - 2}$$

$$= \frac{(x + 2)(x - 2)}{x - 2} + \frac{4}{x - 2}$$

$$= \frac{x^2 - 4}{x - 2} + \frac{4}{x - 2}$$

$$= \frac{x^2}{x - 2}$$

$$= y_1$$

35.

$$\begin{array}{r}
8x + 5 \\
3x - 2 \overline{\smash{)}24x^2 - x - 8} \\
\underline{24x^2 - 16x} \\
15x - 8 \\
\underline{15x - 10} \\
2
\end{array}$$

Thus, $\dfrac{24x^2 - x - 8}{3x - 2} = 8x + 5 + \dfrac{2}{3x - 2}$.

37.

$$\begin{array}{r}
x^2 - 2 \\
x^2 - 1 \overline{\smash{)}x^4 - 3x^2 + 2} \\
\underline{x^4 - x^2} \\
-2x^2 + 2 \\
\underline{-2x^2 + 2} \\
0
\end{array}$$

Thus, $\dfrac{x^4 - 3x^2 + 2}{x^2 - 1} = x^2 - 2, \quad (x \neq \pm 1)$.

39.
$$
\begin{array}{r}
x^2 - x + 1 \\
x^2 + 2x \overline{\smash)x^4 + x^3 - x^2 + 2x} \\
\underline{x^4 + 2x^3} \\
-x^3 - x^2 \\
\underline{-x^3 - 2x^2} \\
x^2 + 2x
\end{array}
$$

Thus, $\dfrac{x^4 + x^3 - x^2 + 2x}{x^2 + 2x} = x^2 - x + 1, \qquad (x \ne 0, -2).$

41. $2 \;\Big|$
$$
\begin{array}{r|rrrrr}
 & 0.25 & -4 & 0 & 0 & 0 \\
 & & \frac{1}{2} & -7 & -14 & -28 \\
\hline
 & \frac{1}{4} & -\frac{7}{2} & -7 & -14 & -28
\end{array}
$$

Hence, $\dfrac{0.25x^4 - 4x^3}{x - 2} = 0.25x^4 - 3.5x^2 - 7x - 14 - \dfrac{28}{x - 2}.$

43. $\frac{2}{3} \;\Big|$
$$
\begin{array}{r|rrrrr}
 & 6 & -4 & -27 & 18 & 0 \\
 & & 4 & 0 & -18 & 0 \\
\hline
 & 6 & 0 & -27 & 0 & 0
\end{array}
$$

Thus, $\dfrac{6x^4 - 4x^3 - 27x^2 + 18x}{x - (2/3)} = 6x^3 - 27x.$

45. $f(x) = 2x^3 + 3x^2 - 20x - 21$

(a) $4 \;\Big|$
$$
\begin{array}{r|rrrr}
 & 2 & 3 & -20 & -21 \\
 & & 8 & 44 & 96 \\
\hline
 & 2 & 11 & 24 & 75
\end{array}
$$

No, $x = 4$ is not a zero.

(b) $-1 \;\Big|$
$$
\begin{array}{r|rrrr}
 & 2 & 3 & -20 & -21 \\
 & & -2 & -1 & 21 \\
\hline
 & 2 & 1 & -21 & 0
\end{array}
$$

Yes, $x = -1$ is a zero.

(c) $-\frac{7}{2} \;\Big|$
$$
\begin{array}{r|rrrr}
 & 2 & 3 & -20 & -21 \\
 & & -7 & 14 & 21 \\
\hline
 & 2 & -4 & -6 & 0
\end{array}
$$

Yes, $x = -\frac{7}{2}$ is a zero.

(d) $0 \;\Big|$
$$
\begin{array}{r|rrrr}
 & 2 & 3 & -20 & -21 \\
 & & 0 & 0 & 0 \\
\hline
 & 2 & 3 & -20 & -21
\end{array}
$$

No, $x = 0$ is not a zero.

47. $f(x) = 6(x + 1)^2 \left(x - \dfrac{1}{3}\right)\left(x + \dfrac{1}{2}\right)$ \qquad Multiply by 6 to clear the fractions.

$= (x + 1)^2 \, 3\left(x - \dfrac{1}{3}\right) 2\left(x + \dfrac{1}{2}\right)$

$= (x^2 + 2x + 1)(3x - 1)(2x + 1)$

$= (x^2 + 2x + 1)(6x^2 + x - 1)$

$= 6x^4 + 13x^3 + 7x^2 - x - 1$

Note: $f(x) = a(6x^4 + 13x^3 + 7x^2 - x - 1)$, where a is any real number, has zeros $-1, -1, \frac{1}{3},$ and $-\frac{1}{2}.$

49. $f(x) = 4x^3 - 11x^2 + 10x - 3$

Possible rational zeros: $\pm 1, \pm 3, \pm\frac{1}{2}, \pm\frac{3}{2}, \pm\frac{1}{4}, \pm\frac{3}{4}$. Use a graphing utility to see that $x = 1$ is probably a zero.

$$
\begin{array}{r|rrrr}
1 & 4 & -11 & 10 & -3 \\
 & & 4 & -7 & 3 \\
\hline
 & 4 & -7 & 3 & 0
\end{array}
$$

$4x^3 - 11x^2 + 10x - 3 = (x - 1)(4x^2 - 7x + 3) = (x - 1)^2(4x - 3)$

Thus, the zeros of f are $x = 1$ and $x = \frac{3}{4}$.

51. $f(x) = 6x^3 - 5x^2 + 24x - 20$

Graphing $f(x)$ with a graphing utility suggests that $x = \frac{5}{6}$ is a zero.

$$
\begin{array}{r|rrrr}
\frac{5}{6} & 6 & -5 & 24 & -20 \\
 & & 5 & 0 & 20 \\
\hline
 & 6 & 0 & 24 & 0
\end{array}
$$

The quadratic $6x^2 + 24 = 0$ has complex zeros $x = \pm 2i$. Thus, the zeros are $\frac{5}{6}, 2i, -2i$.

53. $f(x) = 6x^4 - 25x^3 + 14x^2 + 27x - 18$

Possible rational zeros: $\pm 1, \pm 2, \pm 3, \pm 6, \pm 9, \pm 18, \pm\frac{1}{2}, \pm\frac{3}{2}, \pm\frac{9}{2}, \pm\frac{1}{3}, \pm\frac{2}{3}, \pm\frac{1}{6}$. Use a graphing utility to see that $x = -1$ and $x = 3$ are probably zeros.

$$
\begin{array}{r|rrrrr}
-1 & 6 & -25 & 14 & 27 & -18 \\
 & & -6 & 31 & -45 & 18 \\
\hline
 & 6 & -31 & 45 & -18 & 0
\end{array}
$$

$$
\begin{array}{r|rrrr}
3 & 6 & -31 & 45 & -18 \\
 & & 18 & -39 & 18 \\
\hline
 & 6 & -13 & 6 & 0
\end{array}
$$

$6x^4 - 25x^3 + 14x^2 + 27x - 18 = (x + 1)(x - 3)(6x^2 - 13x + 6)$
$$= (x + 1)(x - 3)(3x - 2)(2x - 3)$$

Thus, the zeros of f are $x = -1$, $x = 3$, $x = \frac{2}{3}$, and $x = \frac{3}{2}$.

55. $f(x) = x^4 + 2x + 1$

(a)

(b) The graph has two x-intercepts, so there are two real zeros.

(c) The zeros are $x = -1$ and $x \approx -0.54$.

57. $h(x) = x^3 - 6x^2 + 12x - 10$

(a)

(b) The graph has one x-intercept, so there is one real zero.

(c) $x \approx 3.26$

59. (a) $S = 1.2087 + 0.2896t + 0.1762t^2 - 0.0309t^3 + 0.0013t^4$

The model is a fairly "good fit."

(b) One explanation may be a recession. The model also shows a downturn in sales.

(c) $S(9) - S(11) \approx 0.47$
The actual decrease of 0.90 was more than this.

(d) $S(15) \approx 6.72$

61. $f(x) = \dfrac{-5}{x^2}$

y-axis symmetry
Vertical asymptote: $x = 0$
Horizontal asymptote: $y = 0$

x	± 3	± 2	± 1
y	$-\frac{5}{9}$	$-\frac{5}{4}$	-5

63. $p(x) = \dfrac{x^2}{x^2 + 1}$

Intercept: $(0, 0)$
y-axis symmetry
Horizontal asymptote: $y = 1$

x	± 3	± 2	± 1	0
y	$\frac{9}{10}$	$\frac{4}{5}$	$\frac{1}{2}$	0

65. $f(x) = \dfrac{x}{x^2 + 1}$

Intercept: $(0, 0)$
Origin symmetry
Horizontal asymptote: $y = 0$

x	-2	-1	0	1	2
y	$-\frac{2}{5}$	$-\frac{1}{2}$	0	$\frac{1}{2}$	$\frac{2}{5}$

67. $f(x) = \dfrac{2x^3}{x^2 + 1} = 2x - \dfrac{2x}{x^2 + 1}$

Intercept: $(0, 0)$

Origin symmetry

Slant asymptote: $y = 2x$

x	-2	-1	0	1	2
y	$-\frac{16}{5}$	-1	0	1	$\frac{16}{5}$

69. $s(x) = \dfrac{8x^2}{x^2 + 4}$

Intercept: $(0, 0)$

Horizontal asymptote: $y = 8$

71. $g(x) = \dfrac{x^2 + 1}{x + 1} = x - 1 + \dfrac{2}{x + 1}$

Intercept: $(0, 1)$

Slant asymptote: $y = x - 1$

73. $f(x) = \dfrac{2x^2}{(x + 3)(x - 4)} = \dfrac{2x^2}{x^2 - x - 12}$

This answer in not unique.

75. $\overline{C} = \dfrac{C}{x} = \dfrac{0.5x + 500}{x}, \quad 0 < x$

$= 0.5 + \dfrac{500}{x}$

As x increase, the cost approaches a horizontal asymptote, $\overline{C} = 0.5$.

77. (a)

(b) $N(5) = 304{,}000$

$N(10) \approx 453{,}333$

$N(25) \approx 702{,}222$

(c) The limit is $\frac{60}{0.05} = 1{,}200{,}000$, the horizontal asymptote.

79. The first graph has a hole at $x = -3$. Since there are only a finite number of pixels, you might not see the hole.

❏ Chapter Test for Chapter 3

1. (a) $g(x) = 2 - x^2$ is a reflection in the x-axis followed by a vertical translation 2 units upward.

(b) $g(x) = \left(x - \frac{3}{2}\right)^2$ is a horizontal translation $\frac{3}{2}$ units to the right.

2. $y = x^2 + 4x + 3 = x^2 + 4x + 4 - 1 = (x + 2)^2 - 1$

Vertex: $(-2, -1)$

$y = 0 \implies y = 3$

$y = 0 \implies x^2 + 4x + 3 = 0 \implies (x + 3)(x + 1) = 0 \implies x = -1, -3$

Intercepts: $(0, 3),\ (-1, 0),\ (-3, 0)$

3. Let $y = a(x - h)^2 + k$. The vertex $(3, -6)$ implies that $y = a(x - 3)^2 - 6$. For $(0, 3)$ you obtain

$$3 = a(0 - 3)^2 - 6 = 9a - 6 \implies a = 1.$$

Thus, $y = (x - 3)^2 - 6 = x^2 - 6x + 3$.

4. (a) $y = -\frac{1}{20}x^2 + 3x + 5 = -\frac{1}{20}(x^2 - 60x + 900) + 5 + 45$
$$= -\frac{1}{20}(x - 30)^2 + 50$$

Maximum height: $y = 50$ feet

(b) The term 5 determines the height at which the ball was thrown. Changing the constant term results in a vertical translation of the graph and therefore changes the maximum height.

5.
$$
\begin{array}{r}
3x \\
x^2 + 1 \overline{)\, 3x^3 + 0x^2 + 4x - 1} \\
\underline{3x^3 + 3x } \\
x - 1
\end{array}
$$

$3x + \dfrac{x - 1}{x^2 + 1}$

6.

$$
\begin{array}{r|rrrrr}
2 & 2 & 0 & -5 & 0 & -3 \\
  &   & 4 & 8 & 6 & 12 \\
\hline
  & 2 & 4 & 3 & 6 & 9 \\
\end{array}
$$

$2x^3 + 4x^2 + 3x + 6 + \dfrac{9}{x - 2}$

7. Possible rational zeros:

$\pm 24, \pm 12, \pm 8, \pm 6, \pm 4, \pm 3, \pm 2, \pm 1, \pm \frac{3}{2}, \pm \frac{1}{2}$

Rational zeros: $-2, \frac{3}{2}$

8. Possible rational zeros:

$\pm 2, \pm 1, \pm \frac{2}{3}, \pm \frac{1}{3}$

Rational zeros: $\pm 1, -\frac{2}{3}$

9. Real zeros: $1.380, -0.819$

10. Real zeros: $-1.414, -0.667, 1.414$

11. $(x - 0)(x - 3)(x - (3 + i))(x - (3 - i))$

$x(x - 3)(x^2 - 6x + 10)$

$x^4 - 9x^3 + 28x^2 - 30x$

12. $(x - (1 + \sqrt{3}i))(x - (1 - \sqrt{3}i))(x - 2)(x - 2)$

$(x^2 - 2x + 4)(x^2 - 4x + 4)$

$x^4 - 6x^3 + 16x^2 - 24x + 16$

13.

14.

15. $f(x) = \dfrac{4x^2}{(x - 3)(x + 3)} = \dfrac{4x^2}{x^2 - 9}$

❑ Practice Test for Chapter 3

1. Sketch the graph of $f(x) = x^2 - 6x + 5$ by hand and identify the vertex and the intercepts.

2. Find the number of units x that produce a minimum cost C if $C = 0.01x^2 - 90x + 15,000$.

3. Find the quadratic function that has a maximum at $(1, 7)$ and passes through the point $(2, 5)$.

4. Find two quadratic functions that have x-intercepts $(2, 0)$ and $\left(\frac{4}{3}, 0\right)$.

5. Use the leading Coefficient Test to determine the right-hand and left-hand behavior of the graph of the polynomial function $f(x) = -3x^5 + 2x^3 - 17$.

6. Find all the real zeros of $f(x) = x^5 - 5x^3 + 4x$. Verify your answer with a graphing utility.

7. Find the polynomial function with 0, 3, and -2 as zeros.

8. Sketch $f(x) = x^3 - 12x$ by hand.

9. Divide $3x^4 - 7x^2 + 2x - 10$ by $x - 3$ using long division.

10. Divide $x^3 - 11$ by $x^2 + 2x - 1$.

11. Use synthetic division to divide $3x^5 + 13x^4 + 12x - 1$ by $x + 5$.

12. Use synthetic division to find $f(-6)$ when $f(x) = 7x^3 + 40x^2 - 12x + 15$.

13. Find the real zeros of $f(x) = x^3 - 19x - 30$.

14. Find the real zeros of $f(x) = x^4 + x^3 - 8x^2 - 9x - 9$.

15. List all possible rational zeros of the function $f(x) = 6x^3 - 5x^2 + 4x - 15$.

16. Find the rational zeros of the polynomial $f(x) = x^3 - \frac{20}{3}x^2 + 9x - \frac{10}{3}$. product of linear factors.

17. Write $f(x) = x^4 + x^3 + 5x - 10$ as a

18. Find a polynomial with real coefficients that has 2, $3 + i$, and $3 - 2i$ as zeros.

19. Use synthetic division to show that $3i$ is a zero of $f(x) = x^3 + 4x^2 + 9x + 36$.

20. Find a mathematical model for the statement, "z varies directly as the square of x and inversely as the square root of y".

21. Sketch the graph of $f(x) = \dfrac{x - 1}{2x}$ and label all intercepts and asymptotes.

22. Sketch the graph of $f(x) = \dfrac{3x^2 - 4}{x}$ and label all intercepts and asymptotes.

23. Find all the asymptotes of $f(x) = \dfrac{8x^2 - 9}{x^2 + 1}$.

24. Find all the asymptotes of $f(x) = \dfrac{4x^2 - 2x + 7}{x - 1}$.

25. Sketch the graph of $f(x) = \dfrac{x - 5}{(x - 5)^2}$.

C H A P T E R   4
Exponential and Logarithmic Functions

C H A P T E R   4
Exponential and Logarithmic Functions

Section 4.1   Exponential Functions and Their Graphs

- You should know that a function of the form $y = a^x$, where $a > 0$, $a \neq 1$, is called an exponential function with base a.
- You should be able to graph exponential functions.
- You should be familiar with the number e and the natural exponential function $f(x) = e^x$.
- You should know formulas for compound interest.

    (a) For n compoundings per year: $A = P\left(1 + \dfrac{r}{n}\right)^{nt}$.

    (b) For continuous compoundings: $A = Pe^{rt}$.

Solutions to Odd-Numbered Exercises

1. $(3.4)^{5.6} \approx 946.852$

3. $(1.005)^{400} \approx 7.352$

5. $5^{-\pi} \approx 0.006$

7. $100^{\sqrt{2}} \approx 673.639$

9. $e^{-3/4} \approx 0.472$

11. $f(x) = 3^{x-2}$

$ = 3^x 3^{-2}$

$ = 3^x\left(\dfrac{1}{3^2}\right)$

$ = \dfrac{1}{9}(3^x)$

$ = h(x)$

Thus, $f(x) \neq g(x)$, but $f(x) = h(x)$. You can confirm your answer graphically by graphing f, g, and h in the same viewing rectangle.

13. $f(x) = 16(4^{-x})$ and $f(x) = 16(4^{-x})$

$ = 4^2(4^{-x}) \qquad\qquad\qquad = 16(2^2)^{-x}$

$ = 4^{2-x} \qquad\qquad\qquad\quad = 16(2^{-2x})$

$ = \left(\dfrac{1}{4}\right)^{-(2-x)} \qquad\qquad = h(x)$

$ = \left(\dfrac{1}{4}\right)^{x-2}$

$ = g(x)$

Thus, $f(x) = g(x) = h(x)$. You can confirm your answer graphically by graphing f, g, and h in the same viewing rectangle.

15. $g(x) = 5^x$

x	-2	-1	0	1	2
$g(x)$	$\frac{1}{25}$	$\frac{1}{5}$	1	5	25

Asymptote: $y = 0$
Intercept: $(0, 1)$
Increasing

169

17. $f(x) = \left(\frac{1}{5}\right)^x = 5^{-x}$

x	-2	-1	0	1	2
y	25	5	1	$\frac{1}{5}$	$\frac{1}{25}$

Asymptote: $y = 0$
Intercepts: $(0, 1)$
Decreasing

19. $h(x) = 5^{x-2}$

x	-1	0	1	2	3
y	$\frac{1}{125}$	$\frac{1}{25}$	$\frac{1}{5}$	1	5

Asymptote: $y = 0$
Intercepts: $\left(0, \frac{1}{25}\right)$
Increasing

21. $g(x) = 5^{-x} - 3$

x	-1	0	1	2
y	2	-2	$-2\frac{4}{5}$	$-2\frac{24}{25}$

Asymptote: $y = -3$
Intercepts: $(1, -2), (-0.683, 0)$
Decreasing

23. $f(x) = 2^x$ rises to the right.

Asymptote: $y = 0$
Intercept: $(0, 1)$
Matches graph (c).

25. $f(x) = 2^{-x}$ falls to the right.

Asymptote: $y = 0$
Intercept: $(0, 1)$
Matches graph (e).

27. $f(x) = 2^x - 4$ rises to the right.

Asymptote: $y = -4$
Intercept: $(0, -3)$
Matches graph (g).

29. $f(x) = -2^{x-2} = -(2^{x-2})$ falls to the right.

Asymptote: $y = 0$
Intercept: $(0, -2^{-2}) = \left(0, -\frac{1}{4}\right)$
Matches graph (a).

31. $y = 2^{-x^2}$
Asymptote: $y = 0$

33. $f(x) = 3^{x-2} + 1$
Asymptote: $y = 1$

35. $y = 1.08^{-5x}$

Asymptote: $y = 0$

37. $s(t) = 2e^{0.12t}$

Asymptote: $y = 0$

39. $g(x) = 1 + e^{-x}$

Asymptote: $y = 1$

41. $y = 3^x$ and $y = 4^x$

x	-2	-1	0	1	2
3^x	$\frac{1}{9}$	$\frac{1}{3}$	1	3	9
4^x	$\frac{1}{16}$	$\frac{1}{4}$	1	4	16

(a) $4^x < 3^x$ when $x < 0$.

(b) $4^x > 3^x$ when $x > 0$.

43. $f(x) = 3^x$

(a) $g(x) = f(x - 2) = 3^{x-2}$

Horizontal shift two units to the right

(b) $h(x) = -\frac{1}{2}f(x) = -\frac{1}{2}(3^x)$

Vertical shrink and a reflection about the x-axis

(c) $q(x) = f(-x) + 3 = 3^{-x} + 3$

Reflection about the y-axis and a vertical translation three units upward

45. (a) $f(x) = x^2 e^{-x}$

Decreasing: $(-\infty, 0)$, $(2, \infty)$

Increasing: $(0, 2)$

Relative maximum: $(2, 4e^{-2})$

Relative minimum: $(0, 0)$

(b) $g(x) = x2^{3-x}$

Decreasing: $(1.44, \infty)$

Increasing: $(-\infty, 1.44)$

Relative maximum: $(1.44, 4.25)$

47. The exponential function, $y = e^x$, increases at a faster rate than the polynomial function, $y = x^n$.

49. $f(x) = \left(1 + \dfrac{0.5}{x}\right)^x$ and $g(x) = e^{0.5}$

(Horizontal line)

As $x \to \infty$, $f(x) \to g(x)$.

51. $A = 5000e^{(0.075)(50)} \approx \$212,605.51$

53. $P = \$2500$, $r = 12\%$, $t = 10$ years

Compounded n times per year: $A = 2500\left(1 + \dfrac{0.12}{n}\right)^{10n}$

Compounded continuously: $A = 2500e^{0.12(10)}$

n	1	2	4	12	365	Continuous compounding
A	\$7,764.62	\$8,017.84	\$8,155.09	\$8250.97	\$8298.66	\$8,300.29

55. $P = \$2500$, $r = 12\%$, $t = 20$ years

Compounded n times per year: $A = 2500\left(1 + \dfrac{0.12}{n}\right)^{20n}$

Compounded continuously: $A = 2500e^{0.12(20)}$

n	1	2	4	12	365	Continuous compounding
A	\$24,115.73	\$25,714.29	\$26,602.23	\$27,231.38	\$27,547.07	\$27,557.94

57. $A = Pe^{rt}$

$100,000 = Pe^{0.09t}$

$\dfrac{100,000}{e^{0.09t}} = P$

$P = 100,000e^{-0.09t}$

t	1	10	20	30	40	50
P	\$91,393.12	\$40,656.97	\$16,529.89	\$6,720.55	\$2,732.37	\$1,110.90

59. $P = 100,000\left(1 + \dfrac{0.10}{12}\right)^{-12t}$

t	1	10	20	30	40	50
P	\$90,521.24	\$36,940.70	\$13,646.15	\$5,040.98	\$1,862.17	\$687.90

61. $P = 5000\left(1 - \dfrac{4}{4 + e^{-0.002x}}\right)$

(a)

(b) If $x = 500$, $p \approx \$421.12$

(c) For $x = 600$, $p \approx \$350.13$.

63. $P(t) = 100e^{0.2197t}$

(a) $P(0) \approx 100$

(b) $P(5) \approx 300$

(c) $P(10) \approx 900$

65. $Q = 25\left(\frac{1}{2}\right)^{t/1620}$

(a) When $t = 0$, $Q = 25\left(\frac{1}{2}\right)^{0/1620} = 25(1) = 25$ units.

(b) When $t = 1000$, $Q = 25\left(\frac{1}{2}\right)^{1000/1620} \approx 16.30$ units.

(c)

67. $P = 10,958e^{-0.15h}$

(a), (b)

(c)

h	0	5	10	15	20
P	10,958	5176	2445	1155	546

The model is a "good fit".

(d) $P(8) \approx 3330 \text{ kg/m}^2$

(e) $2000 = 10,958e^{-0.15h}$ when $x \approx 11.3$.

69. (a) $T = -1.239t + 73.021$

The temperature decreases at a slower rate as it approaches the room temperature.

(b) $T = 0.034t^2 - 2.264t + 77.295$
The parabola is increasing when $t = 60$.

(c) $T = 54.438(0.964)^t$

(d) The horizontal asymptote of the exponential is $T = 0$.

71.

When $t = 2$, $v(2) \approx \$11,250$.

73. Since $\sqrt{2} \approx 1.414$ we know that $1 < \sqrt{2} < 2$.

Thus:
$2^1 < 2^{\sqrt{2}} < 2^2$
$2 < 2^{\sqrt{2}} < 4$

75.

77. (a) $f(u + v) = a^{u+v} = a^u \cdot a^v = f(u)f(v)$

(b) $f(2x) = a^{2x} = (a^x)^2 = [f(x)]^2$

Section 4.2   Logarithmic Functions and Their Graphs

■ You should know that a function of the form $y = \log_a x$, where $a > 0$, $a \neq 1$, and $x > 0$, is called a logarithm of x to base a.

■ You should be able to convert from logarithmic form to exponential form and vice versa.

$$y = \log_a x \iff a^y = x$$

■ You should know the following properties of logarithms.

(a) $\log_a 1 = 0$ since $a^0 = 1$.

(b) $\log_a a = 1$ since $a^1 = a$.

(c) $\log_a a^x = x$ since $a^x = a^x$.

(d) If $\log_a x = \log_a y$, then $x = y$.

■ You should know the definition of the natural logarithmic function.

$$\log_e x = \ln x, \ x > 0$$

■ You should know the properties of the natural logarithmic function.

(a) $\ln 1 = 0$ since $e^0 = 1$.

(b) $\ln e = 1$ since $e^1 = e$.

(c) $\ln e^x = x$ since $e^x = e^x$.

(d) If $\ln x = \ln y$, then $x = y$.

■ You should be able to graph logarithmic functions.

Solutions to Odd-Numbered Exercises

1. $\log_4 64 = 3 \implies 4^3 = 64$

3. $\log_7 \frac{1}{49} = -2 \implies 7^{-2} = \frac{1}{49}$

5. $\log_{32} 4 = \frac{2}{5} \implies 32^{2/5} = 4$

7. $\ln 1 = 0 \implies e^0 = 1$

9. $5^3 = 125 \implies \log_5 125 = 3$

11. $81^{1/4} = 3 \implies \log_{81} 3 = \frac{1}{4}$

13. $6^{-2} = \frac{1}{36} \implies \log_6 \frac{1}{36} = -2$

15. $e^3 = 20.0855\ldots \implies \ln 20.0855\ldots = 3$

17. $e^x = 4 \implies \ln 4 = x$

19. $\log_2 16 = \log_2 2^4 = 4$

21. $\log_{16} 4 = \log_{16} 16^{1/2} = \frac{1}{2}$

23. $\log_7 1 = \log_7 7^0 = 0$

25. $\log_{10} 0.01 = \log_{10} 10^{-2} = -2$

27. $\ln e^3 = 3$

29. $\log_a a^2 = 2$

31. $\log_{10} 345 \approx 2.538$

33. $\log_{10} 145 \approx 2.161$

35. $\ln 18.42 \approx 2.913$

37. $\ln(1 + \sqrt{3}) \approx 1.005$

39. $\ln 0.32 \approx -1.139$

41. $f(x) = 3^x$, $g(x) = \log_3 x$

f and g are inverses. Their graphs are reflected about the line $y = x$.

43. $f(x) = e^x$, $g(x) = \ln x$

f and g are inverses. Their graphs are reflected about the line $y = x$.

45. $f(x) = \log_3 x + 2$

Asymptote: $x = 0$

Point on graph: $(1, 2)$

Matches graph (c).

47. $f(x) = -\log_3(x + 2)$

Asymptote: $x = -2$

Point on graph: $(-1, 0)$

Matches graph (d).

49. $f(x) = \log_3(1 - x)$

Asymptote: $x = 1$

Point on graph: $(0, 0)$

Matches graph (b).

51. $f(x) = \log_4 x$

Domain: $x > 0 \implies$ The domain is $(0, \infty)$.

Vertical asymptote: $x = 0$

x-intercept: $(1, 0)$

$y = \log_4 x \implies 4^y = x$

x	$\frac{1}{4}$	1	4	2
y	-1	0	1	$\frac{1}{2}$

53. $h(x) = \log_4(x - 3)$

Domain: $x - 3 > 0$ or $(3, \infty)$

Vertical asymptote: $x = 3$

Intercept: $(4, 0)$

55. $y = -\log_3 x + 2$

Domain: $(0, \infty)$

Vertical asymptote: $x = 0$

x-intercept: $-\log_3 x + 2 = 0$

$\qquad\qquad 2 = \log_3 x$

$\qquad\qquad 3^2 = x$

$\qquad\qquad 9 = x$

The x-intercept is $(9, 0)$.

$y = -\log_2 x + 2$

$\log_3 x = 2 - y \implies 3^{2-y} = x$

x	27	9	3	1	$\frac{1}{3}$
y	-1	0	1	2	3

57. $y = \log_{10}\left(\dfrac{x}{5}\right)$

Domain: $\dfrac{x}{5} > 0 \implies x > 0$

The domain is $(0, \infty)$.

Vertical asymptote: $\dfrac{x}{5} = 0 \implies x = 0$

The vertical asymptote is the y-axis.

x-intercept: $\log_{10}\left(\dfrac{x}{5}\right) = 0$

$$\dfrac{x}{5} = 10^0$$

$$\dfrac{x}{5} = 1 \implies x = 5$$

The x-intercept is $(5, 0)$.

59. $f(x) = \ln(x - 2)$

Domain: $x - 2 > 0 \implies x > 2$

The domain is $(2, \infty)$.

Vertical asymptote: $x - 2 = 0 \implies x = 2$

x-intercept: $0 = \ln(x - 2)$

$$e^0 = x - 2$$

$$3 = x$$

The x-intercept is $(3, 0)$.

61. $g(x) = \ln(-x)$

Domain: $-x > 0 \implies x < 0$

The domain is $(-\infty, 0)$.

Vertical asymptote: $-x = 0 \implies x = 0$

x-intercept: $0 = \ln(-x)$

$$e^0 = -x$$

$$-1 = x$$

The x-intercept is $(-1, 0)$.

63. $f(x) = \dfrac{x}{2} - \ln\dfrac{x}{4}$

Domain: $(0, \infty)$

Increasing on $(2, \infty)$

Decreasing on $(0, 2)$

Relative minimum: $(2, 1.693)$

65. $h(x) = 4x \ln x$

Domain: $(0, \infty)$

Increasing on $(0.368, \infty)$

Decreasing on $(0, 0.368)$

Relative minimum: $(0.368, -1.472)$

67. $t = \dfrac{10 \ln 2}{\ln 67 - \ln 50} \approx 23.68$ years

69. (a) False, y is not an exponential function of x. (y can never be 0.)

(b) True, y could be $\log_2 x$.

(c) True, x could be 2^y.

(d) False, y is not linear. (The points are not collinear.)

71. $y = (x - 1) - \frac{1}{2}(x - 1)^2 + \frac{1}{3}(x - 1)^3 - \frac{1}{4}(x - 1)^4$

The pattern implies that as we take more terms, the graph of y will more closely resemble that of $\ln x$ on the interval $(0, 2)$.

73. $t = \dfrac{\ln K}{0.095}$

(a)

K	1	2	4	6	8	10	12
t	0	7.3	14.6	18.9	21.9	24.2	26.2

(b)

75. (a)

(b)

(c) $P = e^{-0.1499h + 9.3018} \approx 10,957.7 e^{-0.1499h}$

$\ln P = -0.1499h + 9.3018$

77. $y = 10 \ln\left(\dfrac{10 + \sqrt{100 - x^2}}{x}\right) - \sqrt{100 - x^2}$

(a)

Domain: $0 < x \le 10$

(b) Asymptote: $x = 0$

(c) When $x = 2$, $y \approx 13.126$. Since the rope is 10 feet long, the third side of the shaded right triangle is $\sqrt{100 - 2^2} = \sqrt{96}$. Thus, the person is at $13.126 + \sqrt{96} \approx 22.924$.

(d) $p = y + \sqrt{100 - x^2} = 10 \ln\left(\dfrac{10 + \sqrt{100 - x^2}}{x}\right)$

(e)

The position of the person changes most at the beginning.

79. $y = 80.4 - 11 \ln x$

$y(300) = 80.4 - 11 \ln 300 \approx 17.66 \text{ ft}^3/\text{min}$

81. $w = 19,440(\ln 9 - \ln 3) \approx 21,357$ ft-lb

83. $t = 10.042 \ln\left(\dfrac{1316.35}{1316.35 - 1250}\right) \approx 30$ years

85. Total amount $= (1316.35)(30)(12) = \$473,886$

Interest $= 473,886 - 150,000 = \$323,886$

87. (a) $(0, \infty)$

(b) $y = \log_{10} x$

$x = \log_{10} y$

$10^x = y$

$f^{-1}(x) = 10^x$

(c) Since $\log_{10} 1000 = 3$ and $\log_{10} 10,000 = 4$, the interval in which $f(x)$ will be found is $(3, 4)$.

(d) When $f(x)$ is negative, x is in the interval $(0, 1)$.

(e) $0 = \log_{10} 1$

$1 = \log_{10} 10$

$2 = \log_{10} 100$

$3 = \log_{10} 1000$

When $f(x)$ is increased by one unit, x is increased by a factor of 10.

(f) $\quad f(x_1) = 3n \qquad f(x_2) = n$

$\log_{10} x_1 = 3n \qquad \log_{10} x_2 = n$

$\quad x_1 = 10^{3n} \qquad\quad x_2 = 10^n$

$x_1 : x_2 = 10^{3n} : 10^n = 10^{2n} : 1$

Section 4.3   Properties of Logarithms

■ You should know the following properties of logarithms.

(a) $\log_a x = \dfrac{\log_b x}{\log_b a}$

(b) $\log_a (uv) = \log_a u + \log_a v$ $\ln (uv) = \ln u + \ln v$

(c) $\log_a (u/v) = \log_a u - \log_a v$ $\ln (u/v) = \ln u - \ln v$

(d) $\log_a u^n = n \log_a u$ $\ln u^n = n \ln u$

■ You should be able to rewrite logarithmic expressions using these properties.

Solutions to Odd-Numbered Exercises

1. $f(x) = \log_{10} x$

$g(x) = \dfrac{\ln x}{\ln 10}$

$f(x) = g(x)$

3. $\log_3 5 = \dfrac{\log_{10} 5}{\log_{10} 3}$

5. $\log_2 x = \dfrac{\log_{10} x}{\log_{10} 2}$

7. $\log_3 5 = \dfrac{\ln 5}{\ln 3}$

9. $\log_2 x = \dfrac{\ln x}{\ln 2}$

11. $\log_3 7 = \dfrac{\log_{10} 7}{\log_{10} 3} = \dfrac{\ln 7}{\ln 3} \approx 1.771$

13. $\log_{1/2} 4 = \dfrac{\log_{10} 4}{\log_{10}(1/2)} = \dfrac{\ln 4}{\ln(1/2)} = -2.000$

15. $\log_9(0.4) = \dfrac{\log_{10} 0.4}{\log_{10} 9} = \dfrac{\ln 0.4}{\ln 9} \approx -0.417$

17. $\log_{15} 1250 = \dfrac{\log_{10} 1250}{\log_{10} 15} = \dfrac{\ln 1250}{\ln 15} \approx 2.633$

19. $\log_{10} 5x = \log_{10} 5 + \log_{10} x$

21. $\log_{10} \dfrac{5}{x} = \log_{10} 5 - \log_{10} x$

23. $\log_8 x^4 = 4 \log_8 x$

25. $\ln \sqrt{z} = \ln z^{1/2} = \frac{1}{2} \ln z$

27. $\ln xyz = \ln x + \ln y + \ln z$

29. $\ln \sqrt{a - 1} = \frac{1}{2} \ln(a - 1)$

31. $\ln z(z - 1)^2 = \ln z + \ln(z - 1)^2$

$= \ln z + 2 \ln(z - 1)$

33. $\ln \sqrt[3]{\dfrac{x}{y}} = \frac{1}{3} \ln \dfrac{x}{y}$

$= \frac{1}{3} [\ln x - \ln y]$

$= \frac{1}{3} \ln x - \frac{1}{3} \ln y$

35. $\ln \left(\dfrac{x^4 \sqrt{y}}{z^5} \right) = \ln x^4 \sqrt{y} - \ln z^5$

$= \ln x^4 + \ln \sqrt{y} - \ln z^5$

$= 4 \ln x + \frac{1}{2} \ln y - 5 \ln z$

37. $\log_b\left(\dfrac{x^2}{y^2z^3}\right) = \log_b x^2 - \log_b y^2z^3$

$= \log_b x^2 - [\log_b y^2 + \log_b z^3]$

$= 2\log_b x - 2\log_b y - 3\log_b z$

39. $y_1 = \ln[x^3(x + 4)]$

$y_2 = 3\ln x + \ln(x + 4)$

$y_1 = y_2$

41. $\ln x + \ln 2 = \ln 2x$

43. $\log_4 z - \log_4 y = \log_4 \dfrac{z}{y}$

45. $2\log_2(x + 4) = \log_2(x + 4)^2$

47. $\frac{1}{3}\ln 5x = \ln(5x)^{1/3} = \ln\sqrt[3]{5x}$

49. $\ln x - 3\ln(x + 1) = \ln x - \ln(x + 1)^3$

$= \ln \dfrac{x}{(x + 1)^3}$

51. $\ln(x - 2) - \ln(x + 2) = \ln\left(\dfrac{x - 2}{x + 2}\right)$

53. $\ln x - 2[\ln(x + 2) + \ln(x - 2)] = \ln x - 2\ln[(x + 2)(x - 2)]$

$= \ln x - 2\ln(x^2 - 4)$

$= \ln x - \ln(x^2 - 4)^2$

$= \ln \dfrac{x}{(x^2 - 4)^2}$

55. $\dfrac{1}{3}[2\ln(x + 3) + \ln x - \ln(x^2 - 1)] = \dfrac{1}{3}[\ln(x + 3)^2 + \ln x - \ln(x^2 - 1)]$

$= \dfrac{1}{3}[\ln[x(x + 3)^2] - \ln(x^2 - 1)]$

$= \dfrac{1}{3}\ln\dfrac{x(x + 3)^2}{x^2 - 1}$

$= \ln\sqrt[3]{\dfrac{x(x + 3)^2}{x^2 - 1}}$

57. $\dfrac{1}{3}[\ln y + 2\ln(y + 4)] - \ln(y - 1) = \dfrac{1}{3}[\ln y + \ln(y + 4)^2] - \ln(y - 1)$

$= \dfrac{1}{3}\ln[y(y + 4)^2] - \ln(y - 1)$

$= \ln\sqrt[3]{y(y + 4)^2} - \ln(y - 1)$

$= \ln\dfrac{\sqrt[3]{y(y + 4)^2}}{y - 1}$

59. $2\ln 3 - \dfrac{1}{2}\ln(x^2 + 1) = \ln 3^2 - \ln\sqrt{x^2 + 1}$

$= \ln\dfrac{9}{\sqrt{x^2 + 1}}$

61. $y_1 = 2[\ln 8 - \ln(x^2 + 1)]$

$y_2 = \ln\left[\dfrac{64}{(x^2 + 1)^2}\right]$

$y_1 = y_2$

$y_1 = 2[\ln 8 - \ln(x^2 + 1)]$

$\quad = 2\ln\left(\dfrac{8}{x^2 + 1}\right)$

$\quad = \ln\left[\dfrac{64}{(x^2 + 1)^2}\right] = y_2$

63. $y_1 = \ln x^2$

$y_2 = 2 \ln x$

$y_1 = y_2$ for $x > 0$.

They are not equivalent. The domain of $f(x)$ is all real numbers except 0. The domain of $g(x)$ is $x > 0$.

65. $f(x) = \ln \dfrac{x}{2}$

$g(x) = \dfrac{\ln x}{\ln 2}$

$h(x) = \ln x - \ln 2$

$f(x) = h(x)$ by Property 2.

67. $\log_3 9 = 2 \log_3 3 = 2$

69. $\log_4 16^{1.2} = 1.2(\log_4 16) = 1.2(2) = 2.4$

71. $\log_3 (-9)$ is undefined. -9 is not in the domain of $\log_3 x$.

73. $\log_5 75 - \log_5 3 = \log_5 \frac{75}{3} = \log_5 25$

75. $\ln e^2 - \ln e^5 = 2 - 5 = -3$

77. $\log_{10} 0$ is undefined. 0 is not in the domain of $\log_{10} x$.

79. $\ln e^{4.5} = 4.5$

81. $\log_4 8 = \log_4 2^3 = 3 \log_4 2$

$\quad = 3 \log_4 \sqrt{4} = 3\log_4 4^{1/2}$

$\quad = 3\left(\frac{1}{2}\right) \log_4 4 = \frac{3}{2}$

83. $\log_7 \sqrt{70} = \frac{1}{2} \log_7 70 = \frac{1}{2} \log_7(10 \cdot 7)$

$\quad = \frac{1}{2} \log_7 10 + \frac{1}{2} \log_7 7 = \frac{1}{2} \log_7 10 + \frac{1}{2}$

85. $\log_5 \frac{1}{250} = \log_5 1 - \log_5 250 = 0 - \log_5 (125 \cdot 2)$

$\quad = -\log_5(5^3 \cdot 2) = -[\log_5 5^3 + \log_5 2]$

$\quad = -[3 \log_5 5 + \log_5 2] = -3 - \log_5 2$

87. $\ln(5e^6) = \ln 5 + \ln e^6 = \ln 5 + 6 = 6 + \ln 5$

89. $\beta = 10 \log_{10}\left(\dfrac{I}{10^{-16}}\right) = 10[\log_{10} I - \log_{10} 10^{-16}]$

$\qquad = 10[\log_{10} I - (-16) \log_{10} 10]$

$\qquad = 10[\log_{10} I + 16]$

If $I = 10^{-10}$, then $\log_{10} I = \log_{10} 10^{-10} = -10$
and $\beta = 10[-10 + 16] = 60$ db.

91. (a)

(b) The data $(t, T - 21)$ fits the exponential model
$T - 21 = 54.4380(0.9635)^t$. For the original data the
model is $T = 54.4380(0.9635)^t$.

(c) $\ln(T - 21) = -0.03721t + 3.9971$

$\qquad T - 21 = e^{-0.0377t + 3.9971}$

$\qquad\quad T = 21 + 54.44(e^{-0.0377t})$

$\qquad\qquad = 21 + 54.44(0.9635)^t$

(d) $T = \dfrac{4960}{6t + 80} + 21$

93. $f(x) = \log_2 x = \dfrac{\log_{10} x}{\log_{10} 2}$

95. $g(x) = \log_3 x^{1/2} = \dfrac{1}{2} \log_3 x = \dfrac{1}{2} \dfrac{\log_{10} x}{\log_{10} 3}$

97. $f(x) = \ln x$

False, $f(0) \neq 0$ since 0 is not in the domain of $f(x)$. $f(1) = \ln 1 = 0$

99. False, $f(x) - f(2) = \ln x - \ln 2 = \ln \dfrac{x}{2} \neq \ln(x - 2)$.

101. False, $f(u) = 2f(v) \implies \ln u = 2 \ln v \implies \ln u = \ln v^2 \implies u = v^2$.

103. Let $x = \log_b u$ and $y = \log_b v$, then $b^x = u$ and $b^y = v$.

$\qquad \dfrac{u}{v} = \dfrac{b^x}{b^y} = b^{x-y}$

$\qquad \log_b\left(\dfrac{u}{v}\right) = \log_b(b^{x-y}) = x - y = \log_b u - \log_b v$

105. $\dfrac{24xy^{-2}}{16x^{-3}y} = \dfrac{24xx^3}{16yy^2} = \dfrac{3x^4}{2y^3}$

107. $(18x^3y^4)^{-3}(18x^3y^4)^3 = \dfrac{(18x^3y^4)^3}{(18x^3y^4)^3} = 1$ if $x \neq 0, y \neq 0$.

Section 4.4 Solving Exponential and Logarithmic Equations

- ■ To solve an exponential equation, isolate the exponential expression, then take the logarithm of both sides. Then solve for the variable.
  1. $\log_a a^x = x$
  2. $\ln e^x = x$
- ■ To solve a logarithmic equation, rewrite it in exponential form. Then solve for the variable.
  1. $a^{\log_a x} = x$
  2. $e^{\ln x} = x$
- ■ If $a > 0$ and $a \neq 1$ we have the following:
  1. $\log_a x = \log_a y \implies x = y$
  2. $a^x = a^y \implies x = y$
- ■ Use your graphing utility to approximate solutions.

Solutions to Odd-Numbered Exercises

1. $4^{2x-7} = 64$

   (a) $x = 5$

      $4^{2(5)-7} = 4^3 = 64$

      Yes, $x = 5$ is a solution.

   (b) $x = 2$

      $4^{2(2)-7} = 4^{-3} = \frac{1}{64} \neq 64$

      No, $x = 2$ is not a solution.

3. $3e^{x+2} = 75$

   (a) $x = -2 + e^{25}$

      $3e^{(-2+e^{25})+2} = 3e^{e^{25}} \neq 75$

      No, $x = -2 + e^{25}$ is not a solution.

   (b) $x = -2 + \ln 25$

      $3e^{(-2+\ln 25)+2} = 3e^{\ln 25} = 3(25) = 75$

      Yes, $x = -2 + \ln 25$ is a solution.

   (c) $x \approx 1.2189$

      $3e^{1.2189+2} = 3e^{3.2189} \approx 75$

      Yes, $x \approx 1.2189$ is a solution.

5. $\log_4(3x) = 3 \implies 3x = 4^3 \implies 3x = 64$

   (a) $x \approx 20.3560$

      $3(20.3560) = 61.0680 \neq 64$

      No, $x \approx 20.3560$ is not a solution.

   (b) $x = -4$

      $3(-4) = -12 \neq 64$

      No, $x = -4$ is not a solution.

   (c) $x = \frac{64}{3}$

      $3\left(\frac{64}{3}\right) = 64$

      Yes, $x = \frac{64}{3}$ is a solution.

7. $f(x) = g(x)$

   $2^x = 8$

   $2^x = 2^3$

   $x = 3$

   Point of intersection: $(3, 8)$

9. $f(x) = g(x)$

   $\log_3 x = 2$

   $x = 3^2$

   $x = 9$

   Point of intersection: $(9, 2)$

11. $4^x = 16$

   $4^x = 4^2$

   $x = 2$

13. $7^x = \frac{1}{49}$

   $7^x = 7^{-2}$

   $x = -2$

15. $\left(\frac{3}{4}\right)^x = \frac{27}{64}$

   $\left(\frac{3}{4}\right)^x = \left(\frac{3}{4}\right)^3$

   $x = 3$

17. $\log_4 x = 3$

   $x = 4^3$

   $x = 64$

19. $\log_{10} x = -1$
$\quad\quad x = 10^{-1}$
$\quad\quad x = \frac{1}{10}$

21. $\log_{10} 10^{x^2} = x^2$

23. $e^{\ln(5x+2)} = 5x + 2$

25. $e^{\ln x^2} = x^2$

27. $e^x = 10$
$\quad\quad x = \ln 10 \approx 2.303$

29. $7 - 2e^x = 5$
$\quad\quad -2e^x = -2$
$\quad\quad\quad e^x = 1$
$\quad\quad\quad x = \ln 1 = 0$

31. $500e^{-x} = 300$
$\quad\quad e^{-x} = \frac{3}{5}$
$\quad\quad -x = \ln \frac{3}{5}$
$\quad\quad x = -\ln \frac{3}{5} = \ln \frac{5}{3} \approx 0.511$

33. $10^x = 42$
$\quad\quad x = \log_{10} 42 \approx 1.623$

35.

x	0.6	0.7	0.8	0.9	1.0
$f(x)$	6.05	8.17	11.02	14.88	20.09

$x \approx 0.828$

37.

x	5	6	7	8	9
$f(x)$	1756	1598	1338	908	200

$x \approx 8.635$

39. $e^{2x} - 4e^x - 5 = 0$
$\quad (e^x - 5)(e^x + 1) = 0$
$\quad\quad e^x = 5 \text{ or } e^x = -1 \quad\quad \text{(No solution)}$
$\quad\quad\quad\quad x = \ln 5 \approx 1.609$

41. $\quad 3^{2x} = 80$
$\quad \ln 3^{2x} = \ln 80$
$\quad 2x \ln 3 = \ln 80$
$\quad\quad x = \dfrac{\ln 80}{2 \ln 3} \approx 1.994$

43. $5^{-t/2} = 0.20$
$\quad 5^{-t/2} = \dfrac{1}{5}$
$\quad 5^{-t/2} = 5^{-1}$
$\quad -\dfrac{t}{2} = -1$
$\quad\quad t = 2$

45. $\quad\quad 2^{3-x} = 565$
$\quad\quad \ln 2^{3-x} = \ln 565$
$\quad (3 - x) \ln 2 = \ln 565$
$\quad 3 \ln 2 - x \ln 2 = \ln 565$
$\quad\quad -x \ln 2 = \ln 565 - \ln 2^3$
$\quad\quad -x \ln 2 = \ln 8 - \ln 565$
$\quad\quad\quad x = \dfrac{\ln 8 - \ln 565}{\ln 2} \approx -6.142$

47. $8(10^{3x}) = 12$
$\quad 10^{3x} = \dfrac{12}{8}$
$\quad 3x = \log_{10}\left(\dfrac{3}{2}\right)$
$\quad x = \dfrac{1}{3} \log_{10}\left(\dfrac{3}{2}\right) \approx 0.059$

49. Using the root feature for
$$y = \left(1 + \frac{0.10}{12}\right)^{12t} - 2 = 0$$
you obtain $t \approx 6.960$.

51.

zero at $x = -0.427$

53.

zero at $t = 12.207$

55. $\ln x = -3$
$$x = e^{-3} \approx 0.050$$

57. $\ln\sqrt{x + 2} = 1$
$$\sqrt{x + 2} = e^1$$
$$x + 2 = e^2$$
$$x = e^2 - 2 \approx 5.389$$

59. $\log_{10}(x + 4) - \log_{10} x = \log_{10}(x + 2)$
$$\log_{10}\left(\frac{x + 4}{x}\right) = \log_{10}(x + 2)$$
$$\frac{x + 4}{x} = x + 2$$
$$x + 4 = x^2 + 2x$$
$$0 = x^2 + x - 4$$
$$x = \frac{-1 \pm \sqrt{17}}{2} \quad \text{Quadratic Formula}$$

Choosing the positive value of x (the negative value is extraneous), we have $\dfrac{-1 + \sqrt{17}}{2}$.

61.

x	2	3	4	5	6
$f(x)$	1.39	1.79	2.08	12.30	2.49

$x \approx 5.512$

63.

x	12	13	14	15	16
$f(x)$	9.79	10.22	10.63	11.00	11.36

$x \approx 14.988$

65. $\log_{10}(z - 3) = 2$
$$z - 3 = 10^2$$
$$z = 10^2 + 3 = 103$$

67. $2 \ln x = 7$
$$\ln x = \tfrac{7}{2}$$
$$x = e^{7/2} \approx 33.115$$

69. $\ln x + \ln(x - 2) = 1$

$\ln[x(x - 2)] = 1$

$x(x - 2) = e^1$

$x^2 - 2x - e = 0$

$$x = \frac{2 \pm \sqrt{4 + 4e}}{2}$$

$$= \frac{2 \pm 2\sqrt{1 + e}}{3}$$

Using the positive value for x, we have
$x = 1 + \sqrt{1 + e} \approx 2.928$.

73. $\ln(x + 5) = \ln(x - 1) - \ln(x + 1)$.

$$\ln(x + 5) = \ln\left(\frac{x - 1}{x + 1}\right)$$

$$x + 5 = \frac{x - 1}{x + 1}$$

$(x + 5)(x + 1) = x - 1$

$x^2 + 6x + 5 = x - 1$

$x^2 + 5x + 6 = 0$

$(x + 2)(x + 3) = 0$

$x = -2 \text{ or } x = -3$

Both of these solutions are extraneous, so the
equation has no solution.

77. $y_1 = 7$

$y_2 = 2^x$

From the graph we have $x \approx 2.807$.

81. $A = Pe^{rt}$

$2000 = 1000e^{0.085t}$

$2 = e^{0.085t}$

$\ln 2 = 0.085t$

$$\frac{\ln 2}{0.085} = t$$

$t \approx 8.2 \text{ years}$

71. $\log_3 x + \log_3(x^2 - 8) = \log_3 8x$

$\log_3 x(x^2 - 8) = \log_3 8x$

$x(x^2 - 8) = 8x$

$x^3 - 8x = 8x$

$x^3 - 16x = 0$

$x(x + 4)(x - 4) = 0$

$x = 0, \ x = -4 \text{ or } x = 4$

The only solution that is in the domain is $x = 4$.
Both $x = 0$ and $x = -4$ are extraneous.

75. $\ln x + \ln(x^2 + 1) = 8$

$\ln x(x^2 + 1) = 8$

$x(x^2 + 1) = e^8$

$x^3 + x - e^8 = 0$

From the graph we have $x \approx 14.369$.

79. $y_1 = 3$

$y_2 = \ln x$

From the graph
we have
$x \approx 20.806$.

83. *Doubling Time*

$2P = Pe^{rt}$

$2 = e^{rt}$

$\ln 2 = rt$

$$\frac{\ln 2}{r} = t$$

Quadrupling Time

$4P = Pe^{rt}$

$4 = e^{rt}$

$\ln 4 = rt$

$$\frac{\ln 4}{r} = t$$

$$\frac{\ln 2^2}{r} = t$$

$$\frac{2 \ln 2}{r} = t$$

$$2\left(\frac{\ln 2}{r}\right) = t$$

Yes, it takes twice as long to quadruple.

85. $A = Pe^{rt}$

$3000 = 1000e^{0.085t}$

$3 = e^{0.085t}$

$\ln 3 = 0.085t$

$\dfrac{\ln 3}{0.085} = t$

$t \approx 12.9$ years

87. (a)

(b) From the graph we see horizontal asymptotes at $y = 0$ and $y = 100$. These represent the lower and upper percent bounds.

(c) Males:

$$50 = \frac{100}{1 + e^{-0.6114(x - 69.71)}}$$

$1 + e^{-0.6114(x - 69.71)} = 2$

$e^{-0.6114(x - 69.71)} = 1$

$-0.6114(x - 69.71) = \ln 1$

$-0.6114(x - 69.71) = 0$

$x = 69.71$ inches

Females:

$$50 = \frac{100}{1 + e^{-0.66607(x - 64.51)}}$$

$1 + e^{-0.66607(x - 64.51)} = 2$

$e^{-0.66607(x - 64.51)} = 1$

$-0.66607(x - 64.51) = \ln 1$

$-0.66607(x - 64.51) = 0$

$x = 64.51$ inches

89. $p = 500 - 0.5(e^{0.004x})$

(a) $p = 350$

$350 = 500 - 0.5(e^{0.004x})$

$300 = e^{0.004x}$

$0.004x = \ln 300$

$x \approx 1426$ units

(b) $p = 300$

$300 = 500 - 0.5(e^{0.004x})$

$400 = e^{0.004x}$

$0.004x = \ln 400$

$x \approx 1498$ units

91. $V = 6.7e^{-48.1/t},\ t \geq 0$

(a)

(b) As $x \to \infty$, $V \to 6.7$.

Horizontal asymptote: $y = 6.7$
The yield will approach
6.7 million cubic feet per acre.

(c)

$1.3 = 6.7e^{-48.1/t}$

$\dfrac{1.3}{6.7} = e^{-48.1/t}$

$\ln\left(\dfrac{13}{67}\right) = \dfrac{-48.1}{t}$

$t = \dfrac{-48.1}{\ln(13/67)} \approx 29.3$ years

93. $T = 20[1 + 7(2^{-h})]$

(a)

(b) We see a horizontal asymptote at $y = 20$. This represents the room temperature.

(c) $100 = 20[1 + 7(2^{-h})]$

$5 = 1 + 7(2^{-h})$

$4 = 7(2^{-h})$

$\dfrac{4}{7} = 2^{-h}$

$\ln\left(\dfrac{4}{7}\right) = \ln 2^{-h}$

$\ln\left(\dfrac{4}{7}\right) = -h \ln 2$

$\dfrac{\ln(4/7)}{-\ln 2} = h$

$h \approx 0.81$ hour

95. $4x - 3y - 9 = 0$

$-3y = -4x + 9$

$y = \frac{4}{3}x - 3$

Line with slope $\frac{4}{3}$

y-intercept -3

Matches (b).

97. $y = 25 - 2.25x$

Slope: -2.25

y-intercept: 25

Matches (f).

99. $y - 3 = 0$

$y = 3$

Horizontal line

Matches (d).

Section 4.5 Exponential and Logarithmic Models

■ You should be able to solve compound interest problems.

1. $A = P\left(1 + \dfrac{r}{n}\right)^{nt}$

2. $A = Pe^{rt}$

■ You should be able to solve growth and decay problems.

(a) Exponential growth if $b > 0$ and $y = ae^{bx}$.

(b) Exponential decay if $b > 0$ and $y = ae^{-bx}$.

■ You should be able to use the Gaussian model

$y = ae^{-(x-b)^2/c}$.

■ You should be able to use the logistics growth model

$y = \dfrac{a}{1 + be^{-(x-c)/d}}$.

■ You should be able to use the logarithmic models

$y = \ln(ax + b)$ and $y = \log_{10}(ax + b)$.

Solutions to Odd-Numbered Exercises

1. $y = 2e^{x/4}$

This is an exponential growth model. Matches graph (b).

3. $y = \frac{1}{16}(x^2 + 8x + 32)$

This is a quadratic function. It's graph is a parabola. Matches graph (e).

5. $y = \ln(x + 1)$

This is a logarithmic model. Matches graph (f).

7. Since $A = 1000e^{0.12t}$, the time to double is given by $2000 = 1000e^{0.12t}$ and we have

$$t = \frac{\ln 2}{0.12} \approx 5.78 \text{ years.}$$

Amount after 10 years: $A = 1000e^{1.2} \approx \$3320.12$

9. Since $A = 750e^{rt}$ and $A = 1500$ when $t = 7.75$, we have the following.

$$15000 = 750e^{7.75r}$$

$$r = \frac{\ln 2}{7.75} \approx 0.0894 = 8.94\%$$

Amount after 10 years: $A = 750e^{0.0894(10)} \approx \$1833.67$

11. Since $A = 500e^{rt}$ and $A = 1292.85$ when $t = 10$, we have the following.

$$1292.85 = 500e^{10r}$$

$$r = \frac{\ln(1292.85/500)}{10} \approx 0.9095 = 9.5\%$$

The time to double is given by

$$1000 = 500e^{0.095t}$$

$$t = \frac{\ln 2}{0.095} \approx 7.30 \text{ years.}$$

13. Since $A = Pe^{0.045t}$ and $A = 10,000.00$ when $t = 10$, we have the following.

$$10,000.00 = Pe^{0.045(10)}$$

$$\frac{10,000.00}{e^{0.045(10)}} = P \approx 6376.28$$

The time to double is given by

$$t = \frac{\ln 2}{0.045} \approx 15.40 \text{ years.}$$

15.
$$500,000 = P\left(1 + \frac{0.075}{12}\right)^{12(20)}$$

$$\frac{500,000}{\left(1 + \frac{0.075}{12}\right)^{12(20)}} = P = \$112.087.09$$

17. $P = 1000$, $r = 11\%$

(a) $n = 1$

$$t = \frac{\ln 2}{\ln(1 + 0.11)} \approx 6.642 \text{ years}$$

(b) $n = 12$

$$t = \frac{\ln 2}{12 \ln\left(1 + \frac{0.11}{12}\right)} \approx 6.330 \text{ years}$$

(c) $n = 365$

$$t = \frac{\ln 2}{365 \ln\left(1 + \frac{0.11}{365}\right)} \approx 6.302 \text{ years}$$

(d) Continuously

$$t = \frac{\ln 2}{0.11} \approx 6.301 \text{ years}$$

19. $3P = Pe^{rt}$

$3 = e^{rt}$

$\ln 3 = rt$

$\dfrac{\ln 3}{r} = t$

r	2%	4%	6%	8%	10%	12%
$t = \dfrac{\ln 3}{r}$	54.93	27.47	18.31	13.73	10.99	9.16

21. $\qquad 3P = P(1 + r)^t$

$\qquad 3 = (1 + r)^t$

$\qquad \ln 3 = \ln(1 + r)^t$

$\qquad \ln 3 = t\ln(1 + r)$

$\dfrac{\ln 3}{\ln(1 + r)} = t$

r	2%	4%	6%	8%	10%	12%
$t = \dfrac{\ln 3}{\ln(1 + r)}$	55.47	28.01	18.85	14.27	11.53	9.69

23. Continuous compounding results in faster growth.

$A = 1 + 0.075[\![t]\!]$

and $A = e^{0.07t}$

25. $\dfrac{1}{2}C = Ce^{k(1620)}$

$k = \dfrac{\ln 0.5}{1620}$

Given $C = 10$ grams, after 1000 years, we have

$y = Ce^{[(\ln 0.5)/1620](1000)}$

$C \approx 6.52$ grams.

27. $\dfrac{1}{2}C = Ce^{k(5730)}$

$k = \dfrac{\ln 0.5}{5730}$

Given $y = 3$ grams, after 1000 years, we have

$3 = Ce^{[(\ln 0.5)/5730](1000)}$

$C \approx 2.66$ grams.

29. $y = ae^{bx}$

$1 = ae^{b(0)} \implies 1 = a$

$10 = e^{b(3)}$

$\ln 10 = 3b$

$\dfrac{\ln 10}{3} = b \qquad \implies b \approx 0.7675$

Thus, $y = e^{0.7675x}$.

31. $y = ae^{bx}$

$1 = ae^{b(0)} \implies 1 = a$

$\dfrac{1}{4} = e^{b(3)}$

$\ln\left(\dfrac{1}{4}\right) = 3b$

$\dfrac{\ln(1/4)}{3} = b \qquad \implies b \approx -0.4621$

Thus, $y = e^{-0.4621x}$.

33. $\qquad P = 105{,}300e^{0.015t}$

$150{,}000 = 105{,}300e^{0.015t}$

$\ln\frac{1500}{1053} = 0.015t$

$t \approx 23.59$

The population will reach 150,000 during 2013. [Note: 1990 + 23.59.]

35. For 1945, use $t = -45$.

$1350 = 2500d^{k(-45)}$

$\ln\left(\frac{1350}{2500}\right) = -45k \approx 0.0137$

For 2010, use $t = 20$.

$P = 2500e^{0.0137(20)} \approx 3288$ people

37.
$$y = ae^{bt}$$
$$4.22 = ae^{b(0)} \implies a = 4.22$$
$$6.49 = 4.22e^{b(10)}$$
$$\frac{6.49}{4.22} = e^{10b}$$
$$\ln\left(\frac{6.49}{4.22}\right) = 10b \implies b \approx 0.0430$$
$$y = 4.22e^{0.0430t}$$

When $t = 20$,
$y = 4.22e^{0.0430(20)} \approx 9.97$ million.

39.
$$y = ae^{bt}$$
$$3.00 = ae^{b(0)} \implies a = 3$$
$$2.74 = 3e^{b(10)}$$
$$\frac{2.74}{3} = e^{10b}$$
$$\ln\left(\frac{2.74}{3}\right) = 10b \implies b \approx 0.0091$$
$$y = 3e^{-0.0091t}$$

When $t = 20$,
$y = 3e^{-0.0091(20)} \approx 2.50$ million.

41. b is determined by the growth rate. The greater the rate of growth, the greater the value of b.

43.
$$N = 100e^{kt}$$
$$300 = 100e^{5k}$$
$$k = \frac{\ln 3}{5} \approx 0.2197$$
$$N = 100e^{0.2197t}$$
$$200 = 100e^{0.2197t}$$
$$t = \frac{\ln 2}{0.2197} \approx 3.15 \text{ hours}$$

45.
$$y = Ce^{kt}$$
$$\frac{1}{2}C = Ce^{(1620)k}$$
$$\ln\frac{1}{2} = 1620k$$
$$k = \frac{\ln(1/2)}{1620}$$

When $t = 100$, we have
$$y = Ce^{[\ln(1/2)/1620](100)} \approx 0.958C = 95.8\%C.$$

After 100 years, approximately 95.8% of the radioactive radium will remain.

47. $y = ae^{bt}$.
At time $t = 0$,
$$y = 4600 = ae^{b(0)} \implies a = 4600.$$

At time $t = 2$,
$$3000 = 4600e^{b(2)}$$
$$\frac{30}{46} = e^{2b}$$
$$b = \frac{1}{2}\ln\left(\frac{30}{46}\right) \approx -0.2137.$$

After 3 years,
$$y = 4600e^{b(3)}$$
$$= 4600e^{3/2 \ln(30/46)}$$
$$= 4600 \cdot \left(\frac{30}{46}\right)^{3/2} \approx \$2423.$$

49. $S(t) = 100(1 - e^{kt})$

(a)
$$15 = 100(1 - e^{k(1)})$$
$$-85 = -100e^{k}$$
$$k = \ln 0.85$$
$$k \approx -0.1625$$
$$S(t) = 100(1 - e^{-0.1625t})$$

(b)

(c) $S(5) = 100(1 - e^{-0.1625(5)})$
$$\approx 55.625 = 55{,}625 \text{ units}$$

51. $S = 10(1 - e^{kx})$

$x = 5$ (in hundreds), $S = 2.5$ (in thousands)

(a) $2.5 = 10(1 - e^{k(5)})$

$0.25 = 1 - e^{5k}$

$e^{5k} = 0.75$

$5k = \ln 0.75$

$k \approx -0.0575$

$S = 10(1 - e^{-0.0575x})$

(b) When $x = 7$,

$S = 10(1 - e^{-0.0575(7)}) \approx 3.314$
which corresponds to 3314 units.

53. $N = 30(1 - e^{kt})$

(a) $N = 19$, $t = 20$

$19 = 30(1 - e^{20k})$

$20k = \ln\dfrac{11}{30}$

$k \approx -0.050$

$N = 30(1 - e^{-0.050t})$

(b) $N = 25$

$25 = 30(1 - e^{-0.05t})$

$\dfrac{5}{30} = e^{-0.05t}$

$t = -\dfrac{1}{0.05} \ln\dfrac{5}{30} \approx 36$ days

(c) No, this is not a linear function.

55. $R = \log_{10} \dfrac{I}{I_0} = \log_{10} I$ since $I_0 = 1$.

(a) $R = \log_{10} 80{,}500{,}000 \approx 7.91$

(b) $R = \log_{10} 48{,}275{,}000 \approx 7.68$

57. $\beta(I) = \log_{10} \dfrac{I}{I_0}$ where $I_0 = 10^{-16}$ watt/cm^2.

(a) $\beta(10^{-14}) = 10 \log_{10} \dfrac{10^{-14}}{10^{-16}} = 10 \log_{10} 10^2 = 20$ decibels

(b) $\beta(10^{-9}) = 10 \log_{10} \dfrac{10^{-9}}{10^{-16}} = 10 \log_{10} 10^7 = 70$ decibels

(c) $\beta(10^{-6.5}) = 10 \log_{10} \dfrac{10^{-6.5}}{10^{-16}} = 10 \log_{10} 10^{9.5} = 95$ decibels

(d) $\beta(10^{-4}) = 10 \log_{10} \dfrac{10^{-4}}{10^{-16}} = 10 \log_{10} 10^{12} = 120$ decibels

59. $\beta = 10 \log_{10} \dfrac{I}{I_0}$

$10^{\beta/10} = \dfrac{I}{I_0}$

$I = I_0 10^{\beta/10}$

% decrease $= \dfrac{I_0 10^{9.3} - I_0 10^{8.0}}{I_0 10^{9.3}} \times 100 \approx 95\%$

61. pH $= -\log_{10}[H^+] = -\log_{10}[2.3 \times 10^{-5}] \approx 4.64$

63. $5.8 = -\log_{10}[H^+]$

$10^{-5.8} = H^+$

$H^+ \approx 1.58 \times 10^{-6}$ moles per liter

65. pH $= -\log_{10}[H^+]$

$-$pH $= \log_{10}[H^+]$

$10^{-\text{pH}} = [H^+]$

$\dfrac{\text{Hydrogen ion concentration of fruit}}{\text{Hydrogen ion concentration of tablet}} = \dfrac{10^{-2.5}}{10^{-9.5}} = 10^7$

67. Interest: $u = M - \left(M - \dfrac{Pr}{12}\right)\left(1 + \dfrac{r}{12}\right)^{12t}$

Principle: $v = \left(M - \dfrac{Pr}{12}\right)\left(1 + \dfrac{r}{12}\right)^{12t}$

(a) $P = 120{,}000$, $t = 35$, $r = 0/095$, $M = 985.93$

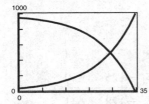

(b) In the early years of the mortgage, the majority of the monthly payment goes toward interest. The principle and interest are nearly equal when $t \approx 27.676 \approx 28$ years.

(c) $P = 120{,}000$, $t = 20$, $r = 0.095$, $M = 1118.56$

The interest is still the majority of the monthly payment in the early years. Now the principle and interest are nearly equal when $t \approx 12.675 \approx 12.7$ years.

69. $t_1 = 40.757 + 0.556s - 15.817 \ln s$

$t_2 = 1.2259 + 0.0023s^2$

(a) Linear Model: $t_3 \approx 0.2729s - 6.0143$

Exponential Model: $t_4 \approx 1.5385e^{1.0291s}$

(b)

(c)

s	30	40	50	60	70	80	90
t_1	3.6	4.7	6.7	9.4	12.5	15.9	19.6
t_2	3.3	4.9	7.0	9.5	12.5	15.9	19.9
t_3	2.2	4.9	7.6	10.4	13.1	15.8	18.5
t_4	3.7	4.9	6.6	8.8	11.8	15.8	21.1

(d) Model t_1: $S_1 = |3.4 - 3.6| + |5 - 4.7| + |7 - 6.7| + |9.3 - 9.4| + |12 - 12.5| +$
$|15.8 - 15.9| + |20 - 19.6| = 1.9$

Model t_2: $S_2 = |3.4 - 3.3| + |5 - 4.9| + |7 - 7| + |9.3 - 9.5| + |12 - 12.5| +$
$|15.8 - 15.9| + |20 - 19.9| = 1.2$

Model t_3: $S_3 = |3.4 - 2.2| + |5 - 4.9| + |7 - 7.6| + |9.3 - 10.4| + |12 - 13.1| +$
$|15.8 - 15.8| + |20 - 18.5| = 5.6$

Model t_4: $S_4 = |3.4 - 3.7| + |5 - 4.9| + |7 - 6.6| + |9.3 - 8.8| + |12 - 11.8| +$
$|15.8 - 15.8| + |20 - 21.1| = 2.6$

t_2, the Quadratic model, is the best fit with the data.

71. Each essay will vary.

73. $t = -2.5 \ln\left(\dfrac{T - 70}{98.6 - 70}\right)$

At 9:00 A.M. we have: $t = -2.5 \ln\left(\dfrac{85.7 - 70}{98.6 - 70}\right) \approx 1.5$ hours.

From this we can conclude that the person died at 7:30 A.M.

75.
$$\frac{3}{2} \begin{array}{|rrrr} 8 & -36 & 54 & -27 \\ & 12 & -36 & 27 \\ \hline 8 & -24 & 18 & 0 \end{array}$$

$$\frac{8x^3 - 36x^2 + 54x - 27}{x - 3/2} = 8x^2 - 24x + 18$$

$$\left(x \neq \frac{3}{2}\right)$$

77.
$$-5 \begin{array}{|rrrrr} 1 & 0 & 0 & -3 & 1 \\ & -5 & 25 & -125 & 640 \\ \hline 1 & -5 & 25 & -128 & 641 \end{array}$$

$$\frac{x^4 - 3x + 1}{x + 5} = x^3 - 5x^2 + 25x - 128 + \frac{641}{x + 5}$$

Section 4.6 Exploring Data: Nonlinear Models

- ■ You should know how to classify scatter plots.
- ■ You should know how to use your calculator or computer to fit a nonlinear model to data.

Solutions to Odd-Numbered Exercises

1. A logarithmic model seems best.

3. A Gaussian model seems best.

5. An exponential model seems best.

7. A Gaussian model seems best.

9. Logarithmic model

11. Exponential model

13. Linear model

15. $y = 3.807(13,057)^x$

17. $y = 8.463(0.7775)^x$

19. $y = 2.083 + 1.257 \ln x$

21. $y = 9.826 - 4.097 \ln x$

23. $y = 1985x^{0.760}$

25. $y = 16.103x^{-3.174}$

27. (a) $y = 38.233d^{1.955}$

(b)

(c) $y = 38.233(2)^{1.955} \approx 148.2$ tons

29. (a) $y = 0.088x + 4.413$

(b) $y = 4.456(1.017)^x$

(c) The linear model is better.

(d) Linear: $y = 0.088(21) + 4.413$

$\qquad = 6.261$ billion

Exponential: $y = 4.456(1.017)^{21}$

$\qquad\qquad \approx 6.349$ billion

31. (a) $y = 5.088x^{0.645}$

(b)

(c) $y = 5.088(50)^{0.645}$

≈ 63.44 million board feet

33. (a) $f = 396.48T^{0.05055}$

(b) 487

(c) $x^{1/2}$

35. (a) $y_1 = 7.01x + 41.14$

$y_2 = 5.31 + 45.83 \ln x$

$y_3 = 51.26(1.08)^x$

$y_4 = 34.00x^{0.513}$

(b)

The linear model seems to best fit the data.

—CONTINUED—

35. —CONTINUED—

(c)

x	y	$y - y_1$	$(y - y_1)^2$	$y - y_2$	$(y - y_2)^2$	$y - y_3$	$(y - y_3)^2$	$y - y_4$	$(y - y_4)^2$
3	63.2	1.03	1.06	7.54	56.86	−1.37	1.88	3.46	11.99
4	68.6	−0.58	0.34	−0.24	0.06	−1.14	1.30	−0.64	0.41
5	73.2	−2.99	8.94	−5.87	34.46	−2.12	4.48	−4.43	19.66
6	83.9	0.70	0.49	−3.53	12.44	2.56	6.54	−1.35	1.81
7	90.3	0.09	0.01	−4.19	17.57	2.45	6.00	−1.96	3.84
8	98.4	1.18	1.39	−2.21	4.89	3.52	12.40	−0.40	0.16
9	107.0	2.77	7.67	0.99	0.98	4.53	20.53	2.04	4.18
10	111.7	0.46	0.21	0.86	0.74	1.03	1.07	0.92	0.84
11	116.8	−1.45	2.10	1.59	2.54	−2.72	7.40	0.46	0.22
12	124.3	−0.96	0.92	5.11	26.08	−4.78	22.86	2.65	7.04

(d) Linear Model

(e) Sum of the squares of the errors

y_1: 23.14, y_2: 156.62, y_3: 84.46, y_4: 50.15

❏ Review Exercises for Chapter 4

Solutions to Odd-Numbered Exercises

1. $f(x) = 4^x$
Intercept: $(0, 1)$
Horizontal asymptote: x-axis
Increasing on: $(-\infty, \infty)$
Matches graph (e).

3. $f(x) = -4^x$
Intercept: $(0, -1)$
Horizontal asymptote: x-axis
Decreasing on: $(-\infty, \infty)$
Matches graph (b).

5. $f(x) = \log_4 x$
Intercept: $(1, 0)$
Vertical asymptote: y-axis
Increasing on: $(0, \infty)$
Matches graph (a).

7. $f(x) = 6^x$
Intercept: $(0, 1)$
Increasing horizontal asymptote: x-axis

9. $g(x) = 6^{-x} = \left(\frac{1}{6}\right)^x$
Intercept: $(0, 1)$
Decreasing horizontal asymptote: x-axis

11. $h(x) = e^{-x/2}$

x	−2	−1	0	1	2
y	2.72	1.65	1	0.61	0.37

13. $f(x) = e^{x+2}$

x	-3	-2	-1	0	1
y	0.37	1	2.72	7.39	20.09

15.

Horizontal asymptote: $y = 8$

17.

Horizontal asymptotes: $y = 0, \ y = 10$

19. $A = 3500\left(1 + \dfrac{0.105}{n}\right)^{10n}$ or $A = 3500e^{(0.105)(10)}$

n	1	2	4	12	365	Continuous Compounding
A	\$9,499.28	\$9,738.91	\$9,867.22	\$9,956.20	\$10,000.27	\$10,001.78

21. $200{,}000 = Pe^{0.08t}$

$$P = \frac{200{,}000}{e^{0.08t}}$$

t	1	10	20	30	40	50
P	\$184,623.27	\$89,865.79	\$40,379.30	\$18,143.59	\$8,152.44	\$3,663.13

23. (a)

(b) $v(2) = 14{,}000\left(\frac{3}{4}\right)^2 = \$7875$

(c) The car depreciates most rapidly at the beginning, which is realistic.

25. $A = 500e^{-0.013t}$

$A = 500e^{-0.013(60)}$

≈ 229.2 units per milliliter

27. $y = 28e^{0.6 - 0.012s}, \quad s \geq 50$

s	50	55	60	65	70
y	28	26.4	24.8	23.4	22.0

29. $g(x) = \log_2 x \implies 2^y = x$

Domain: $(0, \infty)$

Vertical asymptote: $x = 0$

x	$\frac{1}{4}$	$\frac{1}{2}$	1	2	4
y	-2	-1	0	1	2

31. $f(x) = \ln x + 3$

Domain: $(0, \infty)$

Vertical asymptote: $x = 0$

x	1	2	3	$\frac{1}{2}$	$\frac{1}{4}$
$f(x)$	3	3.69	4.10	2.31	1.61

33. $h(x) = \ln(e^{x-1})$

$\quad\quad = (x - 1) \ln e$

$\quad\quad = x - 1$

35. $y = \log_{10}(x^2 + 1)$

37. $\quad 4^3 = 64$

$\log_4 64 = 3$

39. $\log_{10} 1000 = \log_{10} 10^3 = 3$

41. $\log_3 \frac{1}{9} = \log_3 1 - \log_3 9 = -\log_3 3^2 = -2 \log_3 3 = -2$

43. $\ln e^7 = 7$

45. $\ln 1 = 0$ since $e^0 = 1$.

47. $\log_4 9 = \dfrac{\log_{10} 9}{\log_{10} 4} \approx 1.585$

$\log_4 9 = \dfrac{\ln 9}{\ln 4} \approx 1.585$

49. $\log_{12} 200 = \dfrac{\log_{10} 200}{\log_{10} 12} \approx 2.132$

$\log_{12} 200 = \dfrac{\ln 200}{\ln 12} \approx 2.132$

51. $\log_5 5x^2 = \log_5 5 + \log_5 x^2$

$\quad\quad\quad = 1 + 2 \log_5 x$

53. $\log_{10} \dfrac{5\sqrt{y}}{x^2} = \log_{10} 5\sqrt{y} - \log_{10} x^2$

$\quad\quad\quad = \log_{10} 5 + \log_{10} \sqrt{y} - \log_{10} x^2$

$\quad\quad\quad = \log_{10} 5 + \dfrac{1}{2} \log_{10} y - 2 \log_{10} x$

55. $\ln[(x^2 + 1)(x - 1)] = \ln(x^2 + 1) + \ln(x - 1)$

57. $\log_2 5 + \log_2 x = \log_2 5x$

59. $\dfrac{1}{2}\ln|2x-1| - 2\ln|x+1| = \ln\sqrt{|2x-1|} - \ln|x+1|^2$

$$= \ln\dfrac{\sqrt{|2x-1|}}{(x+1)^2}$$

61. $\ln 3 + \dfrac{1}{3}\ln(4-x^2) - \ln x = \ln\left[\dfrac{3(4-x^2)^{1/3}}{x}\right] = \ln\left[\dfrac{3\sqrt[3]{4-x^2}}{x}\right]$

63. True; by the inverse properties, $\log_b b^{2x} = 2x$.

65. False, the domain of $f(x) = \ln x$ is $(0, \infty)$.

67. False; $\ln x + \ln y = \ln(xy) \neq \ln(x+y)$

69. $\log_b 25 = \log_b 5^2 = 2\log_b 5 \approx 2(0.8271) = 1.6542$

71. $\log_b \sqrt{3} = \log_b 3^{1/2} = \frac{1}{2}\log_b 3 \approx \frac{1}{2}(0.5646) = 0.2823$

73. $t = 50\log_{10}\dfrac{18,000}{18,000 - h}$

(a) $0 \le h < 18,000$

(c) The plane climbs at a slower rate as it approaches its absolute ceiling.

(d) If $h = 4000$,

$$t = 50\log_{10}\dfrac{18,000}{18,000 - 4000} \approx 5.46 \text{ minutes.}$$

(b)

Vertical asymptote: $h = 18,000$

75. $e^x = 12$

$x = \ln 12 \approx 2.485$

77. $3e^{-5x} = 132$

$e^{-5x} = 44$

$-5x = \ln 44$

$x = \dfrac{\ln 44}{5} \approx -0.757$

81. $\ln 3x = 8.2$

$3x = e^{8.2}$

$x = \dfrac{e^{8.2}}{3} \approx 1213.650$

79. $\quad e^{2x} - 6x + 8 = 0$

$(e^x - 4)(e^x - 2) = 0$

$e^x = 4 \qquad \text{or} \qquad e^x = 2$

$x = \ln 4 \qquad \text{or} \qquad x = \ln 2$

$x \approx 1.386 \qquad\quad x \approx 0.693$

Extraneous solutions, no solution

83. $\ln x - \ln 3 = 2$

$$\ln\dfrac{x}{3} = 2$$

$$\dfrac{x}{3} = e^2$$

$$x = 3e^2 \approx 22.167$$

85. $\log(x - 1) = \log(x - 2) - \log(x + 2)$

$$\log(x - 1) = \log\left(\frac{x - 2}{x + 2}\right)$$

$$x - 1 = \frac{x - 2}{x + 2}$$

$$(x - 1)(x + 2) = x - 2$$

$$x^2 + x - 2 = 2 - 2$$

$$x^2 = 0$$

$$x = 0$$

Since $x = 0$ is not in the domain of $\ln(x - 1)$ or of $\ln(x - 2)$, it is an extraneous solution. The equation has no solution. You can verify this by graphing each side of the equation and observing that the two curves do not intersect.

87. $2^{0.6x} - 3x = 0$

Graph $y_1 = 2^{0.6x} - 3x$.

The x-intercepts are at $x \approx 0.39$ and at $x \approx 7.48$.

89. $2\ln(x + 3) + 3x = 8$

Graph $y_1 = 2\ln(x + 3) + 3x - 8$.

The x-intercept is at $x \approx 1.64$.

91. $y = ae^{bx}$

$2 = ae^{b(0)} \implies a = 2$

$3 = 2e^{b(4)}$

$1.5 = e^{4b}$

$\ln 1.5 = 4b \implies b \approx 0.1014$

Thus, $y \approx 2e^{0.1014x}$.

93. $y = ae^{bx}$

$4 = ae^{b(0)} = a \implies a = 4$

$\dfrac{1}{2} = 4e^{b(5)}$

$\dfrac{1}{8} = e^{5b}$

$\ln\dfrac{1}{8} = 5b \implies b = -\dfrac{\ln 8}{5} \approx -0.4159$

95. $p = 500 - 0.5e^{0.004x}$

(a) $p = 450$

$450 = 500 - 0.5e^{0.004x}$

$0.5e^{0.004x} = 50$

$e^{0.004x} = 100$

$0.004x = \ln 100$

$x \approx 1151$ units

(b) $p = 400$

$400 = 500 - 0.5e^{0.004x}$

$0.5e^{0.004x} = 100$

$e^{0.004x} = 200$

$0.004x = \ln 200$

$x \approx 1325$ units

97. (a) $t = \dfrac{\ln 2}{r}$

$7.75 = \dfrac{\ln 2}{r}$

$r = \dfrac{\ln 2}{7.75}$

≈ 0.0894

or 8.94%

(b) $A = Pe^{rt}$

$A = 750e^{[(\ln 2)/7.75](10)}$

$\approx \$1834.37$

(c) $A = Pe^{[(\ln 2)/7.75](1)}$

$\approx P(1.0936)$

$= P(1 + 0.0936)$

Effective yield ≈ 0.0936

$= 9.36\%$

99.
$$\beta = 10 \log_{10}\left(\frac{I}{10^{-16}}\right)$$

$$125 = 10 \log_{10}\left(\frac{I}{10^{-16}}\right)$$

$$\frac{125}{10} = \log_{10}\left(\frac{I}{10^{-16}}\right)$$

$$10^{12.5} = \frac{I}{10^{-16}}$$

$$10^{12.5} = 10^{16}I$$

$$10^{12.5}10^{-16} = I$$

$$10^{-3.5} = I$$

101. $y = 234.6839(0.8746)^x$

$= 234.684e^{-0.134x}$

103. (a) $y = 12.907x^{0.5102}$

(b) For 2001, $y = 12.907(21)^{0.5102} \approx 61.0$ billion.

❏ Chapter Test for Chapter 4

1. $f(x) = 2^{-x/3}$

2. $f(x) = \dfrac{1000}{1 + 4e^{-0.2x}}$

These are two
horizontal asymptotes.

$y = 1000$
(to the right)

$y = 0$
(to the left)

3. $200,000 = P\left(1 + \dfrac{0.08}{365}\right)^{(365)20}$

$200,000 = P(4.95216) \implies P = \$40,386.38$

4. $\log_4 64 = 3 \iff 4^3 = 64$

5. $g(x) = \log_3(x - 2) = \dfrac{\ln(x - 3)}{\ln 3}$

6. $\ln\left(\dfrac{6x^2}{\sqrt{x^2 + 1}}\right) = \ln 6x^2 - \ln\sqrt{x^2 + 1}$

$= \ln 6 + \ln x^2 - \ln(x^2 + 1)^{1/2}$

$= \ln 6 + 2 \ln x - \dfrac{1}{2}\ln(x^2 + 1)$

7. $e^{x/2} - 450 = 0 \implies x \approx 12.218$
with a graphing utility. Analytically,

$e^{x/2} = 450$

$\dfrac{x}{2} = \ln 450$

$x = 2 \ln 450 \approx 12.218$.

8. $\left(1 + \dfrac{0.06}{4}\right)^{4t} = 3$

$4t \ln\left(1 + \dfrac{0.06}{4}\right) = \ln 3$

$t = \dfrac{\ln 3}{4 \ln\left(1 + \dfrac{0.06}{4}\right)} \approx 18.447$

9. $5 \ln(x + 4) = 22$

$\ln(x + 4) = \dfrac{22}{5}$

$x + 4 = e^{22/5}$

$x = e^{22/5} - 4 \approx 77.451$

10. $y = ae^{bx} \qquad a = \$28{,}000 \qquad (x = 0)$

$20{,}000 = 28{,}000e^{b(1)} \implies \dfrac{5}{7} = e^b$

$\implies b = \ln \dfrac{5}{7} \approx -0.33647$

$y = 28{,}000e^{(-0.33647)3} \approx \$10{,}204$

11. (a) If $t = 0$, $p(0) = \dfrac{1200}{4} = 300$

(b) $p(5) = \dfrac{1200}{(1 + 3e^{-1})} \approx 570$

(c) Solving $800 = \dfrac{1200}{1 + 3e^{-t/5}}$ graphically, you obtain $t \approx 9$ years.

12. Since the graph is symmetric about the y-axis, the function must be even. Since the graph passes through $(0, 0)$, it must be (c). Also, $y = 6$ is a horizontal asymptote.

13. $y = 5.280 (1.4455)^x$

❑ Practice Test for Chapter 4

1. Solve for x: $x^{3/5} = 8$

2. Solve for x: $3^{x-1} = \frac{1}{81}$

3. Graph $f(x) = 2^{-x}$ by hand.

4. Graph $g(x) = e^x + 1$ by hand.

5. If \$5000 is invested at 9% interest, find the amount after three years if the interest is compounded

   (a) monthly   (b) quarterly   (c) continuously.

6. Write the equation in logarithmic form: $7^{-2} = \frac{1}{49}$

7. Solve for x: $x - 4 = \log_2 \frac{1}{64}$

8. Given $\log_b 2 = 0.3562$ and $\log_b 5 = 0.8271$, evaluate $\log_b \sqrt[4]{8/25}$.

9. Write $5 \ln x - \frac{1}{2} \ln y + 6 \ln z$ as a single logarithm.

10. Using your calculator and the change of base formula, evaluate $\log_9 28$.

11. Use your calculator to solve for N: $\log_{10} N = 0.6646$

12. Graph $y = \log_4 x$ by hand.

13. Determine the domain of $f(x) = \log_3(x^2 - 9)$.

14. Graph $y = \ln(x - 2)$ by hand.

15. True or false: $\dfrac{\ln x}{\ln y} = \ln(x - y)$

16. Solve for x: $5^x = 41$

17. Solve for x: $x - x^2 = \log_5 \frac{1}{25}$

18. Solve for x: $\log_2 x + \log_2(x - 3) = 2$

19. Solve for x: $\dfrac{e^x + e^{-x}}{3} = 4$

20. Six thousand dollars is deposited into a fund at an annual percentage rate of 13%. Find the time required for the investment to double if the interest is compounded continuously.

21. Use a graphing utility to find the points of intersection of the graphs of $y = \ln(3x)$ and $y = e^x - 4$.

22. Use a graphing utility to find the power model $y = ax^b$ for the data $(1, 1)$, $(2, 5)$, $(3, 8)$, and $(4, 17)$.

C H A P T E R 5
Trigonometric Functions

CHAPTER 5
Trigonometric Functions

Section 5.1   Angles and Their Measure

You should know the following basic facts about angles, their measurement, and their applications.

- ■ Types of Angles:
    - (a) Acute: Measure between 0° and 90°.
    - (b) Right: Measure 90°.
    - (c) Obtuse: Measure between 90° and 180°.
    - (d) Straight: Measure 180°.
- ■ α and β are complementary if $\alpha + \beta = 90°$. They are supplementary if $\alpha + \beta = 180°$.
- ■ Two angles in standard position that have the same terminal side are called coterminal angles.
- ■ To convert degrees to radians, use $1° = \pi/180$ radians.
- ■ To convert radians to degrees, use 1 radian $= (180/\pi)°$.
- ■ $1' =$ one minute $= 1/60$ of $1°$
- ■ $1'' =$ one second $= 1/60$ of $1' = 1/3600$ of $1°$
- ■ The length of a circular arc is $s = r\theta$ where θ is measured in radians.
- ■ Speed = distance/time
- ■ Angular speed = $\theta/t = s/rt$

Solutions to Odd-Numbered Exercises

1.

The angle shown is approximately 210°.

3.

The angle shown is approximately −45°.

5. (a) Since $90° < 130° < 180°$, $130°$ lies in Quadrant II.

   (b) Since $270° < 285° < 360°$, $285°$ lies in Quadrant IV.

7. (a) Since $-180° < -132°\ 50' < 90°$, $-132°\ 50'$ lies in Quadrant III.

   (b) Since $-360° < -336° < -270°$, $-336°$ lies in Quadrant I.

9. (a)

   (b)

11. (a)

(b)

13. (a) Coterminal angles for 45°

$45° + 360° = 405°$

$45° - 360° = -315°$

(b) Coterminal angles for $-36°$

$-36° + 360° = 324°$

$-36° - 360° = -396°$

15. (a) Coterminal angles for 300°

$300° + 360° = 660°$

$300° - 360° = -60°$

(b) Coterminal angles for 740°

$740° - 2(360°) = 20°$

$20° - 360° = -340°$

17. (a) $54° \, 45' = 54° + \left(\frac{45}{60}\right)° = 54.75°$

(b) $-128° \, 30' = -128° - \left(\frac{30}{60}\right)° = -128.5°$

19. (a) $85° \, 18' \, 30'' = \left(85 + \frac{18}{60} + \frac{30}{3600}\right)° \approx 85.308°$

(b) $330° \, 25'' = \left(330 + \frac{25}{3600}\right)° \approx 330.007°$

21. (a) $240.6° = 240° + 0.6(60)' = 240° \, 36'$

(b) $-145.8° = 12[145° + 0.8(60')] = -145° \, 48'$

23. (a) $2.5 = 2.5\left(\frac{180}{\pi}\right)° \approx 143.23945° \approx 143° \, 14' \, 22''$

(b) $-3.58 = -3.58\left(\frac{180}{\pi}\right)° \approx -205.11889° \approx -205° \, 7' \, 8''$

25.

The angle shown is approximately 2 radians.

27.

The angle shown is approximately -3 radians.

29. (a) Since $0 < \frac{\pi}{5} < \frac{\pi}{2}$, $\frac{\pi}{5}$ lies in Quadrant I.

(b) Since $\pi < \frac{7\pi}{5} < \frac{3\pi}{2}$, $\frac{7\pi}{5}$ lies in Quadrant III.

31. (a) Since $-\frac{\pi}{2} < -\frac{\pi}{12} < 0$, $-\frac{\pi}{12}$ lies in Quadrant IV.

(b) Since $-\frac{3\pi}{2} < -\frac{11\pi}{9} < -\pi$, $-\frac{11\pi}{9}$ lies in Quadrant II.

33. (a) Since $\pi < 3.5 < \frac{3\pi}{2}$, 3.5 lies in Quadrant III.

(b) Since $\frac{\pi}{2} < 2.25 < \pi$, 2.25 lies in Quadrant II.

35. (a)

(b)

37. (a)

(b)

39. (a) Coterminal angles for $\dfrac{\pi}{12}$

$$\frac{\pi}{12} + 2\pi = \frac{25\pi}{12}$$

$$\frac{\pi}{12} - 2\pi = -\frac{23\pi}{12}$$

(b) Coterminal angles for $\dfrac{2\pi}{3}$

$$\frac{2\pi}{3} + 2\pi = \frac{8\pi}{3}$$

$$\frac{2\pi}{3} - 2\pi = -\frac{4\pi}{3}$$

41. (a) Coterminal angles for $-\dfrac{9\pi}{4}$

$$-\frac{9\pi}{4} + 4\pi = \frac{7\pi}{4}$$

$$\frac{7\pi}{4} - 2\pi = -\frac{\pi}{4}$$

(b) Coterminal angles for $-\dfrac{2\pi}{15}$

$$-\frac{2\pi}{15} + 2\pi = \frac{28\pi}{15}$$

$$-\frac{2\pi}{15} - 2\pi = -\frac{32\pi}{15}$$

43. (a) Complement: $90° - 18° = 72°$

Supplement: $180° - 18° = 162°$

(b) Complement: Not possible; $115°$ is greater than $90°$.

Supplement: $180° - 115° = 65°$

45. (a) Complement: $\dfrac{\pi}{2} - \dfrac{\pi}{3} = \dfrac{\pi}{6}$

Supplement: $\pi - \dfrac{\pi}{3} = \dfrac{2\pi}{3}$

(b) Complement: Not possible; $\dfrac{3\pi}{4}$ is greater than $\dfrac{\pi}{2}$.

Supplement: $\pi - \dfrac{3\pi}{4} = \dfrac{\pi}{4}$

47. (a) $30° = 30\left(\dfrac{\pi}{180}\right) = \dfrac{\pi}{6}$

(b) $150° = 150\left(\dfrac{\pi}{180}\right) = \dfrac{5\pi}{6}$

49. (a) $-20° = -20\left(\dfrac{\pi}{180}\right) = -\dfrac{\pi}{9}$

(b) $-240° = -240\left(\dfrac{\pi}{180}\right) = -\dfrac{4\pi}{3}$

51. (a) $\dfrac{3\pi}{2} = \dfrac{3\pi}{2}\left(\dfrac{180}{\pi}\right)° = 270°$

(b) $\dfrac{7\pi}{6} = \dfrac{7\pi}{6}\left(\dfrac{180}{\pi}\right)° = 210°$

53. (a) $\dfrac{7\pi}{3} = \dfrac{7\pi}{3}\left(\dfrac{180}{\pi}\right)° = 420°$

(b) $-\dfrac{11\pi}{30} = -\dfrac{11\pi}{30}\left(\dfrac{180}{\pi}\right)° = -66°$

55. $115° = 115\left(\dfrac{\pi}{180}\right) \approx 2.007$ radians

57. $-216.35° = -216.35\left(\dfrac{\pi}{180}\right) \approx -3.776$ radians

59. $532° = 532\left(\dfrac{\pi}{180}\right) \approx 9.285$ radians

61. $-0.83° = -0.83\left(\dfrac{\pi}{180}\right) \approx -0.014$ radian

63. $\dfrac{\pi}{7} = \dfrac{\pi}{7}\left(\dfrac{180}{\pi}\right) \approx 25.714°$

65. $\dfrac{15\pi}{8} = \dfrac{15\pi}{8}\left(\dfrac{180}{\pi}\right) = 337.5°$

67. $-4.2\pi = -4.2\pi\left(\dfrac{180}{\pi}\right) = -756°$

69. $-2 = -2\left(\dfrac{180}{\pi}\right) \approx -114.592°$

71. $s = r\theta$

$6 = 5\theta$

$\theta = \frac{6}{5}$ radians

73. $s = r\theta$

$32 = 7\theta$

$\theta = \frac{32}{7} = 4\frac{4}{7}$ radians

75. $s = r\theta$

$4 = 15\theta$

$\theta = \frac{4}{15}$ radian

77. $s = r\theta$

$25 = 14.5\theta$

$\theta = \frac{25}{14.5} \approx 1.724$ radians

79. $s = r\theta$, θ in radians

$s = 15(180)\left(\dfrac{\pi}{180}\right) = 15\pi$ inches

≈ 47.12 inches

81. $s = r\theta$, θ in radians

$s = 6(2) = 12$ meters

83. $\theta = 41° \, 15' \, 42'' - 32° \, 47' \, 9'' = 8° \, 28' \, 33'' \approx 8.47583° \approx 0.14793$ radian

$s = r\theta = 4000(0.14793) \approx 591.72$ miles

85. $\theta = 42° \, 7' \, 15'' - 25° \, 46' \, 37'' = 16° \, 20' \, 38'' \approx 0.2853$ radian

$s = r\theta = 4000(0.2853) \approx 1141.02$ miles

87. $\theta = \dfrac{s}{r} = \dfrac{600}{6378} \approx 0.094$ radian $\approx 5.39°$

89. $\theta = \dfrac{s}{r} = \dfrac{2.5}{6} = \dfrac{25}{60} = \dfrac{5}{12}$ radian

91. (a) 50 miles per hour $= 50(5280)/60 = 4400$ feet per minute

The circumference of the tire is $C = 2.5\pi$ feet.

The number of revolutions per minute is $r = 4400/2.5\pi \approx 560.2$ rev/min.

(b) The angular speed is θ/t.

$\theta = \dfrac{4400}{2.5\pi}(2\pi) = 3520$ radians

Angular speed $= \dfrac{3520 \text{ radians}}{1 \text{ minute}} = 3520$ rad/min

93. 1 radian $= \left(\dfrac{180}{\pi}\right)° \approx 57.3°$, so one radian is much larger than one degree.

95. (a) $\dfrac{\text{Revolutions}}{\text{Second}} = \dfrac{2400}{60} = 40$ rev/sec

Angular speed $= (2\pi)(40) = 80\pi$ rad/sec

(b) Radius of saw blade $= \dfrac{7.5}{2} = 3.75$ in.

Radius in feet $= \dfrac{3.75 \text{ in.}}{12 \text{ in.}} = 0.3125$ ft

Speed $= \dfrac{s}{t} = \dfrac{r\theta}{t} = r\dfrac{\theta}{t}$

$= r(\text{angular speed})$

$= 0.3125(80\pi) = 78.54$ ft/sec

97. (a) Arc length of larger sprocket in feet: $s = r\theta = \left(\dfrac{4}{12}\right)(2\pi) = \dfrac{2\pi}{3}$ feet

The angle θ of the smaller sprocket is $\theta = \dfrac{s}{r} = \dfrac{(2\pi/3)\text{ ft}}{(2/12)\text{ ft}} = 4\pi$.

The arc length of the tire is $s = r\theta = \left(\dfrac{14}{12}\right)(4\pi) = \dfrac{14\pi}{3}$ feet.

$$\text{Speed} = \dfrac{s}{t} = \dfrac{(14\pi/3)\text{ ft}}{1\text{ sec}} = \dfrac{14\pi}{3}\text{ ft/sec}$$

(b) $\left(\dfrac{14\pi}{3}\text{ ft/sec}\right)(3600\text{ sec/hr})\left(\dfrac{1\text{ mile}}{5280\text{ ft}}\right) \approx 10\text{ mi/hr}$

99. $A = \dfrac{1}{2}r^2\theta = \dfrac{1}{2}(10)^2 \cdot \dfrac{\pi}{3} = \dfrac{50}{3}\pi\ m^2$

101. Two angles in standard position are coterminal angles if they have the same initial and terminal sides.

103. $s = r\,\theta \implies \theta = \dfrac{s}{r} = \dfrac{1.2}{4000} = 0.0003$ radians or $0.0172°$

Section 5.2   Right Triangle Trigonometry

- You should know the right triangle definition of trigonometric functions.

   (a) $\sin\theta = \dfrac{\text{opp}}{\text{hyp}}$ (b) $\cos\theta = \dfrac{\text{adj}}{\text{hyp}}$ (c) $\tan\theta = \dfrac{\text{opp}}{\text{adj}}$

   (d) $\csc\theta = \dfrac{\text{hyp}}{\text{opp}}$ (e) $\sec\theta = \dfrac{\text{hyp}}{\text{adj}}$ (f) $\cot\theta = \dfrac{\text{adj}}{\text{opp}}$

- You should know the following identities.

   (a) $\sin\theta = \dfrac{1}{\csc\theta}$ (b) $\csc\theta = \dfrac{1}{\sin\theta}$ (c) $\cos\theta = \dfrac{1}{\sec\theta}$

   (d) $\sec\theta = \dfrac{1}{\cos\theta}$ (e) $\tan\theta = \dfrac{1}{\cot\theta}$ (f) $\cot\theta = \dfrac{1}{\tan\theta}$

   (g) $\tan\theta = \dfrac{\sin\theta}{\cos\theta}$ (h) $\cot\theta = \dfrac{\cos\theta}{\sin\theta}$ (i) $\sin^2\theta + \cos^2\theta = 1$

   (j) $1 + \tan^2\theta = \sec^2\theta$ (k) $1 + \cot^2\theta = \csc^2\theta$

- You should know that two acute angles α and β are complementary if $\alpha + \beta = 90°$, and cofunctions of complementary angles are equal.

- You should know the trigonometric function values of $30°$, $45°$, and $60°$, or be able to construct triangles from which you can determine them.

Solutions to Odd-Numbered Exercises

1.

$\text{adj} = \sqrt{4^2 - 2^2} = \sqrt{12} = 2\sqrt{3}$

$\sin\theta = \dfrac{\text{opp}}{\text{hyp}} = \dfrac{2}{4} = \dfrac{1}{2}$ $\csc\theta = \dfrac{\text{hyp}}{\text{opp}} = \dfrac{4}{2} = 2$

$\cos\theta = \dfrac{\text{adj}}{\text{hyp}} = \dfrac{2\sqrt{3}}{4} = \dfrac{\sqrt{3}}{2}$ $\sec\theta = \dfrac{\text{hyp}}{\text{adj}} = \dfrac{4}{2\sqrt{3}} = \dfrac{2\sqrt{3}}{3}$

$\tan\theta = \dfrac{\text{opp}}{\text{adj}} = \dfrac{2}{2\sqrt{3}} = \dfrac{\sqrt{3}}{3}$ $\cot\theta = \dfrac{\text{adj}}{\text{opp}} = \dfrac{2\sqrt{3}}{2} = \sqrt{3}$

3.

$$hyp = \sqrt{8^2 + 15^2} = 17$$

$$\sin \theta = \frac{opp}{hyp} = \frac{8}{17} \qquad\qquad \csc \theta = \frac{hyp}{opp} = \frac{17}{8}$$

$$\cos \theta = \frac{adj}{hyp} = \frac{15}{17} \qquad\qquad \sec \theta = \frac{hyp}{adj} = \frac{17}{15}$$

$$\tan \theta = \frac{opp}{adj} = \frac{8}{15} \qquad\qquad \cot \theta = \frac{adj}{opp} = \frac{15}{8}$$

5.

$$adj = \sqrt{3^2 - 1^2} = \sqrt{8} = 2\sqrt{2}$$

$$\sin \theta = \frac{opp}{hyp} = \frac{1}{3} \qquad\qquad \csc \theta = \frac{hyp}{opp} = 3$$

$$\cos \theta = \frac{adj}{hyp} = \frac{2\sqrt{2}}{3} \qquad\qquad \sec \theta = \frac{hyp}{adj} = \frac{3}{2\sqrt{2}} = \frac{3\sqrt{2}}{4}$$

$$\tan \theta = \frac{opp}{adj} = \frac{1}{2\sqrt{2}} = \frac{\sqrt{2}}{4} \qquad\qquad \cot \theta = \frac{adj}{opp} = 2\sqrt{2}$$

$$adj = \sqrt{6^2 - 2^2} = \sqrt{32} = 4\sqrt{2}$$

$$\sin \theta = \frac{opp}{hyp} = \frac{2}{6} = \frac{1}{3} \qquad\qquad \csc \theta = \frac{hyp}{opp} = \frac{6}{2} = 3$$

$$\cos \theta = \frac{adj}{hyp} = \frac{4\sqrt{2}}{6} = \frac{2\sqrt{2}}{3} \qquad\qquad \sec \theta = \frac{hyp}{adj} = \frac{6}{4\sqrt{2}} = \frac{3}{2\sqrt{2}} = \frac{3\sqrt{2}}{4}$$

$$\tan \theta = \frac{opp}{adj} = \frac{2}{4\sqrt{2}} = \frac{1}{2\sqrt{2}} = \frac{\sqrt{2}}{4} \qquad\qquad \cot \theta = \frac{adj}{opp} = \frac{4\sqrt{2}}{2} = 2\sqrt{2}$$

The function values are the same since the triangles are similar and the corresponding sides are proportional.

7.

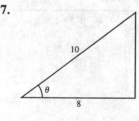

$$opp = \sqrt{10^2 - 8^2} = 6$$

$$\sin \theta = \frac{opp}{hyp} = \frac{6}{10} = \frac{3}{5} \qquad\qquad \csc \theta = \frac{hyp}{opp} = \frac{10}{6} = \frac{5}{3}$$

$$\cos \theta = \frac{adj}{hyp} = \frac{8}{10} = \frac{4}{5} \qquad\qquad \sec \theta = \frac{hyp}{adj} = \frac{10}{8} = \frac{5}{4}$$

$$\tan \theta = \frac{opp}{adj} = \frac{6}{8} = \frac{3}{4} \qquad\qquad \cot \theta = \frac{adj}{opp} = \frac{8}{6} = \frac{4}{3}$$

$$opp = \sqrt{2.5^2 - 2^2} = 1.5$$

$$\sin \theta = \frac{opp}{hyp} = \frac{1.5}{2.5} = \frac{3}{5} \qquad\qquad \csc \theta = \frac{hyp}{opp} = \frac{2.5}{1.5} = \frac{5}{3}$$

$$\cos \theta = \frac{adj}{hyp} = \frac{2}{2.5} = \frac{4}{5} \qquad\qquad \sec \theta = \frac{hyp}{adj} = \frac{2.5}{2} = \frac{5}{4}$$

$$\tan \theta = \frac{opp}{adj} = \frac{1.5}{2} = \frac{3}{4} \qquad\qquad \cot \theta = \frac{adj}{opp} = \frac{2}{0.5} = \frac{4}{3}$$

The function values are the same since the triangles are similar and the corresponding sides are proportional.

9. Given: $\sin \theta = \dfrac{2}{3} = \dfrac{\text{opp}}{\text{hyp}}$

$2^2 + (\text{adj})^2 = 3^2$

$\text{adj} = \sqrt{5}$

$\cos \theta = \dfrac{\sqrt{5}}{3}$

$\tan \theta = \dfrac{2\sqrt{5}}{5}$

$\cot \theta = \dfrac{\sqrt{5}}{2}$

$\sec \theta = \dfrac{3\sqrt{5}}{5}$

$\csc \theta = \dfrac{3}{2}$

11. Given: $\sec \theta = 2 = \dfrac{2}{1} = \dfrac{\text{hyp}}{\text{adj}}$

$(\text{opp})^2 + 1^2 = 2^2$

$\text{opp} = \sqrt{3}$

$\sin \theta = \dfrac{\sqrt{3}}{2}$

$\cos \theta = \dfrac{1}{2}$

$\tan \theta = \sqrt{3}$

$\cot \theta = \dfrac{\sqrt{3}}{3}$

$\csc \theta = \dfrac{2\sqrt{3}}{3}$

13. Given: $\tan \theta = 3 = \dfrac{3}{1} = \dfrac{\text{opp}}{\text{adj}}$

$3^2 + 1^2 = (\text{hyp})^2$

$\text{hyp} = \sqrt{10}$

$\sin \theta = \dfrac{3\sqrt{10}}{10}$

$\cos \theta = \dfrac{\sqrt{10}}{10}$

$\cot \theta = \dfrac{1}{3}$

$\sec \theta = \sqrt{10}$

$\csc \theta = \dfrac{\sqrt{10}}{3}$

15. Given: $\cot \theta = \dfrac{3}{2} = \dfrac{\text{adj}}{\text{opp}}$

$2^2 + 3^2 = (\text{hyp})^2$

$\text{hyp} = \sqrt{13}$

$\sin \theta = \dfrac{2}{\sqrt{13}} = \dfrac{2\sqrt{13}}{13}$

$\cos \theta = \dfrac{3}{\sqrt{13}} = \dfrac{3\sqrt{13}}{13}$

$\tan \theta = \dfrac{2}{3}$

$\csc \theta = \dfrac{\sqrt{13}}{2}$

$\sec \theta = \dfrac{\sqrt{13}}{3}$

17. $\sin 60^\circ = \dfrac{\sqrt{3}}{2}$, $\cos 60^\circ = \dfrac{1}{2}$

(a) $\tan 60^\circ = \dfrac{\sin 60^\circ}{\cos 60^\circ} = \sqrt{3}$

(b) $\sin 30^\circ = \cos 60^\circ = \dfrac{1}{2}$

(c) $\cos 30^\circ = \sin 60^\circ = \dfrac{\sqrt{3}}{2}$

(d) $\cot 60^\circ = \dfrac{\cos 60^\circ}{\sin 60^\circ} = \dfrac{1}{\sqrt{3}} = \dfrac{\sqrt{3}}{3}$

19. $\csc \theta = 3$, $\sec \theta = \dfrac{3\sqrt{2}}{4}$

(a) $\sin \theta = \dfrac{1}{\csc \theta} = \dfrac{1}{3}$

(b) $\cos \theta = \dfrac{1}{\sec \theta} = \dfrac{2\sqrt{2}}{3}$

(c) $\tan \theta = \dfrac{\sin \theta}{\cos \theta} = \dfrac{1/3}{(2\sqrt{2})/3} = \dfrac{\sqrt{2}}{4}$

(d) $\sec(90^\circ - \theta) = \csc \theta = 3$

21. $\cos \alpha = \dfrac{1}{4}$

    (a) $\sec \alpha = \dfrac{1}{\cos \alpha} = 4$

    (b) $\sin^2 \alpha + \cos^2 \alpha = 1$

$$\sin^2 \alpha + \left(\dfrac{1}{4}\right)^2 = 1$$

$$\sin^2 \alpha = \dfrac{15}{16}$$

$$\sin \alpha = \pm\dfrac{\sqrt{15}}{4}$$

    (c) $\cot \alpha = \dfrac{\cos \alpha}{\sin \alpha} = \pm\dfrac{1/4}{\sqrt{15}/4} = \pm\dfrac{1}{\sqrt{15}} = \pm\dfrac{\sqrt{15}}{15}$

    (d) $\sin(90° - \alpha) = \cos \alpha = \dfrac{1}{4}$

23. $\tan \theta \cot \theta = \tan \theta\left(\dfrac{1}{\tan \theta}\right) = 1$

25. $\tan \alpha \cos \alpha = \left(\dfrac{\sin \alpha}{\cos \alpha}\right)\cos \alpha = \sin \alpha$

27. $(1 + \cos \theta)(1 - \cos \theta) = 1 - \cos^2 \theta$

$$= (\sin^2 \theta + \cos^2 \theta) - \cos^2 \theta$$

$$= \sin^2 \theta$$

29. $(\sec \theta + \tan \theta)(\sec \theta - \tan \theta) = \sec^2 \theta - \tan^2 \theta$

$$= (1 + \tan^2 \theta) - \tan^2 \theta$$

$$= 1$$

31. $\dfrac{\sin \theta}{\cos \theta} + \dfrac{\cos \theta}{\sin \theta} = \dfrac{\sin^2 \theta + \cos^2 \theta}{\sin \theta \cos \theta}$

$$= \dfrac{1}{\sin \theta \cos \theta}$$

$$= \dfrac{1}{\sin \theta} \cdot \dfrac{1}{\cos \theta}$$

$$= \csc \theta \sec \theta$$

33. (a) $\cos 60° = \dfrac{1}{2}$

    (b) $\tan \dfrac{\pi}{6} = \dfrac{1}{\sqrt{3}} = \dfrac{\sqrt{3}}{3}$

35. (a) $\cot 45° = 1$

    (b) $\cos 45° = \dfrac{1}{\sqrt{2}} = \dfrac{\sqrt{2}}{2}$

37. (a) $\sin 10° \approx 0.1736$

    (b) $\cos 80° \approx 0.1736$

    Note: $\cos 80° = \sin(90° - 80°) = \sin 10°$

39. (a) $\sin 16.35° \approx 0.2815$

(b) $\csc 16.35° = \dfrac{1}{\sin 16.35°} \approx 3.5523$

41. (a) $\sec 42° \, 12' = \sec 42.2° = \dfrac{1}{\cos 42.2°} \approx 1.3499$

(b) $\csc 48° \, 7' = \dfrac{1}{\sin\left(48 + \frac{7}{60}\right)°} \approx 1.3432$

43. Make sure that your calculator is in radian mode.

(a) $\cot \dfrac{\pi}{16} = \dfrac{1}{\tan(\pi/16)} \approx 5.0273$

(b) $\tan \dfrac{\pi}{16} \approx 0.1989$

45. Make sure that your calculator is in radian mode.

(a) $\csc 1 = \dfrac{1}{\sin 1} \approx 1.1884$

(b) $\tan \dfrac{1}{2} \approx 0.5463$

47. (a) $\sin \theta = \dfrac{1}{2} \implies \theta = 30° = \dfrac{\pi}{6}$

(b) $\csc \theta = 2 \implies \theta = 30° = \dfrac{\pi}{6}$

49. (a) $\sec \theta = 2 \implies \theta = 60° = \dfrac{\pi}{3}$

(b) $\cot \theta = 1 \implies \theta = 45° = \dfrac{\pi}{4}$

51. (a) $\csc \theta = \dfrac{2\sqrt{3}}{3} \implies \theta = 60° = \dfrac{\pi}{3}$

(b) $\sin \theta = \dfrac{\sqrt{2}}{2} \implies \theta = 45° = \dfrac{\pi}{4}$

53. (a) $\sin \theta = 0.8191 \implies \theta \approx 55° \approx 0.960$ radian

(b) $\cos \theta = 0.0175 \implies \theta \approx 89° \approx 1.553$ radians

55. (a) $\tan \theta = 1.1920 \implies \theta \approx 50° \approx 0.873$ radian

(b) $\tan \theta = 0.4663 \implies \theta \approx 25° \approx 0.436$ radian

57. $\tan 30° = \dfrac{y}{75}$

$\dfrac{\sqrt{3}}{3} = \dfrac{y}{75}$

$75\left(\dfrac{\sqrt{3}}{3}\right) = y$

$25\sqrt{3} = y$

59. $\cot 60° = \dfrac{x}{32}$

$\dfrac{\sqrt{3}}{3} = \dfrac{x}{32}$

$\dfrac{32\sqrt{3}}{3} = x$

61. $\sin 40° = \dfrac{15}{r}$

$r = \dfrac{15}{\sin 40°} \approx 23.3$

63. $\sin 50° = \dfrac{y}{8}$

$y = 8 \sin 50° \approx 6.1$

65. $\dfrac{h}{23} = \dfrac{6}{8}$

$h = \dfrac{138}{8} = \dfrac{69}{4} = 17\frac{1}{4}$ ft

67. (a)

(b) $\sin 75° = \dfrac{x}{30}$

(c) $x = 30 \sin 75° \approx 28.98$ meters

69. Let $x = $ distance from the boat to the shoreline

$$\tan 3° = \frac{60}{x}$$

$$x = \frac{60}{\tan 3°} \approx 1144.87 \text{ feet}$$

71.

$$\sin 30° = \frac{y_1}{56}$$

$$y_1 = (\sin 30°)(56) = \left(\frac{1}{2}\right)(56) = 28$$

$$\cos 30° = \frac{x_1}{56}$$

$$x_1 = \cos 30°(56) = \frac{\sqrt{3}}{2}(56) = 28\sqrt{3}$$

$$(x_1, y_1) = \left(28\sqrt{3}, 28\right)$$

$$\sin 60° = \frac{y_2}{56}$$

$$y_2 = \sin 60°(56) = \left(\frac{\sqrt{3}}{2}\right)(56) = 28\sqrt{3}$$

$$\cos 60° = \frac{x_2}{56}$$

$$x_2 = (\cos 60°)(56) = \left(\frac{1}{2}\right)(56) = 28$$

$$(x_2, y_2) = \left(28, 28\sqrt{3}\right)$$

73. $x \approx 9.397, \ y \approx 3.420$

$$\sin \theta = \frac{y}{10} \approx 0.34$$

$$\cos \theta = \frac{x}{10} \approx 0.94$$

$$\tan \theta = \frac{y}{x} \approx 0.36$$

$$\cot \theta = \frac{x}{y} \approx 2.75$$

$$\sec \theta = \frac{10}{x} \approx 1.06$$

$$\csc \theta = \frac{10}{y} \approx 2.92$$

75. (a)

θ	0	0.1	0.2	0.3	0.4	0.5
$\sin \theta$	0	0.0998	0.1987	0.2955	0.3894	0.4794

(b) In the interval $(0, 0.5]$, $\theta > \sin \theta$.

(c) As $\theta \to 0$, $\sin \theta \to 0$.

77. (a)

θ	0°	20°	40°	60°	80°
$\sin \theta$	0	0.3420	0.6428	0.8660	0.9848
$\cos \theta$	1	0.9397	0.7660	0.5000	0.1736
$\tan \theta$	0	0.3640	0.8391	1.7321	5.6713

(b) Sine and tangent are increasing; cosine is decreasing.

(c) In each case, $\tan \theta = \dfrac{\sin \theta}{\cos \theta}$.

79. (a)

θ	20°	30°	40°	50°	60°	70°
R	170.3	229.5	261.0	261.0	229.5	170.3

(b) The range increases as θ increases from 20° through 40°, and decreases as θ increases from 50° through 70°.

(c) The maximum range should be halfway between 40° and 50°: 45°. You can verify this by analyzing tabular values near 45°.

(d)

θ	43°	44°	45°	46°	47°
R	264.4	264.8	265.0	264.8	264.4

81. True, $\csc x = \dfrac{1}{\sin x} \implies \sin 60° \csc 60° = \sin 60°\left(\dfrac{1}{\sin 60°}\right) = 1$

83. False, $\sin 45° + \cos 45° = \dfrac{\sqrt{2}}{2} + \dfrac{\sqrt{2}}{2} = \sqrt{2} \neq 1$

85. False, $\dfrac{\sin 60°}{\sin 30°} = \dfrac{\cos 30°}{\sin 30°} = \cot 30° \approx 1.7321 \neq \sin 2° = 0.0349$

Section 5.3   Trigonometric Functions of Any Angle

■ Know the Definitions of Trigonometric Functions of Any Angle.

If θ is in standard position, (x, y) a point on the terminal side and $r = \sqrt{x^2 + y^2} \neq 0$, then:

$$\sin \theta = \frac{y}{r} \qquad\qquad \csc \theta = \frac{r}{y}, \ y \neq 0$$

$$\cos \theta = \frac{x}{r} \qquad\qquad \sec \theta = \frac{r}{x}, \ x \neq 0$$

$$\tan \theta = \frac{y}{x}, \ x \neq 0 \qquad \cot \theta = \frac{x}{y}, \ y \neq 0$$

■ You should know the signs of the trigonometric functions in each quadrant.

■ You should know the trigonometric function values of the quadrant angles 0, $\dfrac{\pi}{2}$, π, and $\dfrac{3\pi}{2}$.

■ You should be able to find reference angles.

■ You should be able to evaluate trigonometric functions of any angle. (Use reference angles.)

■ You should know that the period of sine and cosine is 2π.

■ You should know which trigonometric functions are odd and even.

Even: $\cos x$ and $\sec x$

Odd: $\sin x$, $\tan x$, $\cot x$, $\csc x$

Solutions to Odd-Numbered Exercises

1. (a) $(x, y) = (4, 3)$

$r = \sqrt{16 + 9} = 5$

$\sin \theta = \dfrac{y}{r} = \dfrac{3}{5} \qquad \csc \theta = \dfrac{r}{y} = \dfrac{5}{3}$

$\cos \theta = \dfrac{x}{r} = \dfrac{4}{5} \qquad \sec \theta = \dfrac{r}{x} = \dfrac{5}{4}$

$\tan \theta = \dfrac{y}{x} = \dfrac{3}{4} \qquad \cot \theta = \dfrac{x}{y} = \dfrac{4}{3}$

(b) $(x, y) = (-8, -15)$

$r = \sqrt{64 + 225} = 17$

$\sin \theta = \dfrac{y}{r} = -\dfrac{15}{17} \qquad \csc \theta = \dfrac{r}{y} = -\dfrac{17}{15}$

$\cos \theta = \dfrac{x}{r} = -\dfrac{8}{17} \qquad \sec \theta = \dfrac{r}{x} = -\dfrac{17}{8}$

$\tan \theta = \dfrac{y}{x} = \dfrac{15}{8} \qquad \cot \theta = \dfrac{x}{y} = \dfrac{8}{15}$

3. (a) $(x, y) = \left(-\sqrt{3}, -1\right)$

$r = \sqrt{3 + 1} = 2$

$\sin \theta = \dfrac{y}{r} = -\dfrac{1}{2} \qquad \csc \theta = \dfrac{r}{y} = -2$

$\cos \theta = \dfrac{x}{r} = \dfrac{-\sqrt{3}}{2} \qquad \sec \theta = \dfrac{r}{x} = \dfrac{-2\sqrt{3}}{3}$

$\tan \theta = \dfrac{y}{x} = \dfrac{\sqrt{3}}{3} \qquad \cot \theta = \dfrac{x}{y} = \sqrt{3}$

(b) $(x, y) = (-2, 2)$

$r = \sqrt{4 + 4} = 2\sqrt{2}$

$\sin \theta = \dfrac{y}{r} = \dfrac{\sqrt{2}}{2} \qquad \csc \theta = \dfrac{r}{y} = \sqrt{2}$

$\cos \theta = \dfrac{x}{r} = -\dfrac{\sqrt{2}}{2} \qquad \sec \theta = \dfrac{r}{x} = -\sqrt{2}$

$\tan \theta = \dfrac{y}{x} = -1 \qquad \cot \theta = \dfrac{x}{y} = -1$

5. $(x, y) = (7, 24)$

$r = \sqrt{49 + 576} = 25$

$\sin \theta = \dfrac{y}{r} = \dfrac{24}{25} \qquad \csc \theta = \dfrac{r}{y} = \dfrac{25}{24}$

$\cos \theta = \dfrac{x}{r} = \dfrac{7}{25} \qquad \sec \theta = \dfrac{r}{x} = \dfrac{25}{7}$

$\tan \theta = \dfrac{y}{x} = \dfrac{24}{7} \qquad \cot \theta = \dfrac{x}{y} = \dfrac{7}{24}$

7. $(x, y) = (-4, 10)$

$r = \sqrt{16 + 100} = 2\sqrt{29}$

$\sin \theta = \dfrac{y}{r} = \dfrac{5\sqrt{29}}{29} \qquad \csc \theta = \dfrac{r}{y} = \dfrac{\sqrt{29}}{5}$

$\cos \theta = \dfrac{x}{r} = -\dfrac{2\sqrt{29}}{29} \qquad \sec \theta = \dfrac{r}{x} = -\dfrac{\sqrt{29}}{2}$

$\tan \theta = \dfrac{y}{x} = -\dfrac{5}{2} \qquad \cot \theta = \dfrac{x}{y} = -\dfrac{2}{5}$

9. $\sin \theta < 0 \implies \theta$ lies in Quadrant III or in Quadrant IV.

$\cos \theta < 0 \implies \theta$ lies in Quadrant II or in Quadrant III.

$\sin \theta < 0$ *and* $\cos \theta < 0 \implies \theta$ lies in Quadrant III.

11. $\sin \theta > 0 \implies \theta$ lies in Quadrant I or in Quadrant II.

$\tan \theta < 0 \implies \theta$ lies in Quadrant II or in Quadrant IV.

$\sin \theta > 0$ *and* $\tan \theta < 0 \implies \theta$ lies in Quadrant II.

13. $\sin \theta = \dfrac{y}{r} = \dfrac{3}{5} \implies x^2 = 25 - 9 = 16$

θ in Quadrant II $\implies x = -4$

$\sin \theta = \dfrac{y}{r} = \dfrac{3}{5} \qquad \csc \theta = \dfrac{r}{y} = \dfrac{5}{3}$

$\cos \theta = \dfrac{x}{r} = -\dfrac{4}{5} \qquad \sec \theta = \dfrac{r}{x} = -\dfrac{5}{4}$

$\tan \theta = \dfrac{y}{x} = -\dfrac{3}{4} \qquad \cot \theta = \dfrac{x}{y} = -\dfrac{4}{3}$

15. $\sin \theta < 0 \implies y < 0$

$\tan \theta = \dfrac{y}{x} = \dfrac{-15}{8} \implies r = 17$

$\sin \theta = \dfrac{y}{r} = -\dfrac{15}{17} \qquad \csc \theta = \dfrac{r}{y} = -\dfrac{17}{15}$

$\cos \theta = \dfrac{x}{r} = \dfrac{8}{17} \qquad \sec \theta = \dfrac{r}{x} = \dfrac{17}{8}$

$\tan \theta = \dfrac{y}{x} = -\dfrac{15}{8} \qquad \cot \theta = \dfrac{x}{y} = -\dfrac{8}{15}$

17. $\sec\theta = \dfrac{r}{x} = \dfrac{2}{-1} \implies y^2 = 4 - 1 = 3$

$\sin\theta > 0 \implies y = \sqrt{3}$

$\sin\theta = \dfrac{y}{r} = \dfrac{\sqrt{3}}{2} \qquad \csc\theta = \dfrac{r}{y} = \dfrac{2\sqrt{3}}{3}$

$\cos\theta = \dfrac{x}{r} = -\dfrac{1}{2} \qquad \sec\theta = \dfrac{r}{x} = -2$

$\tan\theta = \dfrac{y}{x} = -\sqrt{3} \qquad \cot\theta = \dfrac{x}{y} = -\dfrac{\sqrt{3}}{3}$

19. $\sin\theta = 0 \implies \theta = n\pi$

$\sec\theta = -1 \implies \theta = \pi$

$\sin\theta = \dfrac{y}{r} = \dfrac{0}{r} = 0 \qquad \csc\theta = \dfrac{r}{y}$ is undefined.

$\cos\theta = \dfrac{x}{r} = \dfrac{-r}{r} = -1 \qquad \sec\theta = \dfrac{r}{x} = -1$

$\tan\theta = \dfrac{y}{x} = \dfrac{0}{x} = 0 \qquad \cot\theta = \dfrac{x}{y}$ is undefined.

21. To find a point on the terminal side of θ, use any point on the line $y = -x$ that lies in Quadrant II. $(-1, 1)$ is one such point.

$x = -1,\, y = 1,\, r = \sqrt{2}$

$\sin\theta = \dfrac{1}{\sqrt{2}} = \dfrac{\sqrt{2}}{2} \qquad \csc\theta = \sqrt{2}$

$\cos\theta = -\dfrac{1}{\sqrt{2}} = -\dfrac{\sqrt{2}}{2} \qquad \sec\theta = -\sqrt{2}$

$\tan\theta = -1 \qquad\qquad \cot\theta = -1$

23. To find a point on the terminal side of θ, use any point on the line $y = 2x$ that lies in Quadrant III. $(-1, -2)$ is one such point.

$x = -1,\, y = -2,\, r = \sqrt{5}$

$\sin\theta = -\dfrac{2}{\sqrt{5}} = -\dfrac{2\sqrt{5}}{5} \qquad \csc\theta = \dfrac{\sqrt{5}}{-2} = -\dfrac{\sqrt{5}}{2}$

$\cos\theta = -\dfrac{1}{\sqrt{5}} = -\dfrac{\sqrt{5}}{5} \qquad \sec\theta = \dfrac{\sqrt{5}}{-1} = -\sqrt{5}$

$\tan\theta = \dfrac{-2}{-1} = 2 \qquad\qquad \cot\theta = \dfrac{-1}{-2} = \dfrac{1}{2}$

25. $(x, y) = (-1, 0)$

$\cos\pi = \dfrac{x}{r} = \dfrac{-1}{1} = -1$

27. $(x, y) = (-1, 0)$

$\sec\pi = \dfrac{r}{x} = \dfrac{1}{-1} = -1$

29. $(x, y) = (0, 1)$

$\cot\dfrac{\pi}{2} = \dfrac{x}{y} = \dfrac{0}{1} = 0$

31. $\theta = 203°$

$\theta' = 203° - 180° = 23°$

33. $\theta = -245°$

$360° - 245° = 115°$ (coterminal angle)

$\theta' = 180° - 115° = 65°$

35. $\theta = \dfrac{2\pi}{3}$

$\theta = \pi - \dfrac{2\pi}{3} = \dfrac{\pi}{3}$

37. $\theta = 3.5$

$\theta' = 3.5 - \pi$

39. $\theta' = 45°$, Quadrant III

$$\sin 225° = -\sin 45° = -\frac{\sqrt{2}}{2}$$

$$\cos 225° = -\cos 45° = -\frac{\sqrt{2}}{2}$$

$$\tan 225° = \tan 45° = 1$$

41. $\theta' = 30°$, Quadrant I

$$\sin 750° = \sin 30° = \frac{1}{2}$$

$$\cos 750° = \cos 30° = \frac{\sqrt{3}}{2}$$

$$\tan 750° = \tan 30° = \frac{\sqrt{3}}{3}$$

43. $\theta' = \frac{\pi}{3}$, Quadrant III

$$\sin \frac{4\pi}{3} = -\sin \frac{\pi}{3} = -\frac{\sqrt{3}}{2}$$

$$\cos \frac{4\pi}{3} = -\cos \frac{\pi}{3} = -\frac{1}{2}$$

$$\tan \frac{4\pi}{3} = \tan \frac{\pi}{3} = \sqrt{3}$$

45. $\theta' = \frac{\pi}{6}$, Quadrant IV

$$\sin\left(-\frac{\pi}{6}\right) = -\sin \frac{\pi}{6} = -\frac{1}{2}$$

$$\cos\left(-\frac{\pi}{6}\right) = \cos \frac{\pi}{6} = \frac{\sqrt{3}}{2}$$

$$\tan\left(-\frac{\pi}{6}\right) = -\tan \frac{\pi}{6} = -\frac{\sqrt{3}}{3}$$

47. $\theta' = \frac{\pi}{4}$, Quadrant II

$$\sin \frac{11\pi}{4} = \sin \frac{\pi}{4} = \frac{\sqrt{2}}{2}$$

$$\cos \frac{11\pi}{4} = -\cos \frac{\pi}{4} = -\frac{\sqrt{2}}{2}$$

$$\tan \frac{11\pi}{4} = -\tan \frac{\pi}{4} = -1$$

49. $\sin 10° \approx 0.1736$

51. $\cos(-110°) \approx -0.3420$

53. $\tan 240° \approx 1.7321$

55. $\tan \frac{\pi}{9} \approx 0.3640$

57. $\sin 0.65 \approx 0.6052$

59.

θ	0°	20°	40°	60°	80°
$\sec \theta$	1	1.0642	1.3054	2	5.7588
$\sec(-\theta)$	1	1.0642	1.3054	2	5.7588
$\tan \theta$	0	0.3640	0.8391	1.7321	5.6713
$\tan(-\theta)$	0	−0.3640	−0.8391	−1.7321	5.6713

The secant is an even function and the tangent is an odd function.

61. (a)

θ	0	0.3	0.6	0.9	1.2	1.5
$\cos\left(\frac{3\pi}{2} - \theta\right)$	0	−0.2955	−0.5646	−0.7833	−0.9320	−0.9975
$-\sin \theta$	0	−0.2955	−0.5646	−0.7833	−0.9320	−0.9975

(b) $\cos\left(\frac{3\pi}{2} - \theta\right) = -\sin \theta$

63. (a) $\sin \theta = \dfrac{1}{2} \implies$ reference angle is 30° or $\dfrac{\pi}{6}$ and θ is in Quadrant I or Quadrant II.

Values in degrees: 30°, 150°

Values in radian: $\dfrac{\pi}{6}, \dfrac{5\pi}{6}$

(b) $\sin \theta = -\dfrac{1}{2} \implies$ reference angle is 30° or $\dfrac{\pi}{6}$ and θ is in Quadrant III or Quadrant IV.

Values in degrees: 210°, 330°

Values in radians: $\dfrac{7\pi}{6}, \dfrac{11\pi}{6}$

65. (a) $\csc \theta = \dfrac{2\sqrt{3}}{3} \implies$ reference angle is 60° or $\dfrac{\pi}{3}$ and θ is in Quadrant I or Quadrant II.

Values in degrees: 60°, 120°

Values in radians: $\dfrac{\pi}{3}, \dfrac{2\pi}{3}$

(b) $\cot \theta = -1 \implies$ reference angle is 45° or $\dfrac{\pi}{4}$ and θ is in Quadrant III or Quadrant IV.

Values in degrees: 135°, 315°

Values in radians: $\dfrac{3\pi}{4}, \dfrac{7\pi}{4}$

67. $\sin \theta = 0.8191$

Quadrant I: $\theta = \sin^{-1} 0.8191 \approx 54.99°$

Quadrant II: $\theta = 180° - \sin^{-1} 0.8191 \approx 125.01°$

69. $\cos \theta = 0.9848 \implies \theta \approx 0.175$

Quadrant I: $\theta = \cos^{-1}(0.9848) \approx 0.175$

Quadrant IV: $\theta = 2\pi - \theta' \approx 6.109$

71. $\tan \theta = 1.192 \implies \theta' \approx 0.873$

Quadrant I: $\theta = \tan^{-1} 1.192 \approx 0.873$

Quadrant III: $\theta = \pi + \theta' \approx 4.014$

73.
$$\sin \theta = -\frac{3}{5}$$
$$\sin^2 \theta + \cos^2 \theta = 1$$
$$\cos^2 \theta = 1 - \sin^2 \theta$$
$$\cos^2 \theta = 1 - \left(-\frac{3}{5}\right)^2$$
$$\cos^2 \theta = 1 - \frac{9}{25}$$
$$\cos^2 \theta = \frac{16}{25}$$

$\cos \theta > 0$ in Quadrant IV.

$$\cos \theta = \frac{4}{5}$$

75. $\tan \theta = \dfrac{3}{2}$

$$\sec^2 \theta = 1 + \tan^2 \theta$$
$$\sec^2 \theta = 1 + \left(\frac{3}{2}\right)^2$$
$$\sec^2 \theta = 1 + \frac{9}{4}$$
$$\sec^2 \theta = \frac{13}{4}$$

$\sec \theta < 0$ in Quadrant III.

$$\sec \theta = -\frac{\sqrt{13}}{2}$$

77. $\cos \theta = \dfrac{5}{8}$

$$\cos \theta = \frac{1}{\sec \theta} \implies \sec \theta = \frac{1}{\cos \theta}$$
$$\sec \theta = \frac{1}{5/8} = \frac{8}{5}$$

79. $\left(\dfrac{\sqrt{2}}{2}, \dfrac{\sqrt{2}}{2}\right)$ corresponds to $t = \dfrac{\pi}{4}$ on the unit circle.

$\sin \dfrac{\pi}{4} = \dfrac{\sqrt{2}}{2}$ since $\sin \ t = y$.

$\cos \dfrac{\pi}{4} = \dfrac{\sqrt{2}}{2}$ since $\cos \ t = x$.

$\tan \dfrac{\pi}{4} = 1$ since $\tan \ t = \dfrac{y}{x}$.

81. $\left(-\dfrac{\sqrt{3}}{2}, \dfrac{1}{2}\right)$ corresponds to $t = \dfrac{5\pi}{6}$ on the unit circle.

$\sin \dfrac{5\pi}{6} = \dfrac{1}{2}$ since $\sin \ t = y$.

$\cos \dfrac{5\pi}{6} = -\dfrac{\sqrt{3}}{2}$ since $\cos \ t = x$.

$\tan \dfrac{5\pi}{6} = -\dfrac{1}{\sqrt{3}} = \dfrac{-\sqrt{3}}{3}$ since $\tan \ t = \dfrac{y}{x}$.

83. $\left(-\dfrac{1}{2}, -\dfrac{\sqrt{3}}{2}\right)$ corresponds to $t = \dfrac{4\pi}{3}$ on the unit circle.

$\sin \dfrac{4\pi}{3} = -\dfrac{\sqrt{3}}{2}$ since $\sin \ t = y$.

$\cos \dfrac{4\pi}{3} = -\dfrac{1}{2}$ since $\cos \ t = x$.

$\tan \dfrac{4\pi}{3} = \sqrt{3}$ since $\tan \ t = \dfrac{y}{x}$.

85. $(0, -1)$ corresponds to $t = \dfrac{3\pi}{2}$ on the unit circle.

$\sin \dfrac{3\pi}{2} = -1$ since $\sin \ t = y$.

$\cos \dfrac{3\pi}{2} = 0$ since $\cos \ t = x$.

$\tan \dfrac{3\pi}{2}$ is undefined since $\tan \ t = \dfrac{y}{x}$.

87. (a) $\sin 5 \approx -1$

    (b) $\cos 2 \approx -0.4$

89. (a) $\sin t = 0.25$ (b) $\cos t = -0.25$

       $t \approx 0.25$ or 2.89 $t \approx 1.82$ or 4.46

91. $h(t) = f(t)g(t)$

     $h(-t) = f(-t)g(-t)$

           $= -f(t)g(t)$

           $= -h(t)$

Therefore, $h(t)$ is odd.

93. (a) $t = 1$

$$T = 45 - 23 \cos\left[\dfrac{2\pi}{365}(1 - 32)\right] \approx 25.2°\, F$$

    (b) $t = 185$

$$T = 45 - 23 \cos\left[\dfrac{2\pi}{365}(185 - 32)\right] \approx 65.1°\, F$$

    (c) $t = 291$

$$T = 45 - 23 \cos\left[\dfrac{2\pi}{365}(291 - 32)\right] \approx 50.8°\, F$$

95. $y(t) = 2e^{-t} \cos 6t$

    (a) $y(0) = 2e^{-0}\cos(6(0)) = 2$

    (b)

t	0.50	1.02	1.54	2.07	2.59
y	-1.2	0.71	-0.42	0.25	-0.15

    (c) Friction within the system dampens the oscillations and is modeled by the factor e^{-t}.

    (d) Using the zoom and trace feature, or root feature, you obtain $t = 0.26$ and $t = 0.79$.

97. $I = 5e^{-2t} \sin t$

     $I(0.7) = 5e^{-1.4} \sin 0.7 \approx 0.79$

99. $y = 2^{x-1}$

x	-1	0	1	2	3
y	$\frac{1}{4}$	$\frac{1}{2}$	1	2	4

103. $y = \ln(x - 1)$

Domain: $x - 1 > 0 \implies x > 1$

x	1.1	1.5	2	3	4
y	-2.30	-0.69	0	0.69	1.10

Section 5.4   Graphs of Sine and Cosine Functions

- You should be able to graph $y = a \sin(bx - c)$ and $y = a \cos(bx - c)$.
- Amplitude: $|a|$
- Period: $\dfrac{2\pi}{|b|}$
- Shift: Solve $bx - c = 0$ and $bx - c = 2\pi$.
- Key increments: $\dfrac{1}{4}$ (period)

Solutions to Odd-Numbered Exercises

1. $y = 3 \sin 2x$

Period: $\dfrac{2\pi}{2} = \pi$

Amplitude: $|3| = 3$

> Xmin = -2π
> Xmax = 2π
> Xscl = π/2
> Ymin = -4
> Ymax = 4
> Yscl = 1

3. $y = \dfrac{5}{2} \cos \dfrac{x}{2}$

Period: $\dfrac{2\pi}{1/2} = 4\pi$

Amplitude $\left|\dfrac{5}{2}\right| = \dfrac{5}{2}$

> Xmin = -4π
> Xmax = 4π
> Xscl = π
> Ymin = -3
> Ymax = 3
> Yscl = 1

5. $y = \dfrac{2}{3} \sin \pi x$

Period: $\dfrac{2\pi}{\pi} - 2$

Amplitude: $\left|\dfrac{2}{3}\right| - \dfrac{2}{3}$

> Xmin = -π
> Xmax = π
> Xscl = π/2
> Ymin = -1
> Ymax = 1
> Yscl = .5

7. $y = -2 \sin x$

Period: $\dfrac{2\pi}{1} = 2\pi$

Amplitude: $|-2| = 2$

9. $y = 3 \sin 10x$

Period: $\dfrac{2\pi}{10} = \dfrac{\pi}{5}$

Amplitude: $|3| = 3$

11. $y = \dfrac{1}{2} \cos \dfrac{2\pi}{3}$

Period: $\dfrac{2\pi}{2/3} = 3\pi$

Amplitude: $\left|\dfrac{1}{2}\right| = \dfrac{1}{2}$

13. $y = 3 \sin 4\pi x$

Period: $\dfrac{2\pi}{4\pi} = \dfrac{1}{2}$

Amplitude: $|3| = 3$

15. $f(x) = \sin x$

$g(x) = \sin(x - \pi)$

The graph of g is a horizontal shift to the right π units of the graph of f (a phase shift).

17. $f(x) = \cos 2x$

$g(x) = -\cos 2x$

The graph of g is a reflection in the x-axis of the graph of f.

19. $f(x) = \cos x$

$g(x) = -3 \cos x$

The graph of g is three times the amplitude of f, and reflected in the x-axis.

23. The graph of g has twice the amplitude as the graph of f. The period is the same.

27. $y_1 = \frac{1}{2} \sin x$; $y_2 = \frac{3}{2} \sin x$; $y_3 = -3 \sin x$

Changing the value of a changes the amplitude.

31. $f(x) = -2 \sin x$

Period: 2π

Amplitude: 2

$g(x) = 4 \sin x$

Period: 2π

Amplitude: 4 upward.

35. $f(x) = -\frac{1}{2} \sin \frac{x}{2}$

Period: 4π

Amplitude: $\frac{1}{2}$

$g(x) = 3 - \frac{1}{2} \sin \frac{x}{2}$ is the graph of $f(x)$ shifted vertically three units upward.

21. $f(x) = \sin x$

$f(x) = 2 + \sin x$

The graph of g is a vertical shift upward of 2 units of the graph of f.

25. The graph of g is a horizontal shift π units to the right of the graph of f.

29. $y_1 = \sin\left(\frac{1}{2}x\right)$; $y_2 = \sin\left(\frac{3}{2}x\right)$; $y_3 = \sin(4x)$

Changing the value of b changes the period.

33. $f(x) = \cos x$

Period: 2π

Amplitude: 1

$g(x) = 1 + \cos x$ is a vertical shift of the graph of $f(x)$ one unit upward.

37. $f(x) = 2 \cos x$

Period: 2π

Amplitude: 2

$g(x) = 2 \cos(x + \pi)$ is the graph of $f(x)$ shifted π units to the left.

39. Since sine and cosine are cofunctions and x and $x - (\pi/2)$ are complementary, we have

$$\sin x = \cos\left(x - \frac{\pi}{2}\right).$$

Period: 2π

Amplitude: 1

41. $f(x) = \cos x$

$$g(x) = -\sin\left(x - \frac{\pi}{2}\right) = \sin\left(\frac{\pi}{2} - x\right) = \cos x$$

Thus, $f(x) = g(x)$.

43. $y = -2 \sin 6x$; $a = -2$, $b = 6$, $c = 0$

Period: $\dfrac{2\pi}{6} = \dfrac{\pi}{3}$

Amplitude: $|-2| = 2$

Key points: $(0, 0), \left(\dfrac{\pi}{12}, -2\right), \left(\dfrac{\pi}{6}, 0\right), \left(\dfrac{\pi}{4}, 2\right), \left(\dfrac{\pi}{3}, 0\right)$

45. $y = \cos 2\pi x$

Period: $\dfrac{2\pi}{2\pi} = 1$

Amplitude: 1

Key points: $(1, 0), \left(0, \dfrac{1}{4}\right), \left(-1, \dfrac{1}{2}\right), \left(0, \dfrac{3}{4}\right), (1, 1)$

47. $y = -\sin\dfrac{2\pi x}{3}$; $a = -1, b = \dfrac{2\pi}{3}, c = 0$

Period: $\dfrac{2\pi}{2\pi/3} = 3$

Amplitude: 1

Key points: $(0, 0), \left(\dfrac{3}{4}, -1\right), \left(\dfrac{3}{2}, 0\right), \left(\dfrac{9}{4}, 1\right), (3, 0)$

49. $y = \sin\left(x - \dfrac{\pi}{4}\right)$; $a = 1, b = 1, c = \dfrac{\pi}{4}$

Period: 2π

Amplitude: 1

Shift: Set $x - \dfrac{\pi}{4} = 0$ and $x - \dfrac{\pi}{4} = 2\pi$

$$\pi = \frac{\pi}{4} \qquad\qquad \pi = \frac{9\pi}{4}$$

Key points: $\left(\dfrac{\pi}{4}, 0\right), \left(\dfrac{3\pi}{4}, 1\right), \left(\dfrac{5\pi}{4}, 0\right), \left(\dfrac{7\pi}{4}, -1\right), \left(\dfrac{9\pi}{4}, 0\right)$

51. $y = 3 \cos(x + \pi)$

Period: 2π

Amplitude: 3

Shift: Set $x + \pi = 0$ and $x + \pi = 2\pi$

$\qquad x = -\pi \qquad\quad x = \pi$

Key points: $(3, -\pi)$, $\left(0, -\dfrac{\pi}{2}\right)$, $(-3, 0)$, $\left(0, \dfrac{\pi}{2}\right)$, $(3, \pi)$

53. $y = \dfrac{1}{10} \cos(60\pi x)$; $a = \dfrac{1}{10}$, $b = 60\pi$, $c = 0$

Period: $\dfrac{2\pi}{60\pi} = \dfrac{1}{30}$

Amplitude: $\dfrac{1}{10}$

Key points: $\left(0, \dfrac{1}{10}\right)$, $\left(\dfrac{1}{120}, 0\right)$, $\left(\dfrac{1}{60}, -\dfrac{1}{10}\right)$, $\left(\dfrac{1}{40}, 0\right)$, $\left(\dfrac{1}{30}, \dfrac{1}{10}\right)$

55. $y = 2 - \sin \dfrac{2\pi x}{3}$

Vertical shift 2 units upward of the graph in Exercise #47.

57. $y = 3 \cos(x + \pi) - 3$

Vertical shift 2 units downward of the graph in Exercise #51.

59. $y = \dfrac{2}{3} \cos\left(\dfrac{x}{2} - \dfrac{\pi}{4}\right)$; $a = \dfrac{2}{3}$, $b = \dfrac{1}{2}$, $c = \dfrac{\pi}{4}$

Period: 4π

Amplitude: $\dfrac{2}{3}$

Shift: Set $\dfrac{x}{2} - \dfrac{\pi}{4} = 0$ and $\dfrac{x}{2} - \dfrac{\pi}{4} = 2\pi$

$\qquad\quad x = \dfrac{\pi}{2} \qquad\qquad x = \dfrac{9\pi}{2}$

Key points: $\left(\dfrac{\pi}{2}, \dfrac{2}{3}\right)$, $\left(\dfrac{3\pi}{2}, 0\right)$, $\left(\dfrac{5\pi}{2}, \dfrac{-2}{3}\right)$, $\left(\dfrac{7\pi}{2}, 0\right)$, $\left(\dfrac{9\pi}{2}, \dfrac{2}{3}\right)$

61. $y = -2 \sin(4x + \pi)$

63. $y = \cos\left(2\pi x - \dfrac{\pi}{2}\right) + 1$

65. $y = -0.1 \sin\left(\dfrac{\pi x}{10} + \pi\right)$

67. $y = 5 \cos(\pi - 2x) + 2$

69. $f(x) = a \cos x + d$

Amplitude: $\frac{1}{2}[8 - 0] = 4$

Since $f(x)$ is the graph of $g(x) = 4 \cos x$ reflected about the x-axis and shifted vertically 4 units upward, we have $a = -4$ and $d = 4$. Thus, $f(x) = -4 \cos x + 4 = 4 - 4 \cos x$.

71. $y = a \sin(bx - c)$

Amplitude: $|a| = |3|$.

Since the graph is reflected about the x-axis, we have $a = -3$.

Period: $\dfrac{2\pi}{b} = \pi \implies b = 2$

Phase shift: $c = 0$

Thus, $y = -3 \sin 2x$.

73. $y = a \sin(bx + c)$

Amplitude: $a = 1$

Period: $2\pi \implies b = 1$

Phase shift: $bx + c = 0$ when $x = \dfrac{\pi}{4}$

$$(1)\frac{\pi}{4} + c = 0 \implies c = -\frac{\pi}{4}$$

Thus, $y = \sin\left(x - \dfrac{\pi}{4}\right)$.

75. $y_1 = \sin x$

$y_2 = -\dfrac{1}{2}$

In the interval $[-2\pi, 2\pi]$, $\sin x = -\dfrac{1}{2}$ when

$$x = -\frac{5\pi}{6}, -\frac{\pi}{6}, \frac{7\pi}{6}, \frac{11\pi}{6}.$$

77. $y_1 = \cos x$

$y_2 = \dfrac{\sqrt{2}}{2}$

In the interval $[-2\pi, 2\pi]$, $\cos x = \dfrac{\sqrt{2}}{2}$ when $x = \pm\dfrac{\pi}{4}, \pm\dfrac{7\pi}{4}$.

79. (a) $h(x) = \cos^2 x$ is even.   (b) $g(x) = \sin^2 x$ is even.   (c) $h(x) = \sin x \cos x$ is odd.

81. $y = 0.85 \sin \dfrac{\pi t}{3}$

(a)

(b) Time for one cycle = one period = $\dfrac{2\pi}{\pi/3} = 6$ sec

(c) Cycles per min = $\dfrac{60}{6} = 10$ cycles per min

83. (a) $\sin x \approx x - \dfrac{x^3}{3!} + \dfrac{x^5}{5!}$

Near $x = 0$ the graphs are approximately the same.

(b) $\cos x \approx 1 - \dfrac{x^2}{2!} + \dfrac{x^5}{5!}$

Near $x = 0$ the graphs are approximately the same.

(c) $\sin x \approx x - \dfrac{x^3}{3!} + \dfrac{x^5}{5!} - \dfrac{x^7}{7!}$

$\cos x \approx 1 - \dfrac{x^2}{2!} + \dfrac{x^4}{4!} - \dfrac{x^6}{6!}$

The accuracy is increased.

85. $S = 22.3 - 3.4 \cos \dfrac{\pi t}{6}, \ 1 \le t \le 12$

Maximum sales: June

Minimum sales: December

87. $C = 30.3 + 21.6 \sin \left(\dfrac{2\pi t}{365} + 10.9 \right)$

(a) period = $\dfrac{2\pi}{b} = \dfrac{2\pi}{(2\pi/365)} = 365$ days

This is to be expected: 365 days = 1 year

(b) The constant 30.3 gallons is the average daily fuel consumption.

(c)

Consumption exceeds 40 gallons/day when $124 \le x \le 252$. (Graph C together with $y = 40$).

89. (a) A model for Chicago is

$$C(t) = 56.35 + 27.35 \sin\left(\frac{\pi t}{6} + 4.19\right).$$

(b)

(c)

The model is a good fit for most months.

(d) Use the constant term of each model to estimate the average annual temperature.

Honolulu: 84.40°

Chicago: 56.35°

The model is a good fit.

(e) Each model has a period of 12. This corresponds to the 12 months in a year.

(f) Chicago has a greater variability in temperatures during the year. The amplitude of each model indicates this variability.

Section 5.5 Graphs of Other Trigonometric Functions

■ You should be able to graph:

   $y = a \tan(bx - c)$ $y = a \cot(bx - c)$

   $y = a \sec(bx - c)$ $y = a \csc(bx - c)$

■ When graphing $y = a \sec(bx - c)$ or $y = a \csc(bx - c)$ you should know to first graph $y = a \cos(bx - c)$ or $y = a \sin(bx - c)$ since

   (a) The intercepts of sine and cosine are vertical asymptotes of cosecant and secant.

   (b) The maximums of sine and cosine are local minimums of cosecant and secant.

   (c) The minimums of sine and cosine are local maximums of cosecant and secant.

■ You should be able to graph using a damping factor.

Solutions to Odd-Numbered Exercises

1. $y = \sec \dfrac{x}{2}$

Period: $\dfrac{2\pi}{1/2} = 4\pi$

Matches graph (g).

5. $y = \cot \dfrac{\pi x}{2}$

Period: $\dfrac{\pi}{\pi/2} = 2$

Matches graph (b).

3. $y = \tan 2x$

Period: $\dfrac{\pi}{2}$

Matches graph (f).

7. $y = -\csc x$

Period: 2π

Matches graph (e).

9. $y = \dfrac{1}{3}\tan x$

Period: π

Two consecutive asymptotes:

$x = -\dfrac{\pi}{x}$ and $x = \dfrac{\pi}{2}$

x	$-\dfrac{\pi}{4}$	0	$\dfrac{\pi}{4}$
y	$-\dfrac{1}{3}$	0	$\dfrac{1}{3}$

13. $y = -\dfrac{1}{2}\sec x$

Graph $y = -\dfrac{1}{2}\cos x$ first.

Period: 2π

One cycle: 0 to 27

17. $y = \sec \pi x - 1$

Reflect the graph in Exercise #15 about the
x-axis and then shift it vertically down one unit.

11. $y = \tan 2x$

Period: $\dfrac{\pi}{2}$

Two consecutive asymptotes:

$2x = -\dfrac{\pi}{2} \implies x = -\dfrac{\pi}{4}$

$2x = \dfrac{\pi}{2} \implies x = \dfrac{\pi}{4}$

x	$-\dfrac{\pi}{8}$	0	$\dfrac{\pi}{8}$
y	-1	0	1

15. $y = -\sec \pi x$

Graph $y = -\cos \pi x$ first.

Period: $\dfrac{2\pi}{\pi} = 2$

One cycle: 0 to 2

19. $y = \csc \dfrac{x}{2}$

Graph $y = \sin \dfrac{x}{2}$ first.

Period: $\dfrac{2\pi}{1/2} = 4\pi$

One cycle: 0 to 4π

21. $y = \cot \dfrac{x}{2}$

Period: $\dfrac{\pi}{1/2} = 2\pi$

Two consecutive asymptotes:

$\dfrac{x}{2} = 0 \implies x = 0$

$\dfrac{x}{2} = \pi \implies x = 2\pi$

x	$\dfrac{\pi}{2}$	π	$\dfrac{3\pi}{2}$
y	1	0	-1

23. $y = \dfrac{1}{2} \sec 2x$

Graph $y = \dfrac{1}{2} \cos 2x$ first.

Period: $\dfrac{2\pi}{2} = \pi$

One cycle: 0 to π

25. $y = \tan \dfrac{\pi x}{4}$

Period: $\dfrac{\pi}{\pi/4} = 4$

Two consecutive asymptotes:

$\dfrac{\pi x}{4} = -\dfrac{\pi}{2} \implies x = -2$

$\dfrac{\pi x}{4} = \dfrac{\pi}{2} \implies x = 2$

x	-1	0	1
y	-1	0	1

27. $y = \csc(\pi - x)$

Graph $y = \sin(\pi - x)$ first.

Period: 2π

Shift: Set $\pi - x = 0$ and $\pi - x = 2\pi$

$\qquad\qquad x = \pi \qquad\qquad x = -\pi$

29. $y = 2 \cot\left(x + \dfrac{\pi}{2}\right)$

Graph $y = \dfrac{2}{\tan\left(x + \dfrac{\pi}{2}\right)}$

Period: π

Shift: Set $x + \dfrac{\pi}{2} = 0$ and $\pi + \dfrac{\pi}{2} = \pi$

$\qquad\qquad x = -\dfrac{\pi}{2} \qquad\qquad x = \dfrac{\pi}{2}$

31. $y = \tan\dfrac{x}{3}$

33. $y = -2 \sec 4x$

$\qquad = \dfrac{-2}{\cos 4x}$

35. $y = \tan\left(x - \dfrac{\pi}{4}\right)$

37. $y = \dfrac{1}{4}\cot\left(x - \dfrac{\pi}{2}\right)$

$\qquad = \dfrac{1}{4\tan(x - \pi/2)}$

39. $y = 2 \sec(2x - \pi)$

$\qquad y = \dfrac{2}{\cos(2x - \pi)}$

41. $\tan x = 1$

$\qquad x = -\dfrac{7\pi}{4}, \ -\dfrac{3\pi}{4}, \ \dfrac{\pi}{4}, \ \dfrac{5\pi}{4}$

43. $\sec x = -2$

$\qquad x = \pm\dfrac{2\pi}{3}, \ \pm\dfrac{4\pi}{3}$

45. The graph of $f(x) = \sec x$ has y-axis symmetry. Thus, the function is even.

47. As $x \to \dfrac{\pi}{2}$ from the left, $f(x) = \tan x \to \infty$.

As $x \to \dfrac{\pi}{2}$ from the right, $f(x) = \tan x \to -\infty$.

49. $f(x) = 2 \sin x$

$g(x) = \dfrac{1}{2} \csc x$

(a)

(b) $f > g$ on the interval, $\dfrac{\pi}{6} < x < \dfrac{5\pi}{6}$

(c) As $x \to \pi, f(x) = 2 \sin x \to 0$ and

$g(x) = \dfrac{1}{2} \csc x \to \infty$ since $g(x)$ is the reciprocal of

$f(x)$.

51. $y_1 = \sin x \csc x$ and $y_2 = 1$

$\sin x \csc x = \sin x \left(\dfrac{1}{\sin x} \right) = 1, \sin x \neq 0$

53. $y_1 = \dfrac{\cos x}{\sin x}$ and $y_2 = \cot x = \dfrac{1}{\tan x}$

$\cot x = \dfrac{\cos x}{\sin x}$

55. $f(x) = x \cos x$

As $x \to 0, f(x) \to 0$.

Matches graph (d).

57. $g(x) = |x| \sin x$

As $x \to 0, g(x) \to 0$.

Matches graph (b).

59. $f(x) = \sin x + \cos \left(x + \dfrac{\pi}{2} \right), g(x) = 0$

$f(x) = g(x)$

The graph is the line $y = 0$.

61. $f(x) = \sin^2 x, g(x) = \dfrac{1}{2} (1 - \cos 2x)$

$f(x) = g(x)$

63. $f(x) = 2^{-x/4} \cos \pi x$

$-2^{-x/4} \leq f(x) \leq 2^{-2x/4}$

The damping factor is $y = 2^{-x/4}$.

As $x \to \infty, f \to 0$

65. $g(x) = e^{-x^2/2} \sin x$

$-e^{-x^2/2} \leq g(x) \leq e^{-x^2/2}$

The damping factor is $y = e^{-x^2/2}$.

As $x \to \infty, g \to 0$

67. $\tan x = \dfrac{5}{d}$

$d = \dfrac{5}{\tan x} = 5 \cot x$

69. As the predator population increases, the number of prey decrease. When the number of prey is small, the number of predators decreases.

71. (a)

(b) The displacement function is periodic, but damped. It approaches 0 as t increases.

73. $\tan x \approx x + \dfrac{2x^3}{3!} + \dfrac{16x^5}{5!}$

The graphs are approximately the same when x is near zero. As x gets larger, the graphs are further apart.

75. (a) $y_1 = \dfrac{4}{\pi}\left(\sin(\pi x) + \dfrac{1}{3}\sin 3(\pi x)\right)$

$y_2 = \dfrac{4}{\pi}\left(\sin(\pi x) + \dfrac{1}{3}\sin 3(\pi x) + \dfrac{1}{5}\sin 5(\pi x)\right)$

(b) $y_3 = \dfrac{4}{\pi}\left(\sin(\pi x) + \dfrac{1}{3}\sin 3(\pi x) + \dfrac{1}{5}\sin 5(\pi x) + \dfrac{1}{7}\sin 7(\pi x)\right)$

(c) $y_4 = \dfrac{4}{\pi}\left(\sin(\pi x) + \dfrac{1}{3}\sin 3(\pi x) + \dfrac{1}{5}\sin 5(\pi x) + \dfrac{1}{7}\sin 7(\pi x) + \dfrac{1}{9}\sin 9(\pi x)\right)$

77. $y = \dfrac{6}{x} + \cos x,\ x > 0$

As $x \to 0,\ y \to \infty$.

79. (a) Yes. For each t there corresponds one and only one value of y.

(b) 1.27 oscillations per sec

(c) $y = 12(0.2231)^t \cos 8t$

(d) $y = 12e^{-1.5t} \cos 8t$

(e)

81. (a) 850 rev/min

(b) The direction of the saw is reversed.

(c) $L = 60\left[\left(\dfrac{\pi}{2} + \phi\right) + \cot\phi\right],\ 0 < f < \dfrac{\pi}{2}$

(d)

ϕ	0.3	0.6	0.9	1.2	1.5
L	306.2	217.9	195.9	189.6	188.5

(e) Straight line lengths change faster.

(f)

83. Graphing $y = \dfrac{300}{1 + e^{-x}} - 100$, you see that $x \approx -0.639$ is the only root. Analytically,

$$\dfrac{300}{1 + e^{-x}} = 100$$

$$3 = 1 + e^{-x}$$

$$2 = e^{-x}$$

$$\ln 2 = -x \implies x = -\ln 2 \approx -0.693.$$

85. $\log_8 x + \log_8(x - 1) = \tfrac{1}{3}$

$\log_8 x(x - 1) = \tfrac{1}{3}$

$8^{1/3} = x(x - 1)$

$x^2 - x - 2 = 0$

$(x - 2)(x + 1) = 0 \implies x = 2 (x = -1$ is not in the domain.)

Section 5.6   Inverse Trigonometric Functions

■ You should know the definitions, domains, and ranges of $y = \arcsin x$, $y = \arccos x$, and $y = \arctan x$.

Function	Domain	Range
$y = \arcsin x \implies x = \sin y$	$-1 \le x \le 1$	$-\dfrac{\pi}{2} \le y \le \dfrac{\pi}{2}$
$y = \arccos x \implies x = \cos y$	$-1 \le x \le 1$	$0 \le y \le \pi$
$y = \arctan x \implies x = \tan y$	$-\infty < x < \infty$	$-\dfrac{\pi}{2} < x < \dfrac{\pi}{2}$

■ You should know the inverse properties of the inverse trigonometric functions.

$\sin(\arcsin x) = x,\ -1 \le x \le 1$ and $\arcsin(\sin y) = y,\ -\dfrac{\pi}{2} \le y \le \dfrac{\pi}{2}$

$\cos(\arccos x) = x,\ -1 \le x \le 1$ and $\arccos(\cos y) = y,\ 0 \le y \le \pi$

$\tan(\arctan x) = x$ and $\arctan(\tan y) = y,\ -\dfrac{\pi}{2} < y < \dfrac{\pi}{2}$

■ You should be able to use the triangle technique to convert trigonometric functions of inverse trigonometric functions into algebraic expressions.

Solutions to Odd-Numbered Exercises

1. (a)

x	−1.0	−0.8	−0.6	−0.4	−0.2
y	−1.5708	−0.9273	−0.6435	−0.4115	−0.2014

x	0	0.2	0.4	0.6	0.8	1
y	0	0.2014	0.4115	0.6435	0.9273	1.5708

(b)

(c)

(d) $(0, 0)$, Symmetric to the origin

3. (a)

x	−10	−8	−6	−4	−2
y	−1.4711	−1.4464	−1.4056	−1.3258	−1.1071

x	0	2	4	6	8	10
y	0	1.1071	1.3258	1.4056	1.4464	1.4711

(b)

(c)

(d) Horizontal asymptotes: $y = \pm\dfrac{\pi}{2}$

5. $y = \arctan x$

$$\tan\left(-\frac{\pi}{6}\right) = -\frac{\sqrt{3}}{3} \implies \left(-\frac{\sqrt{3}}{3}, -\frac{\pi}{6}\right)$$

$$\arctan(-\sqrt{3}) = -\frac{\pi}{3} \implies \left(-\sqrt{3}, -\frac{\pi}{3}\right)$$

$$\tan\left(\frac{\pi}{4}\right) = 1 \implies \left(1, \frac{\pi}{4}\right)$$

7. (a) $y = \arcsin\dfrac{1}{2} \implies \sin y = \dfrac{1}{2}$ for $-\dfrac{\pi}{2} \le y \le \dfrac{\pi}{2} \implies y = \dfrac{\pi}{6}$

(b) $y = \arcsin 0 \implies \sin y = 0 \implies y = 0$

9. (a) $y = \arctan\dfrac{\sqrt{3}}{3} \implies \tan y = \dfrac{\sqrt{3}}{3}$ for $-\dfrac{\pi}{2} < y < \dfrac{\pi}{2} \implies y = \dfrac{\pi}{6}$

(b) $y = \arctan(-1) \implies \tan y = -1 \implies y = -\dfrac{\pi}{4}$

11. (a) $y = \arctan(-\sqrt{3}) \implies \tan y = \sqrt{3}$ for $-\dfrac{\pi}{2} < y < \dfrac{\pi}{2} \implies y = -\dfrac{\pi}{3}$

(b) $y = \arctan \sqrt{3} \implies \tan y = \sqrt{3} \implies y = \dfrac{\pi}{3}$

13. (a) $y = \arcsin \dfrac{\sqrt{3}}{2} \implies \sin y = \dfrac{\sqrt{3}}{2}$ for $-\dfrac{\pi}{2} \le y \le \dfrac{\pi}{2} \implies y = \dfrac{\pi}{3}$

(b) $y = \arctan\left(\dfrac{-\sqrt{3}}{3}\right) \implies \tan y = \dfrac{-\sqrt{3}}{3} \implies y = -\dfrac{\pi}{6}$

15. (a) $\arccos 0.28 = \cos^{-1} 0.28 \approx 1.29$ (b) $\arcsin 0.45 \approx 0.47$

17. (a) $\arctan(-3) = \tan^{-1}(-3) \approx -1.25$ (b) $\arctan 15 \approx 1.50$

19. (a) $\arccos(-0.41) = \cos^{-1}(-0.41) \approx 1.99$ (b) $\arcsin(-0.125) \approx -0.13$

21. $f(x) = \tan x$ and $g(x) = \arctan x$

Graph: $y_1 = \tan x$

        $y_2 = \tan^{-1} x$

        $y_3 = x$

23. $\tan \theta = \dfrac{x}{4}$

    $\theta = \arctan \dfrac{x}{4}$

25. $\sin \theta = \dfrac{x+2}{5}$

    $\theta = \arcsin\left(\dfrac{x+2}{5}\right)$

27. $\sin(\arcsin 0.3) = 0.3$

29. $\cos[\arccos(-0.1)] = -0.1$

31. $\arcsin(\sin 3\pi) = \arcsin(0) = 0$

Note: 3π is not in the range of the arcsine function.

33. Let $y = \arctan \dfrac{3}{4}$. Then,

$\tan y = \dfrac{3}{4},\ 0 < y < \dfrac{\pi}{2}$

and $\sin y = \dfrac{3}{5}$.

35. Let $y = \arctan 2$. Then,

$\tan y = 2 = \dfrac{2}{1},\ 0 < y < \dfrac{\pi}{2}$

and $\cos y = \dfrac{1}{\sqrt{5}} = \dfrac{\sqrt{5}}{5}$.

37. Let $y = \arcsin \dfrac{5}{13}$. Then,

$\sin y = \dfrac{5}{13}, \quad 0 < y < \dfrac{\pi}{2}$

and $\cos y = \dfrac{12}{13}$.

39. Let $y = \arctan\left(-\dfrac{3}{5}\right)$. Then,

$\tan y = -\dfrac{3}{5}, \quad -\dfrac{\pi}{2} < y < 0$

and $\sec y = \dfrac{\sqrt{34}}{5}$.

41. Let $y = \arccos\left(-\dfrac{2}{3}\right)$. Then,

$\cos y = -\dfrac{2}{3}, \quad -\dfrac{\pi}{2} < y < \pi$

and $\sin y = \dfrac{\sqrt{5}}{3}$.

43. Let $y = \arctan x$. Then,

$\tan y = x$

and $\cot y = \dfrac{1}{x}$.

45. Let $y = \arcsin(2x)$. Then,

$\sin y = 2x = \dfrac{2x}{1}$

and $\cos y = \sqrt{1 - 4x^2}$.

47. Let $y = \arccos x$. Then,

$$\cos y = x = \frac{x}{1}$$

and $\sin y = \sqrt{1 - x^2}$.

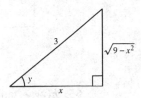

49. Let $y = \arccos\left(\dfrac{x}{3}\right)$. Then,

$$\cos y = \frac{x}{3}$$

and $\tan y = \dfrac{\sqrt{9 - x^2}}{x}$.

51. Let $y = \arctan \dfrac{x}{\sqrt{2}}$. Then,

$$\tan y = \frac{x}{\sqrt{2}}$$

and $\csc y = \dfrac{\sqrt{x^2 + 2}}{x}$.

53. $f(x) = \sin(\arctan 2x)$, $g(x) = \dfrac{2x}{\sqrt{1 + 4x^2}}$

Let $y = \arctan 2x$. Then,

$$\tan y = 2x = \frac{2x}{1}$$

and $\sin y = \dfrac{2x}{\sqrt{1 + 4x^2}}$.

$$g(x) = \frac{2x}{\sqrt{1 + 4x^2}} = f(x)$$

The graph has horizontal asymptotes at $y = \pm 1$.

55. Let $y = \arctan \dfrac{9}{x}$. Then,

$$\tan y = \frac{9}{x} \text{ and } \sin y = \frac{9}{\sqrt{x^2 + 81}}.$$

Thus, $y = \arcsin \dfrac{9}{\sqrt{x^2 + 81}}$.

57. Let $y = \arccos \dfrac{3}{\sqrt{x^2 - 2x + 10}}$. Then,

$$\cos y = \frac{3}{\sqrt{x^2 - 2x + 10}} = \frac{3}{\sqrt{(x - 1)^2 + 9}}$$

and $\sin y = \dfrac{|x - 1|}{\sqrt{(x - 1)^2 + 9}}$.

Thus, $y = \arcsin \dfrac{|x - 1|}{\sqrt{(x - 1)^2 + 9}} = \arcsin \dfrac{|x - 1|}{\sqrt{x^2 - 2x + 10}}$.

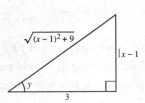

59. $y = 2 \arccos x$

Domain: $-1 \le x \le 1$

Range: $0 \le y \le 2\pi$

Vertical stretch of $f(x) = \arccos x$

61. The graph of $f(x) = \arcsin(x - 1)$ is a horizontal translation of the graph of $y = \arcsin x$ by one unit.

63. $f(x) = \arctan 2x$

Domain: all real numbers

Range: $-\dfrac{\pi}{2} < y < \dfrac{\pi}{2}$

65. $h(v) = \tan(\arccos v) = \dfrac{\sqrt{1 - v^2}}{v}$

Domain: $-1 \le v \le 1$, $v \ne 0$

Range: all real numbers

67. $f(t) = 3\cos 2t + 3\sin 2t = \sqrt{3^2 + 3^2}\, \sin\!\left(2t + \arctan\dfrac{3}{3}\right)$

$\qquad\qquad = 3\sqrt{2}\,\sin(2t + \arctan 1)$

$\qquad\qquad = 3\sqrt{2}\,\sin\!\left(2t + \dfrac{\pi}{4}\right)$

The graphs are the same.

69. $f(x) = \sin x$, $f^{-1}(x) = \arcsin x$

(a) $f \circ f^{-1} = f(f^{-1}(x)) = f(\arcsin x) = \sin(\arcsin x)$

$\quad f^{-1} \circ f = f^{-1}(f(x)) = f^{-1}(\sin x) = \arcsin(\sin x)$

(b) Both the domain and range of $f \circ f^{-1} = \sin(\arcsin x)$ are the intervals of $[-1, 1]$.

The domain of $f^{-1} \circ f$ is all real numbers. The range is still the interval $[-1, 1]$.

Neither graph is the line $y = x$ because of these domain/range restrictions.

71. (a) $\sin \theta = \dfrac{10}{s}$

$\theta = \arcsin \dfrac{10}{s}$

(b) $s = 48$: $\theta = \arcsin \dfrac{10}{48} \approx 0.21$

$s = 24$: $\theta = \arcsin \dfrac{10}{24} \approx 0.43$

73. $\beta = \arctan \dfrac{3x}{x^2 + 4}$

(a)

(b) β is maximum when $x = 2$.

(c) The graph has a horizontal asymptote at $\beta = 0$.
As x increases, β decreases.

75. (a) $\tan \theta = \dfrac{5}{x}$

$\theta = \arctan \dfrac{5}{x}$

(b) $x = 10$: $\theta = \arctan \dfrac{5}{10} \approx 26.6° = 0.46$ rad

$x = 3$: $\theta = \arctan \dfrac{5}{3} \approx 59.0° = 1.03$ rad

77. $y = \text{arccot } x$ if and only if $\cot y = x$.

Domain: $-\infty < x < \infty$

Range: $0 < x < \pi$

79. $y = \text{arccsc } x$ if and only if $\csc y = x$.

Domain: $(-\infty, -1] \cup [1, \infty)$

Range: $\left[-\dfrac{\pi}{2}, 0 \right) \cup \left(0, \dfrac{\pi}{2} \right]$

81. Let $y = \arcsin(-x)$. Then,

$\sin y = -x$

$-\sin y = x$

$\sin(-y) = x$

$-y = \arcsin x$

$y = -\arcsin x.$

Therefore, $\arcsin(-x) = -\arcsin x$.

83. $y = \pi - \arccos x$

$\cos y = \cos(\pi - \arccos x)$

$\cos y = \cos \pi \cos(\arccos x) + \sin \pi \sin(\arccos x)$

$\cos y = -x$

$y = \arccos(-x)$

85. Let $\alpha = \arcsin x$ and $\beta = \arccos x$. Then, $\sin \alpha = x$ and $\cos \beta = x$. Thus, $\sin \alpha = \cos \beta$ which implies that α and β are complementary angles and we have

$$\alpha + \beta = \dfrac{\pi}{2}$$

$$\arcsin x + \arccos x = \dfrac{\pi}{2}.$$

87. Now: Cost = 23,500 + 725 = \$24,225

Wait a month: Cost = 23,500 (1.04) = \$24,440

The customer should buy now and save \$215.

89. Let x = the number of people presently in the group. Each person's share is now $\dfrac{250,000}{x}$. If two more join the group, each person's share would then be $\dfrac{250,000}{x + 2}$.

$$\boxed{\begin{array}{c}\text{Share per person with} \\ \text{two more people}\end{array}} = \boxed{\begin{array}{c}\text{Original share} \\ \text{per person}\end{array}} - 6250$$

$$\frac{250,000}{x + 2} = \frac{250,000}{x} - 6250$$

$$250,000x = 250,000(x + 2) - 6250x(x + 2)$$

$$250,000x = 250,000x + 500,000 - 6250x^2 - 12500x$$

$$6250x^2 + 12500x - 500,000 = 0$$

$$6250(x^2 + 2x - 80) = 0$$

$$6250(x + 10)(x - 8) = 0$$

$$x = -10 \quad \text{or} \quad x = 8$$

Not possible

There were 8 people in the original group.

Section 5.7   Applications and Models

■   You should be able to solve right triangles.

■   You should be able to solve right triangle applications.

■   You should be able to solve applications of simple harmonic motion: $d = a \sin wt$ or $d = a \cos wt$

Solutions to Odd-Numbered Exercises

1. Given: $A = 20°$, $b = 10$

$$\tan A = \frac{a}{b} \implies a = b \tan A = 10 \tan 20° \approx 3.64$$

$$\cos A = \frac{a}{c} \implies c = \frac{a}{\cos A} = \frac{10}{\cos 20°} \approx 10.64$$

$$B = 90° - 20° = 70°$$

3. Given: $B = 71°$, $b = 24$

$$\tan B = \frac{b}{a} \implies a = \frac{b}{\tan B} = \frac{24}{\tan 71°} \approx 8.26$$

$$\sin B = \frac{b}{c} \implies c = \frac{b}{\sin B} = \frac{24}{\sin 71°} \approx 25.38$$

$$A = 90° - 71° = 19°$$

5. Given: $a = 6$, $b = 10$

$c^2 = a^2 + b^2 \implies c = \sqrt{36 + 100}$

$\qquad\qquad\qquad = 2\sqrt{34} \approx 11.66$

$\tan A = \dfrac{a}{b} = \dfrac{6}{10} \implies A = \arctan \dfrac{3}{5} \approx 30.96°$

$B = 90° - 30.964° = 59.04°$

7. $b = 16$, $c = 52$

$a = \sqrt{52^2 - 16^2}$

$\quad = \sqrt{2448} = 12\sqrt{17} \approx 49.48$

$\cos A = \dfrac{16}{52}$

$\qquad A = \arccos \dfrac{16}{52} \approx 72.08°$

$\qquad B = 90 - 72.08 \approx 17.92$

9. $A = 12° \, 15'$, $c = 430.5$

$B = 90° - 12° \, 15' = 77° \, 45'$

$\sin 12° \, 15' = \dfrac{a}{430.5}$

$\qquad a = 430.5 \sin 12° \, 15' \approx 91.34$

$\cos 12° \, 15' = \dfrac{b}{430.5}$

$\qquad b = 430.5 \cos 12° \, 15' \approx 420.70$

11. $\tan \theta = \dfrac{h}{\frac{1}{2}b} \implies h = \dfrac{1}{2}b \tan \theta$

$\qquad h = \dfrac{1}{2}b \tan \theta$

$\qquad h = \dfrac{1}{2}(4) \tan 52° \approx 2.56$ in.

13. (a) $\tan \theta = \dfrac{60}{L}$

$\qquad L = \dfrac{60}{\tan \theta}$

$\qquad = 60 \cot \theta$

(b)

θ	10°	20°	30°	40°	50°
L	340	165	104	72	50

(c) No, the shadow lengths do not increase in equal increments. The cotangent function is not linear.

15. (a) $\sin \theta = \dfrac{h}{20}$

$\qquad h = 20 \sin \theta$

(b)

θ	60°	65°	70°	75°	80°
h	17.3	18.1	18.8	19.3	19.7

17. (a)

(b) Let the height of the church $= x$ and the height of the church and steeple $= y$. Then:

$\tan 35° = \dfrac{x}{50}$ and $\tan 47° \, 40' = \dfrac{y}{50}$

$x = 50 \tan 35°$ and $y = 50 \tan 47° \, 40'$

$h = y - x = 50(\tan 47° \, 40' - \tan 35°)$

(c) $h \approx 19.9$ feet

19. $\sin 34° = \dfrac{x}{4000}$

$x = 4000 \sin 34°$

≈ 2236.8 feet

21. $\tan \theta = \dfrac{75}{50}$

$\theta = \arctan \dfrac{3}{2} \approx 56.3°$

23. $\sin \theta = \dfrac{4000}{4150}$

$\theta = \arcsin\left(\dfrac{4000}{4150}\right)$

$\theta \approx 74.5°$

$\alpha = 90° - 74.5° = 15.5°$

25. Since the airplane speed is

$$\left(275 \,\dfrac{\text{ft}}{\text{sec}}\right)\left(60 \,\dfrac{\text{sec}}{\text{min}}\right) = 16{,}500 \,\dfrac{\text{ft}}{\text{min}},$$

after one minute its distance travelled is 16,500 feet.

$\sin 18° = \dfrac{a}{16{,}500}$

$a = 16{,}500 \sin 18°$

≈ 5099 ft

27. $\sin 10.5° = \dfrac{x}{4}$

$x = 4 \sin 10.5°$

≈ 0.73 mile

29. The plane has traveled $1.5(550) = 825$ miles.

$\sin 38° = \dfrac{a}{825} \Rightarrow a \approx 508$ miles north

$\cos 38° = \dfrac{b}{825} \Rightarrow b \approx 650$ miles east

31. $\theta = 32°, \ \phi = 68°$

(a) $\alpha = 90° - 32° = 58°$

Bearing from A to C: N 58° E

(b) $\beta = \theta = 32°$

$\gamma = 90° - \phi = 22°$

$C = \beta + \gamma = 54°$

$\tan C = \dfrac{d}{50} \Rightarrow \tan 54° = \dfrac{d}{50} \Rightarrow d \approx 68.82$ yd

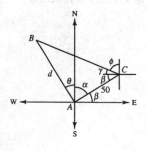

33. $\tan \theta = \dfrac{45}{30} \implies \theta \approx 56.3°$

Bearing: N 56.3° W

35. $\tan 6.5° = \dfrac{350}{d} \implies d \approx 3071.91$ ft

$\tan 4° = \dfrac{350}{D} \implies D \approx 5005.23$ ft

Distance between ships: $D - d \approx 1933.3$ ft

37. $\tan 57° = \dfrac{a}{x} \implies x = a \cot 57°$

$\tan 16° = \dfrac{a}{x + (55/6)}$

$\tan 16° = \dfrac{a}{a \cot 57° + (55/6)}$

$\cot 16° = \dfrac{a \cot 57° + (55/6)}{a}$

$a \cot 16° - a \cot 57° = \dfrac{55}{6} \implies a \approx 3.23$ miles

$\approx 17{,}054$ ft

39. $L_1: \ 3x - 2y = 5 \implies y = \dfrac{3}{2}x - \dfrac{5}{2} \implies m_1 = \dfrac{3}{2}$

$L_2: \ x - y = 1 \implies y = -x + 1 \implies m_2 = -1$

$\tan \alpha = \left| \dfrac{-1 - (3/2)}{1 + (-1)(3/2)} \right| = \left| \dfrac{-5/2}{-1/2} \right| = 5$

$\alpha = \arctan 5 \approx 78.7°$

41. The diagonal of the base has a length of $\sqrt{a^2 + a^2} = \sqrt{2}a$.

Now, we have:

$\tan \theta = \dfrac{a}{\sqrt{2}a} = \dfrac{1}{\sqrt{2}}$

$\theta = \arctan \dfrac{1}{\sqrt{2}}$

$\theta \approx 35.3°$

43. $\cos 30° = \dfrac{b}{r}$

$b = \cos 30° r$

$b = \dfrac{\sqrt{3}r}{2}$

$y = 2b = 2\left(\dfrac{\sqrt{3}r}{2} \right) = \sqrt{3}r$

45. $\sin 36° = \dfrac{d}{25} \implies d \approx 14.6946$

Length of side: $2d \approx 29.4$ inches

47. $\tan 35° = \dfrac{a}{10}$

$a = 10 \tan 35° \approx 7$

$\cos 33° = \dfrac{10}{c}$

$c = \dfrac{10}{\cos 35°} \approx 12.2$

49. $d = 4 \cos 8\pi t$

(a) Maximum displacement = amplitude = 4

(b) Frequency $= \dfrac{\omega}{2\pi} = \dfrac{8\pi}{2\pi}$

$\qquad\qquad = 4$ cycles per unit of time

(c) $8\pi t = \dfrac{\pi}{2} \implies t = \dfrac{1}{16}$

51. $d = \dfrac{1}{16} \sin 120\pi t$

(a) Maximum displacement = amplitude = $\dfrac{1}{16}$

(b) Frequency $= \dfrac{\omega}{2\pi} = \dfrac{120\pi}{2\pi}$

$\qquad\qquad = 60$ cycles per unit of time

(c) $120\pi t = \pi \implies t = \dfrac{1}{120}$

53. $d = 0$ when $t = 0$, $a = 4$, Period $= 2$

Use $d = a \sin \omega t$ since $d = 0$ when $t = 0$

$\dfrac{2\pi}{\omega} = 2 \implies \omega = \pi$

Thus, $d = 4 \sin \pi t$.

55. $d = 3$ when $t = 0$, $a = 3$, Period $= 1.5$

Use $d = a \cos \omega t$ since $d = 3$ when $t = 0$

$\dfrac{2\pi}{\omega} = 1.5 \implies \omega = \dfrac{4\pi}{3}$

Thus, $d = 3 \cos\left(\dfrac{4\pi}{3}t\right) = 3 \cos\left(\dfrac{4\pi t}{3}\right)$.

57. $d = a \sin \omega t$

$\text{Period} = \dfrac{2\pi}{\omega} = \dfrac{1}{\text{frequency}}$

$\dfrac{2\pi}{\omega} = \dfrac{1}{264}$

$\omega = 2\pi(264) = 528\pi$

59. $y = \dfrac{1}{4} \cos 16t$, $t > 0$

(a)

(b) Period: $\dfrac{2\pi}{16} = \dfrac{\pi}{8}$ seconds

(c) $\dfrac{1}{4} \cos 16t = 0$ when $16t = \dfrac{\pi}{2} \implies t = \dfrac{\pi}{32}$ seconds.

61. $S(t) = 18.09 + 1.41 \sin\left(\dfrac{\pi t}{6} + 4.60\right)$

(a)

(b) The period is 12 months, which corresponds to 1 year.

(c) The amplitude is 1.41. This gives the maximum change in time from the average time (18.09) of sunset.

63. (a)

(b) $a = \dfrac{1}{2}(14.30 - 1.70) = 6.3$

$\dfrac{2\pi}{b} = 12 \implies b = \dfrac{\pi}{6}$

Shift: $d = 14.3 - 6.3 = 8$

$S = d + a \cos bt$

$S = 8 + 6.3 \cos\left(\dfrac{\pi t}{6}\right)$

The model is a good fit.

(c) Period: $\dfrac{2\pi}{\pi/6} = 12$

This corresponds to the 12 months in a year. Since the sales of outerwear is seasonal, this is reasonable.

(d) The amplitude represents the maximum displacement from the average sale of 8 million dollars. Sales are greatest in December (cold weather + Christmas) and least in June.

❏ Review Exercises for Chapter 5

Solutions to Odd-Numbered Exercises

1. $\theta = \dfrac{11\pi}{4}$

Coterminal angles: $\dfrac{11\pi}{4} - 2\pi = \dfrac{3\pi}{4}$

$\dfrac{3\pi}{4} - 2\pi = -\dfrac{5\pi}{4}$

3. $\theta = -110°$

Coterminal angles: $-110° + 360° = 250°$

$-110° - 360° = -470°$

5. $135°\, 16'\, 45'' = \left(135 + \dfrac{16}{60} + \dfrac{45}{3600}\right)° \approx 135.28°$

7. $5°\, 22'\, 53'' = \left(5 + \dfrac{22}{60} + \dfrac{53}{3600}\right)° \approx 5.38°$

9. $135.27° = 135° + (0.27)(60)'$
$= 135° + 16' + 0.2(60)''$
$= 135°\, 16'\, 12''$

11. $-85.15° = -[85° + (0.15)(60)'] = -85°\, 9'$

13. $\dfrac{5\pi\,\text{rad}}{7} = \dfrac{5\pi\,\text{rad}}{7} \cdot \dfrac{180°}{\pi\,\text{rad}} \approx 128.57°$

15. $-3.5\,\text{rad} = -3.5\,\text{rad} \cdot \dfrac{180°}{\pi\,\text{rad}} \approx -200.54°$

17. $480° = 480° \cdot \dfrac{\pi \, \text{rad}}{180°} = \dfrac{8\pi}{3} \, \text{rad} \approx 8.3776 \, \text{rad}$

19. $-33° \, 45' = -33.75° = -33.75° \cdot \dfrac{\pi \, \text{rad}}{180°} = -\dfrac{3\pi}{16} \, \text{rad} \approx -0.5890 \, \text{rad}$

21. $252°$ is in Quadrant III.

Reference angle $= 252° - 180° = 72°$

23. $-\dfrac{6\pi}{5}$ is in Quadrant II and is coterminal to $\dfrac{4\pi}{5}$.

Reference angle $= \pi - \dfrac{4\pi}{5} = \dfrac{\pi}{5}$

25. $s = r\theta \implies \theta = \dfrac{s}{r} = \dfrac{25}{12}$

27. $s = r\theta = (20)(2.41) = 48.20$

29. The hypotenuse is $\sqrt{12^2 + 10^2} = \sqrt{244} = 2\sqrt{61}$.

$\sin\theta = \dfrac{\text{opp}}{\text{hyp}} = \dfrac{10}{2\sqrt{61}} = \dfrac{5}{\sqrt{61}} = \dfrac{5\sqrt{61}}{61}$ $\cos\theta = \dfrac{\text{adj}}{\text{hyp}} = \dfrac{12}{2\sqrt{61}} = \dfrac{6}{\sqrt{61}} = \dfrac{6\sqrt{61}}{61}$

$\csc\theta = \dfrac{1}{\sin\theta} = \dfrac{\sqrt{61}}{5}$ $\sec\theta = \dfrac{1}{\cos\theta} = \dfrac{\sqrt{61}}{6}$

$\tan\theta = \dfrac{\text{opp}}{\text{adj}} = \dfrac{10}{12} = \dfrac{5}{6}$ $\cot\theta = \dfrac{1}{\tan\theta} = \dfrac{6}{5}$

31. The opposite side is $\sqrt{6^2 - 4^2} = \sqrt{36 - 16} = \sqrt{20} = 2\sqrt{5}$.

$\sin\theta = \dfrac{\text{opp}}{\text{hyp}} = \dfrac{2\sqrt{5}}{6} = \dfrac{\sqrt{5}}{3}$ $\cos\theta = \dfrac{\text{adj}}{\text{hyp}} = \dfrac{4}{6} = \dfrac{2}{3}$

$\csc\theta = \dfrac{1}{\sin\theta} = \dfrac{3}{\sqrt{5}} = \dfrac{3\sqrt{5}}{5}$ $\sec\theta = \dfrac{1}{\cos\theta} = \dfrac{3}{2}$

$\tan\theta = \dfrac{\text{opp}}{\text{adj}} = \dfrac{2\sqrt{5}}{4} = \dfrac{\sqrt{5}}{2}$ $\cot\theta = \dfrac{1}{\tan\theta} = \dfrac{2}{\sqrt{5}} = \dfrac{2\sqrt{5}}{5}$

33. $x = 12, y = 16$

$r = \sqrt{144 + 256} = \sqrt{400} = 20$

$\sin\theta = \dfrac{y}{r} = \dfrac{4}{5}$ $\csc\theta = \dfrac{r}{y} = \dfrac{5}{4}$

$\cos\theta = \dfrac{x}{r} = \dfrac{3}{5}$ $\sec\theta = \dfrac{r}{x} = \dfrac{5}{3}$

$\tan\theta = \dfrac{y}{x} = \dfrac{4}{3}$ $\cot\theta = \dfrac{x}{y} = \dfrac{3}{4}$

35. $x = -7, y = 2, r = \sqrt{49 + 4} = \sqrt{53}$

$\sin\theta = \dfrac{y}{r} = \dfrac{2}{\sqrt{53}} = \dfrac{2\sqrt{53}}{53}$ $\csc\theta = \dfrac{\sqrt{53}}{2}$

$\cos\theta = \dfrac{x}{r} = -\dfrac{7}{\sqrt{53}} = -\dfrac{7\sqrt{53}}{53}$ $\sec\theta = -\dfrac{\sqrt{53}}{7}$

$\tan\theta = \dfrac{y}{x} = -\dfrac{2}{7}$ $\cot\theta = -\dfrac{7}{2}$

37. $x = -4, y = -6, r = \sqrt{16 + 36} = 2\sqrt{13}$

$\sin\theta = \dfrac{y}{r} = \dfrac{-6}{2\sqrt{13}} = -\dfrac{3\sqrt{13}}{13}$ $\csc\theta = -\dfrac{\sqrt{13}}{3}$

$\cos\theta = \dfrac{x}{r} = \dfrac{-4}{2\sqrt{13}} = -\dfrac{2\sqrt{13}}{13}$ $\sec\theta = -\dfrac{\sqrt{13}}{2}$

$\tan\theta = \dfrac{y}{x} = \dfrac{-6}{-4} = \dfrac{3}{2}$ $\cot\theta = \dfrac{2}{3}$

39. $\sec\theta = \dfrac{6}{5}$, $\tan\theta < 0 \implies \theta$ is in Quadrant IV.

$r = 6$, $x = 5$, $y = -\sqrt{36 - 25} = -\sqrt{11}$

$\sin\theta = \dfrac{y}{r} = -\dfrac{\sqrt{11}}{6}$ $\qquad$ $\csc\theta = -\dfrac{6\sqrt{11}}{11}$

$\cos\theta = \dfrac{x}{r} = \dfrac{5}{6}$ $\qquad$ $\sec\theta = \dfrac{6}{5}$

$\tan\theta = \dfrac{y}{x} = -\dfrac{\sqrt{11}}{5}$ $\qquad$ $\cot\theta = -\dfrac{5\sqrt{11}}{11}$

41. $\sin\theta = \dfrac{3}{8}$, $\cos\theta < 0 \implies \theta$ is in Quadrant II.

$y = 3$, $r = 8$, $x = -\sqrt{55}$

$\sin\theta = \dfrac{y}{r} = \dfrac{3}{8}$ $\qquad$ $\csc\theta = \dfrac{8}{3}$

$\cos\theta = \dfrac{x}{r} = -\dfrac{\sqrt{55}}{8}$ $\qquad$ $\sec\theta = -\dfrac{8}{\sqrt{55}} = -\dfrac{8\sqrt{55}}{55}$

$\tan\theta = \dfrac{y}{x} = -\dfrac{3}{\sqrt{55}} = -\dfrac{3\sqrt{55}}{55}$ $\qquad$ $\cot\theta = -\dfrac{\sqrt{55}}{3}$

43. $\tan\dfrac{\pi}{3} = \sqrt{3}$ $\qquad\qquad$ **45.** $\sin\dfrac{5\pi}{3} = -\sin\dfrac{\pi}{3} = -\dfrac{\sqrt{3}}{2}$ $\qquad\qquad$ **47.** $\cos 495° = -\cos 45° = -\dfrac{\sqrt{2}}{2}$

49. $\tan 33° \approx 0.65$ $\qquad\qquad\qquad\qquad$ **51.** $\sec\dfrac{12\pi}{5} = \dfrac{1}{\cos(12\pi/5)} \approx 3.24$

53. $\cos\theta = -\dfrac{\sqrt{2}}{2} \implies \theta$ is in Quadrant II or III. $\qquad$ **55.** $\csc\theta = -2 \implies \theta$ is in Quadrant III or IV.

Reference angle: $\dfrac{\pi}{4}$ $\qquad\qquad\qquad\qquad\qquad\qquad\qquad$ Reference angle: $\dfrac{\pi}{6}$

$\theta = \dfrac{3\pi}{4}, \dfrac{5\pi}{4}$ or $\theta = 135°, 225°$ $\qquad\qquad\qquad$ $\theta = \dfrac{7\pi}{6}, \dfrac{11\pi}{6}$ or $\theta = 210°, 330°$

57. $\sin\theta = 0.8387 \implies \theta$ is in Quadrant I or II. $\qquad$ **59.** $\sec\theta = -1.0353$, θ is in Quadrant II or III.

$\qquad = \arcsin 0.8387$ $\qquad\qquad\qquad\qquad\qquad\qquad$ Reference angle: $15.0°$

$\theta \approx 0.9949$ rad or $0.9949 \cdot \dfrac{180}{\pi} = 57.0°$ $\qquad\qquad$ $\theta = 165.0°$ or $165° \cdot \dfrac{\pi}{180°} \approx 2.8798$ rad

$\theta \approx \pi - 0.9949 \approx 2.1467$ rad or $\qquad\qquad\qquad$ $\theta = 195.0°$ or $195° \cdot \dfrac{\pi}{180°} \approx 3.4034$ rad

$2.1467 \cdot \dfrac{180}{\pi} = 123.0°$

61. Period: 2, amplitude: 5 $\qquad\qquad\qquad\qquad$ **63.** Period: $3.14 \approx \pi$, amplitude: 3.4

65. $y = 3 \cos 2\pi x$

Amplitude: 3

Period: $\dfrac{2\pi}{2\pi} = 1$

67. $f(x) = 5 \sin \dfrac{2x}{5}$

Amplitude: 5

Period: $\dfrac{2\pi}{2/5} = 5\pi$

69. $f(x) = -\dfrac{1}{4} \cos \dfrac{\pi x}{4}$

Amplitude: $\left| -\dfrac{1}{4} \right| = \dfrac{1}{4}$

Period: $\dfrac{2\pi}{\pi/4} = 8$

71. $g(t) = \dfrac{5}{2} \sin(t - \pi)$

Amplitude: $\dfrac{5}{2}$

Period: 2π

Shift:

$t - \pi = 0$ and $t - \pi = 2\pi$

$\quad\quad t = \pi \quad\quad\quad\quad t = 3\pi$

73. $h(t) = \tan\left(t - \dfrac{\pi}{4}\right)$

Period: π

Two consecutive asymptotes: $t - \dfrac{\pi}{4} = -\dfrac{\pi}{2}$ and $t - \dfrac{\pi}{4} = \dfrac{\pi}{2}$

$\quad\quad\quad\quad\quad\quad\quad\quad\quad t = -\dfrac{\pi}{4} \quad\quad\quad\quad t = \dfrac{3\pi}{4}$

t	0	$\dfrac{\pi}{4}$	$\dfrac{\pi}{2}$
$h(t)$	-1	0	1

75. $f(t) = \csc\left(3t - \dfrac{\pi}{2}\right)$

Graph: $y = \sin\left(3t - \dfrac{\pi}{2}\right)$ first.

Period: $\dfrac{2\pi}{3}$

Shift: $3t - \dfrac{\pi}{2} = 0$ and $3t - \dfrac{\pi}{2} = 2\pi$

$\quad\quad\quad\quad t = \dfrac{\pi}{6} \quad\quad\quad\quad t = \dfrac{5\pi}{6}$

77. $y = \arcsin\dfrac{x}{2}$

Domain: $-2 \le x \le 2$

Range: $-\dfrac{\pi}{2} \le y \le \dfrac{\pi}{2}$

79. $f(x) = \dfrac{x}{4} - \sin x$

Not periodic

81. $f(x) = \dfrac{\pi}{2} + \arctan x$

Not periodic

83. $h(\theta) = \theta \sin \pi\theta$

Not periodic

85. $f(t) = 2.5e^{-t/4} \sin 2\pi t$

$-2.5e^{-t/4} \le f(t) \le 2.5e^{-t/4}$

Not periodic

87. $g(x) = 3\left(\sin\dfrac{\pi x}{3} + 1\right)$

Period: $\dfrac{2\pi}{\pi/3} = 6$

89. $f(x) = e^{\sin x}$

The graph is periodic.

Maximum: $\left(\dfrac{\pi}{2},\, e\right)$

Minimum: $\left(\dfrac{3\pi}{2},\, e^{-1}\right)$

91. $g(x) = 2 \sin x \cos^2 x$

The graph is periodic.

Relative minimum: $\left(\dfrac{\pi}{2}, 0\right)$, $(3.76, -0.77)$, $(5.67, -0.77)$

Relative maximum: $(0.61, 0.77)$, $(2.53, 0.77)$, $\left(\dfrac{3\pi}{2}, 0\right)$

93. $f(x) = -2 \cos\left(x - \dfrac{\pi}{4}\right)$ **95.** $f(x) = -4 \cos\left(2x - \dfrac{\pi}{2}\right)$ **97.** $f(x) = \dfrac{1}{2}\tan\dfrac{x}{2}$

99. Let $y = \arcsin(x - 1)$. Then,

$\sin y = (x - 1) = \dfrac{x - 1}{1}$ and

$\sec y = \dfrac{1}{\sqrt{-x^2 + 2x}} = \dfrac{\sqrt{-x^2 + 2x}}{-x^2 + 2x}$.

101. Let $y = \arccos\dfrac{x^2}{4 - x^2}$ Then

$\cos y = \dfrac{x}{4 - x^2}$ and

$\sin y = \dfrac{\sqrt{(4 - x^2)^2 - (x^2)^2}}{4 - x^2}$

$= \dfrac{\sqrt{16 - 8x^2}}{4 - x^2}$

$= \dfrac{2\sqrt{4 - 2x^2}}{4 - x^2}$.

103. $\sin 50° = \dfrac{h}{12}$

$h = 12 \sin 50°$

≈ 9.2 m

105. $\tan 25° = \dfrac{h}{2.5}$

$h = 2.5 \tan 25°$

≈ 1.2 miles

107. $\tan 1°\,10' = \dfrac{a}{3.5}$

$a = 3.5 \tan 1°\,10'$

≈ 0.071 km

109. (a) $\tan \theta = \dfrac{x}{12}$

$x = 12 \tan \theta$

Area = Area of triangle − Area of sector

$= \left(\dfrac{1}{2}bh\right) - \left(\dfrac{1}{2}r^2\theta\right)$

$= \dfrac{1}{2}(12)(12 \tan \theta) - \dfrac{1}{2}(12^2)(\theta)$

$= 72 \tan \theta - 72\theta$

$= 72(\tan \theta - \theta)$

(b)

As $\theta \to \dfrac{\pi}{2}$, $A \to \infty$. The area increases without

bound as θ approaches $\dfrac{\pi}{2}$.

❑ **Chapter Test for Chapter 5**

1. (a)

(b) $\dfrac{5\pi}{4} + 2\pi = \dfrac{13\pi}{4}$; $\dfrac{5\pi}{4} - 2\pi = -\dfrac{3\pi}{4}$

(c) $\dfrac{5\pi}{4} \cdot \dfrac{180}{\pi} = 225°$

2. $(90{,}000 \text{ meters/hr})\left(\dfrac{1}{60}\text{ hr/min}\right)\left(\dfrac{2\pi\text{ rad}}{2\pi\left(\frac{1}{2}\right)\text{ meters}}\right) = 3000 \text{ rad/min}$

3. $\sin \theta = \dfrac{4}{\sqrt{17}} = \dfrac{4\sqrt{17}}{17}$ $\csc \theta = \dfrac{\sqrt{17}}{4}$

   $\cos \theta = -\dfrac{1}{\sqrt{17}} = -\dfrac{\sqrt{17}}{17}$ $\sec \theta = -\sqrt{17}$

   $\tan \theta = -4$ $\cot \theta = -\dfrac{1}{4}$

4. $\tan \theta = \dfrac{3}{2} > 0 \;\Rightarrow\; \theta$ is in Quadrant I or III.

   $\cot \theta = \dfrac{2}{3}$

   $\sin \theta = \pm\dfrac{3}{\sqrt{13}} = \pm\dfrac{3\sqrt{13}}{13}$ $\cos \theta = \pm\dfrac{2}{\sqrt{13}} = \pm\dfrac{2\sqrt{13}}{13}$

   $\csc \theta = \pm\dfrac{\sqrt{13}}{3}$ $\sec \theta = \pm\dfrac{\sqrt{13}}{2}$

5. $\theta = 290° \;\Rightarrow\; \theta' = 70°$

6. $\sec \theta = \dfrac{1}{\cos \theta} < 0 \;\Rightarrow\;$ Quadrants II or III

   $\tan \theta > 0 \;\Rightarrow\;$ Quadrants I or III

   Hence, Quadrant III.

7. If $\cos \theta = -\dfrac{\sqrt{13}}{2}$, then θ is in Quadrant II or III.

   $\theta = 150°, \ 210°$

8. $\csc \theta = \dfrac{1}{\sin \theta} = 1.030 \;\Rightarrow\; \sin \theta = \dfrac{1}{1.030}$ and θ in Quadrant I or II. Using a calculator, $\theta = 1.33,$
   1.81 radians.

9. Amplitude: 2, shifted $\dfrac{\pi}{4}$ to the right.

10.

Period: $\dfrac{\pi}{2}$

11.

Period is 2

12.

Not periodic

13. Amplitude = 2, reflected in x-axis $\implies$ $a = -2$.

Period 4π and shifted to the right: $y = -2\sin\left(\dfrac{x}{2} - \dfrac{\pi}{4}\right)$

14. Let $u = \arccos\dfrac{2}{3}$ $\implies$ $\cos u = \dfrac{2}{3}$.

Then $\tan\left(\arccos\dfrac{2}{3}\right) = \tan u = \dfrac{\sqrt{5}}{2}$.

15.

16. $(18)(3) = 54$ miles from port

$\sin 16° = -\dfrac{x}{54} \implies x = -14.88$

$\cos 16° = \dfrac{y}{54} \implies y = 51.91$

Position: $(-14.88, 51.91)$

❏ Practice Test for Chapter 5

1 Express 350° in radian measure.

2. Express $(5\pi)/9$ in degree measure.

3. Convert 135° 14′ 12″ to decimal form.

4. Convert −22.569° to D° M′ S″ form.

5. If $\cos \theta = \frac{2}{3}$, use the trigonometric identities to find $\tan \theta$.

6. Find θ given $\sin \theta = 0.9063$.

7. Solve for x in the figure below.

8. Find the magnitude of the reference angle for $\theta = (6\pi)/5$.

9. Evaluate csc 3.92.

10. Find $\sec \theta$ given that θ lies in Quadrant III and $\tan \theta = 6$.

11. Graph $y = 3 \sin \dfrac{\pi}{2}$.

12. Graph $y = -2 \cos(x - \pi)$.

13. Graph $y = \tan 2x$.

14. Graph $y = -\csc\left(x + \dfrac{\pi}{4}\right)$.

15. Graph $y = 2x + \sin x$, using a graphing calculator.

16. Graph $y = 3x \cos x$, using a graphing calculator.

17. Evaluate arcsin 1.

18. Evaluate arctan(−3).

19. Evaluate $\sin\left(\arccos\dfrac{4}{\sqrt{35}}\right)$.

20. Write an algebraic expression for $\cos\left(\arcsin\dfrac{x}{4}\right)$.

For Exercises 21–23, solve the right triangle.

21. $A = 40°$, $c = 12$

22. $B = 6.84°$, $a = 21.3$

23. $a = 5$, $b = 9$

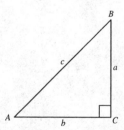

24. A 20-foot ladder leans against the side of a barn. Find the height of the top of the ladder if the angle of elevation of the ladder is 67°.

25. An observer in a lighthouse 250 feet above sea level spots a ship off the shore. If the angle of depression to the ship is 5°, how far out is the ship?

C H A P T E R   6
Analytic Trigonometry

CHAPTER 6
Analytic Trigonometry

Section 6.1   Using Fundamental Identities

■ You should know the fundamental trigonometric identities.

(a) Reciprocal Identities

$$\sin u = \frac{1}{\csc u} \qquad\qquad \csc u = \frac{1}{\sin u}$$

$$\cos u = \frac{1}{\sec u} \qquad\qquad \sec u = \frac{1}{\cos u}$$

$$\tan u = \frac{1}{\cot u} = \frac{\sin u}{\cos u} \qquad \cot u = \frac{1}{\tan u} = \frac{\cos u}{\sin u}$$

(b) Pythagorean Identities

$$\sin^2 u + \cos^2 u = 1$$
$$1 + \tan^2 u = \sec^2 u$$
$$1 + \cot^2 u = \csc^2 u$$

(c) Cofunction Identities

$$\sin\left(\frac{\pi}{2} - u\right) = \cos u \qquad \cos\left(\frac{\pi}{2} - u\right) = \sin u$$

$$\tan\left(\frac{\pi}{2} - u\right) = \cot u \qquad \cot\left(\frac{\pi}{2} - u\right) = \tan u$$

$$\sec\left(\frac{\pi}{2} - u\right) = \csc u \qquad \csc\left(\frac{\pi}{2} - u\right) = \sec u$$

(d) Negative Angle Identities

$$\sin(-x) = -\sin x \qquad \csc(-x) = -\csc x$$
$$\cos(-x) = \cos x \qquad \sec(-x) = \sec x$$
$$\tan(-x) = -\tan x \qquad \cot(-x) = -\cot x$$

■ You should be able to use these fundamental identities to find function values.

■ You should be able to convert trigonometric expressions to equivalent forms by using the fundamental identities.

■ You should be able to check your answers with a graphing utility.

Solutions to Odd-Numbered Exercises

1. $\sin x = \dfrac{1}{2}$, $\cos x = \dfrac{\sqrt{3}}{2} \implies x$ is in

Quadrant I.

$\tan x = \dfrac{\sin x}{\cos x} = \dfrac{1/2}{\sqrt{3}/2} = \dfrac{1}{\sqrt{3}} = \dfrac{\sqrt{3}}{3}$

$\cot x = \dfrac{1}{\tan x} = \sqrt{3}$

$\sec x = \dfrac{1}{\cos x} = \dfrac{2}{\sqrt{3}} = \dfrac{2\sqrt{3}}{3}$

$\csc x = \dfrac{1}{\sin x} = 2$

3. $\sec \theta = \sqrt{2}$, $\sin \theta = -\dfrac{\sqrt{2}}{2} \implies \theta$ is in

Quadrant IV.

$\cos \theta = \dfrac{1}{\sec \theta} = \dfrac{1}{\sqrt{2}} = \dfrac{\sqrt{2}}{2}$

$\tan \theta = \dfrac{\sin \theta}{\cos \theta} = \dfrac{-\sqrt{2}/2}{\sqrt{2}/2} = -1$

$\cot \theta = \dfrac{1}{\tan \theta} = -1$

$\csc \theta = -\sqrt{2}$

5. $\tan x = \dfrac{5}{12}$, $\sec x = -\dfrac{13}{12} \implies x$ is in

Quadrant III.

$\cos x = \dfrac{1}{\sec x} = -\dfrac{12}{13}$

$\sin x = -\sqrt{1 - \cos^2 x} = -\sqrt{1 - \dfrac{144}{169}} = -\dfrac{5}{13}$

$\cot x = \dfrac{1}{\tan x} = \dfrac{12}{5}$

$\csc x = \dfrac{1}{\sin x} = -\dfrac{13}{5}$

7. $\sec \phi = -1$, $\sin \phi = 0 \implies \phi = \pi$

$\cos \phi = -1$

$\tan \phi = 0$

$\cot \phi$ is undefined.

$\csc \phi$ is undefined.

9. $\sin(-x) = -\sin x = -\dfrac{2}{3} \implies \sin x = \dfrac{2}{3}$

$\sin x = \dfrac{2}{3}$, $\tan x = -\dfrac{2\sqrt{5}}{5} \implies x$ is in

Quadrant II.

$\cos x = -\sqrt{1 - \sin^2 x} = -\sqrt{1 - \dfrac{4}{9}} = -\dfrac{\sqrt{5}}{3}$

$\cot x = \dfrac{1}{\tan x} = -\dfrac{\sqrt{5}}{2}$

$\sec x = \dfrac{1}{\cos x} = -\dfrac{3\sqrt{5}}{5}$

$\csc x = \dfrac{1}{\sin x} = \dfrac{3}{2}$

11. $\tan \theta = 2$, $\sin \theta < 0 \implies \theta$ is in Quadrant III.

$\sec \theta = -\sqrt{\tan^2 \theta + 1} = -\sqrt{4 + 1} = -\sqrt{5}$

$\cos \theta = \dfrac{1}{\sec \theta} = -\dfrac{1}{\sqrt{5}} = -\dfrac{\sqrt{5}}{5}$

$\sin \theta = -\sqrt{1 - \cos^2 \theta}$

$\qquad = -\sqrt{1 - \dfrac{1}{5}} = -\dfrac{2}{\sqrt{5}} = -\dfrac{2\sqrt{5}}{5}$

$\csc \theta = \dfrac{1}{\sin \theta} = -\dfrac{\sqrt{5}}{2}$

$\cot \theta = \dfrac{1}{\tan \theta} = \dfrac{1}{2}$

13. $\sin \theta = -1$, $\cot \theta = 0 \implies \theta = \dfrac{3\pi}{2}$

$\cos \theta = \sqrt{1 - \sin^2 \theta} = 0$

$\sec \theta$ is undefined.

$\tan \theta$ is undefined.

$\csc \theta = -1$

15. By looking at the basic graphs of $\sin x$ and $\csc x$, we

see that as $x \to \dfrac{\pi^-}{2}$, $\sin x \to 1$ and $\csc x \to 1$.

17. By looking at the basic graphs of $\tan x$ and $\cot x$, we see that as $x \rightarrow \dfrac{\pi^-}{2}$, $\tan x \rightarrow \infty$ and $\cot x \rightarrow 0$.

19. $\sec x \cos x = \sec x \cdot \dfrac{1}{\sec x} = 1$

The expression is matched with (d).

21. $\tan^2 x - \sec^2 x = \tan^2 x - (\tan^2 x + 1) = -1$

The expression is matched with (a).

23. $\dfrac{\sin(-x)}{\cos(-x)} = \dfrac{-\sin x}{\cos x} = -\tan x$

The expression is matched with (e).

25. $\sin x \sec x = \sin x \cdot \dfrac{1}{\cos x} = \tan x$

The expression is matched with (b).

27. $\sec^4 x - \tan^4 x = (\sec^2 x + \tan^2 x)(\sec^2 x - \tan^2 x)$

$\qquad = (\sec^2 x + \tan^2 x)(1) = \sec^2 x + \tan^2 x$

The expression is matched with (f).

29. $\dfrac{\sec^2 x - 1}{\sin^2 x} = \dfrac{\tan^2 x}{\sin^2 x} = \dfrac{\sin^2 x}{\cos^2 x} \cdot \dfrac{1}{\sin^2 x} = \sec^2 x$

The expression is matched with (e).

31. $\tan \phi \csc \phi = \dfrac{\sin \phi}{\cos \phi} \cdot \dfrac{1}{\sin \phi} = \dfrac{1}{\cos \phi} = \sec \phi$

33. $\cos \beta \tan \beta = \cos \beta \left(\dfrac{\sin \beta}{\cos \beta} \right)$

$\qquad\qquad = \sin \beta$

35. $\dfrac{\cot x}{\csc x} = \dfrac{\cos x / \sin x}{1 / \sin x}$

$\qquad = \dfrac{\cos x}{\sin x} \cdot \dfrac{\sin x}{1} = \cos x$

37. $\sec \alpha \dfrac{\sin \alpha}{\tan \alpha} = \dfrac{1}{\cos \alpha}(\sin \alpha) \cot \alpha$

$\qquad = \dfrac{1}{\cos \alpha}(\sin \alpha) \left(\dfrac{\cos \alpha}{\sin \alpha} \right) = 1$

39. $\dfrac{\sin(-x)}{\cos x} = -\dfrac{\sin x}{\cos x} = -\tan x$

41. $\cos \left(\dfrac{\pi}{2} - x \right) \sec x = (\sin x)(\sec x)$

$\qquad\qquad = (\sin x) \left(\dfrac{1}{\cos x} \right)$

$\qquad\qquad = \dfrac{\sin x}{\cos x}$

$\qquad\qquad = \tan x$

43. $\dfrac{\cos^2 y}{1 - \sin y} = \dfrac{1 - \sin^2 y}{1 - \sin y}$

$\qquad = \dfrac{(1 + \sin y)(1 - \sin y)}{1 - \sin y}$

$\qquad = 1 + \sin y$

45. $\tan^2 x - \tan^2 x \sin^2 x = \tan^2 x(1 - \sin^2 x)$

$\qquad\qquad = \tan^2 x \cos^2 x$

$\qquad\qquad = \dfrac{\sin^2 x}{\cos^2 x} \cdot \cos^2 x$

$\qquad\qquad = \sin^2 x$

47. $\sin^2 x \sec^2 x - \sin^2 x = \sin^2 x(\sec^2 x - 1)$
$$= \sin^2 x \tan^2 x$$

49. $\tan^4 x + 2\tan^2 x + 1 = (\tan^2 x + 1)^2$
$$= (\sec^2 x)^2$$
$$= \sec^4 x$$

51. $\sin^4 x - \cos^4 x = (\sin^2 x + \cos^2 x)(\sin^2 x - \cos^2 x)$
$$= (1)(\sin^2 x - \cos^2 x)$$
$$= \sin^2 x - \cos^2 x$$

53. $(\sin x + \cos x)^2 = \sin^2 x + 2\sin x \cos x + \cos^2 x$
$$= (\sin^2 x + \cos^2 x) + 2\sin x \cos x$$
$$= 1 + 2\sin x \cos x$$

55. $(\sec x + 1)(\sec x - 1) = \sec^2 x - 1 = \tan^2 x$

57. $\dfrac{1}{1 + \cos x} + \dfrac{1}{1 - \cos x} = \dfrac{1 - \cos x + 1 + \cos x}{(1 + \cos x)(1 - \cos x)}$
$$= \dfrac{2}{1 - \cos^2 x}$$
$$= \dfrac{2}{\sin^2 x}$$
$$= 2\csc^2 x$$

59. $\dfrac{\cos x}{1 + \sin x} + \dfrac{1 + \sin x}{\cos x} = \dfrac{\cos^2 x + (1 + \sin x)^2}{\cos x(1 + \sin x)}$
$$= \dfrac{2 + 2\sin x}{\cos x(1 + \sin x)}$$
$$= \dfrac{2(1 + \sin x)}{\cos x(1 + \sin x)}$$
$$= \dfrac{2}{\cos x}$$
$$= 2\sec x$$

61. $\dfrac{\sin^2 y}{1 - \cos y} = \dfrac{1 - \cos^2 y}{1 - \cos y}$
$$= \dfrac{(1 + \cos y)(1 - \cos y)}{1 - \cos y}$$
$$= 1 + \cos y$$

63. $\dfrac{3}{\sec x - \tan x} \cdot \dfrac{\sec x + \tan x}{\sec x + \tan x} = \dfrac{3(\sec x + \tan x)}{\sec^2 x - \tan^2 x}$
$$= \dfrac{3(\sec x + \tan x)}{1}$$
$$= 3(\sec x + \tan x)$$

65. $y_1 = \cos\left(\dfrac{\pi}{2} - x\right)$, $y_2 = \sin x$

x	0.2	0.4	0.6	0.8	1.0	1.2	1.4
y_1	0.1987	0.3894	0.5646	0.7174	0.8415	0.9320	0.9854
y_2	0.1987	0.3894	0.5646	0.7174	0.8415	0.9320	0.9854

Conclusion: $y_1 = y_2$

67. $y_1 = \dfrac{\cos x}{1 - \sin x}$, $y_2 = \dfrac{1 + \sin x}{\cos x}$

x	0.2	0.4	0.6	0.8	1.0	1.2	1.4
y_1	1.2230	1.5085	1.8958	2.4650	3.4082	5.3319	11.6814
y_2	1.2230	1.5085	1.8958	2.4650	3.4082	5.3319	11.6814

Conclusion: $y_1 = y_2$

69. $y_1 = \cos x \cot x + \sin x = \csc x$

71. $\sqrt{25 - x^2} = \sqrt{25 - (5\sin\theta)^2}$, $x - 5\sin\theta$

$\qquad = \sqrt{25 - 25\sin^2\theta}$

$\qquad = \sqrt{25(1 - \sin^2\theta)}$

$\qquad = \sqrt{25\cos^2\theta}$

$\qquad = 5\cos\theta$

73. $\sqrt{x^2 - 9} = \sqrt{(3\sec\theta)^2 - 9}$, $x = 3\sec\theta$

$\qquad = \sqrt{9\sec^2\theta - 9}$

$\qquad = \sqrt{9(\sec^2\theta - 1)}$

$\qquad = \sqrt{9\tan^2\theta}$

$\qquad = 3\tan\theta$

75. $\sqrt{x^2 + 25} = \sqrt{(5\tan\theta)^2 + 25}$, $x = 5\tan\theta$

$\qquad = \sqrt{25\tan^2\theta + 25}$

$\qquad = \sqrt{25(\tan^2\theta + 1)}$

$\qquad = \sqrt{25\sec^2\theta}$

$\qquad = 5\sec\theta$

77. $\sin\theta = \sqrt{1 - \cos^2\theta}$

Let $y_1 = \sin x$ and $y_2 = \sqrt{1 - \cos^2 x}$, $0 \le x \le 2\pi$.

$y_1 = y_2$ for $0 \le x \le \pi$, so we have

$\sin\theta = \sqrt{1 - \cos^2\theta}$ for $0 \le \theta \le \pi$.

79. $\sec \theta = \sqrt{1 + \tan^2 \theta}$

Let $y_1 = \dfrac{1}{\cos x}$ and $y_2 = \sqrt{1 + \tan^2 x}$, $0 \le x \le 2\pi$.

$y_1 = y_2$ for $0 \le x < \dfrac{\pi}{2}$ and $\dfrac{3\pi}{2} < x < 2\pi$, so we have

$\sin \theta = \sqrt{1 + \tan^2 \theta}$ for $0 \le \theta < \dfrac{\pi}{2}$ and $\dfrac{3\pi}{2} < \theta < 2\pi$.

81. $\ln|\cos \theta| - \ln|\sin \theta| = \ln \dfrac{|\cos \theta|}{|\sin \theta|} = \ln|\cot \theta|$

83. False; $\dfrac{\sin k\theta}{\cos k\theta} = \tan k\theta$

85. True; $\sin \theta \csc \theta = \sin \theta\left(\dfrac{1}{\sin \theta}\right) = 1$,

provided $\sin \theta \ne 0$.

87. (a) $\csc^2 132° - \cot^2 132° \approx 1.8107 - 0.8107 = 1$

(b) $\csc^2 \dfrac{2\pi}{7} - \cot^2 \dfrac{2\pi}{7} \approx 1.6360 - 0.6360 = 1$

89. $\cos\left(\dfrac{\pi}{2} - \theta\right) = \sin \theta$

(a) $\theta = 80°$

$\cos(90° - 80°) = \sin 80°$

$0.9848 = 0.9848$

(b) $\theta = 0.8$

$\cos\left(\dfrac{\pi}{2} - 0.8\right) = \sin 0.8$

$0.7174 = 0.7174$

91. Since $\sin^2 \theta + \cos^2 \theta = 1$ and $\cos^2 \theta = 1 - \sin^2 \theta$:

$\cos \theta = \pm\sqrt{1 - \sin^2 \theta}$

$\tan \theta = \dfrac{\sin \theta}{\cos \theta} = \pm\dfrac{\sin \theta}{\sqrt{1 - \sin^2 \theta}}$

$\cot \theta = \dfrac{1}{\tan \theta} = \pm\dfrac{\sqrt{1 - \sin^2 \theta}}{\sin \theta}$

$\sec \theta = \dfrac{1}{\cos \theta} = \pm\dfrac{1}{\sqrt{1 - \sin^2 \theta}}$

$\csc \theta = \dfrac{1}{\sin \theta}$

The sign depends on the choice of θ.

93. Seward has the greater variation in daylight hours because the coefficient of cosine is larger. The coefficients 6.4 and 1.9 determine the difference between the greatest and least number of daylight hours.

Section 6.2   Verifying Trigonometric Identities

- You should know the difference between an expression, a conditional equation, and an identity.
- You should be able to solve trigonometric identities, using the following techniques.
  (a) Work with *one* side at a time. Do not "cross" the equal sign.
  (b) Use algebraic techniques such as combining fractions, factoring expressions, rationalizing denominators, and squaring binomials.
  (c) Use the fundamental identities.
  (d) Convert all the terms into sines and cosines.

Solutions to Odd-Numbered Exercises

1. $\sin t \csc t = \sin t \left(\dfrac{1}{\sin t} \right) = 1$

3. $\dfrac{\sec^2 x}{\tan x} = \dfrac{1}{\cos^2 x} \cdot \dfrac{\cos x}{\sin x}$

$$= \dfrac{1}{\cos x} \cdot \dfrac{1}{\sin x}$$

$$= \sec x \csc x$$

5. $\cos^2 \beta - \sin^2 \beta = (1 - \sin^2 \beta) - \sin^2 \beta$

$$= 1 - 2 \sin^2 \beta$$

7. $\tan^2 \theta + 4 = (\sec^2 \theta - 1) + 4$

$$= \sec^2 \theta + 3$$

9. $\cos x + \sin x \tan x = \cos x + \sin x \cdot \dfrac{\sin x}{\cos x}$

$$= \dfrac{\cos^2 x + \sin^2 x}{\cos x}$$

$$= \dfrac{1}{\cos x}$$

$$= \sec x$$

11.

x	0.2	0.4	0.6	0.8	1.0	1.2	1.4
y_1	4.835	2.1785	1.2064	0.6767	0.3469	0.1409	0.0293
y_2	4.835	2.1785	1.2064	0.6767	0.3469	0.1409	0.0293

$\dfrac{1}{\sec x \tan x} = \cos x \cdot \dfrac{\cos x}{\sin x}$

$$= \dfrac{\cos^2 x}{\sin x}$$

$$= \dfrac{1 - \sin^2 x}{\sin x}$$

$$= \dfrac{1}{\sin x} - \sin x$$

$$= \csc x - \sin x$$

13.

x	0.2	0.4	0.6	0.8	1.0	1.2	1.4
y_1	4.835	2.1785	1.2064	0.6767	0.3469	0.1409	0.0293
y_2	4.835	2.1785	1.2064	0.6767	0.3469	0.1409	0.0293

$\csc x - \sin x = \dfrac{1}{\sin x} - \sin x$

$$= \dfrac{1 - \sin^2 x}{\sin x}$$

$$= \dfrac{\cos^2 x}{\sin x}$$

$$= \cos x \cdot \dfrac{\cos x}{\sin x}$$

$$= \cos x \cdot \cot x$$

15.

x	0.2	0.4	0.6	0.8	1.0	1.2	1.4
y_1	1.0203	1.0857	1.2116	1.4353	1.8508	2.7597	5.8835
y_2	1.0203	1.0857	1.2116	1.4353	1.8508	2.7597	5.8835

$$\cos x + \sin x \tan x$$
$$= \cos x + \sin x \cdot \frac{\sin x}{\cos x}$$
$$= \frac{\cos^2 x + \sin^2 x}{\cos x}$$
$$= \frac{1}{\cos x}$$
$$= \sec x$$

17.

x	0.2	0.4	0.6	0.8	1.0	1.2	1.4
y_1	5.1359	2.7880	2.1458	2.0009	2.1995	2.9609	5.9704
y_2	5.1359	2.7880	2.1458	2.0009	2.1995	2.9609	5.9704

$$\frac{1}{\tan x} + \frac{1}{\cot x} = \frac{\cot x + \tan x}{\tan x \cdot \cot x}$$
$$= \cot x + \tan x$$

19. $\sin^{1/2} x \cos x - \sin^{5/2} x \cos x = \sin^{1/2} x \cos x(1 - \sin^2 x) = \sin^{1/2} x \cos x \cdot \cos^2 x = \cos^3 x \sqrt{\sin x}$

21. $\cos\left(\dfrac{\pi}{2} - x\right)\csc x = \sin x\left(\dfrac{1}{\sin x}\right) = 1$

23. $\dfrac{\csc(-x)}{\sec(-x)} = \dfrac{1/\sin(-x)}{1/\cos(-x)}$

$$= \frac{\cos(-x)}{\sin(-x)}$$
$$= \frac{\cos x}{-\sin x}$$
$$= -\cot x$$

25. $\dfrac{\cos(-\theta)}{1 + \sin(-\theta)} = \dfrac{\cos \theta}{1 - \sin \theta} \cdot \dfrac{1 + \sin \theta}{1 + \sin \theta}$

$$= \frac{\cos \theta(1 + \sin \theta)}{1 - \sin^2 \theta}$$
$$= \frac{\cos \theta(1 + \sin \theta)}{\cos^2 \theta}$$
$$= \frac{1 + \sin \theta}{\cos \theta}$$
$$= \frac{1}{\cos \theta} + \frac{\sin \theta}{\cos \theta}$$
$$= \sec \theta + \tan \theta$$

27. $\dfrac{\sin x \cos y + \cos x \sin y}{\cos x \cos y - \sin x \sin y} = \dfrac{\dfrac{\sin x \cos y}{\cos x \cos y} + \dfrac{\cos x \sin y}{\cos x \cos y}}{\dfrac{\cos x \cos y}{\cos x \cos y} - \dfrac{\sin x \sin y}{\cos x \cos y}} = \dfrac{\tan x + \tan y}{1 - \tan x \tan y}$

29. $\dfrac{\tan x + \cot y}{\tan x \cot y} = \dfrac{\dfrac{1}{\cot x} + \dfrac{1}{\tan y}}{\dfrac{1}{\cot x} \cdot \dfrac{1}{\tan y}} = \dfrac{\dfrac{\tan y + \cot x}{\cot x \cdot \tan y}}{\dfrac{1}{\cot x \cdot \tan y}} = \tan y + \cot x$

31. $\sqrt{\dfrac{1 + \sin \theta}{1 - \sin \theta}} = \sqrt{\dfrac{1 + \sin \theta}{1 - \sin \theta} \cdot \dfrac{1 + \sin \theta}{1 + \sin \theta}}$

Note: Check your answer with a graphing utility. What happens if you leave off the absolute value?

$\phantom{\sqrt{\dfrac{1 + \sin \theta}{1 - \sin \theta}}} = \sqrt{\dfrac{(1 + \sin \theta)^2}{1 - \sin^2 \theta}}$

$\phantom{\sqrt{\dfrac{1 + \sin \theta}{1 - \sin \theta}}} = \sqrt{\dfrac{(1 + \sin \theta)^2}{\cos^2 \theta}}$

$\phantom{\sqrt{\dfrac{1 + \sin \theta}{1 - \sin \theta}}} = \dfrac{1 + \sin \theta}{|\cos \theta|}$

33. $\sin^2 x + \sin^2\left(\dfrac{\pi}{2} - x\right) = \sin^2 x + \cos^2 x = 1$

35. $\csc x \cos\left(\dfrac{\pi}{2} - x\right) = \dfrac{1}{\sin x} \cdot \sin x = 1$

37. $2\sec^2 x - 2\sec^2 x \sin^2 x - \sin^2 x - \cos^2 x = 2\sec^2 x(1 - \sin^2 x) - (\sin^2 x + \cos^2 x)$

$ = 2\sec^2 x(\cos^2 x) - 1$

$ = 2 \cdot \dfrac{1}{\cos^2 x} \cdot \cos^2 x - 1$

$ = 2 - 1$

$ = 1$

39. $2 + \cos^2 x - 3\cos^4 x = (1 - \cos^2 x)(2 + 3\cos^2 x)$

$ = \sin^2 x(2 + 3\cos^2 x)$

41. $\csc^4 x - 2\csc^2 x + 1 = (\csc^2 x - 1)^2$

$ = (\cot^2 x)^2 = \cot^4 x$

43. $\sec^4 \theta - \tan^4 \theta = (\sec^2 \theta + \tan^2 \theta)(\sec^2 \theta - \tan^2 \theta)$

$ = (1 + \tan^2 \theta + \tan^2 \theta)(1)$

$ = 1 + 2\tan^2 \theta$

45. $\dfrac{\sin \beta}{1 - \cos \beta} \cdot \dfrac{1 + \cos \beta}{1 + \cos \beta} = \dfrac{\sin \beta(1 + \cos \beta)}{1 - \cos^2 \beta}$

$$= \dfrac{\sin \beta(1 + \cos \beta)}{\sin^2 \beta} = \dfrac{1 + \cos \beta}{\sin \beta}$$

47. $\dfrac{\tan^3 \alpha - 1}{\tan \alpha - 1} = \dfrac{(\tan \alpha - 1)(\tan^2 \alpha + \tan \alpha + 1)}{\tan \alpha - 1} = \tan^2 \alpha + \tan \alpha + 1$

49. It appears that $y_1 = 1$. Analytically,

$$\dfrac{1}{\cot x + 1} + \dfrac{1}{\tan x + 1} = \dfrac{\tan x + 1 + \cot x + 1}{(\cot x + 1)(\tan x + 1)}$$

$$= \dfrac{\tan x + \cot x + 2}{\cot x \tan x + \cot x + \tan x + 1}$$

$$= \dfrac{\tan x + \cot x + 2}{\tan x + \cot x + 2}$$

$$= 1.$$

51. It appears that $y_1 = \sin x$. Analytically,

$$\dfrac{1}{\sin x} - \dfrac{\cos^2 x}{\sin x} = \dfrac{1 - \cos^2 x}{\sin x} = \dfrac{\sin^2 x}{\sin x} = \sin x.$$

53. $\ln|\tan \theta| = \ln\left|\dfrac{\sin \theta}{\cos \theta}\right|$

$$= \ln \dfrac{|\sin \theta|}{|\cos \theta|}$$

$$= \ln|\sin \theta| - \ln|\cos \theta|$$

55. $-\ln(1 + \cos \theta) = \ln(1 + \cos \theta)^{-1}$

$$= \ln \dfrac{1}{1 + \cos \theta} \cdot \dfrac{1 - \cos \theta}{1 - \cos \theta}$$

$$= \ln \dfrac{1 - \cos \theta}{1 - \cos^2 \theta}$$

$$= \ln \dfrac{1 - \cos \theta}{\sin^2 \theta}$$

$$= \ln(1 - \cos \theta) - \ln \sin^2 \theta$$

$$= \ln(1 - \cos \theta) - 2 \ln|\sin \theta|$$

57. $\sqrt{\tan^2 \theta} = |\tan \theta|$

$\sqrt{\tan^2 \theta} \neq \tan \theta$ if θ lies in Quadrant II or IV.

One such angle is $\theta = \dfrac{3\pi}{4}$.

59. $|\tan \theta| = \sqrt{\sec^2 \theta - 1}$.

One such value is $x = \dfrac{3\pi}{4}$.

61. $\sin^2 25 + \sin^2 65 = \sin^2 25 + \cos^2 25° = 1$

63. $\cos^2 20° + \cos^2 52° + \cos^2 38° + \cos^2 70° = \cos^2 20° + \cos^2 52^2 + \sin^2(90° - 38°) + \sin^2(90° - 70°)$

$$= \cos^2 20° + \cos^2 52^2 + \sin^2 52° + \sin^2 20°$$

$$= (\cos^2 20° + \sin^2 20°) + (\cos^2 52° + \sin^2 52°)$$

$$= 1 + 1$$

$$= 2$$

65. When n is even,

$$\cos\left[\frac{(2n + 1)\pi}{2}\right] = \cos \frac{\pi}{2} = 0.$$

When n is odd,

$$\cos\left[\frac{(2n + 1)\pi}{2}\right] = \cos \frac{3\pi}{2} = 0.$$

Thus, $\cos\left[\dfrac{(2n + 1)\pi}{2}\right] = 0$ for all integers n.

67. $\mu W \cos \theta = W \sin \theta$

$$\mu = \frac{W \sin \theta}{W \cos \theta} = \frac{\sin \theta}{\cos \theta} = \tan \theta$$

Section 6.3   Solving Trigonometric Equations

- You should be able to identify and solve trigonometric equations.
- A trigonometric equation is a conditional equation. It is true for a specific set of values.
- To solve trigonometric equations, use algebraic techniques such as collecting like terms, taking square roots, factoring, squaring, converting to quadratic form, using formulas, and using inverse functions. Study the examples in this section.
- Use your graphing utility to calculate solutions and verify results.

Solutions to Odd-Numbered Exercises

1. $y = \sin \dfrac{\pi x}{2} + 1$

From the graph in the textbook we see that the curve has x-intercepts at $x = -1$ and at $x = 3$.

3. $y = \tan^2\left(\dfrac{\pi x}{6}\right) - 3$

From the graph in the textbook we see that the curve has x-intercepts at $x = \pm 2$.

5. $2 \cos x - 1 = 0$

    (a) $2 \cos \dfrac{\pi}{3} - 1 = 2 \left(\dfrac{1}{2} \right) - 1 = 0$

    (b) $2 \cos \dfrac{5\pi}{3} - 1 = 2 \left(\dfrac{1}{2} \right) - 1 = 0$

7. $3 \tan^2 2x - 1 = 0$

    (a) $3 \left[\tan 2 \left(\dfrac{\pi}{12} \right) \right]^2 - 1 = 3 \tan^2 \dfrac{\pi}{6} - 1$

                  $= 3 \left(\dfrac{1}{\sqrt{3}} \right)^2 - 1$

                   $= 0$

    (b) $3 \left[\tan 2 \left(\dfrac{5\pi}{12} \right) \right]^2 - 1 = 3 \tan^2 \dfrac{5\pi}{6} - 1$

                  $= 3 \left(-\dfrac{1}{\sqrt{3}} \right)^2 - 1$

                   $= 0$

9. $2 \sin^2 x - \sin x - 1 = 0$

    (a) $2 \sin^2 \dfrac{\pi}{2} - \sin \dfrac{\pi}{2} - 1 = 2(1)^2 - 1 - 1$

                        $= 0$

    (b) $2 \sin^2 \dfrac{7\pi}{6} - \sin \dfrac{7\pi}{6} - 1 = 2 \left(-\dfrac{1}{2} \right)^2 - \left(-\dfrac{1}{2} \right) - 1$

                             $= \dfrac{1}{2} + \dfrac{1}{2} - 1$

                             $= 0$

11. $2 \cos x + 1 = 0$

    $2 \cos x = -1$

    $\cos x = -\dfrac{1}{2}$

    $x = \dfrac{2\pi}{3} + 2n\pi$

    or $x = \dfrac{4\pi}{3} + 2n\pi$

13. $\sqrt{3} \csc x - 2 = 0$

    $\sqrt{3} \csc x = 2$

    $\csc x = \dfrac{2}{\sqrt{3}}$

    $x = \dfrac{\pi}{3} + 2n\pi$

    or $x = \dfrac{2\pi}{3} + 2n\pi$

15. $3 \sec^2 x - 4 = 0$

    $\sec x = \pm \dfrac{2}{\sqrt{3}}$

    $x = \dfrac{\pi}{6} + n\pi$

    or $x = \dfrac{5\pi}{6} + n\pi$

17. $2 \sin^2 2x = 1$

    $\sin 2x = \pm \dfrac{1}{\sqrt{2}} = \pm \dfrac{\sqrt{2}}{2}$

    $2x = \dfrac{\pi}{4} + 2n\pi, \ 2x = \dfrac{3\pi}{4} + 2n\pi, \ 2x = \dfrac{5\pi}{4} + 2n\pi, \ 2x = \dfrac{7\pi}{4} + 2n\pi,$

    $2x = \dfrac{9\pi}{4} + 2n\pi, \ 2x = \dfrac{11\pi}{4} + 2n\pi, \ 2x = \dfrac{13\pi}{4} + 2n\pi, \ 2x = \dfrac{15\pi}{4} + 2n\pi$

    Thus, $x = \dfrac{\pi}{8} + n\pi, \ \dfrac{3\pi}{8} + n\pi, \ \dfrac{5\pi}{8} + n\pi, \ \dfrac{7\pi}{8} + n\pi.$

19. $4 \sin^2 - 3 = 0$

$$\sin x = \pm \frac{\sqrt{3}}{2}$$

$$x = \frac{x}{3} + n\pi$$

or $x = \frac{2\pi}{3} + n\pi$

21.
$$\sin^2 x = 3 \cos^2 x$$
$$\sin^2 x - 3(1 - \sin^2 x) = 0$$
$$4 \sin^2 x = 3$$
$$\sin x = \pm \frac{\sqrt{3}}{2}$$
$$x = \frac{\pi}{3} + n\pi$$
or $x = \frac{2\pi}{3} + n\pi$

23. $(3 \tan^2 x - 1)(\tan^2 x - 3) = 0$

$3 \tan^2 x - 1 = 0$ or $\tan^2 x - 3 = 0$

$\tan x = \pm \dfrac{1}{\sqrt{3}}$ $\tan x = \pm \sqrt{3}$

$x = \dfrac{\pi}{6} + n\pi$ $x = \dfrac{\pi}{3} + n\pi$

or $x = \dfrac{5\pi}{6} + n\pi$ or $x = \dfrac{2\pi}{3} + n\pi$

25. $\cos^3 x = \cos x$

$\cos^3 x - \cos x = 0$

$\cos x(\cos^2 x - 1) = 0$

$\cos x = 0$ or $\cos^2 x - 1 = 0$

$x = \dfrac{\pi}{2}, \dfrac{3\pi}{2}$ $\cos x = \pm 1$

                $x = 0, \pi$

27. $3 \tan^3 x - \tan x = 0$

$\tan x(3 \tan^2 x - 1) = 0$

$\tan x = 0$ or $3 \tan^2 x - 1 = 0$

$x = 0, \pi$ $\tan x = \pm \dfrac{\sqrt{3}}{3}$

           $x = \dfrac{\pi}{6}, \dfrac{5\pi}{6}, \dfrac{7\pi}{6}, \dfrac{11\pi}{6}$

29. $\sec^2 x - \sec x - 2 = 0$

$(\sec x - 2)(\sec x + 1) = 0$

$\sec x - 2 = 0$ or $\sec x + 1 = 0$

$\sec x = 2$ $\sec x = -1$

$x = \dfrac{\pi}{3}, \dfrac{5\pi}{3}$ $x = \pi$

31. $2 \sin x + \csc x = 0$

$$2 \sin x + \frac{1}{\sin x} = 0$$

$$2 \sin^2 x + 1 = 0$$

Since $2 \sin^2 x + 1 > 0$, there are no solutions.

33. $\csc x + \cot x = 1$

$$\frac{1}{\sin x} + \frac{\cos x}{\sin x} = 1$$

$$1 + \cos x = \sin x$$

$$(1 + \cos x)^2 = \sin^2 x$$

$$1 + 2 \cos x + \cos^2 x = 1 - \cos^2 x$$

$$2 \cos^2 x + 2 \cos x = 0$$

$$\cos x(\cos x + 1) = 0$$

$\cos x = 0$ or $\cos x = -1$

$x = \dfrac{\pi}{2}, \dfrac{3\pi}{2}$ $x = \pi$

($3\pi/2$ is extraneous.)   (π is extraneous.)

$x = \pi/2$ is the only solution.

35. $\cos\left(\dfrac{x}{2}\right) = \dfrac{\sqrt{2}}{2}$

$$\dfrac{x}{2} = \dfrac{\pi}{4} + 2n\pi$$

$$x = \dfrac{\pi}{2} + 4n\pi$$

$$x = \dfrac{\pi}{2}$$

37. $\dfrac{1 + \cos x}{1 - \cos x} = 0$

$$1 + \cos x = 0$$

$$\cos x = -1$$

$$x = \pi$$

39.
$$2\sec^2 x + \tan^2 x - 3 = 0$$
$$2(\tan^2 x + 1) + \tan^2 x - 3 = 0$$
$$3\tan^2 x - 1 = 0$$
$$\tan x = \pm\dfrac{\sqrt{3}}{3}$$
$$x = \dfrac{\pi}{6}, \dfrac{5\pi}{6}, \dfrac{7\pi}{6}, \dfrac{11\pi}{6}$$

41. $\dfrac{\cos x \cot x}{1 - \sin x} = 3$

Graph $y = \dfrac{\cos x}{(1 - \sin x)\tan x} - 3.$

The solutions are approximately
$x \approx 0.5236,\ x \approx 2.6180$

43. $4\sin^3 x + 2\sin^2 x - 2\sin x - 1 = 0$

Graph $y = 4\sin^3 x + 2\sin^2 x - 2\sin x - 1.$

By altering the y-range to Ymin $= -.5$ and Ymax $= .5$, you see that there are 6 solutions:
0.7854, 2.3562, 3.6652, 3.9270, 5.4978, 5.7596.

45. $2\sin x - x = 0$

Graph $y_1 = 2\sin x - x.$

The x-intercepts occur at $x = 0$ and $x \approx 1.8955.$

47. $\sec^2 x + 0.5\tan x - 1 = 0$

Graph $y_1 = \dfrac{1}{(\cos x)^2} + 0.5\tan x - 1.$

The x-intercepts occur at $x = 0,\ x \approx 2.6779,$
$x = 3.1416$ and $x \approx 5.8195.$

49. $12 \sin^2 x - 13 \sin x + 3 = 0$

$(3 \sin x - 1)(4 \sin x - 3) = 0$

$3 \sin x - 1 = 0$ or $4 \sin x - 3 = 0$

$\sin x = \frac{1}{3}$ $\sin x = \frac{3}{4}$

$x = 0.3398,\ 2.8081$ $x = 0.8481,\ 2.2935$

Graph $y_1 = 12 \sin^2 x + 13 \sin x + 3$.

The x-intercepts occur at $x \approx 0.3398$, $x \approx 0.8481$, $x \approx 2.2935$, and $x \approx 2.8018$.

51. (a)

x	0	1	2	3	4	5	6
$f(x)$	Undef.	0.83	-1.36	-2.93	-4.46	-6.34	-13.02

The zero is in the interval $(1, 2)$ since f changes signs in the interval.

(b)

The interval is the same as part (a).

(c) 1.3065

53. (a)

x	0	1	2	3	4	5	6
$f(x)$	-1	1.39	1.65	-0.70	-1.94	-2.00	-1.48

The zeros are in the intervals $(0, 1)$ and $(2, 3)$ since f changes signs in these intervals.

(b)

The interval is the same as part (a).

(c) 0.4271, 2.7145

55. (a) $f(x) = \sin x + \cos x$

Maximum: $\left(\dfrac{\pi}{4},\ \sqrt{2}\right)$

Minimum: $\left(\dfrac{5\pi}{4},\ -\sqrt{2}\right)$

(b) $\cos x - \sin x = 0$

$$\cos x = \sin x$$

$$1 = \frac{\sin x}{\cos x}$$

$$\tan x = 1$$

$$x = \frac{\pi}{4},\ \frac{5\pi}{4}$$

$$f\left(\frac{\pi}{4}\right) = \sin \frac{\pi}{4} + \cos \frac{\pi}{4} = \frac{\sqrt{2}}{2} + \frac{\sqrt{2}}{2} = \sqrt{2}$$

$$f\left(\frac{5\pi}{4}\right) = \sin \frac{5\pi}{4} + \cos \frac{5\pi}{4} = -\sin \frac{\pi}{4} + \left(-\cos \frac{\pi}{4}\right) = -\frac{\sqrt{2}}{2} - \frac{\sqrt{2}}{2} = -\sqrt{2}$$

Therefore, the maximum point in the interval $[0, 2\pi)$ is $\left(\pi/4,\ \sqrt{2}\right)$ and the minimum point is $\left(5\pi/4,\ -\sqrt{2}\right)$.

57. $f(x) = \tan \dfrac{\pi x}{4}$. $\tan 0 = 0$, but 0 is not positive. By graphing $y = \tan \dfrac{\pi x}{4} - x$, you see that the smallest positive fixed point is $x = 1$.

59. $f(x) = \cos \dfrac{1}{x}$

(a) The domain of $f(x)$ is all real numbers except 0.

(b) The graph has y-axis symmetry and a horizontal asymptote at $y = 1$.

(c) As $x \to 0$, $f(x)$ oscillates between -1 and 1.

(d) There are an infinite number of solutions in the interval $[-1, 1]$.

(e) The greatest solution appears to occur at $x \approx 0.6366$.

61.
$$y = \frac{1}{12}(\cos 8t - 3 \sin 8t)$$

$$\frac{1}{12}(\cos 8t - 3 \sin 8t) = 0$$

$$\cos 8t = 3 \sin 8t$$

$$\frac{1}{3} = \tan 8t$$

$$8t = 0.32175 + n\pi$$

$$t = 0.04 + \frac{n\pi}{8}$$

In the interval $0 \le t \le 1$, $t = 0.04$, 0.43, and 0.83.

63. $r = \dfrac{1}{32} v_0{}^2 \sin 2\theta$, $r = 300$, $v_0 = 100$

$$300 = \frac{1}{32}(100)^2 \sin 2\theta$$

$$\sin 2\theta = 0.96$$

$$2\theta \approx 1.287 \qquad \text{or} \quad 2\theta = \pi - 1.287 \approx 1.855$$

$$\theta \approx 0.6435 \approx 37° \qquad \theta \approx 0.928 \approx 53°$$

65. $A = 2x \cos x$, $-\dfrac{\pi}{2} < x < \dfrac{\pi}{2}$

(a)

(b) $A \geq 1$ for $0.6 < x < 1.1$

The maximum area of $A \approx 1.12$ occurs when $x \approx 0.86$.

67. (a)

(b) By checking the graphs we see that

   (iii) $r = 1.05 \sin[0.95(t + 6.32)] + 6.20$ best fits the data.

(c) The constant term gives the rate of 6.20%.

(d) Period: $\dfrac{2\pi}{0.95} \approx 7$ years

(e) $r \approx 6.00$ when $t \approx 10.4$ which corresponds to late 2000.

Section 6.4   Sum and Difference Formulas

■ You should memorize the sum and difference formulas.

   $\sin(u \pm v) = \sin u \cos v \pm \cos u \sin v$

   $\cos(u \pm v) = \cos u \cos v \mp \sin u \sin v$

   $\tan(u \pm v) = \dfrac{\tan u \pm \tan v}{1 \mp \tan u \tan v}$

■ You should be able to use these formulas to find the values of the trigonometric functions of angles whose sums or differences are special angles.

■ You should be able to use these formulas to solve trigonometric equations.

Solutions to Odd-Numbered Exercises

1. (a) $\cos\left(\dfrac{\pi}{4} + \dfrac{\pi}{3}\right) = \cos\dfrac{\pi}{4}\cos\dfrac{\pi}{3} - \sin\dfrac{\pi}{4}\sin\dfrac{\pi}{3}$

$= \dfrac{\sqrt{2}}{2} \cdot \dfrac{1}{2} - \dfrac{\sqrt{2}}{2} \cdot \dfrac{\sqrt{3}}{2}$

$= \dfrac{\sqrt{2} - \sqrt{6}}{4}$

(b) $\cos\dfrac{\pi}{4} + \cos\dfrac{\pi}{3} = \dfrac{\sqrt{2}}{2} + \dfrac{1}{2} = \dfrac{\sqrt{2} + 1}{2}$

3. (a) $\sin\left(\dfrac{7\pi}{6} - \dfrac{\pi}{3}\right) = \sin\dfrac{5\pi}{6} = \sin\dfrac{\pi}{6} = \dfrac{1}{2}$

(b) $\sin\dfrac{7\pi}{6} - \sin\dfrac{\pi}{3} = -\dfrac{1}{2} - \dfrac{\sqrt{3}}{2} = \dfrac{-1 - \sqrt{3}}{2}$

5. Both statements are false. Parts (a) and (b) are unequal in Exercises 1–4.

7. $\sin 75° = \sin(30° + 45°)$

$= \sin 30° \cos 45° + \sin 45° \cos 30°$

$= \dfrac{1}{2} \cdot \dfrac{\sqrt{2}}{2} + \dfrac{\sqrt{2}}{2} \cdot \dfrac{\sqrt{3}}{2}$

$= \dfrac{\sqrt{2}}{4}(1 + \sqrt{3})$

$\cos 75° = \cos(30° + 45°)$

$= \cos 30° \cos 45° - \sin 30° \sin 45°$

$= \dfrac{\sqrt{3}}{2} \cdot \dfrac{\sqrt{2}}{2} - \dfrac{1}{2} \cdot \dfrac{\sqrt{2}}{2}$

$= \dfrac{\sqrt{2}}{4}(\sqrt{3} - 1)$

$\tan 75° = \tan(30° + 45°)$

$= \dfrac{\tan 30° + \tan 45°}{1 - \tan 30° \tan 45°}$

$= \dfrac{(\sqrt{3}/3) + 1}{1 - (\sqrt{3}/3)} = \dfrac{\sqrt{3} + 3}{3 - \sqrt{3}} \cdot \dfrac{3 + \sqrt{3}}{3 + \sqrt{3}}$

$= \dfrac{6\sqrt{3} + 12}{6} = \sqrt{3} + 2$

9. $\sin 105° = \sin(60° + 45°)$

$= \sin 60° \cos 45° + \sin 45° \cos 60°$

$= \dfrac{\sqrt{3}}{2} \cdot \dfrac{\sqrt{2}}{2} + \dfrac{\sqrt{2}}{2} \cdot \dfrac{1}{2}$

$= \dfrac{\sqrt{2}}{4}(\sqrt{3} + 1)$

$\cos 105° = \cos(60° + 45°)$

$= \cos 60° \cos 45° - \sin 60° \sin 45°$

$= \dfrac{1}{2} \cdot \dfrac{\sqrt{2}}{2} - \dfrac{\sqrt{3}}{2} \cdot \dfrac{\sqrt{2}}{2}$

$= \dfrac{\sqrt{2}}{4}(1 - \sqrt{3})$

$\tan 105° = \tan(60° + 45°)$

$= \dfrac{\tan 60° + \tan 45°}{1 - \tan 60° \tan 45°}$

$= \dfrac{\sqrt{3} + 1}{1 - \sqrt{3}} = \dfrac{\sqrt{3} + 1}{1 - \sqrt{3}} \cdot \dfrac{1 + \sqrt{3}}{1 + \sqrt{3}}$

$= \dfrac{4 + 2\sqrt{3}}{-2} = -2 - \sqrt{3}$

11. $\sin 195° = \sin(225° - 30°)$

$= \sin 225° \cos 30° - \sin 30° \cos 225°$

$= -\sin 45° \cos 30° + \sin 30° \cos 45°$

$= -\dfrac{\sqrt{2}}{2} \cdot \dfrac{\sqrt{3}}{2} + \dfrac{\sqrt{2}}{2} \cdot \dfrac{1}{2}$

$= \dfrac{\sqrt{2}}{4}(1 - \sqrt{3})$

$\cos 195° = \cos(225° - 30°)$

$= \cos 225° \cos 30° + \sin 225° \sin 30°$

$= -\cos 45° \cos 30° - \sin 45° \sin 30°$

$= \dfrac{\sqrt{2}}{2} \cdot \dfrac{\sqrt{2}}{2} - \dfrac{\sqrt{2}}{2} \cdot \dfrac{1}{2}$

$= -\dfrac{\sqrt{2}}{4}(\sqrt{3} + 1)$

$\tan 195° = \tan(225° - 30°)$

$= \dfrac{\tan 225° - \tan 30°}{1 + \tan 225° \tan 30°}$

$= \dfrac{\tan 45° - \tan 30°}{1 + \tan 45° \tan 30°}$

$= \dfrac{1 - (\sqrt{3}/3)}{1 + (\sqrt{3}/3)} = \dfrac{\sqrt{3}}{3 + \sqrt{3}} \cdot \dfrac{3 - \sqrt{3}}{3 - \sqrt{3}}$

$= \dfrac{12 - 6\sqrt{3}}{6} = 2 - \sqrt{3}$

13. $\sin\dfrac{11\pi}{12} = \sin\left(\dfrac{3\pi}{4} + \dfrac{\pi}{6}\right)$

$= \sin\dfrac{3\pi}{4}\cos\dfrac{\pi}{6} + \sin\dfrac{\pi}{6}\cos\dfrac{3\pi}{4}$

$= -\dfrac{\sqrt{2}}{2}\cdot\dfrac{\sqrt{3}}{2} + \dfrac{1}{2}\left(-\dfrac{\sqrt{2}}{2}\right)$

$= \dfrac{\sqrt{2}}{4}(\sqrt{3} - 1)$

$\cos\dfrac{11\pi}{12} = \cos\left(\dfrac{3\pi}{4} + \dfrac{\pi}{6}\right)$

$= \cos\dfrac{3\pi}{4}\cos\dfrac{\pi}{6} - \sin\dfrac{3\pi}{4}\sin\dfrac{\pi}{6}$

$= \dfrac{\sqrt{2}}{2}\cdot\dfrac{\sqrt{3}}{2} - \dfrac{\sqrt{2}}{2}\cdot\dfrac{1}{2}$

$= -\dfrac{\sqrt{2}}{4}(\sqrt{3} + 1)$

$\tan\dfrac{11\pi}{4} = \tan\left(\dfrac{3\pi}{4} + \dfrac{\pi}{6}\right)$

$= \dfrac{\tan(3\pi/4) - \tan(\pi/6)}{1 - \tan(3\pi/4)\tan(\pi/6)}$

$= \dfrac{-1 + (\sqrt{3}/3)}{1 - (-1)(\sqrt{3}/3)}$

$= \dfrac{-3 + \sqrt{3}}{3 + \sqrt{3}}\cdot\dfrac{3 - \sqrt{3}}{3 - \sqrt{3}}$

$= \dfrac{-12 + 6\sqrt{3}}{6} = -2 + \sqrt{3}$

15. $\sin\dfrac{17\pi}{12} = \sin\left(\dfrac{9\pi}{4} - \dfrac{5\pi}{6}\right)$

$= \sin\dfrac{9\pi}{4}\cos\dfrac{5\pi}{6} - \sin\dfrac{5\pi}{6}\cos\dfrac{9\pi}{4}$

$= \dfrac{\sqrt{2}}{2}\left(-\dfrac{\sqrt{3}}{2}\right) - \left(\dfrac{1}{2}\right)\left(\dfrac{\sqrt{2}}{2}\right)$

$= -\dfrac{\sqrt{2}}{4}(\sqrt{3} + 1)$

$\cos\dfrac{17\pi}{12} = \cos\left(\dfrac{9\pi}{4} - \dfrac{5\pi}{6}\right)$

$= \cos\dfrac{9\pi}{4}\cos\dfrac{5\pi}{6} + \sin\dfrac{9\pi}{4}\sin\dfrac{5\pi}{6}$

$= \dfrac{\sqrt{2}}{2}\left(-\dfrac{\sqrt{3}}{2}\right) + \dfrac{\sqrt{2}}{2}\left(\dfrac{1}{2}\right)$

$= \dfrac{\sqrt{2}}{4}\left(1 - \sqrt{3}\right)$

$\tan\dfrac{17\pi}{4} = \tan\left(\dfrac{9\pi}{4} - \dfrac{5\pi}{6}\right)$

$= \dfrac{\tan(9\pi/4) - \tan(5\pi/6)}{1 + \tan(9\pi/4)\tan(5\pi/6)}$

$= \dfrac{1 - (-\sqrt{3}/3)}{1 + (-\sqrt{3}/3)}$

$= \dfrac{3 + \sqrt{3}}{3 - \sqrt{3}}\cdot\dfrac{3 + \sqrt{3}}{3 + \sqrt{3}}$

$= \dfrac{12 + 6\sqrt{3}}{6} = 2 + \sqrt{3}$

17. $\cos 25° \cos 15° - \sin 25° \sin 15° = \cos(25° + 15°) = \cos 40°$

19. $\sin 230° \cos 30° - \cos 230° \sin 30° = \sin(230° - 30°) = \sin 200°$

21. $\dfrac{\tan 325° - \tan 86°}{1 + \tan 325° \tan 86°} = \tan(325° - 86°) = \tan 239°$

23. $\sin 3 \cos 1.2 - \cos 3 \sin 1.2 = \sin(3 - 1.2) = \sin 1.8$

25. $\dfrac{\tan 2x + \tan x}{1 - \tan 2x \tan x} = \tan(2x + x) = \tan 3x$

27.

x	0.2	0.4	0.6	0.8	1.0	1.2	1.4
y_1	0.9801	0.9211	0.8253	0.6967	0.5403	0.3624	0.1700
y_2	0.9801	0.9211	0.8253	0.6967	0.5403	0.3624	0.1700

$$y_1 = \sin\left(\frac{\pi}{2} + x\right)$$
$$= \sin\frac{\pi}{2}\cos x + \sin x \cdot \cos\frac{\pi}{2}$$
$$= \cos x$$
$$= y_2$$

29.

x	0.2	0.4	0.6	0.8	1.0	1.2	1.4
y_1	0.6621	0.7978	0.9017	0.9696	0.9989	0.9883	0.9384
y_2	0.6621	0.7978	0.9017	0.9696	0.9989	0.9883	0.9384

$$y_1 = \sin\left(\frac{\pi}{6} + x\right)$$
$$= \sin\frac{\pi}{6}\cos x + \sin x \cdot \cos\frac{\pi}{6}$$
$$= \frac{1}{2}\cos x + \frac{\sqrt{3}}{2}\sin x$$
$$= \frac{1}{2}(\cos x + \sqrt{3}\sin x)$$
$$= y_2$$

31.

x	0.2	0.4	0.6	0.8	1.0	1.2	1.4
y_1	0.9605	0.8484	0.6812	0.4854	0.2919	0.1313	0.0289
y_2	0.9605	0.8484	0.6812	0.4854	0.2919	0.1313	0.0289

$$y_1 = \cos(x + \pi)\cos(x - \pi)$$
$$= (\cos x \cdot \cos \pi - \sin x \cdot \sin \pi)$$
$$[\cos x \cos \pi + \sin x \sin \pi]$$
$$= [-\cos x][-\cos x]$$
$$= \cos^2 x$$
$$= y_2$$

For Exercises 33–35, we have:

$$\sin u = \tfrac{5}{13},\ u \text{ is in Quadrant I} \implies \cos u = \tfrac{12}{13}$$
$$\cos v = -\tfrac{3}{5},\ v \text{ is in Quadrant II} \implies \sin v = \tfrac{4}{5}$$

33. $\sin(u + v) = \sin u \cos v + \cos u \sin v$
$$= \left(\tfrac{5}{13}\right)\left(-\tfrac{3}{5}\right) + \left(\tfrac{12}{13}\right)\left(\tfrac{4}{5}\right)$$
$$= \tfrac{33}{65}$$

35. $\cos(u + v) = \cos u \cos v - \sin u \sin v$
$$= \left(\tfrac{12}{13}\right)\left(-\tfrac{3}{5}\right) - \left(\tfrac{5}{13}\right)\left(\tfrac{4}{5}\right)$$
$$= \tfrac{-56}{65}$$

For Exercises 37–39, we have:

$\sin u = \frac{7}{25}$, *u* is in Quadrant II $\implies$ $\cos u = \frac{-24}{25}$

$\cos v = \frac{4}{5}$, *v* is in Quadrant IV $\implies$ $\sin v = -\frac{3}{5}$

37. $\cos(u + v) = \cos u \cdot \cos v - \sin u \cdot \sin v$

$$= \left(-\frac{24}{25}\right)\left(\frac{4}{5}\right) - \left(\frac{7}{25}\right)\left(-\frac{3}{5}\right)$$

$$= \frac{-96 + 21}{125} = \frac{-75}{125} = \frac{-3}{5}$$

39. $\sin(v - u) = \sin u \cdot \cos v - \sin u \cdot \cos v$

$$= \left(-\frac{3}{5}\right)\left(-\frac{24}{25}\right) - \left(\frac{7}{25}\right)\left(\frac{4}{5}\right)$$

$$= \frac{72 - 28}{125} = \frac{44}{125}$$

41. $\cos(\pi - \theta) + \sin\left(\frac{\pi}{2} + \theta\right) = \cos \pi \cos \theta + \sin \pi \sin \theta + \sin \frac{\pi}{2} \cos \theta + \sin \theta \cos \frac{\pi}{2}$

$$= (-1)(\cos \theta) + (0)(\sin \theta) + (1)(\cos \theta) + (\sin \theta)(0) = -\cos \theta + \cos \theta = 0$$

43. $\sin(x + y) + \sin(x - y) = \sin x \cos y + \sin y \cos x + \sin x \cos y - \sin y \cos x = 2 \sin x \cos y$

45. $\cos(n\pi + \theta) = \cos n\pi \cos \theta - \sin n\pi \sin \theta$

$$= (-1)^n (\cos \theta) - (0)(\sin \theta)$$

$$= (-1)^n (\cos \theta), \text{ where } n \text{ is an integer.}$$

47. $C = \arctan \dfrac{b}{a} \implies \tan C = \dfrac{b}{a} \implies \sin C = \dfrac{b}{\sqrt{a^2 + b^2}}, \cos C = \dfrac{a}{\sqrt{a^2 + b^2}}$

$$\sqrt{a^2 + b^2} \sin(B\theta + C) = \sqrt{a^2 + b^2}\left(\sin B\theta \cdot \frac{a}{\sqrt{a^2 + b^2}} + \frac{b}{\sqrt{a^2 + b^2}} \cdot \cos B\theta\right) = a \sin B\theta + b \cos B\theta$$

49. The graph of $g(x) = \cos(\pi + x)$ looks like that of $f(x) = -\cos x$. Analytic

$$g(x) = \cos(\pi + x) = \cos \pi \cdot \cos x - \sin \pi \cdot \sin x = -\cos x.$$

51. $\sin \theta + \cos \theta$

$a = 1, b = 1, B = 1$

(a) $C = \arctan \dfrac{b}{a} = \arctan 1 = \dfrac{\pi}{4}$

$\sin \theta + \cos \theta = \sqrt{a^2 + b^2} \sin(B\theta + C)$

$$= \sqrt{2} \sin\left(\theta + \frac{\pi}{4}\right)$$

(b) $C = \arctan \dfrac{a}{b} = \arctan 1 = \dfrac{\pi}{4}$

$\sin \theta + \cos \theta = \sqrt{a^2 + b^2} \cos(B\theta - C)$

$$= \sqrt{2} \cos\left(\theta - \frac{\pi}{4}\right)$$

53. $12 \sin 3\theta + 5 \cos 3\theta$

$a = 12, b = 5, B = 3$

(a) $C = \arctan \dfrac{b}{a} = \arctan \dfrac{5}{12} \approx 0.3948$

$12 \sin 3\theta + 5 \cos 3\theta = \sqrt{a^2 + b^2} \sin(B\theta + C)$

$$\approx 13 \sin(3\theta + 0.3948)$$

(b) $C = \arctan \dfrac{a}{b} = \arctan \dfrac{12}{5} \approx 1.1760$

$12 \sin 3\theta + 5 \cos 3\theta = \sqrt{a^2 + b^2} \cos(B\theta - C)$

$$\approx 13 \cos(3\theta - 1.1760)$$

55. $C = \arctan \dfrac{b}{a} = \dfrac{\pi}{2} \implies a = 0$

$\sqrt{a^2 + b^2} = 2 \implies b = 2$

$B = 1$

$2 \sin\left(\theta + \dfrac{\pi}{2}\right) = (0)(\sin \theta) + (2)(\cos \theta) = 2 \cos \theta$

57. $\sin(\arcsin x + \arccos x) = \sin(\arcsin x) \cos(\arccos x) + \sin(\arccos x) \cos(\arcsin x)$

$$= x \cdot x + \sqrt{1 - x^2} \cdot \sqrt{1 - x^2}$$

$$= x^2 + 1 - x^2$$

$$= 1$$

$\theta = \arcsin x$

$\theta = \arccos x$

59.
$$\sin\left(x + \dfrac{\pi}{3}\right) + \sin\left(x - \dfrac{\pi}{3}\right) = 1$$

$$\sin x \cos \dfrac{\pi}{3} + \cos x \sin \dfrac{\pi}{3} + \sin x \cos \dfrac{\pi}{3} - \cos x \sin \dfrac{\pi}{3} = 1$$

$$2 \sin x(0.5) = 1$$

$$\sin x = 1$$

$$x = \dfrac{\pi}{2}$$

61.
$$\cos\left(x + \dfrac{\pi}{4}\right) - \cos\left(x - \dfrac{\pi}{4}\right) = 1$$

$$\cos x \cos \dfrac{\pi}{4} - \sin x \sin \dfrac{\pi}{4} - \left(\cos x \cos \dfrac{\pi}{4} + \sin x \sin \dfrac{\pi}{4}\right) = 1$$

$$-2 \sin x\left(\dfrac{\sqrt{2}}{2}\right) = 1$$

$$-\sqrt{2} \sin x = 1$$

$$\sin x = -\dfrac{1}{\sqrt{2}}$$

$$\sin x = -\dfrac{\sqrt{2}}{2}$$

$$x = \dfrac{5\pi}{4}, \dfrac{7\pi}{4}$$

63. Graph $y_1 = \cos\left(x + \dfrac{\pi}{4}\right) + \cos\left(x - \dfrac{\pi}{4}\right)$ and $y_2 = 1$.

The points of intersection occur at $x = \dfrac{\pi}{4}$ and $x = \dfrac{7\pi}{4}$.

65. $y_1 + y_2 = A \cos 2\pi\left(\dfrac{t}{T} - \dfrac{x}{\lambda}\right) + A \cos 2\pi\left(\dfrac{t}{T} + \dfrac{x}{\lambda}\right)$

$$= A\left[\cos\left(\dfrac{2\pi t}{T}\right)\cos\left(\dfrac{2\pi x}{\lambda}\right) + \sin\left(\dfrac{2\pi t}{T}\right)\sin\left(\dfrac{2\pi x}{\lambda}\right)\right] + A\left[\cos\left(\dfrac{2\pi t}{T}\right)\cos\left(\dfrac{2\pi x}{\lambda}\right) - \sin\left(\dfrac{2\pi t}{T}\right)\sin\left(\dfrac{2\pi x}{\lambda}\right)\right]$$

$$= 2A \cos\left(\dfrac{2\pi t}{T}\right)\cos\left(\dfrac{2\pi x}{\lambda}\right)$$

67. $y = \dfrac{1}{3}\sin 2t + \dfrac{1}{4}\cos 2t$

(a)

(b) $a = \dfrac{1}{3}$, $b = \dfrac{1}{4}$, $B = 2$

$C = \arctan \dfrac{b}{a} = \arctan \dfrac{3}{4} \approx 0.6435$

$y \approx \sqrt{\left(\tfrac{1}{3}\right)^2 + \left(\tfrac{1}{4}\right)^2}\, \sin\,(2t + 0.6435)$

$= \dfrac{5}{12}\sin(2t + 0.6435)$

(c) Amplitude: $\dfrac{5}{12}$

(d) Frequency: $\dfrac{1}{\text{period}} = \dfrac{b}{2\pi} = \dfrac{2}{2\pi} = \dfrac{1}{\pi}$

69. $f(h) = \dfrac{\cos\left(\dfrac{\pi}{6} + h\right) - \cos\dfrac{\pi}{6}}{h}$

$g(h) = \cos\dfrac{\pi}{6}\left(\dfrac{\cos h - 1}{h}\right) - \sin\dfrac{\pi}{6}\left(\dfrac{\sin h}{h}\right)$

(a) The domains are both $(-\infty, 0)$, $(0, \infty)$.

(b)

h	0.01	0.02	0.05	0.1	0.2	0.5
$f(h)$	-0.5043	-0.5086	-0.5214	-0.5424	-0.5830	-0.6915
$g(h)$	-0.5043	-0.5086	-0.5214	-0.5424	-0.5830	-0.6915

—CONTINUED—

69. —CONTINUED—

(c)

(d) The values tend to $y = -\dfrac{1}{2}$.

Section 6.5   Multiple-Angle and Product-Sum Formulas

■ You should know the following double-angle formulas.

(a) $\sin 2u = 2 \sin u \cos u$

(b) $\cos 2u = \cos^2 u - \sin^2 u$

$\quad\quad\quad = 2 \cos^2 u - 1$

$\quad\quad\quad = 1 - 2 \sin^2 u$

(c) $\tan 2u = \dfrac{2 \tan u}{1 - \tan^2 u}$

■ You should be able to reduce the power of a trigonometric function.

(a) $\sin^2 u = \dfrac{1 - \cos 2u}{2}$ (b) $\cos^2 u = \dfrac{1 + \cos 2u}{2}$ (c) $\tan^2 u = \dfrac{1 - \cos 2u}{1 + \cos 2u}$

■ You should be able to use the half-angle formulas.

(a) $\sin \dfrac{u}{2} = \pm\sqrt{\dfrac{1 - \cos u}{2}}$ (b) $\cos \dfrac{u}{2} = \pm\sqrt{\dfrac{1 + \cos u}{2}}$ (c) $\tan \dfrac{u}{2} = \dfrac{1 - \cos u}{\sin u} = \dfrac{\sin u}{1 + \cos u}$

■ You should be able to use the product-sum formulas.

(a) $\sin u \sin v = \dfrac{1}{2}[\cos(u - v) - \cos(u + v)]$ (b) $\cos u \cos v = \dfrac{1}{2}[\cos(u - v) + \cos(u + v)]$

(c) $\sin u \cos v = \dfrac{1}{2}[\sin(u + v) + \sin(u - v)]$ (d) $\cos u \sin v = \dfrac{1}{2}[\sin(u + v) - \sin(u - v)]$

■ You should be able to use the sum-product formulas.

(a) $\sin x + \sin y = 2 \sin\left(\dfrac{x + y}{2}\right)\cos\left(\dfrac{x - y}{2}\right)$ (b) $\sin x - \sin y = 2 \cos\left(\dfrac{x + y}{2}\right)\sin\left(\dfrac{x - y}{2}\right)$

(c) $\cos x + \cos y = 2 \cos\left(\dfrac{x + y}{2}\right)\cos\left(\dfrac{x - y}{2}\right)$ (d) $\cos x - \cos y = -2 \sin\left(\dfrac{x + y}{2}\right)\sin\left(\dfrac{x - y}{2}\right)$

Solutions to Odd-Numbered Exercises

Figure for Exercises 1–7

$$\sin \theta = \tfrac{3}{5}$$
$$\cos \theta = \tfrac{4}{5}$$
$$\tan \theta = \tfrac{3}{4}$$

1. $\sin \theta = \tfrac{3}{5}$

3. $\cos 2\theta = 2 \cos^2 \theta - 1$
$$= 2\left(\tfrac{4}{5}\right)^2 - 1$$
$$= \tfrac{32}{25} - \tfrac{25}{25}$$
$$= \tfrac{7}{25}$$

5. $\tan 2\theta = \dfrac{2 \tan \theta}{1 - \tan^2 \theta}$
$$= \dfrac{2(3/4)}{1 - (3/4)^2}$$
$$= \dfrac{3/2}{1 - (9/16)}$$
$$= \dfrac{3}{2} \cdot \dfrac{16}{7}$$
$$- \dfrac{24}{7}$$

7. $\csc 2\theta = \dfrac{1}{\sin 2\theta}$
$$= \dfrac{1}{2 \sin \theta \cos \theta}$$
$$= \dfrac{1}{2(3/5)(4/5)}$$
$$= \dfrac{25}{24}$$

9. $\quad\quad \sin 2x - \sin x = 0$
$$2 \sin x \cos x - \sin x = 0$$
$$\sin x(2 \cos x - 1) = 0$$
$$\sin x = 0 \quad \text{ or } \quad 2 \cos x - 1 = 0$$
$$x = 0, \pi \quad\quad\quad \cos x = \tfrac{1}{2}$$
$$x = \tfrac{\pi}{3}, \tfrac{5\pi}{3}$$
$$x = 0, \tfrac{\pi}{3}, \pi, \tfrac{5\pi}{3}$$

11. $4 \sin x \cos x = 1$
$$2 \sin 2x = 1$$
$$\sin 2x = \tfrac{1}{2}$$
$$2x = \tfrac{\pi}{6} + 2n\pi \quad \text{or} \quad 2x = \tfrac{5\pi}{6} + 2n\pi$$
$$x = \tfrac{\pi}{12} + n\pi \quad\quad\quad x = \tfrac{5\pi}{12} + n\pi$$
$$x = \tfrac{\pi}{12}, \tfrac{13\pi}{12} \quad\quad\quad x = \tfrac{5\pi}{12}, \tfrac{17\pi}{12}$$

13.
$$\cos 2x = \cos x$$
$$\cos^2 x - \sin^2 x = \cos x$$
$$\cos^2 x(1 - \cos^2 x) - \cos x = 0$$
$$2\cos^2 x - \cos x - 1 = 0$$
$$(2\cos x + 1)(\cos x - 1) = 0$$
$$2\cos x + 1 = 0 \qquad \text{or} \quad \cos x - 1 = 0$$

$$\cos x = -\frac{1}{2} \qquad\qquad \cos x = 1$$

$$x = \frac{2\pi}{3}, \frac{4\pi}{3} \qquad\qquad x = 0$$

15.
$$\tan 2x - \cot x = 0$$
$$\frac{2\tan x}{1 - \tan^2 x} = \cot x$$
$$2\tan x = \cot x(1 - \tan^2 x)$$
$$2\tan x = \cot x - \cot x \tan^2 x$$
$$2\tan x = \cot x - \tan x$$
$$3\tan x = \cot x$$
$$3\tan x - \cot x = 0$$
$$3\tan x - \frac{1}{\tan x} = 0$$
$$\frac{3\tan^2 x - 1}{\tan x} = 0$$
$$\frac{1}{\tan x}(3\tan^2 x - 1) = 0$$
$$\cot x(3\tan^2 x - 1) = 0$$
$$\cot x = 0 \qquad \text{or} \quad 3\tan^2 x - 1 = 0$$

$$x = \frac{\pi}{2}, \frac{3\pi}{2} \qquad\qquad \tan^2 x = \frac{1}{3}$$

$$\tan x = \pm\frac{\sqrt{3}}{3}$$

$$x = \frac{\pi}{6}, \frac{5\pi}{6}, \frac{7\pi}{6}, \frac{11\pi}{6}$$

$$x = \frac{\pi}{6}, \frac{\pi}{2}, \frac{5\pi}{6}, \frac{7\pi}{6}, \frac{3\pi}{2}, \frac{11\pi}{6}$$

17.
$$\sin 4x = -2\sin 2x$$
$$\sin 4x + 2\sin 2x = 0$$
$$2\sin 2x \cos 2x + 2\sin 2x = 0$$
$$2\sin 2x(\cos 2x + 1) = 0$$
$$2\sin 2x = 0 \qquad \text{or} \quad \cos 2x + 1 = 0$$
$$\sin 2x = 0 \qquad\qquad \cos 2x = -1$$
$$2x = n\pi \qquad\qquad 2x = \pi + 2n\pi$$

$$x = \frac{n}{2}\pi \qquad\qquad x = \frac{\pi}{2} + n\pi$$

$$x = 0, \frac{\pi}{2}, \pi, \frac{3\pi}{2} \qquad\qquad x = \frac{\pi}{2}, \frac{3\pi}{2}$$

19. $f(x) = 6\sin x \cos x$
$$= 3(2\sin x \cos x)$$
$$= 3\sin 2x$$

21. $g(x) = 4 - 8\sin^2 x$
$$= 4(1 - 2\sin^2 x)$$
$$= 4\cos 2x$$

23. $\sin u = \dfrac{3}{5}, \ 0 < u < \dfrac{\pi}{2} \ \Rightarrow \ \cos v = \dfrac{4}{5}$

$\sin 2u = 2 \sin u \cos u = 2 \cdot \dfrac{3}{5} \cdot \dfrac{4}{5} = \dfrac{24}{25}$

$\cos 2u = \cos^2 u - \sin^2 u = \dfrac{16}{25} - \dfrac{9}{25} = \dfrac{7}{25}$

$\tan 2u = \dfrac{2 \tan u}{1 - \tan^2 u} = \dfrac{2(3/4)}{1 - (9/16)} = \dfrac{24}{7}$

25. $\tan u = \dfrac{1}{2}, \ \pi < u < \dfrac{3\pi}{2} \ \Rightarrow \ \sin u = -\dfrac{1}{\sqrt{5}}$ and

$$\cos u = -\dfrac{2}{\sqrt{5}}$$

$\sin 2u = 2 \sin u \cos u = 2\left(-\dfrac{1}{\sqrt{5}}\right)\left(-\dfrac{2}{\sqrt{5}}\right) = \dfrac{4}{5}$

$\cos 2u = \cos^2 u - \sin^2 u = \left(\dfrac{2}{\sqrt{5}}\right)^2 - \left(-\dfrac{1}{\sqrt{5}}\right)^2 = \dfrac{3}{5}$

$\tan 2u = \dfrac{2 \tan u}{1 - \tan^2 u} = \dfrac{2(1/2)}{1 - (1/4)} = \dfrac{4}{3}$

27. $\cos^4 x = (\cos^2 x)(\cos^2 x) = \left(\dfrac{1 + \cos 2x}{2}\right)\left(\dfrac{1 + \cos 2x}{2}\right) = \dfrac{1 + 2 \cos 2x + \cos^2 2x}{4}$

$$= \dfrac{1 + 2 \cos 2x + (1 + \cos 4x)/2}{4}$$

$$= \dfrac{2 + 4 \cos 2x + 1 + \cos 4x}{8}$$

$$= \dfrac{3 + 4 \cos 2x + \cos 4x}{8}$$

$$= \dfrac{1}{8}(3 + 4 \cos 2x + \cos 4x)$$

29. $(\sin^2 x)(\cos^2 x) = \left(\dfrac{1 - \cos 2x}{2}\right)\left(\dfrac{1 + \cos 2x}{2}\right)$

$$= \dfrac{1 - \cos^2 2x}{4}$$

$$= \dfrac{1}{4}\left(1 - \dfrac{1 + \cos 4x}{2}\right)$$

$$= \dfrac{1}{8}(2 - 1 - \cos 4x)$$

$$= \dfrac{1}{8}(1 - \cos 4x)$$

31. $\sin^2 x \cos^4 x = \sin^2 x \cos^2 x \cos^2 x = \left(\dfrac{1 - \cos 2x}{2}\right)\left(\dfrac{1 + \cos 2x}{2}\right)\left(\dfrac{1 + \cos 2x}{2}\right)$

$$= \dfrac{1}{8}(1 - \cos 2x)(1 + \cos 2x)(1 + \cos 2x)$$

$$= \dfrac{1}{8}(1 - \cos^2 2x)(1 + \cos 2x)$$

$$= \dfrac{1}{8}(1 + \cos 2x - \cos^2 2x - \cos^3 2x)$$

$$= \dfrac{1}{8}\left[1 + \cos 2x - \left(\dfrac{1 + \cos 4x}{2}\right) - \cos 2x\left(\dfrac{1 + \cos 4x}{2}\right)\right]$$

$$= \dfrac{1}{16}[2 + 2\cos 2x - 1 - \cos 4x - \cos 2x - \cos 2x \cos 4x]$$

$$= \dfrac{1}{16}\left[1 + \cos 2x - \cos 4x - \left(\dfrac{1}{2}\cos 2x + \dfrac{1}{2}\cos 6x\right)\right]$$

$$= \dfrac{1}{32}(2 + 2\cos 2x - 2\cos 4x - \cos 2x - \cos 6x)$$

$$= \dfrac{1}{32}(2 + \cos 2x - 2\cos 4x - \cos 6x)$$

Figure for Exercises 33 – 37

$\sin \theta = \frac{5}{13}$

$\cos \theta = \frac{12}{13}$

33. $\cos \dfrac{\theta}{2} = \sqrt{\dfrac{1 + \cos \theta}{2}} = \sqrt{\dfrac{1 + (12/13)}{2}} = \sqrt{\dfrac{25}{26}} = \dfrac{5}{\sqrt{26}}$

35. $\tan \dfrac{\theta}{2} = \dfrac{\sin \theta}{1 + \cos \theta} = \dfrac{5/13}{1 + (12/13)} = \dfrac{5}{25} = \dfrac{1}{5}$

37. $\csc \dfrac{\theta}{2} = \dfrac{1}{\sin(\theta/2)} = \dfrac{1}{\sqrt{(1 - \cos \theta/2)}} = \dfrac{1}{\sqrt{\left(1 - \frac{12}{13}\right)/2}} = \dfrac{1}{\sqrt{1/26}} = \sqrt{26}$

39. $\sin 105° = \sin\left(\dfrac{1}{2} \cdot 210°\right) = \sqrt{\dfrac{1 - \cos 210°}{2}} = \sqrt{\dfrac{1 + (\sqrt{3}/2)}{2}} = \dfrac{1}{2}\sqrt{2 + \sqrt{3}}$

$\cos 105° = \cos\left(\dfrac{1}{2} \cdot 210°\right) = \sqrt{\dfrac{1 + \cos 210°}{2}} = \sqrt{\dfrac{1 - (\sqrt{3}/2)}{2}} = -\dfrac{1}{2}\sqrt{2 - \sqrt{3}}$

$\tan 105° = \tan\left(\dfrac{1}{2} \cdot 210°\right) = \dfrac{\sin 210°}{1 + \cos 210°} = \dfrac{-1/2}{1 - (\sqrt{3}/2)} = -2 - \sqrt{3}$

41. $\sin 112° 30' = \sin\left(\frac{1}{2} \cdot 225°\right) = \sqrt{\frac{1 - \cos 225°}{2}} = \sqrt{\frac{1 + (\sqrt{2}/2)}{2}} = \frac{1}{2}\sqrt{2 + \sqrt{2}}$

$\cos 112° 30' = \cos\left(\frac{1}{2} \cdot 225°\right) = -\sqrt{\frac{1 + \cos 225°}{2}} = -\sqrt{\frac{1 - (\sqrt{2}/2)}{2}} = -\frac{1}{2}\sqrt{2 - \sqrt{2}}$

$\tan 112° 30' = \tan\left(\frac{1}{2} \cdot 225°\right) = \frac{\sin 225°}{1 + \cos 225°} = \frac{-\sqrt{2}/2}{1 - (\sqrt{2}/2)} = -1 - \sqrt{2}$

43. $\sin\frac{\pi}{8} = \sin\left[\frac{1}{2}\left(\frac{\pi}{4}\right)\right] = \sqrt{\frac{1 - \cos(\pi/4)}{2}} = \frac{1}{2}\sqrt{2 - \sqrt{2}}$

$\cos\frac{\pi}{8} = \cos\left[\frac{1}{2}\left(\frac{\pi}{4}\right)\right] = \sqrt{\frac{1 + \cos(\pi/4)}{2}} = \frac{1}{2}\sqrt{2 + \sqrt{2}}$

$\tan\frac{\pi}{8} = \tan\left[\frac{1}{2}\left(\frac{\pi}{4}\right)\right] = \frac{\sin(\pi/4)}{1 + \cos(\pi/4)} = \frac{\sqrt{2}/2}{1 + (\sqrt{2}/2)} = \sqrt{2} - 1$

45. $\sin u = \frac{5}{13}, \quad \frac{\pi}{2} < u < \pi \implies \cos u = -\frac{12}{13}$

$\sin\left(\frac{u}{2}\right) = \sqrt{\frac{1 - \cos u}{2}} = \sqrt{\frac{1 + (12/13)}{2}} = \frac{5\sqrt{26}}{26}$

$\cos\left(\frac{u}{2}\right) = \sqrt{\frac{1 + \cos u}{2}} = \sqrt{\frac{1 - (12/13)}{2}} = \frac{\sqrt{26}}{26}$

$\tan\left(\frac{u}{2}\right) = \frac{\sin u}{1 + \cos u} = \frac{5/13}{1 - (12/13)} = \frac{5}{1} = 5$

47. $\tan u = -\frac{5}{8}, \quad \frac{3\pi}{2} < u < 2\pi \implies \sin u = -\frac{8}{\sqrt{89}} \text{ and } \cos u = \frac{5}{\sqrt{89}}$

$\sin\left(\frac{u}{2}\right) = \sqrt{\frac{1 - \cos u}{2}} = \sqrt{\frac{1 - (8/\sqrt{89})}{2}} \sqrt{\frac{\sqrt{89} - 8}{2\sqrt{89}}} = \sqrt{\frac{89 - 8\sqrt{89}}{178}}$

$\cos\left(\frac{u}{2}\right) = -\sqrt{\frac{1 + \cos u}{2}} = -\sqrt{\frac{1 + (8/\sqrt{89})}{2}} = -\sqrt{\frac{\sqrt{89} + 8}{2\sqrt{89}}} = -\sqrt{\frac{89 + 8\sqrt{89}}{178}}$

$\tan\left(\frac{u}{2}\right) = \frac{1 - \cos u}{\sin u} = \frac{1 - (8/\sqrt{89})}{-5/\sqrt{89}} = \frac{8 - \sqrt{89}}{5}$

49. $\sqrt{\frac{1 - \cos 6x}{2}} = |\sin 3x|$

51. $-\sqrt{\frac{1 - \cos 8x}{1 + \cos 8x}} = -\frac{\sqrt{(1 - \cos 8x)/2}}{\sqrt{(1 + \cos 8x)/2}}$

$= -\left|\frac{\sin 4x}{\cos 4x}\right|$

$= -|\tan 4x|$

53. $\sin \dfrac{x}{2} + \cos x = 0$

$\pm \sqrt{\dfrac{1 - \cos x}{2}} = -\cos x$

$\dfrac{1 - \cos x}{2} = \cos^2 x$

$0 = 2\cos^2 x + \cos x - 1$

$\quad = (2\cos x - 1)(\cos x + 1)$

$\cos x = \dfrac{1}{2} \quad$ or $\quad \cos x = -1$

$x = \dfrac{\pi}{3}, \dfrac{5\pi}{3} \qquad\qquad x = \pi$

By checking these values in the original equations, we see that $x = \pi/3$ and $x = 5\pi/3$ are extraneous, and $x = \pi$ is the only solution.

55. $\cos \dfrac{x}{2} - \sin x = 0$

$\pm \sqrt{\dfrac{1 + \cos x}{2}} = \sin x$

$\dfrac{1 + \cos x}{2} = \sin^2 x$

$1 + \cos x = 2\sin^2 x$

$1 + \cos x = 2 - 2\cos^2 x$

$2\cos^2 x + \cos x - 1 = 0$

$2\cos x - 1)(\cos x + 1) = 0$

$2\cos x - 1 = 0 \quad$ or $\quad \cos x + 1 = 0$

$\cos x = \dfrac{1}{2} \qquad\qquad \cos x = -1$

$x = \dfrac{\pi}{3}, \dfrac{5\pi}{3} \qquad\qquad x = \pi$

$x = \dfrac{\pi}{3}, \ \pi, \ \dfrac{5\pi}{3}$

$\pi/3, \ \pi,$ and $5\pi/3$ are all solutions to the equation.

57. $6 \sin \dfrac{\pi}{4} \cos \dfrac{\pi}{4} = 6 \cdot \dfrac{1}{2}\left[\sin\left(\dfrac{\pi}{4} + \dfrac{\pi}{4}\right) + \sin\left(\dfrac{\pi}{4} - \dfrac{\pi}{4}\right)\right] = 3\left(\sin \dfrac{\pi}{2} + \sin 0\right)$

59. $\sin 5\theta \cos 3\theta = \tfrac{1}{2}[\sin(5\theta + 3\theta) + \sin(5\theta - 3\theta) = \tfrac{1}{2}(\sin 8\theta + \sin 2\theta)$

61. $5\cos(-5\beta)\cos 3\beta = 5 \cdot \tfrac{1}{2}[\cos(-5\beta - 3\beta) + \cos(-5\beta + 3\beta)] = \tfrac{5}{2}[\cos(-8\beta) + \cos(-2\beta)]$

$\qquad\qquad = \tfrac{5}{2}(\cos 8\beta + \cos 2\beta)$

63. $\sin 60° + \sin 30° = 2\sin\left(\dfrac{60° + 30°}{2}\right)\cos\left(\dfrac{60° - 30°}{2}\right) = 2\sin 45° \cos 15°$

65. $\cos \dfrac{3\pi}{4} - \cos \dfrac{\pi}{4} = -2\sin\left(\dfrac{(3\pi/4) + (\pi/4)}{2}\right) + \left(\dfrac{(3\pi/4) - (\pi/4)}{2}\right) = -2\sin \dfrac{\pi}{2}\sin \dfrac{\pi}{4}$

67. $\cos 6x + \cos 2x = 2\cos\left(\dfrac{6x + 2x}{2}\right)\cos\left(\dfrac{6x - 2x}{2}\right) = 2\cos 4x \cos 2x$

69. $\sin(\alpha + \beta) - \sin(\alpha - \beta) = 2\cos\left(\dfrac{\alpha + \beta + \alpha - \beta}{2}\right)\sin\left(\dfrac{\alpha + \beta - \alpha + \beta}{2}\right) = 2\cos \alpha \sin \beta$

71. $\cos(\phi + 2\pi) + \cos \phi = 2\cos\left(\dfrac{\phi + 2\pi + \phi}{2}\right)\cos\left(\dfrac{\phi + 2\pi - \phi}{2}\right) = 2\cos(\phi + \pi)\cos \pi$

73. $\sin 6x + \sin 2x = 0$

$$2\sin\left(\frac{6x + 2x}{2}\right)\cos\left(\frac{6x - 2x}{2}\right) = 0$$

$$x = 0, \frac{\pi}{4}, \frac{\pi}{2}, \frac{3\pi}{4}, \pi, \frac{5\pi}{4}, \frac{3\pi}{2}, \frac{7\pi}{4}$$

$\sin 4x = 0$ or $\cos 2x = 0$

$4x = n\pi$ $2x = \frac{\pi}{2} + n\pi$

$x = \frac{n\pi}{4}$ $x = \frac{\pi}{4} + \frac{n\pi}{2}$

In the interval we have

$$x = 0, \frac{\pi}{4}, \frac{\pi}{2}, \frac{3\pi}{4}, \pi, \frac{5\pi}{4}, \frac{3\pi}{2}, \frac{7\pi}{4}.$$

75. $\dfrac{\cos 2x}{\sin 3x - \sin x} - 1 = 0$

$$\frac{\cos 2x}{\sin 3x - \sin x} = 1$$

$$\frac{\cos 2x}{2\cos 2x \sin x} = 1$$

$$2\sin x = 1$$

$$\sin x = \frac{1}{2}$$

$$x = \frac{\pi}{6}, \frac{5\pi}{6}$$

77. $\sin^2 \alpha = \left(\frac{5}{13}\right)^2 = \frac{25}{169}$

$\sin^2 \alpha = 1 - \cos^2 \alpha = 1 - \left(\frac{12}{13}\right)^2 = 1 - \frac{144}{169} = \frac{25}{169}$

79. $\sin \alpha \cos \beta = \left(\frac{5}{13}\right)\left(\frac{4}{5}\right) = \frac{4}{13}$

$\sin \alpha \cos \beta = \cos\left(\frac{\pi}{2} - \alpha\right)\sin\left(\frac{\pi}{2} - \beta\right) = \left(\frac{5}{13}\right)\left(\frac{4}{5}\right) = \frac{4}{13}$

81. $\csc 2\theta = \dfrac{1}{\sin 2\theta}$

$$= \frac{1}{2\sin\theta\cos\theta}$$

$$= \frac{1}{\sin 2\theta} \cdot \frac{1}{2\cos\theta}$$

$$= \frac{\csc\theta}{2\cos\theta}$$

83. $\cos^2 2\alpha - \sin^2 2\alpha = \cos[2(2\alpha)]$

$$= \cos 4\alpha$$

85. $(\sin x + \cos x)^2 = \sin^2 x + 2\sin x \cos x + \cos^2 x$

$$= (\sin^2 x + \cos^2 x) + 2\sin x \cos x$$

$$= 1 + \sin 2x$$

87. $1 + \cos 10y = 1 + \cos^2 5y - \sin^2 5y$

$$= 1 + \cos^2 5y - (1 - \cos^2 5y)$$

$$= 2\cos^2 5y$$

89. $\sec \dfrac{u}{2} = \pm \sqrt{\dfrac{1}{\cos(u/2)}}$

$\quad = \pm \sqrt{\dfrac{2}{1 + \cos u}}$

$\quad = \pm \sqrt{\dfrac{2 \sin u}{\sin u(1 + \cos u)}}$

$\quad = \pm \sqrt{\dfrac{2 \sin u}{\sin u + \sin u \cos u}}$

$\quad = \pm \sqrt{\dfrac{(2 \sin u)/(\cos u)}{(\sin u)/(\cos u) + (\sin u \cos u)/(\cos u)}}$

$\quad = \pm \sqrt{\dfrac{2 \tan u}{\tan u + \sin u}}$

93 $\dfrac{\cos 4x - \cos 2x}{2 \sin 3x} = \dfrac{-2 \sin\left(\dfrac{4x + 2x}{2}\right) \sin\left(\dfrac{4x - 2x}{2}\right)}{2 \sin 3x}$

$\quad = \dfrac{-2 \sin 3x \sin x}{2 \sin 3x}$

$\quad = -\sin x$

95. $\sin^2 x = \dfrac{1 - \cos 2x}{2} = \dfrac{1}{2} - \dfrac{\cos 2x}{2}$

97. (a) $y = 4 \sin \dfrac{x}{2} + \cos x$

Maximum: $(\pi, 3)$

91. $\cos 3\beta = \cos(2\beta + \beta)$

$\quad = \cos 2\beta \cos \beta - \sin 2\beta \sin \beta$

$\quad = (\cos^2 \beta - \sin^2 \beta) \cos \beta - 2 \sin \beta \cos \beta \sin \beta$

$\quad = \cos^3 \beta - \sin^2 \beta \cos \beta - 2 \sin^2 \beta \cos \beta$

$\quad = \cos^3 \beta - 3 \sin^2 \beta \cos \beta$

(b) $\quad 2 \cos \dfrac{x}{2} - \sin x = 0$

$2\left(\pm \sqrt{\dfrac{1 + \cos x}{2}}\right) = \sin x$

$4\left(\dfrac{1 + \cos x}{2}\right) = \sin^2 x$

$2(1 + \cos x) = 1 - \cos^2 x$

$\cos^2 x + 2 \cos x + 1 = 0$

$(\cos x + 1)^2 = 0$

$\cos x = -1$

$x = \pi$

99. $f(x) = 2 \sin x \left[2 \cos^2\left(\dfrac{x}{2}\right) - 1 \right]$

(a)

(b) The graph appears to be that of $y = \sin 2x$.

(c) $2 \sin x \left[2 \cos^2\left(\dfrac{x}{2}\right) - 1 \right] = 2 \sin x \left[2 \dfrac{1 + \cos x}{2} - 1 \right]$

$\qquad\qquad = 2 \sin x \, [\cos x]$

$\qquad\qquad = \sin 2x$

101. $f(x) = \sin^4 x + \cos^4 x$

(a) From Exercise 27:

$\sin^4 x + \cos^4 x = \tfrac{1}{8}(3 - 4 \cos 2x + \cos 4x) + \tfrac{1}{8}(3 + 4 \cos 2x + \cos 4x)$

$\qquad\qquad\qquad = \tfrac{1}{8}(6 + 2 \cos 4x)$

$\qquad\qquad\qquad = \tfrac{1}{4}(3 + \cos 4x)$

(b) $\sin^4 x + \cos^4 x = (\sin^2 x)^2 + \cos^4 x$

$\qquad\qquad\qquad = (1 - \cos^2 x)^2 + \cos^4 x$

$\qquad\qquad\qquad = 1 - 2 \cos^2 x + \cos^4 x + \cos^4 x$

$\qquad\qquad\qquad = 2 \cos^4 x - 2 \cos^2 x + 1$

(c) $\sin^4 x + \cos^4 x = \sin^4 x + 2 \sin^2 x \cos^2 x + \cos^4 x - 2 \sin^2 x \cos^2 x$

$\qquad\qquad\qquad = (\sin^2 x + \cos^2 x)^2 - 2 \sin^2 x \cos^2 x$

$\qquad\qquad\qquad = 1 - 2 \sin^2 x \cos^2 x$

(d) $\sin^4 x + \cos^4 x = 1 - 2 \sin^2 x \cos^2 x$

$\qquad\qquad\qquad = 1 - (2 \sin x \cos x)^2 \left(\tfrac{1}{2}\right)$

$\qquad\qquad\qquad = 1 - \tfrac{1}{2} \sin^2(2x)$

(e) The expression has been rewritten four different ways. Hence, there is often more than one way to write a correct answer.

103. $\sin(2 \arcsin x) = 2 \sin(\arcsin x) \cos(\arcsin x) = 2x \sqrt{1 - x^2}$

❑ Review Exercises for Chapter 6

Solutions to Odd-Numbered Exercises

1. $\dfrac{1}{\cos^2 x + 1} = \dfrac{1}{\csc^2 x} = \sin^2 x$

3. $\dfrac{\sin^2 \alpha - \cos^2 \alpha}{\sin^2 \alpha - \sin \alpha \cos \alpha} = \dfrac{(\sin \alpha + \cos \alpha)(\sin \alpha - \cos \alpha)}{\sin \alpha(\sin \alpha - \cos \alpha)}$

$\qquad\qquad\qquad = \dfrac{\sin \alpha + \cos \alpha}{\sin \alpha}$

$\qquad\qquad\qquad = 1 + \cot \alpha$

5. $\tan^2 \theta(\csc^2 \theta - 1) = \tan^2 \theta(\cot^2 \theta)$

$$= \tan^2 \theta\left(\frac{1}{\tan^2 \theta}\right)$$

$$= 1$$

7. $\dfrac{2 \tan(x + 1)}{1 - \tan^2(x + 1)} = \tan[2(x + 1)]$

$$= \tan(2x + 2)$$

9. $\tan x(1 - \sin^2 x) = \tan x \cos^2 x$

$$= \frac{\sin x}{\cos x} \cdot \cos^2 x$$

$$= \sin x \cos x$$

$$= \frac{1}{2}(2 \sin x \cos x)$$

$$= \frac{1}{2} \sin 2x$$

11. $\sec^2 x \cot x - \cot x = \cot x(\sec^2 x - 1)$

$$= \cot x \tan^2 x$$

$$= \frac{1}{\tan x} \tan^2 x$$

$$= \tan x$$

13. $\sin^5 x \cos^2 x = \sin^4 x \cos^2 x \sin x$

$$= (1 - \cos^2 x)^2 \cos^2 x \sin x$$

$$= (1 - 2 \cos^2 x + \cos^4 x) \cos^2 x \sin x$$

$$= (\cos^2 x - 2 \cos^4 x + \cos^6 x) \sin x$$

15. $\sin 3\theta \sin \theta = \frac{1}{2}[\cos(3\theta - \theta) - \cos(3\theta + \theta)]$

$$= \frac{1}{2}(\cos 2\theta - \cos 4\theta)$$

17. $\sqrt{\dfrac{1 - \sin \theta}{1 + \sin \theta}} = \sqrt{\dfrac{1 - \sin \theta}{1 + \sin \theta} \cdot \dfrac{1 - \sin \theta}{1 - \sin \theta}}$

$$= \sqrt{\frac{(1 - \sin \theta)^2}{1 - \sin^2 \theta}} = \sqrt{\frac{(1 - \sin \theta)^2}{\cos^2 \theta}} = \frac{|1 - \sin \theta|}{|\cos \theta|} = \frac{1 - \sin \theta}{|\cos \theta|}$$

Note: We can drop the absolute value on $1 - \sin \theta$ since it is always nonnegative.

19. $\cos 3x = \cos(2x + x)$

$$= \cos 2x \cos x - \sin 2x \sin x$$

$$= (\cos^2 x - \sin^2 x) \cos x - 2 \sin x \cos x \sin x$$

$$= \cos^3 x - 3 \sin^2 x \cos x$$

$$= \cos^3 x - 3 \cos x(1 - \cos^2 x)$$

$$= \cos^3 x - 3 \cos x + 3 \cos^3 x$$

$$= 4 \cos^3 x - 3 \cos x$$

21. $\cot\left(\dfrac{\pi}{2} - x\right) = \dfrac{\cos[(\pi/2) - x]}{\sin[(\pi/2) - x]}$

$$= \frac{\cos(\pi/2) \cos x + \sin(\pi/2) \sin x}{\sin(\pi/2) \cos x - \sin x \cos(\pi/2)}$$

$$= \frac{\sin x}{\cos x}$$

$$= \tan x$$

23. $\dfrac{\sec x - 1}{\tan x} = \dfrac{(1/\cos x) - 1}{\sin x/\cos x} = \dfrac{1 - \cos x}{\sin x} = \tan \dfrac{x}{2}$

25. $2 \sin y \cos y \sec 2y = (\sin 2y)(\sec 2y)$

$\qquad\qquad\qquad\qquad = \dfrac{\sin 2y}{\cos 2y}$

$\qquad\qquad\qquad\qquad = \tan 2y$

27. $\sin\!\left(x - \dfrac{3\pi}{2}\right) = \sin x \cos \dfrac{3\pi}{2} - \sin \dfrac{3\pi}{2} \cos x$

$\qquad\qquad\qquad = (\sin x)(0) - (-1)(\cos x)$

$\qquad\qquad\qquad = \cos x$

29. $\dfrac{1 - \cos 2x}{1 + \cos 2x} = \dfrac{1 - (1 - 2\sin^2 x)}{1 + (2\cos^2 x - 1)}$

$\qquad\qquad\qquad = \dfrac{2\sin^2 x}{2\cos^2 x}$

$\qquad\qquad\qquad = \tan^2 x$

31. $\sin \dfrac{5\pi}{12} = \sin\!\left(\dfrac{2\pi}{3} - \dfrac{\pi}{4}\right)$

$\qquad\quad = \sin\!\left(\dfrac{2\pi}{3}\right) \cos\!\left(\dfrac{\pi}{4}\right) - \cos \dfrac{2\pi}{3} \sin\!\left(\dfrac{\pi}{4}\right)$

$\qquad\quad = \left(\dfrac{\sqrt{3}}{2}\right)\!\left(\dfrac{\sqrt{2}}{2}\right) - \left(-\dfrac{1}{2}\right)\!\left(\dfrac{\sqrt{2}}{2}\right)$

$\qquad\quad = \dfrac{\sqrt{2}}{4}\left(\sqrt{3} + 1\right)$

33. $\cos(157° \, 30') = \cos \dfrac{315°}{2} = -\sqrt{\dfrac{1 + \cos 315°}{2}} = -\sqrt{\dfrac{1 + \cos 45°}{2}}$

$\qquad\qquad = -\sqrt{\dfrac{1 + \sqrt{2}/2}{2}} = -\sqrt{\dfrac{2 + \sqrt{2}}{4}} = -\dfrac{1}{2}\sqrt{2 + \sqrt{2}}$

For Exercises 35–39:

$$\sin u = \frac{3}{4}, \; u \text{ in Quadrant II} \;\Rightarrow\; \cos u = -\frac{\sqrt{7}}{4}$$

$$\cos v = -\frac{5}{13}, \; v \text{ in Quadrant II} \;\Rightarrow\; \sin v = \frac{12}{13}$$

35. $\sin(u + v) = \sin u \cos v + \cos u \sin v$

$\qquad\qquad = \left(\dfrac{3}{4}\right)\!\left(-\dfrac{5}{13}\right) + \left(-\dfrac{\sqrt{7}}{4}\right)\!\left(\dfrac{12}{13}\right)$

$\qquad\qquad = -\dfrac{15}{52} - \dfrac{12\sqrt{7}}{52}$

$\qquad\qquad = \dfrac{-3(5 + 4\sqrt{7})}{52}$

37. $\cos(u - v) = \cos u \cos v + \sin u \sin v$

$\qquad\qquad = \left(-\dfrac{\sqrt{7}}{4}\right)\!\left(-\dfrac{5}{13}\right) + \left(\dfrac{3}{4}\right)\!\left(\dfrac{12}{13}\right)$

$\qquad\qquad = \dfrac{5\sqrt{7} + 36}{52}$

39. $\cos \dfrac{u}{2} = \sqrt{\dfrac{1 + \cos u}{2}}$

$\qquad = \sqrt{\dfrac{1 + (-\sqrt{7}/4)}{2}}$

$\qquad = \sqrt{\dfrac{4 - \sqrt{7}}{8}}$

$\qquad = \dfrac{1}{4}\sqrt{2(4 - \sqrt{7})}$

41. If $\dfrac{\pi}{2} < \theta < \pi$, then $\cos \dfrac{\theta}{2} < 0$. False, if

$\dfrac{\pi}{2} < \theta < \pi \implies \dfrac{\pi}{4} < \dfrac{\theta}{2} < \dfrac{\pi}{2}$,

which is in Quadrant I $\implies \cos(\theta/2) > 0$.

43. $4 \sin(-x) \cos(-x) = -2 \sin 2x$. True.

$\quad 4 \sin(-x) \cos(-x) = 4(-\sin x)(\cos x) = -4 \sin x \cos x = -2(2 \sin x \cos x) = -2 \sin 2x$

45. $\qquad \sin x - \tan x = 0$

$\qquad \sin x - \dfrac{\sin x}{\cos x} = 0$

$\quad \sin x \cos x - \sin x = 0$

$\qquad \sin x(\cos x - 1) = 0$

$\quad \sin x = 0 \quad$ or $\quad \cos x - 1 = 0$

$\quad x = 0, \pi \qquad\qquad \cos x = 1$

$\qquad\qquad\qquad\qquad\qquad x = 0$

47. $\qquad \sin 2x + \sqrt{2}\sin x = 0$

$\quad 2 \sin x \cos x + \sqrt{2}\sin x = 0$

$\qquad \sin x(2 \cos x + \sqrt{2}) = 0$

$\quad \sin x = 0 \quad$ or $\quad 2 \cos x + \sqrt{2} = 0$

$\quad x = 0, \pi \qquad\qquad \cos x = -\dfrac{\sqrt{2}}{2}$

$\qquad\qquad\qquad\qquad x = \dfrac{3\pi}{4}, \dfrac{5\pi}{4}$

49. $\qquad \cos^2 x + \sin x = 1$

$\quad 1 - \sin^2 x + \sin x = 1$

$\qquad \sin x(\sin x - 1) = 0$

$\quad \sin x = 0 \quad$ or $\quad \sin x = 1$

$\quad x = 0, \pi \qquad\qquad x = \dfrac{\pi}{2}$

51. $\qquad \dfrac{1 + \sin x}{\cos x} + \dfrac{\cos x}{1 + \sin x} = 4$

$\qquad (1 + \sin x)^2 + \cos^2 x = 4 \cos x(1 + \sin x)$

$\quad 1 + 2 \sin x + \sin^2 x + \cos^2 x = 4 \cos x(1 + \sin x)$

$\quad 2 + 2 \sin x = 4 \cos x(1 + \sin x) = 0$

$\qquad 2(1 + \sin x)(1 - 2 \cos x) = 0$

$\quad 1 + \sin x = 0 \quad$ or $\quad 1 - 2 \cos x = 0$

$\qquad \sin x = -1 \qquad\qquad \cos x = \dfrac{1}{2}$

$\qquad x = \dfrac{3\pi}{2} \qquad\qquad x = \dfrac{\pi}{3}, \dfrac{5\pi}{3}$

(extraneous solution)

53.
$$\tan^3 x - \tan^2 x + 3 \tan x - 3 = 0$$
$$\tan^2 x(\tan x - 1) + 3(\tan x - 1) = 0$$
$$(\tan^2 x + 3)(\tan x - 1) = 0$$
$$\tan^2 x + 3 = 0 \quad \text{or} \quad \tan x - 1 = 1$$
$$\text{(No solution)} \quad \text{or} \quad \tan x = 1$$
$$x = \frac{\pi}{4}, \frac{5\pi}{4}$$

55. False, $\sin \theta = \frac{1}{2}$ has an infinite number of solutions but is not an identity.

57.
$$\cos 3\theta + \cos 2\theta = 2 \cos\left(\frac{3\theta + 2\theta}{2}\right) \cos\left(\frac{3\theta - 2\theta}{2}\right)$$
$$= 2 \cos \frac{5\theta}{2} \cos \frac{\theta}{2}$$

59.
$$\sin 3\alpha \sin 2\alpha = \frac{1}{2}[\cos(3\alpha - 2\alpha) - \cos(3\alpha + 2\alpha)]$$
$$= \frac{1}{2}(\cos \alpha - \cos 5\alpha)$$

61.
$$\cos(2 \arccos 2x) = \cos 2\theta$$
$$= \cos^2 \theta - \sin^2 \theta$$
$$= (2x)^2 - \left(\sqrt{1 - 4x^2}\right)^2$$
$$= 4x^2 - (1 - 4x^2)$$
$$= 8x^2 - 1$$

$\theta = \arccos 2x$

63.
$$\sin^{-1/2} \cos x = \frac{\cos x}{\sin^{1/2} x}$$
$$= \frac{\cos x}{\sqrt{\sin x}} \cdot \frac{\sqrt{\sin x}}{\sqrt{\sin x}}$$
$$= \frac{\cos x}{\sin x} \sqrt{\sin x}$$
$$= \cot x \sqrt{\sin x}$$

65. $y = 1.5 \sin 8t - 0.5 \cos 8t$

(a) $a = \dfrac{3}{2}, \ b = -\dfrac{1}{2}, \ B = 8, \ C = \arctan\left(-\dfrac{1/2}{3/2}\right)$

$$y = \sqrt{(3/2)^2 + (1/2)^2} \sin\left(8t + \arctan{-\frac{1}{3}}\right)$$

$$y = \frac{1}{2}\sqrt{10} \sin\left(8t - \arctan\frac{1}{3}\right)$$

(b)

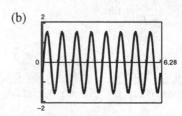

(c) The amplitude is $\dfrac{\sqrt{10}}{2}$.

(d) Frequency $= \dfrac{1}{\text{period}} = \dfrac{4}{\pi}$

❑ Chapter Test for Chapter 6

1. θ is in Quadrant III.

$$\tan^2\theta + 1 = \sec^2\theta \implies \frac{9}{4} + 1 = \sec^2\theta \implies \sec\theta = -\frac{\sqrt{13}}{2}$$

$$\cos\theta = -\frac{2}{\sqrt{13}}$$

$$\sin\theta = (\tan\theta)(\cos\theta) = \frac{3}{2}\left(-\frac{2}{\sqrt{13}}\right) = \frac{-3}{\sqrt{13}}$$

$$\csc\theta = \frac{-\sqrt{13}}{3}$$

$$\cot\theta = \frac{1}{\tan\theta} = \frac{2}{3}$$

2. $\csc^2\beta(1 - \cos^2\beta) = \dfrac{1}{\sin^2\beta} \cdot \sin^2\beta = 1$

3. $\dfrac{\sec^4 x - \tan^4 x}{\sec^2 x + \tan^2 x} = \dfrac{[(\sec^2 x) + (\tan^2 x)][\sec^2 x - \tan^2 x]}{\sec^2 x + \tan^2 x} = \sec^2 x - \tan^2 x = 1$

4. $\dfrac{\cos\theta}{\sin\theta} + \dfrac{\sin\theta}{\cos\theta} = \dfrac{\cos^2\theta + \sin^2\theta}{\sin\theta\cos\theta} = \dfrac{1}{\sin\theta\cos\theta}$

5. Since $\tan^2\theta = \sec^2\theta - 1$ for all θ, then $\tan\theta = -\sqrt{\sec^2\theta - 1}$ in Quadrants II and IV. Thus, $\pi/2 < \theta \le \pi$ and $3\pi/2 < \theta < 2\pi$.

6.

The graph appears equal.

Analytically, $y_1 = \cos x + \sin x \tan x$

$\qquad\qquad\qquad = \cos x + \sin x(\sin x/\cos x)$

$\qquad\qquad\qquad = \dfrac{\cos^2 x + \sin^2 x}{\cos x}$

$\qquad\qquad\qquad = \dfrac{1}{\cos x}$

$\qquad\qquad\qquad = \sec x = y_2$

7. $\sin\theta \cdot \sec\theta = \sin\theta\dfrac{1}{\cos\theta} = \tan\theta$

8. $\sec^2\theta\tan^2\theta + \sec^2\theta = \sec^2\theta(\tan^2\theta + 1) = \sec^4\theta$

9. $\dfrac{\csc\alpha + \sec\alpha}{\sin\alpha + \cos\alpha} = \dfrac{\dfrac{1}{\sin\alpha} + \dfrac{1}{\cos\alpha}}{\sin\alpha + \cos\alpha} = \dfrac{\dfrac{\cos\alpha + \sin\alpha}{\sin\alpha \cdot \cos\alpha}}{(\sin\alpha + \cos\alpha)}$

$\qquad\qquad\qquad\quad = \dfrac{1}{\sin\alpha\cos\alpha} = \dfrac{\cos^2\alpha + \sin^2\alpha}{\sin\alpha\cos\alpha}$

$\qquad\qquad\qquad\quad = \dfrac{\cos\alpha}{\sin\alpha} + \dfrac{\sin\alpha}{\cos\alpha} = \cot\alpha + \tan\alpha$

10. $\cos\left(x + \dfrac{\pi}{2}\right) = \cos x \cos \dfrac{\pi}{2} - \sin x \sin \dfrac{\pi}{2}$

$$= 0 - \sin x = -\sin x$$

11. $\sin(n\pi + \theta) = \sin n\pi \cdot \cos \theta + \sin \theta \cdot \cos n\pi$

$$= \cos n\pi \cdot \sin \theta$$

$$= (-1)^n \sin \theta$$

12. $(\sin x + \cos x)^2 = \sin^2 x + \cos^2 x + 2 \sin x \cos x$

$$= 1 + \sin 2x$$

13. $\tan^2 x + \tan x = 0$

$\tan x(\tan x + 1) = 0$

$\tan x = 0 \implies x = 0, \pi$

$\tan x + 1 = 0 \implies \tan x = -1 \implies x = \dfrac{3\pi}{4}, \dfrac{7\pi}{4}$

14. $\sin 2\alpha - \cos \alpha = 0$

$2 \sin \alpha \cos \alpha - \cos \alpha = 0$

$\cos \alpha(2 \sin \alpha - 1) = 0$

$\cos \alpha = 0 \implies \alpha = \dfrac{\pi}{2}, \dfrac{3\pi}{2}$

$2 \sin \alpha - 1 = 0 \implies \sin \alpha = \dfrac{1}{2} \implies \alpha = \dfrac{\pi}{6}, \dfrac{5\pi}{6}$

15. $4 \cos^2 x - 3 = 0$

$$\cos^2 x = \dfrac{3}{4}$$

$$\cos x = \pm\dfrac{\sqrt{3}}{2}$$

$$x = \dfrac{\pi}{6}, \dfrac{5\pi}{6}, \dfrac{7\pi}{6}, \dfrac{11\pi}{6}$$

16. $\csc^2 x - \csc x - 2 = 0$

$(\csc x - 2)(\csc x + 1) = 0$

$\csc x - 2 = 0 \implies \csc x = 2 \rightarrow \sin x - \dfrac{1}{2} \implies x = \dfrac{\pi}{6}, \dfrac{5\pi}{6}$

$\csc x + 1 = 0 \implies \csc x = -1 \implies \sin x = -1 \implies x = \dfrac{3\pi}{2}$

17. Let $y = 3 \cos x - x$. The zeros are $-2.938, -2.663, 1.170$.

18. Since $|\cos x| \le 1$, $|\cos^2 x + \cos x| \le 2$ for all x.

19. $\cos 105° = \cos(135° - 30°) = \cos 135° \cos 30° + \sin 135° \sin 30°$

$$= \left(-\dfrac{\sqrt{2}}{2}\right)\left(\dfrac{\sqrt{3}}{2}\right) + \left(\dfrac{\sqrt{2}}{2}\right)\dfrac{1}{2}$$

$$= -\dfrac{\sqrt{6}}{4} + \dfrac{\sqrt{2}}{4} = \dfrac{\sqrt{2} - \sqrt{6}}{4}$$

20. $\sin 2u = 2 \sin u \cos u = 2\dfrac{2}{\sqrt{5}} \cdot \dfrac{1}{\sqrt{5}} = \dfrac{4}{5}$

$$\tan 2u = \dfrac{2 \tan u}{1 - \tan^2 u} = \dfrac{2(2)}{1 - 2^2} = -\dfrac{4}{3}$$

❑ Practice Test for Chapter 6

1 Find the value of the other five trigonometric functions, given $\tan x = \frac{4}{11}$, $\sec x < 0$.

2. Simplify $\dfrac{\sec^2 x + \csc^2 x}{\csc^2 x(1 + \tan^2 x)}$.

3. Rewrite as a single logarithm and simplify $\ln|\tan \theta| - \ln|\cot \theta|$.

4. True or false:

$$\cos\left(\frac{\pi}{2} - x\right) = \frac{1}{\csc x}$$

5. Factor and simplify: $\sin^4 x + (\sin^2 x) \cos^2 x$

6. Multiply and simplify: $(\csc x + 1)(\csc x - 1)$

7. Rationalize the denominator and simplify:

$$\frac{\cos^2 x}{1 - \sin x}$$

8. Verify:

$$\frac{1 + \cos \theta}{\sin \theta} + \frac{\sin \theta}{1 + \cos \theta} = 2 \csc \theta$$

9. Verify:

$$\tan^4 x + 2 \tan^2 x + 1 = \sec^4 x$$

10. Use the sum or difference formulas to determine:

    (a) $\sin 105°$ (b) $\tan 15°$

11. Simplify: $(\sin 42°) \cos 38° - (\cos 42°) \sin 38°$

12. Verify $\tan\left(\theta + \dfrac{\pi}{4}\right) = \dfrac{1 + \tan \theta}{1 - \tan \theta}$.

13. Write $\sin(\arcsin x - \arccos x)$ as an algebraic expression in x.

14. Use the double-angle formulas to determine:

    (a) $\cos 120°$ (b) $\tan 300°$

15. Use the half-angle formulas to determine:

    (a) $\sin 22.5°$ (b) $\tan \dfrac{\pi}{12}$

16. Given $\sin = 4/5$, θ lies in Quadrant II, find $\cos \theta/2$.

17. Use the power-reducing identities to write $(\sin^2 x) \cos^2 x$ in terms of the first power of cosine.

18. Rewrite as a sum: $6(\sin 5\theta) \cos 2\theta$.

19. Rewrite as a product:

$$\sin(x + \pi) + \sin(x - \pi).$$

20. Verify $\dfrac{\sin 9x + \sin 5x}{\cos 9x - \cos 5x} = -\cot 2x$.

21. Verify:

$$(\cos u) \sin v = \tfrac{1}{2}[\sin(u + v) - \sin(u - v)].$$

22. Find all solutions in the interval $[0, 2\pi)$:

$$4 \sin^2 x = 1$$

23. Find all solutions in the interval $[0, 2\pi)$:

$$\tan^2 \theta + \left(\sqrt{3} - 1\right) \tan \theta - \sqrt{3} = 0$$

24. Find all solutions in the interval $[0, 2\pi)$:

$$\sin 2x = \cos x$$

25. Use the Quadratic Formula to find all solutions in the interval $[0, 2\pi)$:

$$\tan^2 x - 6 \tan x + 4 = 0$$

CHAPTER 7
Additional Topics in Trigonometry

CHAPTER 7
Additional Topics in Trigonometry

Section 7.1   Law of Sines

■ If ABC is any oblique triangle with sides a, b, and c, then the Law of Sines says

$$\frac{a}{\sin A} = \frac{b}{\sin B} = \frac{c}{\sin C}.$$

■ You should be able to use the Law of Sines to solve an oblique triangle for the remaining three parts, given:

(a) Two angles and any side (AAS or ASA)

(b) Two sides and an angle opposite one of them (SSA)

   1. If A is acute and $h = b \sin A$:

     (a) $a < h$, no triangle is possible.

     (b) $a = h$ or $a > b$, one triangle is possible.

     (c) $h < a < b$, two triangles are possible.

   2. If A is obtuse and $h = b \sin A$:

     (a) $a \le b$, no triangle is possible.

     (b) $a > b$, one triangle is possible.

■ The area of any triangle equals one-half the product of the lengths of two sides times the sine of their included angle.

$$A = \tfrac{1}{2}ab \sin C = \tfrac{1}{2}ac \sin B = \tfrac{1}{2}bc \sin A$$

Solutions to Odd-Numbered Exercises

1. Given: $A = 30°$, $B = 45°$, $a = 20$

$C = 180° - A - B = 105°$

$b = \dfrac{a}{\sin A}(\sin B) = \dfrac{20 \sin 45°}{\sin 30°} = 20\sqrt{2} \approx 28.28$

$c = \dfrac{a}{\sin A}(\sin C) = \dfrac{20 \sin 105°}{\sin 30°} \approx 38.64$

3. Given: $A = 10°$, $B = 60°$, $a = 7.5$

$C = 180° - A - B = 110°$

$b = \dfrac{a}{\sin A}(\sin B) = \dfrac{7.5}{\sin 10°} = (\sin 60°) \approx 37.40$

$c = \dfrac{a}{\sin A}(\sin C) = \dfrac{7.5}{\sin 10°}(\sin 110°) \approx 40.59$

5. Given: $A = 36°$, $a = 8$, $b = 5$

$\sin B = \dfrac{b \sin A}{a} = \dfrac{5 \sin 36°}{8} \approx 0.36737 \implies B \approx 21.55°$

$C = 180 - A - B \approx 180° - 36° - 21.55 = 122.45°$

$c = \dfrac{a}{\sin A}(\sin C) = \dfrac{8}{\sin 36°}(\sin 122.45°) \approx 11.49$

7. Given: $A = 150°$, $C = 20°$, $a = 200$

$B = 180° - A - C = 180° - 150° - 20° = 10°$

$b = \dfrac{a}{\sin A}(\sin B) = \dfrac{200}{\sin 150°}(\sin 10°) \approx 69.46$

$c = \dfrac{a}{\sin A}(\sin C) = \dfrac{200}{\sin 150°}(\sin 20°) \approx 136.81$

9. Given: $A = 83° \, 20'$, $C = 54.6°$, $c = 18.1$

$B = 180° - A - C = 180° - 80° \, 20' - 54° \, 36' = 42° \, 4'$

$a = \dfrac{c}{\sin C}(\sin A) = \dfrac{18.1}{\sin 54.6°}(\sin 83° \, 20') \approx 22.05$

$b = \dfrac{c}{\sin C}(\sin B) = \dfrac{18.1}{\sin 54.6°}(\sin 42° \, 4') \approx 14.88$

11. Given: $B = 15° \, 30'$, $a = 4.5$, $b = 6.8$

$\sin A = \dfrac{a \sin B}{b} = \dfrac{4.5 \sin 15° \, 30'}{6.8} \approx 0.17685 \implies A \approx 10° \, 11'$

$C = 180° - A - B \approx 180° - 10° \, 11' - 15.5° = 154° \, 19'$

$c = \dfrac{b}{\sin B}(\sin C) = \dfrac{6.8}{\sin 15° \, 30'}(\sin 154° \, 19') \approx 11.03$

13. Given: $A = 110° \, 15'$, $a = 48$, $b = 16$

$\sin B = \dfrac{b \sin A}{a} = \dfrac{16 \sin 110° \, 15'}{48} \approx 0.31273 \implies B \approx 18° \, 13'$

$C = 180° - A - B \approx 180° - 110° \, 15' - 18° \, 13' = 51° \, 32'$

$c = \dfrac{a}{\sin A}(\sin C) = \dfrac{48}{\sin 110° \, 15'}(\sin 51° \, 32') \approx 40.05$

15. Given: $a = 4.5$, $b = 12.8$, $A = 58°$

$h = 12.8 \sin 58° \approx 10.86$

Since $a < h$, no triangle is formed.

17. Given: $a = 4.5$, $b = 5$, $A = 58°$

$\sin B = \dfrac{b \sin A}{a} = \dfrac{5 \sin 58°}{4.5} \approx 0.9423 \implies B = 70.4°$ or $B = 109.6°$

<u>Case 1</u>

$B \approx 70.4°$

$C \approx 180° - 70.4° - 58° = 51.6°$

$c \approx \dfrac{4.5}{\sin 58°}(\sin 51.6°) \approx 4.16$

<u>Case 2</u>

$B \approx 109.6°$

$C \approx 180° - 109.6° - 58° = 12.4°$

$c \approx \dfrac{4.5}{\sin 58°}(\sin 12.4°) \approx 1.14$

19. Given: $A = 36°$, $a = 5$

(a) One solution if $b \leq 5$ or $b = \dfrac{5}{\sin 36°}$.

(b) Two solutions if $5 < b < \dfrac{5}{\sin 36°}$.

(c) No solution if $b > \dfrac{5}{\sin 36°}$.

21. (a)

(b) $\dfrac{16}{\sin 70°} = \dfrac{h}{\sin 32°}$

(c) $h = \dfrac{16 \sin 32°}{\sin 70°} \approx 9$ meters

25. Given: $A = 74° - 28° = 46°$,

$B = 180° - 41° - 74° = 65°, \ c = 100$

$C = 180° - 46° - 65° = 69°$

$a = \dfrac{c}{\sin C}(\sin A) = \dfrac{100}{\sin 69°}(\sin 46°) \approx 77$ meters

27. (a)

$\dfrac{18.8°}{} \ \dfrac{17.5°}{}$ z

9000 ft   y

(c) $\dfrac{y}{\sin 71.2°} = \dfrac{x}{\sin 90°}$

$y = x \sin 71.2° \approx 119289.1261 \sin 71.2°$

≈ 112924.963 feet ≈ 21.4 miles

23. $\dfrac{\sin(42° - \theta)}{10} = \dfrac{\sin 48°}{17}$

$\sin(42° - \theta) \approx 0.43714$

$\theta \approx 16.1°$

(b) $\dfrac{x}{\sin 17.5°} = \dfrac{9000}{\sin 1.3°}$

$x \approx 1198289.1261$ feet ≈ 22.6 miles

(d) $z = x \sin 18.8° \approx 119289.1261 \sin 18.8°$

$\approx 38,442.8$ feet

29. $A = 65° - 28° = 37°$

$c = 30$

$B = 180° - 16.5° - 65° = 98.5°$

$C = 180° - 37° - 98.5° = 44.5°$

$a = \dfrac{c}{\sin C}(\sin A) = \dfrac{30}{\sin 44.5°}(\sin 37°) \approx 25.8$ km to B

$b = \dfrac{c}{\sin C}(\sin B) = \dfrac{30}{\sin 44.5°}(\sin 98.5°) \approx 42.3$ km to A

31. $A = 90° - 62° = 28°$,

$B = 90° + 38° = 128°, \ c = 5$

$C = 180° - 128° - 28° = 24°$

$a = \dfrac{c}{\sin C}(\sin A) = \dfrac{5}{\sin 24°}(\sin 28°) \approx 5.77$

$d = a \sin(90° - 38°) \approx 5.77 \sin 52° \approx 4.55$ miles

33. (a) $\dfrac{\sin \alpha}{9} = \dfrac{\sin \beta}{18}$

$\sin \alpha = 0.5 \sin \beta$

$\alpha = \arcsin(0.5 \sin \beta)$

(b)

Domain: $0 < \beta < \pi$

Range: $0 < c \le \pi/6$

(c) $\gamma = \pi - \alpha - \beta - \pi - \beta - \arcsin(0.5 \sin \beta)$

$\dfrac{c}{\sin \gamma} = \dfrac{18}{\sin \beta}$

$c = \dfrac{18 \sin \gamma}{\sin \beta} = \dfrac{18 \sin[\pi - \beta - \arcsin(0.5 \sin \beta)]}{\sin \beta}$

(d)

Domain: $0 < \beta < \pi$

Range: $9 < c < 27$

(e)

β	0	0.4	0.8	1.2	1.6	2.0	2.4	2.8
α	0	0.1960	0.3669	0.4848	0.5234	0.4720	0.3445	0.1683
c	Undef.	25.95	23.07	19.19	15.33	12.29	10.31	9.27

As $\beta \to 0$, $c \to 27$.

As $\beta \to \pi$, $c \to 9$.

35. Area $= \frac{1}{2}ab \sin C = \frac{1}{2}(4)(6) \sin 120° \approx 10.4$

37. Area $= \frac{1}{2}bc \sin A = \frac{1}{2}(57)(85) \sin 43° \, 45' \approx 1675.2$

39. Area $= \frac{1}{2}ac \sin B = \frac{1}{2}(62)(20) \sin 130° \approx 474.9$

41. (a) $A = \dfrac{1}{2}(30)(20) \sin\left(\theta + \dfrac{\theta}{2}\right) - \dfrac{1}{2}(8)(20) \sin \dfrac{\theta}{2} - \dfrac{1}{2}(8)(30) \sin \theta$

$= 300 \sin \dfrac{3\theta}{2} - 80 \sin \dfrac{\theta}{2} - 120 \sin \theta$

$= 20\left[15 \sin \dfrac{3\theta}{2} - 4 \sin \dfrac{\theta}{2} - 6 \sin \theta \right]$

(b)

(c) Domain: $0 \le \theta \le 1.6690$

The domain would increase in length and the area would increase if the 8 centimeter line segment were decreased.

Section 7.2   Law of Cosines

■   If ABC is any oblique triangle with sides a, b, and c, then the Law of Cosines says:

(a) $a^2 = b^2 + c^2 - 2bc \cos A$ or $\cos A = \dfrac{b^2 + c^2 - a^2}{2bc}$

(b) $b^2 = a^2 + c^2 - 2ac \cos B$ or $\cos B = \dfrac{a^2 + c^2 - b^2}{2ac}$

(c) $c^2 = a^2 + b^2 - 2ab \cos C$ or $\cos C = \dfrac{a^2 + b^2 - c^2}{2ab}$

■   You should be able to use the Law of Cosines to solve an oblique triangle for the remaining three parts, given:

(a) Three sides (SSS)

(b) Two sides and their included angle (SAS)

■   Given any triangle with sides of length a, b, and c, then the area of the triangle is

$$\text{Area} = \sqrt{s(s-a)(s-b)(s-c)}, \text{ where } s = \frac{a+b+c}{2}. \quad \text{(Heron's Formula)}$$

Solutions to Odd-Numbered Exercises

1. Given: $a = 6$, $b = 8$, $c = 12$

$\cos A = \dfrac{b^2 + c^2 - a^2}{2bc} = \dfrac{64 + 144 - 36}{2(8)(12)} \approx 0.8958 \implies A \approx 26.4°$

$\sin B = \dfrac{b \sin A}{a} \approx \dfrac{8 \sin 26.4°}{6} \approx 0.5928 \implies B \approx 36.3°$

$C \approx 180° - 26.4° - 36.3° = 117.3°$

3. Given: $A = 30°$, $b = 15$, $c = 30$

$a^2 = b^2 + c^2 - 2bc \cos A$

$\quad = 225 + 900 - 2(15)(30) \cos 30° \approx 18.5897$

$a \approx 18.6$

$\cos B = \dfrac{a^2 + c^2 - b^2}{2ac} \approx \dfrac{(18.6)^2 + 900 - 225}{2(18.6)(30)} \approx 0.9148$

$B \approx 23.8°$

$C \approx 180° - 30° - 23.8° = 126.2°$

5. Given: $a = 9$, $b = 12$, $c = 15$

$\cos C = \dfrac{a^2 + b^2 - c^2}{2ab} = \dfrac{81 + 144 - 225}{2(9)(12)} = 0 \implies C = 90°$

$\sin A = \dfrac{9}{15} = \dfrac{3}{5} \implies A \approx 36.9°$

$B \approx 180° - 90° - 36.9° = 53.1°$

7. Given: $a = 75.4$, $b = 52$, $c = 52$

$$\cos A = \frac{b^2 + c^2 - a^2}{2bc} = \frac{52^2 + 52^2 - 75.4^2}{2(52)(52)} = -0.05125 \implies A = 92.9°$$

$$\sin B = \frac{b \sin A}{a} = \frac{52(0.9987)}{75.4} \approx 0.68875 \implies B \approx 43.53°$$

$$C = B \approx 43.53°$$

9. Given: $B = 8° 45'$, $a = 25$, $c = 15$

$$b^2 = a^2 + c^2 - 2ac \cos B \approx 625 + 225 - 2(25)(15)(0.9884) \approx 108.7 \implies b \approx 10.4$$

$$\sin C = \frac{c \sin B}{b} = \frac{15(0.1521)}{10.43} \approx 0.2188 \implies C \approx 12.64° \approx 12° 38'$$

$$A \approx 180° - 8° 45' - 12° 38' = 158° 37'$$

11.

$$d^2 = 4^2 + 6^2 - 2(4)(6) \cos 30°$$

$$d \approx 3.23$$

$$2\phi = 360° - 2(30°)$$

$$\phi = 150°$$

$$c^2 = 4^2 + 6^2 - 2(4)(6) \cos 150°$$

$$c \approx 9.67$$

13.

$$\cos \phi = \frac{10^2 + 14^2 - 20^2}{2(10)(14)}$$

$$\phi \approx 111.8$$

$$2\theta \approx 360° - 2(111.80°)$$

$$\theta = 68.2°$$

$$d^2 = 10^2 + 14^2 - 2(10)(14) \cos 68.2°$$

$$d \approx 13.86$$

15.
$$\cos \alpha = \frac{(9)^2 + (10)^2 - (6)^2}{2(9)(10)}$$

$$\alpha = 36.3°$$

$$\cos \beta = \frac{6^2 + 10^2 - 9^2}{2(6)(10)}$$

$$\beta \approx 62.7°$$

$$z = 180° - \alpha - \beta \approx 80.9$$

$$\mu = 180° - z \approx 99.1$$

$$b^2 = 9^2 + 6^2 - 2(9)(6)(\cos 99.0°)$$

$$b \approx 11.58$$

$$\cos \omega = \frac{9^2 + 11.58^2 - 6^2}{2(9)(11.58)}$$

$$\omega \approx 30.8°$$

$$\theta = \alpha + \omega \approx 67.1°$$

$$\cos x = \frac{6^2 + 11.58^2 - 9^2}{2(6)(11.58)}$$

$$x \approx 50.1$$

$$\phi = \beta + x \approx 112.8°$$

17.

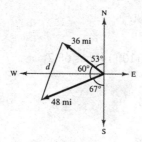

$B = 105° + 32° = 137°$

$b^2 = a^2 + c^2 - 2ac \cdot \cos B$

$\quad = 648^2 + 810^2 - 2(648)(810) \cos(137°)$

$\quad = 1,843,749.862$

$b = 1357.8$ miles

From the Law of Sines, $\dfrac{a}{\sin A} = \dfrac{b}{\sin B} \implies \sin A = \dfrac{a}{b}\sin B = \dfrac{648}{1357.8}\sin(137°) \approx 0.32548$

$\implies A \approx 19° \implies$ Bearing N 56° E

19.

$b^2 = 250^2 + 300^2 - 2(250)(300) \cos 100°$

$b \approx 422.5$ meters

21. $C = 180° - 53° - 67° = 60°$

$c^2 = a^2 + b^2 - 2ab \cos C = 36^2 + 48^2 - 2(36)(48)(0.5) = 1872$

$c \approx 43.3$ mi

23. (a) $\cos \theta = \dfrac{273^2 + 178^2 - 235^2}{2(273)(178)}$

$\qquad \theta \approx 58.4°$

$\qquad$ Bearing: N 58.4° W

(b) $\cos \phi = \dfrac{235^2 + 178^2 - 273^2}{2(235)(178)}$

$\qquad \phi \approx 81.5°$

$\qquad$ Bearing: S 81.5° W

25. $d^2 = 60^2 + 90^2 - 2(60)(90) \cos 45° \approx 4063 \implies d \approx 63.7$ ft

27. $\overline{RS} = \sqrt{8^2 + 10^2} = \sqrt{164} = 2\sqrt{41} \approx 12.8$ ft

$\overline{PQ} = \frac{1}{2}\sqrt{16^2 + 10^2} = \frac{1}{2}\sqrt{356} = \sqrt{89} \approx 9.4$ ft

$\tan P = \frac{10}{16}$

$\quad P = \arctan \frac{5}{8} \approx 32.0°$

$\quad \overline{QS} = \sqrt{8^2 + 9.4^2 - 2(8)(9.4)\cos 32°} \approx \sqrt{24.81} \approx 5.0$ ft

29. (a) $7^2 = 1.5^2 + x^2 - 2(1.5)(x)\cos\theta$

$\quad 49 = 2.25 + x^2 - 3x\cos\theta$

(b) $\qquad x^2 - 3x\cos\theta = 46.75$

$\quad x^2 - 3x\cos\theta + \left(\dfrac{3\cos\theta}{2}\right)^2 = 46.75 + \left(\dfrac{3\cos\theta}{2}\right)^2$

$\quad \left[x - \dfrac{3\cos\theta}{2}\right]^2 = \dfrac{187}{4} - \dfrac{9\cos^2\theta}{4}$

$\quad x - \dfrac{3\cos\theta}{2} = \pm\sqrt{\dfrac{187 + 9\cos^2\theta}{4}}$

Choosing the positive values of x, we have

$x = \frac{1}{2}\left(3\cos\theta + \sqrt{9\cos^2\theta + 187}\right)$.

(c)

(d) $x = \dfrac{1}{2}\left(3\cos\pi + \sqrt{9\cos^2\pi + 187}\right)$

$\quad = 5.5$

$\quad \approx 6$ inches

31. $A = 180° - 40° - 20° = 120°$

$\dfrac{x}{\sin 20°} = \dfrac{7}{\sin 120°}$

$\quad x = \dfrac{7\sin 20°}{\sin 120°}$

$\quad x = 2.76$ feet

33. $a = 25$, $b = 55$, $c = 72$, $s - \dfrac{25 + 55 + 72}{2} = 76$

(a) $A = \sqrt{(76)(76 - 25)(76 - 55)(76 - 72)} \approx 570.60$

(b) $\cos C = \dfrac{a^2 + b^2 - c^2}{2ab} = \dfrac{25^2 + 55^2 - 72^2}{2(25)(55)} \implies C \approx 123.905°$

$\quad 2R = \dfrac{c}{\sin C} \approx \dfrac{72}{\sin 123.905°} \implies R \approx 43.3754$

$\quad A = \pi R^2 \approx 5910.67$

(c) $r = \sqrt{\dfrac{(s - a)(s - b)(s - c)}{s}} = \sqrt{\dfrac{(51)(21)(4)}{76}} \approx 7.5079$

$\quad A = \pi r^2 \approx 177.09$

35. $a = 5$, $b = 7$, $c = 10 \implies s = \dfrac{a + b + c}{2} = 11$

Area $= \sqrt{s(s - a)(s - b)(s - c)} = \sqrt{11(6)(4)(1)} \approx 16.25$

37. $a = 12$, $b = 15$, $c = 9 \implies s = \dfrac{12 + 15 + 9}{2} = 18$

Area $= \sqrt{18(6)(3)(9)} = 54$

39. $a = 20$, $b = 20$, $c = 10 \implies s = \dfrac{20 + 20 + 10}{2} = 25$

Area $= \sqrt{25(5)(5)(15)} \approx 96.82$

41. $\dfrac{1}{2}bc(1 + \cos A) = \dfrac{1}{2}bc\left[1 + \dfrac{b^2 + c^2 - a^2}{2bc}\right]$

$\qquad\qquad = \dfrac{1}{2}bc\left[\dfrac{2bc + b^2 + c^2 - a^2}{2bc}\right]$

$\qquad\qquad = \dfrac{1}{4}[(b + c)^2 - a^2]$

$\qquad\qquad = \dfrac{1}{4}[(b + c) + a][(b + c) - a]$

$\qquad\qquad = \dfrac{b + c + a}{2} \cdot \dfrac{b + c - a}{2}$

$\qquad\qquad = \dfrac{a + b + c}{2} \cdot \dfrac{-a + b + c}{2}$

Section 7.3   Vectors in the Plane

- A vector **v** is the collection of all directed line segments that are equivalent to a given directed line segment $\overrightarrow{PQ}$.

- You should be able to *geometrically* perform the operations of vector addition and scalar multiplication.

- The component form of the vector with initial point $P = (p_1, p_2)$ and terminal point $Q = (q_1, q_2)$ is
  $$\overrightarrow{PQ} = \langle q_1 - p_1, q_2 - p_2 \rangle = \langle v_1, v_2 \rangle = \mathbf{v}.$$

- The magnitude of $\mathbf{v} = \langle v_1, v_2 \rangle$ is given by $\|\mathbf{v}\| = \sqrt{v_1{}^2 + v_2{}^2}$.

- You should be able to perform the operations of scalar multiplication and vector addition in component form.

- You should know the following properties of vector addition and scalar multiplication.

  (a) $\mathbf{u} + \mathbf{v} = \mathbf{v} + \mathbf{u}$

  (b) $(\mathbf{u} + \mathbf{v}) + \mathbf{w} = \mathbf{u} + (\mathbf{v} + \mathbf{w})$

  (c) $\mathbf{u} + \mathbf{0} = \mathbf{u}$

  (d) $\mathbf{u} + (-\mathbf{u}) = \mathbf{0}$

  (e) $c(d\mathbf{u}) = (cd)\mathbf{u}$

  (f) $(c + d)\mathbf{u} = c\mathbf{u} + d\mathbf{u}$

  (g) $c(\mathbf{u} + \mathbf{v}) = c\mathbf{u} + c\mathbf{v}$

  (h) $1(\mathbf{u}) = \mathbf{u}$, $0\mathbf{u} = \mathbf{0}$

  (i) $\|c\mathbf{v}\| = |c| \, \|\mathbf{v}\|$

- A unit vector in the direction of **v** is given $\mathbf{u} = \dfrac{\mathbf{v}}{\|\mathbf{v}\|}$.

- The standard unit vectors are $\mathbf{i} = \langle 1, 0 \rangle$ and $\mathbf{j} = \langle 0, 1 \rangle$. $\mathbf{v} = \langle v_1, v_2 \rangle$ can be written as $\mathbf{v} = v_1\mathbf{i} + v_2\mathbf{j}$.

- A vector **v** with magnitude $\|\mathbf{v}\|$ and direction θ can be written as $\mathbf{v} = a\mathbf{i} + b\mathbf{j} = \mathbf{v}(\cos \theta)\mathbf{i} + \mathbf{v}(\sin \theta)\mathbf{j}$ where $\tan \theta = b/a$.

Solutions to Odd-Numbered Exercises

1. Initial point:$(0, 0)$
Terminal point: $(4, 3)$

$\mathbf{v} = \langle 4 - 0, 3 - 0 \rangle = \langle 4, 3 \rangle$

$\|\mathbf{v}\| = \sqrt{4^2 + 3^2} = 5$

3. Initial point: $(2, 2)$
Terminal point: $(-1, 4)$

$\mathbf{v} = \langle -1 - 2, 4 - 2 \rangle = \langle -3, 2 \rangle$

$\|\mathbf{v}\| = \sqrt{(-3)^2 + 2^2} = \sqrt{13}$

5. Initial point: $(3, -2)$
Terminal point: $(3, 3)$

$\mathbf{v} = \langle 3 - 3, 3 - (-2) \rangle = \langle 0, 5 \rangle$

$\|\mathbf{v}\| = 5$

7. Initial point: $\left(\dfrac{5}{2}, 1 \right)$

Terminal point: $\left(-2, -\dfrac{3}{2} \right)$

$\mathbf{v} = \left\langle -2 - \dfrac{5}{2}, -\dfrac{3}{2} - 1 \right\rangle = \left\langle -\dfrac{9}{2}, -\dfrac{5}{2} \right\rangle$

$\|\mathbf{v}\| = \sqrt{\left(-\dfrac{9}{2} \right)^2 + \left(-\dfrac{5}{2} \right)^2} = \sqrt{\dfrac{81 + 25}{4}} = \dfrac{1}{2}\sqrt{106}$

9. Initial point: $(-3, -5)$
Terminal point: $(5, 1)$

$\mathbf{v} = \langle 5 - (-3), 1 - (-5) \rangle = \langle 8, 6 \rangle$

$\|\mathbf{v}\| = \sqrt{8^2 + 6^2} = \sqrt{100} = 10$

11.

13.

15.

17. $\mathbf{u} = \langle 1, 2 \rangle$, $\mathbf{v} = \langle 3, 1 \rangle$

(a) $\mathbf{u} + \mathbf{v} = \langle 4, 3 \rangle$

(b) $\mathbf{u} - \mathbf{v} = \langle -2, 1 \rangle$

(c) $2\mathbf{u} - 3\mathbf{v} = \langle 2, 4 \rangle - \langle 9, 3 \rangle = \langle -7, 1 \rangle$

19. $\mathbf{u} = \mathbf{i} + \mathbf{j}$, $\mathbf{v} = 2\mathbf{i} - 3\mathbf{j}$

(a) $\mathbf{u} + \mathbf{v} = 3\mathbf{i} - 2\mathbf{j}$

(b) $\mathbf{u} - \mathbf{v} = -\mathbf{i} + 4\mathbf{j}$

(c) $2\mathbf{u} - 3\mathbf{v} = (2\mathbf{i} + 2\mathbf{j}) - (6\mathbf{i} - 9\mathbf{j})$

$= -4\mathbf{i} + 11\mathbf{j}$

21. $\mathbf{u} = \dfrac{1}{\|\mathbf{v}\|}\mathbf{v}$

$= \dfrac{1}{\sqrt{5^2 + 0^2}}\langle 5, 0 \rangle$

$= \dfrac{1}{5}\langle 5, 0 \rangle$

$= \langle 1, 0 \rangle$

23. $\mathbf{u} = \dfrac{1}{\|\mathbf{v}\|}\mathbf{v}$

$= \dfrac{1}{\sqrt{(-2)^2 + 2^2}}\langle -2, 2 \rangle$

$= \dfrac{1}{2\sqrt{2}}\langle -2, 2 \rangle$

$= \left\langle -\dfrac{1}{\sqrt{2}}, \dfrac{1}{\sqrt{2}} \right\rangle$

25. $\mathbf{u} = \dfrac{1}{\|\mathbf{v}\|}\mathbf{v}$

$= \dfrac{1}{\sqrt{16 + 9}}(4\mathbf{i} - 3\mathbf{j}) = \dfrac{1}{5}(4\mathbf{i} - 3\mathbf{j})$

$= \dfrac{4}{5}\mathbf{i} - \dfrac{3}{5}\mathbf{j}$

27. $\mathbf{u} = \dfrac{1}{\|\mathbf{v}\|}\mathbf{v} = \dfrac{1}{2}(2\mathbf{j}) = \mathbf{j}$

29. $5\left(\dfrac{1}{\|\mathbf{v}\|}\mathbf{v}\right) = 5\left(\dfrac{1}{\sqrt{3^2 + 3^2}}\langle 3, 3\rangle\right)$

$\qquad = 5\left(\dfrac{1}{3\sqrt{2}}\langle 3, 3\rangle\right)$

$\qquad = \left\langle \dfrac{5}{\sqrt{2}}, \dfrac{5}{\sqrt{2}}\right\rangle$

31. $7\left(\dfrac{1}{\|\mathbf{v}\|}\mathbf{v}\right) = 7\left(\dfrac{1}{\sqrt{(-3)^2 + 4^2}}\langle -3, 4\rangle\right)$

$\qquad = \dfrac{7}{5}\langle -3, 4\rangle$

$\qquad = \left\langle -\dfrac{21}{5}, \dfrac{28}{5}\right\rangle$

33. $\mathbf{v} = \frac{3}{2}\mathbf{u}$

$\qquad = \frac{3}{2}(2\mathbf{i} - \mathbf{j})$

$\qquad = 3\mathbf{i} - \frac{3}{2}\mathbf{j} = \langle 3, -\frac{3}{2}\rangle$

35. $\mathbf{v} = \mathbf{u} + 2\mathbf{w}$

$\qquad = (2\mathbf{i} - \mathbf{j}) + 2(\mathbf{i} + 2\mathbf{j})$

$\qquad = 4\mathbf{i} + 3\mathbf{j} = \langle 4, 3\rangle$

37. $\mathbf{v} = \frac{1}{2}(3\mathbf{u} + \mathbf{w})$

$\qquad = \frac{1}{2}(6\mathbf{i} - 3\mathbf{j} + \mathbf{i} + 2\mathbf{j})$

$\qquad = \frac{7}{2}\mathbf{i} - \frac{1}{2}\mathbf{j} = \langle \frac{7}{2}, -\frac{1}{2}\rangle$

39. $\mathbf{v} = 5(\cos 30°\mathbf{i} + \sin 30°\mathbf{j})$

$\qquad \|\mathbf{v}\| = 5, \ \theta = 30°$

41. $\mathbf{v} = 6\mathbf{i} - 6\mathbf{j}$

$\qquad \|\mathbf{v}\| = \sqrt{6^2 + (-6)^2} = \sqrt{72} = 6\sqrt{2}$

$\qquad \tan \theta = \dfrac{-6}{6} = -1$

Since $\mathbf{v}$ lies in Quadrant IV, $\theta = 315°$.

43. $\mathbf{v} = \langle 3\cos 0°, \ 3\sin 0°\rangle$

$\qquad = \langle 3, 0\rangle$

45. $\mathbf{v} = \langle 3\sqrt{2}\cos 150°, \ 3\sqrt{2}\sin 150°\rangle$

$\qquad = \left\langle -\dfrac{3\sqrt{6}}{2}, \dfrac{3\sqrt{2}}{2}\right\rangle$

47. $\mathbf{v} = 2\left(\dfrac{1}{\sqrt{3^2 + 1^2}}\right)(\mathbf{i} + 3\mathbf{j})$

$\qquad = \dfrac{2}{\sqrt{10}}(\mathbf{i} + 3\mathbf{j})$

$\qquad = \dfrac{\sqrt{10}}{5}\mathbf{i} + \dfrac{3\sqrt{10}}{5}\mathbf{j} = \left\langle \dfrac{\sqrt{10}}{5}, \dfrac{3\sqrt{10}}{5}\right\rangle$

49. $\mathbf{u} = \langle 5 \cos 0°, 5 \sin 0° \rangle = \langle 5, 0 \rangle$

$\mathbf{v} = \langle 5 \cos 90°, 5 \sin 90° \rangle = \langle 0, 5 \rangle$

$\mathbf{u} + \mathbf{v} = \langle 5, 5 \rangle$

51. $\mathbf{u} = \langle 20 \cos 45°, 20 \sin 45° \rangle = \langle 10\sqrt{2}, 10\sqrt{2} \rangle$

$\mathbf{v} = \langle 50 \cos 180°, 50 \sin 180° \rangle = \langle -50, 0 \rangle$

$\mathbf{u} + \mathbf{v} = \langle 10\sqrt{2} - 50, 10\sqrt{2} \rangle$

53. $\mathbf{v} = \mathbf{i} + \mathbf{j}$

$\mathbf{w} = 2(\mathbf{i} - \mathbf{j})$

$\mathbf{u} = \mathbf{v} - \mathbf{w} = -\mathbf{i} + 3\mathbf{j}$

$\|\mathbf{v}\| = \sqrt{2}$

$\|\mathbf{w}\| = 2\sqrt{2}$

$\|\mathbf{v} - \mathbf{w}\| = \sqrt{10}$

$\cos \alpha = \dfrac{\|\mathbf{v}\|^2 + \|\mathbf{w}\|^2 - \|\mathbf{v} - \mathbf{w}\|^2}{2\|\mathbf{v}\|\,\|\mathbf{w}\|} = \dfrac{2 + 8 - 10}{2\sqrt{2} \cdot 2\sqrt{2}} = 0$

$\alpha = 90°$

55. $\mathbf{v} = \mathbf{i} + \mathbf{j}$

$\mathbf{w} = 3\mathbf{i} - \mathbf{j}$

$\mathbf{u} = \mathbf{v} - \mathbf{w} = -2\mathbf{i} + 2\mathbf{j}$

$\cos \alpha = \dfrac{\|\mathbf{v}\|^2 + \|\mathbf{w}\|^2 - \|\mathbf{v} - \mathbf{w}\|^2}{2\|\mathbf{v}\|\,\|\mathbf{w}\|} = \dfrac{2 + 10 - 8}{2\sqrt{2}\,\sqrt{10}} \approx 0.4472$

$\alpha = 63.4°$

57. Force One: $\mathbf{u} = 45\mathbf{i}$

Force Two: $\mathbf{v} = 60 \cos \theta \mathbf{i} + 60 \sin \theta \mathbf{j}$

Resultant Force: $\mathbf{u} + \mathbf{v} = (45 + 60 \cos \theta)\mathbf{i} + 60 \sin \theta \mathbf{j}$

$\|\mathbf{u} + \mathbf{v}\| = \sqrt{(45 + 60 \cos \theta)^2 + (60 \sin \theta)^2} = 90$

$2025 + 5400 \cos \theta + 3600 = 8100$

$5400 \cos \theta = 2475$

$\cos \theta = \dfrac{2475}{5400} \approx 0.4583$

$\theta \approx 62.7°$

59. (a) The angle between them is $0°$.

(b) The angle between them is $180°$.

(c) No. At most it can be equal to the sum when the angle between them is $0°$.

61. (a) $\mathbf{u} = 220\mathbf{i}, \quad \mathbf{v} = 150 \cos 30°\mathbf{i} + 150 \sin 30°\mathbf{j}$

$\mathbf{u} + \mathbf{v} = (220 + 75\sqrt{3})\mathbf{i} + 75\mathbf{j}$

$\|\mathbf{u} + \mathbf{v}\| = \sqrt{(220 + 75\sqrt{3})^2 + 75^2} \approx 357.85$ newtons

$\tan \theta = \dfrac{75}{220 + 75\sqrt{3}} \implies \theta \approx 12.1°$

—CONTINUED—

61. —CONTINUED—

(b) $\mathbf{u} + \mathbf{v} = 220\mathbf{i} + (150\cos\theta\mathbf{i} + 150\sin\theta\mathbf{j})$

$$M = \|\mathbf{u} + \mathbf{v}\| = \sqrt{(220^2 + 150^2(\cos^2\theta + \sin^2\theta) + 2(220)(150)\cos\theta}$$

$$= \sqrt{70{,}900 + 66{,}000\cos\theta}$$

$$= 10\sqrt{709 + 660\cos\theta}$$

$$\alpha = \arctan\left(\frac{15\sin\theta}{22 + 15\cos\theta}\right)$$

(c)

θ	0°	30°	60°	90°	120°	150°	180°
M	370.0	357.9	322.3	266.3	194.7	117.2	70.0
α	0°	12.1°	23.8°	34.3°	41.9°	39.8°	0°

(d)

(e) For increasing θ the two vectors tend to work against each other resulting in a decrease in the magnitude of the resultant.

63.
$$\mathbf{u} = (75\cos 30°)\mathbf{i} + (75\sin 30)\mathbf{j} \approx 64.95\mathbf{i} + 37.5\mathbf{j}$$
$$\mathbf{v} = (100\cos 45°)\mathbf{i} + (100\sin 45°)\mathbf{j} \approx 70.71\mathbf{i} + 70.71\mathbf{j}$$
$$\mathbf{w} = (125\cos 120°)\mathbf{i} + (125\sin 120°)\mathbf{j} \approx -62.5\mathbf{i} + 108.3\mathbf{j}$$
$$\mathbf{u} + \mathbf{v} + \mathbf{w} = 73.16\mathbf{i} + 216.5\mathbf{j}$$
$$\|\mathbf{u} + \mathbf{v} + \mathbf{w}\| = 228.5 \text{ pounds}$$
$$\tan\theta = \frac{216.5}{73.16} \approx 2.9592 \approx 71.3°$$

65.

$$\mathbf{u} = 400\cos 25°\mathbf{i} + 400\sin 25°\mathbf{j}$$
$$\mathbf{v} = 300\cos 70°\mathbf{i} + 300\sin 70°\mathbf{j}$$
$$\mathbf{u} + \mathbf{v} \approx 465.13\mathbf{i} + 450.96\mathbf{j}$$
$$\|\mathbf{u} + \mathbf{v}\| \approx \sqrt{(465.13)^2 + (450.96)^2} \approx 647.8$$
$$\alpha = \arctan\left(\frac{450.96}{465.13}\right) \approx 44.1°$$

67. Horizontal component of velocity:
$80\cos 40° \approx 61.28$ ft/sec
Vertical component of velocity:
$80\sin 40° \approx 51.42$ ft/sec

69. Cable $\overrightarrow{AC}$: $\mathbf{u} = \|\mathbf{u}\|(\cos 50°\mathbf{i} - \sin 50°\mathbf{j})$
Cable $\overrightarrow{BC}$: $\mathbf{u} = \|\mathbf{u}\|(\cos 30°\mathbf{i} - \sin 30°\mathbf{j})$
Resultant: $\mathbf{u} + \mathbf{v} = -1000\mathbf{j}$
$$\|\mathbf{u}\|\cos 50° - \|\mathbf{v}\|\cos 30° = 0$$
$$-\|\mathbf{u}\|\sin 50° - \|\mathbf{v}\|\sin 30° = -2000$$
Solving this system of equations yields:
$$T_{AC} = \|\mathbf{u}\| \approx 1758.8 \text{ pounds}$$
$$T_{BC} = \|\mathbf{v}\| \approx 1305.4 \text{ pounds}$$

71. (a) Tow line 1: $\mathbf{u} = \|\mathbf{u}\| (\cos 20°\mathbf{i} + \sin 20°\mathbf{j})$

Tow line 2: $\mathbf{v} = \|\mathbf{u}\| (\cos(-20°)\mathbf{i} + \sin(-20°)\mathbf{j})$

Resultant: $\mathbf{u} + \mathbf{v} = 6000\mathbf{i} = [\|\mathbf{u}\| \cos 20° + \|\mathbf{u}\| \cos(-20°)]\mathbf{i}$

$$\Longrightarrow \quad 6000 = 2\|\mathbf{u}\| \cos 20°$$

$$\Longrightarrow \quad \|\mathbf{u}\| \approx 3192.5 \text{ lb}$$

(b) $\mathbf{u} + \mathbf{v} = 6000\mathbf{i} = 2\|\mathbf{u}\| \cos \theta \Longrightarrow T = \|\mathbf{u}\| = 3000 \sec \theta$

(c)

θ	10°	20°	30°	40°	50°	60°
T	3046.3	3192.5	3464.1	2916.2	4667.2	6000.0

(d)

(e) The tension increases because the component in the direction of the motion of the barge decreases.

73. Airspeed: $\mathbf{u} = (875 \cos 32°)\mathbf{i} - (875 \sin 32°)\mathbf{j}$

Groundspeed: $\mathbf{v} = (800 \cos 40°)\mathbf{i} - (800 \sin 40°)\mathbf{j}$

Wind: $\mathbf{w} = \mathbf{v} - \mathbf{u} = (800 \cos 40° - 875 \cos 32°)\mathbf{j} + (-800 \sin 40° + 875 \sin 32°)\mathbf{j}$

$$\approx -129.2065\mathbf{i} - 50.5507\mathbf{j}$$

Wind speed: $\|\mathbf{w}\| \approx \sqrt{(-129.2065)^2 + (-50.5507)}$

$$\approx 138.7 \text{ kilometers per hour}$$

Wind direction: $\tan \theta = \dfrac{-50.5507}{-129.2065}$

$$\theta \approx 21.4°$$

N 21.4° E

75. $W = FD = (85 \cos 60°)(20)$ **77.** True   **79.** False, $a = b = 0$.

$$= 850 \text{ ft/lb}$$

81. Let $\mathbf{v} = (\cos \theta)\mathbf{i} + (\sin \theta)\mathbf{j}$

$\|\mathbf{v}\| = \sqrt{\cos^2 \theta + \sin^2 \theta} = \sqrt{1} = 1$

Therefore, $\mathbf{v}$ is a unit vector for any value of θ.

83. $\mathbf{u} = \langle 5 - 1, 2 - 6 \rangle = \langle 4, -4 \rangle$

$\mathbf{v} = \langle 9 - 4, 4 - 5 \rangle = \langle 5, -1 \rangle$

$\mathbf{u} - \mathbf{v} = \langle -1, -3 \rangle$

$\mathbf{v} - \mathbf{u} = \langle 1, 3 \rangle$

Section 7.4   Vectors and Dot Products

■ Know the definition of the dot product of $\mathbf{u} = \langle u_1, u_2 \rangle$ and $\mathbf{v} = \langle v_1, v_2 \rangle$.

$\mathbf{u} \cdot \mathbf{v} = u_1v_1 + u_2v_2$

■ Know the following properties of the dot product:

1. $\mathbf{u} \cdot \mathbf{v} = \mathbf{v} \cdot \mathbf{u}$

2. $\mathbf{0} \cdot \mathbf{v} = 0$

3. $\mathbf{u} \cdot (\mathbf{v} + \mathbf{w}) = \mathbf{u} \cdot \mathbf{v} + \mathbf{u} \cdot \mathbf{w}$

4. $\mathbf{v} \cdot \mathbf{v} = \|\mathbf{v}\|^2$

5. $c(\mathbf{u} \cdot \mathbf{v}) = c\mathbf{u} \cdot \mathbf{v} = \mathbf{u} \cdot c\mathbf{v}$

■ If θ is the angle between two nonzero vectors $\mathbf{u}$ and $\mathbf{v}$, then

$$\cos \theta = \frac{\mathbf{u} \cdot \mathbf{v}}{\|\mathbf{u}\| \|\mathbf{v}\|}.$$

■ The vectors $\mathbf{u}$ and $\mathbf{v}$ are orthogonal if $\mathbf{u} \cdot \mathbf{v} = 0$.

■ Know the definition of vector components. $\mathbf{u} = \mathbf{w}_1 + \mathbf{w}_2$ where $\mathbf{w}_1$ and $\mathbf{w}_2$ are orthogonal, and $\mathbf{w}_1$ is parallel to $\mathbf{v}$. $\mathbf{w}_1$ is called the projection of $\mathbf{u}$ onto $\mathbf{v}$ and is denoted by

$$\mathbf{w}_1 = \text{proj}_{\mathbf{v}}\mathbf{u} = \left(\frac{\mathbf{u} \cdot \mathbf{v}}{\|\mathbf{v}\|^2}\right)\mathbf{v}.$$

Then we have $\mathbf{w}_2 = \mathbf{u} - \mathbf{w}_1$.

■ Know the definition of work.

1. Projection form: $W = \|\text{proj}_{\overrightarrow{PQ}} \mathbf{F}\| \|PQ\|$

2. Dot product form: $W = \mathbf{F} \cdot \overrightarrow{PQ}$

Solutions to Odd-Numbered Exercises

1. $\mathbf{u} = \langle 3, 4 \rangle$, $\mathbf{v} = \langle 2, -3 \rangle$

$\mathbf{u} \cdot \mathbf{v} = 3(2) + 4(-3) = -6$

3. $\mathbf{u} = 4\mathbf{i} - 2\mathbf{j}$, $\mathbf{v} = \mathbf{i} - \mathbf{j}$

$\mathbf{u} \cdot \mathbf{v} = 4(1) + (-2)(-1) = 6$

5. $\mathbf{u} = \langle 2, 2 \rangle$

$\mathbf{u} \cdot \mathbf{u} = 2(2) + 2(2) = 8$

The result is a scalar.

7. $\mathbf{u} = \langle 2, 2 \rangle$, $\mathbf{v} = \langle -3, 4 \rangle$

$(\mathbf{u} \cdot \mathbf{v})\mathbf{v} = [(2)(-3) + 2(4)] \langle -3, 4 \rangle = 2\langle -3, 4 \rangle = \langle -6, 8 \rangle$

The result is a vector.

9. $\mathbf{u} = \langle -5, 12 \rangle$

$\|\mathbf{u}\| = \sqrt{\mathbf{u} \cdot \mathbf{u}} = \sqrt{(-5)^2 + 12^2} = 13$

11. $\mathbf{u} = 20\mathbf{i} + 25\mathbf{j}$

$\|\mathbf{u}\| = \sqrt{(20)^2 + (25)^2} = \sqrt{1025} = 5\sqrt{41}$

13. $\mathbf{u} = \langle 1245, 2600 \rangle$, $\mathbf{v} = \langle 12.20, 8.50 \rangle$

$\mathbf{u} \cdot \mathbf{v} = 1245(12.20) + 2600(8.50) = \$37,289$

This gives the total revenue that can be earned by selling all of the units.

15. $\mathbf{u} = \langle 1, 0 \rangle$, $\mathbf{v} = \langle 0, -2 \rangle$

$$\cos \theta = \frac{\mathbf{u} \cdot \mathbf{v}}{\|\mathbf{u}\| \, \|\mathbf{v}\|} = \frac{0}{(1)(2)} = 0$$

$$\theta = 90°$$

17. $\mathbf{u} = 3\mathbf{i} + 4\mathbf{j}$, $\mathbf{v} = -2\mathbf{j}$

$$\cos \theta = \frac{\mathbf{u} \cdot \mathbf{v}}{\|\mathbf{u}\| \, \|\mathbf{v}\|} = -\frac{8}{(5)(2)}$$

$$\theta = \arccos\left(-\frac{4}{5}\right)$$

$$\theta \approx 143.13°$$

19. $\mathbf{u} = \left(\cos \dfrac{\pi}{3}\right)\mathbf{i} + \left(\sin \dfrac{\pi}{3}\right)\mathbf{j} = \dfrac{1}{2}\mathbf{i} + \dfrac{\sqrt{3}}{2}\mathbf{j}$

$\mathbf{v} = \left(\cos \dfrac{3\pi}{4}\right)\mathbf{i} + \left(\sin \dfrac{3\pi}{4}\right)\mathbf{j} = -\dfrac{\sqrt{2}}{2}\mathbf{i} + \dfrac{\sqrt{2}}{2}\mathbf{j}$

$\|\mathbf{u}\| = \|\mathbf{v}\| = 1$

$$\cos \theta = \frac{\mathbf{u} \cdot \mathbf{v}}{\|\mathbf{u}\| \, \|\mathbf{v}\|} = \mathbf{u} \cdot \mathbf{v} = \left(\frac{1}{2}\right)\left(-\frac{\sqrt{2}}{2}\right) + \left(\frac{\sqrt{3}}{2}\right)\left(\frac{\sqrt{2}}{2}\right) = \frac{-\sqrt{2} + \sqrt{6}}{4}$$

$$\theta = \arccos\left(\frac{-\sqrt{2} + \sqrt{6}}{4}\right) = 75° = \frac{5\pi}{12}$$

21. $\mathbf{u} = 3\mathbf{i} + 4\mathbf{j}$, $\mathbf{v} = -7\mathbf{i} + 5\mathbf{j}$

$$\cos \theta = \frac{\mathbf{u} \cdot \mathbf{v}}{\|\mathbf{u}\| \, \|\mathbf{v}\|} = -\frac{1}{(5)(\sqrt{74})} \implies \theta \approx 91.33°$$

23. $\mathbf{u} = 5\mathbf{i} + 5\mathbf{j}$, $\mathbf{v} = -6\mathbf{i} + 6\mathbf{j}$

$$\cos \theta = \frac{\mathbf{u} \cdot \mathbf{v}}{\|\mathbf{u}\| \, \|\mathbf{v}\|} = 0 \implies \theta = 90°$$

25. $P = (1, 2)$, $Q = (3, 4)$, $R = (2, 5)$

$\overrightarrow{PQ} = \langle 2, 2 \rangle$, $\overrightarrow{PR} = \langle 1, 3 \rangle$, $\overrightarrow{QR} = \langle -1, -1 \rangle$

$$\cos \alpha = \frac{\overrightarrow{PQ} \cdot \overrightarrow{PR}}{\|\overrightarrow{PQ}\| \, \|\overrightarrow{PR}\|} = \frac{8}{(2\sqrt{2})(\sqrt{10})} \implies \alpha = \arccos \frac{2}{\sqrt{5}} \approx 26.6°$$

$$\cos \beta = \frac{\overrightarrow{PQ} \cdot \overrightarrow{QR}}{\|\overrightarrow{PQ}\| \, \|\overrightarrow{QR}\|} = 0 \implies \beta = 90°. \text{ Thus, } \gamma = 180° - 26.6° - 90° = 63.4°.$$

27. $\mathbf{u} \cdot \mathbf{v} = \|\mathbf{u}\| \, \|\mathbf{v}\| \cos \theta$

$$= (4)(10) \cos \frac{2\pi}{3}$$

$$= 40\left(-\frac{1}{2}\right)$$

$$= -20$$

29. $\mathbf{u} = \langle -12, 30 \rangle$, $\mathbf{v} = \left\langle \dfrac{1}{2}, -\dfrac{5}{4} \right\rangle$

$\mathbf{u} = -24\mathbf{v} \implies \mathbf{u}$ and $\mathbf{v}$ are parallel.

31. $\mathbf{u} = \frac{1}{4}(3\mathbf{i} - \mathbf{j})$, $\mathbf{v} = 5\mathbf{i} + 6\mathbf{j}$

$\mathbf{u} \neq k\mathbf{v} \implies$ Not parallel

$\mathbf{u} \cdot \mathbf{v} \neq 0 \implies$ Not orthogonal

Neither

33. $\mathbf{u} = 2\mathbf{i} - 2\mathbf{j}$, $\mathbf{v} = -\mathbf{i} - \mathbf{j}$

$\mathbf{u} \cdot \mathbf{v} = 0 \implies \mathbf{u}$ and $\mathbf{v}$ are orthogonal.

35. $\mathbf{u} = \langle 3, 4 \rangle$, $\mathbf{v} = \langle 8, 2 \rangle$

$\mathbf{w}_1 = \text{proj}_\mathbf{v}\mathbf{u} = \left(\dfrac{\mathbf{u} \cdot \mathbf{v}}{\|\mathbf{v}\|^2}\right)\mathbf{v} = \left(\dfrac{32}{68}\right)\mathbf{v} = \dfrac{8}{17}\langle 8, 2 \rangle = \dfrac{16}{17}\langle 4, 1 \rangle$

$\mathbf{w}_2 = \mathbf{u} - \mathbf{w}_1 = \langle 3, 4 \rangle - \dfrac{16}{17}\langle 4, 1 \rangle = \dfrac{13}{17}\langle -1, 4 \rangle$

37. $\mathbf{u} = \langle 0, 3 \rangle$, $\mathbf{v} = \langle 2, 15 \rangle$

$\mathbf{w}_1 = \text{proj}_\mathbf{v}\mathbf{u} = \left(\dfrac{\mathbf{u} \cdot \mathbf{v}}{\|\mathbf{v}\|^2}\right)\mathbf{v} = \dfrac{45}{229}\langle 2, 15 \rangle$

$\mathbf{w}_2 = \mathbf{u} - \mathbf{w}_1 = \langle 0, 3 \rangle - \dfrac{45}{229}\langle 2, 15 \rangle = \left\langle -\dfrac{90}{229}, \dfrac{12}{229} \right\rangle = \dfrac{6}{229}\langle -15, 2 \rangle$

39. $\text{proj}_\mathbf{v}\mathbf{u} = \mathbf{u}$ since they are parallel.

$\text{proj}_\mathbf{v}\mathbf{u} = \dfrac{\mathbf{u} \cdot \mathbf{v}}{\|\mathbf{v}\|^2}\mathbf{v} = \dfrac{18 + 18}{36 + 16}\mathbf{v} = \dfrac{26}{52}\langle 6, 4 \rangle = \langle 3, 2 \rangle = \mathbf{u}$

41. $\text{proj}_\mathbf{v}\mathbf{u} = \mathbf{0}$ since they are perpendicular.

$\text{proj}_\mathbf{v}\mathbf{u} = \dfrac{\mathbf{u} \cdot \mathbf{v}}{\|\mathbf{v}\|^2}\mathbf{v} = \mathbf{0}$, since $\mathbf{u} \cdot \mathbf{v} = 0$.

43. $\mathbf{u} = \langle 3, 5 \rangle$

For $\mathbf{v}$ to be orthogonal to $\mathbf{u}$, $\mathbf{u} \cdot \mathbf{v}$ must equal 0.

Two possibilities: $\langle -5, 3 \rangle$ and $\langle 5, -3 \rangle$.

45. $\mathbf{u} = \frac{1}{2}\mathbf{i} - \frac{2}{3}\mathbf{j}$

For $\mathbf{u}$ and $\mathbf{v}$ to be orthogonal, $\mathbf{u} \cdot \mathbf{v}$ must equal 0.

Two possibilities: $\frac{2}{3}\mathbf{i} + \frac{1}{2}\mathbf{j}$ and $-\frac{2}{3}\mathbf{i} - \frac{1}{2}\mathbf{j}$.

47. (a) $\mathbf{F} = -36{,}000\mathbf{j}$ Gravitational force

$\mathbf{v} = (\cos 10°)\mathbf{i} + (\sin 10°)\mathbf{j}$

$\mathbf{w}_1 = \text{proj}_\mathbf{v}\mathbf{F} = \left(\dfrac{\mathbf{F} \cdot \mathbf{v}}{\|\mathbf{v}\|^2}\right)\mathbf{v} = (\mathbf{F} \cdot \mathbf{v})\mathbf{v} \approx -6251.3\mathbf{v}$

The magnitude of this force is 6251.3, therefore a force of 6251.3 pounds is needed to keep the truck from rolling down the hill.

(b) $\mathbf{w}_2 = \mathbf{F} - \mathbf{w}_1 = -36{,}000\mathbf{j} + 6251.3\,(\cos 10°\mathbf{i} + \sin 10°\mathbf{j})$

$= [(6251.3 \cos 10°)\mathbf{i} + (6251.3 \sin 10° - 36{,}000)\mathbf{j}]$

$\|\mathbf{w}_2\| \approx 35{,}453.1$ pounds

49. (a) $\mathbf{u} \cdot \mathbf{v} = 0 \implies \mathbf{u}$ and $\mathbf{v}$ are orthogonal and $\theta = \dfrac{\pi}{2}$.

(b) $\mathbf{u} \cdot \mathbf{v} > 0 \implies \cos \theta > 0 \implies 0 \le \theta < \dfrac{\pi}{2}$

(c) $\mathbf{u} \cdot \mathbf{v} < 0 \implies \cos \theta < 0 \implies \dfrac{\pi}{2} < \theta \le \pi$

51. $w = (245)(3) = 735$ Newton-meters

53. $w = (\cos 30°)(45)(20) \approx 779.4$ foot-pounds

55. $w = \|\text{proj}_{\overrightarrow{PQ}}\mathbf{v}\|\,\|\overrightarrow{PQ}\|$ where $\overrightarrow{PQ} = \langle 4, 7 \rangle$ and $\mathbf{v} = \langle 1, 4 \rangle$.

$\text{proj}_{\overrightarrow{PQ}}\mathbf{v} = \left(\dfrac{\mathbf{v} \cdot \overrightarrow{PQ}}{\|\overrightarrow{PQ}\|^2}\right)\overrightarrow{PQ} = \left(\dfrac{32}{65}\right)\langle 4, 7 \rangle$

$w = \|\text{proj}_{\overrightarrow{PQ}}\mathbf{v}\|\,\|\overrightarrow{PQ}\| = \left(\dfrac{32\sqrt{65}}{65}\right)(\sqrt{65}) = 32$

57. Since $\text{proj}_v\mathbf{u}$ is a scalar multiple of $\mathbf{v}$, you can write $\text{proj}_v\mathbf{u} = \alpha\mathbf{v}$. If $\alpha > 0$, then $\cos\theta > 0$ and

$$\|\text{proj}_v\mathbf{u}\| = \|\alpha\mathbf{v}\| = \|\mathbf{u}\|\cos\theta$$

$$= \frac{\|\mathbf{u}\|\,\|\mathbf{v}\|\cos\theta}{\|\mathbf{v}\|}$$

$$= \frac{\mathbf{u}\cdot\mathbf{v}}{\|\mathbf{v}\|}$$

Thus, $\alpha = \dfrac{\mathbf{u}\cdot\mathbf{v}}{\|\mathbf{v}\|^2}$ and $\text{proj}_v\mathbf{u} = \dfrac{\mathbf{u}\cdot\mathbf{v}}{\|\mathbf{v}\|^2}\mathbf{v}$.

59. Use the Law of Cosines on the triangle.

$$\|\mathbf{u}-\mathbf{v}\|^2 = \|\mathbf{u}\|^2 + \|\mathbf{v}\|^2 - 2\|\mathbf{u}\|\,\|\mathbf{v}\|\cos\theta$$

$$= \|\mathbf{u}\|^2 + \|\mathbf{v}\|^2 - 2\,\mathbf{u}\cdot\mathbf{v}$$

61. $\mathbf{u}\cdot(c\mathbf{v}+d\mathbf{w}) = \mathbf{u}\cdot(c\mathbf{v}) + \mathbf{u}\cdot(d\mathbf{w})$

$\qquad = c(\mathbf{u}\cdot\mathbf{v}) + d(\mathbf{u}\cdot\mathbf{w})$

$\qquad = c0 + d0 = 0$

63. (a) $1 - \dfrac{1}{x^2} = \dfrac{x^2-1}{x^2}$

(b) $1 - \dfrac{1}{\sec^2 x} = \dfrac{\sec^2 x - 1}{\sec^2 x} = \dfrac{\tan^2 x}{\sec^2 x} = \sin^2 x$

65. (a) $\dfrac{y}{1+z} + \dfrac{1+z}{y} = \dfrac{y^2+(1+z)^2}{(1+z)y}$

(b) $\dfrac{\sin x}{1+\cos x} + \dfrac{1+\cos x}{\sin x} = \dfrac{\sin^2 x + (1+\cos x)^2}{\sin x(1+\cos x)}$

$\qquad\qquad = \dfrac{\sin^2 x + 1 + 2\cos x + \cos^2 x}{\sin x(1+\cos x)} = \dfrac{2+2\cos x}{\sin x(1+\cos x)} = \dfrac{2}{\sin x} = 2\csc x$

Section 7.5   DeMoivre's Theorem

- ■ You should be able to graphically represent complex numbers.

- ■ The absolute value of the complex numbers $z = a + bi$ is $|z| = \sqrt{a^2+b^2}$.

- ■ The trigonometric form of the complex number $z = a + bi$ is $z = r(\cos\theta + i\sin\theta)$ where

  (a) $a = r\cos\theta$ (b) $b = r\sin\theta$

  (c) $r = \sqrt{a^2+b^2}$; r is called the modulus of z.   (d) $\tan\theta = b/a$; θ is called the argument of z.

- ■ Given $z_1 = r_1(\cos\theta_1 + i\sin\theta_1)$ and $z_2 = r_2(\cos\theta_2 + i\sin\theta_2)$:

  (a) $z_1 z_2 = r_1 r_2[\cos(\theta_1+\theta_2) + i\sin(\theta_1+\theta_2)]$

  (b) $\dfrac{z_1}{z_2} = \dfrac{r_1}{r_2}[\cos(\theta_1-\theta_2) + i\sin(\theta_1-\theta_2)]$, $z_2 \neq 0$

- ■ You should know DeMoivre's Theorem: If $z = r(\cos\theta + i\sin\theta)$, then for any positive integer n,

  $$z^n = r^n(\cos n\theta + i\sin n\theta).$$

- ■ You should know that for any positive integer n, $z = r(\cos\theta + i\sin\theta)$ has n distinct nth roots given by

  $$\sqrt[n]{r}\left[\cos\left(\frac{\theta+2\pi k}{n}\right) + i\sin\left(\frac{\theta+2\pi k}{n}\right)\right]$$

  where $k = 0, 1, 2, \ldots, n-1$.

Solutions to Odd-Numbered Exercises

1. $|-5i| = \sqrt{0^2 + (-5)^2}$

$= \sqrt{25} = 5$

3. $|-4 + 4i| = \sqrt{(-4)^2 + (4)^2}$

$= \sqrt{32} = 4\sqrt{2}$

5. $|6 - 7i| = \sqrt{6^2 + (-7)^2}$

$= \sqrt{85}$

7. $z = 3i$

$r = \sqrt{0^2 + 3^2} = \sqrt{9} = 3$

$\tan\theta = \dfrac{3}{0}$, undefined $\Rightarrow \theta = \dfrac{\pi}{2}$

$z = 3\left(\cos\dfrac{\pi}{2} + i\sin\dfrac{\pi}{2}\right)$

9. $z = -2 - 2i$

$r = \sqrt{(-2)^2 + (-2)^2} = \sqrt{8} = 2\sqrt{2}$

$\tan\theta = \dfrac{-2}{-2} = 1$, θ is in Quadrant III.

$\theta = \dfrac{5\pi}{4}$

$z = 2\sqrt{2}\left(\cos\dfrac{5\pi}{4} + i\sin\dfrac{5\pi}{4}\right)$

11. $z = 3 - 3i$

$r = \sqrt{3^2 + (-3)^2} = \sqrt{18} = 3\sqrt{2}$

$\tan\theta = \dfrac{-3}{3} = -1 \Rightarrow \theta = \dfrac{7\pi}{4}$

$z = 3\sqrt{2}\left(\cos\dfrac{7\pi}{4} + i\sin\dfrac{7\pi}{4}\right)$

13. $z = \sqrt{3} + i$

$r = \sqrt{\left(\sqrt{3}\right)^2 + 1^2} = \sqrt{4} = 2$

$\tan\theta = \dfrac{1}{\sqrt{3}} = \dfrac{\sqrt{3}}{3} \Rightarrow \theta = \dfrac{\pi}{6}$

$z = 2\left(\cos\dfrac{\pi}{6} + i\sin\dfrac{\pi}{6}\right)$

15. $z = -2(1 + \sqrt{3}i)$

$r = \sqrt{(-2)^2 + (-2\sqrt{3})^2} = \sqrt{16} = 4$

$\tan\theta = \dfrac{\sqrt{3}}{1} = \sqrt{3} \Rightarrow \theta = \dfrac{4\pi}{3}$

$z = 4\left(\cos\dfrac{4\pi}{3} + i\sin\dfrac{4\pi}{3}\right)$

17. $z = 0 + 6i$

$r = \sqrt{0^2 + (6)^2} = \sqrt{36} = 6$

$\tan\theta = \dfrac{6}{0}$, undefined $\Rightarrow \theta = \dfrac{\pi}{2}$

$z = 6\left(\cos\dfrac{\pi}{2} + i\sin\dfrac{\pi}{2}\right)$

19. $z = -7 + 4i$

$r = \sqrt{(-7)^2 + (4)^2} = \sqrt{65}$

$\tan \theta = \dfrac{4}{-7} \;\Rightarrow\; \theta = 2.62$

$z \approx \sqrt{65}(\cos 2.62 + i \sin 2.62)$

21. $z = 7 + 0i$

$r = \sqrt{(7)^2 + (0)^2} = \sqrt{49} = 7$

$\tan \theta = \dfrac{0}{7} = 0 \;\Longrightarrow\; \theta = 0$

$z = 7(\cos 0 + i \sin 0)$

23. $z = 1 + 6i$

$r = \sqrt{1^2 + (6)^2} = \sqrt{37}$

$\tan \theta = \dfrac{6}{1} = 6 \;\Rightarrow\; \theta = 1.41$

$z \approx \sqrt{37}(\cos 1.41 + i \sin 1.41)$

25. $z = -3 - i$

$r = \sqrt{(-3)^2 + (-1)^2} = \sqrt{10}$

$\tan \theta = \dfrac{-1}{-3} = \dfrac{1}{3} \;\Longrightarrow\; \theta \approx 3.46$

$z \approx \sqrt{10}(\cos 3.46 + i \sin 3.46)$

27. $5 + 2i \approx 5.39 \angle 0.38$

$= 5.39(\cos 0.38 + i \sin 0.38)$

29. $3\sqrt{2} - 7i \approx 8.19 \angle -1.0259 \approx 8.19 \angle 5.26$

$= 8.19(\cos 5.26 + i \sin 5.26)$

31. $2(\cos 150° + i \sin 150°) = \left[-\dfrac{\sqrt{3}}{2} + i\left(\dfrac{1}{2}\right) \right]$

$= -\sqrt{3} + i$

33. $\dfrac{3}{2}(\cos 300° + i \sin 300°) = \dfrac{3}{2}\left[\dfrac{1}{2} + i\left(-\dfrac{\sqrt{3}}{2} \right) \right]$

$= \dfrac{3}{4} - \dfrac{3\sqrt{3}}{4}i$

35. $3.75\left(\cos\dfrac{3\pi}{4} + i\sin\dfrac{3\pi}{4}\right) = -\dfrac{15\sqrt{2}}{8} + \dfrac{15\sqrt{2}}{8}i$

37. $4\left(\cos\dfrac{3\pi}{2} + i\sin\dfrac{3\pi}{2}\right) = 4(0 - i) = -4i$

39. $3[\cos(18°\,45') + i\sin(18°\,45')] \approx 2.8408 + 0.9643i$

41. $5\left(\cos\dfrac{\pi}{9} + i\sin\dfrac{\pi}{9}\right) \approx 4.70 + 1.71i$

43. $12\left(\cos\dfrac{3\pi}{5} + i\sin\dfrac{3\pi}{5}\right) \approx -3.71 + 11.41i$

45.

The absolute value of each power is 1.

47. $\left[3\left(\cos\dfrac{\pi}{3} + i\sin\dfrac{\pi}{3}\right)\right]\left[4\left(\cos\dfrac{\pi}{6} + i\sin\dfrac{\pi}{6}\right)\right] = (3)(4)\left[\cos\left(\dfrac{\pi}{3} + \dfrac{\pi}{6}\right) + i\sin\left(\dfrac{\pi}{6} + \dfrac{\pi}{3}\right)\right]$

$$= 12\left(\cos\dfrac{\pi}{2} + i\sin\dfrac{\pi}{2}\right)$$

49. $\left[\tfrac{5}{3}(\cos 140° + i\sin 140°)\right]\left[\tfrac{2}{3}(\cos 60° + i\sin 60°)\right] = \left(\tfrac{5}{3}\right)\left(\tfrac{2}{3}\right)[\cos(140° + 60°) + i\sin(140° + 60°)]$

$$= \tfrac{10}{9}(\cos 200° + i\sin 200°)$$

51. $[0.45(\cos 310° + i\sin 310°)][0.60(\cos 200° + i\sin 200°)] = (0.45)(0.60)[\cos(310° + 200°) + i\sin(310° + 200°)]$

$$= 0.27(\cos 510° + i\sin 510°)$$

$$= 0.27(\cos 150° + i\sin 150°)$$

53. $\dfrac{\cos 40° + i\sin 40°}{\cos 10° + i\sin 10°} = \cos(40° - 10°) + i\sin(40° - 10°) = \cos 30° + i\sin 30°$

55. $\dfrac{2(\cos 120° + i\sin 120°)}{4(\cos 40° + i\sin 40°)} = \dfrac{1}{2}[\cos(120° - 40°) + i\sin(120° - 40°)]$

$$= \dfrac{1}{2}(\cos 80° + i\sin 80°)$$

57. $\dfrac{12(\cos 52° + i \sin 52°)}{3(\cos 110° + i \sin 110°)} = 4[\cos(52° - 110°) + i \sin(52° - 110°)]$

$$= 4[\cos(-58°) + i \sin(-58°)]$$

59. (a) $2 + 2i = 2\sqrt{2}(\cos 45° + i \sin 45°)$

$\quad\quad 1 - i = \sqrt{2}[\cos(-45°) + i \sin(-45°)]$

(b) $(2 + 2i)(1 - i) = [2\sqrt{2}(\cos 45° + i \sin 45°)][\sqrt{2}(\cos(-45°) + i \sin(-45°))] = 4(\cos 0° + i \sin 0°) = 4.$

(c) $(2 + 2i)(1 - i) = 2 - 2i + 2i - 2i^2 = 2 + 2 = 4$

61. (a) $-2i = 2[\cos(-90°) + i \sin(-90°)]$

$\quad\quad 1 + i = \sqrt{2}(\cos 45° + i \sin 45°)$

(b) $-2i(1 + i) = 2[\cos(-90°) + i \sin(-90°)][\sqrt{2}(\cos 45° + i \sin 45°)]$

$$= 2\sqrt{2}[\cos(-45°) + i \sin(-45°)]$$

$$= 2\sqrt{2}\left[\frac{1}{\sqrt{2}} - \frac{1}{\sqrt{2}}i\right] = 2 - 2i$$

(c) $-2i(1 + i) = -2i - 2i^2 = -2i + 2 = 2 - 2i$

63. (a) $\quad\quad 5 = 5(\cos 0° + i \sin 0°)$

$\quad\quad 2 + 3i \approx \sqrt{13}(\cos 56.31° + i \sin 56.31°)$

(b) $\dfrac{5}{2 + 3i} \approx \dfrac{5(\cos 0° + i \sin 0°)}{\sqrt{13}(\cos 56.31° + i \sin 56.31°)} = \dfrac{5\sqrt{13}}{13}(\cos -56.31° + i \sin -56.31) \approx 0.7692 - 1.154i$

(c) $\dfrac{5}{2 + 3i} = \dfrac{5}{2 + 3i} \cdot \dfrac{2 - 3i}{2 - 3i} = \dfrac{10 - 15i}{13} = \dfrac{10}{13} - \dfrac{15}{13}i \approx 0.7692 - 1.154i$

65. $\dfrac{z_1}{z_2} = \dfrac{r_1(\cos \theta_1 + i \sin \theta_1)}{r_2(\cos \theta_2 + i \sin \theta_2)} \cdot \dfrac{\cos \theta_2 - i \sin \theta_2}{\cos \theta_2 - i \sin \theta_2}$

$$= \dfrac{r_1}{r_2(\cos^2 \theta_2 + \sin^2 \theta_2)}[\cos \theta_1 \cos \theta_2 + \sin \theta_1 \sin \theta_2 + i(\sin \theta_1 \cos \theta_2 - \sin \theta_2 \cos \theta_1)]$$

$$= \dfrac{r_1}{r_2}[\cos(\theta_1 - \theta_2) + i \sin(\theta_1 - \theta_2)]$$

67. (a) $z\bar{z} = [r(\cos \theta + i \sin \theta)][r(\cos(-\theta) + i \sin(-\theta)]$

$$= r^2[\cos(\theta - \theta) + i \sin(\theta - \theta)]$$

$$= r^2[\cos 0 + i \sin 0]$$

$$= r^2$$

(b) $\dfrac{z}{\bar{z}} = \dfrac{r(\cos \theta + i \sin \theta)}{r[\cos(-\theta) + i \sin(-\theta)]}$

$$= \dfrac{r}{r}[\cos(\theta - (-\theta)) + i \sin(\theta - (-\theta))]$$

$$= \cos 2\theta + i \sin 2\theta$$

69. Let $z = x + iy$ such that:

$$|z| = 2 \implies 2 = \sqrt{x^2 + y^2}$$

$$\implies 4 = x^2 + y^2: \text{circle with radius of 2}$$

71. $(1 + i)^5 = \left[\sqrt{2}\left(\cos\frac{\pi}{4} + i\sin\frac{\pi}{4}\right)\right]^5$

$= (\sqrt{2})^5\left(\cos\frac{5\pi}{4} + i\sin\frac{5\pi}{4}\right)$

$= 4\sqrt{2}\left(-\frac{\sqrt{2}}{2} - \frac{\sqrt{2}}{2}i\right)$

$= -4 - 4i$

73. $(-1 + i)^{10} = \left[\sqrt{2}\left(\cos\frac{3\pi}{4} + i\sin\frac{3\pi}{4}\right)\right]^{10}$

$= (\sqrt{2})^{10}\left(\cos\frac{30\pi}{4} + i\sin\frac{30\pi}{4}\right)$

$= 32\left[\cos\left(\frac{3\pi}{2} + 6\pi\right) + i\sin\left(\frac{3\pi}{2} + 6\pi\right)\right]$

$= 32\left(\cos\frac{3\pi}{2} + i\sin\frac{3\pi}{2}\right)$

$= 32[0 + i(-1)]$

$= -32i$

75. $2(\sqrt{3} + i)^7 = 2\left[2\left(\cos\frac{\pi}{6} + i\sin\frac{\pi}{6}\right)\right]^7$

$= 2\left[2^7\left(\cos\frac{7\pi}{6} + i\sin\frac{7\pi}{6}\right)\right]$

$= 256\left(-\frac{\sqrt{3}}{2} - \frac{1}{2}i\right)$

$= -128\sqrt{3} - 128i$

77. $[5(\cos 20° + i\sin 20°)]^3 = 5^3(\cos 60° + i\sin 60°) = \dfrac{125}{2} + \dfrac{125\sqrt{3}}{2}i$

79. $\left(\cos\frac{5\pi}{4} + i\sin\frac{5\pi}{4}\right)^{10} = \cos\frac{25\pi}{2} + i\sin\frac{25\pi}{2}$

$= \cos\left(12\pi + \frac{\pi}{2}\right) + i\sin\left(12\pi + \frac{\pi}{2}\right) = \cos\frac{\pi}{2} + i\sin\frac{\pi}{2} = i$

81. $[5(\cos 3.2 + i\sin 3.2)]^4 = 5^4(\cos 12.8 + i\sin 12.8)$

$\approx 608.02 + 144.69i$

83. $(3 - 2i)^5 = -597 - 122i$

85. $[3(\cos 15° + i\sin 15°)]^4 = 81(\cos 60° + i\sin 60°)$

$= \dfrac{81}{2} + \dfrac{81\sqrt{3}}{2}i$

87. $\left[-\frac{1}{2}(1 + \sqrt{3}i)\right]^6 = \left[\cos\frac{4\pi}{3} + i\sin\frac{4\pi}{3}\right]^6$

$= \cos 8\pi + i\sin 8\pi$

$= 1$

89. (a) In trigonometric form we have: $2(\cos 30° + i \sin 30°)$

$$2(\cos 150° + i \sin 150°)$$

$$2(\cos 270° + i \sin 270°)$$

(b) There are three roots evenly spaced around a circle of radius 2. Therefore, they represent the cube roots of some number of modulus 8. Cubing them shows that they are all cube roots of $8i$.

(c) $[2(\cos 30° + i \sin 30°)]^3 = 8i$

$[2(\cos 150° + i \sin 150°)]^3 = 8i$

$[2(\cos 270° + i \sin 270°)]^3 = 8i$

91. (a) Square roots of $5(\cos 120° + i \sin 120°)$:

$$\sqrt{5}\left[\cos\left(\frac{120° + 360°k}{2}\right) + i \sin\left(\frac{120° + 360°k}{2}\right)\right], \; k = 0, 1$$

$$\sqrt{5}(\cos 60° + i \sin 60°)$$

$$\sqrt{5}(\cos 240° + i \sin 240°)$$

(c) $\dfrac{\sqrt{5}}{2} + \dfrac{\sqrt{15}}{2}i, \; -\dfrac{\sqrt{5}}{2} - \dfrac{\sqrt{15}}{2}i$

(b)

93. (a) Fourth roots of $16\left(\cos\dfrac{4\pi}{3} + i \sin\dfrac{4\pi}{3}\right)$:

$$\sqrt[4]{16}\left[\cos\left(\frac{(4\pi/3) + 2k\pi}{4}\right) + i \sin\left(\frac{(4\pi/3) + 2k\pi}{4}\right)\right], \; k = 0, 1, 2, 3$$

$$2\left(\cos\frac{\pi}{3} + i \sin\frac{\pi}{3}\right)$$

$$2\left(\cos\frac{5\pi}{6} + i \sin\frac{5\pi}{6}\right)$$

$$2\left(\cos\frac{4\pi}{3} + i \sin\frac{4\pi}{3}\right)$$

$$2\left(\cos\frac{11\pi}{6} + i \sin\frac{11\pi}{6}\right)$$

(c) $1 + \sqrt{3}i, \; -\sqrt{3} + i, \; -1 - \sqrt{3}i, \; \sqrt{3} - i$

(b)

95. (a) Square roots of $-25i = 25\left(\cos\dfrac{3\pi}{2} + i \sin\dfrac{3\pi}{2}\right)$:

$$\sqrt{25}\left[\cos\left(\frac{(3\pi/2) + 2k\pi}{2}\right) + i \sin\left(\frac{(3\pi/2) + 2k\pi}{2}\right)\right], \; k = 0, 1$$

$$5\left(\cos\frac{3\pi}{4} + i \sin\frac{3\pi}{4}\right)$$

$$5\left(\cos\frac{7\pi}{4} + i \sin\frac{7\pi}{4}\right)$$

(c) $-\dfrac{5\sqrt{2}}{2} + \dfrac{5\sqrt{2}}{2}i, \; \dfrac{5\sqrt{2}}{2} - \dfrac{5\sqrt{2}}{2}i$

(b)

97. (a) Cube roots of $-\dfrac{125}{3}(1 + \sqrt{3}i) = 125\left(\cos\dfrac{4\pi}{3} + i\sin\dfrac{4\pi}{3}\right)$:

$$\sqrt[3]{125}\left[\cos\left(\dfrac{(4\pi/3) + 2k\pi}{3}\right) + i\sin\left(\dfrac{(4\pi/3) + 2k\pi}{3}\right)\right], \; k = 0, 1, 2$$

$$5\left(\cos\dfrac{4\pi}{9} + i\sin\dfrac{4\pi}{9}\right)$$

$$5\left(\cos\dfrac{10\pi}{9} + i\sin\dfrac{10\pi}{9}\right)$$

$$2\left(\cos\dfrac{16\pi}{9} + i\sin\dfrac{16\pi}{9}\right)$$

(b)

(c) $0.8682 + 4.924i, \; -4.698 - 1.710i, \; 3.830 - 3.214i$

99. (a) Cube roots of $8 = 8(\cos 0 + i\sin 0)$:

$$\sqrt[3]{8}\left[\cos\left(\dfrac{2k\pi}{3}\right) + i\sin\left(\dfrac{2k\pi}{3}\right)\right], \; k = 0, 1, 2, 3$$

$$2(\cos 0 + i\sin 0)$$

$$2\left(\cos\dfrac{2\pi}{3} + i\sin\dfrac{2\pi}{3}\right)$$

$$2\left(\cos\dfrac{4\pi}{3} + i\sin\dfrac{4\pi}{3}\right)$$

(c) $2, \; -1 + \sqrt{3}i, \; -1 - \sqrt{3}i$

(b)

101. (a) Fifth roots of $1 = \cos 0 + i\sin 0$:

$$\cos\dfrac{2k\pi}{5} + i\sin\dfrac{2k\pi}{5}, k = 0, 1, 2, 3, 4$$

$$\cos 0 + i\sin 0$$

$$\cos\dfrac{2\pi}{5} + i\sin\dfrac{2\pi}{5}$$

$$\cos\dfrac{4\pi}{5} + i\sin\dfrac{4\pi}{5}$$

$$\cos\dfrac{6\pi}{5} + i\sin\dfrac{6\pi}{5}$$

$$\cos\dfrac{8\pi}{5} + i\sin\dfrac{8\pi}{5}$$

(b)

(c) $1, 0.3090 + 0.9511i, -0.8090 + 0.5878i, -0.8090 - 0.5878i, 0.3090 - 0.9511i$

103. (a) Cube roots of $-125 = 125(\cos 180° + i\sin 180°)$ are:

$$5(\cos 60° + i\sin 60°)$$

$$5(\cos 180° + i\sin 180°)$$

$$5(\cos 300° + i\sin 300°)$$

(b)

(c) $\dfrac{5}{2} + \dfrac{5\sqrt{3}}{2}i, \; -5, \; \dfrac{5}{2} - \dfrac{5\sqrt{3}}{2}i$

105. (a) Fifth roots of $128(-1 + i) = 128\sqrt{2}(\cos 135° + i \sin 135°)$ are:

$$2\sqrt[5]{4\sqrt{2}} (\cos 27° + i \sin 27°)$$

$$2\sqrt[5]{4\sqrt{2}} (\cos 99° + i \sin 99°)$$

$$2\sqrt[5]{4\sqrt{2}} (\cos 171° + i \sin 171°)$$

$$2\sqrt[5]{4\sqrt{2}} (\cos 243° + i \sin 243°)$$

$$2\sqrt[5]{4\sqrt{2}} (\cos 315° + i \sin 315°)$$

(b)

(c) $2.52 + 1.28i, -0.44 + 2.79i, -2.79 + 0.44i,$
$-1.28 - 252i, 2 - 2i$

107. $x^4 - i = 0$

$x^4 = i$

The solutions are the fourth roots of $i = \cos \dfrac{\pi}{2} + i \sin \dfrac{\pi}{2}$:

$$\sqrt[4]{1}\left[\cos\left(\frac{(\pi/2) + 2k\pi}{4}\right) + i \sin\left(\frac{(\pi/2) + 2k\pi}{4}\right)\right], \quad k = 0, 1, 2, 3$$

$$\cos \frac{\pi}{8} + i \sin \frac{\pi}{8}$$

$$\cos \frac{5\pi}{8} + i \sin \frac{5\pi}{8}$$

$$\cos \frac{9\pi}{8} + i \sin \frac{9\pi}{8}$$

$$\cos \frac{13\pi}{8} + i \sin \frac{13\pi}{8}$$

109. $x^5 + 243 = 0$

$x^5 = -243$

The solutions are the fifth roots of $-243 = 243(\cos \pi + i \sin \pi)$:

$$\sqrt[5]{243}\left[\cos\left(\frac{\pi + 2k\pi}{5}\right) + i \sin\left(\frac{\pi + 2k\pi}{5}\right)\right], \quad k = 0, 1, 2, 3, 4$$

$$3\left(\cos \frac{\pi}{5} + i \sin \frac{\pi}{5}\right)$$

$$3\left(\cos \frac{3\pi}{5} + i \sin \frac{3\pi}{5}\right)$$

$$3(\cos \pi + i \sin \pi) = -3$$

$$3\left(\cos \frac{7\pi}{5} + i \sin \frac{7\pi}{5}\right)$$

$$3\left(\cos \frac{9\pi}{5} + i \sin \frac{9\pi}{5}\right)$$

111. $x^3 + 64i = 0$

$$x^3 = -64i$$

The solutions are the fifth roots of $-64i$:

$$\sqrt[3]{64}\left[\cos\left(\frac{(3\pi/2) + 2k\pi}{3}\right) + i\sin\left(\frac{(3\pi/2) + 2k\pi}{3}\right)\right], \; k = 0, 1, 2$$

$$4\left(\cos\frac{\pi}{2} + i\sin\frac{\pi}{2}\right) = 4i$$

$$4\left(\cos\frac{7\pi}{6} + i\sin\frac{7\pi}{6}\right) = -2\sqrt{3} - 2i$$

$$4\left(\cos\frac{11\pi}{6} + i\sin\frac{11\pi}{6}\right) = 2\sqrt{3} - 2i$$

113. $x^3 - (1 - i) = 0$

$$x^3 = 1 - i = \sqrt{2}(\cos 315° + i\sin 315°)$$

The solutions are the cube roots of $1 - i$:

$$\sqrt[3]{\sqrt{2}}\left[\cos\left(\frac{315° + 360°k}{3}\right) + i\sin\left(\frac{315° + 360°k}{3}\right)\right], \; k = 0, 1, 2$$

$$\sqrt[6]{2}(\cos 105° + i\sin 105°)$$

$$\sqrt[6]{2}(\cos 225° + i\sin 225°)$$

$$\sqrt[6]{2}(\cos 345° + i\sin 345°)$$

115. $\sin 28.1° = \dfrac{h}{18} \implies h = 18\sin 28.1° \approx 8.48$

❑ Review Exercises for Chapter 7

Solutions to Odd-Numbered Exercises

1. Given: $a = 5, \; b = 8, \; c = 10$

$$\cos C = \frac{a^2 + b^2 - c^2}{2ab} = \frac{25 + 64 - 100}{80} \approx -0.1375 \implies C \approx 97.9°$$

$$\sin A = \frac{a\sin C}{c} \approx \frac{5(0.9905)}{10} \approx 0.4953 \implies A \approx 29.7°$$

$$\sin B = \frac{b\sin C}{c} \approx \frac{8(0.9905)}{10} \approx 0.7924 \implies B \approx 52.4°$$

3. Given: $A = 12°, \; B = 58°, \; a = 5$

$$C = 180° - A - B = 180° - 12° - 58° = 110°$$

$$b = \frac{a\sin B}{\sin A} = \frac{5\sin 58°}{\sin 12°} \approx \frac{5(0.8480)}{0.2079} \approx 20.4$$

$$c = \frac{a\sin C}{\sin A} = \frac{5\sin 110°}{\sin 12°} \approx \frac{5(0.9397)}{0.2079} \approx 22.6$$

5. Given: $B = 110°$, $a = 4$, $c = 4$

$$b^2 = a^2 + c^2 - 2ac \cos B \approx 16 + 16 - 2(4)(4)(-0.3420) \approx 42.94 \implies b \approx 6.6$$

$$\sin A = \frac{a \sin B}{b} = \frac{4 \sin 110°}{6.6} \approx \frac{4(0.9397)}{6.6} \approx 0.5736 \implies A \approx 35°$$

$$c = a \implies C = A \approx 35°$$

7. Given: $A = 75°$, $a = 2.5$, $b = 16.5$

$$\sin B = \frac{b \sin A}{a} = \frac{16.5 \sin 75°}{2.5} \approx \frac{16.5(0.9659)}{2.5} \approx 5.375 \implies \text{no triangle formed}$$

No solution

9. Given: $B = 115°$, $a = 7$, $b = 14.5$

$$\sin A = \frac{a \sin B}{b} = \frac{7 \sin 115°}{14.5} \approx \frac{7(0.9063)}{14.5} \approx 0.4375 \implies A \approx 25.9°$$

$$C \approx 180° - 115° - 25.9° = 39.1°$$

$$c^2 = a^2 + b^2 - 2ab \cos C \approx 7^2 + 14.5^2 - 2(7)(14.5)(0.7760) \approx 101.7 \implies c \approx 10.1$$

11. Given: $A = 15°$, $a = 5$, $b = 10$

$$\sin B = \frac{b \sin A}{a} = \frac{10 \sin 15°}{5} \approx \frac{10(0.2588)}{5} \approx 0.5176 \implies B \approx 31.2° \text{ or } 148.8°$$

Case 1: $B \approx 31.2°$

$$C \approx 180° - 15° - 31.2° = 133.8°$$

$$c = \frac{a \sin C}{\sin A} \approx 13.9$$

Case 2: $B \approx 148.8°$

$$C \approx 180° - 15° - 148.8° = 16.2°$$

$$c = \frac{a \sin C}{\sin A} \approx 5.39$$

13. Given: $B = 150°$, $a = 10$, $c = 20$

$$b^2 = a^2 + c^2 - 2ac \cos B \approx 100 + 400 - 400(-0.8660) \approx 846.4 \implies b \approx 29.1$$

$$\sin C = \frac{c \sin B}{b} \approx \frac{20(0.5)}{29.09} \approx 0.3437 \implies C \approx 20.1°$$

$$\sin A = \frac{a \sin B}{b} \approx \frac{10(0.5)}{29.09} \approx 0.1719 \implies A \approx 9.9°$$

15. Given: $B = 25°$, $a = 6.2$, $b = 4$

$$\sin A = \frac{a \sin B}{b} \approx 0.6551 \implies A \approx 40.9° \text{ or } 139.1°$$

Case 1: $A \approx 40.9°$

$$C \approx 180° - 25° - 40.9° = 114.1°$$

$$c \approx 8.6$$

Case 2: $A \approx 139.1°$

$$C \approx 180° - 25° - 139.1° = 15.9°$$

$$c \approx 2.6$$

17. $a = 4$, $b = 5$, $c = 7$

$$s = \frac{a + b + c}{2} = \frac{4 + 5 + 7}{2} = 8$$

$$\text{Area} = \sqrt{s(s - a)(s - b)(s - c)}$$

$$= \sqrt{8(4)(3)(1)} \approx 9.798$$

19. $A = 27°$, $b = 5$, $c = 8$

$$\text{Area} = \frac{1}{2}bc \sin A = \frac{1}{2}(5)(8)(0.4540) = 9.08$$

21. $\alpha = 180° - 31° = 149°$

$\phi = 180° - 149° - 17° = 14°$

$x = \dfrac{50 \sin 17°}{\sin \phi} = \dfrac{50 \sin 17°}{\sin 14°} \approx 60.43$

$h = x \sin 31°$

$\approx 50.43(0.5150) \approx 31.1$ meters

23. $\sin 28° = \dfrac{h}{75}$

$h = 75 \sin 28° \approx 35.21$ feet

$\cos 28° = \dfrac{x}{75}$

$x = 75 \cos 28° \approx 66.2211$ feet

$\tan 45° = \dfrac{H}{x}$

$H = x \tan 45° \approx 66.22$ feet

Height of tree: $H - h \approx 31$ feet

25. $d^2 = 850^2 + 1060^2 - 2(850)(1060) \cos 72°$

$\approx 1,289,251$

$d \approx 1135$ miles

27. The height is given by

$h = a \cdot \sin 55° \approx 14.6$ m.

29. Initial point: $(-5, 4)$
Terminal point: $(2, -1)$

$\mathbf{v} = \langle 2 - (-5), -1, -4 \rangle = \langle 7, -5 \rangle$

31. Initial point: $(0, 10)$
Terminal point: $(7, 3)$

$\mathbf{v} = \langle 7 - 0, 3 - 10 \rangle = \langle 7, -7 \rangle$

33. $\langle 8 \cos 120°, 8 \sin 120° \rangle = (-4, 4\sqrt{3})$

35. $\mathbf{v} = -10\mathbf{i} + 10\mathbf{j}$

$\|\mathbf{v}\| = \sqrt{(-10)^2 + (10)^2} = \sqrt{200} = 10\sqrt{2}$

$\tan \theta = \dfrac{10}{-10} = -1 \implies \theta = 135°$ since

$\mathbf{v}$ is in Quadrant II.

$\mathbf{v} = 10\sqrt{2}(\mathbf{i} \sin 135° + \mathbf{j} \cos 135°)$

37. $\mathbf{u} = 6\mathbf{i} - 5\mathbf{j}$

$\dfrac{1}{\|\mathbf{u}\|}\mathbf{u} = \dfrac{1}{\sqrt{6^2 + 5^2}}(6\mathbf{i} - 5\mathbf{j}) = \dfrac{6}{\sqrt{61}}\mathbf{i} - \dfrac{5}{\sqrt{61}}\mathbf{j}$

$= \left\langle \dfrac{6}{\sqrt{61}}, -\dfrac{5}{\sqrt{61}} \right\rangle$

39. $\mathbf{u} = 6\mathbf{i} - 5\mathbf{j}, \quad \mathbf{v} = 10\mathbf{i} + 3\mathbf{j}$

$4\mathbf{u} - 5\mathbf{v} = (24\mathbf{i} - 20\mathbf{j}) - (50\mathbf{i} + 15\mathbf{j}) = -26\mathbf{i} - 35\mathbf{j}$

$$= \langle -26, -35 \rangle$$

41. $\mathbf{u} = 15[(\cos 20°)\mathbf{i} + (\sin 20°)\mathbf{j}]$

$\mathbf{v} = 20[(\cos 63°)\mathbf{i} + (\sin 63°)\mathbf{j}]$

$\mathbf{u} + \mathbf{v} \approx 23.1752\mathbf{i} + 22.9504\mathbf{j}$

$\|\mathbf{u} + \mathbf{v}\| \approx 32.62$

$\|\mathbf{u} + \mathbf{v}\| = \dfrac{22.9504}{23.1752} \implies \theta \approx 44.72°$

43. $\tan \alpha = \frac{12}{5} \implies \sin \alpha = \frac{12}{13}$ and $\cos \alpha = \frac{5}{13}$

$\tan \beta = \frac{3}{4} \implies \sin(180 - \beta) = \frac{3}{5}$ and $\cos(180° - \beta) = -\frac{4}{5}$

$\mathbf{u} = 250\left(\frac{5}{13}\mathbf{i} + \frac{12}{13}\mathbf{j}\right)$

$\mathbf{v} = 100\left(-\frac{4}{5}\mathbf{i} + \frac{3}{5}\mathbf{j}\right)$

$\mathbf{w} = 200(0\mathbf{i} - \mathbf{j})$

$\mathbf{r} = \mathbf{u} + \mathbf{v} + \mathbf{w} = \left(\frac{1250}{13} - 80 + 0\right)\mathbf{i} + \left(\frac{3000}{13} + 60 - 200\right)\mathbf{j} = \frac{210}{13}\mathbf{i} + \frac{1180}{13}\mathbf{j}$

$\|\mathbf{r}\| = \sqrt{\left(\frac{210}{13}\right)^2 + \left(\frac{1180}{13}\right)^2} \approx 92.2$

$\tan \theta = \frac{1180}{210} \implies \theta \approx 79.9°$

45. Rope One: $\mathbf{u} = \|\mathbf{u}\|(\cos 30°\mathbf{i} - \sin 30°\mathbf{j}) = \|\mathbf{u}\|\left(\dfrac{\sqrt{3}}{2}\mathbf{i} - \dfrac{1}{2}\mathbf{j}\right)$

Rope Two: $\mathbf{v} = \|\mathbf{u}\|(-\cos 30°\mathbf{i} - \sin 30°\mathbf{j}) - \|\mathbf{u}\|\left(-\dfrac{\sqrt{3}}{2}\mathbf{i} - \dfrac{1}{2}\mathbf{j}\right)$

Resultant: $\mathbf{u} + \mathbf{v} = -\|\mathbf{u}\|\mathbf{j} = -180\mathbf{j}$

$\|\mathbf{u}\| = 180$

Therefore, the tension on each rope is $\|\mathbf{u}\| = 180$ lb.

47. Force $= 500 \sin 12° \approx 104$ lbs

49. Airspeed: $\mathbf{u} = 724(\cos 60°\mathbf{i} + \sin 60°\mathbf{j})$

$$= 362(\mathbf{i} + \sqrt{3}\mathbf{j})$$

Wind: $\mathbf{w} = 32\mathbf{i}$

Groundspeed $= \mathbf{u} + \mathbf{w} = (394\mathbf{i} + 362\sqrt{3}\mathbf{j})$

$\|\mathbf{u} + \mathbf{w}\| = \sqrt{(394)^2 + (362\sqrt{3})^2} \approx 740.5$ km/hr

$\tan \theta = \dfrac{362\sqrt{3}}{394} \implies \theta \approx 57.9°$

Bearing: N 32.1° E

51. $P(7, -4), Q(-3, 2)$

$$\overrightarrow{PQ} = \langle -3 - 7, 2 - (-4) \rangle = \langle -10, 6 \rangle$$

$$\|\overrightarrow{PQ}\| = \sqrt{(-10)^2 + (6)^2} = \sqrt{136} = 2\sqrt{34}$$

$$\frac{\overrightarrow{PQ}}{\|\overrightarrow{PQ}\|} = \frac{1}{2\sqrt{34}}\langle -10, 6 \rangle = \frac{1}{\sqrt{34}}\langle -5, 3 \rangle$$

53. $\mathbf{u} = \langle 39, -12 \rangle, \mathbf{v} = \langle -26, 8 \rangle$

$$\mathbf{u} \cdot \mathbf{v} = 39(-26) + (-12)(8) = -1110 \neq 0 \implies \mathbf{u} \text{ and } \mathbf{v} \text{ are not orthogonal.}$$

$$\mathbf{v} = -\tfrac{2}{3}\mathbf{u} \implies \mathbf{u} \text{ and } \mathbf{v} \text{ are parallel.}$$

55. $\mathbf{u} = \cos\dfrac{7\pi}{4}\mathbf{i} + \sin\dfrac{7\pi}{4}\mathbf{j} = \left\langle \dfrac{1}{\sqrt{2}}, -\dfrac{1}{\sqrt{2}} \right\rangle$

$$\mathbf{v} = \cos\frac{5\pi}{6}\mathbf{i} + \sin\frac{5\pi}{6}\mathbf{j} = \left\langle -\frac{\sqrt{3}}{2}, \frac{1}{2} \right\rangle$$

$$\cos\theta = \frac{\mathbf{u} \cdot \mathbf{v}}{\|\mathbf{u}\|\,\|\mathbf{v}\|} = \frac{\dfrac{-\sqrt{3}}{2\sqrt{2}} - \dfrac{1}{2\sqrt{2}}}{(1)(1)} \approx -0.966 \implies \theta \approx 165° \text{ or } \frac{11\pi}{12}$$

57. $\mathbf{u} = \langle 2\sqrt{2}, -4 \rangle, \mathbf{v} = \langle -\sqrt{2}, 1 \rangle$

$$\cos\theta = \frac{\mathbf{u} \cdot \mathbf{v}}{\|\mathbf{u}\|\,\|\mathbf{v}\|} = \frac{-8}{(\sqrt{24})(\sqrt{3})} \implies \theta \approx 160.5°$$

59.

$$\cos\theta = \frac{\mathbf{u} \cdot \mathbf{v}}{\|\mathbf{u}\|\,\|\mathbf{v}\|} = 0 \implies \theta = 90°$$

61.

$$\cos\theta = \frac{\mathbf{u} \cdot \mathbf{v}}{\|\mathbf{u}\|\,\|\mathbf{v}\|} = \frac{70 - 15}{\sqrt{74}\sqrt{109}} \approx 0.612 \implies \theta \approx 52.2°$$

63. $\mathbf{u} = \langle -4, 3 \rangle, \mathbf{v} = \langle -8, -2 \rangle$

$$\text{proj}_{\mathbf{v}}\mathbf{u} = \left(\frac{\mathbf{u} \cdot \mathbf{v}}{\|\mathbf{v}\|^2}\right)\mathbf{v} = \left(\frac{26}{68}\right)\langle -8, -2 \rangle$$

$$= -\frac{13}{17}\langle 4, 1 \rangle$$

65. $\text{proj}_{\mathbf{v}}\mathbf{u} = \left(\dfrac{\mathbf{u} \cdot \mathbf{v}}{\|\mathbf{v}\|^2}\right)\mathbf{v} = \dfrac{-5}{2}\langle 1, -1 \rangle$

67. $z = -3 = 3(\cos 180° + i\sin 180°)$

69. $z = 5 - 2i, \ r = \sqrt{25 + 4} = \sqrt{29}, \ \theta = \arctan\left(-\tfrac{2}{5}\right) \approx 338.2°$

$$z = \sqrt{29}(\cos 338.2° + i\sin 338.2°)$$

71. $5 - 5i$

$$r = \sqrt{5^2 + (-5)^2} = \sqrt{50} = 5\sqrt{2}$$

$\tan \theta = \dfrac{-5}{5} - -1 \implies \theta \approx 315°$ since the complex number is in Quadrant IV.

$$5 - 5i = 5\sqrt{2}(\cos 315° + i \sin 315°)$$

73. $5 + 12i$

$$r = \sqrt{5^2 + 12^2} = \sqrt{169} = 13$$

$\tan \theta = \frac{12}{5} \implies \theta \approx 67.8°$ since the number is in Quadrant I.

$$5 + 12i \approx 13(\cos 67.38° + i \sin 67.38°)$$

75. $100(\cos 240° + i \sin 240°) = 100\left(-\dfrac{1}{2} - \dfrac{\sqrt{3}}{2}i\right)$

$$= -50 - 50\sqrt{3}i$$

77. $13(\cos 0 + i \sin 0) = 13(1 + 0i) = 13$

79. (a) $z_1 = 2\sqrt{3} - 2i = 4(\cos 330° + i \sin 330°)$

$z_2 = -10i = 10(\cos 270° + i \sin 270°)$

(b) $z_1 z_2 = [4(\cos 330° + i \sin 330°)][10(\cos 270° + i \sin 270°)]$

$$= 40(\cos 600° + i \sin 600°)$$

$$= 40(\cos 240° + i \sin 240°)$$

$$\approx -20.00 - 34.64i$$

$$\dfrac{z_1}{z_2} = \dfrac{4(\cos 330° + i \sin 330°)}{10(\cos 270° + i \sin 270°)}$$

$$= \dfrac{2}{5}(\cos 60° + i \sin 60°)$$

81. $\left[5\left(\cos \dfrac{\pi}{12} + i \sin \dfrac{\pi}{12}\right)\right]^4 = 5^4\left(\dfrac{4\pi}{12} + i \sin \dfrac{4\pi}{12}\right)$

$$= 625\left(\cos \dfrac{\pi}{3} + i \sin \dfrac{\pi}{3}\right)$$

$$= 625\left(\dfrac{1}{2} + \dfrac{\sqrt{3}}{2}i\right)$$

$$= \dfrac{625}{2} + \dfrac{625\sqrt{3}}{2}i$$

83. $(2 + 3i)^6 = [\sqrt{13}(\cos 56.3° + i \sin 56.3°)]^6$

$$= 13^3(\cos 337.9° + i \sin 337.9°)$$

$$\approx 13^3(0.9263 - 0.3769i)$$

$$\approx 2035 - 828i$$

85. (a) The trigonometric form of the three roots shown is:

$4(\cos 60° + i \sin 60°)$

$4(\cos 180° + i \sin 180°)$

$4(\cos 300° + i \sin 300°)$

(b) Since there are three evenly spaced roots on the circle of radius 4, they are cube roots of a complex number of modulus $4^3 = 64$. Cubing them yields -64.

(c) $[4(\cos 60° + i \sin 60°)]^3 = -64$

$[4(\cos 180° + i \sin 180°)]^3 = -64$

$[4(\cos 300° + i \sin 300°)]^3 = -64$

87. (a) 2

2(cos 72° + *i* sin 72°)

2(cos 144° + *i* sin 144°)

2(cos 216° + *i* sin 216°)

2(cos 288° + *i* sin 288°)

(b) Since there are five equally spaced roots on the circle of radius 2, they are fifth roots of a complex number of modulus $32 = 2^5$.

89. Sixth roots of $-729i = 729\left(\cos\dfrac{3\pi}{2} + i\sin\dfrac{3\pi}{2}\right)$:

$$\sqrt[6]{729}\left(\cos\dfrac{(3\pi/2) + 2k\pi}{6} + i\sin\dfrac{(3\pi/2) + 2k\pi}{6}\right), k = 1, 2, 3, 4, 5$$

$$3\left(\cos\dfrac{\pi}{4} + i\sin\dfrac{\pi}{4}\right)$$

$$3\left(\cos\dfrac{7\pi}{12} + i\sin\dfrac{7\pi}{12}\right)$$

$$3\left(\cos\dfrac{11\pi}{12} + i\sin\dfrac{11\pi}{12}\right)$$

$$3\left(\cos\dfrac{5\pi}{4} + i\sin\dfrac{5\pi}{4}\right)$$

$$3\left(\cos\dfrac{19\pi}{12} + i\sin\dfrac{19\pi}{12}\right)$$

$$3\left(\cos\dfrac{23\pi}{12} + i\sin\dfrac{23\pi}{12}\right)$$

91. $x^4 + 81 = 0$

$$x^4 = -81$$

$$-81 = 81(\cos\pi + i\sin\pi)$$

$$\sqrt[4]{-81} = \sqrt[4]{81}\left[\cos\left(\dfrac{\pi + 2\pi k}{4}\right) + i\sin\left(\dfrac{\pi + 2\pi k}{4}\right)\right], k = 1, 2, 3$$

$$3\left(\cos\dfrac{\pi}{4} + i\sin\dfrac{\pi}{4}\right) = \dfrac{3\sqrt{2}}{2} + \dfrac{3\sqrt{2}}{2}i$$

$$3\left(\cos\dfrac{3\pi}{4} + i\sin\dfrac{3\pi}{4}\right) = -\dfrac{3\sqrt{2}}{2} + \dfrac{3\sqrt{2}}{2}i$$

$$3\left(\cos\dfrac{5\pi}{4} + i\sin\dfrac{5\pi}{4}\right) = -\dfrac{3\sqrt{2}}{2} - \dfrac{3\sqrt{2}}{2}i$$

$$3\left(\cos\dfrac{7\pi}{4} + i\sin\dfrac{7\pi}{4}\right) = \dfrac{3\sqrt{2}}{2} - \dfrac{3\sqrt{2}}{2}i$$

93. $x^3 + 8i = 0$

$\qquad x^3 = -8i$

$\qquad -8i = 8\left(\cos\dfrac{3\pi}{2} + i\sin\dfrac{3\pi}{2}\right)$

$\sqrt[3]{-8i} = \sqrt[3]{8}\left[\cos\dfrac{(3\pi/2) + 2\pi k}{3} + i\sin\dfrac{(3\pi/2) + 2\pi k}{3}\right]$, $k = 0, 1, 2$

$2\left(\cos\dfrac{\pi}{2} + i\sin\dfrac{\pi}{2}\right) = 2i$

$2\left(\cos\dfrac{7\pi}{6} + i\sin\dfrac{7\pi}{6}\right) = -\sqrt{3} - i$

$2\left(\cos\dfrac{11\pi}{6} + i\sin\dfrac{11\pi}{6}\right) = \sqrt{3} - i$

❑ Cumulative Test for Chapters 5–7

1. (a)

(b) $-120° + 360° = 240°$

(c) $-120° \cdot \dfrac{\pi}{180}\dfrac{\text{rad}}{\text{deg}} = -\dfrac{2\pi}{3}$

(d) $\theta' = 60°$

(e) $\sin\theta = -\dfrac{\sqrt{3}}{2}, \quad \cos\theta = -\dfrac{1}{2}, \quad \tan\theta = \sqrt{3}$

$\quad\csc\theta = -\dfrac{2}{\sqrt{3}} = -\dfrac{2\sqrt{3}}{3}, \quad \sec\theta = -2,$

$\quad\cot\theta = \dfrac{1}{\sqrt{3}} = \dfrac{\sqrt{3}}{3}$

2. 2.35 radians $\left(\dfrac{180}{\pi}\right) \approx 134.6°$

3. $\tan\theta = -\dfrac{4}{3} \implies \sec^2\theta = \tan^2\theta + 1 = \dfrac{16}{9} + 1 = \dfrac{25}{9}$

$\implies \sec\theta = \dfrac{5}{3}$ (Quadrant IV) $\implies \cos\theta = \dfrac{3}{5}$

4 (a)

(b)

5. Amplitude: -3
Cosine curve reflected about the x-axis.
Period: $2 \implies h(x) = -3\cos(\pi x)$
Answer: $a = -3, b = \pi, c = 0$

6. Let $u = \arccos 2x \implies \cos u = 2x$. Then:

$$\sin(\arccos 2x) = \sin u$$
$$= \sqrt{1 - 4x^2}$$

7.
$$\frac{\sin\theta - 1}{\cos\theta} - \frac{\cos\theta}{\sin\theta - 1} = \frac{\sin^2\theta - 2\sin\theta + 1 - \cos^2\theta}{\cos\theta(\sin\theta - 1)}$$
$$= \frac{\sin^2\theta - 2\sin\theta + \sin^2\theta}{\cos\theta(\sin\theta - 1)}$$
$$= \frac{2\sin\theta(\sin\theta - 1)}{\cos\theta(\sin\theta - 1)} = 2\tan\theta$$

8. (a) $\cot^2\alpha(\sec^2\alpha - 1) = \cot^2\alpha(\tan^2\alpha) = 1$

(b) $\sin(x + y)\sin(x - y) = [\sin x\cos y + \cos x\sin y][\sin x\cos y - \sin y\cos x]$
$$= \sin^2 x\cos^2 y - \sin^2 y\cos^2 x$$
$$= \sin^2 x(1 - \sin^2 y) - \sin^2 y(1 - \sin^2 x)$$
$$= \sin^2 x - \sin^2 x\sin^2 y - \sin^2 y + \sin^2 y\sin^2 x$$
$$= \sin^2 x - \sin^2 y$$

9. (a) $\quad 2\cos^2\beta - \cos\beta = 0$
$$\cos\beta(2\cos\beta - 1) = 0$$
$$\cos\beta = 0 \implies \beta = \frac{\pi}{2}, \frac{3\pi}{2}$$
$$2\cos\beta - 1 = 0 \implies \cos\beta = \frac{1}{2} \implies \beta = \frac{\pi}{3}, \frac{5\pi}{3}$$

(b) $3\tan^2\theta - \cot\theta = 0$
$$3\tan\theta - \frac{1}{\tan\theta} = 0$$
$$3\tan^2\theta - 1 = 0$$
$$\tan\theta = \pm\frac{1}{\sqrt{3}} \implies \theta = \frac{\pi}{6}, \frac{5\pi}{6}, \frac{7\pi}{6}, \frac{11\pi}{6}$$

10. (a) By the Law of Sines,
$$\frac{a}{\sin A} = \frac{b}{\sin B}$$
$$\frac{9}{\sin 30°} = \frac{8}{\sin B}$$
$$\sin B = \frac{8}{9}\sin 30° = \frac{8}{9}\left(\frac{1}{2}\right) = \frac{4}{9}.$$

Hence, $B \approx 26.4°$, and $C = 180° - 30° - 26.4° = 123.6°$. Finally,
$$\frac{c}{\sin C} = \frac{a}{\sin A} \implies c = 9\frac{\sin(123.6°)}{\sin 30°} \approx 15.$$

(b) $a^2 = b^2 + c^2 - 2bc \cdot \cos A = 8^2 + 10^2 - 2(8)(10)\cos 30° = 25.44 \implies a \approx 5.0$. Then,
$$\frac{b}{\sin B} = \frac{a}{\sin A} \implies \sin B = \frac{b\sin A}{a} \approx \frac{8 \cdot \sin 30°}{5.0} = 0.793 \implies B \approx 52.5°.$$

(c) Finally, $C = 180° - A - B \approx 97.5°$.

11. $r = \sqrt{(-2)^2 + 2^2} = 2\sqrt{2} : -2 + 2i = 2\sqrt{2}(\cos 135° + i \sin 135°)$

12. $[4(\cos 30° + i \sin 30°)][6(\cos 120° + i \sin 120°)] = 24(\cos(30 + 120°) + i \sin(30° + 120°))$

$$= 24(\cos 150° + i \sin 150°)$$

$$= 24\left(-\frac{\sqrt{3}}{2} + i\frac{1}{2}\right) = -12\sqrt{3} + 12i$$

13. $1 = 1(\cos 0 + i \sin 0)$

$$\cos\left(\frac{0 + 2\pi k}{3}\right) + i \sin\left(\frac{0 + 2\pi k}{3}\right)$$

$k = 0 : \cos 0 + i \sin 0 = 1$

$k = 1 : \cos \dfrac{2\pi}{3} + i \sin \dfrac{2\pi}{3} = -\dfrac{1}{2} + \dfrac{\sqrt{3}}{2}i$

$k = 2 : \cos \dfrac{4\pi}{3} + i \sin \dfrac{4\pi}{3} = -\dfrac{1}{2} - \dfrac{\sqrt{3}}{2}i$

14. $\tan 18° = \dfrac{h}{200}$

$\tan 16° 45' = \dfrac{k}{200}$

Hence, $f = h - k = 200 \tan 18° - 200 \tan 16° 45'$

$$\approx 4.8 \approx 5 \text{ feet.}$$

15. Add the two vectors:

$500(\cos 60\mathbf{i} + \sin 60\mathbf{j}) + 50(\cos 30\mathbf{i} + \sin 30\mathbf{j}) = \left(250 + 25\sqrt{3}\right)\mathbf{i} + \left(250\sqrt{3} + 25\right)\mathbf{j}$

$\tan \theta = \dfrac{250\sqrt{3} + 25}{250 + 25\sqrt{3}} \approx 1.56 \Rightarrow \theta \approx 57.4$

Direction: N 32.6° E

Speed $= \sqrt{\left(250 + 25\sqrt{3}\right)^2 + \left(250\sqrt{3} + 25\right)^2} \approx 543.9 \text{ km/hr}$

❑ Practice Test for Chapter 7

For Exercises 1 and 2, use the Law of Sines to find the remaining sides and angles of the triangle.

1. $A = 40°$, $B = 12°$, $b = 100$

2. $C = 150°$, $a = 5$, $c = 20$

3. Find the area of the triangle: $a = 3$, $b = 6$, $C = 130°$.

4. Determine the number of solutions to the triangle: $1 = 10$, $b = 35$, $A = 22.5°$.

For Exercises 5 and 6, use the Law of Cosines to find the remaining sides and angles off the triangle.

5. $a = 49$, $b = 53$, $c = 38$

6. $C = 29°$, $a = 100$, $b = 300$

7. Use Heron's Formula to find the area of the triangle: $a = 4.1$, $b = 6.8$, $c = 5.5$.

8. A ship travels 40 miles due east, then adjusts its course 12° southward. After traveling 70 miles in that direction, how far is the ship from its point of departure?

9. $\mathbf{w}$ is $4\mathbf{u} - 7\mathbf{v}$ where $\mathbf{u} = 3\mathbf{i} + \mathbf{j}$ and $\mathbf{v} = -\mathbf{i} + 2\mathbf{j}$. Find $\mathbf{w}$.

10. Find a unit vector in the direction of $\mathbf{v} = 5\mathbf{i} - 3\mathbf{j}$.

11. Find the dot product and the angle between $\mathbf{u} = 6\mathbf{i} + 5\mathbf{j}$ and $\mathbf{v} = 2\mathbf{i} - 3\mathbf{j}$.

12. $\mathbf{v}$ is a vector of magnitude 4 making an angle of 30° with the positive x-axis. Find $\mathbf{v}$ in component form.

13. Find the projection of $\mathbf{u}$ onto $\mathbf{v}$ given $\mathbf{u} = \langle 3, -1 \rangle$ and $\mathbf{v} = \langle -2, 4 \rangle$.

14. Give the trigonometric form of $z = 5 - 5i$.

15. Give the standard form of $z = 6(\cos 225° + i \sin 225°)$

16. Multiply $[7 \cos 23° + i \sin 23°)][4(\cos 7° + i \sin 7°)]$.

17. Divide $\dfrac{9\left(\cos \dfrac{5\pi}{4} + i \sin \dfrac{5\pi}{4}\right)}{3(\cos \pi + i \sin \pi)}$.

18. Find $(2 + 2i)^8$.

19. Find the cube roots of $8\left(\cos \dfrac{\pi}{3} + i \sin \dfrac{\pi}{3}\right)$.

20. Find all the solutions to $x^4 + i = 0$.

CHAPTER 8
Systems of Equations and Inequalities

CHAPTER 8
Systems of Equations and Inequalities

Section 8.1   Solving Systems of Equations

- You should be able to solve systems of equations by the method of substitution.
    1. Solve one of the equations for one of the variables.
    2. Substitute this expression into the other equation and solve.
    3. Back-substitute into the first equation to find the value of the other variable.
    4. Check your answer in each of the original equations.
- You should be able to find solutions graphically. (See Example 5 in textbook.)

Solutions to Odd-Numbered Exercises

1. $2x + y = 6$ Equation 1

$-x + y = 0$ Equation 2

Solve for y in Equation 1: $y = 6 - 2x$

Substitute for y in Equation 2: $-x + (6 - 2x) = 0$

Solve for x: $-3x + 6 = 0 \implies x = 2$

Back-substitute $x = 2$: $y = 6 - 2(2) = 2$

Answer: $(2, 2)$

3. $x - y = -4$ Equation 1

$x^2 - y = -2$ Equation 2

Solve for y in Equation 1: $y = x + 4$

Substitute for y in Equation 2: $x^2 - (x + 4) = -2$

Solve for x: $x^2 - x - 2 = 0 \implies (x + 1)(x - 2) = 0 \implies x = -1, 2$

Back-substitute $x = -1$: $y = -1 + 4 = 3$

Back-substitute $x = 2$: $y = 2 + 4 = 6$

Answers: $(-1, 3), (2, 6)$

5. $x - 3y = 15$ Equation 1

$x^2 + y^2 = 25$ Equation 2

Solve for x in Equation 1: $x = 3y + 15$

Substitute for x in Equation 2: $(3y + 15)^2 + y^2 = 25$

Solve for y: $10y^2 + 90y + 200 = 0 \implies y^2 + 9y + 20 = 0 \implies (y + 5)(y + 4) = 0 \implies y = -5, -4$

Back-substitute $y = -5$: $x = 3(-5) + 15 = 0$

Back-substitute $y = -4$: $x = 3(-4) + 15 = 3$

Answers: $(0, -5), (3, -4)$

7. $x^2 + y = 0$ Equation 1

$x^2 - 4x - y = 0$ Equation 2

Solve for y in Equation 1: $y = -x^2$

Substitute for y in Equation 2: $x^2 - 4x - (-x^2) = 0$

Solve for x: $2x^2 - 4x = 0 \implies 2x(x - 2) = 0 \implies x = 0, 2$

Back-substitute $x = 0$: $y = -0^2 = 0$

Back-substitute $x = 2$: $y = -2^2 = -4$

Answers: $(0, 0), (2, -4)$

9. $x - 6y = -8$ Equation 1

$x^2 - 4y^3 = 0$ Equation 2

Solve for x in Equation 1: $x = 6y - 8$

Substitute for x in Equation 2: $(6y - 8)^2 - 4y^3 = 0$

Solve for y: $-4y^3 + 36y^2 - 96y + 64 = 0$

$$y^3 - 9y^2 + 24y - 16 = 0$$

$$(y - 1)(y - 4)^2 = 0 \implies y = 1, 4$$

Back-substitute $y = 1$: $x = 6(1) - 8 = -2$

Back-substitute $y = 4$: $x = 6(4) - 8 = 16$

Answers: $(-2, 1), (16, 4)$

11. $x - y = 0$ Equation 1

$5x - 3y = 10$ Equation 2

Substitute for y in Equation 2: $5x - 3x = 10$

Solve for x: $2x = 10 \implies x = 5$

Back-substitute in Equation 1: $y = x = 5$

Answer: $(5, 5)$

13. $2x - y + 2 = 0$ Equation 1

$4x + y - 5 = 0$ Equation 2

Solve for y in Equation 1: $y = 2x + 2$

Substitute for y in Equation 2: $4x + (2x + 2) - 5 = 0$

Solve for x: $4x + (2x + 2) - 5 = 0 \implies 6x - 3 = 0 \implies x = \frac{1}{2}$

Back-substitute $x = \frac{1}{2}$: $y = 2x + 2 = 2\left(\frac{1}{2}\right) + 2 = 3$

Answer: $\left(\frac{1}{2}, 3\right)$

15. $1.5x + 0.8y = 2.3 \implies 15x + 8y = 23$

$\qquad 0.3x - 0.2y = 0.1 \implies 3x - 2y = 1$

Solve for y in Equation 2: $-2y = 1 - 3x$

$$y = \frac{3x - 1}{2}$$

Substitute for y in Equation 1: $15x + 8\left(\dfrac{3x - 1}{2}\right) = 23$

$$15x + 12x - 4 = 23$$

$$27x = 27$$

$$x = 1$$

Then, $y = \dfrac{3x - 1}{2} = \dfrac{3(1) - 1}{2} = 1.$

17. $\frac{1}{5}x + \frac{1}{2}y = 8 \qquad$ Equation 1

$\qquad x + y = 20 \qquad$ Equation 2

Solve for x in Equation 2: $x = 20 - y$

Substitute for x in Equation 1: $\frac{1}{5}(20 - y) + \frac{1}{2}y = 8$

Solve for y: $4 + \frac{3}{10}y = 8 \implies y = \frac{40}{3}$

Back-substitute $y = \frac{40}{3}$: $x = 20 - y = 20 - \frac{40}{3} = \frac{20}{3}$

Answer: $\left(\frac{20}{3}, \frac{40}{3}\right)$

19. $2x - y = 4 \qquad$ Equation 1

$\qquad -4x + 2y = -12 \qquad$ Equation 2

Solve for y in Equation 1: $y = 2x - 4$

Substitute for y in Equation 2: $-4x + 2(2x - 4) = -12$

Solve for x: $-8 \neq -12$ Inconsistent

No Solution

21. $x - y = 0 \qquad$ Equation 1

$\qquad 2x + y = 0 \qquad$ Equation 2

Solve for y in Equation 1: $y = x$

Substitute for y in Equation 2: $2x + x = 0$

Solve for x: $3x = 0 \implies x = 0$

Back-substitute $x = 0$: $y = x = 0$

Answer: $(0, 0)$

23. $-x + 2y = 2$

$\qquad 3x + y = 15$

Point of intersection: $(4, 3)$

25. $x - 3y = -2$

$5x + 3y = 17$

Point of intersection: $\left(\frac{5}{2}, \frac{3}{2}\right)$

27. $x + y = 4$

$x^2 + y^2 - 4x = 0$

Points of intersection: $(2, 2), (4, 0)$

29. $7x + 8y = 24 \implies y_1 = -\frac{7}{8}x + 3$

$x - 8y = 8 \implies y_2 = \frac{1}{8}x - 1$

Point of intersection: $\left(4, -\frac{1}{2}\right)$

31. $2x - y + 3 = 0 \implies y_1 = 2x + 3$

$x^2 + y^2 - 4x = 0 \implies y_2 = \sqrt{4x - x^2}, \ y_3 = -\sqrt{4x - x^2}$

No points of intersection

33. $x^2 + y^2 = 8 \implies y_1 = \sqrt{8 - x^2}$ and $y_2 = -\sqrt{8 - x^2}$

$y = x^2 \implies y_3 = x^2$

Points of intersection: $\left(\pm\sqrt{\dfrac{-1 + \sqrt{33}}{2}}, \dfrac{-1 + \sqrt{33}}{2}\right) \approx (\pm 1.54, 2.37)$

35.
$$y = e^x$$
$$x - y + 1 = 0 \implies y = x + 1$$

Point of intersection: $(0, 1)$

37. $y = \sqrt{x}$
$$y = x$$

Points of intersection: $(0, 0)$, $(1, 1)$

39. $x^2 + y^2 = 169 \implies y_1 = \sqrt{169 - x^2}$ and $y_2 = -\sqrt{169 - x^2}$

$x^2 - 8y = 104 \implies y_3 = \frac{1}{8}x^2 - 13$

Points of intersection: $(0, -13)$, $(\pm 12, 5)$

41. $y = 2x$ Equation 1

$y = x^2 + 1$ Equation 2

Substitute for y in Equation 2: $2x = x^2 + 1$

Solve for x: $x^2 - 2x + 1 = (x - 1)^2 = 0 \implies x = 1$

Back-substitute $x = 1$ in Equation 1: $y = 2x = 2$

Answer: $(1, 2)$

43. $3x - 7y + 6 = 0$ Equation 1

$x^2 - y^2 = 4$ Equation 2

Solve for y in Equation 1: $y = \dfrac{3x + 6}{7}$

Solve for y in Equation 2: $x^2 - \left(\dfrac{3x + 6}{7}\right)^2 = 4$

Solve for x: $x^2 - \left(\dfrac{9x^2 + 36x + 36}{49}\right) = 4$

$$49x^2 - (9x^2 + 36x + 36) = 196$$
$$40x^2 - 36x - 232 = 0$$

$10x^2 - 9x - 58 = 0 \implies x = \dfrac{9 \pm \sqrt{81 + 40(58)}}{20} \implies x = \dfrac{29}{10}, -2$

Back-substitute $x = \dfrac{29}{10}$: $y = \dfrac{3x + 6}{7} = \dfrac{3(29/10) + 6}{7} = \dfrac{21}{10}$

Back-substitute $x = -2$: $y = \dfrac{3x + 6}{7} = 0$

Answers: $\left(\dfrac{29}{10}, \dfrac{21}{10}\right)$, $(-2, 0)$

45. $x - 2y = 4$ Equation 1

$x^2 - y = 0$ Equation 2

Solve for y in Equation 2: $y = x^2$

Substitute for y in Equation 1: $x - 2x^2 = 4$

Solve for x: $0 = 2x^2 - x + 4$

No real solutions, the discriminant in the Quadratic Formula is negative.

Inconsistent, No solution

47. $y - e^{-x} = 1 \implies y = e^{-x} + 1$

$y - \ln x = 3 \implies y = \ln x + 3$

Point of intersection: Approximately $(0.287, 1.75)$

49. $y = x^4 - 2x^2 + 1$ Equation 1

$y = 1 - x^2$ Equation 2

Substitute for y in Equation 1: $1 - x^2 = x^4 - 2x^2 + 1$

Solve for x: $x^4 - x^2 = 0 \implies x^2(x^2 - 1) = 0$

$\implies x = 0, \pm 1$

Back-substitute $x = 0$: $1 - x^2 = 1$

Back-substitute $x = 1$: $1 - x^2 = 1 - 1^2 = 0$

Back-substitute $x = -1$: $1 - x^2 = 1 - (-1)^2 = 0$

Answers: $(0, 1), (\pm 1, 0)$

51. $xy - 1 = 0$ Equation 1

$2x - 4y + 7 = 0$ Equation 2

Solve for y in Equation 1: $y = \dfrac{1}{x}$

Substitute for y in Equation 2: $2x - 4\left(\dfrac{1}{x}\right) + 7 = 0$

Solve for x: $2x^2 - 4 + 7x = 0 \implies (2x - 1)(x + 4) = 0 \implies x = \dfrac{1}{2}, -4$

Back-substitute $x = \dfrac{1}{2}$: $y = \dfrac{1}{1/2} = 2$

Back-substitute $x = -4$: $y = \dfrac{1}{-4} = -\dfrac{1}{4}$

Answers: $\left(\dfrac{1}{2}, 2\right), \left(-4, -\dfrac{1}{4}\right)$

53. The system has no solution if you arrive at a false statement, ie. $4 = 8$, or you have a quadratic equation with a negative discriminant, which would yield imaginary roots.

55. (a) $C = 8650x + 250,000, \; R = 9950x$

$R = C$

$9950x = 8650x + 250,000$

$1300x = 250,000$

$x \approx 192$ units

(b)

57. (a) $C = 2.65x + 350{,}000,\ R = 4.15x$

  $R = C$

  $4.15x = 2.65x + 350{,}000$

  $1.50x = 350{,}000$

  $x \approx 233{,}333$ units

(b)

59. (a) $C = 3.45x + 16{,}000,\ R = 5.95x$

  (c) $R = C$

  $5.95x = 3.45x + 16{,}000$

  $2.50x = 16{,}000$

  $x \approx 6400$ units

(b)

61. $x +\quad\ y = 20{,}000$

  $0.065x + 0.085y = 1600$

  Graphing $y_1 = 20{,}000 - x$ and

  $y_2 = (1600 - 0.065x)\dfrac{1}{0.085}$

  you will see that the point of intersection
  occurs when $x = \$5000$.

63. $0.06x = 0.03x + 250$

  $0.03x = 250$

  $x \approx \$8333.33$

  To make the straight commission offer better, you
  would have to sell more than $\$8333.33$ per week.

65. Supply: $p = 1.45 + 0.00014x^2$

  Demand: $p = (2.388 - 0.007x)^2$

  The two graphs intersect at $x = 100$ bushels.

67. $2l + 2w = 30 \implies l + w = 15$

  $l = w + 3 \implies (w + 3) + 2 = 15$

  $\qquad\qquad\qquad\qquad 2w = 12$

  $\qquad\qquad\qquad\qquad\ w = 6$

$l = w + 3 = 9$

Dimensions: 6 meters $\times$ 9 meters

69. $2l + 2w = 42 \implies l + w = 21$

  $\qquad w = \tfrac{3}{4}l \implies l + \tfrac{3}{4}l = 21$

  $\qquad\qquad\qquad\qquad \tfrac{7}{4}l = 21$

  $\qquad\qquad\qquad\qquad\ l = 12$

$w = \tfrac{3}{4},\ l = 9$

Dimensions: 9 inches $\times$ 12 inches

71. $2l + 2w = 40 \implies l + w = 20 \implies w = 20 - l$

  $lw = 96 \implies l(20 - l) = 96$

  $\qquad\qquad\qquad 20l - l^2 = 96$

  $\qquad\qquad\quad 0 = l^2 - 20l + 96$

  $\qquad\qquad\quad 0 = (l - 8)(l - 12)$

  $\qquad\qquad\quad l = 8 \text{ or } l = 12$

$w = 12,\ w = 8$

Since the length is supposed to be greater than the width, we have $l = 12$ miles and $w = 8$ miles.

73. (a) The line $y = 2x$ intersects the parabola $y = x^2$ at two points, $(0, 0)$ and $(2, 4)$.

(b) The line $y = 0$ intersects $y = x^2$ at $(0, 0)$ only.

(c) The line $y = x - 2$ does not intersect $y = x^2$.

75. $(0, 6.6), (1, 6.8), (2, 7.1), (3, 7.1)$

(a) Linear model: $f(t) = 0.18t + 6.63$

Quadratic model:
$g(t) = -0.05t^2 + 0.33t + 6.58$

(b)

(c) Points of intersection: $(0.382, 6.70), (2.618, 7.10)$

(d) Linear model when $t = 4$:
$f(4) = 7.35$ million short tons

Quadratic model when $t = 4$:
$g(4) = 7.1$ million short tons

Since the sale of newsprint has been slowly decreasing (more papers are on-line now and many people would rather listen to the news than read it) the Quadratic model is probably more accurate.

77. $(-2, 7), (5, 5)$

$$m = \frac{5 - 7}{5 - (-2)} = -\frac{2}{7}$$

$$y - 7 = -\frac{2}{7}(x - (-2))$$

$$7y - 49 = -2x - 4$$

$$2x + 7y - 45 = 0$$

79. $(6, 3), (10, 3)$

$$m = \frac{3 - 3}{10 - 6} = 0 \implies \text{The line is horizontal.}$$

$$y = 3 \implies y - 3 = 0$$

81. $\left(\frac{3}{5}, 0\right), (4, 6)$

$$m = \frac{6 - 0}{4 - \frac{3}{5}} = \frac{6}{\frac{17}{5}} = \frac{30}{17}$$

$$y - 6 = \frac{30}{17}(x - 4)$$

$$17y - 102 = 30x - 120$$

$$0 = 30x - 17y - 18$$

Section 8.2 Systems of Linear Equations in Two Variables

> ■ You should be able to solve a linear system by the method of elimination.
>
> 1. Obtain coefficients for either x or y that differ only in sign. This is done by multiplying all the terms of one or both equations by appropriate constants.
>
> 2. Add the equations to eliminate one of the variables and then solve for the remaining variable.
>
> 3. Use back-substitution into either original equation and solve for the other variable.
>
> 4. Check your answer.
>
> ■ You should know that for a system of two linear equations, one of the following is true.
>
> (a) There are infinitely many solutions; the lines are identical. The system is consistent.
>
> (b) There is no solution; the lines are parallel. The system is inconsistent.
>
> (c) There is one solution; the lines intersect at one point. The system is consistent.

Solutions to Odd-Numbered Exercises

1. $2x + y = 5$ Equation 1

    $x - y = 1$ Equation 2

Add to eliminate y: $3x = 6 \implies x = 2$

Substitute $x = 2$ in Equation 2: $2 - y = 1 \implies y = 1$

Answer: $(2, 1)$

3. $x + y = 0$ Equation 1

    $3x + 2y = 1$ Equation 2

Multiply Equation 1 by -2: $-2x - 2y = 0$

Add this to Equation 2 to eliminate y: $x = 1$

Substitute $x = 1$ in Equation 1: $1 + y = 0 \implies y = -1$

Answer: $(1, -1)$

5. $x - y = 2$ Equation 1

    $-2x + 2y = 5$ Equation 2

Multiply Equation 1 by 2: $2x - 2y = 4$

Add this to Equation 2: $0 = 9$

There are no solutions.

7. $3x - 2y = 5$ Equation 1

$-6x + 4y = -10$ Equation 2

Multiply Equation 1 by 2 and add to Equation 2: $0 = 0$

The equations are dependent. There are infinitely many solutions.

9. $9x + 3y = 1$ Equation 1

$3x - 6y = 5$ Equation 2

Multiply Equation 2 by (-3): $9x + 3y = 1$

$-9x + 18y = -15$

Add to eliminate x: $21y = -14 \implies y = -\frac{2}{3}$

Substitute $y = -\frac{2}{3}$ in Equation 1: $9x + 3\left(-\frac{2}{3}\right) = 1$

$x = \frac{1}{3}$

Answer: $\left(\frac{1}{3}, -\frac{2}{3}\right)$

11. $x + 2y = 4$ Equation 1

$x - 2y = 1$ Equation 2

Add to eliminate y:

$2x = 5$

$x = \frac{5}{2}$

Substitute $x = \frac{5}{2}$ in Equation 1:

$\frac{5}{2} + 2y = 4 \implies y = \frac{3}{4}$

Answer: $\left(\frac{5}{2}, \frac{3}{4}\right)$

13. $2x + 3y = 18$ Equation 1

$5x - y = 11$ Equation 2

Multiply Equation 2 by 3: $15x - 3y = 33$

Add this to Equation 1 to eliminate y:

$17x = 51 \implies x = 3$

Substitute $x = 3$ in Equation 1:

$6 + 3y = 18 \implies y = 4$

Answer: $(3, 4)$

15. $3x + 2y = 10$ Equation 1

$2x + 5y = 3$ Equation 2

Multiply Equation 1 by 2 and Equation 2 by (-3):

$6x + 4y = 20$

$-6x - 15y = -9$

Add to eliminate x: $-11y = 1 \implies y = -1$

Substitute $y = -1$ in Equation 1:

$3x - 2 = 10 \implies x = 4$

Answer: $(4, -1)$

17. $2u + v = 120$ Equation 1

$u + 2v = 120$ Equation 2

Multiply Equation 2 by (-2):

$-2u - 4v = -240$

Add this to Equation 1 to eliminate u:

$-3v = -120$

$v = 40$

Substitute $v = 40$ in Equation 2:

$u + 80 = 120 \implies u = 40$

Answer: $(40, 40)$

19. $6r - 5s = 3$

$10r - 12s = 5$

Multiply Equation 1 by 5 and Equation 2 by (-3):

$30r - 25s = 15$

$-30r + 36s = -15$

Add to eliminate r: $11s = 0$

$s = 0$

Substitute $s = 0$ in Equation 1: $6r - 5(0) = 3$

$r = \frac{1}{2}$

Answer: $\left(\frac{1}{2}, 0\right)$

21. $\dfrac{x}{4} + \dfrac{y}{6} = 1$ \qquad Equation 1

$x - y = 3$ \qquad Equation 2

Multiply Equation 1 by 6: $\dfrac{3}{2}x + y = 6$

Add this to Equation 2 to eliminate y:

$\dfrac{5}{2}x = 9 \implies x = \dfrac{18}{5}$

Substitute $x = \dfrac{18}{5}$ in Equation 2:

$\dfrac{18}{5} - y = 3$

$y = \dfrac{3}{5}$

Answer: $\left(\dfrac{18}{5}, \dfrac{3}{5}\right)$

23. $\dfrac{x+3}{4} + \dfrac{y-1}{3} = 1$ \qquad Equation 1

$2x - y = 12$ \qquad Equation 2

Multiply Equation 1 by 12 and Equation 2 by 4

$3x + 4y = 7$

$8x - 4y = 48$

Add to eliminate y: $11x = 55 \implies x = 5$

Substitute $x = 5$ into Equation 2:

$2(5) - y = 12 \implies y = -2$

Answer: $(5, -2)$

25. $2.5x - 3y = 1.5$ \qquad Equation 1

$10x - 12y = 6$ \qquad Equation 2

Multiply Equation 1 by (-4):

$-10x + 12y = -6$

Add this to Equation 2 to eliminate x:

$0 = 0$ (Dependents)

The solution set consists of all points lying on the line

$10x - 12y = 6$.

Let $x = a$, then $y = \frac{5}{6}a - \frac{1}{2}$.

Answer: $\left(a, \frac{5}{6}a - \frac{1}{2}\right)$, where a is any real number. Infinitely many solutions.

27. $0.05x - 0.03y = 0.21$ \qquad Equation 1

$0.07x + 0.02y = 0.16$ \qquad Equation 2

Multiply Equation 1 by 200 and Equation 2 by 300:

$10x - 6y = 42$

$21x + 6y = 48$

Add to eliminate y: $31x = 90$

$x = \frac{90}{31}$

Substitute $x = \frac{90}{31}$ in Equation 2:

$0.07\left(\frac{90}{31}\right) + 0.02y = 0.16$

$y = -\frac{67}{31}$

Answer: $\left(\frac{90}{31}, -\frac{67}{31}\right)$

29. $4b + 3m = 3$ Equation 1

   $3b + 11m = 13$ Equation 2

Multiply Equation 1 by 3 and Equation 2 by (-4):

$$12b + 9m = 9$$

$$-12b - 44m = -52$$

Add to eliminate b: $-35m = -43$

$$m = \frac{43}{35}$$

Substitute $m = \frac{43}{35}$ in Equation 1: $5b + 3\left(\frac{43}{35}\right) = 3 \implies b = -\frac{6}{35}$

Answer: $\left(-\frac{6}{35}, \frac{43}{35}\right)$

31. $\frac{1}{5}x - \frac{1}{3}y = 1$

     $-3x + 5y = 9$

The lines are parallel.
The system is inconsistent.

33. $2x - 5y = 0$

     $x - y = 3$

The system is consistent. There is one solution.

35. $8x + 9y = 42$

     $6x - y = 16$

Solution: $(3, 2)$

37. $4y = -8$

     $7x - 2y = 25$

Solution: $(3, -2)$

39. $3x - 5y = 7$ Equation 1

   $2x + y = 9$ Equation 2

Multiply Equation 2 by 5:

$$10x + 5y = 45$$

Add this to Equation 1:

$$13x = 52 \implies x = 4$$

Back-substitute $x = 4$ into Equation 2:

$$2(4) + y = 9 \implies y = 1$$

Solution: $(4, 1)$

41. $y = 2x - 5$ Equation 1

   $y = 5x - 11$ Equation 2

Since both equations are solved for y, set them equal to one another and solve for x.

$$2x - 5 = 5x - 11$$

$$6 = 3x$$

$$2 = x$$

Back-substitute $x = 2$ into Equation 1:

$$y = 2(2) - 5 = -1$$

Solution: $(2, -1)$

43. There are infinitely many systems that have the solution $\left(3, \frac{5}{2}\right)$. One possible system is:

$$2(3) + 2\left(\tfrac{5}{2}\right) = 11 \implies 2x + 2y = 11$$

$$3 - 4\left(\tfrac{5}{2}\right) = -7 \implies x - 4y = -7$$

45. $100y - x = 200$ Equation 1

   $99y - x = -198$ Equation 2

Subtract Equation 2 from Equation 1 to eliminate x: $y = 398$

Substitute $y = 398$ into Equation 1:

   $100(398) - x = 200 \implies x = 39{,}600$

Solution: $(39{,}600, \ 398)$

The lines are not parallel. The scale on the axes must be changed to see the point of intersection.

47. No, it is not possible for a consistent system of linear equations to have exactly two solutions. Either the lines will intersect once or they will coincide and then the system would have infinite solutions.

49. $4x - 8y = -3$ Equation 1

   $2x + ky = 16$ Equation 2

Multiply Equation 2 by -2: $-4x - 2ky = -32$

Add this to Equation 1: $-8y - 2ky = -35$

The system in inconsistent if $-8y - 2ky = 0$. This occurs when $k = -4$.

Note that for $k = -4$, the two original equations represent parallel lines.

51. Let $x =$ the ground speed and $y =$ the wind speed.

$$\begin{array}{ll} 3.6(x - y) = 1800 & \text{Equation 1} \\ 6(x + y) = 1800 & \text{Equation 2} \end{array}$$

$$\begin{array}{rcl} x - y &=& 500 \\ x + y &=& 600 \\ \hline 2x &=& 1100 \\ \\ x &=& 550 \\ 550 + y &=& 600 \\ y &=& 50 \end{array}$$

Answer: $x = 550$ mph, $y = 50$ mph

53. Let $x =$ the number of liters at 20%, $y =$ the number of liters at 50%.

(a) $x + y = 10$

   $0.2x + 0.5y = 0.3(10)$

(b) As x increases, y decreases.

(c) $\begin{array}{ll} -2 & \text{Equation 1} \\ 10 & \text{Equation 2} \end{array}$ $\begin{array}{rcl} -2x - 2y &=& -20 \\ 2x + 5y &=& 30 \\ \hline 3y &=& 10 \end{array}$

$$y = \frac{10}{3}$$

$$x + \frac{10}{3} = 10$$

$$x = \frac{20}{3}$$

Answer: $x = 6\frac{2}{3}$ liters at 20%, $y = 3\frac{1}{3}$ liters at 50%

55. Let x = amount invested at 10.5%, y = amount invested at 12%.

$$x + \quad y = 12{,}000 \quad \text{Equation 1} \qquad -12x - 12y = -144{,}000$$
$$0.105x + 0.12y = \quad 1350 \quad \text{Equation 2} \qquad \underline{10.5x + 12y = \quad 135{,}000}$$
$$-1.5x \qquad = \qquad -9000$$

$$x \qquad = \qquad 6000$$
$$6000 + \quad y = 12{,}000$$
$$y = \quad 6000$$

Answer: y = \$6000 at 12%, x = \$6000 at 10.5%.

57. Let x = number of adult tickets sold, y = number of child tickets sold.

$$x + \quad y = \quad 500 \qquad \text{Equation 1} \qquad -4x - 4y = -2000.00$$
$$7.5x + 4y = \$3312.50 \qquad \text{Equation 2} \qquad \underline{7.5x + 4y = \quad 3312.50}$$
$$3.5x \qquad = \quad 1312.50$$

$$x \qquad = 375$$
$$375 + \quad y = 500$$
$$y = 125$$

Answer: x = 375 adult tickets, y = 125 child tickets

59. Let x = distance one person drives,

y = distance other person drives.

$$x + y = 300 \qquad \qquad \text{Equation 1}$$
$$y = 3x \qquad \qquad \text{Equation 2}$$
$$x + 3x = 300 \qquad \qquad \text{Use substitution.}$$
$$4x = 300$$
$$x = 75$$
$$y = 3x = 225$$

Answer: 75 km and 225 km

61. $\quad 5b + 10a = 20.2 \quad \Longrightarrow \quad -10b - 20a = -40.4$
$\qquad 10b + 30a = 50.1 \quad \Longrightarrow \quad \underline{10b + 30a = \quad 50.1}$
$$10a = \quad 9.7$$
$$a = 0.97$$
$$b = 2.10$$

Least squares regression line:

$$y = 0.97x + 2.10$$

63. $\quad 7b + 21a = \quad 35.1 \quad \Longrightarrow \quad -21b - 63a = -105.3$
$\qquad 21b + 91a = 114.2 \quad \Longrightarrow \quad \underline{21b + 91a = \quad 114.2}$
$$28a = \quad 8.9$$

$$a = \frac{89}{280}$$
$$b = \frac{1137}{280}$$

Least squares regression line: $y = \frac{1}{280}(89x + 1137) \approx 0.318x + 4.061$

65. $(-2, 0)$, $(0, 1)$, $(2, 3)$

$3b = 4 \implies b = \frac{4}{3}$

$8a = 6 \implies a = \frac{3}{4}$

Least squares regression line:

$y = \frac{3}{4}x + \frac{4}{3}$

67. $(0, 4)$, $(1, 3)$, $(1, 1)$, $(2, 0)$

$4b + 4a = 8 \implies \quad 4b + 4a = \quad 8$

$4b + 6a = 4 \implies \quad \underline{-4b - 6a = -4}$

$\qquad\qquad\qquad\qquad -2a = \quad 4$

$a = -2$

$b = 4$

Least squares regression line: $y = -2x + 4$

69. $(1.0, 32)$, $(1.5, 41)$, $(2.0, 48)$, $(2.5, 53)$

$n = 4$, $\displaystyle\sum_{i=1}^{4} x_i = 7$, $\displaystyle\sum_{i=1}^{4} y_i = 174$, $\displaystyle\sum_{i=1}^{4} x_i^2 = 13.5$, $\displaystyle\sum_{i=1}^{4} x_i y_i = 322$

$4b + \quad 7a = 174 \implies \quad 28b + 49a = \quad 1218$

$7b + 13.5a = 322 \implies \quad \underline{-28b - 54a = -1288}$

$\qquad\qquad\qquad\qquad\qquad -5a = \qquad -70$

$\qquad\qquad\qquad\qquad\qquad\quad a = 14$

$\qquad\qquad\qquad\qquad\qquad\quad b = 19$

$y = ax + b$

$y = 14x + 19$

When $x = 1.6$, $y = 14(1.6) + 19 = 41.4$ bushels per acre.

71.   Demand = Supply

$\qquad 50 - 0.5 = 0.125x$

$\qquad\qquad 50 = 0.625x$

$\qquad\qquad\quad x = 80$ units

$\qquad\qquad\quad p = \$10$

Answer: $(80, 10)$

73.   Demand = Supply

$140 - 0.00002x = 80 + 0.00001x$

$\qquad\qquad 60 = 0.00003x$

$\qquad\qquad\quad x = 2{,}000{,}000$ units

$\qquad\qquad\quad p = \$100.00$

Answer: $(2{,}000{,}000, 100)$

75. Multiply the first equation by $(\cos x)$ and the second by $(-\sin x)$.

$\quad u \sin x(\cos x) + v(\cos x)(\cos x) = 0(\cos x)$

$\quad u \cos x(-\sin x) - v \sin x(-\sin x) = \sec x(-\sin x)$

Adding,

$\quad v \cos^2 x + v \sin^2 x = -\sec x \cdot \sin x$

$\quad v(\cos^2 x + \sin^2 x) = -\tan x$

$\qquad\qquad\qquad v = -\tan x.$

Finally,

$\qquad u \sin x + v \cos x = 0$

$\implies u \sin x - \tan x \cos x = 0$

$\qquad \implies u \sin x = \sin x \implies u = 1.$

77. Subtracting the two equations:

$$vxe^x - v(x + 1)e^x = -e^x \ln x$$

$$vxe^x - vxe^x - ve^x = -e^x \ln x$$

$$ve^x = e^x \ln x$$

$$v = \ln x$$

Finally, $ue^x + vxe^x = ue^x + \ln x \cdot x \cdot e^x = 0$

$$\Rightarrow \quad ue^x = -x \ln x \cdot e^x$$

$$\Rightarrow \quad u = -x \ln x$$

81. The domain of $h(x) = \sqrt{25 - x^2}$ is:

$$25 - x^2 \geq 0$$

$$x^2 \leq 25$$

$$-5 \leq x \leq 5$$

79. The domain of $f(x) = x^2 - 2x$ is all real numbers.

Section 8.3   Multivariable Linear Systems

> ■ You should know the operations that lead to equivalent systems of linear equations:
>
> (a) Interchange any two equations.
>
> (b) Multiply all terms of an equation by a nonzero constant.
>
> (c) Replace an equation by the sum of itself and a constant multiple of any other equation in the system.
>
> ■ You should be able to use the method of elimination.

Solutions to Odd-Numbered Exercises

1.
$$2x - y + 5z = 24 \quad \text{Equation 1}$$
$$y + 2z = 6 \quad \text{Equation 2}$$
$$z = 4 \quad \text{Equation 3}$$

Back-substitute $z = 4$ into Equation 2.

$$y + 2(4) = 6$$

$$z = -2$$

Back-substitute $y = -2$ and $z = 4$ into Equation 1.

$$2x - (-2) + 5(4) = 24$$

$$2x + 22 = 24$$

$$x = 1$$

Answer: $(1, -2, 4)$

3.
$$2x + y - 3z = 10 \quad \text{Equation 1}$$
$$y = 2 \quad \text{Equation 2}$$
$$y - z = 4 \quad \text{Equation 3}$$

Back-substitute $y = 2$ into Equation 3.

$$2 - z = 4$$

$$z = -2$$

Back-substitute $y = 2$ and $z = -2$ into Equation 1.

$$2x + 2 - 3(-2) = 10$$

$$2x + 8 = 10$$

$$x = 1$$

Answer: $(1, 2, -2)$

5. $4x - 2y + z = 8$ Equation 1

           $2z = 4$ Equation 2

      $-y + z = 4$ Equation 3

From Equation 2 we have $z = 2$. Back-substitute $z = 2$ into Equation 3.

$$-y + 2 = 4$$

$$y = -2$$

Back-substitute $y = -2$ and $z = 2$ into Equation 1.

$$4x - 2(-2) + 2 = 8$$

$$4x + 6 = 8$$

$$x = \tfrac{1}{2}$$

Answer: $\left(\tfrac{1}{2}, -2, 2\right)$

7. $x - 2y + 3z = 5$ Equation 1

   $-x + 3y - 5z = 4$ Equation 2

   $2x \quad\ - 3z = 0$ Equation 3

Add Equation 1 to Equation 2.

$$y - 2z = 9$$

This is the first step in putting the system in row-echelon form.

9. $x + y + z = 6$ Equation 1

   $2x - y + z = 3$ Equation 2

   $3x \quad\ - z = 0$ Equation 3

$x + y + z = 6$

$\quad\ -3y - z = -9$ -2Eq.1 + Eq.2

$x - 3y - 4z = -18$ -3Eq.1 + Eq.3

$x + y + z = 6$

$\quad\ -3y - z = -9$

$\qquad\qquad -3z = -9$ $-$Eq.2 + Eq.3

$-3z = -9 \implies z = 3$

$-3y - 3 = -9 \implies y = 2$

$x + 2 + 3 = 6 \implies x = 1$

Answer: $(1, 2, 3)$

11. $2x \qquad\ + 2z = 2$ Equation 1

   $5x + 3y \qquad = 4$ Equation 2

        $3y - 4z = 4$ Equation 3

$x + 3y - 4z = 0$ -2Eq.1 + Eq.2

$2x \qquad\ + 2z = 2$ Interchange

$\qquad 3y - 4z = 4$ the equations.

$x + 3y - 4z = 0$

$\quad\ -6y + 10z = 2$ -2Eq.1 + Eq.2

$\qquad 3y - 4z = 4$

$x + 3y - 4z = 0$

$\quad\ -6y + 10z = 2$

$\qquad\qquad\qquad z = 5$ $\tfrac{1}{2}$Eq.2 + Eq.3

$$z = 5$$

$-6y + 10(5) = 2 \implies y = 8$

$x + 3(8) - 4(5) = 0 \implies x = -4$

Answer: $(-4, 8, 5)$

13.
$$\begin{aligned} 3x + 3y \quad\;\;\; &= \;\;\; 9 \\ 2x \quad\;\; - 3z &= \;\; 10 \\ 6y + 4z &= -12 \end{aligned}$$
Interchange the equations.

$$\begin{aligned} x + y \quad\;\;\; &= \; 3 \\ 2x \quad\;\; - 3z &= 10 \\ 6y + 4z &= -12 \end{aligned}$$
$\frac{1}{3}$Eq.1

$$\begin{aligned} x + y \quad\;\;\; &= \; 3 \\ -2y - 3z &= \; 4 \\ 6y + 4z &= -12 \end{aligned}$$
-2Eq.1 + Eq.2

$$\begin{aligned} x + y \quad\;\;\; &= 3 \\ -2y - 3z &= 4 \\ -5z &= 0 \end{aligned}$$
3Eq.2 + Eq.3

$$-5x = 0 \;\;\Longrightarrow\;\; z = 0$$
$$-2y - 3(0) = 4 \;\;\Longrightarrow\;\; y = -2$$
$$x - 2 = 3 \;\;\Longrightarrow\;\; x = 5$$

Answer: $(5, -2, 0)$

17.
$$\begin{aligned} 3x + 3y + 5z &= 1 \\ 3x + 5y + 9z &= 0 \\ 5x + 9y + 17z &= 0 \end{aligned}$$

$$\begin{aligned} 6x + 6y + 10z &= 2 \\ 3x + 5y + 9z &= 0 \\ 5x + 9y + 17z &= 0 \end{aligned}$$
2 Eq.1

$$\begin{aligned} x - 3y - 7z &= 2 \\ 3x + 5y + 9z &= 0 \\ 5x + 9y + 17z &= 0 \end{aligned}$$
$-$Eq.3 + Eq.1

$$\begin{aligned} x - 3y - 7z &= 2 \\ 14y + 30z &= -6 \\ 24y + 52z &= -10 \end{aligned}$$
-3Eq.1 + Eq.2
-5Eq.1 + Eq.3

15.
$$\begin{aligned} x + y - 2z &= 3 \\ 3x - 2y + 4z &= 1 \\ 2x - 3y + 6z &= 8 \end{aligned}$$
Interchange the equations.

$$\begin{aligned} x + y - 2z &= 3 \\ -5y + 10z &= -8 \\ -5y + 10z &= 2 \end{aligned}$$
-3Eq.1 + Eq.2
-2Eq.1 + Eq.3

$$\begin{aligned} x + y - 2z &= 3 \\ -5y + 10z &= -8 \\ 0 &= 10 \end{aligned}$$
$\rightarrow \leftarrow -$Eq.2 + Eq.3

No solution, inconsistent

$$\begin{aligned} x - 3y - 7z &= 2 \\ 84y + 180z &= -36 \\ 84y + 182z &= -35 \end{aligned}$$
6Eq.2
3.5Eq.3

$$\begin{aligned} x - 3y - 7z &= 2 \\ 84y + 180z &= -36 \\ 2z &= 1 \end{aligned}$$
$-$Eq.2 + Eq.3

$$2z = 1 \;\Longrightarrow\; x = \tfrac{1}{2}$$
$$84y + 180\left(\tfrac{1}{2}\right) = -36 \;\Longrightarrow\; y = -\tfrac{3}{2}$$
$$x - 3\left(-\tfrac{3}{2}\right) - 7\left(\tfrac{1}{2}\right) = 2 \;\Longrightarrow\; x = 1$$

Answer: $\left(1, -\tfrac{3}{2}, \tfrac{1}{2}\right)$

19.
$$x + 2y - 7z = -4$$
$$2x + y + z = 13$$
$$3x + 9y - 36z = -33$$

$$x + 2y - 7z = -4$$
$$-3y + 15z = 21 \quad -2\text{Eq.1} + \text{Eq.2}$$
$$3y - 15z = -21 \quad -3\text{Eq.1} + \text{Eq.3}$$

$$x + 2y - 1z = -4$$
$$-3y + 15z = 21$$
$$0 = 0 \quad \text{Eq.2} + \text{Eq.3}$$

$$x + 2y - 7z = -4$$
$$y - 5z = -7 \quad \tfrac{1}{3}\text{Eq.2}$$

$$x + 3z = 10 \quad -2\text{Eq.2} + \text{Eq.1}$$
$$y - 5z = -7$$

Let $z = a$, then:
$$y = 5a - 7$$
$$x = -3a + 10$$
Answer: $(-3a + 10, 5a - 7, a)$

21.
$$3x - 3y + 6z = 6$$
$$x + 2y - z = 5$$
$$5x - 8y + 13z = 7$$

$$x - y + 2z = 2 \qquad \tfrac{1}{3}\text{Eq.1}$$
$$3y - 3z = 3 \qquad -\text{Eq.1} + \text{Eq.2}$$
$$-3y + 3z = -3 \qquad -5\text{Eq.1} + \text{Eq.3}$$

$$x - y + 2z = 2$$
$$y - z = 1 \qquad \tfrac{1}{3}\text{Eq.2}$$
$$0 = 0 \qquad \text{Eq.2} + \text{Eq.3}$$

$$x + z = 3 \qquad \text{Eq.2} + \text{Eq.1}$$
$$y - z = 1$$

Let $z = a$, then:
$$y = a + 1$$
$$x = -a + 3$$
Answer: $(-a + 3, a + 1, a)$

23.
$$x - 2y + 5z = 2$$
$$4x - z = 0$$
Let $z = a$, then $x = \tfrac{1}{4}a$.
$$\tfrac{1}{4}a - 2y + 5a = 2$$
$$a - 8y + 20a = 8$$
$$-8y = -21a + 8$$
$$y = \tfrac{21}{8}a - 1$$
Answer: $\left(\tfrac{1}{4}a, \tfrac{21}{8}a - 1, a\right)$

To avoid fractions, we could go back and let $z = 8a$, then $4x - 8a = 0 \implies x = 2a$.
$$2a - 2y + 5(8a) = 2$$
$$-2y + 42a = 2$$
$$y = 21a - 1$$
Answer: $(2a, 21a - 1, 8a)$

25.
$$2x - 3y + z = -2$$
$$-4x + 9y = 7$$

$$2x - 3y + z = -2$$
$$3y + 2z = 3 \qquad 2\text{Eq.1} + \text{Eq.2}$$

$$2x + 3z = 1 \qquad \text{Eq.2} + \text{Eq.1}$$
$$3y + 2z = 3$$

Let $x = a$, then:
$$y = -\tfrac{2}{3}a + 1$$
$$x = -\tfrac{3}{2}a + \tfrac{1}{2}$$
Answer: $\left(-\tfrac{3}{2}a + \tfrac{1}{2}, -\tfrac{2}{3}a + 1, a\right)$

27.

$$\begin{aligned}
x \qquad\quad + 3w &= 4 \\
2y - \;z - \;w &= 0 \\
3y \qquad - 2w &= 1 \\
2x - y + 4z \qquad &= 5
\end{aligned}$$

$$\begin{aligned}
x \qquad\quad + 3w &= 4 \\
2y - \;z - \;w &= 0 \\
3y \qquad - 2w &= 1 \\
-\;y + 4z - 6w &= -3 \qquad -2\text{Eq.1} + \text{Eq.4}
\end{aligned}$$

$$\begin{aligned}
x \qquad\quad + 3w &= 4 \\
y - 4z + 6w &= 3 \qquad -\text{Eq.4 and} \\
2y - \;z - \;w &= 0 \qquad \text{interchange} \\
3y \qquad - 2w &= 1 \qquad \text{the equations.}
\end{aligned}$$

$$\begin{aligned}
x \qquad\quad + 3w &= 4 \\
y - 4z + 6w &= 3 \\
7z - 13w &= -6 \qquad -\text{Eq.2} + \text{Eq.3} \\
12z - 20w &= -8 \qquad -3\text{Eq.2} + \text{Eq.4}
\end{aligned}$$

$$\begin{aligned}
x \qquad\quad + 3w &= 4 \\
y - 4z + 6w &= 3 \\
z + 3w &= -2 \qquad -\tfrac{1}{2}\text{Eq.4} + \text{Eq.3} \\
12z - 20w &= -8
\end{aligned}$$

$$\begin{aligned}
x \qquad\quad + 3w &= 4 \\
y - 4z + 6w &= 3 \\
z - 3w &= -2 \\
16w &= 16 \qquad -12\text{Eq.3} + \text{Eq.4}
\end{aligned}$$

$$\begin{aligned}
16w &= 16 \Longrightarrow w = 1 \\
z - 3(1) &= -2 \Longrightarrow z = 1 \\
y - 4(1) + 6(1) &= 3 \Longrightarrow y = 1 \\
x + 3(1) &= 4 \Longrightarrow x = 1
\end{aligned}$$

Answer: $(1, 1, 1, 1)$

29.

$$\begin{aligned}
x \qquad + 4z &= 1 \\
x + y + 10z &= 10 \\
2x - y + 2z &= -5
\end{aligned}$$

$$\begin{aligned}
x \qquad + 4z &= 1 \\
y + 6z &= 9 \qquad -\text{Eq.1} + \text{Eq.2} \\
-y - 6z &= -7 \qquad -2\text{Eq.1} + \text{Eq.3}
\end{aligned}$$

$$\begin{aligned}
x \qquad + 4z &= 1 \\
y + 6z &= 9 \\
0 &= 2 \qquad \rightarrow \leftarrow \text{Eq.2} + \text{Eq.3}
\end{aligned}$$

No solution, inconsistent.

31.

$$\begin{aligned}
2x + 3y \qquad &= 0 \\
4x + 3y - \;z &= 0 \\
8x + 3y + 3z &= 0
\end{aligned}$$

$$\begin{aligned}
2x + 3y \qquad &= 0 \\
-3y - \;z &= 0 \qquad -2\text{Eq.1} + \text{Eq.2} \\
-9y + 3z &= 0 \qquad -4\text{Eq.1} + \text{Eq.3}
\end{aligned}$$

$$\begin{aligned}
2x + 3y \qquad &= 0 \\
-3y - \;z &= 0 \\
6z &= 0 \qquad -3\text{Eq.2} + \text{Eq.3}
\end{aligned}$$

$$\begin{aligned}
6z &= 0 \Longrightarrow z = 0 \\
-3y - 0 &= 0 \Longrightarrow y = 0 \\
2x + 3(0) &= 0 \Longrightarrow x = 0
\end{aligned}$$

Answer: $(0, 0, 0)$

33.

$$\begin{aligned}
23x + 4y - \;z &= 0 \qquad \text{Interchange} \\
12x + 5y + \;z &= 0 \qquad \text{the equations.}
\end{aligned}$$

$$\begin{aligned}
x + 6y + 3z &= 0 \qquad 2\text{Eq.2} - \text{Eq.1} \\
-67y - 35z &= 0 \qquad -12\text{Eq.1} + \text{Eq.2}
\end{aligned}$$

To avoid fractions, let $z = 67a$, then:

$$\begin{aligned}
-67y - 35(67a) &= 0 \\
y &= -35a \\
x + 6(-35a) + 3(67a) &= 0 \\
x &= 9a
\end{aligned}$$

Answer: $(9a, -35a, 67a)$

35. No, they are not equivalent. The constant in the second equation should be -11 and the coefficient of z in the third equation should be 2.

37. There are an infinite number of linear systems that has $(4, -1, 2)$ as their solution.
One such system is as follows:

$$3(4) + (-1) - (2) = 9 \implies 3x + y - z = 9$$
$$(4) + 2(-1) - (2) = 0 \implies x + 2y - z = 0$$
$$-(4) + (-1) + 3(2) = 1 \implies -x + y + 3z = 1$$

39. $y = ax^2 + bx + c$ passing through $(0, 0), (2, -2), (4, 0)$

$(0, \ 0): \ 0 = \qquad c$

$(2, -2): -2 = \ 4a + 2b + c \implies -1 = 2a + b$

$(4, \ 0): \ 0 = 16a + 4b + c \implies \ 0 = 4a + b$

Answer: $a = \frac{1}{2}, b = -2, c = 0$

The equation of the parabola is $y = \frac{1}{2}x^2 - 2x$.

41. $y = ax^2 + bx + c$ passing through $(2, 0), (3, -1), (4, 0)$

$(2, \ 0): \ 0 = \ 4a + 2b + c$

$(3, -1): -1 = \ 9a + 3b + c \implies -1 = 5a + b$

$(4, \ 0): \ 0 = 16a + 4b + c \implies \ 0 = 12a + 2b$

Answer: $a = 1, b = -6, c = 8$

The equation of the parabola is $y = x^2 - 6x + 8$.

43. $x^2 + y^2 + Dx + Ey + F = 0$ passing through $(0, 0), (2, 2), (4, 0)$

$(0, 0): \qquad\qquad F = 0$

$(2, 2): \ 8 + 2D + 2E + F = 0 \implies D + E = -4$

$(4, 0): 16 + 4D \qquad + F = 0 \implies D = -4 \text{ and } E = 0$

The equation of the circle is $x^2 + y^2 - 4x = 0$.

To graph, let $y_1 = \sqrt{4x - x^2}$ and $y_2 = -\sqrt{4x - x^2}$.

45. $x^2 + y^2 + Dx + Ey + F = 0$ passing through $(-3, -1), (2, 4), (-6, 8)$

$(-3, -1): \ 10 - 3D - E + F = 0 \implies \ 10 = \ 3D + E - F$

$(\ 2, \ 4): \ 20 + 2D + 4E + F = 0 \implies \ 20 = -2D - 4E - F$

$(-6, \ 8): 100 - 6D + 8E + F = 0 \implies 100 = \ 6D - 8E - F$

Answer: $D = 6, E = -8, F = 0$

The equation of the circle is $x^2 + y^2 + 6x - 8y = 0$. To graph, complete the squares first, then solve for y.

$$(x^2 + 6x + 9) + (y^2 - 8y + 16) = 0 + 9 + 16$$
$$(x + 3)^2 + (y - 4)^2 = 25$$
$$(y - 4)^2 = 25 - (x + 3)^2$$
$$y - 4 = \pm\sqrt{25 - (x + 3)^2}$$
$$y = 4 \pm \sqrt{25 - (x + 3)^2}$$

Let $y_1 = 4 + \sqrt{25 - (x + 3)^2}$ and $y_2 = 4 - \sqrt{25 - (x + 3)^2}$.

47. $s = \frac{1}{2}at^2 + v_0t + s_0$

$(1, 128), (2, 80), (3, 0)$

$128 = \frac{1}{2}a + v_0 + s_0 \implies a + 2v_0 + 2s_0 = 256$

$80 = 2a + 2v_0 + s_0 \implies 2a + 2v_0 + s_0 = 80$

$0 = \frac{9}{2}a + 3v_0 + s_0 \implies 9a + 6v_0 + 2s_0 = 0$

Solving this system yields $a = -32$, $v_0 = 0$, $s_0 = 144$.

Thus, $s = \frac{1}{2}(-32)t^2 + (0)t + 144$

$\qquad = -16t^2 + 144.$

49. $s = \frac{1}{2}at^2 + v_0t + s_0$

$(1, 452), (2, 260), (3, 116)$

$452 = \frac{1}{2}a + v_0 + s_0 \implies a + 2v_0 + 2s_0 = 904$

$260 = 2a + 2v_0 + s_0 \implies 2a + 2v_0 + s_0 = 260$

$116 = \frac{9}{2}a + 3v_0 + s_0 \implies 9a + 6v_0 + 2s_0 = 232$

Solving this system yields $a = 48$, $v_0 = -264$, $s_0 = 692$.

Thus, $s = \frac{1}{2}(48)t^2 + (-264)t + 692$

$\qquad = 24t^2 - 264t + 692.$

51. Let x = amount at 5%.

Let y = amount at 6%.

Let z = amount at 7%.

$$x + y + z = 16{,}000$$
$$0.05x + 0.06y + 0.07z = 990$$
$$x + 3000 = z$$
$$y + 2000 = z$$

$$(z - 3000) + (z - 2000) + z = 16{,}000$$
$$3z = 21{,}000$$
$$z = 7000$$

$x = 4000$, $y = 5000$

Check: $0.05(4000) + 0.06(5000) + 0.07(7000) = 990$

Answer: $x = \$4000$ at 5%, $y = \$5000$ at 6%, $z = \$7000$ at 7%

53. Let x = amount at 8%.

Let y = amount at 9%.

Let z = amount at 10%.

$$x + y + z = 775,000$$
$$0.08x + 0.09y + 0.10z = 67,000$$
$$x = 4z$$

$$y + 5z = 775,000$$
$$0.09y + 0.42z = 67,000$$
$$z \approx 91,666.67$$
$$y = 775,000 - 5z = 316,666.67$$
$$x = 4z = 366,666.67$$

Answer: x = \$366,666.67 at 8%

y = \$316,666.67 at 9%

z = \$91,666.67 at 10%

55. Let C = amount in certificates of deposit.

Let M = amount in municipal bonds.

Let B = amount in blue-chip stocks.

Let G = amount in growth or speculative stocks.

$$C + M + B + G = 500,000$$
$$0.10C + 0.08M + 0.12B + 0.13G = 0.10(500,000)$$
$$B + G = \tfrac{1}{4}(500,000)$$

This system has infinitely many solutions.

Let $G = s$, then $B = 125,000 - s$

$$M = 125,000 + \tfrac{1}{2}s$$
$$C = 250,000 - \tfrac{1}{2}s.$$

Answer:
$\left(250,000 - \tfrac{1}{2}s,\ 125,000 + \tfrac{1}{2}s,\ 125,000 - s,\ s\right),$
where $0 \le s \le 125,000$.

One possible solution is to let $s = 50,000$.

Certificates of deposit: \$225,000

Municipal bonds: \$150,000

Blue-chip stocks: \$75,000

Growth or speculative stocks: \$50,000

57. Let x = gallons of spray X.

Let y = gallons of spray Y.

Let z = gallons of spray Z.

Chemical A: $\tfrac{1}{5}x + \tfrac{1}{2}z = 12$
Chemical B: $\tfrac{2}{5}x + \tfrac{1}{2}z = 16$ $\Big\} \Rightarrow x = 20,\ z = 16$
Chemical C: $\tfrac{2}{5}x + y = 26 \Rightarrow y = 18$

Answer: 20 liters of spray X

18 liters of spray Y

16 liters of spray Z

59.

Truck	Product	
	A	B
Large	6	3
Medium	4	4
Small	0	3

Possible solutions:

(1) 4 medium trucks

(2) 2 large trucks, 1 medium truck, 2 small trucks

(3) 3 large trucks, 1 medium truck, 1 small truck

(4) 3 large trucks, 3 small trucks

61.

$$t_1 - 2t_2 = 0$$
$$t_1 \qquad 2a = 128 \Rightarrow 2t_2 - 2a = 128$$
$$t_2 + a = 32 \Rightarrow -2t_2 - 2a = -64$$
$$\overline{\qquad\qquad -4a = 64}$$

$$a = -16$$
$$t_2 = 48$$
$$t_1 = 96$$

Answer: $t_1 = 96$ lb, $t_2 = 48$ lb, $a = -16$ ft/sec^2

63.

Four points are:
(6, 0, 0), (0, 4, 0), (0, 0, 3), (4, 0, 1)

65.

Four points are:
(2, 0, 0), (0, 4, 0), (0, 0, 4), (0, 2, 2)

67. Least squares regression parabola through $(-4, 5)$, $(-2, 6)$, $(2, 6)$, $(4, 2)$

$n = 4$

$\sum x_i = 0$ $\qquad$ $\sum y_i = 19$

$\sum x_i^2 = 40$ $\qquad$ $\sum x_i^3 = 0$

$\sum x_i^4 = 544$ $\qquad$ $\sum x_i y_i = -12$

$\sum x_i^2 y_i = 160$

$$4c \quad + \quad 40a = \quad 19$$
$$40b \qquad\quad = -12$$
$$40c \quad + \, 544a = \, 160$$

Solving this system yields $a = -\frac{5}{24}$, $b = -\frac{3}{10}$, and $c = \frac{41}{6}$. Thus, $y = -\frac{5}{24}x^2 - \frac{3}{10}x + \frac{41}{6}$.

69. Least squares regression parabola through $(0, 0)$, $(2, 2)$, $(3, 6)$, $(4, 12)$

$n = 4$

$\sum x_i = 9$ $\qquad$ $\sum y_i = 20$

$\sum x_i^2 = 29$ $\qquad$ $\sum x_i^3 = 99$

$\sum x_i^4 = 353$ $\qquad$ $\sum x_i y_i = 70$

$\sum x_i^2 y_i = 254$

$$4c + \quad 9b + \quad 29a = \quad 20$$
$$9c + \, 29b + \quad 99a = \quad 70$$
$$29c + \, 99b + \, 353a = 254$$

Solving this system yields $a = 1$, $b = -1$, and $c = 0$. Thus, $y = x^2 - x$.

71. (a) Least squares regression parabola through $(20, 25)$, $(30, 55)$, $(40, 105)$, $(50, 188)$, $(60, 300)$

$n = 5$

$\sum x_i = 200$ $\qquad$ $\sum y_i = 673$

$\sum x_i^2 = 9000$ $\qquad$ $\sum x_i^3 = 440{,}000$

$\sum x_i^4 = 22{,}740{,}000$ $\qquad$ $\sum x_i y_i = 33{,}750$

$\sum x_i^2 y_i = 1{,}777{,}500$

$$5c + \qquad 200b + \qquad\quad 9000a = \qquad 673$$
$$200c + \quad 9000b + \quad 440{,}000a = \quad 33{,}750$$
$$9000c + 440{,}000b + 22{,}740{,}000a = 1{,}777{,}500$$

Solving this system yields $a \approx 0.14$, $b \approx -4.43$, and $c \approx 58.40$. Thus, $y = 0.14x^2 - 4.43x + 58.40$.

(b)   When $x = 70$, $y \approx 434.3$ feet.

73. $\left.\begin{array}{r} y + \quad \lambda = 0 \\ x + \lambda = 0 \end{array}\right\} \implies x = y = -\lambda$

$$x + y - 10 = 0 \implies 2x - 10 = 0$$
$$x = 5$$
$$y = 5$$
$$\lambda = -5$$

75. $2x - 2x\lambda = 0 \implies x = x\lambda$

$-2y + \lambda = 0 \implies 2y = \lambda$

$y - x^2 = 0 \implies y = x^2$

From the first equation, $x = 0$ or $\lambda = 1$. If $x = 0$, then $y = 0^2 = 0$ and $\lambda = 0$. If $x \neq 0$, then

$\lambda = 1 \implies y = \frac{1}{2}$ and $x = \pm\sqrt{\frac{1}{2}}$.

Thus, the solutions are:

(1) $x = y = \lambda = 0$

(2) $x = \dfrac{\sqrt{2}}{2}$, $y = \dfrac{1}{2}$, $\lambda = 1$

(3) $x = -\dfrac{\sqrt{2}}{2}$, $y = \dfrac{1}{2}$, $\lambda = 1$

77. The slope represents the average increase in sales per year.

79. $(0.075)(85) = 6.375$

81. $(0.005)(n) = 400$
$n = 80,000$

Section 8.4   Partial Fractions

■ You should know how to decompose a rational function $\dfrac{N(x)}{D(x)}$ into partial fractions.

(a) If the fraction is improper, divide to obtain

$$\frac{N(x)}{D(x)} = p(x) + \frac{N_1(x)}{D(x)}$$

where $p(x)$ is a polynomial.

(b) Factor the denominator completely into linear and irreducible (over the reals) quadratic factors.

(c) For each factor of the form $(px + q)^m$, the partial fraction decomposition includes the terms

$$\frac{A_1}{(px + q)} + \frac{A_2}{(px + q)^2} + \cdots + \frac{A_m}{(px + q)^m}.$$

(d) For each factor of the form $(ax^2 + bx + c)^n$, the partial fraction decomposition includes the terms

$$\frac{B_1 x + C_1}{ax^2 + bx + c} + \frac{B_2 x + C_2}{(ax^2 + bx + c)^2} + \cdots + \frac{B_n x + C_n}{(ax^2 + bx + c)^n}.$$

■ You should know how to determine the values of the constants in the numerators.

(a) Set $\dfrac{N_1(x)}{D(x)}$ = partial fraction decomposition.

(b) Multiply both sides by $D(x)$. This is called the basic equation.

(c) For distinct linear factors, substitute the roots of the distinct linear factors into the basic equation.

(d) For repeated linear factors, use the coefficients found in part (c) to rewrite the basic equation. Then use other values of x to solve for the remaining coefficients.

(e) For quadratic factors, expand the basic equation, collect like terms, and then equate the coefficients of like terms.

Solutions to Odd-Numbered Exercises

1. $\dfrac{7}{x^2 - 14x} = \dfrac{7}{x(x - 14)} = \dfrac{A}{x} + \dfrac{B}{x - 14}$

3. $\dfrac{12}{x^3 - 10x^2} = \dfrac{12}{x^2(x - 10)} = \dfrac{A}{x} + \dfrac{B}{x^2} + \dfrac{C}{x - 10}$

5. $\dfrac{2x - 3}{x^3 + 10x} = \dfrac{2x - 3}{x(x^2 + 10)} = \dfrac{A}{x} + \dfrac{Bx + C}{x^2 + 10}$

7 $\dfrac{1}{x^2 - 1} = \dfrac{A}{x + 1} + \dfrac{B}{x - 1}$

$1 = A(x - 1) + B(x + 1)$

Let $x = -1$: $1 = -2A \implies A = -\dfrac{1}{2}$

Let $x = 1$: $1 = 2B \implies B = \dfrac{1}{2}$

$\dfrac{1}{x^2 - 1} = \dfrac{1/2}{x - 1} - \dfrac{1/2}{x + 1} = \dfrac{1}{2}\left[\dfrac{1}{x - 1} - \dfrac{1}{x + 1}\right]$

9. $\dfrac{1}{x^2 + x} = \dfrac{A}{x} + \dfrac{B}{x + 1}$

$1 = A(x + 1) + Bx$

Let $x = 0$: $1 = A$

Let $x = -1$: $1 = -B \implies B = -1$

$\dfrac{1}{x^2 + x} = \dfrac{1}{x} - \dfrac{1}{x + 1}$

11. $\dfrac{1}{2x^2 + x} = \dfrac{A}{2x + 1} + \dfrac{B}{x}$

$\qquad 1 = Ax + B(2x + 1)$

Let $x = -\dfrac{1}{2}$: $1 = -\dfrac{1}{2}A \implies A = -2$

Let $x = 0$: $1 = B$

$\dfrac{1}{2x^2 + x} = \dfrac{1}{x} - \dfrac{2}{2x + 1}$

15. $\dfrac{x^2 + 12x + 12}{x^3 - 4x} = \dfrac{A}{x} + \dfrac{B}{x + 2} + \dfrac{C}{x - 2}$

$x^2 + 12x + 12 = A(x + 2)(x - 2) + Bx(x - 2) + Cx(x + 2)$

Let $x = 0$: $12 = -4A \implies A = -3$

Let $x = -2$: $-8 = 8B \implies B = -1$

Let $x = 2$: $40 = 8C \implies C = 5$

$\dfrac{x^2 + 12x + 12}{x^3 - 4x} = -\dfrac{3}{x} - \dfrac{1}{x + 2} + \dfrac{5}{x - 2}$

17. $\dfrac{4x^2 + 2x - 1}{x^2(x + 1)} = \dfrac{A}{x} + \dfrac{B}{x^2} + \dfrac{C}{x + 1}$

$4x^2 + 2x - 1 = Ax(x + 1) + B(x + 1) + Cx^2$

Let $x = 0$: $-1 = B$

Let $x = -1$: $1 = C$

Let $x = 1$: $5 = 2A + 2B + C$

$\qquad\qquad 5 = 2A - 2 + 1$

$\qquad\qquad 6 = 2A$

$\qquad\qquad 3 = A$

$\dfrac{4x^2 + 2x - 1}{x^2(x + 1)} = \dfrac{3}{x} - \dfrac{1}{x^2} + \dfrac{1}{x + 1}$

19. $\dfrac{3x}{(x - 3)^2} = \dfrac{A}{x - 3} + \dfrac{B}{(x - 3)^2}$

$\qquad 3x = A(x - 3) + B$

Let $x = 3$: $9 = B$

Let $x = 0$: $0 = -3A + B$

$\qquad\qquad 0 = -3A + 9$

$\qquad\qquad 3 = A$

$\dfrac{3x}{(x - 3)^2} = \dfrac{3}{x - 3} + \dfrac{9}{(x - 3)^2}$

13. $\dfrac{3}{x^2 + x - 2} = \dfrac{A}{x - 1} + \dfrac{B}{x + 2}$

$\qquad 3 = A(x + 2) + B(x - 1)$

Let $x = 1$: $3 = 3A \implies A = 1$

Let $x = -2$: $3 = -3B \implies B = -1$

$\dfrac{3}{x^2 + x - 2} = \dfrac{1}{x - 1} - \dfrac{1}{x + 2}$

21. $\dfrac{x^2 - 1}{x(x^2 + 1)} = \dfrac{A}{x} + \dfrac{Bx + C}{x^2 + 1}$

$\qquad x^2 - 1 = A(x^2 + 1) + (Bx + C)x$

Let $x = 0$: $-1 = A$

$x^2 - 1 = Ax^2 + A + Bx^2 + Cx$

$\qquad\quad = -x^2 - 1 + Bx^2 + Cx$

$\qquad\quad = x^2(B - 1) + Cx - 1$

Equating coefficients of like powers:

$1 = B - 1, 2 = B,$ and $0 = C$

$\dfrac{x^2 - 1}{x(x^2 + 1)} = -\dfrac{1}{x} + \dfrac{2x}{x^2 + 1}$

23. $\dfrac{x^2}{x^4 - 2x^2 - 8} = \dfrac{x^2}{(x^2 - 4)(x^2 + 2)} = \dfrac{A}{x + 2} + \dfrac{B}{x - 2} + \dfrac{Cx + D}{x^2 + 2}$

$x^2 = A(x - 2)(x^2 + 2) + B(x + 2)(x^2 + 2) + (Cx + D)(x^2 - 4)$

Let $x = -2$: $4 = -24A \implies A = -\dfrac{1}{6}$

Let $x = 2$: $4 = 24B \implies B = \dfrac{1}{6}$

$x^2 = -\dfrac{1}{6}(x - 2)(x^2 + 2) + \dfrac{1}{6}(x + 2)(x^2 + 2) + (Cx + D)(x^2 - 4)$

$x^2 = -\dfrac{1}{6}x^3 + \dfrac{1}{3}x^2 - \dfrac{1}{3}x + \dfrac{2}{3} + \dfrac{1}{6}x^3 + \dfrac{1}{3}x^2 + \dfrac{1}{3}x + \dfrac{2}{3} + Cx^3 + Dx^2 - 4Cx - 4D$

$x^2 = Cx^3 + \left(\dfrac{2}{3} + D\right)x^2 - 4Cx + \left(\dfrac{4}{3} - 4D\right)$

Equating coefficients of like powers:

$$C \implies 0$$

$$1 = \dfrac{2}{3} + D \implies D = \dfrac{1}{3}$$

$\dfrac{x^2}{x^4 - 2x^2 - 8} = -\dfrac{1}{6(x - 2)} + \dfrac{1}{6(x + 2)} + \dfrac{1}{3(x^2 + 2)}$

25. $\dfrac{x}{16x^4 - 1} = \dfrac{A}{2x + 1} + \dfrac{B}{2x - 1} + \dfrac{Cx + D}{4x^2 + 1}$

$x = A(2x - 1)(4x^2 + 1) + B(2x + 1)(4x^2 + 1) + (Cx + D)(2x + 1)(2x - 1)$

Let $x = -\dfrac{1}{2}$: $-\dfrac{1}{2} = -4A \implies A = \dfrac{1}{8}$

Let $x = \dfrac{1}{2}$: $\dfrac{1}{2} - 4B \implies B = \dfrac{1}{8}$

Let $x = 0$: $0 = -A + B - D$

$$0 = -\dfrac{1}{8} + \dfrac{1}{8} - D$$

$$0 = D$$

Let $x = 1$: $1 = 5A + 15B + 3C + 3D$

$$1 = \dfrac{5}{8} + \dfrac{15}{8} + 3C + 0$$

$$-\dfrac{1}{2} = C$$

$\dfrac{x}{16x^4 - 1} = \dfrac{1/8}{2x + 1} + \dfrac{1/8}{2x - 1} - \dfrac{x/2}{4x^2 + 1} = \dfrac{1}{8(2x + 1)} + \dfrac{1}{8(2x - 1)} - \dfrac{x}{2(4x^2 + 1)}$

27. $\dfrac{x^2 + 5}{(x + 1)(x^2 - 2x + 3)} = \dfrac{A}{x + 1} + \dfrac{Bx + C}{x^2 - 2x + 3}$

$$x^2 + 5 = A(x^2 - 2x + 3) + (Bx + C)(x + 1)$$

Let $x = -1$: $6 = 6A \implies A = 1$

$x^2 + 5 = x^2 - 2x + 3 + Bx^2 + Bx + Cx + C$

$\qquad = x^2(1 + B) + x(-2 + B + C) + (3 + C)$

Equating coefficients of like powers:

$1 = 1 + B, \quad 0 = -2 + B + C, \quad$ and $5 = 3 + C$

$0 = B \qquad\quad 0 = -2 + 0 + C \qquad 2 = C$

$\qquad\qquad\qquad\quad 2 = C$

$\dfrac{x^2 + 5}{(x + 1)(x^2 - 2x + 3)} = \dfrac{1}{x + 1} + \dfrac{2}{x^2 - 2x + 3}$

29. $\dfrac{x^4}{(x - 1)^3} = \dfrac{x^4}{x^3 - 3x^2 + 3x - 1} = x + 3 + \dfrac{6x^2 - 8x + 3}{(x - 1)^3}$

$\dfrac{6x^2 - 8x + 3}{(x - 1)^3} = \dfrac{A}{x - 1} + \dfrac{B}{(x - 1)^2} + \dfrac{C}{(x - 1)^3}$

$6x^2 - 8x + 3 = A(x - 1)^2 + B(x - 1) + C$

Let $x = 1$: $1 = C$

$6x^2 - 8x + 3 = Ax^2 - 2Ax + A + Bx - B + 1$

$6x^2 - 8x + 3 = Ax^2 + (-2A + B)x + (A - B + 1)$

Equating coefficients of like powers:

$6 = A, \quad -8 = -2A + B$ and $3 = A - B + 1$

$\qquad\qquad -8 = -12 + B \qquad 3 = 6 - B + 1$

$\qquad\qquad\quad\; 4 = B \qquad\qquad\; 4 = B$

$\dfrac{x^4}{(x - 1)^3} = x + 3 + \dfrac{6}{x - 1} + \dfrac{4}{(x - 1)^2} + \dfrac{1}{(x - 1)^3}$

31. $\dfrac{5 - x}{2x^2 + x - 1} = \dfrac{A}{2x - 1} + \dfrac{B}{x + 1}$

$\qquad -x + 5 = A(x + 1) + B(2x - 1)$

Let $x = \dfrac{1}{2}$: $\dfrac{9}{2} = \dfrac{3}{2}A \implies A = 3$

Let $x = -1$: $6 = -3B \implies B = -2$

$\dfrac{5 - x}{2x^2 + x - 1} = \dfrac{3}{2x - 1} - \dfrac{2}{x + 1}$

33. $\dfrac{x-1}{x^3+x^2}=\dfrac{A}{x}+\dfrac{B}{x^2}+\dfrac{C}{x+1}$

$x-1=Ax(x+1)+B(x+1)+Cx^2$

Let $x=-1$: $-2=C$

Let $x=0$: $-1=B$

Let $x=1$: $0=2A+2B+C$

$\qquad\qquad 0=2A-2-2$

$\qquad\qquad 2=A$

$\dfrac{x-1}{x^3+x^2}=\dfrac{2}{x}-\dfrac{1}{x^2}-\dfrac{2}{x+1}$

35. $\dfrac{x^2+x+2}{(x^2+2)^2}=\dfrac{Ax+B}{x^2+2}+\dfrac{Cx+D}{(x^2+2)^2}$

$x^2+x+2=(Ax+B)(x^2+2)+Cx+D$

$x^2+x+2=Ax^3+Bx^2+(2A+C)x+(2B+D)$

Equating coefficient of like powers:

$0=A$

$1=B$

$1=2A+C\implies C=1$

$2=2B+D\implies D=0$

$\dfrac{x^2+x+2}{(x^2+2)^2}=\dfrac{1}{x^2+2}+\dfrac{x}{(x^2+2)^2}$

37. $\dfrac{2x^3-4x^2-15x+5}{x^2-2x-8}=2x+\dfrac{x+5}{(x+2)(x-4)}$

$\dfrac{x+5}{(x+2)(x-4)}=\dfrac{A}{x+2}+\dfrac{B}{x-4}$

$x+5=A(x-4)+B(x+2)$

Let $x=-2$: $3=-6A\implies A=-\dfrac{1}{2}$

Let $x=4$: $9=6B\implies B=\dfrac{3}{2}$

$\dfrac{2x^3-4x^2-15x+5}{x^2-2x-8}=2x+\dfrac{1}{2}\left[\dfrac{3}{x-4}-\dfrac{1}{x+2}\right]$

39. $\dfrac{1}{a^2-x^2}=\dfrac{A}{a+x}+\dfrac{B}{a-x}$, a is a constant

$1=A(a-x)+B(a+x)$

Let $x=-a$: $1=2aA\implies A=\dfrac{1}{2a}$

Let $x=a$: $1=2aB\implies B=\dfrac{1}{2a}$

$\dfrac{1}{a^2-x^2}=\dfrac{1}{2a}\left[\dfrac{1}{a+x}+\dfrac{1}{a-x}\right]$

41. $\dfrac{1}{y(a-y)}=\dfrac{A}{y}+\dfrac{B}{a-y}$

$1=A(a-y)+By$

Let $y=0$: $1=aA\implies A=\dfrac{1}{a}$

Let $y=a$: $1=aB\implies B=\dfrac{1}{a}$

$\dfrac{1}{y(a-y)}=\dfrac{1}{a}\left(\dfrac{1}{y}+\dfrac{1}{a-y}\right)$

43. $\dfrac{x - 12}{x(x - 4)} = \dfrac{A}{x} + \dfrac{B}{x - 4}$

$x - 12 = A(x - 4) + Bx$

Let $x = 0$: $-12 = -4A \implies A = 3$

Let $x = 4$: $-8 = 4B \implies B = -2$

$\dfrac{x - 12}{x(x - 4)} = \dfrac{3}{x} - \dfrac{2}{x - 4}$

$y = \dfrac{x - 12}{x(x - 4)}$

Vertical asymptotes: $x = 0$ and $x = 4$

$y = \dfrac{3}{x}$

Vertical asymptote: $x = 0$

$y = -\dfrac{2}{x - 4}$

Vertical asymptote: $x = 4$

The combination of the vertical asymptotes of the terms of the decompositions are the same as the vertical asymptotes of the rational function.

45. $\dfrac{2(4x - 3)}{x^2 - 9} = \dfrac{A}{x - 3} + \dfrac{B}{x + 3}$

$2(4x - 3) = A(x + 3) + B(x - 3)$

Let $x = 3$: $18 = 6A \implies A = 3$

Let $x = -3$: $-30 = -6B \implies B = 5$

$\dfrac{2(4x - 3)}{x^2 - 9} = \dfrac{3}{x - 3} + \dfrac{5}{x + 3}$

$y = \dfrac{2(4x - 3)}{x^2 - 9}$

Vertical asymptotes: $x = \pm 3$

$y = \dfrac{3}{x - 3}$

Vertical asymptote: $x = 3$

$y = \dfrac{5}{x + 3}$

Vertical asymptote: $y = -3$

The combination of the vertical asymptotes of the terms of the decompositions are the same as the vertical asymptotes of the rational function.

47. (a) $\dfrac{2000(4-3x)}{(11-7x)(7-4x)} = \dfrac{A}{11-7x} + \dfrac{B}{7-4x}, \quad 0 \le x \le 1$

$$2000(4-3x) = A(7-4x) + B(11-7x)$$

Let $x = \dfrac{11}{7}$: $-\dfrac{10{,}000}{7} = \dfrac{5}{7}A \implies A = -2000$

Let $x = \dfrac{7}{4}$: $-2500 = -\dfrac{5}{4}B \implies B = 2000$

$$\dfrac{2000(4-3x)}{(11-7x)(7-4x)} = \dfrac{-2000}{11-7x} + \dfrac{2000}{7-4x} = \dfrac{2000}{7-4x} - \dfrac{2000}{11-7x}$$

(b) $y_1 = \dfrac{2000}{7-4x}$

$y_2 = \dfrac{2000}{11-7x}$

Section 8.5   Systems of Inequalities

- You should be able to sketch the graph of an inequality in two variables:

    (a) Replace the inequality with an equal sign and graph the equation. Use a dashed line for < or >, a solid line for ≤ or ≥.

    (b) Test a point in each region formed by the graph. If the point satisfies the inequality, shade the whole region.

Solutions to Odd-Numbered Exercises

1. $x < 2$

Vertical boundary

Matches graph (g).

3. $2x + 3y \ge 6$

$\quad y \ge -\dfrac{2}{3}x + 2$

Line with negative slope

Matches (a).

5. $x^2 + y^2 < 9$

Circular boundary

Matches (e).

7. $xy > 1$ or $y > \dfrac{1}{x}$

Matches (f).

9. $x \ge 2$

Using a solid line, graph the vertical line $x = 2$ and shade to the right of this line.

11. $y \geq -1$

Using a solid line, graph the horizontal line $y = -1$ and shade above this line.

13. $y < 2 - x$

Using a dashed line, graph $y = 2 - x$, and then shade below the line. (Use $(0, 0)$ as a test point.)

15. $2y - x \geq 4$

Using a solid line, graph $2y - x = 4$, and then shade above the line. (Use $(0, 0)$ as a test point.)

17. $y^2 - x < 0$

$$y^2 < x$$

Using a dashed line, graph the parabola $y^2 = x$, and then shade inside. (Use $(1, 0)$ as a test point.)

19. $y \leq \dfrac{1}{1 + x^2}$

Using a solid line, graph $y = \dfrac{1}{1 + x^2}$, and then shade below the curve. (Use $(0, 0)$ as a test point.)

21. $y \geq \dfrac{2}{3}x - 1$

23. $x^2 + 5y - 10 \leq 0$

$$y \leq 2 - \frac{x^2}{5}$$

25. The line through $(-4, 0)$ and $(0, 2)$ is $y = (1/2)x + 2$. For the shaded region below the line, we have $y \leq (1/2)x + 2$.

27. The line through $(0, 2)$ and $(3, 0)$ is $y = -\frac{2}{3}x + 2$. For the shaded region above the line, we have:

$$y \geq -\frac{2}{3}x + 2$$

$$3y \geq -2x + 6$$

$$2x + 3y \geq 6$$

$$\frac{x}{3} + \frac{y}{2} \geq 1$$

29. The boundary is given by the function $y = 4 - |x|$. Hence, $y < 4 - |x|$.

31. $x + y \leq 1$

   $-x + y \leq 1$

   $y \geq 0$

First, find the points of intersection of each pair of equations.

Vertex A	*Vertex B*	*Vertex C*
$x + y = 1$	$x + y = 1$	$-x + y = 1$
$-x + y = 1$	$y = 0$	$y = 0$
$(0, 1)$	$(1, 0)$	$(-1, 0)$

33. $x + y \leq 5$

   $x \geq 2$

   $y \geq 0$

First, find the points of intersection of each pair of equations.

Vertex A	*Vertex B*	*Vertex C*
$x + y = 5$	$x + y = 5$	$x = 2$
$x = 2$	$y = 0$	$y = 0$
$(2, 3)$	$(5, 0)$	$(2, 0)$

35. $-3x + 2y < 6$

   $x - 4y > -2$

   $2x + y < 3$

First, find the points of intersection of each pair of equations.

Vertex A	*Vertex B*	*Vertex C*
$-3x + 2y = 6$	$-3x + 2y = 6$	$x - 4y = -2$
$x - 4y = -2$	$2x + y = 3$	$2x + y = 3$
$(-2, 0)$	$(0, 3)$	$\left(\frac{10}{9}, \frac{7}{9}\right)$

37. $2x + y > 2$

   $6x + 3y < 2$

The lines are parallel. There are no points of intersection. There is no region in common to both inequalities.

39. $\quad x \qquad \geq 1$

$\qquad x - 2y \leq 3$

$\qquad 3x + 2y \geq 9$

$\qquad x + \ y \leq 6$

First, find the points of intersection of each pair of equations.

Vertex A	Vertex B	Vertex C
$x = 1$	$x = 1$	$x = 1$
$x - 2y = 3$	$3x + 2y = 9$	$x + y = 6$
$(1, -1)$	$(1, 3)$	$(1, 5)$

Vertex D	Vertex E	Vertex F
$x - 2y = 3$	$x - 2y = 3$	$3x + 2y = 9$
$3x + 2y = 9$	$x + \ y = 6$	$x + \ y = 6$
$(3, 0)$	$(5, 1)$	$(-3, 9)$

By shading each inequality, we find that the vertices of the region are $(1, 5)$, $(1, 3)$, $(3, 0)$, and $(5, 1)$.

41. $x^2 + y^2 \leq 9$

$\qquad x^2 + y^2 \geq 1$

There are no points of intersection. The region in common to both inequalities is the region between the circles.

43. $x > y^2$

$\qquad x < y + 2$

Points of intersection:

$$y^2 = y + 2$$

$$y^2 - y - 2 = 0$$

$$(y + 1)(y - 2) = 0$$

$$y = -1, 2$$

$(1, -1), (4, 2)$

45. $y \leq \sqrt{3x} + 1$

$\qquad y \geq x^2 + 1$

47. $y < x^3 - 2x + 1$

$\qquad y > -2x$

$\qquad x \leq 1$

49. $x^2 y \ge 1$

$0 < x \le 4$

$y \le 4$

51. $y \le -x + 4 \implies \dfrac{x}{4} + \dfrac{y}{4} \le 1$

$x \ge 0 \qquad\qquad x \ge 0$

$y \ge 0 \qquad\qquad y \ge 0$

53. $(0, 4), (4, 0)$

Line: $y \ge 4 - x$

$(0, 2), (3, 1)$

Line: $y \ge 2 - \dfrac{1}{3}x$

$x \ge 0, \ y \ge 0$

55. $x^2 + y^2 \le 16$

$x \ge 0$

$y \ge 0$

57. Rectangular region with vertices at $(2, 1), (5, 1), (5, 7),$ and $(2, 7)$

$x \ge 2$

$x \le 5$

$y \ge 1$

$y \le 7$

Thus, $2 \le x \le 5, 1 \le y \le 7$.

59. Triangle with vertices at $(0, 0), (5, 0), (2, 3)$

$(0, 0), (5, 0)$

Line: $y \ge 0$

$(0, 0), (2, 3)$

Line: $y \le \dfrac{3}{2}x$

$(2, 3), (5, 0)$

Line: $y \le -x + 5$

61. Account constraints:

$x \ge 5000$

$y \ge 5000$

$2x \le y$

$x + y \le 20{,}000$

63. Assembly center constraint: $x + \dfrac{3}{2}y \le 12$

Finishing center constraint: $\dfrac{4}{3}x + \dfrac{3}{2}y \le 15$

Point of intersection: $(9, 2)$

Physical constraints: $x \ge 0$ and $y \ge 0$

65. x = number of ounces of food X

y = number of ounces of food Y

Calcium: $20x + 10y \geq 280$

Iron: $15x + 10y \geq 160$

Vitamin B: $10x + 20y \geq 180$

$$x \geq 0$$

$$y \geq 0$$

67. $xy \geq 500$ Body-building space

$2x + \pi y \geq 125$ Track (Two semi-circles and two lengths)

$x \geq 0$ Physical constraint

$y \geq 0$ Physical constraint

69.   Demand = Supply

$50 - 0.5x = 0.125x$

$50 = 0.625x$

$80 = x$

$10 = p$

Point of equilibrium: (80, 10)

The consumer surplus is the area of the triangle bounded by

$p \leq 50 - 0.5x$

$p \geq 10$

$x \geq 0.$

Consumer surplus = $\frac{1}{2}$(base)(height) = $\frac{1}{2}$(80)(40) = \$1600

The producer surplus is the area of the triangle bounded by

$p \geq 0.125x$

$p \leq 10$

$x \geq 0.$

Producer surplus = $\frac{1}{2}$(base)(height) = $\frac{1}{2}$(80)(10) = \$400

71. Demand = Supply

$300 - x = 100 + x$

$x = 100$

Consumer surplus = 5000

Producer surplus = 5000

73. Test a point on either side of the boundary.

Section 8.6   Linear Programming

■ To solve a linear programming problem:
1. Sketch the solution set for the system of constraints.
2. Find the vertices of the region.
3. Test the objective function at each of the vertices.

Solutions to Odd-Numbered Exercises

1. $z = 4x + 5y$

At $(0, 6)$: $z = 4(0) + 5(6) = 30$

At $(0, 0)$: $z = 4(0) + 5(0) = 0$

At $(6, 0)$: $z = 4(6) + 5(0) = 24$

The minimum value is 0 at $(0, 0)$.

The maximum value is 30 at $(0, 6)$.

3. $z = 10x + 6y$

At $(0, 6)$: $z = 10(0) + 6(6) = 36$

At $(0, 0)$: $z = 10(0) + 6(0) = 0$

At $(6, 0)$: $z = 10(6) + 6(0) = 60$

The minimum value is 0 at $(0, 0)$.

The maximum value is 60 at $(6, 0)$.

5. $z = 3x + 2y$

At $(0, 5)$: $z = 3(0) + 2(5) = 10$

At $(4, 0)$: $z = 3(4) + 2(0) = 12$

At $(3, 4)$: $z = 3(3) + 2(4) = 17$

At $(0, 0)$: $z = 3(0) + 2(0) = 0$

The minimum value is 0 at $(0, 0)$.

The maximum value is 17 at $(3, 4)$.

7. $z = 5x + 0.5y$

At $(0, 5)$: $z = 5(0) + \frac{5}{2} = \frac{5}{2}$

At $(4, 0)$: $z = 5(4) + \frac{0}{2} = 20$

At $(3, 4)$: $z = 5(3) + \frac{4}{2} = 17$

At $(0, 0)$: $z = 5(0) + \frac{0}{2} = 0$

The minimum value is 0 at $(0, 0)$.

The maximum value is 20 at $(4, 0)$.

9. $z = 10x + 7y$

At $(0, 45)$: $z = 10(0) + 7(45) = 315$

At $(30, 45)$: $z = 10(30) + 7(45) = 615$

At $(60, 20)$: $z = 10(60) + 7(20) = 740$

At $(60, 0)$: $z = 10(60) + 7(0) = 600$

At $(0, 0)$: $z = 10(0) + 7(0) = 0$

The minimum value is 0 at $(0, 0)$.

The maximum value is 740 at $(60, 20)$.

11. $z = 25x + 30y$

At $(0, 45)$: $z = 25(0) + 30(45) = 1350$

At $(30, 45)$: $z = 25(30) + 30(45) = 2100$

At $(60, 20)$: $z = 25(60) + 30(20) = 2100$

At $(60, 0)$: $z = 25(60) + 30(0) = 1500$

At $(0, 0)$: $z = 25(0) + 30(0) = 0$

The minimum value is 0 at $(0, 0)$.

The maximum value is 2100 at any point along the line segment connecting $(30, 45)$ and $(60, 20)$.

13. $z = 6x + 10y$

At $(0, 2)$: $z = 6(0) + 10(2) = 20$

At $(5, 0)$: $z = 6(5) + 10(0) = 30$

At $(0, 0)$: $z = 6(0) + 10(0) = 0$

The minimum value is 0 at $(0, 0)$.

The maximum value is 30 at $(5, 0)$.

15. $z = 9z + 24y$

At $(0, 2)$: $z = 9(0) + 24(2) = 48$

At $(5, 0)$: $z = 9(5) + 24(0) = 45$

At $(0, 0)$: $z = 9(0) + 24(0) = 0$

The minimum value is 0 at $(0, 0)$.

The maximum value is 48 at $(0, 2)$.

17. $z = 4x + 5y$

At $(10, 0)$: $z = 4(10) + 5(0) = 40$

At $(5, 3)$: $z = 4(5) + 5(3) = 35$

At $(0, 8)$: $z = 4(0) + 5(8) = 40$

The minimum value is 35 at $(5, 3)$.

C is unbounded. Therefore, there is no maximum.

19. $z = 2x + 7y$

At $(10, 0)$: $z = 2(10) + 7(0) = 20$

At $(5, 3)$: $z = 2(5) + 7(3) = 31$

At $(0, 8)$: $z = 2(0) + 7(8) = 56$

The minimum value is 20 at $(10, 0)$.

C is unbounded. Therefore, there is no maximum.

21. $z = 4x + y$

At $(36, 0)$: $z = 4(36) + 0 = 144$

At $(40, 0)$: $z = 4(40) + 0 = 160$

At $(24, 8)$: $z = 4(24) + 8 = 104$

The minimum value is 104 at $(24, 8)$.

The maximum value is 160 at $(40, 0)$.

23. $z = x + 4y$

At $(36, 0)$: $z = 36 + 4(0) = 36$

At $(40, 0)$: $z = 40 + 4(0) = 40$

At $(24, 8)$: $z = 24 + 4(8) = 56$

The minimum value is 36 at $(36, 0)$.

The maximum value is 56 at $(24, 8)$.

25. $z = 2x + 3y$

At $(36, 0)$: $z = 2(36) + 3(0) = 72$

At $(40, 0)$: $z = 2(40) + 3(0) = 80$

At $(24, 8)$: $z = 2(24) + 3(8) = 72$

Minimum at any point on the line segment joining $(36, 0)$ and $(24, 8)$: 72.

Maximum at $(40, 0)$: 80.

27. $z = 2x + y$

At $(0, 10)$: $z = 2(0) + (10) = 10$

At $(3, 6)$: $z = 2(3) + (6)$ $= 12$

At $(5, 0)$: $z = 2(5) + (0)$ $= 10$

At $(0, 0)$: $z = 2(0) + (0)$ $= 0$

The maximum value is 12 at $(3, 6)$.

29. $z = x + y$

At $(0, 10)$: $z = (0) + (10) = 10$

At $(3, 6)$: $z = (3) + (6)$ $= 9$

At $(5, 0)$: $z = (5) + (0)$ $= 5$

At $(0, 0)$: $z = (0) + (0)$ $= 0$

The maximum value is 10 at $(0, 10)$.

31. $z = x + 5y$

At $(0, 5)$: $z = 0 + 5(5) = 25$

At $(4, 4)$: $z = 4 + 5(4) = 24$

At $(5, 3)$: $z = 5 + 5(3) = 20$

At $(7, 0)$: $z = 7 + 5(0) = 7$

The maximum value is 25 at $(0, 5)$.

33. $z = 4x + 5y$

At $(0, 5)$: $z = 4(0) + 5(5) = 25$

At $(4, 4)$: $z = 4(4) + 5(4) = 36$

At $(5, 3)$: $z = 4(5) + 5(3) = 35$

At $(7, 0)$: $z = 4(7) + 5(0) = 28$

The maximum valve is 36 at $(4, 4)$.

35. There are an infinite number of objective functions that would have a maximum at $(0, 4)$.
One such objective function is $z = x + 5y$.

37. There are an infinite number of objective functions that would have a maximum at $(5, 0)$.
One such objective function is $z = 4x + y$.

39. $x =$ number of \$250 models

$y =$ number of \$400 models

Constraints: $250x + 400y \leq 70{,}000$

$$x + y \leq 250$$

$$x \geq 0$$

$$y \geq 0$$

Objective function: $P = 45x + 50y$

Vertices: $(0, 175)$, $(200, 50)$, $(250, 0)$, $(0, 0)$

—CONTINUED—

39. —CONTINUED—

At $(0, 175)$: $P = 45(0) + 50(175) = 8750$

At $(200, 50)$: $P = 45(200) + 50(50) = 11,500$

At $(250, 0)$: $P = 45(250) + 50(0) = 11,250$

At $(0, 0)$: $P = 45(0) + 50(0) = 0$

To maximize the profit, the merchant should stock 200 units of the model costing $250 and 50 units of the model costing $400. Then the maximum profit would be $11,500.

41. $x = $ fraction of type A

$y = $ fraction of type B

Constraints: $80x + 92y \leq 90$

$\qquad\qquad x + y \leq 1$

$\qquad\qquad\quad x \leq 0$

$\qquad\qquad\quad y \leq 0$

Objective function: $C = 1.13x + 1.28y$

Vertices: $\left(\frac{1}{6}, \frac{5}{6}\right)$

At $\left(\frac{1}{6}, \frac{5}{6}\right)$: $C = (1.13)\left(\frac{1}{6}\right) + (1.28)\left(\frac{5}{6}\right) = 1.255$

The minimum cost is $1.26 and occurs with a mixture that is $\frac{1}{6}$ A and $\frac{5}{6}$ B.

43. Objective function: $R = 1000x + 300y$

At $(0, 0)$: $R = 1000(0) + 300(0) = 0$

At $(0, 40)$: $R = 1000(0) + 300(40) = 12,000$

At $(8, 8)$: $R = 1000(8) + 300(8) = 10,400$

At $(9, 0)$: $R = 1000(9) + 300(0) = 9000$

The revenue will be maximum ($12,000) if the firm does 0 audits and 40 tax returns.

45. $x = $ fraction of Model A

$y = $ fraction of Model B

Constraints: $\qquad 2.5x + 3y \leq 4000$

$\qquad\qquad\qquad 2x + y \leq 2500$

$\qquad\qquad 0.75x + 1.25y \leq 1500$

$\qquad\qquad\qquad\qquad x \leq 0$

$\qquad\qquad\qquad\qquad y \leq 0$

Objective function: $P = 50x + 52y$

Vertices: $(0, 0)$, $(0, 1200)$, $\left(\frac{4000}{7}, \frac{6000}{7}\right)$, $(1000, 500)$, $(1250, 0)$

At $(0, 0)$: $P = (50)(0) + 52(0) = 0$

At $(0, 1200)$: $P = 50(0) + 52(1200) = 62,400$

At $\left(\frac{4000}{7}, \frac{6000}{7}\right)$: $P = 50\left(\frac{4000}{7}\right) + 52\left(\frac{6000}{7}\right) \approx 73,142.86$

At $(1000, 500)$: $P = 50(1000) + 52(500) = 76,000$

At $(1250, 0)$: $P = 50(1250) + 52(0) = 62,500$

The maximum profit ($76,000) occurs when 1000 units of Model A and 500 units of Model B are produced.

47. Objective function: $z = 2.5x + y$

Constraints: $x \geq 0, y \geq 0, 3x + 5y \leq 15, 5x + 2y \leq 10$

At $(0, 0)$: $z = 0$

At $(2, 0)$: $z = 5$

At $\left(\frac{20}{19}, \frac{45}{19}\right)$: $z = \frac{95}{19} = 5$

At $(0, 3)$: $z = 3$

z is the maximum at any point on the line $5x + 2y = 10$ between the points $(2, 0)$ and $\left(\frac{20}{19}, \frac{45}{19}\right)$.

49. Objective function: $z = -x + 2y$

Constraints: $x \geq 0, y \geq 0, x \leq 10, x + y \leq 7$

At $(0, 0)$: $z = -0 + 2(0) = \quad 0$

At $(0, 7)$: $z = -0 + 2(7) = \quad 14$

At $(7, 0)$: $z = -7 + 2(0) = -7$

The constraint $x \leq 10$ is extraneous.
The maximum value of 14 occurs at $(0, 7)$.

51. Objective function: $z = 3x + 4y$

Constraints: $x \geq 0, y \geq 0, x + y \leq 1, 2x + y \leq 4$
The constraint $2x + y \leq 4$ is extraneous.
The maximum value of $z = 4$ occurs at $(0, 1)$.

53. Constraints: $x \geq 0, y \geq 0, x + 3y \leq 15, 4x + y \leq 16$

Vertex	Value of $z = 3x + ty$
$(0, 0)$	$z = 0$
$(0, 5)$	$z = 5t$
$(3, 4)$	$z = 9 + 4t$
$(4, 0)$	$z = 12$

(a) For the maximum value to be at $(0, 5)$, $z = 5t$ must be greater than

$z = 9 + 4t$ and $z = 12$.

$5t > 9 + 4t$ and $5t > 12$

$t > 9$ $\qquad\qquad t > \frac{12}{5}$

Thus, $t > 9$.

(b) For the maximum value to be at $(3, 4)$, $z = 9 + 4t$ must be greater than $z = 5t$ and $z = 12$.

$9 + 4t > 5t$ and $9 + 4t > 12$

$9 > t$ $\qquad\qquad t > 3$

$\qquad\qquad\qquad t > \frac{3}{4}$

Thus, $\frac{3}{4} < t < 9$.

55. $\dfrac{\dfrac{9}{x}}{\left(\dfrac{6}{x}+2\right)} = \dfrac{\dfrac{9}{x}}{\dfrac{6+2x}{x}} = \dfrac{9}{x} \cdot \dfrac{x}{2(3+x)} = \dfrac{9}{2(3+x)} = \dfrac{9}{2(x+3)}, x \neq 0$

57. $\dfrac{\left(\dfrac{4}{x^2-9}+\dfrac{2}{x-2}\right)}{\left(\dfrac{1}{x+3}+\dfrac{1}{x-3}\right)} = \dfrac{\dfrac{4(x-2)+2(x^2-9)}{(x-2)(x^2-9)}}{\dfrac{(x-3)+(x+3)}{x^2-9}}$

$\qquad = \dfrac{2x^2+4x-26}{(x-2)(x^2-9)} \cdot \dfrac{x^2-9}{2x}$

$\qquad = \dfrac{2(x^2+2x-13)}{(x-2)(2x)}$

$\qquad = \dfrac{x^2+2x-13}{x(x-2)}, x \neq \pm 3$

❑ Review Exercises for Chapter 8

Solutions to Odd-Numbered Exercises

1. $x + y = 2 \implies \qquad\qquad y = 2 - x$
$x - y = 0 \implies x - (2 - x) = 0$
$\qquad\qquad\qquad 2x - 2 = 0$
$\qquad\qquad\qquad\qquad x = 1$
$\qquad\qquad\qquad\qquad y = 2 - 1 = 1$

Solution: $(1, 1)$

3. $x^2 - y^2 = 9$
$x - y = 1 \implies \quad x = y + 1$
$\qquad\qquad (y + 1)^2 - y^2 = 9$
$\qquad\qquad\qquad 2y + 1 = 9$
$\qquad\qquad\qquad\qquad y = 4$
$\qquad\qquad\qquad\qquad x = 5$

Solution: $(5, 4)$

5. $y = 2x^2$
$y = x^4 - 2x^2 \implies 2x^2 = x^4 - 2x^2$
$\qquad\qquad\qquad\quad 0 = x^4 - 4x^2$
$\qquad\qquad\qquad\quad 0 = x^2(x^2 - 4)$
$\qquad\qquad\qquad\quad 0 = x^2(x + 2)(x - 2)$
$\qquad\qquad\qquad\quad x = 0, x = -2, x = 2$
$\qquad\qquad\qquad\quad y = 0, y = 8, y = 8$

Solutions: $(0, 0), (-2, 8), (2, 8)$

7. $y^2 - 2y + x = 0 \implies (y - 1)^2 = 1 - x \implies y = 1 \pm \sqrt{1 - x}$
$\qquad x + y = 0 \implies \qquad\qquad y = -x$

Points of intersection: $(0, 0)$ and $(-3, 3)$

9. $y = 2(6 - x)$

$y = 2^{x-2}$

Point of intersection: $(4, 4)$

11. $2x - y = 2 \implies 16x - 8y = 16$

$\underline{6x + 8y = 39 \implies 6x + 8y = 39}$

$22x = 55$

$x = \frac{55}{22} = \frac{5}{2}$

$y = 3$

Solution: $\left(\frac{5}{2}, 3\right)$

13. $0.2x + 0.3y = 0.14 \implies 20x + 30y = 14 \implies 20x + 30y = 14$

$0.4x + 0.5y = 0.20 \implies 4x + 5y = 2 \implies \underline{-20x - 25y = -10}$

$5y = 4$

$y = \frac{4}{5}$

$x = -\frac{1}{2}$

Solution: $\left(-\frac{1}{2}, \frac{4}{5}\right)$ or $(-0.5, 0.8)$

15. $3x - 2y = 0 \implies 3x - 2y = 0$

$3x + 2(y + 5) = 10 \implies \underline{3x + 2y = 0}$

$6x = 0$

$x = 0$

$y = 0$

Solution: $(0, 0)$

17. $1.25x - 2y = 3.5 \implies 5x - 8y = 14$

$5x - 8y = 14 \implies \underline{-5x + 8y = -14}$

$0 = 0$

Infinite solutions

Let $y = a$, then $5x - 8a = 14 \implies x = \frac{14}{5} + \frac{8}{5}a$.

Solution: $\left(\frac{14}{5} + \frac{8}{5}a, a\right)$

19. There are infinite linear systems with the solution $\left(\frac{4}{3}, 3\right)$. One possible solution is:

$3\left(\frac{4}{3}\right) + 3 = 7 \implies 3x + y = 7$

$-6\left(\frac{4}{3}\right) + 3(3) = 1 \implies -6x + 3y = 1$

21. Revenue $= 4.95x$

Cost $= 2.85x + 10,000$

Break even when Revenue = Cost

$4.95x = 2.85x + 10,000$

$2.10x = 10,000$

$x \approx 4762$ units

23. Let $x =$ speed of the slower plane.

Let $y =$ speed of the faster plane.

Then, distance of first plane + distance of second plane = 275 miles.

(rate of first plane)(time) + (rate of second plane)(time) = 275 miles

$x\left(\frac{40}{60}\right) + y\left(\frac{40}{60}\right) = 275$

$y = x + 25$

$\frac{2}{3}x + \frac{2}{3}(x + 25) = 275$

$4x + 50 = 825$

$4x = 775$

$x = 193.75$ mph

$y = x + 25 = 218.75$ mph

25.   Demand = Supply

$$37 - 0.0002x = 22 + 0.00001x$$

$$15 = 0.00021x$$

$$x = \frac{500,000}{7}$$

Point of equilibrium: $p = \frac{159}{7}$

$$\left(\frac{500,000}{7}, \frac{159}{7}\right)$$

27.

$$\begin{array}{rcr} x + 3y - z &=& 13 \\ 2x - 5z &=& 23 \\ 4x - y - 2z &=& 14 \end{array}$$

$$\begin{array}{rcr} x + 3y - z &=& 13 \\ - 6y - 3z &=& -3 \\ - 13y + 2z &=& -38 \end{array}$$

$$\begin{array}{rcr} x + 3y - z &=& 13 \\ - 6y - 3z &=& -3 \\ \frac{17}{2}z &=& -\frac{63}{2} \end{array}$$

$$\frac{17}{2}z = -\frac{63}{2} \implies z = -\frac{63}{17}$$

$$-6y - 3\left(-\frac{63}{17}\right) = -3 \implies y = \frac{40}{17}$$

$$x + 3\left(\frac{40}{17}\right) - \left(-\frac{63}{17}\right) = 13 \implies x = \frac{38}{17}$$

Solution: $\left(\frac{38}{17}, \frac{40}{17}, -\frac{63}{17}\right)$

29.

$$\begin{array}{rcr} x - 2y + z &=& -6 \\ 2x - 3y &=& -7 \\ -x + 3y - 3z &=& 11 \end{array}$$

$$\begin{array}{rcll} x - 2y + z &=& -6 & \\ y - 2z &=& 5 & -2\text{Eq.1} + \text{Eq.2} \\ y - 2z &=& 5 & \text{Eq.1} + \text{Eq.3} \end{array}$$

$$\begin{array}{rcll} x - 2y + z &=& -6 & \\ y - 2z &=& 5 & \\ 0 &=& 0 & -\text{Eq.2} + \text{Eq.3} \end{array}$$

Let $z = a$, then $y = 2a + 5$.

$$x - 2(2a + 5) + a = -6$$

$$x - 3a - 10 = -6$$

$$x = 3a + 4$$

Solution: $(3a + 4, 2a + 5, a)$ where a is any real number.

31.   There are an infinite number of linear systems with the solution $(4, -1, 3)$. One possible system is as follows:

$$2(4) + (-1) - 2(3) = 1 \implies 2x + y - 2z = 1$$

$$(4) + (-1) - (3) = 0 \implies x + y - z = 0$$

$$2(4) - 3(-1) - 2(3) = 5 \implies 2x - 3y - 2z = 5$$

33. $y = ax^2 + bx + c$ through $(0, -5)$, $(1, -2)$, and $(2, 5)$

$$\begin{array}{rcll} (0, -5): -5 &=& + c & \\ (1, -2): -2 &=& a + b + c & \implies a + b = 3 \\ (2, 5): 5 &=& 4a + 2b + c & \implies 2a + b = 5 \end{array}$$

$$\begin{array}{rcr} 2a + b &=& 5 \\ -a - b &=& -3 \\ \hline a &=& 2 \end{array}$$

$$b = 1$$

The equation of the parabola is $y = 2x^2 + x - 5$.

35. x = amount invested at 7%

y = amount invested at 9%

z = amount invested at 11%

$$\begin{aligned}
x + y + z &= 20{,}000 \\
0.07x + 0.09y + 0.11z &= 1780 \\
x - y &= 3000 \\
x - z &= 1000
\end{aligned}$$

Solution: $x = \$8000$, $y = \$5000$, $z = \$7000$

37. $\dfrac{4 - x}{x^2 + 6x + 8} = \dfrac{A}{x + 2} + \dfrac{B}{x + 4}$

$4 - x = A(x + 4) + B(x + 2)$

Let $x = -2$: $6 = 2A \implies A = 3$

Let $x = -4$: $8 = -2B \implies B = -4$

$\dfrac{4 - x}{x^2 + 6x + 8} = \dfrac{3}{x + 2} - \dfrac{4}{x + 4}$

39. $\dfrac{x^2}{x^2 + 2x - 15} = 1 - \dfrac{2x - 15}{x^2 + 2x - 15} = 1 + \dfrac{A}{x + 5} + \dfrac{B}{x - 3}$

$-2x + 15 = A(x - 3) + B(x + 5)$

Let $x = -5$: $25 = -8A \implies A = -\dfrac{25}{8}$

Let $x = 3$: $9 = 8B \implies B = \dfrac{9}{8}$

$\dfrac{x^2}{x^2 + 2x - 15} = 1 + \dfrac{9}{8(x - 3)} - \dfrac{25}{8(x + 5)}$

41. $\dfrac{x^2 + 2x}{x^3 - x^2 + x - 1} = \dfrac{A}{x - 1} + \dfrac{Bx + C}{x^2 + 1}$

$x^2 + 2x = A(x^2 + 1) + (Bx + C)(x - 1)$

Let $x = 1$: $3 = 2A \implies A = \dfrac{3}{2}$

Let $x = 0$: $0 = A - C \implies C = \dfrac{3}{2}$

Let $x = 2$: $8 = 5A + 2B + C$

$8 = \left(\dfrac{15}{2}\right) + 2B + \left(\dfrac{3}{2}\right) \implies B = -\dfrac{1}{2}$

$\dfrac{x^2 + 2x}{x^3 - x^2 + x - 1} = \dfrac{3/2}{x - 1} + \dfrac{-(1/2)x + 3/2}{x^2 + 1} = \dfrac{1}{2}\left(\dfrac{3}{x - 1} - \dfrac{x - 3}{x^2 + 1}\right)$

43. $x + 2y \le 160$

$3x + y \le 180$

$x \ge 0$

$y \ge 0$

Vertex A	Vertex B	Vertex C	Vertex D	Vertex E	Vertex F
$x + 2y = 160$	$x + 2y = 160$	$3x + y = 180$	$x = 0$	$x + 2y = 160$	$3x + y = 180$
$3x + y = 180$	$x = 0$	$y = 0$	$y = 0$	$y = 0$	$x = 0$
$(40, 60)$	$(0, 80)$	$(60, 0)$	$(0, 0)$	$(160, 0)$	$(0, 180)$
				Outside the region	Outside the region

45. $3x + 2y \geq 24$

$x + 2y \geq 12$

$2 \leq x \leq 15$

$y \leq 15$

Vertex A	*Vertex B*	*Vertex C*
$3x + 2y = 24$	$3x + 2y = 24$	$3x + 2y = 24$
$x + 2y = 12$	$x = 2$	$x = 15$
$(6, 3)$	$(2, 9)$	$\left(15, -\frac{21}{2}\right)$
		Outside the region

Vertex D	*Vertex E*
$3x + 2y = 24$	$x + 2y = 12$
$y = 15$	$x = 2$
$(-2, 15)$	$(2, 5)$
Outside the region	Outside the region

Vertex F	*Vertex G*	*Vertex H*	*Vertex I*
$x + 2y = 12$	$x + 2y = 12$	$x = 2$	$x = 15$
$x = 15$	$y = 15$	$y = 15$	$y = 15$
$\left(15, -\frac{3}{2}\right)$	$(-18, 15)$	$(2, 15)$	$(15, 15)$
	Outside the region		

47. $y < x + 1$

$y > x^2 - 1$

Vertices:

$x + 1 = x^2 - 1$

$\quad 0 = x^2 - x - 2 = (x + 1)(x - 2)$

$x = -1 \quad$ or $\quad x = 2$

$y = 0 \qquad\quad y = 3$

$(-1, 0) \qquad (2, 3)$

49. $2x - 3y \geq 0$

$2x - y \leq 8$

$y \geq 0$

Vertex A	*Vertex B*	*Vertex C*
$2x - 3y = 0$	$2x - 3y = 0$	$2x - y = 8$
$2x - y = 8$	$y = 0$	$y = 0$
$(6, 4)$	$(0, 0)$	$(4, 0)$

51

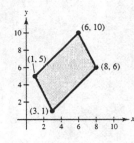

Line through $(1, 5), (3, 1)$: $2x + y = 7$

Line through $(1, 5), (6, 10)$: $-x + y = 4$

Line through $(6, 10), (8, 6)$: $2x + y = 22$

Line through $(8, 6), (3, 1)$: $-x + y = -2$

System of inequalities:

$$-x + y \le 4$$
$$2x + y \le 22$$
$$-x + y \ge -2$$
$$2x + y \ge 7$$

53. Let $x =$ the number of bushels for Harrisburg, and $y =$ the number of bushels for Philadelphia.

$$x \ge 400$$
$$y \ge 600$$
$$x + y \le 1500$$

55.   Demand = Supply

$$160 - 0.001x = 70 + 0.002x$$
$$90 = 0.003x$$
$$x = 300,000 \text{ units}$$
$$p = \$130$$

Point of equilibrium: $(300,000, 130)$

Consumer surplus: $\frac{1}{2}(300,000)(30) = \$4,500,000$

Producer surplus: $\frac{1}{2}(300,000)(60) = \$9,000,000$

57. Maximize $z = 3x + 4y$ subject to the following constraints.

$$x \ge 0$$
$$y \ge 0$$
$$2x + 5y \le 50$$
$$4x + y \le 28$$

Vertex	Value of $z = 3x + 4y$
$(0, 0)$	$z = 0$
$(0, 10)$	$x = 40$
$(5, 8)$	$z = 47$, maximum value
$(7, 0)$	$z = 21$

59. Minimize $z = 1.75x + 2.25y$ subject to the following constraints.

$$2x + y \geq 25$$
$$3x + 2y \geq 45$$
$$x \geq 0$$
$$y \geq 0$$

Vertex	Value of $z = 1.75x + 2.25y$
$(0, 25)$	$z = 56.25$
$(5, 15)$	$z = 42.5$
$(15, 0)$	$z = 26.25$, minimum value

61. Let $x =$ number of haircuts.

Let $y =$ number of perms.

Maximize $R = 17x + 60y$ subject to the following constraints.

$$x \geq 0$$
$$y \geq 0$$
$$\left(\tfrac{20}{60}\right)x + \left(\tfrac{70}{60}\right)y \leq 24 \implies 2x + 7y \leq 144$$

Vertex	Value of $R = 17x + 60y$
$(0, 0)$	$R = 0$
$(72, 0)$	$R = 1224$
$\left(0, \tfrac{144}{7}\right)$	$R \approx 1234.29$, maximum value

The revenue is maximum when $y = \frac{144}{7} \approx 20$ perms. (Round down since the student cannot work more than 24 hours. Note: Since we rounded down, the student would have enough time left to do 2 haircuts.)

63. Let $x =$ the number of bags of Brand X, and $y =$ the number of bags of Brand Y.

Objective function: Minimize $C = 15x + 30y$.

Constraints: $8x + 2y \geq 16$

$$x + y \geq 5$$
$$2x + 7y \geq 20$$
$$x \geq 0, y \geq 0$$

Vertex	Value of $C = 15x + 30y$
$(0, 8)$	$C = 15(0) + 30(8) = 240$
$(1, 4)$	$C = 15(1) + 30(4) = 135$
$(3, 2)$	$C = 15(3) + 30(2) = 105$, minimum value
$(10, 0)$	$C = 15(10) + 30(0) = 150$

To minimize cost, use three bags of Brand X and two bags of Brand Y. The cost per bag is $\frac{105}{5} = \$21$.

65. You want the equations to be multiples of each other. Multiply Equation 1 by $\frac{2}{3}$.

$$2x - \tfrac{10}{3}y = \tfrac{16}{3} \implies k_1 = -\tfrac{10}{3}, \ k_2 = \tfrac{16}{3}$$
$$2x + k_1 y = k_2$$

❏ Chapter Test for Chapter 8

1. $x - y = 4$
$3x + 2y = 2$

Solve the first equation for x.
$x = y + 4$
Substitute into the second equation.
$3(y + 4) + 2y = 2$
$3y + 12 + 2y = 2$
$\quad\quad\quad 5y = -10$
$\quad\quad\quad\quad y = -2$
Substitute y back into rewritten first equation.
$x = -2 + 4 = 2$

Solution: $(2, -2)$

2. $y = x - 1$
$y = (x - 1)^3$

Substitute the first equation into the second equation.
$x - 1 = (x - 1)^3$
$x - 1 = x^3 - 3x^2 + 3x - 1$
$\quad\quad 0 = x^3 - 3x^2 + 2x$
$\quad\quad 0 = x(x - 2)(x - 1)$
$\quad\quad x = 0, 2, 1$
Substitute each of these values into the first equation.
$x = 0$: $y = 0 - 1 = -1$
$x = 2$: $y = 2 - 1 = 1$
$x = 1$: $y = 1 - 1 = 0$
Solutions: $(0, -1)$, $(2, 1)$, $(1, 0)$

3. $2x - y^2 = 0$
$x - y = 4$

Solve the second equation for x.
$x = y + 4$
Substitute into the first equation.
$2(y + 4) - y^2 = 0$
$-y^2 + 2y + 8 = 0$
$y^2 - 2y - 8 = 0$
$(y - 4)(y + 2) = 0$
$\quad\quad\quad\quad y = 4, -2$
Substitute each of these values into the rewritten second equation.
$y = \quad 4$: $x = 4 + 4 = 8$
$y = -2$: $x = -2 + 4 = 2$
Solutions: $(8, 4)$, $(2, -2)$

4. $2x - 3y = 0$
$2x + 3y = 12$ $\Rightarrow$ $\begin{array}{l} y = \frac{2}{3}x \\ y = -\frac{2}{3}x + 4 \end{array}$

Solution: $(3, 2)$

5. $y = 9 - x^2$
$y = x + 3$

Solutions: $(-3, 0)$, $(2, 5)$

6. $y = \log_3 x$
$y = -\frac{1}{3}x + 2$

Solution: $(3, 1)$

7.
$\begin{array}{r} 2x + 3y = 17 \\ 5x - 4y = -15 \end{array}$

$\begin{array}{r} 8x + 12y = 68 \\ 15x - 12y = -45 \\ \hline 23x \quad\quad = 23 \\ x = 1 \end{array}$

$2(1) + 3y = 17$
$\quad\quad\quad 3y = 15$
$\quad\quad\quad\ y = 5$

Solution: $(1, 5)$

8. $x - 2y + 3z = 11$
$2x \quad\quad - z = 3$
$\quad\quad 3y + z = -8$
Add -2 times the first equation to the second equation.
$x - 2y + 3z = 11$
$\quad\quad 4y - 7z = -19$
$\quad\quad 3y + z = -8$
Add -3 times the second equation to 4 times the third equation.
$x - 2y + 3z = 11$
$\quad\quad 4y - 7z = -19$
$\quad\quad\quad\quad 25z = 25$
Solve for each variable.
$z = 1 \quad 4y - 7(1) = -19$
$\quad\quad\quad\quad\quad\quad\ y = -3$
$x - 2(-3) + 3(1) = 11$
$\quad\quad\quad\quad\quad\quad x = 2$
Solution: $(2, -3, 1)$

9. Using the equations: $ax + by = c$
$\quad\quad\quad\quad\quad\quad dx + ey = f$
choose values for the coefficients a, b, d, and e. Substitute $\frac{4}{3}$ for x and -5 for y and solve for c and f. Use the values for a, b, c, d, e, and f for the system of linear equations. Answers will vary.

10. $(0, 6)$: $6 = a(0)^2 + b(0) + c$
          $6 = c$
   $(-2, 2)$: $2 = a(-2)^2 + b(-2) + c$
          $2 = 4a - 2b + c$
   $\left(3, \frac{9}{2}\right)$: $\frac{9}{2} = a(3)^2 + b(3) + c$
          $9 = 18a + 6b + 2c$

   $4a - 2b + c = 2$
  $18a + 6b + 2c = 9$
          $c = 6$

Add 9 times the first equation to -2 times the second equation.

$4a - 2b + c = 2$
$ -30b + 5c = 0$
$ c = 6$

Solve for b and a.

$-30b + 5(6) = 0$ $4a - 2(1) + 6 = 2$
     $b = 1$ $a = -\frac{1}{2}$

Parabola: $y = -\frac{1}{2}x^2 + x + 6$

13. The line connecting the points $(0, 15)$ and $(9, 12)$:

$$y - 15 = \frac{15 - 12}{0 - 9}(x - 0)$$

$$y = -\frac{1}{3}x + 15$$

The line connecting the points $(9, 12)$ and $(12, 5)$:

$$y - 12 = \frac{12 - 5}{9 - 12}(x - 9)$$

$$y = -\frac{7}{3}x + 33$$

The line connecting the points $(12, 5)$ and $(12, 0)$:

$x = 12$

Set of inequalities to describe the region:

$y \le -\frac{1}{3}x + 15$

$y \le -\frac{7}{3}x + 33$

$y \ge 0$

$x \ge 0$

$x \le 12$

11. $2x + y \le 4$ $y \le -2x + 4$
$2x - y \ge 0$ $\Rightarrow$ $y \le 2x$
    $x \ge 0$ $x \ge 0$

12. $y < -x^4 + x^2 + 4$
    $y > 4x$

14. Begin by graphing the constraints.

      $x \ge 0$
      $y \ge 0$
   $x + 4y \le 3$
  $3x + 2y \le 36$

Vertex	Value of Objective Function
$(0, 0)$	$z = 20(0) + 12(0) = 0$
$(0, 8)$	$z = 20(0) + 12(8) = 96$
$(8, 6)$	$z = 20(8) + 12(6) = 232$
$(12, 0)$	$z = 20(12) + 12(0) = 240$

At $(12, 0)$ the maximum value of the objective function is 240.

15. Let x be the number of \$275 models. Let y be the number of \$400 models. The total monthly demand will not exceed 300 units: $x + y \le 300$. The amount invested is no more than \$100,000 in inventory: $275x + 400y \le 100,000$. x and y must be non-negative numbers: $x \ge 0$, $y \ge 0$. The objective function that will maximize profit is $z = 55x + 75y$.

Graph the constraints: $x + y \le 300$
            $275x + 400y \le 100,000$
                     $x \ge 0$
                     $y \ge 0$

Vertex	Value of the Objective Function
$(0, 0)$	$z = 55(0) + 75(0) = 0$
$(0, 250)$	$z = 55(0) + 75(250) = 18{,}750$
$(160, 140)$	$z = 55(160) + 75(140) = 19{,}300$
$(300, 0)$	$z = 55(300) + 75(0) = 16{,}500$

A maximum profit is obtained when 160 units of the \$275 model and 140 units of the \$400 model are stocked.

❏ Practice Test for Chapter 8

For Exercises 1–3, solve the given system by the method of substitution.

1. $x + y = 1$

   $3x - y = 15$

2. $x - 3y = -3$

   $x^2 + 6y = 5$

3. $x + y + z = 6$

   $2x - y + 3z = 0$

   $5x + 2y - z = -3$

4. Find the two numbers whose sum is 110 and product is 2800.

5. Find the dimensions of a rectangle if its perimeter is 170 feet and its area is 2800 square feet.

For Exercises 6–7, solve the linear system by elimination.

6. $2x + 15y = 4$

   $x - 3y = 23$

7. $x + y = 2$

   $38x - 19y = 7$

8. Use a graphing utility to graph the two equations. Use the graph to approximate the solution of the system. Verify your answer analytically.

   $0.4x + 0.5y = 0.112$

   $0.3x - 0.7y = -0.131$

9. Herbert invests $17,000 in two funds that pay 11% and 13% simple interest, respectively. If he receives $2080 in yearly interest, how much is invested in each fund?

10. Find the least squares regression line for the points $(4, 3)$, $(1, 1)$, $(-1, -2)$, and $(-2, -1)$.

For Exercises 11–13, solve the system of equations.

11. $\begin{aligned} x + y \qquad\;\; &= -2 \\ 2x - y + z &= 11 \\ 4y - 3z &= -20 \end{aligned}$

12. $\begin{aligned} 4x - y + 5z &= 4 \\ 2x + y - z &= 0 \\ 2x + 4y + 8z &= 0 \end{aligned}$

13. $\begin{aligned} 3x + 2y - z &= 5 \\ 6x - y + 5z &= 2 \end{aligned}$

14. Find the equation of the parabola $y = ax^2 + bx + c$ passing through the points $(0, -1)$, $(1, 4)$ and $(2, 13)$.

15. Find the position equation $s = \frac{1}{2}at^2 + v_0 t + s_0$ given that $s = 12$ feet after 1 second, $s = 5$ feet after 2 seconds, and $s = 4$ after 3 seconds.

16. Graph $x^2 + y^2 \geq 9$.

17. Graph the solution of the system.

$$x + y \leq 6$$
$$x \geq 2$$
$$y \geq 0$$

18. Derive a set of inequalities to describe the triangle with vertices $(0, 0)$, $(0, 7)$, and $(2, 3)$.

19. Find the maximum value of the objective function, $z = 30z + 26y$, subject to the following constraints.

$$x \geq 0$$
$$y \geq 0$$
$$2x + 3y \leq 21$$
$$5x + 3y \leq 30$$

20. Graph the system of inequalities.

$$x^2 + y^2 \leq 4$$
$$(x - 2)^2 + y^2 \geq 4$$

CHAPTER 9
Matrices and Determinants

CHAPTER 9
Matrices and Determinants

Section 9.1   Matrices and Systems of Equations

- You should be able to use elementary row operations to produce a row-echelon form (or reduced row-echelon form) of a matrix.

  1. Interchange two rows

  2. Multiply a row by a nonzero constant

  3. Add a multiple of one row to another row

- You should be able to use either Gaussian elimination with back-substitution or Gauss-Jordan elimination to solve a system of linear equations.

Solutions to Odd-Numbered Exercises

1. Since the matrix has three rows and two columns, its order is 3×2.

3. Since the matrix has three rows and one column, its order is 3×1.

5. Since the matrix has two rows and two columns, its order is 2×2.

7. $4x - 3y = -5$
$-x + 3y = 12$

$$\begin{bmatrix} 4 & -3 & \vdots & -5 \\ -1 & 3 & \vdots & 12 \end{bmatrix}$$

9. $x + 10y - 2z = 2$
$5x - 3y + 4z = 0$
$2x + y = 6$

$$\begin{bmatrix} 1 & 10 & -2 & \vdots & 2 \\ 5 & -3 & 4 & \vdots & 0 \\ 2 & 1 & 0 & \vdots & 6 \end{bmatrix}$$

11. $$\begin{bmatrix} 1 & 2 & \vdots & 7 \\ 2 & -3 & \vdots & 4 \end{bmatrix}$$

$x + 2y = 7$
$2x - 3y = 4$

13. $$\begin{bmatrix} 2 & 0 & 5 & \vdots & -12 \\ 0 & 1 & -2 & \vdots & 7 \\ 6 & 3 & 0 & \vdots & 2 \end{bmatrix}$$

$2x + 5z = -12$
$y - 2z = 7$
$6x + 3y = 2$

15. $$\begin{bmatrix} 1 & 0 & 0 & 0 \\ 0 & 1 & 1 & 5 \\ 0 & 0 & 0 & 0 \end{bmatrix}$$

This matrix is in reduced row-echelon form.

17. $$\begin{bmatrix} 2 & 0 & 4 & 0 \\ 0 & -1 & 3 & 6 \\ 0 & 0 & 1 & 5 \end{bmatrix}$$

The first nonzero entries in rows one and two are not one. The matrix is not in row-echelon form.

19. $$\begin{bmatrix} 1 & 4 & 3 \\ 2 & 10 & 5 \end{bmatrix}$$

$-2R_1 + R_2 \rightarrow \begin{bmatrix} 1 & 4 & 3 \\ 0 & \boxed{2} & -1 \end{bmatrix}$

21.
$$\begin{bmatrix} 1 & 1 & 4 & -1 \\ 3 & 8 & 10 & 3 \\ -2 & 1 & 12 & 6 \end{bmatrix}$$

$$\begin{matrix} \\ -3R_1 + R_2 \rightarrow \\ 2R_1 + R_3 \rightarrow \end{matrix} \begin{bmatrix} 1 & 1 & 4 & -1 \\ 0 & 5 & \boxed{-2} & \boxed{6} \\ 0 & 3 & \boxed{20} & \boxed{4} \end{bmatrix}$$

$$\begin{matrix} \\ \tfrac{1}{5}R_2 \rightarrow \\ \\ \end{matrix} \begin{bmatrix} 1 & 1 & 4 & -1 \\ 0 & 1 & \boxed{-\tfrac{2}{5}} & \boxed{\tfrac{6}{5}} \\ 0 & 3 & \boxed{20} & \boxed{4} \end{bmatrix}$$

23. $\begin{bmatrix} 1 & 2 & 3 \\ 2 & -1 & -4 \\ 3 & 1 & -1 \end{bmatrix}$

(a) $\begin{bmatrix} 1 & 2 & 3 \\ 0 & -5 & -10 \\ 3 & 1 & -1 \end{bmatrix}$ (b) $\begin{bmatrix} 1 & 2 & 3 \\ 0 & -5 & -10 \\ 0 & -5 & -10 \end{bmatrix}$ (c) $\begin{bmatrix} 1 & 2 & 3 \\ 0 & -5 & -10 \\ 0 & 0 & 0 \end{bmatrix}$

(d) $\begin{bmatrix} 1 & 2 & 3 \\ 0 & 1 & 2 \\ 0 & 0 & 0 \end{bmatrix}$ (e) $\begin{bmatrix} 1 & 0 & -1 \\ 0 & 1 & 2 \\ 0 & 0 & 0 \end{bmatrix}$ This matrix is in reduced row-echelon form.

25.
$$\begin{bmatrix} 1 & 1 & 0 & 5 \\ -2 & -1 & 2 & -10 \\ 3 & 6 & 7 & 14 \end{bmatrix}$$

$$\begin{matrix} \\ 2R_1 + R_2 \rightarrow \\ 3R_1 + R_3 \rightarrow \end{matrix} \begin{bmatrix} 1 & 1 & 0 & 5 \\ 0 & 1 & 2 & 0 \\ 0 & 3 & 7 & -1 \end{bmatrix}$$

$$\begin{matrix} \\ -3R_2 + R_3 \rightarrow \\ \\ \end{matrix} \begin{bmatrix} 1 & 1 & 0 & 5 \\ 0 & 1 & 2 & 0 \\ 0 & 0 & 1 & -1 \end{bmatrix}$$

27.
$$\begin{bmatrix} 1 & -1 & -1 & 1 \\ 5 & -4 & 1 & 8 \\ -6 & 8 & 18 & 0 \end{bmatrix}$$

$$\begin{matrix} \\ -5R_1 + R_2 \rightarrow \\ 6R_1 + R_3 \rightarrow \end{matrix} \begin{bmatrix} 1 & -1 & -1 & 1 \\ 0 & 1 & 6 & 3 \\ 0 & 2 & 12 & 6 \end{bmatrix}$$

$$\begin{matrix} \\ \\ -2R_2 + R_3 \rightarrow \end{matrix} \begin{bmatrix} 1 & -1 & -1 & 1 \\ 0 & 1 & 6 & 3 \\ 0 & 0 & 0 & 0 \end{bmatrix}$$

29. $\begin{bmatrix} 3 & 3 & 3 \\ -1 & 0 & -4 \\ 2 & 4 & -2 \end{bmatrix}$

$\frac{1}{3}R_1 \rightarrow \begin{bmatrix} 1 & 1 & 1 \\ -1 & 0 & -4 \\ 2 & 4 & -2 \end{bmatrix}$

$\begin{matrix} -R_2 + R_1 \rightarrow \\ -2R_1 + R_3 \rightarrow \end{matrix} \begin{bmatrix} 1 & 1 & 1 \\ 0 & 1 & -3 \\ 0 & 2 & -4 \end{bmatrix}$

$\begin{matrix} -R_2 + R_1 \rightarrow \\ -2R_2 + R_3 \rightarrow \end{matrix} \begin{bmatrix} 1 & 0 & 4 \\ 0 & 1 & -3 \\ 0 & 0 & 2 \end{bmatrix}$

$\frac{1}{2}R_3 \rightarrow \begin{bmatrix} 1 & 0 & 4 \\ 0 & 1 & -3 \\ 0 & 0 & 1 \end{bmatrix}$

$\begin{matrix} -4R_3 + R_1 \rightarrow \\ 3R_3 + R_2 \rightarrow \end{matrix} \begin{bmatrix} 1 & 0 & 0 \\ 0 & 1 & 0 \\ 0 & 0 & 1 \end{bmatrix}$

31. $\begin{bmatrix} 1 & 2 & 3 & -5 \\ 1 & 2 & 4 & -9 \\ -2 & -4 & -4 & 3 \\ 4 & 8 & 11 & -14 \end{bmatrix}$

$\begin{matrix} -R_1 + R_2 \rightarrow \\ 2R_1 + R_3 \rightarrow \\ -4R_1 + R_4 \rightarrow \end{matrix} \begin{bmatrix} 1 & 2 & 3 & -5 \\ 0 & 0 & 1 & -4 \\ 0 & 0 & 2 & -7 \\ 0 & 0 & -1 & 6 \end{bmatrix}$

$\begin{matrix} -3R_2 + R_1 \rightarrow \\ \\ -2R_2 + R_3 \rightarrow \\ R_2 + R_4 \rightarrow \end{matrix} \begin{bmatrix} 1 & 2 & 0 & 7 \\ 0 & 0 & 1 & -4 \\ 0 & 0 & 0 & 1 \\ 0 & 0 & 0 & 2 \end{bmatrix}$

$\begin{matrix} -7R_3 + R_1 \rightarrow \\ 4R_3 + R_2 \rightarrow \\ \\ -2R_3 + R_4 \rightarrow \end{matrix} \begin{bmatrix} 1 & 2 & 0 & 0 \\ 0 & 0 & 1 & 0 \\ 0 & 0 & 0 & 1 \\ 0 & 0 & 0 & 0 \end{bmatrix}$

33. $\quad x - 2y = 4$
$\qquad\qquad y = -3$

$x - 2(-3) = 4$
$\qquad\quad x = -2$

Answer: $(-2, -3)$

35. $\quad x - y + 2z = 4$
$\qquad\quad y - z = 2$
$\qquad\qquad\quad z = -2$

$\qquad\quad y - (-2) = 2$
$\qquad\qquad\quad y = 0$

$x - 0 + 2(-2) = 4$
$\qquad\qquad\quad x = 8$

Answer: $(8, 0, -2)$

37. $\begin{bmatrix} 1 & 0 & \vdots & 7 \\ 0 & 1 & \vdots & -5 \end{bmatrix}$

$x = 7$
$y = -5$
Answer: $(7, -5)$

39. $\begin{bmatrix} 1 & 0 & 0 & \vdots & -4 \\ 0 & 1 & 0 & \vdots & -8 \\ 0 & 0 & 1 & \vdots & 2 \end{bmatrix}$

$x = -4$
$y = -8$
$z = 2$
Answer: $(-4, -8, 2)$

41. $x + 2y = 7$

$2x + \ y = 8$

$$\begin{bmatrix} 1 & 2 & \vdots & 7 \\ 2 & 1 & \vdots & 8 \end{bmatrix}$$

$$-2R_1 + R_2 \rightarrow \begin{bmatrix} 1 & 2 & \vdots & 7 \\ 0 & -3 & \vdots & -6 \end{bmatrix}$$

$$-\tfrac{1}{3}R_2 \rightarrow \begin{bmatrix} 1 & 2 & \vdots & 7 \\ 0 & 1 & \vdots & 2 \end{bmatrix}$$

$$y = 2$$

$$x + 2(2) = 7 \implies x = 3$$

Answer: $(3, 2)$

43. $-3x + 5y = -22$

$3x + 4y = \ \ \ 4$

$4x - 8y = \ \ \ 32$

$$\begin{bmatrix} -3 & 5 & \vdots & -22 \\ 3 & 4 & \vdots & 4 \\ 4 & -8 & \vdots & 32 \end{bmatrix}$$

$$R_3 + R_1 \rightarrow \begin{bmatrix} 1 & -3 & \vdots & 10 \\ 3 & 4 & \vdots & 4 \\ 4 & -8 & \vdots & 32 \end{bmatrix}$$

$$\begin{matrix} -3R_1 + R_2 \rightarrow \\ -4R_1 + R_3 \rightarrow \end{matrix} \begin{bmatrix} 1 & -3 & \vdots & 10 \\ 0 & 13 & \vdots & -26 \\ 0 & 4 & \vdots & -8 \end{bmatrix}$$

$$\begin{matrix} \tfrac{1}{13}R_2 \rightarrow \\ -4R_2 + R_3 \rightarrow \end{matrix} \begin{bmatrix} 1 & -3 & \vdots & 10 \\ 0 & 1 & \vdots & -2 \\ 0 & 0 & \vdots & 0 \end{bmatrix}$$

$$y = -2$$

$$x - 3(-2) = 10 \implies x = \ \ 4$$

Answer: $(4, -2)$

45. $8x - 4y = 7$

$5x + 2y = 1$

$$\begin{bmatrix} 8 & -4 & \vdots & 7 \\ 5 & 2 & \vdots & 1 \end{bmatrix}$$

$$\begin{matrix} 3R_1 \rightarrow \\ 5R_2 \rightarrow \end{matrix} \begin{bmatrix} 24 & -12 & \vdots & 21 \\ 25 & 10 & \vdots & 5 \end{bmatrix}$$

$$-R_2 + R_1 \rightarrow \begin{bmatrix} -1 & -22 & \vdots & 16 \\ 25 & 10 & \vdots & 5 \end{bmatrix}$$

$$25R_1 + R_2 \rightarrow \begin{bmatrix} -1 & -22 & \vdots & 16 \\ 0 & -540 & \vdots & 405 \end{bmatrix}$$

$$\begin{matrix} -R_1 \rightarrow \\ -\tfrac{1}{540}R_2 \rightarrow \end{matrix} \begin{bmatrix} 1 & 22 & \vdots & -16 \\ 0 & 1 & \vdots & -\tfrac{3}{4} \end{bmatrix}$$

$$y = -\tfrac{3}{4}$$

$$x + 22\left(-\tfrac{3}{4}\right) = -16 \implies x = \tfrac{1}{2}$$

Answer: $\left(\tfrac{1}{2}, -\tfrac{3}{4}\right)$

47. $-x + 2y = 1.5$

$2x - 4y = 3.0$

$$\begin{bmatrix} -1 & 2 & \vdots & 1.5 \\ 2 & -4 & \vdots & 3.0 \end{bmatrix}$$

$$2R_1 + R_2 \rightarrow \begin{bmatrix} -1 & 2 & \vdots & 1.5 \\ 0 & 0 & \vdots & 6.0 \end{bmatrix}$$

The system is inconsistent and there is no solution.

49. $x \quad\quad - 3z = -2$

$3x + y - 2z = 5$

$2x + 2y + z = 4$

$$\begin{bmatrix} 1 & 0 & -3 & \vdots & -2 \\ 3 & 1 & -2 & \vdots & 5 \\ 2 & 2 & 1 & \vdots & 4 \end{bmatrix}$$

$$\begin{matrix} \\ -3R_1 + R_2 \rightarrow \\ -2R_1 + R_3 \rightarrow \end{matrix} \begin{bmatrix} 1 & 0 & -3 & \vdots & -2 \\ 0 & 1 & 7 & \vdots & 11 \\ 0 & 2 & 7 & \vdots & 8 \end{bmatrix}$$

$$\begin{matrix} \\ \\ -2R_2 + R_3 \rightarrow \end{matrix} \begin{bmatrix} 1 & 0 & -3 & \vdots & -2 \\ 0 & 1 & 7 & \vdots & 11 \\ 0 & 0 & -7 & \vdots & -14 \end{bmatrix}$$

$$\begin{matrix} \\ \\ -\frac{1}{7}R_3 \rightarrow \end{matrix} \begin{bmatrix} 1 & 0 & -3 & \vdots & -2 \\ 0 & 1 & 7 & \vdots & 11 \\ 0 & 0 & 1 & \vdots & 2 \end{bmatrix}$$

$z = 2$

$y + 7(2) = 11 \Longrightarrow y = -3$

$x - 3(2) = -2 \Longrightarrow x = 4$

Answer: $(4, -3, 2)$

51. $x + y - 5z = 3$

$x \quad\quad - 2z = 1$

$2x - y - z = 0$

$$\begin{bmatrix} 1 & 1 & -5 & \vdots & 3 \\ 1 & 0 & -2 & \vdots & 1 \\ 2 & -1 & -1 & \vdots & 0 \end{bmatrix}$$

$$\begin{matrix} \\ -R_1 + R_2 \rightarrow \\ -2R_1 + R_3 \rightarrow \end{matrix} \begin{bmatrix} 1 & 1 & -5 & \vdots & 3 \\ 0 & -1 & 3 & \vdots & -2 \\ 0 & -3 & 9 & \vdots & -6 \end{bmatrix}$$

$$\begin{matrix} \\ \\ -3R_2 + R_3 \rightarrow \end{matrix} \begin{bmatrix} 1 & 1 & -5 & \vdots & 3 \\ 0 & -1 & 3 & \vdots & -2 \\ 0 & 0 & 0 & \vdots & 0 \end{bmatrix}$$

$$\begin{matrix} R_2 + R_1 \rightarrow \\ -R_2 \rightarrow \\ \\ \end{matrix} \begin{bmatrix} 1 & 0 & -2 & \vdots & 1 \\ 0 & 1 & -3 & \vdots & 2 \\ 0 & 0 & 0 & \vdots & 0 \end{bmatrix}$$

$z = a$

$y - 3a = 2 \implies y = 3a + 2$

$x - 2a = 1 \implies x = 2a + 1$

Answer: $(2a + 1, 3a + 2, a)$

53. $x + 2y + \;z = \;8$

$\quad 3x + 7y + 6z = 26$

$$\begin{bmatrix} 1 & 2 & 1 & \vdots & 8 \\ 3 & 7 & 6 & \vdots & 26 \end{bmatrix}$$

$$-3R_1 + R_2 \rightarrow \begin{bmatrix} 1 & 2 & 1 & \vdots & 8 \\ 0 & 1 & 3 & \vdots & 2 \end{bmatrix}$$

$$-2R_2 + R_1 \rightarrow \begin{bmatrix} 1 & 0 & -5 & \vdots & 4 \\ 0 & 1 & 3 & \vdots & 2 \end{bmatrix}$$

$$z = \;a$$

$y + 3a = 2 \implies y = -3a + 2$

$x - 5a = 4 \implies x = 5a + 4$

Answer: $(5a + 4, -3a + 2, a)$

55. $\quad x + 2y = 0$

$\quad -x - \;y = 0$

$$\begin{bmatrix} 1 & 2 & \vdots & 0 \\ -1 & -1 & \vdots & 0 \end{bmatrix}$$

$$R_1 + R_2 \rightarrow \begin{bmatrix} 1 & 2 & \vdots & 0 \\ 0 & 1 & \vdots & 0 \end{bmatrix}$$

$$y = 0$$

$x + 2(0) = 0 \implies$

$$x = 0$$

Answer: $(0, 0)$

57. $3x + 3y + 12z = \;6$

$\quad\;\; x + \;\;y + \;\;4z = \;2$

$\quad 2x + 5y + 20z = 10$

$\quad -x + 2y + \;\;8z = \;4$

$z = a$

$y = -4a + 2$

$x = 0$

Answer: $(0, -4a + 2, a)$

$$\begin{bmatrix} 3 & 3 & 12 & \vdots & 6 \\ 1 & 1 & 4 & \vdots & 2 \\ 2 & 5 & 20 & \vdots & 10 \\ -1 & 2 & 8 & \vdots & 4 \end{bmatrix} \implies \begin{bmatrix} 1 & 0 & 0 & \vdots & 0 \\ 0 & 0 & 0 & \vdots & 0 \\ 0 & 1 & 4 & \vdots & 2 \\ 0 & 0 & 0 & \vdots & 0 \end{bmatrix}$$

59. $2x + y - z + 2w = -6$
$3x + 4y \quad\quad + w = 1$
$x + 5y + 2z + 6w = -3$
$5x + 2y - z - w = 3$

$$\begin{bmatrix} 2 & 1 & -1 & 2 & \vdots & -6 \\ 3 & 4 & 0 & 1 & \vdots & 1 \\ 1 & 5 & 2 & 6 & \vdots & -3 \\ 5 & 2 & -1 & -1 & \vdots & 3 \end{bmatrix} \Rightarrow \begin{bmatrix} 1 & 5 & 2 & 6 & \vdots & -3 \\ 0 & 1 & -1 & -3 & \vdots & 2 \\ 0 & 0 & 238 & 629 & \vdots & -306 \\ 0 & 0 & 0 & -71 & \vdots & 142 \end{bmatrix}$$

$x \approx 1$

$y \approx 0$

$z \approx 4$

$w \approx -2$

Answer: $(1, 0, 4\ -2)$

61. $x + y + z = 0$
$2x + 3y + z = 0$
$3x + 5y + z = 0$

$$\begin{bmatrix} 1 & 1 & 1 & \vdots & 0 \\ 2 & 3 & 1 & \vdots & 0 \\ 3 & 5 & 1 & \vdots & 0 \end{bmatrix} \Rightarrow \begin{bmatrix} 1 & 0 & 2 & \vdots & 0 \\ 0 & 1 & -1 & \vdots & 0 \\ 0 & 0 & 0 & \vdots & 0 \end{bmatrix}$$

$z = a$

$y = a$

$x = -2a$

Answer: $(-2a, a, a)$

63. $z = a$
$y = -4a + 1$
$x = -3a - 2$

One possible solution is:

$$x + y + 7z = (-3a - 2) + (-4a + 1) + 7a = -1$$
$$x + 2y + 11z = (-3a - 2) + 2(-4a + 1) + 11a = 0$$
$$2x + y + 10z = 2(-3a - 2) + (-4a + 1) + 10a = -3$$

65. $x =$ amount at 8%
$y =$ amount at 9%
$z =$ amount at 12%

$x + y + z = 1,500,000$
$0.08x + 0.09y + 0.12z = 133,000$
$x \quad\quad - 4z = 0$

$$\begin{bmatrix} 1 & 1 & 1 & \vdots & 1,500,000 \\ 0.08 & 0.09 & 0.12 & \vdots & 133,000 \\ 1 & 0 & -4 & \vdots & 0 \end{bmatrix}$$

$$\begin{matrix} \\ -0.08R_1 + R_2 \rightarrow \\ -R_1 + R_3 \rightarrow \end{matrix} \begin{bmatrix} 1 & 1 & 1 & \vdots & 1,500,000 \\ 0 & 0.01 & 0.04 & \vdots & 13,000 \\ 0 & -1 & -5 & \vdots & -1,500,000 \end{bmatrix}$$

$$\begin{matrix} \\ 100R_2 \\ R_2 + R_3 \end{matrix} \begin{bmatrix} 1 & 1 & 1 & \vdots & 1,500,000 \\ 0 & 1 & 4 & \vdots & 1,300,000 \\ 0 & 0 & -1 & \vdots & -200,000 \end{bmatrix}$$

$$-z = -200,000 \implies z = 200,000$$
$$y + 4(200,000) = 1,300,000 \implies y = 500,000$$
$$x + (500,000) + (200,000) = 1,500,000 \implies x = 800,000$$

Answer: \$800,000 at 8%, \$500,000 at 9%, \$200,000 at 12%

67. $\dfrac{4x^2}{(x+1)^2(x-1)} = \dfrac{A}{x-1} + \dfrac{B}{x+1} + \dfrac{C}{(x+1)^2}$

$4x^2 = A(x+1)^2 + B(x+1)(x-1) + C(x-1)$

Let $x = 1$: $4 = 4A \implies A = 1$

Let $x = -1$: $4 = -2C \implies C = -2$

Let $x = 0$: $0 = A - B - C \implies 0 = 1 - B - (-2)$

$\implies B = 3$

Thus, $\dfrac{4x^2}{(x+1)^2(x-1)} = \dfrac{1}{x-1} + \dfrac{3}{x+1} - \dfrac{2}{(x+1)^2}$.

69. $f(x) = ax^2 + bx + c$

$f(1) = a + b + c = 8$

$f(2) = 4a + 2b + c = 13$

$f(3) = 9a + 3b + c = 20$

$$\begin{bmatrix} 1 & 1 & 1 & \vdots & 8 \\ 4 & 2 & 1 & \vdots & 13 \\ 9 & 3 & 1 & \vdots & 20 \end{bmatrix}$$

$$\begin{matrix} \\ -4R_1 + R_2 \longrightarrow \\ -9R_1 + R_3 \longrightarrow \end{matrix} \begin{bmatrix} 1 & 1 & 1 & \vdots & 8 \\ 0 & -2 & -3 & \vdots & -19 \\ 0 & -6 & -8 & \vdots & -52 \end{bmatrix}$$

$$\begin{matrix} \\ -\tfrac{1}{2}R_2 \longrightarrow \\ -3R_2 + R_3 \longrightarrow \end{matrix} \begin{bmatrix} 1 & 1 & 1 & \vdots & 8 \\ 0 & 1 & \tfrac{3}{2} & \vdots & \tfrac{19}{2} \\ 0 & 0 & 1 & \vdots & 5 \end{bmatrix}$$

$c = 5$

$b + \tfrac{3}{2}(5) = \tfrac{19}{2} \implies b = 2$

$a + 2 + 5 = 8 \implies a = 1$

Answer: $y = x^2 + 2x + 5$

71. $f(x) = ax^3 + bx^2 + cx + d$

$f(-2) = -8a + 4b - 2c + d = 2$

$f(-1) = -a + b - c + d = -\tfrac{1}{4}$

$f(1) = a + b + c + d = -\tfrac{7}{4}$

$f(2) = 8a + 4b + 2c + d = 2$

Solving this system, you obtain

$a = \tfrac{1}{4}$, $b = 1$, $c = -1$ and $d = -2$.

Thus, $y = \tfrac{1}{4}x^3 + x^2 - x - 2$.

73. $f(x) = ax^4 + bx^3 + cx^2 + dx + e$

$f(-2) = 16a - 8b + 4c - 2d + e = 0$

$f(-1) = a - b + c - d + e = 3$

$f(0) = e = 0$

$f(1) = a + b + c + d + e = 3$

$f(2) = 16a + 8b + 4c + 2d + e = 0$

Solving this system, you obtain

$a = -1$, $b = 0$, $c = 4$, $d = e = 0$.

Thus, $y = -x^4 + 4x^2$.

75. (a) The points are $(0, 670)$, $(1, 280)$, $(2, 231)$.

If $y = at^2 + bt + c$, then:

$670 = c$

$280 = a + b + c$

$231 = 4a + 2b + c$

Solving this system, you obtain

$a = 170.5$, $b = -560.5$ and $c = 670$.

Thus, $y = 170.5t^2 - 560.5t + 670$.

(b)

(c) For 1993, $t = 3$ and $y = 523$.

77. (a) $x_1 + x_3 = 600$

$x_1 = x_2 + x_4 \implies x_1 - x_2 - x_4 = 0$

$x_2 + x_5 = 500$

$x_3 + x_6 = 600$

$x_4 + x_7 = x_6 \implies x_4 - x_6 + x_7 = 0$

$x_5 + x_7 = 500$

$$\begin{bmatrix} 1 & 0 & 1 & 0 & 0 & 0 & 0 & \vdots & 600 \\ 1 & -1 & 0 & -1 & 0 & 0 & 0 & \vdots & 0 \\ 0 & 1 & 0 & 0 & 1 & 0 & 0 & \vdots & 500 \\ 0 & 0 & 1 & 0 & 0 & 1 & 0 & \vdots & 600 \\ 0 & 0 & 0 & 1 & 0 & -1 & 1 & \vdots & 0 \\ 0 & 0 & 0 & 0 & 1 & 0 & 1 & \vdots & 500 \end{bmatrix}$$

$$\begin{matrix} \\ -R_1 + R_2 \to \\ R_2 + R_3 \to \\ R_3 + R_4 \to \\ R_4 + R_5 \to \\ -R_5 + R_6 \to \end{matrix} \begin{bmatrix} 1 & 0 & 1 & 0 & 0 & 0 & 0 & \vdots & 600 \\ 0 & -1 & -1 & -1 & 0 & 0 & 0 & \vdots & -600 \\ 0 & 0 & -1 & -1 & 1 & 0 & 0 & \vdots & -100 \\ 0 & 0 & 0 & -1 & 1 & 1 & 0 & \vdots & 500 \\ 0 & 0 & 0 & 0 & 1 & 0 & 1 & \vdots & 500 \\ 0 & 0 & 0 & 0 & 0 & 0 & 0 & \vdots & 0 \end{bmatrix}$$

$$\begin{matrix} \\ -R_3 + R_2 \to \\ -R_4 + R_3 \to \\ -R_4 \to \\ \\ \end{matrix} \begin{bmatrix} 1 & 0 & 1 & 0 & 0 & 0 & 0 & \vdots & 600 \\ 0 & -1 & 0 & 0 & -1 & 0 & 0 & \vdots & -500 \\ 0 & 0 & -1 & 0 & 0 & -1 & 0 & \vdots & -600 \\ 0 & 0 & 0 & 1 & -1 & -1 & 0 & \vdots & -500 \\ 0 & 0 & 0 & 0 & 1 & 0 & 1 & \vdots & 500 \\ 0 & 0 & 0 & 0 & 0 & 0 & 0 & \vdots & 0 \end{bmatrix}$$

Let $x_7 = t$ and $x_6 = s$, then:

$x_5 = 500 - t$

$x_4 = -500 + s + (500 - t) = s - t$

$x_3 = 600 - s$

$x_2 = 500 - (500 - t) = t$

$x_1 = 600 - (600 - s) = s$

(b) If $x_6 = x_7 = 0$, then $s = t = 0$, and

$x_1 = 0$

$x_2 = 0$

$x_3 = 600$

$x_4 = 0$

$x_5 = 500$

$x_6 = x_7 = 0$

(c) If $x_5 = 1000$ and $x_6 = 0$, then $s = 0$ and $t = -500$.

Thus, $x_1 = 0$

$x_2 = -500$

$x_3 = 600$

$x_4 = 500$

$x_5 = 1000$

$x_6 = 0$

$x_7 = -500$

79. (a) $200 + x_2 = x_1 \implies -x_1 - x_2 = 200$

$x_2 + 100 = x_4 \implies -x_2 + x_4 = 100$

$x_4 + 200 = x_3 \implies x_3 - x_4 = 200$

$x_1 + 100 = x_3 \implies x_1 - x_3 = -100$

Solving this system, you obtain:

$x_1 = 100 + t$

$x_2 = -100 + t$

$x_3 = 200 + t$

$x_4 = t$

(b) If $x_4 = 0$, then $t = 0$ and

$x_1 = 100, x_2 = -100, x_3 = 200.$

(c) f $x_4 = 100$, then $t = 100$ and $x_1 = 200, x_2 = 0,$

$x_3 = 300.$

81. For the year 2002, $t = 22$ and

$s = 1.279 - 0.0049(20) = 1.1712$ minutes (Men)

$s = 1.411 - 0.0078(20) = 1.2394$ minutes (Women).

83. $f(x) = 2^{x-1}$

x	-1	0	1	2	3
y	$\frac{1}{4}$	$\frac{1}{2}$	1	2	4

85. $h(x) = \log_2(x - 1) \implies 2^y = x - 1 \implies 2^y + 1 = x$

x	$\frac{3}{2}$	2	3	5	9
y	-1	0	1	2	3

Section 9.2   Operations with Matrices

- $A = B$ if and only if they have the same order and $a_{ij} = h_{ij}$
- You should be able to perform the operations of matrix addition, scalar multiplication, and matrix multiplication.
- Some properties of matrix addition and scalar multiplication are:

    (a) $A + B = B + A$

    (b) $A + (B + C) = (A + B) + C$

    (c) $(cd)A = c(dA)$

    (d) $1A = A$

    (e) $c(A + B) = cA + cB$

    (f) $(c + d)A = cA + dA$

- Some properties of matrix multiplication are:

    (a) $A(BC) = (AB)C$

    (b) $A(B + C) = AB + AC$

    (c) $(A + B)C = AC + BC$

    (d) $c(AB) = (cA)B = A(cB)$

- You should remember that $AB \neq BA$ in general.

Solutions to Odd-Numbered Exercises

1. $x = -4$, $y = 22$

3. $2x + 1 = 5$, $3y - 5 = 4$
$$x = 2, \ y = 3$$

5. (a) $A + B = \begin{bmatrix} 1 & -1 \\ 2 & -1 \end{bmatrix} + \begin{bmatrix} 2 & -1 \\ -1 & 8 \end{bmatrix} = \begin{bmatrix} 1+2 & -1-1 \\ 2-1 & -1+8 \end{bmatrix} = \begin{bmatrix} 3 & -2 \\ 1 & 7 \end{bmatrix}$

(b) $A - B = \begin{bmatrix} 1 & -1 \\ 2 & -1 \end{bmatrix} - \begin{bmatrix} 2 & -1 \\ -1 & 8 \end{bmatrix} = \begin{bmatrix} 1-2 & -1+1 \\ 2+1 & -1-8 \end{bmatrix} = \begin{bmatrix} -1 & 0 \\ 3 & -9 \end{bmatrix}$

(c) $3A = 3\begin{bmatrix} 1 & -1 \\ 2 & -1 \end{bmatrix} = \begin{bmatrix} 3(1) & 3(-1) \\ 3(2) & 3(-1) \end{bmatrix} = \begin{bmatrix} 3 & -3 \\ 6 & -3 \end{bmatrix}$

(d) $3A - 2B = \begin{bmatrix} 3 & -3 \\ 6 & -3 \end{bmatrix} - 2\begin{bmatrix} 2 & -1 \\ -1 & 8 \end{bmatrix} = \begin{bmatrix} 3 & -3 \\ 6 & -3 \end{bmatrix} + \begin{bmatrix} -4 & 2 \\ 2 & -16 \end{bmatrix} = \begin{bmatrix} -1 & -1 \\ 8 & -19 \end{bmatrix}$

7. $A = \begin{bmatrix} 6 & -1 \\ 2 & 4 \\ -3 & 5 \end{bmatrix}$, $B = \begin{bmatrix} 1 & 4 \\ -1 & 5 \\ 1 & 10 \end{bmatrix}$

(a) $A + B = \begin{bmatrix} 7 & 3 \\ 1 & 9 \\ -2 & 15 \end{bmatrix}$ (b) $A - B = \begin{bmatrix} 5 & -5 \\ 3 & -1 \\ -4 & -5 \end{bmatrix}$ (c) $3A = \begin{bmatrix} 18 & -3 \\ 6 & 12 \\ -9 & 15 \end{bmatrix}$

(d) $3A - 2B = \begin{bmatrix} 18 & -3 \\ 6 & 12 \\ -9 & 15 \end{bmatrix} - \begin{bmatrix} 2 & 8 \\ -2 & 10 \\ 2 & 20 \end{bmatrix} = \begin{bmatrix} 16 & -11 \\ 8 & 2 \\ -11 & -5 \end{bmatrix}$

9. $A = \begin{bmatrix} 2 & 2 & -1 & 0 & 1 \\ 1 & 1 & -2 & 0 & -1 \end{bmatrix}$, $B = \begin{bmatrix} 1 & 1 & -1 & 1 & 0 \\ -3 & 4 & 9 & -6 & -7 \end{bmatrix}$

(a) $A + B = \begin{bmatrix} 3 & 3 & -2 & 1 & 1 \\ -2 & 5 & 7 & -6 & -8 \end{bmatrix}$

(b) $A - B = \begin{bmatrix} 1 & 1 & 0 & -1 & 1 \\ 4 & -3 & -11 & 6 & 6 \end{bmatrix}$

(c) $3A = \begin{bmatrix} 6 & 6 & -3 & 0 & 3 \\ 3 & 3 & -6 & 0 & -3 \end{bmatrix}$

(d) $3A - 2B = \begin{bmatrix} 6 & 6 & -3 & 0 & 3 \\ 3 & 3 & -6 & 0 & -3 \end{bmatrix} - \begin{bmatrix} 2 & 2 & -2 & 2 & 0 \\ -6 & 8 & 18 & -12 & -14 \end{bmatrix} = \begin{bmatrix} 4 & 4 & -1 & -2 & 3 \\ 9 & -5 & -24 & 12 & 11 \end{bmatrix}$

11. $X = 3\begin{bmatrix} -2 & -1 \\ 1 & 0 \\ 3 & 4 \end{bmatrix} - 2\begin{bmatrix} 0 & 3 \\ 2 & 0 \\ -4 & -1 \end{bmatrix} = \begin{bmatrix} -6 & -3 \\ 3 & 0 \\ 9 & -12 \end{bmatrix} - \begin{bmatrix} 0 & 6 \\ 4 & 0 \\ -8 & -2 \end{bmatrix} = \begin{bmatrix} -6 & -9 \\ -1 & 0 \\ 17 & -10 \end{bmatrix}$

13. $X = -\frac{3}{2}A + \frac{1}{2}B = -\frac{3}{2}\begin{bmatrix} -2 & -1 \\ 1 & 0 \\ 3 & -4 \end{bmatrix} + \frac{1}{2}\begin{bmatrix} 0 & 3 \\ 2 & 0 \\ -4 & -1 \end{bmatrix} = \begin{bmatrix} 3 & 3 \\ -\frac{1}{2} & 0 \\ -\frac{13}{2} & \frac{11}{2} \end{bmatrix}$

15. (a) $AB = \begin{bmatrix} 1 & 2 \\ 4 & 2 \end{bmatrix}\begin{bmatrix} 2 & -1 \\ -1 & 8 \end{bmatrix} = \begin{bmatrix} 2-2 & -1+16 \\ 8-2 & -4+16 \end{bmatrix} = \begin{bmatrix} 0 & 15 \\ 6 & 12 \end{bmatrix}$

(b) $BA = \begin{bmatrix} 2 & -1 \\ -1 & 8 \end{bmatrix}\begin{bmatrix} 1 & 2 \\ 4 & 2 \end{bmatrix} = \begin{bmatrix} 2-4 & 4-2 \\ -1+32 & -2+16 \end{bmatrix} = \begin{bmatrix} -2 & 2 \\ 31 & 14 \end{bmatrix}$

(c) $A^2 = \begin{bmatrix} 1 & 2 \\ 4 & 2 \end{bmatrix}\begin{bmatrix} 1 & 2 \\ 4 & 2 \end{bmatrix} = \begin{bmatrix} 1+8 & 2+4 \\ 4+8 & 8+4 \end{bmatrix} = \begin{bmatrix} 9 & 6 \\ 12 & 12 \end{bmatrix}$

17. (a) $AB = \begin{bmatrix} 3 & -1 \\ 1 & 3 \end{bmatrix}\begin{bmatrix} 1 & -3 \\ 3 & 1 \end{bmatrix} = \begin{bmatrix} 3-3 & -9-1 \\ 1+9 & -3+3 \end{bmatrix} = \begin{bmatrix} 0 & -10 \\ 10 & 0 \end{bmatrix}$

(b) $BA = \begin{bmatrix} 1 & -3 \\ 3 & 1 \end{bmatrix}\begin{bmatrix} 3 & -1 \\ 1 & 3 \end{bmatrix} = \begin{bmatrix} 3-3 & -1-9 \\ 9+1 & -3+3 \end{bmatrix} = \begin{bmatrix} 0 & -10 \\ 10 & 0 \end{bmatrix}$

(c) $A^2 = \begin{bmatrix} 3 & -1 \\ 1 & 3 \end{bmatrix}\begin{bmatrix} 3 & -1 \\ 1 & 3 \end{bmatrix} = \begin{bmatrix} 9-1 & -3-3 \\ 3=3 & -1+9 \end{bmatrix} = \begin{bmatrix} 8 & -6 \\ 6 & 8 \end{bmatrix}$

19. (a) $AB = \begin{bmatrix} 1 & -1 & 7 \\ 2 & -1 & 8 \\ 3 & 1 & -1 \end{bmatrix}\begin{bmatrix} 1 & 1 & 2 \\ 2 & 1 & 1 \\ 1 & -3 & 2 \end{bmatrix} = \begin{bmatrix} 1-2+7 & 1-1-21 & 2-1+14 \\ 2-2+8 & 2-1-24 & 4-1+16 \\ 3+2-1 & 3+1+3 & 6+1-2 \end{bmatrix} = \begin{bmatrix} 6 & -21 & 15 \\ 8 & -23 & 19 \\ 4 & 7 & 5 \end{bmatrix}$

(b) $BA = \begin{bmatrix} 1 & 1 & 2 \\ 2 & 1 & 1 \\ 1 & -3 & 2 \end{bmatrix}\begin{bmatrix} 1 & -1 & 7 \\ 2 & -1 & 8 \\ 3 & 1 & -1 \end{bmatrix} = \begin{bmatrix} 1+2+6 & -1-1+2 & 7+8-2 \\ 2+2+3 & -2-1+1 & 14+8-1 \\ 1-6+6 & -1+3+2 & 7-24-2 \end{bmatrix} = \begin{bmatrix} 9 & 0 & 13 \\ 7 & -2 & 21 \\ 1 & 4 & -19 \end{bmatrix}$

(c) $A^2 = \begin{bmatrix} 1 & -1 & 7 \\ 2 & -1 & 8 \\ 3 & 1 & -1 \end{bmatrix}\begin{bmatrix} 1 & -1 & 7 \\ 2 & -1 & 8 \\ 3 & 1 & -1 \end{bmatrix} = \begin{bmatrix} 1-2+21 & -1+1+7 & 7-8-7 \\ 2-2+24 & -2+1+8 & 14-8-8 \\ 3+2-3 & -3-1-1 & 21+8+1 \end{bmatrix} = \begin{bmatrix} 20 & 7 & -8 \\ 24 & 7 & -2 \\ 2 & -5 & 30 \end{bmatrix}$

21. A is 3×2 and B is $3 \times 3 \implies AB$ is not defined.

23. A is 3×2, B is $2 \times 2 \implies AB$ is 3×2.

$AB = \begin{bmatrix} -1 & 3 \\ 4 & -5 \\ 0 & 2 \end{bmatrix}\begin{bmatrix} 1 & 2 \\ 0 & 7 \end{bmatrix} = \begin{bmatrix} -1 & 19 \\ 4 & -27 \\ 0 & 14 \end{bmatrix}$

25. A is 3×3, B is $3 \times 3 \implies AB$ is 3×3.

$AB = \begin{bmatrix} 5 & 0 & 0 \\ 0 & -8 & 0 \\ 0 & 0 & 7 \end{bmatrix}\begin{bmatrix} \frac{1}{5} & 0 & 0 \\ 0 & -\frac{1}{8} & 0 \\ 0 & 0 & \frac{1}{2} \end{bmatrix} = \begin{bmatrix} 1 & 0 & 0 \\ 0 & 1 & 0 \\ 0 & 0 & \frac{7}{2} \end{bmatrix}$

27. $\begin{bmatrix} 0 & 0 & 5 \\ 0 & 0 & -3 \\ 0 & 0 & 4 \end{bmatrix}\begin{bmatrix} 6 & -11 & 4 \\ 8 & 16 & 4 \\ 0 & 0 & 0 \end{bmatrix} = \begin{bmatrix} 0 & 0 & 0 \\ 0 & 0 & 0 \\ 0 & 0 & 0 \end{bmatrix}$

29. $\begin{bmatrix} 5 & 6 & -3 \\ -2 & 5 & 1 \\ 10 & -5 & 5 \end{bmatrix}\begin{bmatrix} 1 & -1 & 2 \\ 8 & 1 & 4 \\ 4 & -2 & 9 \end{bmatrix} = \begin{bmatrix} 41 & 7 & 7 \\ 42 & 5 & 25 \\ -10 & -25 & 45 \end{bmatrix}$

31. $\begin{bmatrix} -3 & 8 & -6 & 8 \\ -12 & 15 & 9 & 6 \\ 5 & -1 & 1 & 5 \end{bmatrix} \begin{bmatrix} 3 & 1 & 6 \\ 24 & 15 & 14 \\ 16 & 10 & 21 \\ 8 & -4 & 10 \end{bmatrix} = \begin{bmatrix} 151 & 25 & 48 \\ 516 & 279 & 387 \\ 47 & -20 & 87 \end{bmatrix}$

33. A is 2×4 and B is $2 \times 4 \implies AB$ is not defined.

35. $A = \begin{bmatrix} -1 & 1 \\ -2 & 1 \end{bmatrix}$, $X = \begin{bmatrix} x \\ y \end{bmatrix}$, $B = \begin{bmatrix} 4 \\ 0 \end{bmatrix}$

By Gauss-Jordan elimination on

$$\begin{bmatrix} -1 & 1 & \vdots & 4 \\ -2 & 1 & \vdots & 0 \end{bmatrix}$$

$$\begin{matrix} -R_1 \rightarrow \\ 2R_1 + R_2 \rightarrow \end{matrix} \begin{bmatrix} 1 & -1 & \vdots & -4 \\ 0 & -1 & \vdots & -8 \end{bmatrix}$$

$$\begin{matrix} R_2 + R_1 \rightarrow \\ -R_2 \rightarrow \end{matrix} \begin{bmatrix} 1 & 0 & \vdots & 4 \\ 0 & 1 & \vdots & 8 \end{bmatrix},$$

we have $x = 4$ and $y = 8$.

37. $A = \begin{bmatrix} 2 & 3 \\ 1 & 4 \end{bmatrix}$, $X = \begin{bmatrix} x \\ y \end{bmatrix}$, $B = \begin{bmatrix} 5 \\ 10 \end{bmatrix}$

By Gauss-Jordan elimination on

$$\begin{bmatrix} 1 & 4 & \vdots & 10 \\ 2 & 3 & \vdots & 5 \end{bmatrix}$$

$$-2R_1 + R_2 \rightarrow \begin{bmatrix} 1 & 4 & \vdots & 10 \\ 0 & -5 & \vdots & -15 \end{bmatrix}$$

$$\begin{matrix} -4R_2 + R_1 \rightarrow \\ -\frac{1}{5}R_2 \rightarrow \end{matrix} \begin{bmatrix} 1 & 0 & \vdots & -2 \\ 0 & 1 & \vdots & 3 \end{bmatrix},$$

we have $x = -2$ and $y = 3$.

39. $A = \begin{bmatrix} 2 & 0 \\ 4 & 5 \end{bmatrix}$

$f(A) = A^2 - 5A + 2 = \begin{bmatrix} 2 & 0 \\ 4 & 5 \end{bmatrix}\begin{bmatrix} 2 & 0 \\ 4 & 5 \end{bmatrix} - 5\begin{bmatrix} 2 & 4 \\ 0 & 5 \end{bmatrix} + 2\begin{bmatrix} 1 & 0 \\ 0 & 1 \end{bmatrix} = \begin{bmatrix} -4 & 0 \\ 8 & 2 \end{bmatrix}$

41. $A = \begin{bmatrix} 3 & 1 & 4 \\ 0 & 2 & 6 \\ 0 & 0 & 5 \end{bmatrix}$

$f(A) = \begin{bmatrix} 3 & 1 & 4 \\ 0 & 2 & 6 \\ 0 & 0 & 5 \end{bmatrix}^3 - 10\begin{bmatrix} 3 & 1 & 4 \\ 0 & 2 & 6 \\ 0 & 0 & 5 \end{bmatrix}^2 + 31\begin{bmatrix} 3 & 1 & 4 \\ 0 & 2 & 6 \\ 0 & 0 & 5 \end{bmatrix} - 30\begin{bmatrix} 1 & 0 & 0 \\ 0 & 1 & 0 \\ 0 & 0 & 1 \end{bmatrix} = \begin{bmatrix} 0 & 0 & 0 \\ 0 & 0 & 0 \\ 0 & 0 & 0 \end{bmatrix}$

43. $AC = \begin{bmatrix} 0 & 1 \\ 0 & 1 \end{bmatrix} \begin{bmatrix} 2 & 3 \\ 2 & 3 \end{bmatrix} = \begin{bmatrix} 2 & 3 \\ 2 & 3 \end{bmatrix}$

$BC = \begin{bmatrix} 1 & 0 \\ 1 & 0 \end{bmatrix} \begin{bmatrix} 2 & 3 \\ 2 & 3 \end{bmatrix} = \begin{bmatrix} 2 & 3 \\ 2 & 3 \end{bmatrix}$

$AC = BC$, but $A \neq B$.

For 45–53, A is of order 2×3, B is of order 2×3, C is of order 3×2 and D is of order 2×2.

45. $A + 2C$ is not possible. A and C are not of the same order.

47. AB is not possible. The number of columns of A does not equal the number of rows of B.

49. $BC - D$ is possible. The resulting order is 2×2.

51. (CA) is 3×3 so $(CA)D$ is not possible.

53. $D(A - 3B)$ is possible. The resulting order is 2×3.

55. $1.20 \begin{bmatrix} 60 & 40 & 20 \\ 30 & 90 & 60 \end{bmatrix} = \begin{bmatrix} 72 & 48 & 24 \\ 36 & 108 & 72 \end{bmatrix}$

57. $BA = [3.75 \quad 7.00] \begin{bmatrix} 100 & 75 & 75 \\ 125 & 150 & 100 \end{bmatrix} = [\$1250.00 \quad \$1331.25 \quad \$981.25]$

The entries in the last matrix represent the profit for both crops at each of the three outlets.

59. $A^2 = \begin{bmatrix} i & 0 \\ 0 & i \end{bmatrix} \begin{bmatrix} i & 0 \\ 0 & i \end{bmatrix} = \begin{bmatrix} -1 & 0 \\ 0 & -1 \end{bmatrix}$ and $i^2 = -1$

$A^3 = A^2 A = \begin{bmatrix} -1 & 0 \\ 0 & -1 \end{bmatrix} \begin{bmatrix} i & 0 \\ 0 & i \end{bmatrix} = \begin{bmatrix} -i & 0 \\ 0 & -i \end{bmatrix}$ and $i^3 = -i$

$A^4 = A^3 A = \begin{bmatrix} -i & 0 \\ 0 & -i \end{bmatrix} \begin{bmatrix} i & 0 \\ 0 & i \end{bmatrix} = \begin{bmatrix} 1 & 0 \\ 0 & 1 \end{bmatrix}$ and $i^4 = 1$

61. $ST = \begin{bmatrix} 3 & 2 & 2 & 3 & 0 \\ 0 & 2 & 3 & 4 & 3 \\ 4 & 2 & 1 & 3 & 2 \end{bmatrix} \begin{bmatrix} 840 & 1100 \\ 1200 & 1350 \\ 1450 & 1650 \\ 2650 & 3000 \\ 3050 & 3200 \end{bmatrix} = \begin{bmatrix} \$15,770 & \$18,300 \\ \$26,500 & \$29,250 \\ \$21,260 & \$24,150 \end{bmatrix}$

The entries represent the wholesale and retail prices of the inventory at each outlet.

63. $P^2 = \begin{bmatrix} 0.6 & 0.1 & 0.1 \\ 0.2 & 0.7 & 0.1 \\ 0.2 & 0.2 & 0.8 \end{bmatrix} \begin{bmatrix} 0.6 & 0.1 & 0.1 \\ 0.2 & 0.7 & 0.1 \\ 0.2 & 0.2 & 0.8 \end{bmatrix} = \begin{bmatrix} 0.40 & 0.15 & 0.15 \\ 0.28 & 0.53 & 0.17 \\ 0.32 & 0.32 & 0.68 \end{bmatrix}$

This product represents the changes in party affiliation after *two* elections.

65. The product of two diagonal matrices of the same order is a diagonal matrix whose entries are the products of the corresponding diagonal entries of A and B.

67. $\log_4 \sqrt{32} = \log_4 2^{5/2} = \log_4 4^{5/4} = \frac{5}{4} \log_4 4 = \frac{5}{4}$

Section 9.3 The Inverse of a Square Matrix

■ You should be able to find the inverse, if it exists, of a square matrix.

(a) Write the $n \times 2n$ matrix that consists of the given matrix A on the left and the $n \times n$ identity matrix I on the right to obtain $[A \ \vdots \ I]$. Note that we separate the matrices A and I by a dotted line. We call this process **adjoining** the matrices A and I.

(b) If possible, row reduce A to I using elementary row operations of the *entire* matrix $[A \ \vdots \ I]$. The result will be the matrix $[I \ \vdots \ A]$. If this is not possible, then A is not invertible.

(c) Check your work by multiplying to see that $AA^{-1} = I = A^{-1}A$.

■ You should be able to use inverse matrices to solve systems of equation.

■ You should be able to find inverses using a graphing utility.

Solutions to Odd-Numbered Exercises

1. $AB = \begin{bmatrix} 2 & 1 \\ 5 & 3 \end{bmatrix} \begin{bmatrix} 3 & -1 \\ -5 & 2 \end{bmatrix} = \begin{bmatrix} 2(3) + 1(-5) & 2(-1) + 1(2) \\ 5(3) + 3(-5) & 5(-1) + 3(2) \end{bmatrix} = \begin{bmatrix} 1 & 0 \\ 0 & 1 \end{bmatrix}$

$BA = \begin{bmatrix} 3 & -1 \\ -5 & 2 \end{bmatrix} \begin{bmatrix} 2 & 1 \\ 5 & 3 \end{bmatrix} = \begin{bmatrix} 3(2) + (-1)(5) & 3(1) + (-1)(3) \\ -5(2) + 2(5) & -5(1) + 2(3) \end{bmatrix} = \begin{bmatrix} 1 & 0 \\ 0 & 1 \end{bmatrix}$

3. $AB = \begin{bmatrix} 1 & 2 \\ 3 & 4 \end{bmatrix} \begin{bmatrix} -2 & 1 \\ \frac{3}{2} & -\frac{1}{2} \end{bmatrix} = \begin{bmatrix} -2 + 3 & 1 - 1 \\ -6 + 6 & 3 - 2 \end{bmatrix} = \begin{bmatrix} 1 & 0 \\ 0 & 1 \end{bmatrix}$

$BA = \begin{bmatrix} -2 & 1 \\ \frac{3}{2} & -\frac{1}{2} \end{bmatrix} \begin{bmatrix} 1 & 2 \\ 3 & 4 \end{bmatrix} = \begin{bmatrix} -2 + 3 & -4 + 4 \\ \frac{3}{2} - \frac{3}{2} & 3 - 2 \end{bmatrix} = \begin{bmatrix} 1 & 0 \\ 0 & 1 \end{bmatrix}$

5. $AB = \frac{1}{3} \begin{bmatrix} -2 & 2 & 3 \\ 1 & -1 & 0 \\ 0 & 1 & 4 \end{bmatrix} \begin{bmatrix} -4 & -5 & 3 \\ -4 & -8 & 3 \\ 1 & 2 & 0 \end{bmatrix} = \frac{1}{3} \begin{bmatrix} -8 + 8 + 3 & 10 - 16 + 6 & -6 + 6 \\ -4 + 4 & -5 + 8 & 3 - 3 \\ -4 + 4 & -8 + 8 & 3 \end{bmatrix}$

$= \frac{1}{3} \begin{bmatrix} 3 & 0 & 0 \\ 0 & 3 & 0 \\ 0 & 0 & 3 \end{bmatrix} = \begin{bmatrix} 1 & 0 & 0 \\ 0 & 1 & 0 \\ 0 & 0 & 1 \end{bmatrix}$

$BA = \frac{1}{3} \begin{bmatrix} -4 & -5 & 3 \\ -4 & -8 & 3 \\ 1 & 2 & 0 \end{bmatrix} \begin{bmatrix} -2 & 2 & 3 \\ 1 & -1 & 0 \\ 0 & 1 & 4 \end{bmatrix} = \frac{1}{3} \begin{bmatrix} 8 - 5 & -8 + 5 + 3 & -12 + 12 \\ 8 - 8 & -8 + 8 + 3 & -12 + 12 \\ -2 + 2 & 2 - 2 & 3 \end{bmatrix} = \begin{bmatrix} 1 & 0 & 0 \\ 0 & 1 & 0 \\ 0 & 0 & 1 \end{bmatrix}$

7. $AB = \begin{bmatrix} 2 & 0 & 1 & 1 \\ 3 & 0 & 0 & 1 \\ -1 & 1 & -2 & 1 \\ 4 & -1 & 1 & 0 \end{bmatrix} \begin{bmatrix} -1 & 2 & -1 & -1 \\ -4 & 9 & -5 & -6 \\ 0 & 1 & -1 & -1 \\ 3 & -5 & 3 & 3 \end{bmatrix} = \begin{bmatrix} 1 & 0 & 0 & 0 \\ 0 & 1 & 0 & 0 \\ 0 & 0 & 1 & 0 \\ 0 & 0 & 0 & 1 \end{bmatrix}$

$BA = \begin{bmatrix} -1 & 2 & -1 & -1 \\ -4 & 9 & -5 & -6 \\ 0 & 1 & -1 & -1 \\ 3 & -5 & 3 & 3 \end{bmatrix} \begin{bmatrix} 2 & 0 & 1 & 1 \\ 3 & 0 & 0 & 1 \\ -1 & 1 & -2 & 1 \\ 4 & -1 & 1 & 0 \end{bmatrix} = \begin{bmatrix} 1 & 0 & 0 & 0 \\ 0 & 1 & 0 & 0 \\ 0 & 0 & 1 & 0 \\ 0 & 0 & 0 & 1 \end{bmatrix}$

9. $[A \;\vdots\; I] = \begin{bmatrix} 2 & 0 & \vdots & 1 & 0 \\ 0 & 3 & \vdots & 0 & 1 \end{bmatrix}$

$$\begin{matrix} \frac{1}{2}R_1 \to \\ \frac{1}{3}R_2 \to \end{matrix} \begin{bmatrix} 1 & 0 & \vdots & \frac{1}{2} & 0 \\ 0 & 1 & \vdots & 0 & \frac{1}{3} \end{bmatrix} = [I \;\vdots\; A^{-1}]$$

$$A^{-1} = \begin{bmatrix} \frac{1}{2} & 0 \\ 0 & \frac{1}{3} \end{bmatrix} = \frac{1}{6}\begin{bmatrix} 3 & 0 \\ 0 & 2 \end{bmatrix}$$

11. $[A \;\vdots\; I] = \begin{bmatrix} 1 & -2 & \vdots & 1 & 0 \\ 2 & -3 & \vdots & 0 & 1 \end{bmatrix}$

$$-2R_1 + R_2 \to \begin{bmatrix} 1 & -2 & \vdots & 1 & 0 \\ 0 & 1 & \vdots & -2 & 1 \end{bmatrix}$$

$$2R_2 + R_1 \to \begin{bmatrix} 1 & 0 & \vdots & -3 & 2 \\ 0 & 1 & \vdots & -2 & 1 \end{bmatrix} = [I \;\vdots\; A^{-1}]$$

$$A^{-1} = \begin{bmatrix} -3 & 2 \\ -2 & 1 \end{bmatrix}$$

13. $[A \;\vdots\; I] = \begin{bmatrix} -1 & 1 & \vdots & 1 & 0 \\ -2 & 1 & \vdots & 0 & 1 \end{bmatrix}$

$$-2R_1 + R_2 \to \begin{bmatrix} -1 & 1 & \vdots & 1 & 0 \\ 0 & -1 & \vdots & -2 & 1 \end{bmatrix}$$

$$R_2 + R_1 \to \begin{bmatrix} -1 & 0 & \vdots & -1 & 1 \\ 0 & -1 & \vdots & -2 & 1 \end{bmatrix}$$

$$\begin{matrix} -R_1 \to \\ -R_2 \to \end{matrix} \begin{bmatrix} 1 & 0 & \vdots & 1 & -1 \\ 0 & 1 & \vdots & 2 & -1 \end{bmatrix} = [I \;\vdots\; A^{-1}]$$

$$A^{-1} = \begin{bmatrix} 1 & -1 \\ 2 & -1 \end{bmatrix}$$

15. $[A \;\vdots\; I] = \begin{bmatrix} 2 & 4 & \vdots & 1 & 0 \\ 4 & 8 & \vdots & 0 & 1 \end{bmatrix}$

$$-2R_1 + R_2 \to \begin{bmatrix} 2 & 4 & \vdots & 1 & 0 \\ 0 & 0 & \vdots & -2 & 1 \end{bmatrix}$$

The two zeros in the second row imply that the inverse does not exist.

17. $A = \begin{bmatrix} 2 & 7 & 1 \\ -3 & -9 & 2 \end{bmatrix}$

A has no inverse because it is not square.

19.

$$\begin{bmatrix} 1 & 1 & 1 & \vdots & 1 & 0 & 0 \\ 3 & 5 & 4 & \vdots & 0 & 1 & 0 \\ 3 & 6 & 5 & \vdots & 0 & 0 & 1 \end{bmatrix}$$

$$\begin{matrix} \\ -3R_1 + R_2 \rightarrow \\ -3R_1 + R_3 \rightarrow \end{matrix} \begin{bmatrix} 1 & 1 & 1 & \vdots & 1 & 0 & 0 \\ 0 & 2 & 1 & \vdots & -3 & 1 & 0 \\ 0 & 3 & 2 & \vdots & -3 & 0 & 1 \end{bmatrix}$$

$$\begin{matrix} -R_2 + R_1 \rightarrow \\ \frac{1}{2}R_2 \rightarrow \\ -3R_2 + R_3 \rightarrow \end{matrix} \begin{bmatrix} 1 & 0 & \frac{1}{2} & \vdots & \frac{5}{2} & -\frac{1}{2} & 0 \\ 0 & 1 & \frac{1}{2} & \vdots & -\frac{3}{2} & \frac{1}{2} & 0 \\ 0 & 0 & \frac{1}{2} & \vdots & \frac{3}{2} & -\frac{3}{2} & 1 \end{bmatrix}$$

$$\begin{matrix} -R_3 + R_1 \rightarrow \\ -R_3 + R_2 \rightarrow \\ 2R_3 \rightarrow \end{matrix} \begin{bmatrix} 1 & 0 & 0 & \vdots & 1 & 1 & -1 \\ 0 & 1 & 0 & \vdots & -3 & 2 & -1 \\ 0 & 0 & 1 & \vdots & 3 & -3 & 2 \end{bmatrix}$$

$$A^{-1} = \begin{bmatrix} 1 & 1 & -1 \\ -3 & 2 & -1 \\ 3 & -3 & 2 \end{bmatrix}$$

21. $[A \; \vdots \; I] = \begin{bmatrix} 1 & 0 & 0 & \vdots & 1 & 0 & 0 \\ 3 & 4 & 0 & \vdots & 0 & 1 & 0 \\ 2 & 5 & 5 & \vdots & 0 & 0 & 1 \end{bmatrix}$

$$\begin{matrix} \\ -3R_1 + R_2 \rightarrow \\ -2R_1 + R_3 \rightarrow \end{matrix} \begin{bmatrix} 1 & 0 & 0 & \vdots & 1 & 0 & 0 \\ 0 & 4 & 0 & \vdots & -3 & 1 & 0 \\ 0 & 5 & 5 & \vdots & -2 & 0 & 1 \end{bmatrix}$$

$$\begin{matrix} \\ \\ -\frac{5}{4}R_2 + R_3 \rightarrow \end{matrix} \begin{bmatrix} 1 & 0 & 0 & \vdots & 1 & 0 & 0 \\ 0 & 4 & 0 & \vdots & -3 & 1 & 0 \\ 0 & 0 & 5 & \vdots & \frac{7}{4} & -\frac{5}{4} & 1 \end{bmatrix}$$

$$\begin{matrix} \\ \frac{1}{4}R_2 \rightarrow \\ \frac{1}{5}R_3 \rightarrow \end{matrix} \begin{bmatrix} 1 & 0 & 0 & \vdots & 1 & 0 & 0 \\ 0 & 1 & 0 & \vdots & -\frac{3}{4} & \frac{1}{4} & 0 \\ 0 & 0 & 1 & \vdots & \frac{7}{20} & -\frac{1}{4} & \frac{1}{5} \end{bmatrix}$$

$$= [I \; \vdots \; A^{-1}]$$

$$A^{-1} = \frac{1}{20} \begin{bmatrix} 20 & 0 & 0 \\ -15 & 5 & 0 \\ 7 & -5 & 4 \end{bmatrix} = \begin{bmatrix} 1 & 0 & 0 \\ -0.75 & 0.25 & 0 \\ 0.35 & -0.25 & 0.2 \end{bmatrix}$$

23. $[A \;\vdots\; I] = \begin{bmatrix} -8 & 0 & 0 & 0 & \vdots & 1 & 0 & 0 & 0 \\ 0 & 1 & 0 & 0 & \vdots & 0 & 1 & 0 & 0 \\ 0 & 0 & 4 & 0 & \vdots & 0 & 0 & 1 & 0 \\ 0 & 0 & 0 & -5 & \vdots & 0 & 0 & 0 & 1 \end{bmatrix}$

$\begin{array}{c} -\frac{1}{8}R_1 \to \\ \\ \frac{1}{4}R_3 \to \\ -\frac{1}{5}R_4 \to \end{array} \begin{bmatrix} 1 & 0 & 0 & 0 & \vdots & -\frac{1}{8} & 0 & 0 & 0 \\ 0 & 1 & 0 & 0 & \vdots & 0 & 1 & 0 & 0 \\ 0 & 0 & 1 & 0 & \vdots & 0 & 0 & \frac{1}{4} & 0 \\ 0 & 0 & 0 & 1 & \vdots & 0 & 0 & 0 & -\frac{1}{5} \end{bmatrix}$

$= [I \;\vdots\; A^{-1}]$

$A^{-1} = \begin{bmatrix} -\frac{1}{8} & 0 & 0 & 0 \\ 0 & 1 & 0 & 0 \\ 0 & 0 & \frac{1}{4} & 0 \\ 0 & 0 & 0 & -\frac{1}{5} \end{bmatrix}$

25. $A = \begin{bmatrix} 1 & 2 & -1 \\ 3 & 7 & -10 \\ -5 & -7 & -15 \end{bmatrix}$

$A^{-1} = \begin{bmatrix} -175 & 37 & -13 \\ 95 & -20 & 7 \\ 14 & -3 & 1 \end{bmatrix}$

27. $A = \begin{bmatrix} 1 & 1 & 2 \\ 3 & 1 & 0 \\ -2 & 0 & 3 \end{bmatrix}$

$A^{-1} = \frac{1}{2}\begin{bmatrix} -3 & 3 & 2 \\ 9 & -7 & -6 \\ -2 & 2 & 2 \end{bmatrix}$

29. $A = \begin{bmatrix} 0.1 & 0.2 & 0.3 \\ -0.3 & 0.2 & 0.2 \\ 0.5 & 0.4 & 0.4 \end{bmatrix}$

$A^{-1} = \frac{5}{11}\begin{bmatrix} 0 & -4 & 2 \\ -22 & 11 & 11 \\ 22 & -6 & -8 \end{bmatrix}$

31. $A = \begin{bmatrix} 1 & 0 & 3 & 0 \\ 0 & 2 & 0 & 4 \\ 1 & 0 & 3 & 0 \\ 0 & 2 & 0 & 4 \end{bmatrix}$

A^{-1} does not exist.

33. $A = \begin{bmatrix} 1 & -2 & -1 & -2 \\ 3 & -5 & -2 & -3 \\ 2 & -5 & -2 & -5 \\ -1 & 4 & 4 & 11 \end{bmatrix}$

$A^{-1} = \begin{bmatrix} -24 & 7 & 1 & -2 \\ -10 & 3 & 0 & -1 \\ -29 & 7 & 3 & -2 \\ 12 & -3 & -1 & 1 \end{bmatrix}$

35. $AA^{-1} = \begin{bmatrix} a & b \\ c & d \end{bmatrix} \left(\dfrac{1}{ad - bc} \right) \begin{bmatrix} d & -b \\ -c & a \end{bmatrix} = \dfrac{1}{ad - bc} \begin{bmatrix} a & b \\ c & d \end{bmatrix} \begin{bmatrix} d & -b \\ -c & a \end{bmatrix}$

$\quad = \dfrac{1}{ad - bc} \begin{bmatrix} ad - bc & 0 \\ 0 & ad - bc \end{bmatrix} = \begin{bmatrix} 1 & 0 \\ 0 & 1 \end{bmatrix}$

$\quad A^{-1}A = \dfrac{1}{ad - bc} \begin{bmatrix} d & -b \\ -c & a \end{bmatrix} \begin{bmatrix} a & b \\ c & d \end{bmatrix} = \dfrac{1}{ad - bc} \begin{bmatrix} ad - bc & 0 \\ 0 & ad - bc \end{bmatrix} = \begin{bmatrix} 1 & 0 \\ 0 & 1 \end{bmatrix}$

37. $\begin{bmatrix} x \\ y \end{bmatrix} = \begin{bmatrix} -3 & 2 \\ -2 & 1 \end{bmatrix} \begin{bmatrix} 5 \\ 10 \end{bmatrix} = \begin{bmatrix} 5 \\ 0 \end{bmatrix}$

Answer: $(5, 0)$

39. $\begin{bmatrix} x \\ y \end{bmatrix} = \begin{bmatrix} -3 & 2 \\ -2 & 1 \end{bmatrix} = \begin{bmatrix} 4 \\ 2 \end{bmatrix} = \begin{bmatrix} -8 \\ -6 \end{bmatrix}$

Answer: $(-8, -6)$

41. $\begin{bmatrix} x \\ y \\ z \end{bmatrix} = \begin{bmatrix} 1 & 1 & -1 \\ -3 & 2 & -1 \\ 3 & -3 & 2 \end{bmatrix} \begin{bmatrix} 0 \\ 5 \\ 2 \end{bmatrix} = \begin{bmatrix} 3 \\ 8 \\ -11 \end{bmatrix}$

Answer: $(3, 8, -11)$

43. $\begin{bmatrix} x_1 \\ x_2 \\ x_3 \\ x_4 \end{bmatrix} = \begin{bmatrix} -24 & 7 & 1 & -2 \\ -10 & 3 & 0 & -1 \\ -29 & 7 & 3 & -2 \\ 12 & -3 & -1 & 1 \end{bmatrix} \begin{bmatrix} 0 \\ 1 \\ -1 \\ 2 \end{bmatrix} = \begin{bmatrix} 2 \\ 1 \\ 0 \\ 0 \end{bmatrix}$

Answer: $(2, 1, 0, 0)$

45. $A = \begin{bmatrix} 3 & 4 \\ 5 & 3 \end{bmatrix}$

$\quad A^{-1} = \dfrac{1}{9 - 20} \begin{bmatrix} 3 & -4 \\ -5 & 3 \end{bmatrix}$

$\quad \begin{bmatrix} x \\ y \end{bmatrix} = -\dfrac{1}{11} \begin{bmatrix} 3 & -4 \\ -5 & 3 \end{bmatrix} \begin{bmatrix} -2 \\ 4 \end{bmatrix} = -\dfrac{1}{11} \begin{bmatrix} -22 \\ 22 \end{bmatrix} = \begin{bmatrix} 2 \\ -2 \end{bmatrix}$

Answer: $(2, -2)$

47. $A = \begin{bmatrix} -0.4 & 0.8 \\ 2 & -4 \end{bmatrix}$

$\quad A^{-1} = \dfrac{1}{1.6 - 1.6} \begin{bmatrix} -4 & -0.8 \\ -2 & -0.4 \end{bmatrix} \Rightarrow A^{-1}$ does not exist.

No solution

49. $A = \begin{bmatrix} 3 & 6 \\ 6 & 14 \end{bmatrix}$

$\quad A^{-1} = \dfrac{1}{42 - 36} \begin{bmatrix} 14 & -6 \\ -6 & 3 \end{bmatrix}$

$\quad \begin{bmatrix} x \\ y \end{bmatrix} = \dfrac{1}{6} \begin{bmatrix} 14 & -6 \\ -6 & 3 \end{bmatrix} \begin{bmatrix} 6 \\ 11 \end{bmatrix} = \dfrac{1}{6} \begin{bmatrix} 18 \\ -3 \end{bmatrix} = \begin{bmatrix} 3 \\ -\frac{1}{2} \end{bmatrix}$

Answer: $\left(3, -\frac{1}{2} \right)$

51. $A = \begin{bmatrix} 4 & -1 & 1 \\ 2 & 2 & 3 \\ 5 & -2 & 6 \end{bmatrix}$

$\quad A^{-1} = \frac{1}{55} \begin{bmatrix} 18 & 4 & -5 \\ 3 & 19 & -10 \\ -14 & 3 & 10 \end{bmatrix}$

$\quad \begin{bmatrix} x \\ y \\ z \end{bmatrix} = \frac{1}{55} \begin{bmatrix} 18 & 4 & -5 \\ 3 & 19 & -10 \\ -14 & 3 & 10 \end{bmatrix} \begin{bmatrix} -5 \\ 10 \\ 1 \end{bmatrix} = \frac{1}{55} \begin{bmatrix} -55 \\ 165 \\ 110 \end{bmatrix} = \begin{bmatrix} -1 \\ 3 \\ 2 \end{bmatrix}$

Answer: $(-1, 3, 2)$

53. $A = \begin{bmatrix} 5 & -3 & 2 \\ 2 & 2 & -3 \\ -1 & 7 & -8 \end{bmatrix}$

A^{-1} does not exist.

No solution

55. $A = \begin{bmatrix} 7 & -3 & 0 & 2 \\ -2 & 1 & 0 & -1 \\ 4 & 0 & 1 & -2 \\ -1 & 1 & 0 & -1 \end{bmatrix}$

$A^{-1} = \begin{bmatrix} 0 & -1 & 0 & 1 \\ -1 & -5 & 0 & 3 \\ -2 & -4 & 1 & -2 \\ -1 & -4 & 0 & 1 \end{bmatrix}$

$\begin{bmatrix} x \\ y \\ z \\ w \end{bmatrix} = \begin{bmatrix} 0 & -1 & 0 & 1 \\ -1 & -5 & 0 & 3 \\ -2 & -4 & 1 & -2 \\ -1 & -4 & 0 & 1 \end{bmatrix} \begin{bmatrix} 41 \\ -13 \\ 12 \\ -8 \end{bmatrix} = \begin{bmatrix} 5 \\ 0 \\ -2 \\ 3 \end{bmatrix}$

Answer: $(5, 0, -2, 3)$

For 57–59 use $A = \begin{bmatrix} 1 & 1 & 1 \\ 0.065 & 0.07 & 0.09 \\ 0 & 2 & -1 \end{bmatrix}$ **.Using the methods of this section, we have**

$A^{-1} = \frac{1}{11}\begin{bmatrix} 50 & -600 & -4 \\ -13 & 200 & 5 \\ -26 & 400 & -1 \end{bmatrix}.$

57. $X = A^{-1}B = \frac{1}{11}\begin{bmatrix} 50 & -600 & -4 \\ -13 & 200 & 5 \\ -26 & 400 & -1 \end{bmatrix}\begin{bmatrix} 25,000 \\ 1900 \\ 0 \end{bmatrix} = \begin{bmatrix} 10,000 \\ 5000 \\ 10,000 \end{bmatrix}$

Answer: \$10,000 in AAA bonds, \$5000 in A bonds, \$10,000 in B bonds

59. $X = A^{-1}B = \frac{1}{11}\begin{bmatrix} 50 & -600 & -4 \\ -13 & 200 & 5 \\ -26 & 400 & -1 \end{bmatrix}\begin{bmatrix} 12,000 \\ 835 \\ 0 \end{bmatrix} = \begin{bmatrix} 9000 \\ 1000 \\ 2000 \end{bmatrix}$

Answer: \$9000 in AAA bonds, \$1000 in A bonds, \$2000 in B bonds

61. The inverse matrix remained the same for each system.

63. $A = \begin{bmatrix} 2 & 0 & 4 \\ 0 & 1 & 4 \\ 1 & 1 & -1 \end{bmatrix}$

$A^{-1} = \frac{1}{14}\begin{bmatrix} 5 & -4 & 4 \\ -4 & 6 & 8 \\ 1 & 2 & -2 \end{bmatrix}$

$\begin{bmatrix} I_1 \\ I_2 \\ I_3 \end{bmatrix} = \frac{1}{14}\begin{bmatrix} 5 & -4 & 4 \\ -4 & 6 & 8 \\ 1 & 2 & -2 \end{bmatrix}\begin{bmatrix} 14 \\ 28 \\ 0 \end{bmatrix} = \begin{bmatrix} -3 \\ 8 \\ 5 \end{bmatrix}$

Answer: $I_1 = -3$ amps, $I_2 = 8$ amps, $I_3 = 5$ amps

65. (a) Given $A = \begin{bmatrix} a_{11} & 0 \\ 0 & a_{22} \end{bmatrix}$, $A^{-1} = \begin{bmatrix} \dfrac{1}{a_{11}} & 0 \\ 0 & \dfrac{1}{a_{22}} \end{bmatrix}$.

Given $A = \begin{bmatrix} a_{11} & 0 & 0 \\ 0 & a_{22} & 0 \\ 0 & 0 & a_{33} \end{bmatrix}$, $A^{-1} = \begin{bmatrix} \dfrac{1}{a_{11}} & 0 & 0 \\ 0 & \dfrac{1}{a_{22}} & 0 \\ 0 & 0 & \dfrac{1}{a_{33}} \end{bmatrix}$.

(b) In general, the inverse of the diagonal matrix A is

$$\begin{bmatrix} \dfrac{1}{a_{11}} & 0 & 0 & \cdots & 0 \\ 0 & \dfrac{1}{a_{22}} & 0 & \cdots & 0 \\ 0 & 0 & \dfrac{1}{a_{33}} & \cdots & 0 \\ \vdots & \vdots & \vdots & \vdots & \vdots \\ 0 & 0 & 0 & \cdots & \dfrac{1}{a_{nn}} \end{bmatrix} \quad \text{(assuming } a_{ii} \neq 0\text{)}$$

Section 9.4   The Determinant of a Square Matrix

- ■ You should be able to determine the determinant of a matrix of order 2×2 by using the products of the diagonals.
- ■ You should be able to use expansion by cofactors to find the determinant of a matrix of order 3 or greater.
- ■ The determinant of a triangular matrix equals the product of the entries on the main diagonal.
- ■ You should be able to calculate determinants using a graphing utility.

Solutions to Odd-Numbered Exercises

1. 5

3. $\begin{vmatrix} 2 & 1 \\ 3 & 4 \end{vmatrix} = 2(4) - 1(3) = 8 - 3 = 5$

5. $\begin{vmatrix} 5 & 2 \\ -6 & 3 \end{vmatrix} = 5(3) - 2(-6) = 15 + 12 = 27$

7. $\begin{vmatrix} -7 & 6 \\ \frac{1}{2} & 3 \end{vmatrix} = -7(3) - 6\left(\frac{1}{2}\right) = -21 - 3 = -24$

9. $\begin{vmatrix} 2 & 6 \\ 0 & 3 \end{vmatrix} = 2(3) - 6(0) = 6$

11. $\begin{vmatrix} 2 & -1 & 0 \\ 4 & 2 & 1 \\ 4 & 2 & 1 \end{vmatrix} = 2\begin{vmatrix} 2 & 1 \\ 2 & 1 \end{vmatrix} - 4\begin{vmatrix} -1 & 0 \\ 2 & 1 \end{vmatrix} + 4\begin{vmatrix} -1 & 0 \\ 2 & 1 \end{vmatrix} = 2(0) - 4(-1) + 4(-1) = 0$

13. $\begin{vmatrix} 6 & 3 & -7 \\ 0 & 0 & 0 \\ 4 & -6 & 3 \end{vmatrix} = 0\begin{vmatrix} 3 & -7 \\ -6 & 3 \end{vmatrix} - 0\begin{vmatrix} 6 & -7 \\ 4 & 3 \end{vmatrix} + 0\begin{vmatrix} 6 & 3 \\ 4 & -6 \end{vmatrix} = 0$

15. $\begin{vmatrix} -1 & 2 & 5 \\ 0 & 3 & 4 \\ 0 & 0 & 3 \end{vmatrix} = (-1)(3)(3) = -9$ (Upper Triangular)

17. $\begin{vmatrix} 0.3 & 0.2 & 0.2 \\ 0.2 & 0.2 & 0.2 \\ -0.4 & 0.4 & 0.3 \end{vmatrix} = -0.002$

19. $\begin{vmatrix} 1 & 4 & -2 \\ 3 & 6 & -6 \\ -2 & 1 & 4 \end{vmatrix} = 0$

21. $\begin{bmatrix} 3 & 4 \\ 2 & -5 \end{bmatrix}$

(a) $M_{11} = -5$

$M_{12} = 2$

$M_{21} = 4$

$M_{22} = 3$

(b) $C_{11} = M_{11} = -5$

$C_{12} = -M_{12} = -2$

$C_{21} = -M_{21} = -4$

$C_{22} = M_{22} = 3$

23. $\begin{bmatrix} 3 & -2 & 8 \\ 3 & 2 & -6 \\ -1 & 3 & 6 \end{bmatrix}$

(a) $M_{11} = \begin{vmatrix} 2 & -6 \\ 3 & 4 \end{vmatrix} = 12 + 18 = 30$

$M_{12} = \begin{vmatrix} 3 & -6 \\ -1 & 6 \end{vmatrix} = 18 - 6 = 12$

$M_{13} = \begin{vmatrix} 3 & 2 \\ -1 & 3 \end{vmatrix} = 9 + 2 = 11$

$M_{21} = \begin{vmatrix} -2 & 8 \\ 3 & 6 \end{vmatrix} = -12 - 24 = -36$

$M_{22} = \begin{vmatrix} 3 & 8 \\ -1 & 6 \end{vmatrix} = 18 + 8 = 26$

$M_{23} = \begin{vmatrix} 3 & -2 \\ -1 & 3 \end{vmatrix} = 9 - 2 = 7$

$M_{31} = \begin{vmatrix} -2 & 8 \\ 2 & -6 \end{vmatrix} = 12 - 16 = -4$

$M_{32} = \begin{vmatrix} 3 & 8 \\ 3 & -6 \end{vmatrix} = -18 - 24 = -42$

$M_{33} = \begin{vmatrix} 3 & -2 \\ 3 & 2 \end{vmatrix} = 6 + 6 = 12$

(b) $C_{11} = (-1)^2 M_{11} = 30$

$C_{12} = (-1)^3 M_{12} = -12$

$C_{13} = (-1)^4 M_{13} = 11$

$C_{21} = (-1)^3 M_{21} = 36$

$C_{22} = (-1)^4 M_{22} = 26$

$C_{23} = (-1)^5 M_{23} = -7$

$C_{31} = (-1)^4 M_{31} = -4$

$C_{32} = (-1)^5 M_{32} = 42$

$C_{33} = (-1)^6 M_{33} = 12$

25. (a) $\begin{vmatrix} -3 & 2 & 1 \\ 4 & 5 & 6 \\ 2 & -3 & 1 \end{vmatrix} = -3 \begin{vmatrix} 5 & 6 \\ -3 & 1 \end{vmatrix} - 2 \begin{vmatrix} 4 & 6 \\ 2 & 1 \end{vmatrix} + \begin{vmatrix} 4 & 5 \\ 2 & -3 \end{vmatrix} = -3(23) - 2(-8) - 22 = -75$

(b) $\begin{vmatrix} -3 & 2 & 1 \\ 4 & 5 & 6 \\ 2 & -3 & 1 \end{vmatrix} = -2 \begin{vmatrix} 4 & 6 \\ 2 & 1 \end{vmatrix} + 5 \begin{vmatrix} -3 & 1 \\ 2 & 1 \end{vmatrix} + 3 \begin{vmatrix} -3 & 1 \\ 4 & 6 \end{vmatrix} = -2(-8) + 5(-5) + 3(-22) = -75$

27. (a) $\begin{vmatrix} 5 & 0 & -3 \\ 0 & 12 & 4 \\ 1 & 6 & 3 \end{vmatrix} = 0 \begin{vmatrix} 0 & -3 \\ 6 & 3 \end{vmatrix} + 12 \begin{vmatrix} 5 & -3 \\ 1 & 3 \end{vmatrix} - 4 \begin{vmatrix} 5 & 0 \\ 1 & 6 \end{vmatrix} = 0(18) + 12(18) - 4(30) = 96$

(b) $\begin{vmatrix} 5 & 0 & -3 \\ 0 & 12 & 4 \\ 1 & 6 & 3 \end{vmatrix} = 0 \begin{vmatrix} 0 & 4 \\ 1 & 3 \end{vmatrix} + 12 \begin{vmatrix} 5 & -3 \\ 1 & 3 \end{vmatrix} - 6 \begin{vmatrix} 5 & -3 \\ 0 & 4 \end{vmatrix} = 0(-4) + 12(18) - 6(20) = 96$

29. (a) $\begin{vmatrix} 6 & 0 & -3 & 5 \\ 4 & 13 & 6 & -8 \\ -1 & 0 & 7 & 4 \\ 8 & 6 & 0 & 2 \end{vmatrix} = -4\begin{vmatrix} 0 & -3 & 5 \\ 0 & 7 & 4 \\ 6 & 0 & 2 \end{vmatrix} + 13\begin{vmatrix} 6 & -3 & 5 \\ -1 & 7 & 4 \\ 8 & 0 & 2 \end{vmatrix} - 6\begin{vmatrix} 6 & 0 & 5 \\ -1 & 0 & 4 \\ 8 & 6 & 2 \end{vmatrix} - 8\begin{vmatrix} 6 & 0 & -3 \\ -1 & 0 & 7 \\ 8 & 6 & 0 \end{vmatrix}$

$$= -4(-282) + 13(-298) - 6(-174) - 8(-234) = 170$$

(b) $\begin{vmatrix} 6 & 0 & -3 & 5 \\ 4 & 13 & 6 & -8 \\ -1 & 0 & 7 & 4 \\ 8 & 6 & 0 & 2 \end{vmatrix} = 0\begin{vmatrix} 4 & 6 & -8 \\ -1 & 7 & 4 \\ 8 & 0 & 2 \end{vmatrix} + 13\begin{vmatrix} 6 & -3 & 5 \\ -1 & 7 & 4 \\ 8 & 0 & 2 \end{vmatrix} + 0\begin{vmatrix} 6 & -3 & 5 \\ 4 & 6 & -8 \\ 8 & 0 & 2 \end{vmatrix} + 6\begin{vmatrix} 6 & -3 & 5 \\ 4 & 6 & -8 \\ -1 & 7 & 4 \end{vmatrix}$

$$= 0 + 13(-298) + 0 + 6(674) = 170$$

31. Expand by Column 3.

$$\begin{vmatrix} 1 & 4 & -2 \\ 3 & 2 & 0 \\ -1 & 4 & 3 \end{vmatrix} = -2\begin{vmatrix} 3 & 2 \\ -1 & 4 \end{vmatrix} + 3\begin{vmatrix} 1 & 4 \\ 3 & 2 \end{vmatrix} = -2(14) + 3(-10) = -58$$

33. $\begin{vmatrix} 2 & 4 & 6 \\ 0 & 3 & 1 \\ 0 & 0 & -5 \end{vmatrix} = (2)(3)(-5) = -30$ (Upper Triangular)

35. Expand by Column 3.

$$\begin{vmatrix} 2 & 6 & 6 & 2 \\ 2 & 7 & 3 & 6 \\ 1 & 5 & 0 & 1 \\ 3 & 7 & 0 & 7 \end{vmatrix} = 6\begin{vmatrix} 2 & 7 & 6 \\ 1 & 5 & 1 \\ 3 & 7 & 7 \end{vmatrix} - 3\begin{vmatrix} 2 & 6 & 2 \\ 1 & 5 & 1 \\ 3 & 7 & 7 \end{vmatrix} = 6(-20) - 3(16) = -168$$

37. Expand by Column 1.

$$\begin{vmatrix} 5 & 3 & 0 & 6 \\ 4 & 6 & 4 & 12 \\ 0 & 2 & -3 & 4 \\ 0 & 1 & -2 & 2 \end{vmatrix} = 5\begin{vmatrix} 6 & 4 & 12 \\ 2 & -3 & 4 \\ 1 & -2 & 2 \end{vmatrix} - 4\begin{vmatrix} 3 & 0 & 6 \\ 2 & -3 & 4 \\ 1 & -2 & 2 \end{vmatrix} = 5(0) - 4(0) = 0$$

39. Expand by Column 2.

$$\begin{vmatrix} 3 & 2 & 4 & -1 & 5 \\ -2 & 0 & 1 & 3 & 2 \\ 1 & 0 & 0 & 4 & 0 \\ 6 & 0 & 2 & -1 & 0 \\ 3 & 0 & 5 & 1 & 0 \end{vmatrix} = -2\begin{vmatrix} -2 & 1 & 3 & 2 \\ 1 & 0 & 4 & 0 \\ 6 & 2 & -1 & 0 \\ 3 & 5 & 1 & 0 \end{vmatrix} = (-2)(-2)\begin{vmatrix} 1 & 0 & 4 \\ 6 & 2 & -1 \\ 3 & 5 & 1 \end{vmatrix} = 4(103) = 412$$

41. $\begin{vmatrix} 3 & 8 & -7 \\ 0 & -5 & 4 \\ 8 & 1 & 6 \end{vmatrix} = -126$

43. $\begin{vmatrix} 7 & 0 & -14 \\ -2 & 5 & 4 \\ -6 & 2 & 12 \end{vmatrix} = 0$

45. $\begin{vmatrix} 1 & -1 & 8 & 4 \\ 2 & 6 & 0 & -4 \\ 2 & 0 & 2 & 6 \\ 0 & 2 & 8 & 0 \end{vmatrix} = -336$

47. $\begin{vmatrix} 3 & -2 & 4 & 3 & 1 \\ -1 & 0 & 2 & 1 & 0 \\ 5 & -1 & 0 & 3 & 2 \\ 4 & 7 & -8 & 0 & 0 \\ 1 & 2 & 3 & 0 & 2 \end{vmatrix} = 410$

49. $\begin{vmatrix} w & x \\ y & z \end{vmatrix} = wz - xy$

$-\begin{vmatrix} y & z \\ w & x \end{vmatrix} = -(xy - wz) = wz - xy$

Thus, $\begin{vmatrix} w & x \\ y & z \end{vmatrix} = -\begin{vmatrix} y & z \\ w & x \end{vmatrix}.$

51. $\begin{vmatrix} w & x \\ y & z \end{vmatrix} = wz - xy$

$\begin{vmatrix} w & x + cw \\ y & z + cy \end{vmatrix} = w(z + cy) - y(x + cw) = wz - xy$

Thus, $\begin{vmatrix} w & x \\ y & z \end{vmatrix} = \begin{vmatrix} w & x + cw \\ y & z + cy \end{vmatrix}.$

53. $\begin{vmatrix} 1 & x & x^2 \\ 1 & y & y^2 \\ 1 & z & z^2 \end{vmatrix} = \begin{vmatrix} y & y^2 \\ z & z^2 \end{vmatrix} - \begin{vmatrix} x & x^2 \\ z & z^2 \end{vmatrix} + \begin{vmatrix} x & x^2 \\ y & y^2 \end{vmatrix}$

$= (yz^2 - y^2z) - (xz^2 - x^2z) + (xy^2 - x^2y)$

$= yz^2 - xz^2 - y^2z + x^2z + xy(y - x)$

$= z^2(y - x) - z(y^2 - x^2) + xy(y - x)$

$= z^2(y - x) - z(y - x)(y + x) + xy(y - x)$

$= (y - x)[z^2 - z(y + x) + xy]$

$= (y - x)[z^2 - zy - zx + xy]$

$= (y - x)[z^2 - zx - zy + xy]$

$= (y - x)[z(z - x) - y(z - x)]$

$= (y - x)(z - x)(z - y)$

55. $\begin{vmatrix} x - 1 & 2 \\ 3 & x - 2 \end{vmatrix} = 0$

$(x - 1)(x - 2) - 6 = 0$

$x^2 - 3x - 4 = 0$

$(x + 1)(x - 4) = 0$

$x = -1 \text{ or } x = 4$

57. $\begin{vmatrix} 4u & -1 \\ -1 & 2v \end{vmatrix} = 8uv - 1$

59. $\begin{vmatrix} e^{2x} & e^{3x} \\ 2e^{2x} & 3e^{3x} \end{vmatrix} = 3e^{5x} - 2e^{5x} = e^{5x}$

61. $\begin{vmatrix} x & \ln x \\ 1 & \dfrac{1}{x} \end{vmatrix} = 1 - \ln x$

63. (a) $\begin{vmatrix} -1 & 0 \\ 0 & 3 \end{vmatrix} = -3$

(b) $\begin{vmatrix} 2 & 0 \\ 0 & -1 \end{vmatrix} = -2$

(c) $\begin{bmatrix} -1 & 0 \\ 0 & 3 \end{bmatrix} \begin{bmatrix} 2 & 0 \\ 0 & -1 \end{bmatrix} = \begin{bmatrix} -2 & 0 \\ 0 & -3 \end{bmatrix}$

(d) $\begin{vmatrix} -2 & 0 \\ 0 & -3 \end{vmatrix} = 6$

65. (a) $\begin{vmatrix} -1 & 2 & 1 \\ 1 & 0 & 1 \\ 0 & 1 & 0 \end{vmatrix} = 2$

(b) $\begin{vmatrix} -1 & 0 & 0 \\ 0 & 2 & 0 \\ 0 & 0 & 3 \end{vmatrix} = -6$

(c) $\begin{bmatrix} -1 & 2 & 1 \\ 1 & 0 & 1 \\ 0 & 1 & 0 \end{bmatrix} \begin{bmatrix} -1 & 0 & 0 \\ 0 & 2 & 0 \\ 0 & 0 & 3 \end{bmatrix} = \begin{bmatrix} 1 & 4 & 3 \\ -1 & 0 & 3 \\ 0 & 2 & 0 \end{bmatrix}$

(d) $\begin{vmatrix} 1 & 4 & 3 \\ -1 & 0 & 3 \\ 0 & 2 & 0 \end{vmatrix} = -12$

67. Let $A = \begin{bmatrix} 1 & 3 \\ -2 & 4 \end{bmatrix}$ and $B = \begin{bmatrix} -4 & 0 \\ 3 & 5 \end{bmatrix}$.

$|A| = \begin{vmatrix} 1 & 3 \\ -2 & 4 \end{vmatrix} = 10$, $|B| = \begin{vmatrix} -4 & 0 \\ 3 & 5 \end{vmatrix} = -20$, $|A| + |B| = -10$

$A + B = \begin{bmatrix} -3 & 3 \\ 1 & 9 \end{bmatrix}$, $|A + B| = \begin{vmatrix} -3 & 3 \\ 1 & 9 \end{vmatrix} = -30$

Thus, $|A + B| \neq |A| + |B|$. Your answer may differ, depending on how you choose A and B.

69. A square matrix is a square array of numbers. The determinant of a square matrix is a real number.

71. (a) Columns 2 and 3 are interchanged.

(b) Rows 1 and 3 are interchanged.

73. (a) 5 is factored out of the first row of A.

(b) 4 and 3 are factored out of columns 2 and 3.

Section 9.5   Applications of Matrices and Determinants

- You should be able to find the area of a triangle with vertices (x_1, y_1), (x_2, y_2), and (x_3, y_3).

$$\text{Area} = \pm\frac{1}{2}\begin{vmatrix} x_1 & y_1 & 1 \\ x_2 & y_2 & 1 \\ x_3 & y_3 & 1 \end{vmatrix}$$

  The $\pm$ symbol indicates that the appropriate sign should be chosen so that the area is positive.

- You should be able to test to see if three points, (x_1, y_1), (x_2, y_2), and (x_3, y_3), are collinear.

$$\begin{vmatrix} x_1 & y_1 & 1 \\ x_2 & y_2 & 1 \\ x_3 & y_3 & 1 \end{vmatrix} = 0, \text{ if and only if they are collinear.}$$

- You should be able to find the equation of the line through (x_1, y_1) and (x_2, y_2) by evaluating

$$\begin{vmatrix} x & y & 1 \\ x_1 & y_1 & 1 \\ x_2 & y_2 & 1 \end{vmatrix} = 0.$$

- You should be able to use Cramer's Rule to solve a system of linear equations.

- Now you should be able to solve a system of linear equations by substitution, elimination, elementary row operations on an augmented matrix, using the inverse matrix, or Cramer's Rule.

- You should be able to encode and decode messages by using an invertible $n \times n$ matrix.

Solutions to Odd-Numbered Exercises

1. Vertices: $(-2, -3)$, $(2, -3)$, $(0, 4)$

$$\text{Area} = \frac{1}{2}\begin{vmatrix} -2 & -3 & 1 \\ 2 & -3 & 1 \\ 0 & 4 & 1 \end{vmatrix} = \frac{1}{2}\left(-2\begin{vmatrix} -3 & 1 \\ 4 & 1 \end{vmatrix} - 2\begin{vmatrix} -3 & 1 \\ 4 & 1 \end{vmatrix}\right) = \frac{1}{2}(14 + 14) = 14 \text{ square units}$$

3. Vertices: $(0, 0)$, $(3, 1)$, $(1, 5)$

$$\text{Area} = \frac{1}{2}\begin{vmatrix} 0 & 0 & 1 \\ 3 & 1 & 1 \\ 1 & 5 & 1 \end{vmatrix} = \frac{1}{2}\begin{vmatrix} 3 & 1 \\ 1 & 5 \end{vmatrix} = 7 \text{ square units}$$

5. Vertices: $\left(0, \frac{1}{2}\right)$, $\left(\frac{5}{2}, 0\right)$, $(4, 3)$

$$\text{Area} = \frac{1}{2}\begin{vmatrix} 0 & \frac{1}{2} & 1 \\ \frac{5}{2} & 0 & 1 \\ 4 & 3 & 1 \end{vmatrix} = \frac{1}{2}\left(2 + \frac{15}{2} - \frac{5}{4}\right) = \frac{33}{8} \text{ square units}$$

7. Vertices: $(4, 5)$, $(6, 1)$, $(7, 9)$

$$\text{Area} = \tfrac{1}{2} \begin{vmatrix} 4 & 5 & 1 \\ 6 & 1 & 1 \\ 7 & 9 & 1 \end{vmatrix} = \tfrac{1}{2}(20) = 10 \text{ square units}$$

9. Vertices: $(-3, 5)$, $(2, 6)$, $(3, -5)$

$$\text{Area} = -\tfrac{1}{2} \begin{vmatrix} -3 & 5 & 1 \\ 2 & 6 & 1 \\ 3 & -5 & 1 \end{vmatrix} = -\tfrac{1}{2} \begin{vmatrix} -3 & 5 & 1 \\ 5 & 1 & 0 \\ 6 & -10 & 0 \end{vmatrix} = -\tfrac{1}{2} \begin{vmatrix} 5 & 1 \\ 6 & -10 \end{vmatrix} = 28 \text{ square units}$$

11. $4 = \pm \dfrac{1}{2} \begin{vmatrix} -5 & 1 & 1 \\ 0 & 2 & 1 \\ -2 & x & 1 \end{vmatrix}$

$\pm 8 = -5 \begin{vmatrix} 2 & 1 \\ x & 1 \end{vmatrix} - 2 \begin{vmatrix} 1 & 1 \\ 2 & 1 \end{vmatrix}$

$\pm 8 = -5(2 - x) - 2(-1)$

$\pm 8 = 5x - 8$

$x = \dfrac{8 \pm 8}{5}$

$x = \dfrac{16}{5} \quad \text{OR} \quad x = 0$

13. $3x + 4y = -2$

$5x + 3y = 4$

$x = \dfrac{\begin{vmatrix} -2 & 4 \\ 4 & 3 \end{vmatrix}}{\begin{vmatrix} 3 & 4 \\ 5 & 3 \end{vmatrix}} = \dfrac{-22}{-11} = 2$

$y = \dfrac{\begin{vmatrix} 3 & -2 \\ 5 & 4 \end{vmatrix}}{\begin{vmatrix} 3 & 4 \\ 5 & 3 \end{vmatrix}} = \dfrac{22}{-11} = -2$

Answer: $(2, -2)$

15. $4x - y + z = -5$

$2x + 2y + 3z = 10$

$5x - 2y + 6z = 1$

$D = \begin{vmatrix} 4 & -1 & 1 \\ 2 & 2 & 3 \\ 5 & -2 & 6 \end{vmatrix} = 55$

$x = \dfrac{\begin{vmatrix} -5 & -1 & 1 \\ 10 & 2 & 3 \\ 1 & -2 & 6 \end{vmatrix}}{55} = \dfrac{-55}{55} = -1$

$y = \dfrac{\begin{vmatrix} 4 & -5 & 1 \\ 2 & 10 & 3 \\ 5 & 1 & 6 \end{vmatrix}}{55} = \dfrac{165}{55} = 3$

$z = \dfrac{\begin{vmatrix} 4 & -1 & -5 \\ 2 & 2 & 10 \\ 5 & -2 & 1 \end{vmatrix}}{55} = \dfrac{110}{55} = 2$

Answer: $(-1, 3, 2)$

17. $3x + 3y + 5z = 1$

$3x + 5y + 9z = 2$ $D = \begin{vmatrix} 3 & 3 & 5 \\ 3 & 5 & 9 \\ 5 & 9 & 17 \end{vmatrix} = 4$

$5x + 9y + 17z = 4$

$x = \dfrac{\begin{vmatrix} 1 & 3 & 5 \\ 2 & 5 & 9 \\ 4 & 9 & 17 \end{vmatrix}}{4} = 0, \; y = \dfrac{\begin{vmatrix} 3 & 1 & 5 \\ 3 & 2 & 9 \\ 5 & 4 & 17 \end{vmatrix}}{4} = -\dfrac{1}{2}, \; z = \dfrac{\begin{vmatrix} 3 & 3 & 1 \\ 3 & 5 & 2 \\ 5 & 9 & 4 \end{vmatrix}}{4} = \dfrac{1}{2}$

Answer: $\left(0, -\dfrac{1}{2}, \dfrac{1}{2}\right)$

$\qquad\qquad\quad A \qquad\; B \qquad\; C$

19. Vertices: $(0, 25), \; (10, 0), \; (28, 5)$

Area $= \dfrac{1}{2} \begin{vmatrix} 0 & 25 & 1 \\ 10 & 0 & 1 \\ 28 & 5 & 1 \end{vmatrix} = 250$ square miles

21. Points: $(3, -1), \; (0, -3), \; (12, 5)$

$\begin{vmatrix} 3 & -1 & 1 \\ 0 & -3 & 1 \\ 12 & 5 & 1 \end{vmatrix} = \begin{vmatrix} 3 & -1 & 1 \\ 0 & -3 & 1 \\ 0 & 9 & -3 \end{vmatrix} = 3\begin{vmatrix} -3 & 1 \\ 9 & -3 \end{vmatrix} = 0$

The points are collinear.

23. Points: $\left(2, -\dfrac{1}{2}\right), \; (-4, 4), \; (6, -3)$

$\begin{vmatrix} 2 & -\frac{1}{2} & 1 \\ -4 & 4 & 1 \\ 6 & -3 & 1 \end{vmatrix} = \begin{vmatrix} -4 & \frac{5}{2} & 0 \\ -10 & 7 & 0 \\ 6 & -3 & 1 \end{vmatrix} = 3\begin{vmatrix} -4 & \frac{5}{2} \\ -10 & 7 \end{vmatrix} = -3 \neq 0$

The points are not collinear.

25. Points: $(0, 2), \; (1, 2.4), \; (-1, 1.6)$

$\begin{vmatrix} 0 & 2 & 1 \\ 1 & 2.4 & 1 \\ -1 & 1.6 & 1 \end{vmatrix} = \begin{vmatrix} 0 & 2 & 1 \\ 1 & 2.4 & 1 \\ 0 & 4.0 & 2 \end{vmatrix} = -\begin{vmatrix} 2 & 1 \\ 4 & 2 \end{vmatrix} = 0$

The points are collinear.

27. Points: $(0, 0), \; (5, 3)$

Equation: $\begin{vmatrix} x & y & 1 \\ 0 & 0 & 1 \\ 5 & 3 & 1 \end{vmatrix} = 5y - 3x = 0$ OR $3x - 5y = 0$

29. Points: $(-4, 3), \; (2, 1)$

Equation: $\begin{vmatrix} x & y & 1 \\ -4 & 3 & 1 \\ 2 & 1 & 1 \end{vmatrix} = 3x + 2y - 4 - 6 + 4y - x = 0$ OR $x + 3y - 5 = 0$

31. Points: $\left(-\frac{1}{2}, 3\right)$, $\left(\frac{5}{2}, 1\right)$

Equation: $\begin{vmatrix} x & y & 1 \\ -\frac{1}{2} & 3 & 1 \\ \frac{5}{2} & 1 & 1 \end{vmatrix} = 3x + \frac{5}{2}y - \frac{1}{2} - \frac{15}{2} + \frac{1}{2}y - x = 0$ OR $2x + 3y - 8 = 0$

33.
$$\begin{vmatrix} 2 & -5 & 1 \\ 4 & x & 1 \\ 5 & -2 & 1 \end{vmatrix} = 0$$

$$2\begin{vmatrix} x & 1 \\ -2 & 1 \end{vmatrix} + 5\begin{vmatrix} 4 & 1 \\ 5 & 1 \end{vmatrix} + \begin{vmatrix} 4 & x \\ 5 & -2 \end{vmatrix} = 0$$

$$2(x + 2) + 5(-1) + (-8 - 5x) = 0$$

$$-3x - 9 = 0$$

$$x = -3$$

35. The uncoded row matrices are the rows of the 7×3 matrix on the left.

$$
\begin{matrix}
T & R & 0 \\
U & B & L \\
E & & I \\
N & & R \\
I & V & E \\
R & & C \\
I & T & Y
\end{matrix}
\begin{bmatrix}
20 & 18 & 15 \\
21 & 2 & 12 \\
5 & 0 & 9 \\
14 & 0 & 18 \\
9 & 22 & 5 \\
18 & 0 & 3 \\
9 & 20 & 25
\end{bmatrix}
\begin{bmatrix}
1 & -1 & 0 \\
1 & 0 & -1 \\
-6 & 2 & 3
\end{bmatrix}
=
\begin{bmatrix}
-52 & 10 & 27 \\
-49 & 3 & 34 \\
-49 & 13 & 27 \\
-94 & 22 & 54 \\
1 & 1 & -7 \\
0 & -12 & 9 \\
-121 & 41 & 55
\end{bmatrix}
$$

Answer: $[-52, 10, 27], [-49, 3, 34], [-49, 13, 27], [-94, 22, 54], [1, 1, -7], [0, -12, 9], [-121, 41, 55]$

In Exercises 37–39, use the matrix $A = \begin{bmatrix} 1 & 2 & 2 \\ 3 & 7 & 9 \\ -1 & -4 & -7 \end{bmatrix}$.

37. L A N   D I N G _ S U C C   E S S   F U L

[12 1 14] [4 9 14]   [7 0 19] [21 3 3]   [5 19 19]   [6 21 12]

$[12 \quad 1 \quad 14]A = [\quad 1 \quad -25 \quad -65]$

$[4 \quad 9 \quad 14]A = [\quad 17 \quad 15 \quad -9]$

$[7 \quad 0 \quad 19]A = [-12 \quad -62 \quad -119]$

$[21 \quad 3 \quad 3]A = [\quad 27 \quad 51 \quad 48]$

$[5 \quad 19 \quad 19]A = [\quad 43 \quad 67 \quad 48]$

$[6 \quad 21 \quad 12]A = [\quad 57 \quad 111 \quad 117]$

Cryptogram: 1 −25 −65 17 15 −9 −12 −62 −119 27 51 48 43 67 48 57 111 117

39. H   A   P   P   Y   _   B   I   R   T   H   D   A   Y   _

[8 1 16]   [16 25 0]   [2 9 18]   [20 8 4]   [1 25 0]

$[\ 8\quad 1\quad 16]A = [\ 5\quad -41\quad -87]$

$[16\quad 25\quad 0]A = [91\quad 207\quad 257]$

$[\ 2\quad 9\quad 18]A = [11\quad -5\quad -41]$

$[20\quad 8\quad 4]A = [40\quad 80\quad 84]$

$[\ 1\quad 25\quad 0]A = [76\quad 177\quad 227]$

Cryptogram: $-5\ \ -41\ \ -87\ \ 91\ \ 207\ \ 257\ \ 11\ \ -5\ \ -41\ \ 40\ \ 80\ \ 84\ \ 76\ \ 177\ \ 227$

41. $A^{-1} = \begin{bmatrix} 1 & 2 \\ 3 & 5 \end{bmatrix}^{-1} = \begin{bmatrix} -5 & 2 \\ 3 & -1 \end{bmatrix}$

$$\begin{bmatrix} 11 & 21 \\ 64 & 112 \\ 25 & 50 \\ 29 & 53 \\ 23 & 46 \\ 40 & 75 \\ 55 & 92 \end{bmatrix} \begin{bmatrix} -5 & 2 \\ 3 & -1 \end{bmatrix} = \begin{bmatrix} 8 & 1 \\ 16 & 16 \\ 25 & 0 \\ 14 & 5 \\ 23 & 0 \\ 25 & 5 \\ 1 & 18 \end{bmatrix} \begin{matrix} \text{H} & \text{A} \\ \text{P} & \text{P} \\ \text{Y} & \\ \text{N} & \text{E} \\ \text{W} & \\ \text{Y} & \text{E} \\ \text{A} & \text{R} \end{matrix}$$

Message: HAPPY NEW YEAR

43. $A^{-1} = \begin{bmatrix} 1 & 2 & 2 \\ 3 & 7 & 9 \\ -1 & -4 & -7 \end{bmatrix}^{-1} = \begin{bmatrix} -13 & 6 & 4 \\ 12 & -5 & -3 \\ -5 & 2 & 1 \end{bmatrix}$

$$\begin{bmatrix} 20 & 17 & -15 \\ -12 & -56 & -104 \\ 1 & -25 & -65 \\ 62 & 143 & 181 \end{bmatrix} \begin{bmatrix} -13 & 6 & 4 \\ 12 & -5 & -3 \\ -5 & 2 & 1 \end{bmatrix} = \begin{bmatrix} 19 & 5 & 14 \\ 4 & 0 & 16 \\ 12 & 1 & 14 \\ 5 & 19 & 0 \end{bmatrix} \begin{matrix} \text{S} & \text{E} & \text{N} \\ \text{D} & & \text{P} \\ \text{L} & \text{A} & \text{N} \\ \text{E} & \text{S} & \end{matrix}$$

Message: SEND PLANES

45. Let A be the 2×2 matrix needed to decode the message.

$$\begin{bmatrix} -18 & -18 \\ 1 & 16 \end{bmatrix} A = \begin{bmatrix} 0 & 18 \\ 15 & 14 \end{bmatrix} \begin{matrix} & \text{R} \\ \text{O} & \text{N} \end{matrix}$$

$$A = \begin{bmatrix} -18 & -18 \\ 1 & 16 \end{bmatrix}^{-1} \begin{bmatrix} 0 & 18 \\ 15 & 14 \end{bmatrix} = \begin{bmatrix} -\frac{8}{135} & -\frac{1}{15} \\ \frac{1}{270} & \frac{1}{15} \end{bmatrix} \begin{bmatrix} 0 & 18 \\ 15 & 14 \end{bmatrix} = \begin{bmatrix} -1 & -2 \\ 1 & 1 \end{bmatrix}$$

$$\begin{bmatrix} 8 & 21 \\ -15 & -10 \\ -13 & -13 \\ 5 & 10 \\ 5 & 25 \\ 5 & 19 \\ -1 & 6 \\ 20 & 40 \\ -18 & -18 \\ 1 & 16 \end{bmatrix} \begin{bmatrix} -1 & -2 \\ 1 & 1 \end{bmatrix} = \begin{bmatrix} 13 & 5 \\ 5 & 20 \\ 0 & 13 \\ 5 & 0 \\ 20 & 15 \\ 14 & 9 \\ 7 & 8 \\ 20 & 0 \\ 0 & 18 \\ 15 & 14 \end{bmatrix} \begin{matrix} \text{M} & \text{E} \\ \text{E} & \text{T} \\ & \text{M} \\ \text{E} & \\ \text{T} & \text{O} \\ \text{N} & \text{I} \\ \text{G} & \text{H} \\ \text{T} & \\ & \text{R} \\ \text{O} & \text{N} \end{matrix}$$

Message: MEET ME TONIGHT RON

☐ Review Exercises for Chapter 9

Solutions to Odd-Numbered Exercises

1. $\begin{bmatrix} 3 & -10 & \vdots & 15 \\ 5 & 4 & \vdots & 22 \end{bmatrix}$

3. $\begin{bmatrix} 5 & 1 & 7 & \vdots & -9 \\ 4 & 2 & 0 & \vdots & 10 \\ 9 & 4 & 2 & \vdots & 3 \end{bmatrix}$ $\begin{aligned} 5x + y + 7z &= -9 \\ 4x + 2y \quad\;\; &= 10 \\ 9x + 4y + 2z &= 3 \end{aligned}$

5. $\begin{bmatrix} 0 & 1 & 1 \\ 1 & 2 & 3 \\ 2 & 2 & 2 \end{bmatrix}$

$\begin{matrix} R_1 + R_2 \rightarrow \\ -R_1 + R_2 \rightarrow \\ -2R_1 + R_3 \rightarrow \end{matrix} \begin{bmatrix} 1 & 3 & 4 \\ 0 & -1 & -1 \\ 0 & -4 & -6 \end{bmatrix}$

$\begin{matrix} 3R_2 + R_1 \rightarrow \\ -R_2 \rightarrow \\ -4R_2 + R_3 \rightarrow \end{matrix} \begin{bmatrix} 1 & 0 & 1 \\ 0 & 1 & 1 \\ 0 & 0 & -2 \end{bmatrix}$

$\begin{matrix} -R_3 + R_1 \rightarrow \\ -R_3 + R_2 \rightarrow \\ -\frac{1}{2}R_3 \rightarrow \end{matrix} \begin{bmatrix} 1 & 0 & 0 \\ 0 & 1 & 0 \\ 0 & 0 & 1 \end{bmatrix}$

7. $\begin{bmatrix} 3 & -2 & 1 & 0 \\ 4 & -3 & 0 & 1 \end{bmatrix} \Rightarrow \begin{bmatrix} 1 & 0 & 3 & -2 \\ 0 & 1 & 4 & -3 \end{bmatrix}$

9. $\begin{bmatrix} 1 & 3 & 4 \\ 0 & 1 & 1 \\ 2 & 4 & 6 \end{bmatrix} \Rightarrow \begin{bmatrix} 1 & 0 & 1 \\ 0 & 1 & 1 \\ 0 & 0 & 0 \end{bmatrix}$

11. $\begin{bmatrix} 5 & 4 & \vdots & 2 \\ -1 & 1 & \vdots & -22 \end{bmatrix}$

$\begin{matrix} 4R_2 + R_1 \rightarrow \\ R_1 + R_2 \rightarrow \end{matrix} \begin{bmatrix} 1 & 8 & \vdots & -86 \\ 0 & 9 & \vdots & -108 \end{bmatrix}$

$\begin{matrix} -8R_2 + R_1 \rightarrow \\ \frac{1}{9}R_2 \rightarrow \end{matrix} \begin{bmatrix} 1 & 0 & \vdots & 10 \\ 0 & 1 & \vdots & -12 \end{bmatrix}$

$x = 10, \; y = -12$

Answer: $(10, -12)$

13. $\begin{bmatrix} 2 & 1 & \vdots & 0.3 \\ 3 & -1 & \vdots & -1.3 \end{bmatrix}$

$\begin{matrix} \\ -R_1 + R_2 \rightarrow \end{matrix} \begin{bmatrix} 2 & 1 & \vdots & 0.3 \\ 1 & -2 & \vdots & -1.6 \end{bmatrix}$

$\begin{bmatrix} 1 & -2 & \vdots & -1.6 \\ 2 & 1 & \vdots & 0.3 \end{bmatrix}$

$\begin{matrix} \\ -2R_1 + R_2 \rightarrow \end{matrix} \begin{bmatrix} 1 & -2 & \vdots & -1.6 \\ 0 & 5 & \vdots & 3.5 \end{bmatrix}$

$\begin{matrix} 2R_2 + R_1 \rightarrow \\ \frac{1}{5}R_2 \rightarrow \end{matrix} \begin{bmatrix} 1 & 0 & \vdots & -0.2 \\ 0 & 1 & \vdots & 0.7 \end{bmatrix}$

$x = -0.2, \; y = 0.7$

15.
$$\begin{bmatrix} 2 & 1 & 2 & \vdots & 4 \\ 2 & 2 & 0 & \vdots & 5 \\ 2 & -1 & 6 & \vdots & 2 \end{bmatrix}$$

$$\begin{matrix} \\ -R_1 + R_2 \rightarrow \\ -R_1 + R_3 \rightarrow \end{matrix} \begin{bmatrix} 2 & 1 & 2 & \vdots & 4 \\ 0 & 1 & -2 & \vdots & 1 \\ 0 & -2 & 4 & \vdots & -2 \end{bmatrix}$$

$$\begin{matrix} -R_1 + R_2 \rightarrow \\ \\ -R_1 + R_3 \rightarrow \end{matrix} \begin{bmatrix} 2 & 1 & 2 & \vdots & 4 \\ 0 & 1 & -2 & \vdots & 1 \\ 0 & -2 & 4 & \vdots & -2 \end{bmatrix}$$

Let $z = a$, then $y - 2a = 1 \implies y = 2a + 1$, and $2x + 4a = 3 \implies x = -2a + \frac{3}{2}$.

Answer: $\left(-2a + \frac{3}{2}, 2a + 1, a\right)$

17.
$$\begin{bmatrix} 4 & 4 & 4 & \vdots & 5 \\ 4 & -2 & -8 & \vdots & 1 \\ 5 & 3 & 8 & \vdots & 6 \end{bmatrix}$$

$$\begin{matrix} R_3 - R_1 \rightarrow \\ -4R_1 + R_2 \rightarrow \\ -5R_1 + R_3 \rightarrow \end{matrix} \begin{bmatrix} 1 & -1 & 4 & \vdots & 1 \\ 0 & 2 & -24 & \vdots & -3 \\ 0 & 8 & -12 & \vdots & 1 \end{bmatrix}$$

$$\begin{matrix} R_2 + R_1 \rightarrow \\ \frac{1}{2}R_2 \rightarrow \\ -8R_2 + R_3 \rightarrow \end{matrix} \begin{bmatrix} 1 & 0 & -8 & \vdots & -\frac{1}{2} \\ 0 & 1 & -12 & \vdots & -\frac{3}{2} \\ 0 & 0 & 84 & \vdots & 13 \end{bmatrix}$$

$$\begin{matrix} 8R_3 + R_1 \rightarrow \\ 12R_3 + R_2 \rightarrow \\ \frac{1}{84}R_3 \rightarrow \end{matrix} \begin{bmatrix} 1 & 0 & 0 & \vdots & \frac{31}{42} \\ 0 & 1 & 0 & \vdots & \frac{5}{14} \\ 0 & 0 & 1 & \vdots & \frac{13}{84} \end{bmatrix}$$

$x = \frac{31}{42}, y = \frac{5}{14}, z = \frac{13}{84}$

Answer: $\left(\frac{31}{42}, \frac{5}{14}, \frac{13}{84}\right)$

19.
$$\begin{bmatrix} -1 & 1 & 2 & \vdots & 1 \\ 2 & 3 & 1 & \vdots & -2 \\ 5 & 4 & 2 & \vdots & 4 \end{bmatrix}$$

$$\begin{matrix} -R_1 \rightarrow \\ 2R_1 + R_2 \rightarrow \\ 5R_1 + R_3 \rightarrow \end{matrix} \begin{bmatrix} 1 & -1 & -2 & \vdots & -1 \\ 0 & 5 & 5 & \vdots & 0 \\ 0 & 9 & 12 & \vdots & 9 \end{bmatrix}$$

$$\begin{matrix} R_2 + R_1 \rightarrow \\ \frac{1}{5}R_2 \rightarrow \\ -9R_2 + R_3 \rightarrow \end{matrix} \begin{bmatrix} 1 & 0 & -1 & \vdots & -1 \\ 0 & 1 & 1 & \vdots & 0 \\ 0 & 0 & 3 & \vdots & 9 \end{bmatrix}$$

$$\begin{matrix} R_3 + R_1 \rightarrow \\ -R_3 + R_2 \rightarrow \\ \frac{1}{3}R_3 \rightarrow \end{matrix} \begin{bmatrix} 1 & 0 & 0 & \vdots & 2 \\ 0 & 1 & 0 & \vdots & -3 \\ 0 & 0 & 1 & \vdots & 3 \end{bmatrix}$$

$x = 2, y = -3, z = 3$

Answer: $(2, -3, 3)$

21.
$$\begin{bmatrix} 1 & 2 & 6 & \vdots & 1 \\ 2 & 5 & 15 & \vdots & 4 \\ 3 & 1 & 3 & \vdots & -6 \end{bmatrix}$$

$$\begin{matrix} \\ -2R_1 + R_2 \rightarrow \\ -3R_1 + R_3 \rightarrow \end{matrix} \begin{bmatrix} 1 & 2 & 6 & \vdots & 1 \\ 0 & 1 & 3 & \vdots & 2 \\ 0 & -5 & -15 & \vdots & -9 \end{bmatrix}$$

$$\begin{matrix} -2R_2 + R_1 \rightarrow \\ \\ 5R_2 + R_3 \rightarrow \end{matrix} \begin{bmatrix} 1 & 0 & 0 & \vdots & -3 \\ 0 & 1 & 3 & \vdots & 2 \\ 0 & 0 & 0 & \vdots & 1 \end{bmatrix}$$

$x = -3$

$y + 3z = 2$

$0 = 1$

Inconsistent, no solution

23. If a system of linear equations has a unique solution, the augmented matrix reduces to a form in which the number of rows with nonzero entries on the coefficient side of the matrix equals the number of variables.

25. $\begin{bmatrix} 1 & -3 & \vdots & -2 \\ 1 & 1 & \vdots & 2 \end{bmatrix} \implies \begin{bmatrix} 1 & 0 & \vdots & 1 \\ 0 & 1 & \vdots & 1 \end{bmatrix}$

$x = 1, \ y = 1$

27. $\begin{bmatrix} 1 & 2 & -1 & \vdots & 7 \\ 0 & -1 & -1 & \vdots & 4 \\ 4 & 0 & -1 & \vdots & 16 \end{bmatrix} \implies \begin{bmatrix} 1 & 0 & 0 & \vdots & 3 \\ 0 & 1 & 0 & \vdots & 0 \\ 0 & 0 & 1 & \vdots & -4 \end{bmatrix}$

$x = 3, \ y = 0, \ z = -4$

29. $\begin{bmatrix} 2 & 1 & 0 \\ 0 & 5 & -4 \end{bmatrix} - 3\begin{bmatrix} 5 & 3 & -6 \\ 0 & -2 & 5 \end{bmatrix} = \begin{bmatrix} 2 & 1 & 0 \\ 0 & 5 & -4 \end{bmatrix} - \begin{bmatrix} 15 & 9 & -18 \\ 0 & -6 & 15 \end{bmatrix}$

$$= \begin{bmatrix} -13 & -8 & 18 \\ 0 & 11 & -19 \end{bmatrix}$$

31. $\begin{bmatrix} 1 & 2 \\ 5 & -4 \\ 6 & 0 \end{bmatrix}\begin{bmatrix} 6 & -2 & 8 \\ 4 & 0 & 0 \end{bmatrix} = \begin{bmatrix} 1(6) + 2(4) & 1(-2) + 2(0) & 1(8) + 2(0) \\ 5(6) + (-4)(4) & 5(-2) + (-4)(0) & 5(8) + (-4)(0) \\ 6(6) + (0)(4) & 6(-2) + (0)(0) & 6(8) + (0)(0) \end{bmatrix}$

$$= \begin{bmatrix} 14 & -2 & 8 \\ 14 & -10 & 40 \\ 36 & -12 & 48 \end{bmatrix}$$

33. $\begin{bmatrix} 1 & 5 & 6 \\ 2 & -4 & 0 \end{bmatrix}\begin{bmatrix} 6 & 4 \\ -2 & 0 \\ 8 & 0 \end{bmatrix} = \begin{bmatrix} 1(6) + 5(-2) + 6(8) & 1(4) + 5(0) + 6(0) \\ 2(6) - 4(-2) + 0(8) & 2(4) - 4(0) + 0(0) \end{bmatrix}$

$$= \begin{bmatrix} 44 & 4 \\ 20 & 8 \end{bmatrix}$$

35. $\begin{bmatrix} 1 & 3 & 2 \\ 0 & 2 & -4 \\ 0 & 0 & 3 \end{bmatrix}\begin{bmatrix} 4 & -3 & 2 \\ 0 & 3 & -1 \\ 0 & 0 & 2 \end{bmatrix} = \begin{bmatrix} 1(4) & 1(-3) + 3(3) & 1(2) + 3(-1) + 2(2) \\ 0 & 2(3) & 2(-1) + (-4)(2) \\ 0 & 0 & 3(2) \end{bmatrix}$

$$= \begin{bmatrix} 4 & 6 & 3 \\ 0 & 6 & -10 \\ 0 & 0 & 6 \end{bmatrix}$$

37. $3\begin{bmatrix} 8 & -2 & 5 \\ 1 & 3 & -1 \end{bmatrix} + 6\begin{bmatrix} 4 & -2 & -3 \\ 2 & 7 & 6 \end{bmatrix} = \begin{bmatrix} 48 & -18 & -3 \\ 15 & 51 & 33 \end{bmatrix}$

39. $\begin{bmatrix} 4 & 1 \\ 11 & -7 \\ 12 & 3 \end{bmatrix}\begin{bmatrix} 3 & -5 & 6 \\ 2 & -2 & -2 \end{bmatrix} = \begin{bmatrix} 14 & -22 & 22 \\ 19 & -41 & 80 \\ 42 & -66 & 66 \end{bmatrix}$

41. $X = 3A - 2B = 3\begin{bmatrix} -4 & 0 \\ 1 & -5 \\ -3 & 2 \end{bmatrix} - 2\begin{bmatrix} 1 & 2 \\ -2 & 1 \\ 4 & 4 \end{bmatrix} = \begin{bmatrix} -14 & -4 \\ 7 & -17 \\ -17 & -2 \end{bmatrix}$

43. $X = \frac{1}{3}[B - 2A] = \frac{1}{3}\left(\begin{bmatrix} 1 & 2 \\ -2 & 1 \\ 4 & 4 \end{bmatrix} - 2\begin{bmatrix} -4 & 0 \\ 1 & -5 \\ -3 & 2 \end{bmatrix}\right) = \frac{1}{3}\begin{bmatrix} 9 & 2 \\ -4 & 11 \\ 10 & 0 \end{bmatrix}$

45. $\begin{bmatrix} 5 & 4 \\ -1 & 1 \end{bmatrix}\begin{bmatrix} x \\ y \end{bmatrix} = \begin{bmatrix} 2 \\ -22 \end{bmatrix} \Rightarrow \begin{bmatrix} 5x + 4y \\ -x + y \end{bmatrix} = \begin{bmatrix} 2 \\ -22 \end{bmatrix} \Rightarrow \begin{array}{l} 5x + 4y = 2 \\ -x + y = -22 \end{array}$

47. $\begin{bmatrix} 2 & 6 \\ 3 & -6 \end{bmatrix}^{-1} = \begin{bmatrix} \frac{1}{5} & \frac{1}{5} \\ \frac{1}{10} & -\frac{1}{15} \end{bmatrix}$

49. $\begin{bmatrix} 2 & 0 & 3 \\ -1 & 1 & 1 \\ 2 & -2 & 1 \end{bmatrix}^{-1} = \begin{bmatrix} \frac{1}{2} & -1 & -\frac{1}{2} \\ \frac{1}{2} & -\frac{2}{3} & -\frac{5}{6} \\ 0 & \frac{2}{3} & \frac{1}{3} \end{bmatrix}$

51. $\begin{vmatrix} 50 & -30 \\ 10 & 5 \end{vmatrix} = 50(5) - (-30)(10) = 550$

53. $\begin{vmatrix} 10 & 8 \\ -6 & -4 \end{vmatrix} = 10(-4) - (-6)(8) = -40 + 48 = 8$

55. $\begin{vmatrix} 1 & 0 & -2 \\ 0 & 1 & 0 \\ -2 & 0 & 1 \end{vmatrix} = 1\begin{vmatrix} 1 & -2 \\ -2 & 1 \end{vmatrix} = 1(1) - (-2)(-2) = 1 - 4 = -3$

57. $\begin{vmatrix} 3 & 0 & -4 & 0 \\ 0 & 8 & 1 & 2 \\ 6 & 1 & 8 & 2 \\ 0 & 3 & -4 & 1 \end{vmatrix} = 3\begin{vmatrix} 8 & 1 & 2 \\ 1 & 8 & 2 \\ 3 & -4 & 1 \end{vmatrix} + (-4)\begin{vmatrix} 0 & 8 & 2 \\ 6 & 1 & 2 \\ 0 & 3 & 1 \end{vmatrix}$ (Expansion along Row 1)

$= 3[3(8 - (-8)) - 1(1 - 6) + 2(-4 - 24)] - 4[0 - 6(8 - 6) + 0]$

$= 3[128 + 5 - 56] - 4[-12]$

$= 279$

59. $x + 2y = -1$

$3x + 4y = -5$

$\begin{bmatrix} 1 & 2 \\ 3 & 4 \end{bmatrix}^{-1} = \begin{bmatrix} -2 & 1 \\ \frac{3}{2} & -\frac{1}{2} \end{bmatrix} \Rightarrow \begin{bmatrix} x \\ y \end{bmatrix} = \begin{bmatrix} -2 & 1 \\ \frac{3}{2} & -\frac{1}{2} \end{bmatrix}\begin{bmatrix} -1 \\ -5 \end{bmatrix} = \begin{bmatrix} -3 \\ 1 \end{bmatrix}$

$x = -3, y = 1$

Answer: $(-3, 1)$

61. $-3x - 3y - 4z = 2$

$\quad\quad\quad y + z = -1$

$\quad 4x + 3y + 4z = -1$

$$\begin{bmatrix} -3 & -3 & -4 \\ 0 & 1 & 1 \\ 4 & 3 & 4 \end{bmatrix}^{-1} = \begin{bmatrix} 1 & 0 & 1 \\ 4 & 4 & 3 \\ 4 & -3 & -3 \end{bmatrix} \Rightarrow \begin{bmatrix} x \\ y \\ z \end{bmatrix} = \begin{bmatrix} 1 & 0 & 1 \\ 4 & 4 & 3 \\ -4 & -3 & -3 \end{bmatrix}\begin{bmatrix} 2 \\ -1 \\ -1 \end{bmatrix} = \begin{bmatrix} 1 \\ 1 \\ -2 \end{bmatrix}$$

$x = 1, y = 1, z = -2$

Answer: $(1, 1, -2)$

63. $\quad x + 3y + 2z = 2$

$\quad -2x - 5y - z = 10$

$\quad 2x + 4y = -12$

$$\begin{bmatrix} 1 & 3 & 2 \\ -2 & -5 & -1 \\ 2 & 4 & 0 \end{bmatrix}^{-1} = \begin{bmatrix} 2 & 4 & \frac{7}{2} \\ -1 & -2 & -\frac{3}{2} \\ 1 & 1 & \frac{1}{2} \end{bmatrix} \Rightarrow \begin{bmatrix} x \\ y \\ z \end{bmatrix} = \begin{bmatrix} 2 & 4 & \frac{7}{2} \\ -1 & -2 & -\frac{3}{2} \\ 1 & 1 & \frac{1}{2} \end{bmatrix}\begin{bmatrix} 2 \\ 10 \\ -12 \end{bmatrix} = \begin{bmatrix} 2 \\ -4 \\ 6 \end{bmatrix}$$

$x = 2, y = -4, z = 6$

Answer: $(2, -4, 6)$

65. $-x + y + z = 6$

$\quad 4x - 3y + z = 20$

$\quad 2x - y + 3z = 8$

$$\begin{bmatrix} -1 & 1 & 1 \\ 4 & -3 & 1 \\ 2 & -1 & 3 \end{bmatrix}^{-1} \text{ does not exist.}$$

The system is inconsistent and has no solution.

67. $x = \dfrac{\begin{vmatrix} 5 & 2 \\ 1 & 1 \end{vmatrix}}{\begin{vmatrix} 1 & 2 \\ -1 & 1 \end{vmatrix}} = \dfrac{3}{3} = 1$

$y = \dfrac{\begin{vmatrix} 1 & 5 \\ -1 & 1 \end{vmatrix}}{\begin{vmatrix} 1 & 2 \\ -1 & 1 \end{vmatrix}} = \dfrac{6}{3} = 2$

69. $x = \dfrac{\begin{vmatrix} 11 & 8 \\ 21 & -24 \end{vmatrix}}{\begin{vmatrix} 20 & 8 \\ 12 & -24 \end{vmatrix}} = \dfrac{-432}{-576} = \dfrac{3}{4}$

$y = \dfrac{\begin{vmatrix} 20 & 11 \\ 12 & 21 \end{vmatrix}}{\begin{vmatrix} 20 & 8 \\ 12 & -24 \end{vmatrix}} = \dfrac{288}{-576} = -\dfrac{1}{2}$

71. $x = \dfrac{\begin{vmatrix} 5 & 6 \\ 11 & 14 \end{vmatrix}}{\begin{vmatrix} 3 & 6 \\ 6 & 14 \end{vmatrix}} = \dfrac{4}{6} = \dfrac{2}{3}$

$y = \dfrac{\begin{vmatrix} 3 & 5 \\ 6 & 11 \end{vmatrix}}{\begin{vmatrix} 3 & 6 \\ 6 & 14 \end{vmatrix}} = \dfrac{3}{6} = \dfrac{1}{2}$

73. Cramer's Rule does not apply because the determinant of the coefficient matrix is zero.

75. x = number of carnations

y = number of roses

$$x + \quad y = 12$$
$$0.75x + 1.50y = 12.00$$

$$\begin{bmatrix} 1 & 1 & \vdots & 12 \\ 0.75 & 1.50 & \vdots & 12 \end{bmatrix} -0.75R_1 + R_2 \begin{bmatrix} 1 & 1 & \vdots & 12 \\ 0 & 0.75 & \vdots & 3 \end{bmatrix}$$

$0.75y = 3 \implies y = 4$

$x + (4) = 12 \implies x = 8$

Answer: 8 carnations, 4 roses

77. $(-1, 2), \ (0, 3), \ (1, 6)$

$f(x) = ax^2 + bx + c$

$\left. \begin{array}{l} f(-1) = a - b + c = 2 \implies a - b = -1 \\ f(0) = c = 3 \\ f(1) = a + b + c = 6 \implies a + b = \quad 3 \end{array} \right\} a = 1, b = 2$

Thus, $y = x^2 + 2x + 3$.

79. $13a + \quad 91b = 1107$

$91a + 819b = 8404.7$

(a) $a \approx 59.9, \ b \approx 3.6$

$\quad y = 59.9 + 3.6t$

(b)

(c) The median price of one-family homes sold in the United States has been increasing by an average of 3.6 thousand dollars ($3600) each year.

(d) $y(15) = 59.9 + 3.6(15) = 113.9$ which corresponds to a price of $113,900.

81. $(1, 0), \ (5, 0), \ (5, 8)$

$\text{Area} = \dfrac{1}{2} \begin{vmatrix} 1 & 0 & 1 \\ 5 & 0 & 1 \\ 5 & 8 & 1 \end{vmatrix} = \dfrac{1}{2}(32)$

$\quad\quad = 16$ square units

83. $(1, 2), \ (4, -5), \ (3, 2)$

$\text{Area} = \dfrac{1}{2} \begin{vmatrix} 1 & 2 & 1 \\ 4 & -5 & 1 \\ 3 & 1 & 1 \end{vmatrix} = \dfrac{1}{2}(14)$

$\quad\quad = 7$ square units

85. $(-4, 0), \ (4, 4)$

$\begin{vmatrix} x & y & 1 \\ -4 & 0 & 1 \\ 4 & 4 & 1 \end{vmatrix} = 0$

$-4x + 8y - 16 = 0$

$\quad x - 2y + 4 = 0$

87. $\left(-\dfrac{5}{2}, 3\right), \ \left(\dfrac{7}{2}, 1\right)$

$\begin{vmatrix} x & y & 1 \\ -\dfrac{5}{2} & 3 & 1 \\ \dfrac{7}{2} & 1 & 1 \end{vmatrix} = 0$

$-2x - 6y + 13 = 0$

89. Expansion by Row 3

$$\begin{vmatrix} a_{11} & a_{12} & a_{13} \\ a_{21} & a_{22} & a_{23} \\ a_{31} + c_1 & a_{32} + c_2 & a_{33} + c_3 \end{vmatrix} = (a_{31} + c_1)\begin{vmatrix} a_{12} & a_{13} \\ a_{22} & a_{23} \end{vmatrix} - (a_{32} + c_2)\begin{vmatrix} a_{11} & a_{13} \\ a_{21} & a_{23} \end{vmatrix} + (a_{33} + c_3)\begin{vmatrix} a_{11} & a_{12} \\ a_{21} & a_{22} \end{vmatrix}$$

$$= a_{31}\begin{vmatrix} a_{12} & a_{13} \\ a_{22} & a_{23} \end{vmatrix}$$

$$- a_{32}\begin{vmatrix} a_{11} & a_{13} \\ a_{21} & a_{23} \end{vmatrix} + a_{33}\begin{vmatrix} a_{11} & a_{12} \\ a_{21} & a_{22} \end{vmatrix}$$

$$+ c_1\begin{vmatrix} a_{12} & a_{13} \\ a_{22} & a_{23} \end{vmatrix} - c_2\begin{vmatrix} a_{11} & a_{13} \\ a_{21} & a_{23} \end{vmatrix} + c_3\begin{vmatrix} a_{11} & a_{12} \\ a_{21} & a_{22} \end{vmatrix}$$

$$= \begin{vmatrix} a_{11} & a_{12} & a_{13} \\ a_{21} & a_{22} & a_{23} \\ a_{31} & a_{32} & a_{33} \end{vmatrix} + \begin{vmatrix} a_{11} & a_{12} & a_{13} \\ a_{21} & a_{22} & a_{23} \\ c_1 & c_2 & c_3 \end{vmatrix}$$

Note: Expand each of these matrices by Row 3 to see the previous step.

91. Since each of the three rows is multiplied by 4, $|4A| = 4^3\,|A| = 4^3(2) = 128$.

❏ Chapter Test for Chapter 9

1. $\begin{bmatrix} 1 & -1 & 5 \\ 6 & 2 & 3 \\ 5 & 3 & 3 \end{bmatrix} \Rightarrow \begin{bmatrix} 1 & -1 & 5 \\ 0 & 8 & -27 \\ 0 & 8 & -28 \end{bmatrix}$

$$\Rightarrow \begin{bmatrix} 1 & -1 & 5 \\ 0 & 8 & -27 \\ 0 & 0 & -1 \end{bmatrix}$$

$$\Rightarrow \begin{bmatrix} 1 & -1 & 0 \\ 0 & 8 & 0 \\ 0 & 0 & 1 \end{bmatrix}$$

$$\Rightarrow \begin{bmatrix} 1 & 0 & 0 \\ 0 & 1 & 0 \\ 0 & 0 & 1 \end{bmatrix}$$

2. $\begin{bmatrix} 1 & 0 & -1 & 2 \\ -1 & 1 & 1 & -3 \\ 1 & 1 & -1 & 1 \\ 3 & 2 & -3 & 4 \end{bmatrix} \Rightarrow \begin{bmatrix} 1 & 0 & -1 & 2 \\ 0 & 1 & 0 & -1 \\ 0 & 1 & 0 & -1 \\ 0 & 2 & 0 & -2 \end{bmatrix}$

$$\Rightarrow \begin{bmatrix} 1 & 0 & -1 & 2 \\ 0 & 1 & 0 & -1 \\ 0 & 0 & 0 & 0 \\ 0 & 0 & 0 & 0 \end{bmatrix}$$

3. $\begin{bmatrix} 4 & 3 & -2 & \vdots & 14 \\ -1 & -1 & 2 & \vdots & -5 \\ 3 & 1 & -4 & \vdots & 8 \end{bmatrix} \Rightarrow \begin{bmatrix} 1 & 0 & 0 & \vdots & 1 \\ 0 & 1 & 0 & \vdots & 3 \\ 0 & 0 & 1 & \vdots & -\frac{1}{2} \end{bmatrix} \Rightarrow (x, y, z) = \left(1, 3, -\tfrac{1}{2}\right)$

4. $-2 = a(-2)^2 + b(-2) + c$

$\quad 2 = a(2)^2 + b(2) + c$

$-2 = a(4)^2 + b(4) + c$

$\quad 4a - 2b + c = -2$

$\quad 4a + 2b + c = 2$

$16a + 4b + c = -2$

Row-reducing the augmented matrix yields

$$\begin{bmatrix} 4 & -2 & 1 & \vdots & -2 \\ 4 & 2 & 1 & \vdots & 2 \\ 16 & 4 & 1 & \vdots & -2 \end{bmatrix} \Rightarrow \begin{bmatrix} 1 & 0 & 0 & \vdots & -\frac{1}{2} \\ 0 & 1 & 0 & \vdots & 1 \\ 0 & 0 & 1 & \vdots & 2 \end{bmatrix}.$$

Thus, $y = -\frac{1}{2}x^2 + x + 2$.

5. (a) $A - B = \begin{bmatrix} 5 & 4 & 4 \\ -4 & -4 & 0 \end{bmatrix} - \begin{bmatrix} 4 & -1 & 6 \\ -4 & 0 & -3 \end{bmatrix} = \begin{bmatrix} 1 & 5 & -2 \\ 0 & -4 & 3 \end{bmatrix}$

(b) $3A = 3\begin{bmatrix} 5 & 4 & 4 \\ -4 & -4 & 0 \end{bmatrix} = \begin{bmatrix} 15 & 12 & 12 \\ -12 & -12 & 0 \end{bmatrix}$

(c) $3A - 2B = \begin{bmatrix} 15 & 12 & 12 \\ -12 & -12 & 0 \end{bmatrix} - 2\begin{bmatrix} 4 & -1 & 6 \\ -4 & 0 & -3 \end{bmatrix} = \begin{bmatrix} 7 & 14 & 0 \\ -4 & -12 & 6 \end{bmatrix}$

6. $AB = \begin{bmatrix} 2 & -2 & 6 \\ 3 & -1 & 7 \\ 2 & 0 & -2 \end{bmatrix}\begin{bmatrix} 4 & 4 \\ 3 & 2 \\ 1 & -2 \end{bmatrix} = \begin{bmatrix} 8 & -8 \\ 16 & -4 \\ 6 & 12 \end{bmatrix}$

7. $A^{-1} = \dfrac{1}{ad - bc}\begin{bmatrix} d & -b \\ -c & a \end{bmatrix} = \dfrac{1}{30 - 40}\begin{bmatrix} -5 & -4 \\ -10 & -6 \end{bmatrix} = \dfrac{1}{10}\begin{bmatrix} 5 & 4 \\ 10 & 6 \end{bmatrix} = \begin{bmatrix} \frac{1}{2} & \frac{2}{5} \\ 1 & \frac{3}{5} \end{bmatrix}$

8. $X = A^{-1}B = \begin{bmatrix} \frac{1}{2} & \frac{2}{5} \\ 1 & \frac{3}{5} \end{bmatrix}\begin{bmatrix} 10 \\ 20 \end{bmatrix} = \begin{bmatrix} 13 \\ 22 \end{bmatrix} \implies (x, y) = (13, 22)$

9. $\det(A) = \begin{vmatrix} 4 & 0 & 3 \\ 1 & -8 & 2 \\ 3 & 2 & 2 \end{vmatrix} = 4(-16 - 4) - 0 + 3(2 + 24)$

$$= -80 + 78 = -2$$

10. $\begin{vmatrix} -5 & 0 & 1 \\ 3 & 2 & 1 \\ 4 & 4 & 1 \end{vmatrix} = -5(2 - 4) - 0 + 1(12 - 8) = 10 + 4 = 14$

Area $= \frac{1}{2}(14) = 7$

❑ Practice Test for Chapter 9

1. Write the matrix in reduced row-echelon form.

$$\begin{bmatrix} 1 & -2 & 4 \\ 3 & -5 & 9 \end{bmatrix}$$

For Exercises 2–4, use matrices to solve the system of equations.

2. $3x + 5y = 3$
   $2x - y = -11$

3. $2x + 3y = -3$
   $3x + 2y = 8$
   $x + y = 1$

4. $x \qquad + 3z = -5$
   $2x + y \qquad = 0$
   $3x + y - z = 3$

5. Multiply $\begin{bmatrix} 1 & 4 & 5 \\ 2 & 0 & -3 \end{bmatrix} \begin{bmatrix} 1 & 6 \\ 0 & -7 \\ -1 & 2 \end{bmatrix}$

6. Given $A = \begin{bmatrix} 9 & 1 \\ -4 & 8 \end{bmatrix}$ and $B = \begin{bmatrix} 6 & -2 \\ 3 & 5 \end{bmatrix}$, find $3A - 5B$.

7. Find $f(A)$:

$$f(x) = x^2 - 7x + 8, \ A = \begin{bmatrix} 3 & 0 \\ 7 & 1 \end{bmatrix}$$

8. True or false:

$(A + B)(A + 3B) = A^2 + 4AB + 3B^2$ where A and B are matrices.

(Assume that A^2, AB, and B^2 exist.)

For Exercises 9–10, find the inverse of the matrix, if it exists.

9. $\begin{bmatrix} 1 & 2 \\ 3 & 5 \end{bmatrix}$

10. $\begin{bmatrix} 1 & 1 & 1 \\ 3 & 6 & 5 \\ 6 & 10 & 8 \end{bmatrix}$

11. Use an inverse matrix to solve the systems.

   (a) $x + 2y = 4$
   $3x + 5y = 1$

   (b) $x + 2y = 3$
   $3x + 5y = -2$

For Exercises 12–13, find the determinant of the matrix.

12. $\begin{bmatrix} 6 & -1 \\ 3 & 4 \end{bmatrix}$

13. $\begin{bmatrix} 1 & 3 & -1 \\ 5 & 9 & 0 \\ 6 & 2 & -5 \end{bmatrix}$

14. Use a graphing utility to find the determinant of the matrix.

$$\begin{bmatrix} 1 & 4 & 2 & 3 \\ 0 & 1 & -2 & 0 \\ 3 & 5 & -1 & 1 \\ 2 & 0 & 6 & 1 \end{bmatrix}$$

15. Evaluate $\begin{vmatrix} 6 & 4 & 3 & 0 & 6 \\ 0 & 5 & 1 & 4 & 8 \\ 0 & 0 & 2 & 7 & 3 \\ 0 & 0 & 0 & 9 & 2 \\ 0 & 0 & 0 & 0 & 1 \end{vmatrix}$.

16. Use a determinant to find the area of the triangle with vertices $(0, 7)$, $(5, 0)$, and $(3, 9)$.

17. Use a determinant to find the equation of the line through $(2, 7)$ and $(-1, 4)$.

For Exercises 18–20, use Cramer's Rule to find the indicated value.

18. Find x.

$$6x - 7y = 4$$
$$2x + 5y = 11$$

19. Find z.

$$3x \qquad + z = 1$$
$$y + 4z = 3$$
$$x - y \qquad = 2$$

20. Find y.

$$721.4x - 29.1y = 33.77$$
$$45.9x + 105.6y = 19.85$$

C H A P T E R 1 0
Sequences and Probability

CHAPTER 10
Sequences and Probability

Section 10.1   Sequences and Summation Notation

- Given the general nth term in a sequence, you should be able to find, or list, some of the terms.
- You should be able to find an expression for the nth term of a sequence.
- You should be able to use and evaluate factorials.
- You should be able to use sigma notation for a sum.

Solutions to Odd-Numbered Exercises

1. $a_n = 2n + 1$

$a_1 = 2(1) + 1 = 3$

$a_2 = 2(2) + 1 = 5$

$a_3 = 2(3) + 1 = 7$

$a_4 = 2(4) + 1 = 9$

$a_5 = 2(5) + 1 = 11$

3. $a_n = 2^n$

$a_1 = 2^1 = 2$

$a_2 = 2^2 = 4$

$a_3 = 2^3 = 8$

$a_4 = 2^4 = 16$

$a_5 = 2^5 = 32$

5. $a_n = (-2)^n$

$a_1 = (-2)^1 = -2$

$a_3 = (-2)^2 = 4$

$a_3 = (-2)^3 = -8$

$a_4 = (-2)^4 = 16$

$a_5 = (-2)^5 = -32$

7. $a_n = \dfrac{n + 1}{n}$

$a_1 = \dfrac{1 + 1}{1} = 2$

$a_2 = \dfrac{3}{2}$

$a_3 = \dfrac{4}{3}$

$a_4 = \dfrac{5}{4}$

$a_5 = \dfrac{6}{5}$

9. $a_n = \dfrac{6n}{3n^2 - 1}$

$a_1 = \dfrac{6(1)}{3(1)^2 - 1} = 3$

$a_2 = \dfrac{6(2)}{3(2)^2 - 1} = \dfrac{12}{11}$

$a_3 = \dfrac{6(3)}{3(3)^2 - 1} = \dfrac{9}{13}$

$a_4 = \dfrac{6(4)}{3(4)^2 - 1} = \dfrac{24}{47}$

$a_5 = \dfrac{6(5)}{3(5)^2 - 1} = \dfrac{15}{37}$

11. $a_n = \dfrac{1 + (-1)^n}{n}$

$a_1 = 0$

$a_2 = \dfrac{2}{2} = 1$

$a_3 = 0$

$a_4 = \dfrac{2}{4} = \dfrac{1}{2}$

$a_5 = 0$

13. $a_n = 3 - \dfrac{1}{2^n}$

$a_1 = 3 - \dfrac{1}{2} = \dfrac{5}{2}$

$a_2 = 3 - \dfrac{1}{4} = \dfrac{11}{4}$

$a_3 = 3 - \dfrac{1}{8} = \dfrac{23}{8}$

$a_4 = 3 - \dfrac{1}{16} = \dfrac{47}{16}$

$a_5 = 3 - \dfrac{1}{32} = \dfrac{95}{32}$

15. $a_n = \dfrac{1}{n^{3/2}}$

$a_1 = \dfrac{1}{1} = 1$

$a_2 = \dfrac{1}{2^{3/2}}$

$a_3 = \dfrac{1}{3^{3/2}}$

$a_4 = \dfrac{1}{4^{3/2}} = \dfrac{1}{8}$

$a_5 = \dfrac{1}{5^{3/2}}$

17. $a_n = \dfrac{3^n}{n!}$

$a_1 = \dfrac{3^1}{1!} = \dfrac{3}{1} = 3$

$a_2 = \dfrac{3^2}{2!} = \dfrac{9}{2}$

$a_3 = \dfrac{27}{6} = \dfrac{9}{2}$

$a_4 = \dfrac{81}{24} = \dfrac{27}{8}$

$a_5 = \dfrac{243}{120} = \dfrac{81}{40}$

19. $a_n = \dfrac{(-1)^n}{n^2}$

$a_1 = \dfrac{-1}{1} = -1$

$a_2 = \dfrac{1}{4}$

$a_3 = \dfrac{-1}{9}$

$a_4 = \dfrac{1}{16}$

$a_5 = \dfrac{-1}{25}$

21. $a_n = \dfrac{2}{3}$

$a_1 = \dfrac{2}{3}$

$a_2 = \dfrac{2}{3}$

$a_3 = \dfrac{2}{3}$

$a_4 = \dfrac{2}{3}$

$a_5 = \dfrac{2}{3}$

23. $a_{25} = (-1)^{25}[3(25) - 2] = -73$

25. $a_1 = 28$ and $a_{k+1} = a_k - 4$

$a_1 = 28$

$a_2 = a_1 - 4 = 28 - 4 = 24$

$a_3 = a_2 - 4 = 24 - 4 = 20$

$a_4 = a_3 - 4 = 20 - 4 = 16$

$a_5 = a_4 - 4 = 16 - 4 = 12$

27. $a_1 = 3$ and $a_{k+1} = 2(a_k - 1)$

$a_1 = 3$

$a_2 = 2(a_1 - 1) = 2(3 - 1) = 4$

$a_3 = 2(a_2 - 1) = 2(4 - 1) = 6$

$a_4 = 2(a_3 - 1) = 2(6 - 1) = 10$

$a_5 = 2(a_4 - 1) = 2(10 - 1) = 18$

29. $a_n = \dfrac{2}{3}n$

31. $a_n = 16(-0.5)^{n-1}$

33. $a_n = \dfrac{2n}{n+1}$

35. $a_n = \dfrac{8}{n + 1}$

$a_n \rightarrow 0$ as $n \rightarrow \infty$

$a_1 = 4, \ a_{10} = \dfrac{8}{11}$

Matches graph (c).

37. $a_n = 4(0.5)^{n-1}$

$a_n \rightarrow 0$ as $n \rightarrow \infty$

$a_1 = 4, \ a_{10} \approx 0.008$

Matches graph (d).

39. $\dfrac{4!}{6!} = \dfrac{4!}{6 \cdot 5 \cdot 4!} = \dfrac{1}{30}$

41. $\dfrac{10!}{8!} = \dfrac{10 \cdot 9 \cdot 8!}{8!} = 90$

43. $\dfrac{(n + 1)!}{n!} = \dfrac{(n + 1)n!}{n!} = n + 1$

45. $\dfrac{(2n - 1)!}{(2n + 1)!} = \dfrac{(2n - 1)!}{(2n + 1)(2n)(2n - 1)!}$

$= \dfrac{1}{2n(2n + 1)}$

47. $1, 4, 7, 10, 13, \ldots$

$a_n = 1 + (n - 1)3 = 3n - 2$

49. $0, 3, 8, 15, 24, \ldots$

$a_n = n^2 - 1$

51. $\dfrac{2}{3}, \dfrac{3}{4}, \dfrac{4}{5}, \dfrac{5}{6}, \dfrac{6}{7}, \ldots$

$a_n = \dfrac{n + 1}{n + 2}$

53. $\dfrac{1}{2}, \dfrac{-1}{4}, \dfrac{1}{8}, \dfrac{-1}{16}, \ldots$

$a_n = \dfrac{(-1)^{n+1}}{2^n}$

55. $1 + \dfrac{1}{1}, 1 + \dfrac{1}{2}, 1 + \dfrac{1}{3}, 1 + \dfrac{1}{4}, 1 + \dfrac{1}{5}, \ldots$

$a_n = 1 + \dfrac{1}{n}$

57. $1, \dfrac{1}{2}, \dfrac{1}{6}, \dfrac{1}{24}, \dfrac{1}{120}, \ldots$

$a_n = \dfrac{1}{n!}$

59. $1, -1, 1, -1, 1, \ldots$

$a_n = (-1)^{n+1}$

61. $a_1 = 6$ and $a_{k+1} = a_k + 2$

$a_1 = 6$

$a_2 = a_1 + 2 = 6 + 2 = 8$

$a_3 = a_2 + 2 = 8 + 2 = 10$

$a_4 = a_3 + 2 = 10 + 2 = 12$

$a_5 = a_4 + 2 = 12 + 2 = 14$

In general, $a_n = 2n + 4$.

63. $a_1 = 81$ and $a_{k+1} = \dfrac{1}{3}a_k$

$a_1 = 81$

$a_2 = \dfrac{1}{3}a_1 = \dfrac{1}{3}(81) = 27$

$a_3 = \dfrac{1}{3}a_2 = \dfrac{1}{3}(27) = 9$

$a_4 = \dfrac{1}{3}a_3 = \dfrac{1}{3}(9) = 3$

$a_5 = \dfrac{1}{3}a_4 = \dfrac{1}{3}(3) = 1$

In general, $a_n = 81\left(\dfrac{1}{3}\right)^{n-1} = 81(3)\left(\dfrac{1}{3}\right)^n = \dfrac{253}{3^n}$.

65. $\displaystyle\sum_{i=1}^{5}(2i + 1) = (2 + 1) + (4 + 1) + (6 + 1) + (8 + 1) + (10 + 1) = 35$

67. $\displaystyle\sum_{k=1}^{4}10 = 10 + 10 + 10 + 10 = 40$

69. $\displaystyle\sum_{i=0}^{4}i^2 = 0^2 + 1^2 + 2^2 + 3^2 + 4^2 = 30$

71. $\displaystyle\sum_{k=0}^{3}\frac{1}{k^2+1} = \frac{1}{1} + \frac{1}{1+1} + \frac{1}{1+4} + \frac{1}{9+1} = \frac{9}{5}$

73. $\displaystyle\sum_{i=1}^{4}[(i-1)^2 + (i+1)^3] = [(0)^2 + (2)^3] + [(1)^2 + (3)^3] + [(2)^2 + (4)^3] + [(3)^2 + (5)^3] = 238$

75. $\displaystyle\sum_{i=1}^{4}2^i = 2^1 + 2^2 + 2^3 + 2^4 = 30$

77. $\displaystyle\sum_{j=1}^{6}(24-3j) = 81$

79. $\displaystyle\sum_{k=0}^{4}\frac{(-1)^k}{k+1} = \frac{47}{60}$

81. $\displaystyle\frac{1}{3(1)} + \frac{1}{3(2)} + \frac{1}{3(3)} + \cdots + \frac{1}{3(9)} = \sum_{i=1}^{9}\frac{1}{3i}$

83. $\displaystyle\left[2\left(\frac{1}{8}\right)+3\right] + \left[2\left(\frac{2}{8}\right)+3\right] + \left[2\left(\frac{3}{8}\right)+3\right] + \cdots + \left[2\left(\frac{8}{8}\right)+3\right] = \sum_{i=1}^{8}\left[2\left(\frac{i}{8}\right)+3\right]$

85. $\displaystyle 3 - 9 + 27 - 81 + 243 - 729 = \sum_{i=1}^{6}(-1)^{i+1}3^i$

87. $\displaystyle\frac{1}{1^2} - \frac{1}{2^2} + \frac{1}{3^2} - \frac{1}{4^2} + \cdots + -\frac{1}{20^2} = \sum_{i=1}^{20}\frac{(-1)^{i+1}}{i^2}$

89. $\displaystyle\frac{1}{4} + \frac{3}{8} + \frac{7}{16} + \frac{15}{32} + \frac{31}{64} = \sum_{i=1}^{5}\frac{2i-1}{2^{i+1}}$

91. $A_n = 5000\left(1 + \dfrac{0.08}{4}\right)^n,\ n = 1, 2, 3, \ldots$

    (a) $A_1 = \$5100.00$

        $A_2 = \$5202.00$

        $A_3 = \$5306.04$

        $A_4 = \$5412.16$

        $A_5 = \$5520.40$

        $A_6 = \$5630.81$

        $A_7 = \$5743.43$

        $A_8 = \$5858.30$

    (b) $A_{40} = \$11{,}040.20$

93. $a_n = 510.13 + 16.37n + 3.23n^2,\ n = 1, \ldots, 11$

    $a_1 = 529.73$

    $a_2 = 555.79$

    $a_3 = 588.31$

    $a_4 = 627.29$

    $a_5 = 672.73$

    $a_6 = 724.63$

    $a_7 = 782.99$

    $a_8 = 847.81$

    $a_9 = 919.09$

    $a_{10} = 996.83$

    $a_{11} = 1081.03$

95. $\displaystyle\sum_{n=5}^{14}(129.9 + 0.9n^3) = \$11{,}131.5$ million

97. $a_1 = 1, a_2 = 1, \ a_{k+2} = a_{k+1} + a_k$

$a_1 = 1$	$b_1 = \frac{1}{1} = 1$
$a_2 = 1$	$b_2 = \frac{2}{1} = 2$
$a_3 = 1 + 1 = 2$	$b_3 = \frac{3}{2}$
$a_4 = 2 + 1 = 3$	$b_4 = \frac{5}{3}$
$a_5 = 3 + 2 = 5$	$b_5 = \frac{8}{5}$
$a_6 = 5 + 3 = 8$	$b_6 = \frac{13}{8}$
$a_7 = 8 + 5 = 13$	$b_7 = \frac{21}{13}$
$a_8 = 13 + 8 = 21$	$b_8 = \frac{34}{21}$
$a_9 = 21 + 13 = 34$	$b_9 = \frac{55}{34}$
$a_{10} = 34 + 21 = 55$	$b_{10} = \frac{89}{55}$
$a_{11} = 55 + 34 = 89$	
$a_{12} = 89 + 55 = 144$	

Section 10.2 Arithmetic Sequences

■ You should be able to recognize an arithmetic sequence, find its common difference, and find its nth term.

■ You should be able to find the nth partial sum of an arithmetic sequence with common difference d using the formula

$$S_n = \frac{n}{2}(a_1 + a_n).$$

Solutions to Odd-Numbered Exercises

1. 10, 8, 6, 4, 2, . . .

Arithmetic sequence, $d = -2$

3. 1, 2, 4, 8, 16, 32, . . .

Not an arithmetic sequence

5. $\frac{9}{4}, 2, \frac{7}{4}, \frac{3}{2}, \frac{5}{4}, \ldots$

Arithmetic sequence, $d = -\frac{1}{4}$

7. $-12, -8, -4, 0, 4, \ldots$

Arithmetic sequence, $d = 4$

9. 5.3, 5.7, 6.1, 6.5, 6.9, . . .

Arithmetic sequence, $d = 0.4$

11. $a_n = 5 + 3n$

8, 11, 14, 17, 20

Arithmetic sequence, $d = 3$

13. $a_n = \dfrac{1}{n + 1}$

$\dfrac{1}{2}, \dfrac{1}{3}, \dfrac{1}{4}, \dfrac{1}{5}, \dfrac{1}{6}$

Not an arithmetic sequence

15. $a_n = 100 - 3n$

97, 94, 91, 88, 85

Arithmetic sequence, $d = -3$

17. $a_n = 3 + \dfrac{(-1)^n 2}{n}$

$1, 4, \dfrac{7}{3}, \dfrac{7}{2}, \dfrac{13}{5}$

Not an arithmetic sequence

19. $a_1 = 15, \ a_{k+1} = a_k + 4$

$a_2 = 15 + 4 = 19$

$a_3 = 19 + 4 = 23$

$a_4 = 23 + 4 = 27$

$a_5 = 27 + 4 = 31$

$a_n = 11 + 4n$

21. $a_1 = 200, \ a_{k+1} = a_k - 10$

$a_2 = 200 - 10 = 190$

$a_3 = 190 - 10 = 180$

$a_4 = 180 - 10 = 170$

$a_5 = 170 - 10 = 160$

$a_n = 210 - 10n$

23. $a_1 = \frac{3}{2}, \ a_{k+1} = a_k - \frac{1}{4}$

$a_2 = \frac{3}{2} - \frac{1}{4} = \frac{5}{4}$

$a_3 = \frac{5}{4} - \frac{1}{4} = 1$

$a_4 = 1 - \frac{1}{4} = \frac{3}{4}$

$a_5 = \frac{3}{4} - \frac{1}{4} = \frac{1}{2}$

$a_n = \frac{7}{4} - \frac{1}{4}n$

25. $a_1 = 5, \ d = 6$

$a_1 = 5$

$a_2 = 5 + 6 = 11$

$a_3 = 11 + 6 = 17$

$a_4 = 17 + 6 = 23$

$a_5 = 23 + 6 = 29$

27. $a_1 = -2.6, \ d = -0.4$

$a_1 = -2.6$

$a_2 = -2.6 + (-0.4) = -3.0$

$a_3 = -3.0 + (-0.4) = -3.4$

$a_4 = -3.4 + (-0.4) = -3.8$

$a_5 = -3.8 + (-0.4) = -4.2$

29. $a_1 = 2, \ a_{12} = 46$

$46 = 2 + (12 - 1)d$

$44 = 11d$

$4 = d$

$a_1 = 2$

$a_2 = 2 + 4 = 6$

$a_3 = 6 + 4 = 10$

$a_4 = 10 + 4 = 14$

$a_5 = 14 + 4 = 18$

31. $a_8 = 26, \ a_{12} = 42$

$26 = a_8 = a_1 + (n - 1)d = a_1 + 7d$

$42 = a_{12} = a_1 + (n - 1)d = a_1 + 11d$

Answer: $d = 4, \ a_1 = -2$

$a_1 = -2$

$a_2 = -2 + 4 = 2$

$a_3 = 2 + 4 = 6$

$a_4 = 6 + 4 = 10$

$a_5 = 10 + 4 = 14$

33. $a_1 = 1, \ d = 3$

$a_n = a_1 + (n - 1)d = 1 + (n - 1)(3)$

35. $a_1 = 100, \ d = -8$

$a_n = a_1 + (n - 1)d = 100 + (n - 1)(-8)$

37. $a_1 = x, \ d = 2x$

$a_n = a_1 + (n - 1)d = x + (n - 1)(2x)$

39. $4, \frac{3}{2}, -1, -\frac{7}{2}, \ldots$

$d = -\frac{5}{2}$

$a_n = a_1 + (n - 1)d = 4 + (n - 1)\left(-\frac{5}{2}\right)$

41. $a_1 = 5, \ a_4 = 15$

$a_4 = a_1 + 3d \ \Longrightarrow \ 15 = 5 + 3d \ \Longrightarrow \ d = \frac{10}{3}$

$a_n = a_1 + (n - 1)d = 5 + (n - 1)\left(\frac{10}{3}\right)$

43. $a_3 = 94, \ a_6 = 85$

$a_6 = a_3 + 3d \ \Longrightarrow \ 85 = 94 + 3d \ \Longrightarrow \ d = -3$

$a_1 = a_3 - 2d \ \Longrightarrow \ a_1 = 94 - 2(-3) = 100$

$a_n = a_1 + (n - 1)d = 100 + (n - 1)(-3)$

45. $a_n = -\frac{2}{3}n + 6$

$d = -\frac{2}{3}$ so the sequence is decreasing,

and $a_1 = 5\frac{1}{3}$.

Matches (b).

47. $a_n = 2 + \frac{3}{4}n$

$d = \frac{3}{4}$ so the sequence is increasing,

and $a_1 = 2\frac{3}{4}$.

Matches (c).

49. $a_n = 15 - \frac{3}{2}n$

51. $a_n = 0.2n + 3$

53. Since $a_n = dn + c$, its geometric pattern is linear.

55. $8, 20, 32, 44, \ldots$

$a_1 = 8, \ d = 12, \ n = 10$

$a_{10} = 8 + 9(12) = 116$

$S_{10} = \frac{10}{2}(8 + 116) = 620$

57. $-6, -2, 2, 6, \ldots$

$a_1 = -6, \ d = 4, \ n = 50$

$a_{50} = -6 + 49(4) = 190$

$S_{50} = \frac{50}{2}(-6 + 190) = 4600$

59. $40, 37, 34, 31, \ldots$

$a_1 = 40, d = -3, n = 10$

$a_{10} = 40 + 9(-3) = 13$

$S_{10} = \frac{10}{2}(40 + 13) = 265$

61. $a_1 = 100, \ a_{25} = 220, \ n = 25$

$S_n = \frac{n}{2}[a_1 + a_n]$

$S_{25} = \frac{25}{2}(100 + 220) = 4000$

63. $a_1 = 1, \ a_{50} = 50, \ n = 50$

$\sum_{n=1}^{50} n = \frac{50}{2}(1 + 50) = 1275$

65. $a_1 = 5, \ a_{100} = 500, n = 100$

$\sum_{n=1}^{100} 5n = \frac{100}{2}(5 + 500) = 25,250$

67. $\sum_{n=11}^{30} n - \sum_{n=1}^{10} n = \frac{20}{2}(11 + 30) - \frac{10}{2}(1 + 10) = 355$

69. $a_1 = 4, \ a_{500} = 503, n = 500$

$\sum_{n=1}^{500} (n + 3) = \frac{500}{2}(4 + 503) = 126,750$

71. $a_1 = 7, a_{20} = 45, \ n = 20$

$\sum_{n=1}^{20} (2n + 5) = \frac{20}{2}(7 + 45) = 520$

73. $a_0 = 1000, \ a_{50} = 750, \ n = 51$

$\sum_{n=0}^{50} (100 - 5n) = \frac{51}{2}(1000 + 750) = 44,625$

75. $a_1 = \frac{742}{3}, \ a_{60} = 90, \ n = 60$

$\sum_{i=1}^{60} \left(250 - \frac{8}{3}i\right) = \frac{60}{2}\left(\frac{742}{3} + 90\right) = 10,120$

77. $a_1 = 1, \ a_{100} = 199, \ n = 100$

$\sum_{n=1}^{100} (2n - 1) = \frac{100}{2}(1 + 199) = 10,000$

79. (a) $a_1 = 32,500, \ d = 1500$

$a_6 = a_1 + 5d = 32,500 + 5(1500) = \$40,000$

(b) $S_6 = \frac{6}{2}[32,500 + 40,000] = \$217,500$

81. $a_1 = 20, \ d = 4, \ n = 30$

$a_{30} = 20 + 29(4) = 136$

$S_{30} = \frac{30}{2}(20 + 36) = 2340$ seats

83. $a_1 = 14, a_{18} = 31$

$S_{18} = \frac{18}{2}(14 + 31) = 405$ bricks

85. $a_1 = 25, \ a_2 = 25 + 2 = 27$, etc. $\implies \ d = 2$ and $n = 15$.

$a_{15} = 2(15) + 23 = 53$

$S_{15} = \frac{15}{2}(25 + 53) = \frac{15}{2} \cdot 78 = 585$ seats

87. $(1 + 2 + \cdots + 12) + (1 + 2 + \cdots + 12) = \frac{12}{2}(1 + 12) \times 2 = 12 \cdot 13 = 156$ times

89. (a) $1 + 3 = 4$

$1 + 3 + 5 = 9$

$1 + 3 + 5 + 7 = 16$

$1 + 3 + 5 + 7 + 9 = 25$

$1 + 3 + 5 + 7 + 9 + 11 = 36$

(b) $S_n = n^2$

$S_7 = 1 + 3 + 5 + 7 + 9 + 11 + 13 = 49 = 7^2$

(c) $S_n = \dfrac{n}{2}[1 + (2n - 1)] = \dfrac{n}{2}(2n) = n^2$

91. $S_{20} = \dfrac{20}{2}\{a_1 + [a_1 + (20 - 1)(3)]\} = 650$

$10(2a_1 + 57) = 650$

$2a_1 + 57 = 65$

$2a_1 = 8$

$a_1 = 4$

Section 10.3   Geometric Sequences

- You should be able to identify a geometric sequence, find its common ratio, and find the nth term.
- You should be able to find the nth partial sum of a geometric sequence with common ratio r using the formula.

$$S_n = a_1\left(\frac{1 - r^n}{1 - r}\right)$$

- You should know that if $|r| < 1$, then

$$\sum_{n=1}^{\infty} a_1 r^{n-1} = \frac{a_1}{1 - r}.$$

Solutions to Odd-Numbered Exercises

1. $5, 15, 45, 135, \ldots$

Geometric sequence, $r = 3$

3. $3, 12, 21, 30, \ldots$

Not a geometric sequence

Note: It is an arithmetic sequence
with $d = 9$.

5. $1, -\frac{1}{2}, \frac{1}{4}, -\frac{1}{8}, \ldots$

Geometric sequence, $r = -\frac{1}{2}$

7. $\frac{1}{2}, \frac{2}{3}, \frac{3}{4}, \frac{4}{5}, \ldots$

Not a geometric sequence

9. $1, \frac{1}{2}, \frac{1}{3}, \frac{1}{4}, \ldots$

Not a geometric sequence

11. $a_1 = 2$, $r = 3$

$a_1 = 2$

$a_2 = 2(3) = 6$

$a_3 = 6(3) = 18$

$a_4 = 18(3) = 54$

$a_5 = 54(3) = 162$

13. $a_1 = 1$, $r = \frac{1}{2}$

$a_1 = 1$

$a_2 = 1\left(\frac{1}{2}\right) = \frac{1}{2}$

$a_3 = \frac{1}{2}\left(\frac{1}{2}\right) = \frac{1}{4}$

$a_4 = \frac{1}{4}\left(\frac{1}{2}\right) = \frac{1}{8}$

$a_5 = \frac{1}{8}\left(\frac{1}{2}\right) = \frac{1}{16}$

15. $a_1 = 5$, $r = -\frac{1}{10}$

$a_1 = 5$

$a_2 = 5\left(-\frac{1}{10}\right) = -\frac{1}{2}$

$a_3 = \left(-\frac{1}{2}\right)\left(-\frac{1}{10}\right) = \frac{1}{20}$

$a_4 = \frac{1}{20}\left(-\frac{1}{10}\right) = -\frac{1}{200}$

$a_5 = \left(-\frac{1}{200}\right)\left(-\frac{1}{10}\right) = \frac{1}{2000}$

17. $a_1 = 1$, $r = e$

$a_1 = 1$

$a_2 = 1(e) = e$

$a_3 = (e)(e) = e^2$

$a_4 = (e^2)(e) = e^3$

$a_5 = (e^3)(e) = e^4$

19. $a_1 = 3$, $r = \frac{x}{2}$

$a_1 = 3$

$a_2 = 3\left(\frac{x}{2}\right) = \frac{3x}{2}$

$a_3 = \left(\frac{3x}{2}\right)\left(\frac{x}{2}\right) = \frac{3x^2}{4}$

$a_4 = \left(\frac{3x^3}{4}\right)\left(\frac{x}{2}\right) = \frac{3x^3}{8}$

$a_5 = \left(\frac{3x^3}{8}\right)\left(\frac{x}{2}\right) = \frac{3x^4}{16}$

21. $a_1 = 64$, $a_{k+1} = \frac{1}{2}a_k$

$a_1 = 64$

$a_2 = \frac{1}{2}(64) = 32$

$a_3 = \frac{1}{2}(32) = 16$

$a_4 = \frac{1}{2}(16) = 8$

$a_5 = \frac{1}{2}(8) = 4$

$a_n = 64\left(\frac{1}{2}\right)^{n-1} = 128\left(\frac{1}{2}\right)^n$

23. $a_1 = 4$, $a_{k+1} = 3a_k$

$a_1 = 4$

$a_2 = 3(4) = 12$

$a_3 = 3(12) = 36$

$a_4 = 3(36) = 108$

$a_5 = 3(108) = 324$

$a_n = 4(3)^{n-1} = \frac{4}{3}(3)^n$

25. $a_k = 6$, $a_{k+1} = -\frac{3}{2}a_k$

$a_1 = 6$

$a_2 = -\frac{3}{2}(6) = -9$

$a_3 = -\frac{3}{2}(-9) = \frac{27}{2}$

$a_4 = -\frac{3}{2}\left(\frac{27}{2}\right) = -\frac{81}{4}$

$a_5 = -\frac{3}{2}\left(-\frac{81}{4}\right) = \frac{243}{8}$

$a_n = 6\left(-\frac{3}{2}\right)^{n-1}$

27. $a_1 = 4$, $r = \frac{1}{2}$, $n = 10$

$a_n = a_1 r^{n-1}$

$a_{10} = 4\left(\frac{1}{2}\right)^9 = \left(\frac{1}{2}\right)^7 = \frac{1}{128}$

29. $a_1 = 6$, $r = -\frac{1}{3}$, $n = 12$

$a_n = a_1 r^{n-1}$

$a_{12} = 6\left(-\frac{1}{3}\right)^{11} = \frac{-2}{3^{10}}$

31. $a_1 = 100$, $r = e^x$, $n = 9$

$a_n = a_1 r^{n-1}$

$a_9 = 100(e^x)^8 = 100e^{8x}$

33. $a_1 = 500$, $r = 1.02$, $n = 40$

$a_n = a_1 r^{n-1}$

$a_{40} = 500(1.02)^{39} \approx 1082.37$

35. $a_1 = 16$, $a_4 = \frac{27}{4}$, $n = 3$

$\frac{27}{4} = 16r^3 \implies r = \frac{3}{4}$

$a_n = a_1 r^{n-1}$

$a_3 = 16\left(\frac{3}{4}\right)^2 = 9$

37. $a_2 = a_1 r = -18 \implies a_1 = \frac{-18}{r}$

$a_5 = a_1 r^4 = (a_1 r)r^3 = -18r^3 = \frac{2}{3} \implies r = -\frac{1}{3}$

$a_1 = \frac{-18}{r} = \frac{-18}{-1/3} = 54$

$a_6 = a_1 r^5 = 54\left(\frac{-1}{3}\right)^5 = \frac{54}{243} = -\frac{2}{9}$

39. $a_n = 18\left(\frac{2}{3}\right)^{n-1}$

$r = \frac{2}{3} < 1$, so the sequence is decreasing.

Matches (a).

41. $a_n = 18\left(\frac{3}{2}\right)^{n-1}$

$r = \frac{3}{2} > 1$, so the sequence is increasing.

Matches (b).

43. $a_n = 12(-0.75)^{n-1}$

45. $a_n = 2(1.3)^{n-1}$

47. Given real numbers r between -1 and 1, as the exponent increases, r^n approaches zero.

49. $A = P\left(1 + \dfrac{r}{n}\right)^{nt} = 1000\left(1 + \dfrac{0.10}{n}\right)^{n(10)}$

(a) $n = 1$, $A = 1000(1 + 0.10)^{10} \approx \$2593.74$

(b) $n = 2$, $A = 1000\left(1 + \dfrac{0.10}{2}\right)^{2(10)} \approx \$2653.30$

(c) $n = 4$, $A = 1000\left(1 + \dfrac{0.10}{4}\right)^{4(10)} \approx \$2685.06$

(d) $n = 12$, $A = 1000\left(1 + \dfrac{0.10}{12}\right)^{12(10)} \approx \$2707.04$

(e) $n = 365$, $A = 1000\left(1 + \dfrac{0.10}{365}\right)^{365(10)} \approx \$2717.91$

51. $V_5 = 135,000(0.70)^5 = \$22,689.45$

53. $8, -4, 2, -1, \frac{1}{2}$

$S_1 = 8$

$S_2 = 8 + (-4) = 4$

$S_3 = 8 + (-4) + 2 = 6$

$S_4 = 8 + (-4) + 2 + (-1) = 5$

55. $\displaystyle\sum_{n=1}^{9} 2^{n-1} \;\Rightarrow\; a_1 = 1,\; r = 2$

$S_9 = \dfrac{1(1 - 2^9)}{1 - 2} = 511$

57. $\displaystyle\sum_{i=1}^{7} 64\left(-\frac{1}{2}\right)^{i-1} \;\Rightarrow\; a_1 = 64,\; r = -\frac{1}{2}$

$S_7 = 64\left[\dfrac{1 - (-1/2)^7}{1 - (-1/2)}\right] = \dfrac{128}{3}\left[1 - \left(-\dfrac{1}{2}\right)^7\right] = 43$

59. $\displaystyle\sum_{n=0}^{20} 3\left(\frac{3}{2}\right)^{n} = \sum_{n=1}^{21} 3\left(\frac{3}{2}\right)^{n-1} \;\Rightarrow\; a_1 = 3,\; r = \frac{3}{2}$

$S_{21} = 3\left[\dfrac{1 - (3/2)^{21}}{1 - (3/2)}\right] = -6\left[1 - \left(\dfrac{3}{2}\right)^{21}\right] \approx 29,921.31$

61. $\displaystyle\sum_{i=1}^{10} 8\left(-\frac{1}{4}\right)^{i-1} \implies a_1 = 8, \; r = -\frac{1}{4}$

$S_{10} = 8\left[\dfrac{1 - (-1/4)^{10}}{1 - (-1/4)}\right] = \dfrac{32}{5}\left[1 - \left(-\dfrac{1}{4}\right)^{10}\right] \approx 6.4$

63. $\displaystyle\sum_{n=0}^{5} 300(1.06)^n = \sum_{n=1}^{6} 300(1.06)^{n-1} \implies a_1 = 300, \; r = 1.06$

$S_6 = 300\left[\dfrac{1 - (1.06)^6}{1 - 1.06}\right] \approx 2092.60$

65. $5 + 15 + 45 + \cdots + 3645$

$r = 3$ and $3645 = 5(3)^{n-1} \implies n = 7$

Thus, the sum can be written as $\displaystyle\sum_{n=1}^{7} 5(3)^{n-1}$.

67. $A = \displaystyle\sum_{n=1}^{60} 100\left(1 + \frac{0.10}{12}\right)^n = 100\left(1 + \frac{0.10}{12}\right) \cdot \dfrac{\left[1 - \left(1 + \dfrac{0.10}{12}\right)^{60}\right]}{\left[1 - \left(1 + \dfrac{0.10}{12}\right)\right]} \approx \$7808.24$

69. Let $N = 12t$ be the total number of deposits.

$A = P\left(1 + \dfrac{r}{12}\right) + P\left(1 + \dfrac{r}{12}\right)^2 + \cdots + P\left(1 + \dfrac{r}{12}\right)^N$

$= \left(1 + \dfrac{r}{12}\right)\left[P + P\left(r + \dfrac{r}{12}\right) + \cdots + P\left(1 + \dfrac{r}{12}\right)^{N-1}\right]$

$= P\left(1 + \dfrac{r}{12}\right)\displaystyle\sum_{n=1}^{N}\left(1 + \dfrac{r}{12}\right)^{n-1}$

$= P\left(1 + \dfrac{r}{12}\right)\dfrac{1 - \left(1 + \dfrac{r}{12}\right)^N}{1 - \left(1 + \dfrac{r}{12}\right)}$

$= P\left(1 + \dfrac{r}{12}\right)\left(-\dfrac{12}{r}\right)\left[1 - \left(1 + \dfrac{r}{12}\right)^N\right]$

$= P\left(\dfrac{12}{r} + 1\right)\left[-1 + \left(1 + \dfrac{r}{12}\right)^N\right]$

$= P\left[\left(1 + \dfrac{r}{12}\right)^N - 1\right]\left(1 + \dfrac{12}{r}\right)$

$= P\left[\left(1 + \dfrac{r}{12}\right)^{12t} - 1\right]\left(1 + \dfrac{12}{r}\right)$

71. $P = \$50$, $r = 7\%$, $t = 20$ years

    (a) Compounded monthly: $A = 50\left[\left(1 + \dfrac{0.07}{12}\right)^{12(20)} - 1\right]\left(1 + \dfrac{12}{0.07}\right) \approx \$26{,}198.27$

    (b) Compounded continuously: $A = \dfrac{50e^{0.07/12}(e^{0.07(20)} - 1)}{e^{0.07/12} - 1} \approx \$26{,}263.88$

73. $P = \$100$, $r = 10\%$, $t = 40$ years

    (a) Compounded monthly: $A = 100\left[\left(1 + \dfrac{0.10}{12}\right)^{12(40)} - 1\right]\left(1 + \dfrac{12}{0.10}\right) \approx \$637{,}678.02$

    (b) Compounded continuously: $A = \dfrac{100e^{0.10/12}(e^{(0.10)(40)} - 1)}{e^{0.10/12} - 1} \approx \$645{,}861.43$

75. $P = w \displaystyle\sum_{n=1}^{12t}\left[\left(1 + \dfrac{r}{12}\right)^{-1}\right]^{n}$

$= w\left(1 + \dfrac{r}{12}\right)^{-1}\left[\dfrac{1 - \left(1 + \dfrac{r}{12}\right)^{-12t}}{1 - \left(1 - \dfrac{r}{12}\right)^{-1}}\right]$

$= w\left(\dfrac{1}{1 + \dfrac{r}{12}}\right)\dfrac{\left[1 - \left(1 + \dfrac{r}{12}\right)^{-12t}\right]}{1 - \dfrac{1}{\left(1 + \dfrac{r}{12}\right)}}$

$= w\dfrac{\left[1 - \left(1 + \dfrac{r}{12}\right)^{-12t}\right]}{\left(1 + \dfrac{r}{12}\right)\quad 1}$

$= w\left(\dfrac{12}{r}\right)\left[1 - \left(1 - \dfrac{r}{12}\right)^{-12t}\right]$

77. $\displaystyle\sum_{n=0}^{5}\dfrac{16^2}{4}\left(\dfrac{1}{2}\right)^{n} \approx 126$

Total area of shaded region is approximately 126 square inches

79. $S_n = \displaystyle\sum_{i=1}^{n}0.01(2)^{i-1}$

$S_{29} = \$5{,}368{,}709.11$

$S_{30} = \$10{,}737{,}418.23$

$S_{31} = \$21{,}474{,}836.47$

81. $a_1 = 1$, $r = \dfrac{1}{2}$

$\displaystyle\sum_{n=0}^{\infty}\left(\dfrac{1}{2}\right)^{n} = \dfrac{a_1}{1 - r} = \dfrac{1}{1 - (1/2)} = 2$

83. $a_1 = 1$, $r = -\dfrac{1}{2}$

$\displaystyle\sum_{n=0}^{\infty}\left(-\dfrac{1}{2}\right)^{n} = \sum_{n=1}^{\infty}\left(-\dfrac{1}{2}\right)^{n-1} = \dfrac{a_1}{1 - r} = \dfrac{1}{1 - (-1/2)} = \dfrac{2}{3}$

85. $a_1 = 4$, $r = \dfrac{1}{4}$

$\displaystyle\sum_{n=0}^{\infty}4\left(\dfrac{1}{4}\right)^{n} = \dfrac{a_1}{1 - r} = \dfrac{4}{1 - (1/4)} = \dfrac{16}{3}$

87. $8 + 6 + \dfrac{9}{2} + \dfrac{27}{8} + \cdots = \displaystyle\sum_{n=0}^{\infty} 8\left(\dfrac{3}{4}\right)^n = \dfrac{8}{1 - 3/4} = 32$

89. $0.\overline{36} = \displaystyle\sum_{n=0}^{\infty} 0.36(0.01)^n = \dfrac{0.36}{1 - 0.01} = \dfrac{0.36}{0.99} = \dfrac{36}{99} = \dfrac{4}{11}$

91. $0.3\overline{18} = 0.3 + \displaystyle\sum_{n=0}^{\infty} 0.018(0.01)^n = \dfrac{3}{10} + \dfrac{0.018}{1 - 0.01}$

$\quad = \dfrac{3}{10} + \dfrac{0.018}{0.99} = \dfrac{3}{10} + \dfrac{18}{990} = \dfrac{3}{10} + \dfrac{2}{110}$

$\quad = \dfrac{35}{110} = \dfrac{7}{22}$

93. $f(x) = 6\left[\dfrac{1 - (0.5)^x}{1 - (0.5)}\right], \ \displaystyle\sum_{n=0}^{\infty} 6\left(\dfrac{1}{2}\right)^n = \dfrac{6}{1 - 1/2} = 12$

The horizontal asymptote of $f(x)$ is $y = 12$. This corresponds to the sum of the series.

95. (a) Total distance $= \left[\displaystyle\sum_{n=0}^{\infty} 32(0.81)^n\right] - 16 = \dfrac{32}{1 - 0.81} - 16 \approx 152.42$ feet

$\quad$ (b) $t = 1 + 2\displaystyle\sum_{n=1}^{\infty} (0.9)^n = 1 + 2\left[\dfrac{0.9}{1 - 0.9}\right] = 19$ seconds

97. Time $= \dfrac{\text{Distance}}{\text{Speed}} = \dfrac{200}{50} + \dfrac{200}{42} = 200\left[\dfrac{92}{2100}\right]$ hours

$\quad$ Speed $= \dfrac{\text{Distance}}{\text{Time}} = \dfrac{400}{200\left[\frac{92}{2100}\right]} = \dfrac{2(2100)}{92} \approx 45.65$ mph

99. Your friend mows at the rate of $\frac{1}{4}$ lawns/hour, and your rate is $\frac{1}{6}$ lawns/hour. Together, the time would be

$\quad \dfrac{1}{\frac{1}{4} + \frac{1}{6}} = \dfrac{1}{\frac{10}{24}} = \dfrac{24}{10} = 2.4$ hours.

Section 10.4   Mathematical Induction

- You should be sure that you understand the principle of mathematical induction. If P_n is a statement involving the positive integer n, where P_1 is true and the truth of P_k implies the truth of P_{k+1}, then P_n is true for all positive integers n.
- You should be able to verify (by induction) the formulas for the sums of powers of integers and be able to use these formulas.
- You should be able to work with finite differences.

Solutions to Odd-Numbered Exercises

1. $P_k = \dfrac{5}{k(k+1)}$

$P_{k+1} = \dfrac{5}{(k+1)[(k+1)+1]} = \dfrac{5}{(k+1)(k+2)}$

3. $P_k = \dfrac{k^2(k+1)^2}{4}$

$P_{k+1} = \dfrac{(k+1)^2[(k+1)+1]^2}{4} = \dfrac{(k+1)^2(k+2)^2}{4}$

5. 1. When $n = 1$, $S_1 = 2 = 1(1 + 1)$.

  2. Assume that
  $$S_k = 2 + 4 + 6 + 8 + \cdots + 2k = k(k + 1).$$
  Then,
  $$S_{k+1} = 2 + 4 + 6 + 8 + \cdots + 2k + 2(k + 1)$$
  $$= S_k + 2(k + 1) = k(k + 1) + 2(k + 1) = (k + 1)(k + 2).$$

We conclude by mathematical induction that the formula is valid for all positive integer values of n.

7. 1. When $n = 1$, $S_1 = 2 = \dfrac{1}{2}[5(1) - 1]$.

  2. Assume that
  $$S_k = 2 + 7 + 12 + 17 + \cdots + (5k - 3) = \frac{k}{2}(5k - 1).$$
  Then,
  $$S_{k+1} = 2 + 7 + 12 + 17 + \cdots + (5k - 3) + [5(k + 1) - 3]$$
  $$= S_k + (5k + 5 - 3) = \frac{k}{2}(5k - 1) + 5k + 2$$
  $$= \frac{5k^2 - k + 10k + 4}{2} = \frac{5k^2 + 9k + 4}{2}$$
  $$= \frac{(k + 1)(5k + 4)}{2} = \frac{(k + 1)}{2}[5(k + 1) - 1].$$

We conclude by mathematical induction that the formula is valid for all positive integer values of n.

9. 1. When $n = 1$, $S_1 = 1 = 2^1 - 1$.

    2. Assume that

$$S_k = 1 + 2 + 2^2 + 2^3 + \cdots + 2^{k-1} = 2^k - 1.$$

Then,

$$S_{k+1} = 1 + 2 + 2^2 + 2^3 + \cdots + 2^{k-1} + 2^k$$
$$= S_k + 2^k = 2^k - 1 + 2^k = 2(2^k) - 1 = 2^{k+1} - 1.$$

Therefore, by mathematical induction, the formula is valid for all positive integer values of n.

11. 1. When $n = 1$, $S_1 = 1 = \dfrac{1(1+1)}{2}$.

    2. Assume that

$$S_k = 1 + 2 + 3 + 4 + \cdots + k = \frac{k(k+1)}{2}.$$

Then,

$$S_{k+1} = 1 + 2 + 3 + 4 + \cdots + k + (k+1)$$
$$= S_k + (k+1) = \frac{k(k+1)}{2} + \frac{2(k+1)}{2} = \frac{(k+1)(k+2)}{2}.$$

Therefore, we conclude that this formula holds for all positive integer values of n.

13. 1. When $n = 1$, $S_1 = 1^3 = 1 = \dfrac{1(1+1)^2}{4}$.

    2. Assume that

$$S_k = 1^3 + 2^3 + 3^3 + 4^3 + \cdots + k^3 = \frac{k^2(k+1)^2}{4}.$$

Then,

$$S_{k+1} = 1^3 + 2^3 + 3^3 + 4^3 + \cdots + k^3 + (k+1)^3$$
$$= S_k + (k+1)^3 = \frac{k^2(k+1)^2}{4} + (k+1)^3 = \frac{k^2(k+1)^2 + 4(k+1)^3}{4}$$
$$= \frac{(k+1)^2[k^2 + 4(k+1)]}{4} = \frac{(k+1)^2(k^2 + 4k + 4)}{4} = \frac{(k+1)^2(k+2)^2}{4}.$$

Therefore, we conclude that this formula holds for all positive integer values of n.

15. 1. When $n = 1$, $S_1 = \dfrac{(1)^2(1 + 1)^2(2(1)^2 + 2(1) - 1)}{12} = 1$.

2. Assume that

$$S_k = \sum_{i=1}^{k} i^5 = \frac{k^2(k + 1)^2(2k^2 + 2k - 1)}{12}.$$

Then,

$$S_{k+1} = \sum_{i=1}^{k+1} i^5 = \sum_{i=1}^{k} i^5 + (k + 1)^5$$

$$= \frac{k^2(k + 1)^2(2k^2 + 2k - 1)}{12} + \frac{12(k + 1)^5}{12}$$

$$= \frac{(k + 1)^2[k^2(2k^2 + 2k - 1) + 12(k + 1)^3]}{12}$$

$$= \frac{(k + 1)^2[2k^4 + 2k^3 - k^2 + 12(k^3 + 3k^2 + 3k + 1)]}{12}$$

$$= \frac{(k + 1)^2[2k^4 + 14k^3 + 35k^2 + 36k + 12]}{12}$$

$$= \frac{(k + 1)^2(k^2 + 4k + 4)(2k^2 + 6k + 3)}{12}$$

$$= \frac{(k + 1)^2(k + 2)^2[2(k + 1)^2 + 2(k + 1) - 1]}{12}.$$

Therefore, we conclude that this formula holds for all positive integer values of n.

17. 1. When $n = 1$, $S_1 = 2 = \dfrac{1(2)(3)}{3}$.

2. Assume that

$$S_k = 1(2) + 2(3) + 3(4) + \cdots + k(k + 1) = \frac{k(k + 1)(k + 2)}{3}.$$

Then,

$$S_{k+1} = 1(2) + 2(3) + 3(4) + \cdots + k(k + 1) + (k + 1)(k + 2)$$

$$= S_k + (k + 1)(k + 2) = \frac{k(k + 1)(k + 2)}{3} + \frac{3(k + 1)(k + 2)}{3}$$

$$= \frac{(k + 1)(k + 2)(k + 3)}{3}.$$

Thus, this formula is valid for all positive integer values of n.

19. $\displaystyle\sum_{n=1}^{20} n = \frac{20(20 + 1)}{2} = 210$

21. $\displaystyle\sum_{n=1}^{6} n^2 = \frac{6(6 + 1)[2(6) + 1]}{6} = 91$

23. $\displaystyle\sum_{n=1}^{5} n^4 = \frac{5(5 + 1)(2(5) + 1)(3(5)^2 + 3(5) - 1)}{30} = 979$

25. $\displaystyle\sum_{n=1}^{6} (n^2 - n) = \sum_{n=1}^{6} n^2 - \sum_{n=1}^{6} n = \frac{6(6 + 1)[2(6) + 1]}{6} - \frac{6(6 + 1)}{2} = 91 - 21 = 70$

27. $\displaystyle\sum_{i=1}^{6}(6i - 8i^3) = 6\sum_{i=1}^{6}i - 8\sum_{i=1}^{6}i^3$

$$= 6\left[\frac{9(6+1)}{2}\right] - 8\left[\frac{(6)^2(6+1)^2}{4}\right] = 6(21) - 8(441) = -3402$$

29. $\displaystyle 1 + 5 + 9 + 13 + \cdots = \sum_{n=0}^{\infty}(1 + 4n)$ **31.** $\displaystyle 1 + \frac{9}{10} + \frac{81}{100} + \frac{729}{1000} + \cdots = \sum_{n=1}^{\infty}\left(\frac{9}{10}\right)^{n-1}$

33. $\displaystyle \frac{1}{4} + \frac{1}{12} + \frac{1}{24} + \frac{1}{40} + \cdots + \frac{1}{2n(n-1)} + \cdots = \sum_{n=2}^{\infty}\frac{1}{2n(n-1)}$

35. 1. When $n = 4$, $4! = 24$ and $2^4 = 16$, thus $4! > 2^4$.

     2. Assume $k! > 2^k$, $k > 4$. Then, $(k + 1)! = k!(k + 1) > 2^k(2)$ since $k + 1 > 2$. Thus, $(k + 1)! > 2^{k+1}$.

     Therefore, by mathematical induction, the formula is valid for all integers n such that $n \geq 4$.

37. 1. When $n = 2$, $\dfrac{1}{\sqrt{1}} + \dfrac{1}{\sqrt{2}} \approx 1.707$ and $\sqrt{2} \approx 1.414$, thus $\dfrac{1}{\sqrt{1}} + \dfrac{1}{\sqrt{2}} > \sqrt{2}$.

     2. Assume

$$\frac{1}{\sqrt{1}} + \frac{1}{\sqrt{2}} + \frac{1}{\sqrt{3}} + \cdots + \frac{1}{\sqrt{k}} > \sqrt{k},\ k > 2.$$

     Then,

$$\frac{1}{\sqrt{1}} + \frac{1}{\sqrt{2}} + \frac{1}{\sqrt{3}} + \cdots + \frac{1}{\sqrt{k}} + \frac{1}{\sqrt{k+1}} > \sqrt{k} + \frac{1}{\sqrt{k+1}}.$$

     Now we need to show that

$$\sqrt{k} + \frac{1}{\sqrt{k+1}} > \sqrt{k+1},\ k > 2.$$

     This is true since

$$\sqrt{k(k+1)} > k$$
$$\sqrt{k(k+1)} + 1 > k + 1$$
$$\frac{\sqrt{k(k+1)} + 1}{\sqrt{k+1}} > \frac{k+1}{\sqrt{k+1}}$$
$$\sqrt{k} + \frac{1}{\sqrt{k+1}} > \sqrt{k+1}.$$

     Therefore,

$$\frac{1}{\sqrt{1}} + \frac{1}{\sqrt{2}} + \frac{1}{\sqrt{3}} + \ldots + \frac{1}{\sqrt{k}} + \frac{1}{\sqrt{k+1}} > \sqrt{k+1}.$$

     Therefore, by mathematical induction, the formula is valid for all integers n such that $n \geq 2$.

39. 1. When $n = 1$, $(ab)^1 = a^1b^1 = ab$.

     2. Assume that $(ab)^k = a^k b^k$.

         Then, $(ab)^{k+1} = (ab)^k(ab)$

$$= a^k b^k ab$$
$$= a^{k+1} b^{k+1}.$$

     Thus, $(ab)^n = a^n b^n$.

41. 1. When $n = 1$, $(x_1)^{-1} = x_1^{-1}$.

     2. Assume that

$$(x_1 x_2 x_3 \cdots x_k)^{-1} = x_1^{-1}x_2^{-1}x_3^{-1}\cdots x_k^{-1}.$$

     Then,

$$(x_1 x_2 x_3 \cdots x_k x_{k+1})^{-1} = [(x_1 x_2 x_3 \cdots x_k)x_{k+1}]^{-1}$$
$$= (x_1 x_2 x_3 \ldots x_k)^{-1}x_{k+1}^{-1}$$
$$= x_1^{-1}x_2^{-1}x_3^{-1}\cdots x_k^{-1}x_{k+1}^{-1}.$$

     Thus, the formula is valid.

43. 1. When $n = 1$, $x(y_1) = xy_1$.

2. Assume that

$$x(y_1 + y_2 + \cdots + y_k) = xy_1 + xy_2 + \cdots + xy_k.$$

Then,

$$xy_1 + xy_2 + \cdots + xy_k + xy_{k+1} = x(y_1 + y_2 + \cdots + y_k) + xy_{k+1}$$
$$= x[(y_1 + y_2 + \cdots + y_k) + y_{k+1}]$$
$$= x(y_1 + y_2 + \cdots + y_k + y_{k+1}).$$

Hence, the formula holds.

45. 1. When $n = 1$, $\sin(x + \pi) = \sin x \cdot \cos \pi + \cos x \cdot \sin \pi$

$$= -\sin x = (-1)^1 \sin x.$$

2. Assume $\sin(x + k\pi) = (-1)^k \sin x$.

Then,

$$\sin(x + (k + 1)\pi) = \sin[(x + k\pi) + \pi]$$
$$= \sin(x + k\pi)\cos \pi + \cos(x + k\pi)\sin \pi$$
$$= \sin(x + k\pi)(-1) + 0$$
$$= (-1)(-1)^k \sin x$$
$$= (-1)^{k+1} \sin x.$$

Thus, $\sin(x + n\pi) = (-1)^n \sin x$ for all positive integers n.

47. 1. When $n = 1$, $[1^3 + 3(1)^2 + 2(1)] = 6$ and 3 is a factor.

2. Assume that 3 is a factor of $(k^3 + 3k^2 + 2k)$. Then,

$$[(k + 1)^3 + 3(k + 1)^2 + 2(k + 1)] = k^3 + 3k^2 + 3k + 1 + 3k^2 + 6k + 3 + 2k + 2$$
$$= (k^3 + 3k^2 + 2k) + (3k^2 + 9k + 6)$$
$$= (k^3 + 3k^2 + 2k) + 3(k^2 + 3k + 2).$$

Since 3 is a factor of $(k^3 + 3k^2 + 2k)$ by our assumption, and 3 is a factor of $3(k^2 + 3k + 2)$ then 3 is a factor of the whole sum.

Thus, 3 is a factor of $(n^3 + 3n^2 + 2n)$ for every positive integer n.

49. See the domino illustration and Figure 7.4.

51. $a_0 = 1, a_n = a_{n-1} + 2$

$a_0 = 1$

$a_1 = a_0 + 2 = 1 + 2 = 3$

$a_2 = a_1 + 2 = 3 + 2 = 5$

$a_3 = a_2 + 2 = 5 + 2 = 7$

$a_4 = a_3 + 2 = 7 + 2 = 9$

53. $a_0 = 4, a_1 = 2, a_n = a_{n-1} - a_{n-2}$

$a_0 = 4$

$a_1 = 2$

$a_2 = a_1 - a_0 = 2 - 4 = -2$

$a_3 = a_2 - a_1 = -2 - 2 = -4$

$a_4 = a_3 - a_2 = -4(-2) = -2$

55. $f(1) = 0, a_n = a_{n-1} + 3$

$a_1 = f(1) = 0$

$a_2 = a_1 + 3 = 0 + 3 = 3$

$a_3 = a_2 + 3 = 3 + 3 = 6$

$a_4 = a_3 + 3 = 6 + 3 = 9$

$a_5 = a_4 + 3 = 9 + 3 = 12$

a_n :   0   3   6   9   12

First differences :   3   3   3   3

Second differences :   0   0   0

Since the first differences are equal, the sequence has a linear model.

59. $a_0 = 0, a_n = a_{n-1} + n$

$a_0 = 0$

$a_1 = a_0 + 1 = 0 + 1 = 1$

$a_2 = a_1 + 2 = 1 + 2 = 3$

$a_3 = a_2 + 3 = 3 + 3 = 6$

$a_4 = a_3 + 4 = 6 + 4 = 10$

a_n :   0   1   3   6   10

First differences :   1   2   3   4

Second differences :   1   1   1

Since the second differences are equal, the sequence has a quadratic model.

63. $a_0 = 1, a_n = a_{n-1} + n^2$

$a_0 = 1$

$a_1 = 1 + 1^2 = 2$

$a_2 = 2 + 2^2 = 6$

$a_3 = 6 + 3^2 = 15$

$a_4 = 15 + 4^2 = 31$

a_n :   1   2   6   15   31

First differences :   1   4   9   16

Second differences :   3   5   7

Since neither the first differences, nor the second differences are equal, the sequence does not have a linear or a quadratic model.

57. $f(1) = 3, a_n = a_{n-1} - n$

$a_1 = f(1) = 3$

$a_2 = a_1 - 2 = 3 - 2 = 1$

$a_3 = a_2 - 3 = 1 - 3 = -2$

$a_4 = a_3 - 4 = -2 - 4 = -6$

$a_5 = a_4 - 5 = -6 - 5 = -11$

a_n :   3   1   -2   -6   -11

First differences :   -2   -3   -4   -5

Second differences :   -1   -1   -1

Since the second differences are all the same, the sequence has a quadratic model.

61. $f(1) = 2, a_n = a_{n-1} + 2$

$a_1 = f(1) = 2$

$a_2 = a_1 + 2 = 2 + 2 = 4$

$a_3 = a_2 + 2 = 4 + 2 = 6$

$a_4 = a_3 + 2 = 6 + 2 = 8$

$a_5 = a_4 + 2 = 8 + 2 = 10$

a_n :   2   4   6   8   10

First differences :   2   2   2   2

Second differences :   0   0   0

Since the first differences are equal, the sequence has a linear model.

65. $a_0 = 3, a_1 = 3, a_4 = 15$

Let $a_n = an^2 + bn + c$. Thus

$a_0 = a(0)^2 + b(0) + c = \quad 3 \implies c = 3$

$a_1 = a(1)^2 + b(1) + c = \quad 3 \implies a + b + c = 3$

$$a + b \qquad = 0$$

$a_4 = a(4)^2 + b(4) + c = 15 \implies 16a + 4b + c = 15$

$$16a + 4b \qquad = 12$$

$$4a + \ b \qquad = 3$$

By elimination: $-a - b = 0$

$$\underline{4a + b = 3}$$

$$3a \qquad = 3$$

$$a = 1 \implies b = -1$$

Thus, $a_n = n^2 - n + 3$.

67. $a_0 = -3, a_2 = 1, a_4 = 9$

Let $a_n = an^2 + bn + c$. Then

$a_0 = a(0)^2 + b(0) + c = -3 \implies c = -3$

$a_2 = a(2)^2 + b(2) + c = \quad 1 \implies 4a + 2b + c = 1$

$$4a + 2b \qquad = 4$$

$$2a + \ b \qquad = 2$$

$a_4 = a(4)^2 + b(4) + c = \quad 9 \implies 16a + 4b + c = \ 9$

$$16a + 4b \qquad = 12$$

$$4a + \ b \qquad = 3$$

By elimination: $-2a - b = -2$

$$\underline{4a + b = \quad 3}$$

$$2a \qquad = -1$$

$$a = \ \tfrac{1}{2} \implies b = 1$$

Thus, $a_n = \tfrac{1}{2}n^2 + n - 3$.

69.

$$y = x^2$$

$$-3x + 2y = 2 \quad \implies \quad -3x + 2x^2 = 2$$

$$2x^2 - 3x - 2 = 0$$

$$(2x + 1)(x - 2) = 0$$

$$x = -\tfrac{1}{2} \ \text{ or } x \ = 2$$

$$x = -\tfrac{1}{4} \ \text{ or } x \ = 4$$

Points of intersection: $\left(-\tfrac{1}{2}, \tfrac{1}{4}\right), (2, 4)$

71.
$$x - y \qquad = -1$$
$$x + 2y - 2z = 3$$
$$3x - y + 2z = 3$$

Using an augmented matrix, we have

$$\begin{bmatrix} 1 & -1 & 0 & \vdots & -1 \\ 1 & 2 & -2 & \vdots & 3 \\ 3 & -1 & 2 & \vdots & 3 \end{bmatrix}$$

$$\begin{matrix} \\ -R_1 + R_2 \rightarrow \\ -3R_1 + R_3 \rightarrow \end{matrix} \begin{bmatrix} 1 & -1 & 0 & \vdots & -1 \\ 0 & 3 & -2 & \vdots & 4 \\ 0 & 2 & 2 & \vdots & 6 \end{bmatrix}$$

$$\begin{matrix} \\ -R_3 + R_2 \rightarrow \\ \frac{1}{2}R_3 \rightarrow \end{matrix} \begin{bmatrix} 1 & -1 & 0 & \vdots & -1 \\ 0 & 1 & -4 & \vdots & -2 \\ 0 & 1 & 1 & \vdots & 3 \end{bmatrix}$$

$$\begin{matrix} R_2 + R_1 \rightarrow \\ \\ -R_2 + R_3 \rightarrow \end{matrix} \begin{bmatrix} 1 & 0 & -4 & \vdots & -3 \\ 0 & 1 & -4 & \vdots & -2 \\ 0 & 0 & 5 & \vdots & 5 \end{bmatrix}$$

$$\begin{matrix} 4R_3 + R_1 \rightarrow \\ 4R_3 + R_2 \rightarrow \\ \frac{1}{5}R_3 \rightarrow \end{matrix} \begin{bmatrix} 1 & 0 & 0 & \vdots & 1 \\ 0 & 1 & 0 & \vdots & 2 \\ 0 & 0 & 1 & \vdots & 1 \end{bmatrix}$$

Thus, $x = 1, y = 2, z = 1$.
Answer: $(1, 2, 1)$

Section 10.5   The Binomial Theorem

■ You should be able to use the Binomial Theorem

$$(x + y)^n = x^n + nx^{n-1}y + \frac{n(n-1)}{2!}x^{n-2}y^2 + \cdots + {}_nC_r x^{n-r}y^r + \cdots + y^n$$

where ${}_nC_r = \dfrac{n!}{(n-r)!r!}$, to expand $(x + y)^n$.

■ You should be able to use Pascal's Triangle.

Solutions to Odd-Numbered Exercises

1. ${}_5C_3 = \dfrac{5!}{3!2!} = \dfrac{5 \cdot 4}{2 \cdot 1} = 10$

3. ${}_{12}C_0 = \dfrac{12!}{0!12!} = 1$

5. ${}_{20}C_{15} = \dfrac{20!}{15!5!} = \dfrac{20 \cdot 19 \cdot 18 \cdot 17 \cdot 16}{5 \cdot 4 \cdot 3 \cdot 2 \cdot 1} = 15,504$

7. $_{100}C_{98} = \dfrac{100!}{98!2!} = \dfrac{100 \cdot 99}{2 \cdot 1} = 4950$

9. $_{100}C_2 = \dfrac{100!}{2!98!} = \dfrac{100 \cdot 99}{2 \cdot 1} = 4950$

11. The first and last number in each row is 1. Each number is found by adding the two numbers immediately above it.

13.
```
            1
          1   1
        1   2   1
      1   3   3   1
    1   4   6   4   1
  1   5  10  10   5   1
1   6  15  20  15   6   1
1  7  21  35 (35) 21  7  1
```

$_7C_4 = 35$, the 5th entry in the 8th row.

15.
```
            1
          1   1
        1   2   1
      1   3   3   1
    1   4   6   4   1
  1   5  10  10   5   1
1   6  15  20  15   6   1
1  7  21  35  35  21  7  1
1  8 28 56 70 (56) 28 8 1
```

$_8C_5 = 56$, the 6th entry in the 9th row.

17. $(x + 1)^4 = {}_4C_0 x^4 + {}_4C_1 x^3(1) + {}_4C_2 x(1)^2 + {}_4C_3 x(1)^3 + {}_4C_4(1)^4$

$\qquad = x^4 + 4x^3 + 6x^2 + 4x + 1$

19. $(a + 2)^3 = {}_3C_0 a^3 + {}_3C_1 a^2(2) + {}_3C_2 a(2)^2 + {}_3C_3(2)^3$

$\qquad = a^3 + 3a^2(2) + 3a(2)^2 + (2)^3$

$\qquad = a^3 + 6a^2 + 12a + 8$

21. $(y - 2)^4 = {}_4C_0 y^4 - {}_4C_1 y^3(2) + {}_4C_2 y^2(2)^2 - {}_4C_3 y(2)^3 + {}_4C_4(2)^4$

$\qquad = y^4 - 4y^3(2) + 6y^2(4) - 4y(8) + 16$

$\qquad = y^4 - 8y^3 + 24y^2 - 32y + 16$

23. $(x + y)^5 = {}_5C_0 x^5 + {}_5C_1 x^4 y + {}_5C_2 x^3 y^2 + {}_5C_3 x^2 y^3 + {}_5C_4 xy^4 + {}_5C_5 y^5$

$\qquad = x^5 + 5x^4 y + 10x^3 y^2 + 10x^2 y^3 + 5xy^4 + y^5$

25. $(r + 3s)^6 = {}_6C_0 r^6 + {}_6C_1 r^5(3s) + {}_6C_2 r^4(3s)^2 + {}_6C_3 r^3(3s)^3 + {}_6C_4 r^2(3s)^4$

$\qquad\qquad + {}_6C_5 r(3s)^5 + {}_6C_6(3s)^6$

$\qquad = r^6 + 18r^5 s + 135r^4 s^2 + 540r^3 s^3 + 1215r^2 s^4 + 1458rs^5 + 729s^6$

27. $(x - y)^5 = {}_5C_0 x^5 - {}_5C_1 x^4 y + {}_5C_2 x^3 y^2 - {}_5C_3 x^2 y^3 - {}_5C_4 xy^4 - {}_5C_5 y^5$

$\qquad = x^5 - 5x^4 y + 10x^3 y^2 - 10x^2 y^3 + 5xy^4 - y^5$

29. $(1 - 2x)^3 = {}_3C_0 1^3 - {}_3C_1 1^2(2x) + {}_3C_2 1(2x)^2 - {}_3C_3(2x)^3$

$\qquad = 1 - 3(2x) + 3(2x)^2 - (2x)^3$

$\qquad = 1 - 6x + 12x^2 - 8x^3$

31. $(x^2 + 5)^4 = {}_4C_0(x^2)^4 + {}_4C_1(x^2)^3(5) + {}_4C_2(x^2)^2(5)^2 + {}_4C_3(x^2)(5)^3 + {}_4C_4(5)^4$

$\qquad = x^8 + 4x^6(5) + 6x^4(25) + 4x^2(125) + 625$

$\qquad = x^8 + 20x^6 + 150x^4 + 500x^2 + 625$

33. $\left(\dfrac{1}{x} + y\right)^5 = {}_5C_0\left(\dfrac{1}{x}\right)^5 + {}_5C_1\left(\dfrac{1}{x}\right)^4 y + {}_5C_2\left(\dfrac{1}{x}\right)^3 y^2 + {}_5C_3\left(\dfrac{1}{x}\right)^2 y^3 + {}_5C_4\left(\dfrac{1}{x}\right) y^4 + {}_5C_5 y^5$

$$= \dfrac{1}{x^5} + \dfrac{5y}{x^4} + \dfrac{10y^2}{x^3} + \dfrac{10y^3}{x^2} + \dfrac{5y^4}{x} + y^5$$

35. $2(x - 3)^4 + 5(x - 3)^2 = 2[x^4 - 4(x^3)(3) + 6(x^2)(3^2) - 4(x)(3^3) + 3^4] + 5[x^2 - 2(x)(3) + 3^2]$

$$= 2(x^4 - 12x^3 + 54x^2 - 108x + 81) + 5(x^2 - 6x + 9)$$

$$= 2x^4 - 24x^3 + 113x^2 - 246x + 207$$

37. 5th Row of Pascal's Triangle: 1   5   10   10   5   1

$(2t - s)^5 = 1(2t)^5 + 5(2t)^4(-s) + 10(2t)^3(-s)^2 + 10(2t)^2(-s)^3 + 5(2t)(-s)^4 + 1(-s)^5$

$$= 32t^5 - 80t^4 s + 80t^3 s^2 - 40t^2 s^3 + 10ts^4 - s^5$$

39. 4th Row of Pascal's Triangle: 1   4   6   4   1

$(3 - 2z)^4 = 3^4 - 4(3)^3(2z) + 6(3)^2(2z)^2 - 4(3)(2z)^3 + (2z)^4$

$$= 81 - 216z + 216z^2 - 96z^3 + 16z^4$$

41. The term involving x^5 in the expansion of $(x + 3)^{12}$ is

$${}_{12}C_7 x^5 (3)^7 = \dfrac{12!}{7!5!} \cdot 3^7 x^5 = 1{,}732{,}104 x^5.$$ The coefficient is 1,732,104.

43. The term involving $x^8 y^2$ in the expansion of $(x - 2y)^{10}$ is

$${}_{10}C_2 x^8 (-2y)^2 = \dfrac{10!}{2!8!} \cdot 4x^8 y^2 = 180 x^8 y^2.$$ The coefficient is 180.

45. The coefficient of $x^4 y^5$ in the expansion of $(3x - 2y)^9$ is

$${}_9C_5 (3)^4 (-2)^5 = \dfrac{9!}{5!4!}(81)(-32) = -326{,}592.$$

47. The coefficient of $x^8 y^6 = (x^2)^4 y^6$ in the expansion of $(x^2 + y)^{10}$ is ${}_{10}C_6 = 210$.

49. There are $n + 1$ terms in the expansion of $(x + y)^n$.

51. $\left(\sqrt{x} + 3\right)^4 = \left(\sqrt{x}\right)^4 + 4\left(\sqrt{x}\right)^3(3) + 6\left(\sqrt{x}\right)^2(3)^2 + 4\left(\sqrt{x}\right)(3)^3 + (3)^4$

$$= x^2 + 12x\sqrt{x} + 54x + 108\sqrt{x} + 81$$

$$= x^2 + 12x^{3/2} + 54x + 108x^{1/2} + 81$$

53. $(x^{2/3} - y^{1/3})^3 = (x^{2/3})^3 - 3(x^{2/3})^2 (y^{1/3}) + 3(x^{2/3})(y^{1/3})^2 - (y^{1/3})^3$

$$= x^2 - 3x^{4/3} y^{1/3} + 3x^{2/3} y^{2/3} - y$$

55. $\dfrac{f(x + h) - f(x)}{h} = \dfrac{(x + h)^3 - x^3}{h}$

$$= \dfrac{x^3 + 3x^2 h + 3xh^2 + h^3 - x^3}{h}$$

$$= \dfrac{h(3x^2 + 3xh + h^2)}{h}$$

$$= 3x^2 + 3xh + h^2, \; h \neq 0$$

57. $\dfrac{f(x + h) - f(x)}{h} = \dfrac{\sqrt{x + h} - \sqrt{x}}{h}$

$$= \dfrac{\sqrt{x + h} - \sqrt{x}}{h}$$

59. $(1 + i)^4 = {}_4C_0 1^4 + {}_4C_1(1)^3 i + {}_4C_2(1)^2 i^2 + {}_4C_3 1 \cdot i^3 + {}_4C_4 i^4$

$\qquad = 1 + 4i - 6 - 4i + 1$

$\qquad = -4$

61. $(2 - 3i)^6 = {}_6C_0 2^6 - {}_6C_1 2^5(3i) + {}_6C_2 2^4(3i)^2 - {}_6C_3 2^3(3i)^3 + {}_6C_4 2^2(3i)^4 - {}_6C_5 2(3i)^5 + {}_6C_6(3i)^6$

$\qquad = 64 - 576i - 2160 + 4320i + 4860 - 2916i - 729$

$\qquad = 2035 + 828i$

63. $\left(-\dfrac{1}{2} + \dfrac{\sqrt{3}}{2}i\right)^3 = \dfrac{1}{8}(-1 + \sqrt{3}i)^3$

$\qquad = \dfrac{1}{8}\left[(-1)^3 + 3(-1)^2(\sqrt{3}i) + 3(-1)(\sqrt{3}i)^2 + (\sqrt{3}i)^3\right]$

$\qquad = \dfrac{1}{8}\left[-1 + 3\sqrt{3}i + 9 - 3\sqrt{3}i\right]$

$\qquad = 1$

65. ${}_7C_4\left(\dfrac{1}{2}\right)^4\left(\dfrac{1}{2}\right)^3 = 35\left(\dfrac{1}{16}\right)\left(\dfrac{1}{8}\right) \approx 0.273$

67. ${}_8C_4\left(\dfrac{1}{3}\right)^4\left(\dfrac{2}{3}\right)^4 = 70\left(\dfrac{1}{81}\right)\left(\dfrac{16}{81}\right) \approx 0.171$

69. $(1.02)^8 = (1 + 0.02)^8 = 1 + 8(0.02) + 28(0.02)^2 + 56(0.02)^3 + 70(0.02)^4 + 56(0.02)^5$

$\qquad\qquad\qquad + 28(0.02)^6 + 8(0.02)^7 + (0.02)^8$

$\qquad\qquad = 1 + 0.16 + 0.0112 + 0.000448 + \cdots \approx 1.172$

71. $(2.99)^{12} = (3 - 0.01)^{12}$

$\qquad = 3^{12} - 12(3)^{11}(0.01) + 66(3)^{10}(0.01)^2 - 220(3)^9(0.01)^3 + 495(3)^8(0.01)^4$

$\qquad\quad - 792(3)^7(0.01)^5 + 924(3)^6(0.01)^6 - 792(3)^5(0.01)^7 + 495(3)^4(0.01)^8$

$\qquad\quad - 220(3)^3(0.01)^9 + 66(3)^2(0.01)^{10} - 12(3)(0.01)^{11} + (0.01)^{12}$

$\qquad \approx 510{,}568.785$

73. $f(x) = x^3 - 4x$

$g(x) = f(x + 4)$

$\qquad = (x + 4)^3 - 4(x + 4)$

$\qquad = x^3 + 3x^2(4) + 3x(4)^2 + (4)^3 - 4x - 16$

$\qquad = x^3 + 12x^2 + 48x + 64 - 4x - 16$

$\qquad = x^3 + 12x^2 + 44x + 48$

The graph of g is the same as the graph of f shifted 4 units to the left.

75. $f(x) = -x^2 + 3x + 2$

$g(x) = f(x - 2)$

$\qquad = -(x - 2)^2 + 3(x - 2) + 2$

$\qquad = -x^2 + 4x - 4 + 3x - 6 + 2$

$\qquad = -x^2 + 7x - 8$

The graph of g is the same as the graph of f shifted 2 units to the right

77. $_nC_{n-r} = \dfrac{n!}{[n-(n-r)]!(n-r)!}$

$= \dfrac{n!}{r!(n-r)!}$

$= \dfrac{n!}{(n-r)!r!}$

$= {}_nC_r$

79. $_nC_r + {}_nC_{r-1} = \dfrac{n!}{(n-r)!r!} + \dfrac{n!}{(n-r+1)!(r-1)!}$

$= \dfrac{n!(n-r+1)}{(n-r)!r!(n-r+1)} + \dfrac{n!}{(n-r+1)!(r-1)!r} \cdot r$

$= \dfrac{n!(n-r+1)}{(n-r+1)!r!} + \dfrac{n!r}{(n-r+1)!r!}$

$= \dfrac{n!(n-r+1+r)}{(n-r+1)!r!}$

$= \dfrac{n!(n+1)}{(n-r+1)!r!}$

$= \dfrac{(n+1)!}{(n+1-r)!r!} = {}_{n+1}C_r$

81. (a) $_{12}C_5 = 792$

(b) $(_6C_5)^2 = 36$

(c) $_{11}C_5 + {}_{11}C_4 = 792$

(d) $_6C_5 + {}_6C_5 = 12$

(a) and (c) are equal.

83. $f(x) = (1-x)^3$

$g(x) = 1 - 3x$

$h(x) = 1 - 3x + 3x^2$

$p(x) = 1 - 3x + 3x^2 - x^3$

Since $p(x)$ is the expansion of $f(x)$, they have the same graph.

85. $f(t) = 0.1506t^2 + 0.7361t + 21.1374,\ 0 \le t \le 22$

(a) $g(t) = f(t + 10)$

$= 0.1506(t + 10)^2 + 0.7361(t + 10) + 21.1374$

$= 0.1506(t^2 + 20t + 100) + 0.7361t + 7.361 + 21.1374$

$= 0.1506t^2 + 3.7481t + 43.5584$

(b)

87. $g(x) = f(x) + 8$

$g(x)$ is shifted 8 units up from $f(x)$.

89. $g(x) = f(-x)$

$g(x)$ is the reflection of $f(x)$ in the y-axis.

Section 10.6   Counting Principles

- You should know The Fundamental Counting Principle.

- $_nP_r = \dfrac{n!}{(n-r)!}$ is the number of permutations of n elements taken r at a time.

- Given a set of n objects that has n_1 of one kind, n_2 of a second kind, and so on, the number of distinguishable permutations is
$$\frac{n!}{n_1!n_2!\cdots n_k!}.$$

- $_nC_r = \dfrac{n!}{(n-r)!r!}$ is the number of combinations of n elements taken r at a time.

Solutions to Odd-Numbered Exercises

1. Odd integers: 1, 3, 5, 7, 9, 11
6 ways

3. Prime integers: 2, 3, 5, 7, 11
5 ways

5. Divisible by 4: 4, 8, 12
3 ways

7. Sum is 8: $1 + 7$, $2 + 6$, $3 + 5$, $4 + 4$, $5 + 3$, $6 + 2$, $7 + 1$
7 ways

9. Amplifiers: 2 choices
Compact disc players: 4 choices
Speakers: 6 choices
Total: $2 \cdot 4 \cdot 6 = 48$ ways

11. Chemist: 3 choices
Statistician: 4 choices
Total: $3 \cdot 4 = 12$ ways

13. $2^6 = 64$

15. 1st Position: 2 choices
2nd Position: 3 choices
3rd Position: 2 choices
4th Position: 1 choice
Total: $2 \cdot 3 \cdot 2 \cdot 1 = 12$ ways

Label the four people A, B, C, and D and suppose that A and B are willing to take the first position. The twelve combinations are as follows.

ABCD	BACD
ABDC	BADC
ACBD	BCAD
ACDB	BCDA
ADBC	BDAC
ADCB	BDCA

17. $26 \cdot 26 \cdot 10 \cdot 10 \cdot 10 \cdot 10 = 6{,}760{,}000$

19. (a) $9 \cdot 10 \cdot 10 = 900$

(b) $9 \cdot 9 \cdot 8 = 648$

(c) $9 \cdot 10 \cdot 2 = 180$

(d) $10 \cdot 10 \cdot 10 - 400 = 600$

21. $40^3 = 64,000$

23. (a) $6 \cdot 5 \cdot 4 \cdot 3 \cdot 2 \cdot 1 = 720$

(b) $6 \cdot 1 \cdot 4 \cdot 1 \cdot 2 \cdot 1 = 48$

25. $_nP_r = \dfrac{n!}{(n-r)!}$

So, $_4P_4 = \dfrac{4!}{0!} = 4! = 24.$

27. $_8P_3 = \dfrac{8!}{5!} = 8 \cdot 7 \cdot 6 = 336$

29. $_5P_4 = \dfrac{5!}{1!} = 120$

31. $\qquad 14 \cdot {}_nP_3 = {}_{n+2}P_4 \qquad$ Note $n \geq 3$ for this to be defined.

$$14\left[\frac{n!}{(n-3)!}\right] = \frac{(n+2)!}{(n-2)!}$$

$14n(n-1)(n-2) = (n+2)(n+1)n(n-1) \qquad$ (We can divide here by $n(n-1)$ since $n \neq 0, n \neq 1.$)

$$14n - 28 = n^2 + 3n + 2$$
$$0 = n^2 - 11n + 30$$
$$0 = (n-5)(n-6)$$
$$n = 5 \quad \text{or} \quad n = 6$$

33. $_{20}P_5 = 1,860,480$

35. $_{100}P_3 = 970,200$

37. $_{20}C_5 = 15,504$

39. $_{100}P_{80} \approx 3.836 \times 10^{139}$

This number is too large for some calculators to evaluate.

41.

ABCD	BACD	CABD	DABC
ABDC	BADC	CADB	DACB
ACBD	BCAD	CBAD	DBAC
ACDB	BCDA	CBDA	DBCA
ADBC	BDAC	CDAB	DCAB
ADCB	BDCA	CDBA	DCBA

43. $5! = 120$ ways

45. $_{12}P_4 = \dfrac{12!}{8!} = 12 \cdot 11 \cdot 10 \cdot 9 = 11,880$ ways

47. $\dfrac{7!}{2!1!3!1!} = \dfrac{7!}{2!3!} = 420$

49. $\dfrac{7!}{2!1!1!1!1!1!} = \dfrac{7!}{2!} = 7 \cdot 6 \cdot 5 \cdot 4 \cdot 3 = 2520$

51. $_6C_2 = 15$

The 15 ways are listed below.

AB, AC, AD, AE, AF,

BC, BD, BE, BF, CD,

CE, CF, DE, DF, EF

53. $_{20}C_4 = 4845$ groups

55. $_{40}C_6 = 3,838,380$ ways

57. $_{100}C_4 = 3,921,225$ subsets

59. $_7C_2 = 21$ lines

61. (a) $_8C_4 = \dfrac{8!}{(8-4)!4!} = \dfrac{8!}{4!4!} = \dfrac{8 \cdot 7 \cdot 6 \cdot 5}{4 \cdot 3 \cdot 2} = 70$ ways

   (b) $_3C_2 \cdot {}_5C_2 = \dfrac{3!}{(3-2)!2!} \cdot \dfrac{5!}{(5-2)!2!} = 3 \cdot 10 = 30$ ways

63. (a) $_8C_4 = \dfrac{8!}{4!4!} = 70$ ways

   (b) There are $2^4 = 16$ ways that a group of four can be formed without any couples in the group. Therefore, if at least one couple is to be in the group, there are $70 - 60 = 54$ ways that could occur.

   (c) $2 \cdot 2 \cdot 2 \cdot 2 = 16$ ways

65. $_5C_2 - 5 = 10 - 5 = 5$ diagonals   **67.** $_8C_2 - 8 = 28 - 8 = 20$ diagonals

69. $_nP_{n-1} = \dfrac{n!}{(n-(n-1))!} = \dfrac{n!}{1!} = \dfrac{n!}{0!} = {}_nP_n$

71. $_nC_{n-1} = \dfrac{n!}{[n-(n-1)]!(n-1)!} = \dfrac{n!}{(1)!(n-1)!} = \dfrac{n!}{(n-1)!1!} = {}_nC_1$

73. From the graph of $y = \sqrt{x-3} - x + 6$, you see that there is one zero, $x \approx 8.303$. Analytically,

$$\sqrt{x-3} = x - 6$$
$$x - 3 = x^2 - 12x + 36$$
$$0 = x^2 - 13x + 39.$$

By the Quadratic Formula, $x = \dfrac{13 \pm \sqrt{(-13)^2 - 4(39)}}{2} = \dfrac{13 \pm \sqrt{13}}{2}$.

Selecting the larger solution, $x = \dfrac{13 + \sqrt{13}}{2} \approx 8.303$.

75. $\log_2(x-3) = 5$

$$2^5 = x - 3$$
$$2^5 + 3 = x$$
$$x = 35$$

Section 10.7   Probability

You should know the following basic principles of probability.

■ If an event E has $n(E)$ equally likely outcomes and its sample space has $n(S)$ equally likely outcomes, then the probability of event E is

$$P(E) = \frac{n(E)}{n(S)}, \text{ where } 0 \le P(E) \le 1.$$

■ If A and B are mutually exclusive events, then $P(A \cup B) = P(A) + P(B)$.

   If A and B are not mutually exclusive events, then $P(A \cup B) = P(A) + P(B) - P(A \cap B)$.

■ If A and B are independent events, then the probability that both A and B will occur is $P(A)P(B)$.

■ The probability of the complement of an event A is $P(A') = 1 - P(A)$.

Solutions to Odd-Numbered Exercises

1. $\{(h, 1), (h, 2), (h, 3), (h, 4), (h, 5), (h, 6),$
$(t, 1), (t, 2), (t, 3), (t, 4), (t, 5), (t, 6)\}$

3. $\{ABC, ACB, BAC, BCA, CAB, CBA\}$

5. $\{(A, B), (A, C), (A, D), (A, E), (B, C), (B, D), (B, E), (C, D), (C, E), (D, E)\}$

7. $E = \{HHT, HTH, THH\}$

$P(E) = \dfrac{n(E)}{n(S)} = \dfrac{3}{8}$

9. $E = \{HHH, HHT, HTH, HTT, THH, THT, TTH\}$

$P(E) = \dfrac{n(E)}{n(S)} = \dfrac{7}{8}$

11. $E = \{K, K, K, K, Q, Q, Q, Q, J, J, J, J\}$

$P(E) = \dfrac{n(E)}{n(S)} = \dfrac{12}{52} = \dfrac{3}{13}$

13. $E = \{K, K, Q, Q, J, J\}$

$P(E) = \dfrac{n(E)}{n(S)} = \dfrac{6}{52} = \dfrac{3}{26}$

15. $E = \{(1, 3), (2, 2), (3, 1)\}$

$P(E) = \dfrac{n(E)}{n(S)} = \dfrac{3}{36} = \dfrac{1}{12}$

17. not $E = \{(5, 6), (6, 5), (6, 6)\}$

$n(E) = n(S) - n(\text{not } E) = 36 - 3 = 33$

$P(E) = \dfrac{n(E)}{n(S)} = \dfrac{33}{36} = \dfrac{11}{12}$

19. $E_3 = \{(1, 2), (2, 1)\}, \ n(E_3) = 2$
$E_5 = \{(1, 4), (2, 3), (3, 2), (4, 1)\}, \ n(E_5) = 4$
$E_7 = \{(1, 6), (2, 5), (3, 4), (4, 3), (5, 2), (6, 1)\}, \ n(E_7) = 6$
$E = E_3 \cup E_5 \cup E_7$
$n(E) = 2 + 4 + 6 = 12$

$P(E) = \dfrac{n(E)}{n(s)} = \dfrac{12}{36} = \dfrac{1}{3}$

21. $P(E) = \dfrac{{}_3C_2}{{}_6C_2} = \dfrac{3}{15} = \dfrac{1}{5}$

23. $P(E) = \dfrac{{}_4C_2}{{}_6C_2} = \dfrac{6}{15} = \dfrac{2}{5}$

25. $1 - P(E) = 1 - 0.7 = 0.3$

27. $1 - p = 1 - 0.15 = 0.85$

29. (a) $0.37(2.5) = 0.925$ million $= 925,000$

(b) 0.18

31. (a) $\frac{290}{500} = 0.58$

(b) $\frac{478}{500} = 0.956$

(c) $\frac{2}{500} = 0.004$

33. (a) $\dfrac{672}{1254}$

(b) $\dfrac{582}{1254}$

(c) $\dfrac{672 - 124}{1254} = \dfrac{548}{1254}$

35. $p + p + 2p = 1$

$\qquad\qquad\quad p = 0.25$

Taylor: $0.50 = \dfrac{1}{2}$

Moore: $0.25 = \dfrac{1}{4}$

Jenkins: $0.25 = \dfrac{1}{4}$

37. (a) $\dfrac{{}_{15}C_{10}}{{}_{20}C_{10}} = \dfrac{3003}{184,756} = \dfrac{21}{1292} \approx 0.016$

(b) $\dfrac{{}_{15}C_{8} \cdot {}_{5}C_{2}}{{}_{20}C_{10}} = \dfrac{64,350}{184,756} = \dfrac{225}{646} \approx 0.348$

(c) $\dfrac{{}_{15}C_{9} \cdot {}_{5}C_{1}}{{}_{20}C_{10}} + \dfrac{{}_{15}C_{10}}{{}_{20}C_{10}} = \dfrac{25,025 + 3003}{184,756} = \dfrac{28,028}{184,756} = \dfrac{49}{323} \approx 0.152$

39. Total ways to insert letters: $4! = 24$ ways

4 correct: 1 way

3 correct: not possible

2 correct: 6 ways

1 correct: 8 ways

0 correct: 9 ways

(a) $\dfrac{8}{24} = \dfrac{1}{3}$

(b) $\dfrac{8 + 6 + 1}{24} = \dfrac{15}{24} = \dfrac{5}{8}$

41. (a) $\dfrac{1}{{}_{5}P_{5}} = \dfrac{1}{120}$

(b) $\dfrac{1}{{}_{4}P_{4}} = \dfrac{1}{24}$

43. (a) $\dfrac{4}{52} \cdot \dfrac{4}{52} = \dfrac{1}{169}$

(b) $\dfrac{4}{52} \cdot \dfrac{3}{51} = \dfrac{1}{221}$

45. (a) $\dfrac{{}_{9}C_{4}}{{}_{12}C_{4}} = \dfrac{126}{495} = \dfrac{14}{55}$ (4 good units)

(b) $\dfrac{({}_{9}C_{2})\,({}_{3}C_{2})}{{}_{12}C_{4}} = \dfrac{108}{495} = \dfrac{12}{55}$ (2 good units)

(c) $\dfrac{({}_{9}C_{3})({}_{3}C_{1})}{{}_{12}C_{4}} = \dfrac{252}{495} = \dfrac{28}{55}$ (3 good units)

At least 2 good units: $\dfrac{12}{55} + \dfrac{28}{55} + \dfrac{14}{55} = \dfrac{54}{55}$

47. (a) $P(EE) = \dfrac{15}{30} \cdot \dfrac{15}{30} = \dfrac{1}{4}$

(b) $P(E)$ or $P(OE) = 2\left(\dfrac{15}{30}\right)\left(\dfrac{15}{30}\right) = \dfrac{1}{2}$

(c) $P(N_1 < 10, N_2 < 10) = \dfrac{9}{30} \cdot \dfrac{9}{30} = \dfrac{9}{100}$

(d) $P(N_1 N_1) = \dfrac{30}{30} \cdot \dfrac{1}{30} = \dfrac{1}{30}$

49. (a) $P(SS) = (0.985)^2 \approx 0.9702$

(b) $P(S) = 1 - P(FF) = 1 - (0.015)^2 \approx 0.9998$

(c) $P(FF) = (0.015)^2 \approx 0.0002$

51. (a) $\left(\frac{1}{4}\right)^5 = \frac{1}{1024}$

(b) $\left(\frac{3}{4}\right)^5 = \frac{243}{1024}$

(c) $1 - \frac{243}{1024} = \frac{781}{1024}$

53. $(0.32)^2 = 0.1024$

55. $1 - \dfrac{(45)^2}{(60)^2} = 1 - \left(\dfrac{45}{60}\right)^2 = 1 - \left(\dfrac{3}{4}\right)^2 = 1 - \dfrac{9}{16} = \dfrac{7}{16}$

57. (a) As you consider successive people with distinct birthdays, the probabilities must decrease to take into account the birth dates already used. Since the birth dates of people are independent events, multiply the respective probabilities of distinct birthdays.

(b) $\dfrac{365}{365} \cdot \dfrac{364}{365} \cdot \dfrac{363}{365} \cdot \dfrac{362}{365}$

(c) $P_1 = \dfrac{365}{365} = 1$

$P_2 = \dfrac{365}{365} \cdot \dfrac{364}{365} = \dfrac{364}{365} P_1 = \dfrac{365 - (2-1)}{365} P_1$

$P_3 = \dfrac{365}{365} \cdot \dfrac{364}{365} \cdot \dfrac{363}{365} = \dfrac{363}{365} P_2 = \dfrac{365 - (3-1)}{365} P_2$

$P_n = \dfrac{365}{365} \cdot \dfrac{364}{365} \cdot \dfrac{363}{365} \cdot \ldots \cdot \dfrac{365 - (n-1)}{365} = \dfrac{365 - (n-1)}{365} P_{n-1}$

(d) Q_n is the probability that the birthdays are *not* distinct which is equivalent to at least 2 people having the same birthday.

(e)

n	10	15	20	23	30	40	50
P_n	0.88	0.75	0.59	0.49	0.29	0.11	0.03
Q_n	0.12	0.25	0.41	(0.51)	0.71	0.89	0.97

(f) 23,   See the chart above.

59. $1 - 0.546 = 0.454$

❑ Review Exercises for Chapter 10

Solutions to Odd-Numbered Exercises

1. $a_n = 2 + \dfrac{6}{n}$

$a_1 = 2 + \dfrac{6}{1} = 8$

$a_2 = 2 + \dfrac{6}{2} = 5$

$a_3 = 2 + \dfrac{6}{3} = 4$

$a_4 = 2 + \dfrac{6}{4} = \dfrac{7}{2}$

$a_5 = 2 + \dfrac{6}{5} = \dfrac{16}{5}$

3. $a_n = \dfrac{72}{n!}$

$a_1 = \dfrac{72}{1!} = 72$

$a_2 = \dfrac{72}{2!} = 36$

$a_3 = \dfrac{72}{3!} = 12$

$a_4 = \dfrac{72}{4!} = 3$

$a_5 = \dfrac{72}{5!} = \dfrac{3}{5}$

5. $a_n = \dfrac{3}{2}n$

7. $a_n = \dfrac{3n}{n + 2}$

9. $\dfrac{1}{2(1)} + \dfrac{1}{2(2)} + \dfrac{1}{2(3)} + \cdots + \dfrac{1}{2(20)} = \displaystyle\sum_{k=1}^{20} \dfrac{1}{2k}$

11. $\dfrac{1}{2} + \dfrac{2}{3} + \dfrac{3}{4} + \cdots + \dfrac{9}{10} = \displaystyle\sum_{k=1}^{9} \dfrac{k}{k + 1}$

13. $\displaystyle\sum_{i=1}^{6} 5 = 6(5) = 30$

15. $\displaystyle\sum_{j=1}^{4} \dfrac{6}{j^2} = \dfrac{6}{1^2} + \dfrac{6}{2^2} + \dfrac{6}{3^2} + \dfrac{6}{4^2} + = 6 + \dfrac{3}{2} + \dfrac{2}{3} + \dfrac{3}{8} = \dfrac{205}{24}$

17. $\displaystyle\sum_{k=1}^{10} 2k^3 = 2(1)^3 + 2(2)^3 + 2(3)^3 + \cdots + 2(10)^3 = 6050$

19. $\displaystyle\sum_{n=0}^{10} (n^2 + 3) = \sum_{n=0}^{10} n^2 + \sum_{n=0}^{10} 3 = \dfrac{10(11)(21)}{6} + 11(3) = 418$

21. $a_1 = 3, d = 4$

$a_1 = 3$

$a_2 = 3 + 4 = 7$

$a_3 = 7 + 4 = 11$

$a_4 = 11 + 4 = 15$

$a_5 = 15 + 4 = 19$

23. $a_4 = 10 \quad a_{10} = 28$

$a_{10} = a_4 + 6d$

$28 = 10 + 6d$

$18 = 6d$

$3 = d$

$a_1 = a_4 - 3d$

$a_1 = 10 - 3(3)$

$a_1 = 1$

$a_2 = 1 + 3 = 4$

$a_3 = 4 + 3 = 7$

$a_4 = 7 + 3 = 10$

$a_5 = 10 + 3 = 13$

25. $a_1 = 35, a_{k+1} = a_k - 3$

$a_1 = 35$

$a_2 = a_1 - 3 = 35 - 3 = 32$

$a_3 = a_2 - 3 = 32 - 3 = 29$

$a_4 = a_3 - 3 = 29 - 3 = 26$

$a_5 = a_4 - 3 = 26 - 3 = 23$

$a_n = 35 + (n - 1)(-3) = 38 - 3n$

27. $a_1 = 9, a_{k+1} = a_k + 7$

$a_1 = 9$

$a_2 = a_1 + 7 = 9 + 7 = 16$

$a_3 = a_2 + 7 = 16 + 7 = 23$

$a_4 = a_3 + 7 = 23 + 7 = 30$

$a_5 = a_4 + 7 = 30 + 7 = 37$

$a_n = 9 + (n - 1)(7) = 2 + 7n$

29. $a_n = 100 + (n - 1)(-3) = 103 - 3n$

$$\sum_{n=1}^{20}(103 - 3n) = \sum_{n=1}^{20}103 - 3\sum_{n=1}^{20}n = 20(103) - 3\left[\frac{(20)(21)}{2}\right] = 1430$$

31. $\displaystyle\sum_{j=1}^{10}(2j - 3) = 2\sum_{j=1}^{10}j - \sum_{j=1}^{10}3 = 2\left[\frac{10(11)}{2}\right] - 10(3) = 80$

33. $\displaystyle\sum_{k=1}^{11}\left(\frac{2}{3}k + 4\right) = \frac{2}{3}\sum_{k=1}^{11}k + \sum_{k=1}^{11}4 = \frac{2}{3}\cdot\frac{(11)(12)}{2} + 11(4) = 88$

35. $\displaystyle\sum_{k=1}^{100}5k = 5\left[\frac{(100)(101)}{2}\right] = 25,250$

37. (a) $34,000 + 4(2250) = \$43,000$

(b) $\displaystyle\sum_{k=1}^{5}[34,000 + (k - 1)(2250)] = \sum_{k=1}^{5}(31,750 + 2250k) = \$192,500$

39. $a_1 = 4, \ r = -\frac{1}{4}$

$a_1 = 4$

$a_2 = 4\left(-\frac{1}{4}\right) = -1$

$a_3 = -1\left(-\frac{1}{4}\right) = \frac{1}{4}$

$a_4 = \frac{1}{4}\left(-\frac{1}{4}\right) = -\frac{1}{16}$

$a_5 = -\frac{1}{16}\left(-\frac{1}{4}\right) = \frac{1}{64}$

41. $a_1 = 9$, $a_3 = 4$

$a_3 = a_1 r^2$

$4 = 9r^2$

$\frac{4}{9} = r^2 \implies r = \pm\frac{2}{3}$

$a_1 = 9$	$a_1 = 9$
$a_2 = 9\left(\frac{2}{3}\right) = 6$	$a_2 = 9\left(-\frac{2}{3}\right) = -6$
$a_3 = 6\left(\frac{2}{3}\right) = 4$ OR	$a_3 = 6\left(-\frac{2}{3}\right) = -4$
$a_4 = 4\left(\frac{2}{3}\right) = \frac{8}{3}$	$a_4 = 4\left(-\frac{2}{3}\right) = -\frac{8}{3}$
$a_5 = \frac{8}{3}\left(\frac{2}{3}\right) = \frac{16}{9}$	$a_5 = 4\left(-\frac{2}{3}\right) = -\frac{16}{9}$

43. $a_1 = 120$, $a_{k+1} = \frac{1}{3}a_k$

$a_1 = 120$

$a_2 = \frac{1}{3}(120) = 40$

$a_3 = \frac{1}{3}(40) = \frac{40}{3}$

$a_4 = \frac{1}{3}\left(\frac{40}{3}\right) = \frac{40}{9}$

$a_5 = \frac{1}{3}\left(\frac{40}{9}\right) = \frac{40}{27}$

$a_n = 120\left(\frac{1}{3}\right)^{n-1}$

45. $a_1 = 25$, $a_{k+1} = -\frac{3}{5}a_k$

$a_1 = 25$

$a_2 = -\frac{3}{5}(25) = -15$

$a_3 = -\frac{3}{5}(-15) = 9$

$a_4 = -\frac{3}{5}(9) = -\frac{27}{5}$

$a_5 = -\frac{3}{5}\left(-\frac{27}{5}\right) = \frac{81}{25}$

$a_n = 25\left(-\frac{3}{5}\right)^{n-1}$

47. $a_2 = a_1 r$

$-8 = 16r$

$-\frac{1}{2} = r$

$a_n = 16\left(-\frac{1}{2}\right)^{n-1}$

$\sum_{n=1}^{20} 16\left(-\frac{1}{2}\right)^{n-1} = 16\left[\frac{1 - (-1/2)^{20}}{1 - (-1/2)}\right] \approx 10.67$

49. $\sum_{i=1}^{7} 2^{i-1} = \frac{1 - 2^7}{1 - 2} = 127$

51. $\sum_{i=1}^{\infty} \left(\frac{7}{8}\right)^{i-1} = \frac{1}{1 - 7/8} = 8$

53. $\sum_{k=1}^{\infty} 4\left(\frac{2}{3}\right)^{k-1} = \frac{4}{1 - 2/3} = 12$

55. $\sum_{i=1}^{10} 10\left(\frac{3}{5}\right)^{i-1} \approx 24.849$

57. (a) $a_t = 120{,}000(0.7)^t$

(b) $a_5 = 120{,}000(0.7)^5 = \$20{,}168.40$

59. $A = \sum_{i=1}^{24} 200\left(1 + \frac{0.06}{12}\right)^t \approx \$5111.82$

61. 1. When $n = 1$, $1 = \frac{1}{2}(3(1) - 1)$.

2. Assume that

$S_k = 1 + 4 + \cdots + (3k - 2) = \frac{k}{2}(3k - 1)$.

Then,

$S_{k+1} = 1 + 4 + \cdots + (3k - 2) + (3(k + 1) - 2) = S_k + (3k + 1)$

$= \frac{k}{2}(3k - 1) + (3k + 1) = \frac{k(3k - 1) + 2(3k + 1)}{2}$

$= \frac{3k^2 + 5k + 2}{2} = \frac{(k + 1)(3k + 2)}{2} = \frac{(k + 1)}{2}[3(k + 1) - 1]$.

Therefore, by mathematical induction, the formula is valid for all positive integer values of n.

63. 1. When $n = 1$, $a = a\left(\dfrac{1 - r}{1 - r}\right)$.

  2. Assume that

$$S_k = \sum_{i=0}^{k-1} ar^i = \frac{a(1 - r^k)}{1 - r}.$$

Then,

$$S_{k+1} = \sum_{i=0}^{k} ar^i = \sum_{i=0}^{k-1} ar^i + ar^k = \frac{a(1 - r^k)}{1 - r} + ar^k$$

$$= \frac{a(1 - r^k + r^k - r^{k+1})}{1 - r} = \frac{a(1 - r^{k+1})}{1 - r}.$$

Therefore, by mathematical induction, the formula is valid for all positive integer values of n.

65. $_6C_4 = \dfrac{6!}{2!4!} = 15$

67. $_8P_5 = \dfrac{8!}{3!} = 6720$

69. $\left(\dfrac{x}{2} + y\right)^4 = \left(\dfrac{x}{2}\right)^4 + 4\left(\dfrac{x}{2}\right)^3 y + 6\left(\dfrac{x}{2}\right)^2 y^2 + 4\left(\dfrac{x}{2}\right)y^3 + y^4$

$$= \frac{x^4}{16} + \frac{x^3 y}{2} + \frac{3x^2 y^2}{2} + 2xy^3 + y^4$$

71. $\left(\dfrac{2}{x} - 3x\right)^6 = \left(\dfrac{2}{x}\right)^6 + 6\left(\dfrac{2}{x}\right)^5(-3x) + 15\left(\dfrac{2}{x}\right)^4(-3x)^2 + 20\left(\dfrac{2}{x}\right)^3(-3x)^3$

$$+ 15\left(\dfrac{2}{x}\right)^2(-3x)^4 + 6\left(\dfrac{2}{x}\right)(-3x)^5 + (-3x)^6$$

$$= \frac{64}{x^6} - \frac{576}{x^4} + \frac{2160}{x^2} - 4320 + 4860x^2 - 2916x^4 + 729x^6$$

73. $(5 + 2i)^4 = (5)^4 + 4(5)^3(2i) + 6(5)^2(2i)^2 + 4(5)(2i)^3 + (2i)^4$

$$= 625 + 1000i + 600i^2 + 160i^3 + 16i^4$$

$$= 625 + 1000i - 600 - 160i + 16 = 41 + 840i$$

75. $(26)(26)(10)(26)(26)(26) = 118{,}813{,}760$

77. $\dfrac{10}{10} \cdot \dfrac{1}{9} = \dfrac{1}{9}$

79. Chance of rolling a 3 with one die is $\dfrac{1}{6}$. With two dice

$E = \{(1, 5),\ (2, 4),\ (3, 3),\ (4, 2),\ (5, 1)\}$ and $P(E) = \dfrac{5}{36}$.

The probability of rolling a 3 with one die is higher.

81. $1 - P(HHHHH) = 1 - \left(\dfrac{1}{2}\right)^5 = \dfrac{31}{32}$

83. $P(2 \text{ pairs}) = \dfrac{(_{13}C_2)(_4C_2)(_4C_2)(_{44}C_1)}{(_{52}C_5)} = 0.0475$

❏ Chapter Test for Chapter 10

1. $a_n = \left(-\frac{2}{3}\right)^{n-1}$ $a_1 = \left(-\frac{2}{3}\right)^{1-1} = \left(-\frac{2}{3}\right)^0 = 1$

$a_2 = -\frac{2}{3}$

$a_3 = \left(-\frac{2}{3}\right)^2 = \frac{4}{9}$

$a_4 = \left(-\frac{2}{3}\right)^3 = -\frac{8}{27}$

$a_5 = \left(-\frac{2}{3}\right)^4 = \frac{16}{81}$

2. $a_1 = 12$, $a_{k+1} = a_k + 4$

$a_2 = 12 + 4 = 16$

$a_3 = 16 + 4 = 20$

$a_4 = 20 + 4 = 24$

$a_5 = 24 + 4 = 28$

3. $a_n = dn + c$, $c = a_1 - d = 5000 - (-100) = 5100$

$\implies a_n = -100n + 5100 = 5000 - 100(n - 1)$

4. $a_n = a_1 r^{n-1}$, $a_1 = 4$, $r = \dfrac{1}{2}$ $\implies a_n = 4\left(\dfrac{1}{2}\right)^{n-1}$

5. $\displaystyle\sum_{n=1}^{12} \frac{2}{3n + 1}$

6. $3 + 6 + \cdots + 150 = 3(1 + 2 + \cdots + 50) = 3 \cdot \dfrac{50(51)}{2} = 3825$

7. $2(r) = -3 \implies r = -\dfrac{3}{2}$

8. $r = \dfrac{a_2}{a_1} = 2 \implies S_8 = a_1\left(\dfrac{1 - r^8}{1 - r}\right) = 3\left(\dfrac{1 - 2^8}{1 - 2}\right) = 765$

9. $A_1 = 50\left(1 + \dfrac{0.08}{12}\right)^1 = 50(1.00667)$

$A_{300} = 50\left(1 + \dfrac{0.08}{12}\right)^{300} 50(1.00667)^{300}$

$S_n = 50(1.00667)\left[\dfrac{1 - (1.00667)^{300}}{1 - 1.00667}\right] \approx \$47{,}868.33$

10. $_{20}C_3 = \dfrac{20!}{(17!)(3!)} = \dfrac{20 \cdot 19 \cdot 18 \cdot 17!}{17!\ 3!} = \dfrac{20 \cdot 19 \cdot 18}{6} = 1140$

11. $_8C_3 = \dfrac{8!}{5!\ 3!} = \dfrac{8 \cdot 7 \cdot 6}{3 \cdot 2} = 56$

12. $26 \cdot 10 \cdot 10 \cdot 10 = 26{,}000$ ways

13. $_{25}C_4 = \dfrac{25!}{21!\ 4!} = \dfrac{25 \cdot 24 \cdot 23 \cdot 22}{24} = 12{,}650$ ways

14. There are 6 red face cards $\implies$ probability $= \dfrac{6}{52} = \dfrac{3}{26}$.

15. There are $_2C_4 = 6$ ways to select 2 spark plugs. Only one way corresponds to both being selected. Probability $= \dfrac{1}{6}$.

16. $\dfrac{1}{4!} = \dfrac{1}{24}$

❑ Practice Test for Chapter 10

1. Write out the first five terms of the sequence $a_n = \dfrac{2n}{(n+2)!}$.

2. Write an expression for the nth term of the sequence $\left\{\dfrac{4}{3}, \dfrac{5}{9}, \dfrac{6}{27}, \dfrac{7}{81}, \dfrac{8}{243}, \ldots\right\}$.

3. Find the sum $\displaystyle\sum_{i=1}^{6}(2i - 1)$.

4. Write out the first five terms of the arithmetic sequence where $a_1 = 23$ and $d = -2$.

5. Find a_n for the arithmetic sequence with $a_1 = 12$, $d = 3$, and $n = 50$.

6. Find the sum of the first 200 positive integers.

7. Write out the first five terms of the geometric sequence with $a_1 = 7$ and $r = 2$.

8. Evaluate $\displaystyle\sum_{n=0}^{9} 6\left(\dfrac{2}{3}\right)^n$.

9. Evaluate $\displaystyle\sum_{n=0}^{\infty} (0.03)^n$.

10. Use mathematical induction to prove that $1 + 2 + 3 + 4 + \cdots + n = \dfrac{n(n+1)}{2}$.

11. Use mathematical induction to prove that $n! > 2^n$, $n \geq 4$.

12. Evaluate $_{13}C_4$. Verify with a graphing utility.

13. Expand $(x + 3)^5$.

14. Find the term involving x^7 in $(x - 2)^{12}$.

15. Evaluate $_{30}P_4$.

16. How many ways can six people sit at a table with six chairs?

17. Twelve cars run in a race. How many different ways can they come in first, second, and third place? (Assume that there are no ties.)

18. Two six-sided dice are tossed. Find the probability that the total of the two dice is less than 5.

19. Two cards are selected at random form a deck of 52 playing cards without replacement. Find the probability that the first card is a King and the second card is a black ten.

20. A manufacturer has determined that for every 1000 units it produces, 3 will be faulty. What is the probability that an order of 50 units will have one or more faulty units?

C H A P T E R 11
Topics in Analytic Geometry

CHAPTER 11
Topics in Analytic Geometry

Section 11.1   Conics

You should know the following basic definitions of conic sections.

■ A parabola is the set of all points (x, y) that are equidistant from a fixed line (directrix) and a fixed point (focus) not on the line.

   (a) Standard equation with vertex $(0, 0)$ and directrix $y = -p$ (vertical axis): $x^2 = 4py$

   (b) Standard equation with vertex $(0, 0)$ and directrix $x = -p$ (horizontal axis): $y^2 = 4px$

   (c) The focus lies on the axis p units (directed distance) from the vertex.

■ An ellipse is the set of all points (x, y) the sum of whose distances from two distinct fixed points (foci) is constant.

   (a) Standard equation of an ellipse with center $(0, 0)$, major axis length $2a$, and minor axis length $2b$:

     1. Horizontal major axis: $\dfrac{x^2}{a^2} + \dfrac{y^2}{b^2} = 1$ 2. Vertical major axis: $\dfrac{x^2}{b^2} + \dfrac{y^2}{a^2} = 1$

   (b) The foci lie on the major axis, c units from the center, where a, b, and c are related by the equation $c^2 = a^2 - b^2$.

   (c) The vertices and endpoints of the minor axis are:

     1. Horizontal axis: $(\pm a, 0)$ and $(0, \pm b)$ 2. Vertical axis: $(0, \pm a)$ and $(\pm b, 0)$

■ A hyperbola is the set of all points (x, y) the difference of whose distances from two distinct fixed points (foci) is constant.

   (a) Standard equation of hyperbola with center $(0, 0)$

     1. Horizontal transverse axis: $\dfrac{x^2}{a^2} - \dfrac{y^2}{b^2} = 1$ 2. Vertical transverse axis: $\dfrac{y^2}{a^2} - \dfrac{x^2}{b^2} = 1$

   (b) The vertices and foci are a and c units from the center and $b^2 = c^2 - a^2$.

   (c) The asymptotes of the hyperbola are:

     1. Horizontal transverse axis: $y = \pm \dfrac{b}{a}x$ 2. Vertical transverse axis: $y = \pm \dfrac{a}{b}x$

Solutions to Odd-Numbered Exercises

1. $x^2 = 2y$

Parabola opening upward

Matches (g).

3. $y^2 = 2x$

Parabola opening to the right

Matches (d).

5. $9x^2 + y^2 = 9$

$\dfrac{x^2}{1} + \dfrac{y^2}{9} = 1$

Ellipse with vertical major axis

Matches (h).

7. $9x^2 - y^2 = 9$

$\dfrac{x^2}{1} - \dfrac{y^2}{9} = 1$

Hyperbola with horizontal transverse axis

Matches (e).

9. $y = \frac{1}{2}x^2$

$x^2 = 2y = 4\left(\frac{1}{2}\right)y; \quad p = \frac{1}{2}$

Vertex: $(0, 0)$

Focus: $\left(0, \frac{1}{2}\right)$

11. $y^2 = -6x$

$y^2 = 4\left(-\frac{3}{2}\right)x; \quad p = -\frac{3}{2}$

Vertex: $(0, 0)$

Focus: $\left(-\frac{3}{2}, 0\right)$

13. $x^2 + 8y = 0$

$x^2 = 4(-2)y; \quad p = -2$

Vertex: $(0, 0)$

Focus: $(0, -2)$

15. $y^2 - 8 = 0$ and $x - y + 2 = 0$

$\quad\quad y^2 = 8x \quad\quad\quad\quad y_3 = x + 2$

$\quad\quad y_1 = \sqrt{8x}$

$\quad\quad y_2 = -\sqrt{8x}$

The point of tangency is $(2, 4)$.

17. Focus; $\left(0, -\frac{3}{2}\right)$

$x^2 = 4\left(-\frac{3}{2}\right)y$

$x^2 = -6y$

19. Focus: $(-2, 0)$

$y^2 = 4(-2)x$

$y^2 = -8x$

21. Directrix: $y = -1$

$x^2 = 4(1)y$

$x^2 = 4y$

23. Directrix: $y = 2$

$x^2 = 4(-2)y$

$x^2 = -8y$

25. $y^2 = 4px$

$6^2 = 4p(4)$

$36 = 16p$

$p = \frac{9}{4}$

$y^2 = 4\left(\frac{9}{4}\right)x$

$y^2 = 9x$

27. $x^2 = 4py$

$3^2 = 4p(6)$

$9 = 24p$

$\frac{3}{8} = p$

$x^2 = 4\left(\frac{3}{8}\right)y$

$x^2 = \frac{3}{2}y \quad \text{OR} \quad y = \frac{2}{3}x^2$

Focus: $\left(0, \frac{3}{8}\right)$

29. $x^2 = 4py, \quad p = 3.5$

$x^2 = 4(3.5)y$

$x^2 = 14y$

$y = \frac{1}{14}x^2$

31. (a) $x^2 = 4py$

$32^2 = 4p\left(\frac{1}{12}\right)$

$1024 = \frac{1}{3}p$

$3072 = p$

$x^2 = 4(3072)y$

$y = \frac{x^2}{12{,}288}$

(b) $\dfrac{1}{24} = \dfrac{x^2}{12{,}288}$

$\dfrac{12{,}288}{24} = x^2$

$512 = x^2$

$x \approx 22.6 \text{ feet}$

33. False. If the graph crossed the directrix there would exist points closer to the directrix than to the focus.

35. $\dfrac{x^2}{25} + \dfrac{y^2}{16} = 1$

Horizontal major axis
$a = 5,\ b = 4$
Center: $(0, 0)$
Vertices: $(\pm 5, 0)$

37. $\dfrac{x^2}{16} + \dfrac{y^2}{25} = 1$

Vertical major axis
$a = 5,\ b = 4$
Center: $(0, 0)$
Vertices: $(0, \pm 5)$

39. $\dfrac{x^2}{9} + \dfrac{y^2}{5} = 1$

Horizontal major axis
$a = 3,\ b = \sqrt{5}$
Center: $(0, 0)$
Vertices: $(\pm 3, 0)$

41. $5x^2 + 3y^2 = 15$

$$3y^2 = 15 - 5x^2$$
$$y^2 = 5 - \tfrac{5}{3}x^2$$
$$y = \pm\sqrt{5 - \tfrac{5}{3}x^2}$$

43. Since x is negative, $x = -\tfrac{3}{2}\sqrt{4 - y^2}$ represents the left half of the ellipse.

45. Vertices: $(0, \pm 2) \implies a = 2$

Minor axis of length 2 $\implies b = 1$

Vertical major axis

$$\dfrac{x^2}{b^2} + \dfrac{y^2}{a^2} = 1$$
$$\dfrac{x^2}{1} + \dfrac{y^2}{4} = 1$$

47. Vertices: $(\pm 5, 0) \implies a = 5$

Foci: $(\pm 2, 0) \implies b = \sqrt{5^2 - 2^2} = \sqrt{21}$

Horizontal major axis

$$\dfrac{x^2}{a^2} + \dfrac{y^2}{b^2} = 1$$
$$\dfrac{x^2}{25} + \dfrac{y^2}{21} = 1$$

49. Foci: $(\pm 5, 0) \implies c = 5$

Major axis of length 12 $\implies a = 6$

$$b = \sqrt{6^2 - 5^2} = \sqrt{11}$$

Horizontal major axis

$$\dfrac{x^2}{a^2} + \dfrac{y^2}{b^2} = 1$$
$$\dfrac{x^2}{36} + \dfrac{y^2}{11} = 1$$

51. Vertices: $(0, \pm 5) \implies a = 5$

Vertical major axis

$$\dfrac{x^2}{b^2} + \dfrac{y^2}{25} = 1$$
$$\dfrac{(4)^2}{b^2} + \dfrac{(2)^2}{25} = 1$$
$$\dfrac{400}{21} = b^2$$
$$\dfrac{21x^2}{400} + \dfrac{y^2}{25} = 1$$

53. Let $\dfrac{x^2}{a^2} + \dfrac{y^2}{b^2} = 1$ be the equation of the ellipse. Then $b = 2$ and $a = 3 \implies c^2 = a^2 - b^2 = 9 - 4 = 5$.

Thus, the tacks are placed at $\left(\pm\sqrt{5}, 0\right)$ and the string is 6 feet in length.

55. (a) The length of the string is $2a$.

(b) The path is an ellipse since the sum of the distances from the two fixed points (thumbtacks) is constant ($2a$).

57. No, it is not an ellipse. The exponent on y is not 2.

59. (a) $a + b = 20 \implies b = 20 - a$

$A = \pi ab = \pi a(20 - a)$

(c)

a	8	9	10	11	12	13
A	301.6	311.0	314.2	311.0	301.6	285.9

(d)

The area is maximum when $a = b = 10$ and it is a circle.

(b)
$$264 = \pi a(20 - a)$$
$$\pi a^2 - 20\pi a + 264 = 0$$

$a \approx 14$ OR $a \approx 6$ by the Quadratic Formula

$b = 6$ $b = 14$

Since $a > b$ we choose $a = 14$ and $b = 6$.

$$\frac{x^2}{14^2} + \frac{y^2}{6^2} = 1$$

$$\frac{x^2}{196} + \frac{y^2}{36} = 1$$

61. $\dfrac{x^2}{a^2} + \dfrac{y^2}{4^2} = 1$, $1 \le a \le 8$

The shape changes from an ellipse with a vertical major axis of length 8 and a minor axis of length 2 to a circle with a diameter of 8 and then to an ellipse with a horizontal major axis of length 16 and a minor axis of length 8.

63. $\dfrac{x^2}{4} + \dfrac{y^2}{1} = 1$

$a = 2$, $b = 1$, $c = \sqrt{3}$

Points on the ellipse: $(\pm 2, 0)$, $(0, \pm 1)$

Length of latus recta: $\dfrac{2b^2}{a} = 1$

Additional points: $\left(\sqrt{3}, \pm\dfrac{1}{2}\right)$, $\left(-\sqrt{3}, \pm\dfrac{1}{2}\right)$

65. $9x^2 + 4y^2 = 36$

$\dfrac{x^2}{4} + \dfrac{y^2}{9} = 1$

Points on the ellipse: $(\pm 2, 0)$, $(0, \pm 3)$

Length of latus recta: $\dfrac{2b^2}{a} = \dfrac{2 \cdot 2^2}{3} = \dfrac{8}{3}$

Additional points: $\left(\pm\dfrac{4}{3}, -\sqrt{5}\right)$, $\left(\pm\dfrac{4}{3}, \sqrt{5}\right)$

67. $x^2 - y^2 = 1$

$a = 1, \ b = 1$

Center: $(0, 0)$

Vertices: $(\pm 1, 0)$
Foci: $(\pm \sqrt{2}, 0)$

Asymptotes: $y = \pm x$

69. $\dfrac{y^2}{1} - \dfrac{x^2}{4} = 1$

$a = 1, \ b = 1$

Center: $(0, 0)$

Vertices: $(0, \pm 1)$
Foci: $(0, \pm \sqrt{5})$

Asymptotes: $y = \pm \dfrac{1}{2} x$

71. $\dfrac{y^2}{25} - \dfrac{x^2}{144} = 1$

$a = 5, \ b = 12$

Center: $(0, 0)$

Vertices: $(0, \pm 5)$
Foci: $(0, \pm 13)$

Asymptotes: $y = \pm \dfrac{5}{12} x$

73. $2x^2 - 3y^2 = 6$

$$y^2 = \tfrac{1}{3}(2x^2 - 6)$$

$$y = \pm \sqrt{\tfrac{2}{3}(x^2 - 3)}$$

Asymptotes: $y = \pm \sqrt{\tfrac{2}{3}} x$

75. Since y is negative, $y = -\tfrac{2}{3}\sqrt{x^2 - 9}$ represents the bottom half of the hyperbola.

77. Vertices: $(0, \pm 2) \implies a = 2$
Foci: $(0, \pm 4) \implies c = 4$
$b^2 = c^2 - a^2 = 12$
Vertical transverse axis

$$\dfrac{y^2}{a^2} - \dfrac{x^2}{b^2} = 1$$

$$\dfrac{y^2}{4} - \dfrac{x^2}{12} = 1$$

79. Vertices: $(\pm 1, 0) \implies a = 1$
Asymptotes: $y = \pm 3x$
Horizontal transverse axis

$$3 = \dfrac{b}{a} = \dfrac{b}{1} \implies b = 3$$

$$\dfrac{x^2}{a^2} - \dfrac{y^2}{b^2} = 1$$

$$\dfrac{x^2}{1} - \dfrac{y^2}{9} = 1$$

81. Foci: $(0, \pm 8) \implies c = 8$
Asymptotes: $y = \pm 4x$
Vertical transverse axis

$$4 = \dfrac{a}{b} \implies a = 4b$$

$$16b^2 + b^2 = (8)^2$$

$$b^2 = \dfrac{64}{17} \implies a^2 = \dfrac{1024}{17}$$

$$\dfrac{y^2}{a^2} - \dfrac{x^2}{b^2} = 1$$

$$\dfrac{17y^2}{1024} - \dfrac{17x^2}{64} = 1$$

83. Vertices: $(0, \pm 3) \implies a = 3$
Vertical transverse axis

$$\dfrac{y^2}{9} - \dfrac{x^2}{b^2} = 1$$

$$\dfrac{5^2}{9} - \dfrac{(-2)^2}{b^2} = 1$$

$$b^2 = \dfrac{9}{4}$$

$$\dfrac{y^2}{9} - \dfrac{x^2}{\frac{9}{4}} = 1$$

$$\dfrac{y^2}{9} - \dfrac{4x^2}{9} = 1$$

85. Center: $(0, 0)$

Focus: $(24, 0)$

$$b^2 = c^2 - a^2 = 24^2 - a^2 = 576 - a^2$$

$$\frac{x^2}{a^2} - \frac{y^2}{576 - a^2} = 1$$

$$\frac{24^2}{a^2} - \frac{24^2}{576 - a^2} = 1$$

$$\frac{576}{a^2} - \frac{576}{576 - a^2} = 1$$

$$576(576 - a^2) = 576a^2 = a^2(576 - a^2)$$

$$a^4 - 1728a^2 + 331{,}776 = 0$$

$$a \approx \pm 38.83 \quad \text{OR} \quad a \approx \pm 14.83$$

Since $a < c$ and $c = 24$, we choose $a = 14.83$. The vertex is approximately at $(14.83, 0)$. [Note: By the Quadratic Formula, the exact value of a is $a = 12(\sqrt{5} - 1)$.]

87. Let (x, y) be such that the sum of the distance from $(c, 0)$ and $(-c, 0)$ is $2a$. (Note that this is only deriving the standard form for the ellipse with horizontal major axis.)

$$2a = \sqrt{(x - c)^2 + y^2} + \sqrt{(x + c)^2 + y^2}$$

$$2a - \sqrt{(x + c)^2 + y^2} = \sqrt{(x - c) + y^2}$$

$$4a^2 - 4a\sqrt{(x + c)^2 + y^2} + (x + c)^2 + y^2 = (x - c)^2 + y^2$$

$$4a^2 + 4cx = 4a\sqrt{(x + c)^2 + y^2}$$

$$a^2 + cx = a\sqrt{(x + c)^2 + y^2}$$

$$a^4 + 2a^2cx + c^2x^2 = a^2(x^2 + 2cx + c^2 + y^2)$$

$$a^4 + c^2x^2 = a^2x^2 + a^2c^2 + a^2y^2$$

$$a^2(a^2 - c^2) = (a^2 - c^2)x^2 + a^2y^2$$

Let $b^2 = a^2 - c^2$. Then we have

$$a^2b^2 = b^2x^2 + a^2y^2 \implies 1 = \frac{x^2}{a^2} + \frac{y^2}{b^2}.$$

89. (a) $12x^2 + 7x - 10 = (3x - 2)(4x + 5)$

(b) $25x^3 - 60x^2 + 36x = x(25x^2 - 60x + 36) = x(5x - 6)^2$

(c) $12z^4 + 17z^3 + 5z^2 = z^2(12z^2 + 17z + 5) = z^2(z + 1)(12z + 5)$

(d) $x^3 + 3x^2 - 4x - 12 = x^2(x + 3) - 4(x + 3) = (x + 3)(x^2 - 4)$
$$= (x + 3)(x + 2)(x - 2)$$

91. (Many answers are possible.)

(a) $(x - 0)(x - 3)(x - 4) = x(x^2 - 7x + 12) = x^3 - 7x^2 + 12x$

(b) $(x + 6)(x - 1) = x^2 + 5x - 6$

(c) $(x + 3)(x - 1 - \sqrt{2})(x - 1 + \sqrt{2}) = (x + 3)(x^2 - 2x - 1)$
$$= x^3 + x^2 - 7x - 3$$

(d) $(x - 3)(x - 2 - i)(x - 2 + i) = (x - 3)((x - 2)^2 - i^2))$
$$= (x - 3)(x^2 - 4x + 4 + 1)$$
$$= (x - 3)(x^2 - 4x + 5)$$
$$= x^3 - 7x^2 + 17x - 15$$

93. $g(x) = 6x^4 + 7x^3 - 29x^2 - 28x + 20$

Possible rational zeros: $\pm 1, \pm 2, \pm 4, \pm 5, \pm 10, \pm 20, \pm\frac{1}{2}, \pm\frac{5}{2}, \pm\frac{1}{3}, \pm\frac{2}{3}, \pm\frac{4}{3}, \pm\frac{5}{3}, \pm\frac{10}{3}, \pm\frac{20}{3}, \pm\frac{1}{6}, \pm\frac{5}{6}$

[Note: The actual zeros are $\pm 2, \frac{1}{2}$, and $-\frac{5}{3}$.]

Section 11.2   Translations of Conics

You should know the following basic facts about conic sections.

■   Parabola with Vertex (h, k)

   (a) **Vertex Axis**

      1. Standard equation: $(x - h)^2 = 4p(y - k)$

      2. Focus: $(h, k + p)$

      3. Directrix: $y = k - p$

   (b) **Horizontal Axis**

      1. Standard equation: $(y - k)^2 = 4p(x - h)$

      2. Focus: $(h + p, k)$

      3. Directrix: $x = h - p$

continued

■ Circle with Center (h, k) and Radius r

Standard equation: $(x - h)^2 + (y - k)^2 = r^2$

■ Ellipse with Center (h, k)

(a) Horizontal Major Axis:

1. Standard equation:

$$\frac{(x - h)^2}{a^2} + \frac{(y - k)^2}{b^2} = 1$$

2. Vertices: $(h \pm a, k)$

3. Foci: $(h \pm c, k)$

4. $c^2 = a^2 - b^2$

(b) Vertical Major Axis:

1. Standard equation:

$$\frac{(x - h)^2}{b^2} + \frac{(y - k)^2}{a^2} = 1$$

2. Vertices: $(h, k \pm a)$

3. Foci: $(h, k \pm c)$

4. $c^2 = a^2 - b^2$

■ Hyperbola with Center (h, k)

(a) Horizontal Transverse Axis:

1. Standard equation:

$$\frac{(x - h)^2}{a^2} - \frac{(y - k)^2}{b^2} = 1$$

2. Vertices: $(h \pm a, k)$

3. Foci: $(h \pm c, k)$

4. Asymptotes: $y - k = \pm\dfrac{b}{a}(x - h)$

5. $c^2 = a^2 + b^2$

(b) Vertical Transverse Axis:

1. Standard equation:

$$\frac{(y - h)^2}{a^2} - \frac{(x - k)^2}{b^2} = 1$$

2. Vertices: $(h, k \pm a)$

3. Foci: $(h, k \pm c)$

4. Asymptotes: $y - k = \pm\dfrac{b}{a}(x - h)$

5. $c^2 = a^2 + b^2$

Solutions to Odd-Numbered Exercises

1. $(x - 1)^2 + 8(y + 2) = 0$

$\qquad (x - 1)^2 = 4(-2)(y + 2); p = -2$

Vertex: $(1, -2)$
Focus: $(1, -4)$
Directrix: $y = 0$

3. $\left(y + \frac{1}{2}\right)^2 = 2(x - 5)$

$\left(y + \frac{1}{2}\right)^2 = 4\left(\frac{1}{2}\right)(x - 5); p = \frac{1}{2}$

Vertex: $\left(5, -\frac{1}{2}\right)$
Focus: $\left(\frac{11}{2}, -\frac{1}{2}\right)$
Directrix: $x = \frac{9}{2}$

5. $y = \frac{1}{4}(x^2 - 2x + 5)$

$y = \frac{1}{4}(x - 1)^2 + 1$

$4(y - 1) = (x - 1)^2; p = 1$
Vertex: $(1, 1)$
Focus: $(1, 2)$
Directrix: $y = 0$

7. $y^2 + 6y + 8x + 25 = 0$

$\qquad (y + 3)^2 = 4(-2)(x + 2); p = -2$

Vertex: $(-2, -3)$
Focus: $(-4, -3)$
Directrix: $x = 0$

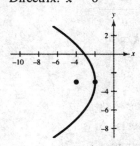

9. $\qquad y = -\frac{1}{6}(x^2 + 4x - 2)$

$\qquad y = -\frac{1}{6}(x + 2)^2 + 1$

$4\left(-\frac{3}{2}\right)(y - 1) = (x + 2)^2; p = -\frac{3}{2}$

Vertex: $(-2, 1)$

Focus: $\left(-2, -\frac{1}{2}\right)$

Directrix: $y = \frac{5}{2}$

11. $y^2 + x + y = 0$

$\left(y + \frac{1}{2}\right)^2 = 4\left(-\frac{1}{4}\right)\left(x - \frac{1}{4}\right); p = -\frac{1}{4}$

Vertex: $\left(\frac{1}{4}, -\frac{1}{2}\right)$

Focus: $\left(0, -\frac{1}{2}\right)$

Directrix: $x = \frac{1}{2}$

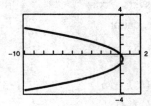

Note: Use $y_1 = -\frac{1}{2} + \sqrt{\frac{1}{4} - x}$

and $y_2 = -\frac{1}{2} - \sqrt{\frac{1}{4} - x}$ in your grapher.

13. Vertex: $(3, 1)$ and opens downward
Passes through $(2, 0)$ and $(4, 0)$

$$y = -(x - 2)(x - 4)$$
$$= -x^2 + 6x - 8$$
$$= -(x - 3)^2 + 1$$
$$(x - 3)^2 = -(y - 1)$$

15. Vertex: $(-2, 0)$ and opens to the right
Passes through $(0, 2)$

$$(y - 0)^2 = 4p(x + 2)$$
$$2^2 = 4p(0 + 2)$$
$$\tfrac{1}{2} = p$$
$$y^2 = 4\left(\tfrac{1}{2}\right)(x + 2)$$
$$y^2 = 2(x + 2)$$

17. Vertex: $(3, 2)$
Focus: $(1, 2)$
Horizontal axis
$p = 1 - 3 = -2$

$$(y - 2)^2 = 4(-2)(x - 3)$$
$$(y - 2)^2 = -8(x - 3)$$

19. Vertex: $(0, 4)$
Directrix: $y = 2$
Vertical axis
$p = 4 - 2 = 2$

$$(x - 0)^2 = 4(2)(y - 4)$$
$$x^2 = 8(y - 4)$$

21. Focus: $(2, 2)$
Directrix: $x = -2$
Horizontal axis
Vertex: $(0, 2)$
$p = 2 - 0 = 2$

$$(y - 2)^2 = 4(2)(x - 0)$$
$$(y - 2)^2 = 8x$$

23. $(y - 3)^2 = 6(x + 1)$

For the upper half of the parabola:

$$y - 3 = +\sqrt{6(x + 1)}$$
$$y = \sqrt{6(x + 1)} + 3$$

25. (a) $V = 17{,}500\sqrt{2}$ mi/hr
$\approx 24{,}750$ mi/hr

(b) $p = -4100$, $(h, k) = (0, 4100)$

$$(x - 0)^2 = 4(-4100)(y - 4100)$$
$$x^2 = -16{,}400(y - 4100)$$

27. $y = -0.08x^2 + x + 4$

(a)

(b) The maximum is at the point $(6.25, 7.125)$.
The range is the x-intercept of ≈ 15.69 feet.

29. $\quad 12x^2 + 20y^2 - 12x + 40y - 37 = 0$

$$12\left(x^2 - x + \frac{1}{4}\right) + 20(y^2 + 2y + 1) = 60$$

$$\frac{\left(x - \frac{1}{2}\right)^2}{5} + \frac{(y + 1)^2}{3} = 1$$

$$a = \sqrt{5}, \ b = \sqrt{3}, \ c = \sqrt{a^2 - b^2} = \sqrt{2}$$

Horizontal major axis

Center: $\left(\dfrac{1}{2}, -1\right)$

Foci: $\left(\dfrac{1}{2} - \sqrt{2}, -1\right)$, $\left(\dfrac{1}{2} + \sqrt{2}, -1\right)$

Vertices: $\left(\dfrac{1}{2} - \sqrt{5}, -1\right)$, $\left(\dfrac{1}{2} - \sqrt{5}, -1\right)$

Note: Use $y_1 = -1 + \sqrt{3 - \frac{3}{5}\left(x - \frac{1}{2}\right)^2}$ and $y_2 = -1 - \sqrt{3 - \frac{3}{5}\left(x - \frac{1}{2}\right)^2}$ in your grapher.

31. $\dfrac{(x-1)^2}{9} + \dfrac{(y-5)^2}{25} = 1$

$a = 5,\; b = 3,\; c = \sqrt{a^2 - b^2} = 4$

Center: $(1, 5)$
Foci: $(1, 1),\; (1, 9)$
Vertices: $(1, 0),\; (1, 10)$

33. $9x^2 + 4y^2 + 36x - 24y + 36 = 0$

$9(x^2 + 4x + 4) + 4(y^2 - 6y + 9) = 36$

$$\dfrac{(x+2)^2}{4} + \dfrac{(y-3)^2}{9} = 1$$

$a = 3,\; b = 2,\; c = \sqrt{a^2 - b^2} = \sqrt{5}$
Vertical major axis
Center: $(-2, 3)$
Foci: $\left(-2, 3 - \sqrt{5}\right),\; \left(-2, 3 + \sqrt{5}\right)$
Vertices: $(-2, 0),\; (-2, 6)$

35. $16x^2 + 25y^2 - 32x + 50y + 16 = 0$

$16(x^2 - 2x + 1) + 25(y^2 + 2y + 1) = 25$

$$\dfrac{(x-1)^2}{25/16} + (y+1)^2 = 1$$

$a = \dfrac{5}{4},\; b = 1,\; c = \sqrt{a^2 - b^2} = \dfrac{3}{4}$

Horizontal major axis
Center: $(1, -1)$

Foci: $\left(\dfrac{1}{4}, -1\right),\; \left(\dfrac{7}{4}, -1\right)$

Vertices: $\left(-\dfrac{1}{4}, -1\right),\; \left(\dfrac{9}{4}, -1\right)$

37. Center: $(2, 3)$
Vertical major axis
$a = 3,\; b = 1$

$$\dfrac{(x-2)^2}{1} + \dfrac{(y-3)^2}{9} = 1$$

39. Center: $(2, 2)$
Horizontal major axis
$a = 3,\; b = 2$

$$\dfrac{(x-2)^2}{9} + \dfrac{(y-2)^2}{4} = 1$$

41. Vertices: $(0, 2),\; (4, 2)$
Minor axis of length 2

$$a = \dfrac{4 - 0}{2} = 2,\; b = \dfrac{2}{2} = 1$$

Center: $(2, 2)$
Horizontal major axis

$$\dfrac{(x-2)^2}{4} + \dfrac{(y-2)^2}{1} = 1$$

43. Foci: $(0, 0)$, $(0, 8)$
Major axis of length 16
$a = 8$, $c = 4$, $b^2 = 48$
Center: $(0, 4)$
Vertical major axis
$$\frac{x^2}{48} + \frac{(y - 4)^2}{64} = 1$$

45. Vertices: $(3, 1)$, $(3, 9)$
Minor axis of length 6
$a = 4$, $b = 3$
Center: $(3, 5)$
Vertical major axis
$$\frac{(x - 3)^2}{9} + \frac{(y - 5)^2}{16} = 1$$

47. Center: $(0, 4)$
$a = 2c$
Vertices: $(-4, 4)$, $(4, 4)$
$a = 4$, $c = 2$, $b^2 = 12$
Horizontal major axis
$$\frac{x^2}{16} + \frac{(y - 4)^2}{12} = 1$$

49. $\dfrac{(x - 3)^2}{9} + \dfrac{y^2}{4} = 1$

$$\frac{(x - 3)^2}{9} = 1 - \frac{y^2}{4}$$

$$(x - 3)^2 = 9\left(\frac{4 - y^2}{4}\right)$$

$$x - 3 = \pm\frac{3}{2}\sqrt{4 - y^2}$$

$$x = 3 \pm \frac{3}{2}\sqrt{4 - y^2}$$

$$x = \frac{3}{2}\left(2 \pm \sqrt{4 - y^2}\right)$$

The right half of the ellipse is $x = \frac{3}{2}\left(2 + \sqrt{4 - y^2}\right)$.

51. Vertices: $(\pm 5, 0)$

$$e = \frac{c}{a} = \frac{3}{5}$$

$$a = 5, \quad c = 3, \quad b = 4$$

$$\frac{x^2}{25} + \frac{y^2}{16} = 1$$

53. $a = 3.666 \times 10^9$

$$e = \frac{c}{a} = 0.248$$

$c = 909{,}168{,}000$

Smallest distance: $a - c = 2{,}756{,}832{,}000$

Greatest distance: $a + c = 4{,}575{,}168{,}000$

55. $\dfrac{x^2}{a^2} + \dfrac{y^2}{b^2} = 1$

(a) Let $e = \dfrac{c}{a}$ be the eccentricity. Then,

$$c^2 = e^2 a^2 \implies a^2 - b^2 = e^2 a^2 \implies b^2 = a^2 - e^2 a^2 = a^2(1 - e^2).$$

So if the center of the ellipse is (h, k),

$$\frac{(x - h)^2}{a^2} + \frac{(y - k)^2}{a^2(1 - e^2)} = 1.$$

(b) Solve for y: $\dfrac{(y - k)^2}{a^2(1 - e^2)} = 1 - \dfrac{(x - h)^2}{a^2} = \dfrac{a^2 - (x - h)^2}{a^2}$

$$(y - k)^2 = (1 - e^2)(a^2 - (x - h)^2)$$

$$y = k \pm \sqrt{(1 - e^2)(a^2 - (x - h)^2)}$$

For $h = 2$, $k = 3$, $a = 2$, graph:

$$y_1 = 3 + \sqrt{(1 - e^2)(4 - (x - 2)^2)}$$

$$y_2 = 3 - \sqrt{(1 - e^2)(4 - (x - 2)^2)}$$

(c) As e approaches 0, the ellipse becomes more circular.

57. $\dfrac{(x-1)^2}{4} - \dfrac{(y+2)^2}{1} = 1$

$a = 2,\ b = 1,\ c = \sqrt{a^2+b^2} = \sqrt{5}$
Center: $(1, -2)$
Horizontal transverse axis
Vertices: $(-1, -2),\ (3, -2)$
Foci: $\left(1 \pm \sqrt{5}, -2\right)$

Asymptotes: $y = \pm\dfrac{1}{2}(x-1) - 2$

59. $(y+6)^2 - (x-2)^2 = 1$

$a = 1,\ b = 1,\ c = \sqrt{a^2+b^2} = \sqrt{2}$
Center: $(2, -6)$
Vertical transverse axis
Vertices: $(2, -5),\ (2, -7)$
Foci: $\left(2, -6 \pm \sqrt{2}\right)$

Asymptotes: $y = \pm(x-2) - 6$

61. $9x^2 - y^2 - 36x - 6y + 18 = 0$

$9(x^2 - 4x + 4) - (y^2 + 6y + 9) = 9$

$(x-2)^2 - \dfrac{(y+3)^2}{9} = 1$

$a = 1,\ b = 3,\ c = \sqrt{a^2+b^2} = \sqrt{10}$
Center: $(2, -3)$
Horizontal transverse axis
Vertices: $(1, -3),\ (3, -3)$
Foci: $\left(2 \pm \sqrt{10}, -3\right)$

Asymptotes: $y = \pm 3(x-2) - 3$

63. $x^2 - 9y^2 + 2x - 54y - 80 = 0$

$(x^2 + 2x + 1) - 9(y^2 + 6y + 9) = 0$

$9(y+3)^2 = (x+1)^2$

$y = \pm\dfrac{1}{3}(x+1) - 3$

The graph of this equation is two lines intersecting at $(-1, -3)$.

65. $9y^2 - x^2 + 2x + 54y + 62 = 0$

$9(y^2 + 6y + 9) - (x^2 - 2x + 1) = 18$

$$\frac{(y + 3)^2}{2} - \frac{(x - 1)^2}{18} = 1$$

$a = \sqrt{2}, \; b = 3\sqrt{2}, \; c = \sqrt{a^2 + b^2} = 2\sqrt{5}$

Center: $(1, -3)$

Vertical transverse axis

Vertices: $\left(1, -3 \pm \sqrt{2}\right)$

Foci: $\left(1, -3 \pm 2\sqrt{5}\right)$

Asymptotes: $y = \pm\dfrac{1}{3}(x - 1) - 3$

Note: Use $y_1 = \dfrac{1}{3}(x - 1) - 3$

$y_2 = -\dfrac{1}{3}(x - 1) - 3$

$y_3 = -3 + \dfrac{1}{3}\sqrt{(x - 1)^2 + 18}$

and $y_4 = -3 - \dfrac{1}{3}\sqrt{(x - 1)^2 + 18}$ in your grapher.

67. Vertices: $(0, 0), \; (0, 2)$

Passes through $\left(\sqrt{3}, 3\right)$

Center: $(0, 1)$

Vertical transverse axis

$$a = 1$$

$$\frac{(y - 1)^2}{1} - \frac{x^2}{b^2} = 1$$

$$\frac{(3 - 1)^2}{1} - \frac{\left(\sqrt{3}\right)^2}{b^2} = 1$$

$$b^2 = 1$$

$$(y - 1)^2 - x^2 = 1$$

69. Vertices: $(1, 2), \; (5, 2)$

Center: $(3, 2)$

Passes through $(0, 0)$

Horizontal transverse axis

$a = 2$

$$\frac{(x - 3)^2}{4} - \frac{(y - 2)^2}{b^2} = 1$$

$$\frac{(0 - 3)^2}{4} - \frac{(0 - 2)^2}{b^2} = 1$$

$$b^2 = \frac{16}{5}$$

$$\frac{(x - 3)^2}{4} - \frac{(y - 2)^2}{16/5} = 1$$

71. Vertices: $(2, 0), \; (6, 0)$

Foci: $(0, 0), \; (8, 0)$

Center: $(4, 0)$

Horizontal transverse axis

$a = 2, \; c = 4, \; b^2 = c^2 - a^2 = 12$

$$\frac{(x - 4)^2}{4} - \frac{y^2}{12} = 1$$

73. Vertices: $(4, 1), \; (4, 9)$

Foci: $(4, 0), \; (4, 10)$

Center: $(4, 5)$

Vertical transverse axis

$a = 4, \; c = 5, \; b^2 = c^2 - a^2 = 9$

$$\frac{(y - 5)^2}{16} - \frac{(x - 4)^2}{9} = 1$$

75. Vertices: $(2, 3)$, $(2, -3)$

Passes through the point $(0, 5)$

Center: $(2, 0)$

Vertical transverse axis

$a = 3$

$$\frac{y^2}{9} - \frac{(x-2)^2}{b^2} = 1$$

$$\frac{5^2}{9} - \frac{(x-2)^2}{b^2} = 1$$

$$b^2 = \frac{9}{4}$$

$$\frac{y^2}{9} - \frac{4(x-2)^2}{9} = 1$$

77. Vertices: $(0, 2)$, $(6, 2)$

Asymptotes: $y = \frac{2}{3}x$, $y = 4 = \frac{2}{3}x$

Center: $(3, 2)$

Horizontal transverse axis

$a = 3$, $b = 2$

$$\frac{(x-3)^2}{9} - \frac{(y-2)^2}{4} = 1$$

79. $\dfrac{(x-3)^2}{4} - \dfrac{(y-1)^2}{9} = 1$

$$(x-3)^2 = \frac{4}{9}[9 + (y-1)^2]$$

$$x - 3 = \pm\frac{2}{3}\sqrt{9 + (y-1)^2}$$

$$x = 3 \pm \frac{2}{3}\sqrt{9 + (y-1)^2}$$

The left half of the hyperbola is

$x = 3 - \dfrac{2}{3}\sqrt{9 + y - 1)^2}$.

81. $x^2 + y^2 - 6x + 4y + 9 = 0$

$$(x-3)^2 + (y+2)^2 = 4$$

Circle

83. $4x^2 - y^2 - 4x - 3 = 0$

$$4\left(x - \frac{1}{2}\right)^2 - y^2 = 4$$

$$\left(x - \frac{1}{2}\right)^2 - \frac{y^2}{4} = 1$$

Hyperbola

85. $4x^2 + 3y^2 + 8x - 24y + 51 = 0$

$$4(x+1)^2 + 3(y-4)^2 = 1$$

$$\frac{(x+1)^2}{1/4} + \frac{(y-4)^2}{1/3} = 1$$

Ellipse

87. $25x^2 - 10x - 200y - 119 = 0$

$$25\left(x - \tfrac{1}{5}\right)^2 = 200\left(y + \tfrac{3}{5}\right)$$

$$\left(x - \tfrac{1}{5}\right)^2 = 8\left(y + \tfrac{3}{5}\right)$$

Parabola

89. $x^2 + 9y^2 = 9 \implies y = \pm\frac{1}{3}\sqrt{9 - x^2}$

$$y = x^2 - 4$$

The approximate points ofof intersection are

$(\pm 2.166, 0.692)$ and $(\pm 1.788, -0.803)$.

91. Center: $(0, 0)$

$2a = 36.23$

$a = 18.115 \implies a^2 \approx 328.15$

$3 = \dfrac{c}{a} \implies 0.97 = \dfrac{c}{18.115}$

$\qquad\qquad c = 17.57155$

$c^2 = a^2 - b^2 \implies b^2 = a^2 - c^2 \approx 19.39$

Thus, the equation of the ellipse to approximately $\dfrac{x^2}{328.15} + \dfrac{y^2}{19.39} = 1$.

Section 11.3 Parametric Equations

- If f and g are continuous functions of t on an interval I, then the set of ordered pairs $(f(t), g(t))$ is a *plane curve C*. The equations $x = f(t)$ and $y = g(t)$ are *parametric equations* for C and t is the *parameter*.
- You should be able to graph plane curves with your graphing utility.
- To eliminate the parameter:
  (a) Solve for t in one equation and substitute into the second equation.
  (b) Use trigonometric identities.
- You should be able to find the parametric equations for a graph.

Solutions to Odd-Numbered Exercises

1. $x = \sqrt{t}, y = 1 - t$

(a)

t	0	1	2	3	4
x	0	1	$\sqrt{2}$	$\sqrt{3}$	2
y	1	0	-1	-2	-3

(b)

(c) $x = \sqrt{t} \implies t = x^2$. Hence, $y = 1 - t = 1 - x^2$.
The graph is the entire parabola rather than just the right half.

3. $x = t, y = -2t$

$y = -2x$

5. $x = 3t - 1, y = 2t + 1$

$y = 2\left(\dfrac{x + 1}{3}\right) + 1$

$y = (4x)^2$

$2x - 3y + 5 = 0$

7. $x = \dfrac{1}{4}t, y = t^2$

$y = (4x)^2$

$y = 16x^2$

9. $x = t + 1, y = t^2$

$y = (x - 1)^2$

11. $x = t^3, y = \dfrac{t^2}{2}$

$y = \dfrac{1}{2}\left(\sqrt[3]{x}\right)^2$

13. $x = 2t \implies t = \dfrac{x}{2}$

$y = |t - 2|$

$y = \left|\dfrac{x}{2} - 2\right| = \dfrac{1}{2}|x - 4|$

15. $x = 3\cos\theta \implies \left(\dfrac{x}{3}\right)^2 = \cos^2\theta$

$y = 3\sin\theta \implies \left(\dfrac{y}{3}\right)^2 = \sin^2\theta$

$\left(\dfrac{x}{3}\right)^2 + \left(\dfrac{y}{3}\right)^2 = 1$

17. $x = 4\sin 2\theta \implies \left(\dfrac{x}{4}\right)^2 = \sin^2 2\theta$

$y = 2\cos 2\theta \implies \left(\dfrac{y}{2}\right)^2 = \cos^2 2\theta$

$\dfrac{x^2}{16} + \dfrac{y^2}{4} = \sin^2 2\theta + \cos^2 2\theta$

$\dfrac{x^2}{16} + \dfrac{y^2}{4} = 1$

Ellipse

19. $x = 4 + 2 \cos \theta \implies \left(\dfrac{x-4}{2}\right)^2 = \cos^2 \theta$

$y = -1 + \sin \theta \qquad (y+1)^2 = \sin^2 \theta$

$\left(\dfrac{x-4}{2}\right)^2 + (y+1)^2 = \cos^2 \theta + \sin^2 \theta$

$\dfrac{(x-4)^2}{4} + (y+1)^2 = 1$

Ellipse

21. $x = 4 + 2 \cos \theta \implies \left(\dfrac{x-4}{2}\right)^2 = \cos^2 \theta$

$y = -1 + 4 \sin \theta \implies \left(\dfrac{y+1}{4}\right)^2 = \sin^2 \theta$

$\left(\dfrac{x-4}{2}\right)^2 + \left(\dfrac{y+1}{4}\right)^2 = 1$

$\dfrac{(x-4)^2}{4} + \dfrac{(y+1)^2}{16} = 1$

Ellipse

23. $x = 4 \sec \theta \implies \left(\dfrac{x}{4}\right)^2 = \sec^2 \theta$

$y = 3 \tan \theta \implies \left(\dfrac{y}{3}\right)^2 = \tan^2 \theta$

$\left(\dfrac{x}{4}\right)^2 - \left(\dfrac{y}{3}\right)^2 = \sec^2 \theta - \tan^2 \theta$

$\dfrac{x^2}{16} - \dfrac{y^2}{9} = 1$

Hyperbola

25. $x = e^{-t} \implies \dfrac{1}{x} = e^t$

$y = e^{3t} \implies y = (e^t)^3$

$y = \left(\dfrac{1}{x}\right)^3$

$y = \dfrac{1}{x^3}, \ x > 0, y > 0$

27. $x = t^3 \qquad \implies x^{1/3} = t$

$y = 3 \ln t \implies y = \ln t^3$

$y = \ln(x^{1/3})^3$

$y = \ln x$

29. By eliminating the parameters in (a)–(d), we get $y = 2x + 1$. They differ from each other in restricted domain and in orientation.

    (a) Domain: $-\infty < x < \infty$
        Orientation: Left to right

    (b) Domain: $-1 \le x \le 1$
        Orientation: Depends on θ

    (c) Domain: $0 < x < \infty$
        Orientation: Right to left

    (d) Domain: $0 < x < \infty$
        Orientation: Left to right

31. $x = x_1 + t(x_2 - x_1)$

$y = y_1 + t(y_2 - y_1)$

$\dfrac{x - x_1}{x_2 - x_1} = t$

$y = y_1 + \left(\dfrac{x - x_1}{x_2 - x_1}\right)(y_2 - y_1)$

$y - y_1 = \dfrac{y_2 - y_1}{x_2 - x_1}(x - x_1)$

Notice that this is the point-slope form of the line,
$y - y_1 = m(x - x_1)$.

33. $x = h + a \cos \theta$

$y = k + b \sin \theta$

$\dfrac{x - h}{a} = \cos \theta, \ \dfrac{y - k}{b} = \sin \theta$

$\dfrac{(x - h)^2}{a^2} + \dfrac{(y - k)^2}{b^2} = 1$

35. From Exercise 31:

$x = 5t$

$y = -2t$

Solution not unique

37. From Exercise 32:

$x = 2 + 4 \cos \theta$

$y = 1 + 4 \sin \theta$

Solution not unique

39. From Exercise 33:

$a = 5, c = 4$, and hence, $b = 3$.

$x = 5 \cos \theta$

$y = 3 \sin \theta$

Center: $(0, 0)$

Solution not unique

41. $y = 3x - 2$

Examples:

$x = t \qquad x = 2t$

$y = 3t - 2 \qquad y = 6t - 2$

43. $x = 2(\theta - \sin \theta)$

$y = 2(1 - \cos \theta)$

45. $x = 3 \cos^3 \theta, \ y = 3 \sin^3 \theta$

47. $x = 2 \cot \theta, \ y = 2 \sin^2 \theta$

49. Matches graph (b).

51. Matches graph (d).

53. $x = (v_0 \cos \theta)t, \ y = h + (v_0 \sin \theta)t - 16t^2$

(a) $100 \text{ miles/hour} = \dfrac{100 \text{ mi/hr} \cdot 5280 \text{ ft/mi}}{3600 \text{ sec/hr}}$

$\qquad\qquad\qquad = 146.67 \text{ ft/sec}$

$\quad x = (146.67 \cos \theta)t$

$\quad y = 3 + (146.67 \sin \theta)t - 16t^2$

(b) $\theta = 15°$

$\quad x = (146.67 \cos 15°)t = 141.7t$

$\quad y = 3 + (146.67 \sin 15°)t - 16t^2$

$\qquad = 3 + 38.0t - 16t^2$

It is not a home run because $y < 10$ when $x = 400$.

(c) $\theta = 23°$

$\quad x = (146.67 \cos 23°)t = 135.0t$

$\quad y = 3 + (146.67 \sin 23°)t - 16t^2$

$\qquad = 3 + 57.3t - 16t^2$

Yes, it is a home run because $y > 10$ when $x = 400$.

(d) $\theta = 19.4°$ is the minimum angle.

55. $y = h + (v_0 \sin \theta)t - 16t^2 \ \text{and} \ t = \dfrac{x}{v_0 \cos \theta}$

$\quad = h + (v_0 \sin \theta)\left(\dfrac{x}{v_0 \cos \theta}\right) - 16\left(\dfrac{x}{v_0 \cos \theta}\right)^2$

$\quad = h + (\tan \theta)x - \dfrac{16 \sec^2 \theta}{v_0^2}x^2$

57. False, the graph of $x = t^2, y = t^2$ is the portion of the line $y = x$ for $x \geq 0$.

Section 11.4 Polar Coordinates

■ In polar coordinates you do not have unique representation of points. The point (r, θ) can be represented by $(r, \theta \pm 2n\pi)$ or by $(-r, \theta \pm (2n + 1)\pi)$ where n is any integer. The pole is represented by $(0, \theta)$ where θ is any angle.

■ To convert from polar coordinates to rectangular coordinates, use the following relationships.

$\quad x = r \cos \theta$

$\quad y = r \sin \theta$

■ To convert from rectangular coordinates to polar coordinates, use the following relationships.

$\quad r = \pm\sqrt{x^2 + y^2}$

$\quad \tan \theta = y/x$

If θ is in the same quadrant as the point (x, y), then r is positive. If θ is in the opposite quadrant as the point (x, y), then r is negative.

■ You should be able to convert rectangular equations to polar form and vice versa.

Solutions to Odd-Numbered Exercises

1. Polar coordinates: $\left(4, \dfrac{\pi}{2}\right)$

$x = 4\cos\left(\dfrac{\pi}{2}\right) = 0$

$y = 4\sin\left(\dfrac{\pi}{2}\right) = 4$

Rectangular coordinates: $(0, 4)$

3. Polar coordinates: $\left(-1, \dfrac{5\pi}{4}\right)$

$x = -1\cos\left(\dfrac{5\pi}{4}\right) = \dfrac{\sqrt{2}}{2}$

$y = -1\sin\left(\dfrac{5\pi}{4}\right) = \dfrac{\sqrt{2}}{2}$

Rectangular coordinates: $\left(\dfrac{\sqrt{2}}{2}, \dfrac{\sqrt{2}}{2}\right)$

5. Polar coordinates: $\left(4, -\dfrac{\pi}{3}\right)$

$x = 4\cos\left(-\dfrac{\pi}{3}\right) = 2$

$y = 4\sin\left(-\dfrac{\pi}{3}\right) = -2\sqrt{3}$

Rectangular coordinates: $\left(2, -2\sqrt{3}\right)$

7. Polar coordinates: $\left(0, -\dfrac{7\pi}{6}\right)$

$x = 0\cos\left(-\dfrac{7\pi}{6}\right) = 0$

$y = 0\sin\left(-\dfrac{7\pi}{6}\right) = 0$

Rectangular coordinates: $(0, 0)$

9. Polar coordinates: $\left(\sqrt{2}, 2.36\right)$

$x = \sqrt{2}\cos(2.36) \approx -1.004$

$y = \sqrt{2}\sin(2.36) \approx 0.996$

Rectangular coordinates: $(-1.004, 0.996)$

11. $(r, \theta) = \left(2, \dfrac{3\pi}{4}\right) \implies (x, y) = (-1.414, 1.414) = \left(-\sqrt{2}, \sqrt{2}\right)$

13. $(r, \theta) = (-4.5, 1.3) \implies (x, y) = (-1.204, -4.336)$

15. Rectangular coordinates: $(1, 1)$

$r = \sqrt{2},\ \tan \theta = 1,\ \theta = \dfrac{\pi}{4}$

Polar coordinates: $\left(\sqrt{2}, \dfrac{\pi}{4}\right),\ \left(-\sqrt{2}, \dfrac{5\pi}{4}\right)$

17. Rectangular coordinates: $(-6, 0)$

$r = 6,\ \tan \theta = 0,\ \theta = 0$

Polar coordinates: $(6, \pi),\ (-6, 0)$

19. Rectangular coordinates: $(-3, 4)$

$r = \sqrt{9 + 16} = 5,\ \tan \theta = -\dfrac{4}{3},\ \theta \approx 2.214$

Polar coordinates: $(5, 2.214),\ (-5, 5.356)$

21. Rectangular coordinates: $\left(-\sqrt{3}, -\sqrt{3}\right)$

$r = \sqrt{3 + 3} = \sqrt{6},\ \tan \theta = 1,\ \theta = \dfrac{\pi}{4}$

Polar coordinates: $\left(\sqrt{6}, \dfrac{5\pi}{4}\right),\ \left(-\sqrt{6}, \dfrac{\pi}{4}\right)$

23. Rectangular coordinates: $(4, 6)$

$r = \sqrt{16 + 36} = 2\sqrt{13},\ \tan \theta = \dfrac{3}{2},\ \theta \approx 0.983$

Polar coordinates: $(2\sqrt{13}, 0.983),\ (-2\sqrt{13}, 4.124)$

25. $(x, y) = (3, -2) \implies r = \sqrt{3^2 + (-2)^2} = \sqrt{13}$

$\theta = \arctan\left(-\dfrac{2}{3}\right) \approx -0.588$

$(r, \theta) \approx \left(\sqrt{13}, -0.588\right)$

27. $(x, y) = \left(\sqrt{3}, 2\right) \implies r = \sqrt{3 + 2^2} = \sqrt{7}$

$$\theta = \arctan\left(\frac{2}{\sqrt{3}}\right) \approx 0.857$$

$(r, \theta) \approx \left(\sqrt{7}, 0.857\right)$

29. $(x, y) = \left(\frac{5}{2}, \frac{4}{3}\right) \implies r = \sqrt{\left(\frac{5}{2}\right)^2 + \left(\frac{4}{3}\right)^2} = \frac{17}{6}$

$$\theta = \arctan\left(\frac{4/3}{5/2}\right) \approx 0.490$$

$(r, \theta) \approx \left(\frac{17}{6}, 0.490\right)$

31. True, the distances from the origin are the same.

33. $x^2 + y^2 = 9$

$r = 3$

35. $x^2 + y^2 - 2ax = 0$

$r^2 - 2ar\cos\theta = 0$

$r(r - 2a\cos\theta) = 0$

$r = 2a\cos\theta$

37. $y = 4$

$r\sin\theta = 4$

$r = 4\csc\theta$

39. $x = 10$

$r\cos\theta = 10$

$r = 10\sec\theta$

41. $3x - y + 2 = 0$

$3r\cos\theta - r\sin\theta + 2 = 0$

$r(3\cos\theta - \sin\theta) = -2$

$$r = \frac{-2}{3\cos\theta - \sin\theta}$$

43. $xy = 4$

$(r\cos\theta)(r\sin\theta) = 4$

$r^2 = 4\ \sec\theta\csc\theta = 8\csc 2\theta$

45. $(x^2 + y^2)^2 - 9(x^2 - y^2) = 0$

$(r^2)^2 - 9(r^2\cos^2\theta - r^2\sin^2\theta) = 0$

$r^2[r^2 - 9(\cos 2\theta)] = 0$

$r^2 = 9\cos 2\theta$

47. $r = 4\sin\theta$

$r^2 = 4r\sin\theta$

$x^2 + y^2 = 4y$

$x^2 + y^2 - 4y = 0$

49. $\theta = \dfrac{\pi}{6}$

$\tan\theta = \dfrac{\sqrt{3}}{3}$

$\dfrac{y}{x} = \dfrac{\sqrt{3}}{3}$

$y = \dfrac{\sqrt{3}}{3}x$

$\sqrt{3}x - 3y = 0$

51. $r = 2\csc\theta$

$r\sin\theta = 2$

$y = 2$

53. $r = 2\sin 3\theta$

$r = 2(3\sin\theta - 4\sin^3\theta)$

$r^4 = 6r^3\sin\theta - 8r^3\sin^3\theta$

$(x^2 + y^2)^2 = 6(x^2 + y^2)y - 8y^3$

$(x^2 + y^2)^2 = 6x^2y - 2y^3$

55. $r = \dfrac{6}{2 - 3\sin\theta}$

$r(2 - 3\sin\theta) = 6$

$2r = 6 + 3r\sin\theta$

$2\left(\pm\sqrt{x^2 + y^2}\right) = 6 + 3y$

$4(x^2 + y^2) = (6 + 3y)^2$

$4x^2 + 4y^2 = 36 + 36y + 9y^2$

$4x^2 - 5y^2 - 36y - 36 = 0$

57. $r = 3$

$r^2 = 9$

$x^2 + y^2 = 9$

59. $\theta = \dfrac{\pi}{4}$

$\tan \theta = \tan \dfrac{\pi}{4}$

$\dfrac{y}{x} = 1$

$y = x$

$x - y = 0$

61. $r = 3 \sec \theta$

$r \cos \theta = 3$

$x = 3$

$x - 3 = 0$

63.

$$r = 2(h \cos \theta + k \sin \theta)$$

$$r = 2\left(h\left(\dfrac{x}{r}\right) + k\left(\dfrac{y}{r}\right) \right)$$

$$r = \dfrac{2hx + 2ky}{r}$$

$$r^2 = 2hx + 2ky$$

$$x^2 + y^2 = 2hx + 2ky$$

$$x^2 - 2hx + y^2 - 2ky = 0$$

$$(x^2 - 2hx + h^2) + (y^2 - 2ky + k^2) = h^2 + k^2$$

$$(x - h)^2 + (y - k)^2 = h^2 + k^2$$

Center: (h, k)

Radius: $\sqrt{h^2 + k^2}$

65. (a) $(r_1, \theta_1) = (x_1, y_1)$ where $x_1 = r_1 \cos \theta_1$ and $y_1 = r_1 \sin \theta_1$.

(r_2, \theta_2) = (x_2, y_2)$ where $x_2 = r_2 \cos \theta_2$ and $y_2 = r_2 \sin \theta_2$.

Then $x_1^2 + y_1^2 = r_1^2 \cos^2 \theta_1 + r_1^2 \sin^2 \theta_1 = r_1^2$ and $x_2^2 + y_2^2 = r_2^2$. Thus,

$$d = \sqrt{(x_1 - x_2)^2 + (y_1 - y_2)^2}$$

$$= \sqrt{x_1^2 - 2x_1x_2 + x_2^2 + y_1^2 - 2y_1y_2 + y_2^2}$$

$$= \sqrt{(x_1^2 + y_1^2) + (x_2^2 + y_2^2) - 2(x_1x_2 + y_1y_2)}$$

$$= \sqrt{r_1^2 + r_2^2 - 2(r_1r_2 \cos \theta_1 \cos \theta_2 + r_1r_2 \sin \theta_1 \sin \theta_2)}$$

$$= \sqrt{r_1^2 + r_2^2 - 2r_1r_2 \cos(\theta_1 - \theta_2)}.$$

(b) If $\theta_1 = \theta_2$, the points are on the same line through the origin. In this case,

$$d = \sqrt{r_1^2 + r_2^2 - 2r_1r_2 \cos(0)} = \sqrt{(r_1 - r_2)^2} = |r_1 - r_2|.$$

(c) If $\theta_1 - \theta_2 = 90°, d = \sqrt{r_1^2 + r_2^2}$, the Pythagorean Theorem.

(d) For instance, $\left(3, \dfrac{\pi}{6}\right), \left(4, \dfrac{\pi}{3}\right)$ gives $d \approx 2.053$ and $\left(-3, \dfrac{7\pi}{6}\right), \left(-4, \dfrac{4\pi}{3}\right)$ gives $d \approx 2.053$. (same!)

67. $D = \begin{vmatrix} 5 & -7 \\ -3 & 1 \end{vmatrix} = 5 - 21 = -16$

$D_x = \begin{vmatrix} -11 & -7 \\ -3 & 1 \end{vmatrix} = -11 - 21 = -32$

$D_y = \begin{vmatrix} 5 & -11 \\ -3 & -3 \end{vmatrix} = -15 - 33 = -48$

$x = \dfrac{D_x}{D} = \dfrac{-32}{-16} = 2$

$y = \dfrac{D_y}{D} = \dfrac{-48}{-16} = 3$

69. $D = \begin{vmatrix} 3 & -2 & 1 \\ 2 & 1 & -3 \\ 1 & -3 & 9 \end{vmatrix} = 35$

$D_x = \begin{vmatrix} 0 & -2 & 1 \\ 0 & 1 & -3 \\ 8 & -3 & 9 \end{vmatrix} = 40$

$D_y = \begin{vmatrix} 3 & 0 & 1 \\ 2 & 0 & -3 \\ 1 & 8 & 9 \end{vmatrix} = 88$

$D_z = \begin{vmatrix} 3 & -2 & 0 \\ 2 & 1 & 0 \\ 1 & -3 & 8 \end{vmatrix} = 56$

$x = \dfrac{D_x}{D} = \dfrac{40}{35} = \dfrac{8}{7}$

$y = \dfrac{D_y}{D} = \dfrac{88}{35}$

$z = \dfrac{D_z}{D} = \dfrac{56}{35} = \dfrac{8}{5}$

71. $D = \begin{vmatrix} 1 & 1 & 1 & -3 \\ 3 & -1 & -2 & 1 \\ -1 & 1 & -1 & 2 \\ 0 & 1 & 0 & 1 \end{vmatrix} = 20$

$D_x = \begin{vmatrix} -8 & 1 & 1 & -3 \\ 7 & -1 & -2 & 1 \\ -2 & 1 & -1 & 2 \\ -6 & 1 & 0 & 1 \end{vmatrix} = 20$

$D_y = \begin{vmatrix} 1 & -8 & 1 & -3 \\ 3 & 7 & -2 & 1 \\ -1 & -2 & -1 & 2 \\ 0 & -6 & 0 & 1 \end{vmatrix} = -80$

$D_z = \begin{vmatrix} 1 & 1 & -8 & -3 \\ 3 & -1 & 7 & 1 \\ -1 & 1 & -2 & 2 \\ 0 & 1 & -6 & 1 \end{vmatrix} = 20$

$D_w = \begin{vmatrix} 1 & 1 & 1 & -8 \\ 3 & -1 & -2 & 7 \\ -1 & 1 & -1 & -2 \\ 0 & 1 & 0 & -6 \end{vmatrix} = 40$

$x = \dfrac{D_x}{D} = \dfrac{20}{20} = 1$

$y = \dfrac{D_y}{D} = -\dfrac{80}{20} = -4$

$z = \dfrac{D_z}{D} = \dfrac{20}{20} = 1$

$w = \dfrac{D_w}{D} = \dfrac{40}{20} = 2$

Section 11.5 Graphs of Polar Equations

■ When graphing polar equations:

1. Test for symmetry

    (a) $\theta = \pi/2$: Replace (r, θ) by $(r, \pi - \theta)$ or $(-r, -\theta)$.

    (b) Polar axis: Replace (r, θ) by $(r, -\theta)$ or $(-r, \pi - \theta)$.

    (c) Pole: Replace (r, θ) by $(r, \pi + \theta)$ or $(-r, \theta)$.

    (d) $r = f(\sin \theta)$ is symmetric with respect to the line $\theta = \pi/2$.

    (e) $r = f(\cos \theta)$ is symmetric with respect to the polar axis.

2. Find the θ values for which $|r|$ is maximum.

3. Find the θ values for which $r = 0$.

4. Know the different types of polar graphs.

    (a) Limaçons   (b) Rose Curves, $n \geq 2$

        $r = a \pm b \cos \theta$ $r = a \cos n\theta$

        $r = a \pm b \sin \theta$ $r = a \sin n\theta$

    (c) Circles   (d) Lemniscates

        $r = a \cos \theta$ $r^2 = a^2 \cos 2\theta$

        $r = a \sin \theta$ $r^2 = a^2 \sin 2\theta$

        $r = a$

■ You should be able to graph polar equations of the form $r = f(\theta)$ with your graphing utility. If your utility does not have a polar mode, use

    $x = f(t) \cos t$

    $y = f(t) \sin t$

in parametric mode.

Solutions to Odd-Numbered Exercises

1. $r = 3 \cos 2\theta$ is a rose curve.   **3.** $r = 2 - \cos \theta$ is a limaçon.   **5.** $r = 6 \sin 2\theta$ is a rose curve.

7. $r = 10 + 6 \cos \theta$

    $\theta = \dfrac{\pi}{2}$: $-r = 10 + 6 \cos(-\theta)$

             $-r = 10 + 6 \cos \theta$

             Not an equivalent equation

    Polar axis: $r = 10 + 6 \cos(-\theta)$

             $r = 10 + 6 \cos \theta$

             Equivalent equation

    Pole: $-r = 10 + 6 \cos \theta$

             Not an equivalent equation

    Answer: Symmetric with respect to polar axis

9. $r = \dfrac{2}{1 + \sin \theta}$

$\theta = \dfrac{\pi}{2}$: $\quad r = \dfrac{2}{1 + \sin(\pi - \theta)}$

$\qquad\qquad r = \dfrac{2}{1 + \sin \pi \cos \theta - \cos \pi \sin \theta}$

$\qquad\qquad r = \dfrac{2}{1 + \sin \theta}$

Equivalent equation

Polar axis: $\quad r = \dfrac{2}{1 + \sin(-\theta)}$

$\qquad\qquad r = \dfrac{2}{1 - \sin \theta}$

Not an equivalent equation

Pole: $\quad -r = \dfrac{2}{1 + \sin \theta}$

Not an equivalent equation

Answer: Symmetric with respect to $\theta = \pi/2$

11. $r = 4 \sec \theta \csc \theta$

$\theta = \dfrac{\pi}{2}$: $\quad -r = 4 \sec(-\theta) \csc(-\theta)$

$\qquad\qquad -r = -4 \sec \theta \csc \theta$

$\qquad\qquad r = 4 \sec \theta \csc \theta$

Equivalent equation

Polar axis: $\quad -r = 4 \sec(\pi - \theta) \csc(\pi - \theta)$

$\qquad\qquad -r = 4(-\sec \theta) \csc \theta$

$\qquad\qquad r = 4 \sec \theta \csc \theta$

Equivalent equation

Pole: $\quad r = 4 \sec(\pi + \theta) \csc(\pi + \theta)$

$\qquad\qquad r = 4(-\sec \theta)(-\csc \theta)$

$\qquad\qquad r = 4 \sec \theta \csc \theta$

Equivalent equation

Answer: Symmetric with respect to $\theta = \pi/2$, pole axis, and pole

13. $|r| = |10(1 - \sin \theta)|$

$\quad = 10|1 - \sin \theta| \le 10(2) = 20$

$|1 - \sin \theta| = 2$

$\quad 1 - \sin \theta = 2$ or $1 - \sin \theta = -2$

$\qquad \sin \theta = -1 \qquad \sin \theta = 3$

$\qquad\quad \theta = \dfrac{3\pi}{2} \qquad$ Not possible

Maximum: $|r| = 20$ when $\theta = \dfrac{3\pi}{2}$.

$r = 0$ when $1 - \sin \theta = 0$

$\qquad\qquad\qquad \sin \theta = 1$

$\qquad\qquad\qquad\quad \theta = \dfrac{\pi}{2}$.

15. $|r| = |4 \cos 3\theta| = 4 |\cos 3\theta| \le 4$

$|\cos 3\theta| = 1$

$\cos 3\theta = \pm 1$

$\theta = 0, \dfrac{\pi}{3}, \dfrac{2\pi}{3}$

Maximum: $|r| = 4$ when $\theta = 0, \dfrac{\pi}{3}, \dfrac{2\pi}{3}$.

$r = 0$ when $\cos 3\theta = 0$

$\theta = \dfrac{\pi}{6}, \dfrac{\pi}{2}, \dfrac{5\pi}{6}$.

17. Circle: $r = 5$

19. $r = \dfrac{\pi}{6}$ is a circle.

21. $r = 3 \sin \theta$

Symmetric with respect to $\theta = \dfrac{\pi}{2}$

Circle with radius of $\dfrac{3}{2}$

23. $r = 3(1 - \cos \theta)$
Cardioid

25. $r = 4 + 4 \sin \theta$
Symmetric with respect to

$\theta = \dfrac{\pi}{2}$

$\dfrac{a}{b} = \dfrac{4}{4} = 1 \implies$ Cardioid

$|r| = 8$ when $\theta = \dfrac{\pi}{2}$.

$r = 0$ when $\theta = \dfrac{3\pi}{2}$.

27. $r = 3 - 2 \cos \theta$
Dimpled limaçon

29. $r = 2 + \sin \theta$
Convex limaçon

31. $r = 2 \cos 3\theta$
Rose curve

33. $r = 3 \sin 2\theta$
Symmetric with respect
to $\theta = \dfrac{\pi}{2}$, polar axis, and pole

Rose curve ($n = 2$) with
4 petals

35. $r = \dfrac{\theta}{2}$

Symmetric with respect
to $\theta = \dfrac{\pi}{2}$ and polar axis
Spiral

37.

39.

41.

43.

45.

47.

49.

51.

53.

55. $r = 3 - 4 \cos \theta, \ 0 \le \theta < 2\pi$

57. $r = 2 + \sin \theta, \ 0 \le \theta < 2\pi$

59. $r = 2 \cos\left(\dfrac{3\theta}{2}\right), \ 0 \le \theta < 4\pi$

61. $r^2 = 4 \sin 2\theta, \ 0 \le \theta < \dfrac{\pi}{2}$

$\left(\text{Use } r_1 = \sqrt{4 \sin 2\theta} \text{ and } r_2 = -\sqrt{4 \sin 2\theta}.\right)$

63. $r = 2 - \sec \theta$

$x = -1$ is an asymptote.

65. $r = \dfrac{2}{\theta}$

$y = 2$ is an asymptote.

67.

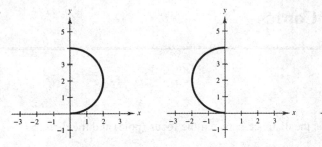

Semicircle   Semicircle   Circle   Semicircle

69. The graph of $r = f(\theta)$ is rotated about the pole through an angle ϕ. Let (r, θ) be any point on the graph of $r = f(\theta)$. Then $(r, \theta + \phi)$ is rotated through the angle ϕ, and since $r = f((\theta + \phi) - \phi) = f(\theta)$, it follows that $(r, \theta + \phi)$ is on the graph of $r = f(\theta - \phi)$.

71. (a) $r = 2 - \sin\left(\theta - \dfrac{\pi}{4}\right)$

$\qquad = 2 - \dfrac{\sqrt{2}}{2}(\sin\theta - \cos\theta)$

(b) $r = 2 - \sin\left(\theta - \dfrac{\pi}{2}\right)$

$\qquad = 2 + \cos\theta$

(c) $r = 2 - \sin(\theta - \pi)$

$\qquad = 2 + \sin\theta$

(d) $r = 2 - \sin\left(\theta - \dfrac{3\pi}{2}\right)$

$\qquad = 2 - \cos\theta$

73. (a) $r = 1 - \sin\theta$

(b) $r = 1 - \sin\left(\theta - \dfrac{\pi}{4}\right)$

75. $r = 2 + k\cos\theta$

$k = 0$

Circle

$k = 1$

Convex limaçon

$k = 2$

Cardioid

$k = 3$

Limaçon with inner loop

Section 11.6   Polar Equations of Conics

■ The graph of a polar equation of the form

$$r = \frac{ep}{1 \pm e \cos \theta} \quad \text{or} \quad r = \frac{ep}{1 \pm e \sin \theta}$$

is a conic, where $e > 0$ is the eccentricity and $|p|$ is the distance between the focus (pole) and the directrix.

(a) If $e < 1$, the graph is an ellipse.

(b) If $e = 1$, the graph is a parabola.

(c) If $e > 1$, the graph is a hyperbola.

■ Guidelines for finding polar equations of conics:

(a) Horizontal directrix above the pole: $r = \dfrac{ep}{1 + e \sin \theta}$

(b) Horizontal directrix below the pole: $r = \dfrac{ep}{1 - e \sin \theta}$

(c) Vertical directrix to the right of the pole: $r = \dfrac{ep}{1 + e \cos \theta}$

(d) Vertical directrix to the left of the pole: $r = \dfrac{ep}{1 - e \cos \theta}$

Solutions to Odd-Numbered Exercises

1.

3.

5. Matches (b).
   (Parabola $e = 1$)

7. Matches (d).
   (Hyperbola $e = 2$)

9. $r = \dfrac{2}{1 - \cos \theta}$

$e = 1$ so the graph is a parabola.

Vertex: $(r, \theta) = (1, \pi)$

11. $r = \dfrac{5}{1 + \sin \theta}$

$e = 1$ so the graph is a parabola.

Vertex: $(r, \theta) = \left(\dfrac{5}{2}, \dfrac{\pi}{2}\right)$

13. $r = \dfrac{2}{2 - \cos\theta} = \dfrac{1}{1 - (1/2)\cos\theta}$

$e = \dfrac{1}{2} < 1$, the graph is an ellipse.

Vertices: $(r, \theta) = (2, 0), \left(\dfrac{2}{3}, \pi\right)$

15. $r = \dfrac{4}{2 + \sin\theta} = \dfrac{2}{1 + (1/2)\sin\theta}$

$e = \dfrac{1}{2} < 1$, the graph is an ellipse.

Vertices: $(r, \theta) = \left(\dfrac{4}{3}, \dfrac{\pi}{2}\right), \left(4, \dfrac{3\pi}{2}\right)$

17. $r = \dfrac{3}{2 + 4\sin\theta} = \dfrac{3/2}{1 + 2\sin\theta}$

$e = 2 > 1$, the graph is a hyperbola.

Vertices: $(r, \theta) = \left(\dfrac{1}{2}, \dfrac{\pi}{2}\right), \left(-\dfrac{3}{2}, \dfrac{3\pi}{2}\right)$

19. $r = \dfrac{3}{2 - 6\cos\theta} = \dfrac{3/2}{1 - 3\cos\theta}$

$e = 3 > 1$, the graph is a hyperbola.

Vertices: $(r, \theta) = \left(-\dfrac{3}{4}, 0\right), \left(\dfrac{3}{8}, \pi\right)$

21.

23.

25.

27.

29.

31. $e = 1, x = -1, p = 1$

Vertical directrix to the left of the pole

$r = \dfrac{1(1)}{1 - 1\cos\theta} = \dfrac{1}{1 - \cos\theta}$

33. $e = \dfrac{1}{2}, y = 1, p = 1$

Horizontal directrix above the pole

$r = \dfrac{(1/2)(1)}{1 + (1/2)\sin\theta} = \dfrac{1}{2 + \sin\theta}$

35. $e = 2, x = 1, p = 1$

Vertical directrix to the right of the pole

$r = \dfrac{2(1)}{1 + 2\cos\theta} = \dfrac{2}{1 + 2\cos\theta}$

37. Vertex: $\left(1, -\dfrac{\pi}{2}\right) \implies e = 1, p = 2$

Horizontal directrix below the pole

$$r = \frac{1(2)}{1 - 1\sin\theta} = \frac{2}{1 - \sin\theta}$$

39. Vertex: $(5, \pi) \implies e = 1, p = 10$

Vertical directrix to the left of the pole

$$r = \frac{1(10)}{1 - 1\cos\theta} = \frac{10}{1 - \cos\theta}$$

41. Center: $(3, \pi)$; $c = 3$, $a = 5$, $e = \dfrac{3}{5}$

Vertical directrix to the right of the pole

$$r = \frac{(3/5)p}{1 + (3/5)\cos\theta} = \frac{3p}{5 + 3\cos\theta}$$

$$2 = \frac{3p}{5 + 3\cos 0}$$

$$p = \frac{16}{3}$$

$$r = \frac{3(16/3)}{5 + 3\cos\theta} = \frac{16}{5 + 3\cos\theta}$$

43. Center: $(8, 0)$; $c = 8$, $a = 12$, $e = \dfrac{2}{3}$

Vertical directrix to the left of the pole

$$r = \frac{(2/3)p}{1 - (2/3)\cos\theta} = \frac{2p}{3 - 2\cos\theta}$$

$$20 = \frac{2p}{3 - 2\cos 0}$$

$$p = 10$$

$$r = \frac{2(10)}{3 - 2\cos\theta} = \frac{20}{3 - 2\cos\theta}$$

45. Center: $\left(5, \dfrac{3\pi}{2}\right)$; $c = 5$, $a = 4$, $e = \dfrac{5}{4}$

Horizontal directrix below the pole

$$r = \frac{(5/4)p}{1 - (5/4)\sin\theta} = \frac{5p}{4 - 5\sin\theta}$$

$$1 = \frac{5p}{4 - 5\sin(3\pi/2)}$$

$$p = \frac{9}{5}$$

$$r = \frac{5(9/5)}{4 - 5\sin\theta} = \frac{9}{4 - 5\sin\theta}$$

47.

$$\frac{x^2}{a^2} + \frac{y^2}{b^2} = 1$$

$$\frac{r^2\cos^2\theta}{a^2} + \frac{r^2\sin^2\theta}{b^2} = 1$$

$$\frac{r^2\cos^2\theta}{a^2} + \frac{r^2(1 - \cos^2\theta)}{b^2} = 1$$

$$r^2 b^2 \cos^2\theta + r^2 a^2 - r^2 a^2 \cos^2\theta = a^2 b^2$$

$$r^2(b^2 - a^2)\cos^2\theta + r^2 a^2 = a^2 b^2$$

For an ellipse, $b^2 - a^2 = -c^2$. Hence,

$$-r^2 c^2 \cos^2\theta + r^2 a^2 = a^2 b^2$$

$$-r^2\left(\frac{c}{a}\right)^2 \cos^2\theta + r^2 = b^2, \quad e = \frac{c}{a}$$

$$-r^2 e^2 \cos^2\theta + r^2 = b^2$$

$$r^2(1 - e^2 \cos^2\theta) = b^2$$

$$r^2 = \frac{b^2}{1 - e^2 \cos^2\theta}.$$

49. $\dfrac{x^2}{169} + \dfrac{y^2}{144} = 1$

$a = 13$, $b = 12$, $c = 5$, $e = \dfrac{5}{13}$

$$r^2 = \frac{144}{1 - (25/169)\cos^2\theta} = \frac{24{,}336}{169 - 25\cos^2\theta}$$

51. $\dfrac{x^2}{9} - \dfrac{y^2}{16} = 1$

$a = 3$, $b = 4$, $c = 5$, $e = \dfrac{5}{3}$

$$r^2 = \frac{-16}{1 - (25/9)\cos^2\theta} = \frac{144}{25\cos^2\theta - 9}$$

53. Hyperbola

One focus: $\left(5, \dfrac{\pi}{2}\right)$

Vertices: $\left(4, \dfrac{\pi}{2}\right), \left(4, -\dfrac{\pi}{2}\right)$

$a = 4, c = 5, b = 3, e = \dfrac{5}{4}$

$$r^2 = \frac{-3^2}{1 - (5/4)^2 \sin^2 \theta} = \frac{-144}{16 - 25 \sin^2 \theta}$$

$$= \frac{144}{25 \sin^2 \theta - 16}$$

55. When $\theta = 0, r = c + a = ea + a = a(1 + e)$.

Therefore,

$$a(1 + e) = \frac{ep}{1 - e \cos 0}$$

$$a(1 + e)(1 - e) = ep$$

$$a(1 - e^2) = ep.$$

Thus, $r = \dfrac{ep}{1 - e \cos \theta} = \dfrac{(1 - e^2)a}{1 - e \cos \theta}.$

57. $r = \dfrac{[1 - (0.0167)^2](92.957 \times 10^6)}{1 - 0.0167 \cos \theta} \approx \dfrac{9.2931 \times 10^7}{1 - 0.0167 \cos \theta}$

Perihelion distance: $r = 92.957 \times 10^6(1 - 0.0167) \approx 9.1405 \times 10^7$

Aphelion distance: $r = 92.957 \times 10^6(1 + 0.0167) \approx 9.4509 \times 10^7$

59. Radius of earth ≈ 4000 miles. Choose $r = \dfrac{ep}{1 - e \cos \theta}.$

Vertices: $(126{,}000, \ 0)$ and $(4119, \ \pi)$

$$a = \frac{126{,}000 + 4119}{2} = 65{,}059.5$$

$$c = 65{,}059.5 - 4119 = 60{,}940.5$$

$$e = \frac{c}{a} = \frac{60{,}940.5}{65{,}059.5} \approx 0.93669$$

$$2a = \frac{ep}{1 - e \cos 0} + \frac{ep}{1 - e \cos(\pi)} = \frac{ep}{1 - e} + \frac{ep}{1 + c} = \frac{2ep}{1 - e^2}$$

Thus, $p = \dfrac{a(1 - e^2)}{e} \approx 8516.4.$

Thus, $r = \dfrac{ep}{1 - e \cos \theta} = \dfrac{(0.93669)(8516.4)}{1 - (0.93669) \cos \theta} \approx \dfrac{7977.22}{1 - 0.9367 \cos \theta}.$

When $\theta = 60°, r \approx 15{,}004.5$ and the distance from the surface of the earth to the satellite is $15{,}004.5 - 4000 = 11{,}004.5$ miles.

❑ **Review Exercises for Chapter 11**

Solutions to Odd-Numbered Exercises

1. $4x^2 + y^2 = 4$

Ellipse

Matches (d).

3. $4x^2 - y^2 = 4$

Hyperbola

Matches (f).

5. $x^2 + 4y^2 = 4$

Ellipse

Matches (c).

7. $4x = y^2$

Parabola

Vertex: $(0, 0)$

Horizontal axis

9. $x^2 - 6x + 2y + 9 = 0$

$$(x - 3)^2 = -2y$$

Parabola

Vertex: $(3, 0)$

Focus: $\left(3, -\frac{1}{2}\right)$

11.
$$x^2 + y^2 - 2x - 4y + 5 = 0$$
$$(x^2 - 2x + 1) + (y^2 - 4y + 4) = -5 + 1 + 4$$
$$(x - 1)^2 + (y - 2)^2 = 0$$

Point: $(1, 2)$

Note: This a degenerate conic—a circle of radius zero.

13. $4x^2 + y^2 = 16$

$$\frac{x^2}{4} + \frac{y^2}{16} = 1$$

Ellipse

Center: $(0, 0)$

Vertices: $(0, -4)$, $(0, 4)$

15. $x^2 + 9y^2 + 10x - 18y + 25 = 0$

$$(x + 5)^2 + 9(y - 1)^2 = 9$$

$$\frac{(x + 5)^2}{9} + (y - 1)^2 = 1$$

Ellipse

Center: $(-5, 1)$

Vertices: $(-8, 1), (-2, 1)$

17. $3x^2 + 2y^2 - 12x + 12y + 29 = 0$

$$3(x^2 - 4x + 4) + 2(y^2 + 6y + 9) = -29 + 12 + 18$$

$$3(x - 2)^2 + 2(y + 3)^2 = 1$$

Ellipse

$$2(y + 3)^2 = 1 - 3(x - 2)^2$$

$$(y + 3) = \pm\sqrt{\tfrac{1}{2} - \tfrac{3}{2}(x - 2)^2}$$

$$y = -3 \pm \sqrt{\tfrac{1}{2} - \tfrac{3}{2}(x - 2)^2}$$

Graph: $y_1 = -3 + \sqrt{\tfrac{1}{2} - \tfrac{3}{2}(x - 2)^2}$

$$y_2 = -3 - \sqrt{\tfrac{1}{2} - \tfrac{3}{2}(x - 2)^2}$$

19. $x^2 - 9y^2 + 10x + 18y + 7 = 0$

$$(x^2 + 10x + 25) - 9(y^2 - 2y + 1) = -7 + 25 - 9$$

$$(x + 5)^2 - 9(y - 1)^2 = 9$$

$$\frac{(x + 5)^2}{9} - (y - 1)^2 = 1$$

Hyperbola

$$(y - 1)^2 = \frac{(x + 5)^2}{9} - 1 = \frac{1}{9}[(x + 5)^2 - 9]$$

$$y - 1 = \pm\frac{1}{3}\sqrt{(x + 5)^2 - 9}$$

$$y = 1 \pm \frac{1}{3}\sqrt{(x + 5)^2 - 9}$$

Graph: $y_1 = 1 + \dfrac{1}{3}\sqrt{(x + 5)^2 - 9}$

$$y_2 = 1 - \frac{1}{3}\sqrt{(x + 5)^2 - 9}$$

21. Vertex: $(4, 2)$

Focus: $(4, 0)$

Vertical axis, $p = -2$

$(x - 4)^2 = 4(-2)(y - 2)$

$(x - 4)^2 = -8(y - 2)$

23. Vertex: $(0, 2)$

Directrix: $x = -3$

$(y - k)^2 = 4px, \quad p = 3$

$(y - 2)^2 = 12x$

25. Vertices: $(-3, 0)$, $(7, 0)$

Foci: $(0, 0)$, $(4, 0)$

Horizontal major axis

Center: $(2, 0)$

$a = 5, c = 2,$

$b = \sqrt{25 - 4} = \sqrt{21}$

$$\frac{(x - h)^2}{a^2} + \frac{(y - k)^2}{b^2} = 1$$

$$\frac{(x - 2)^2}{25} + \frac{y^2}{21} = 1$$

27. Vertices: $(0, \pm 6)$

Passes through $(2, 2)$

Vertical major axis

Center: $(0, 0)$

$a = 6$

$\dfrac{(x - h)^2}{b^2} + \dfrac{(y - k)^2}{a^2} = 1$

$\dfrac{(2 - 0)^2}{b^2} + \dfrac{(2 - 0)^2}{6^2} = 1$

$b^2 = \dfrac{9}{2}$

$\dfrac{2x^2}{9} + \dfrac{y^2}{36} = 1$

29. Vertices: $(0, \pm 1)$

Foci: $(0, \pm 3)$

Vertical transverse axis

Center: $(0, 0)$

$a = 1, c = 3,$

$b = \sqrt{9 - 1} = \sqrt{8}$

$\dfrac{y^2}{1} - \dfrac{x^2}{8} = 1$

31. Foci: $(0, 0), (8, 0)$

Asymptotes: $y = \pm 2(x - 4)$

Horizontal transverse axis

Center: $(4, 0) \implies c = 4$

$\dfrac{b}{a} = 2 \implies b = 2a$

$a^2 + b^2 = c^2$

$a^2 + (2a)^2 = 4^2$

$a^2 = \dfrac{16}{5}$

$b^2 = \dfrac{64}{5}$

$\dfrac{(x - h)^2}{a^2} - \dfrac{(y - k)^2}{b^2} = 1$

$\dfrac{5(x - 4)^2}{16} - \dfrac{5y^2}{64} = 1$

33. Let $y = 12 - cx^2$.

$10 = 12 - c(4)^2$

$2 = 16c$

$c = \frac{1}{8}$

For $y = 0$, $12 - cx^2 = 12 - \frac{1}{8}x^2 = 0 \implies 12 = \frac{1}{8}x^2$
$\implies x = \pm\sqrt{96} = \pm 4\sqrt{6}$. The width is $8\sqrt{6}$.

35. $x = 2t, \; y = 4t$

$t = \dfrac{x}{2}$

$y = 4\left(\dfrac{x}{2}\right) = 2x$

37. $x = 1 + 4t, \; y = 2 - 3t$

$t = \dfrac{x - 1}{4}$

$y = 2 - 3\left(\dfrac{x - 1}{4}\right)$

$3x + 4y = 11$

39. $x = \dfrac{1}{t}, \; y = t^2$

$t = \dfrac{1}{x}$

$y = \dfrac{1}{x^2}$

41. $x = 6 \cos \theta$, $y = 6 \sin \theta$

$\cos \theta = \dfrac{x}{6}$, $\sin \theta = \dfrac{y}{6}$

$\dfrac{x^2}{36} + \dfrac{y^2}{36} = 1$

43. (a) $\dfrac{(x + 3)^2}{16} + \dfrac{(y - 4)^2}{9} = 1$

$x = -3 + 4 \cos \theta$

$y = 4 + 3 \sin \theta$

The solution is not unique.

(b) $\dfrac{y^2}{a^2} - \dfrac{x^2}{b^2} = 1$, $a = 4, c = 5, b = 3$

$\dfrac{y^2}{16} - \dfrac{x^2}{9} = 1$

$x = 3 \tan \theta$, $y = 4 \sec \theta$

45. $r = 3 \cos \theta$

$r^2 = 3r \cos \theta$

$x^2 + y^2 = 3x$

47. $r^2 = \cos 2\theta$

$r^2 = 1 - 2 \sin^2 \theta$

$r^4 = r^2 - 2r^2 \sin^2 \theta$

$(x^2 + y^2)^2 = x^2 + y^2 - 2y^2$

$(x^2 + y^2)^2 - x^2 + y^2 = 0$

49. $(x^2 + y^2)^2 = ax^2 y$

$(r^2)^2 = ar^2 \cos^2 \theta \, r \sin \theta$

$r = a \cos^2 \theta \sin \theta$

51. $r = 4$

Circle of radius 4 centered at the pole

53. $r = 4 \sin 2\theta$

Symmetric with respect to $\theta = \dfrac{\pi}{2}$, polar axis, and pole

Rose curve ($n = 2$) with 4 petals

55. $r = -2 - 2 \cos \theta$

Symmetric with respect to polar axis

$\dfrac{a}{b} = \dfrac{2}{2} = 1 \implies$ Cardioid

57. $r = -3 \cos 2\theta$

Rose curve

59. $r^2 = \cos 2\theta$

Leminscate

61. $r^2 = 4 \sin 2\theta \implies r = \pm 2 \sin 2\theta$

$r_1 = 2 \sin 2\theta$

$r_2 = -2 \sin 2\theta$

63. $r = 3 - 4 \cos \theta$

65. $r = \dfrac{3}{\cos(\theta - (\pi/4))}$

67. Circle symmetric to $\theta = \dfrac{\pi}{2}$

Center: $\left(5, \dfrac{\pi}{2}\right)$

Solution point:

$(0, 0) \implies$ Radius $= 5 \implies a = 10$

$r = a \sin \theta$

$r = 10 \sin \theta$

69. Parabola: $r = \dfrac{ep}{1 - e \cos \theta}, e = 1$

Vertex: $(2, \pi)$

Focus: $(0, 0) \implies p = 4$

$4 = \dfrac{4}{1 - \cos \theta}$

71. Ellipse: $r = \dfrac{ep}{1 - e \cos \theta}$

Vertices: $(5, 0), (1, \pi) \implies a = 3$

One focus: $(0, 0) \implies c = 2$

$e = \dfrac{c}{a} = \dfrac{2}{3}, \ p = \dfrac{5}{2}$

$r = \dfrac{(2/3)(5/2)}{1 - (2/3) \cos \theta} = \dfrac{5/3}{1 - (2/3) \cos \theta} = \dfrac{5}{3 - 2 \cos \theta}$

❑ Cumulative Test for Chapters 8–11

1.
$$y = 3 - x^2$$
$$2(y - 2) = x - 1$$
$$2(3 - x^2 - 2) = x - 1$$
$$-2x^2 - x + 3 = 0$$
$$2x^2 + x - 3 = 0$$
$$(2x + 3)(x - 1) = 0$$

$2x + 3 = 0 \implies x = -\frac{3}{2}, \ y = 3 - \left(-\frac{3}{2}\right)^2 = 3 - \frac{9}{4} = \frac{3}{4} : \left(-\frac{3}{2}, \frac{3}{4}\right)$

$x - 1 = 0 \implies x = 1, \quad y = 3 - 1^2 = 2 : (1, 2)$

2.
$$\begin{bmatrix} 1 & 3 & -2 & \vdots & -7 \\ -2 & 1 & -1 & \vdots & -5 \\ 4 & 1 & 1 & \vdots & 3 \end{bmatrix} \implies \begin{bmatrix} 1 & 3 & -2 & \vdots & -7 \\ 0 & 7 & -5 & \vdots & -19 \\ 0 & -11 & 9 & \vdots & 31 \end{bmatrix}$$

$$\implies \begin{bmatrix} 1 & 3 & -2 & \vdots & -7 \\ 0 & 1 & -\frac{5}{7} & \vdots & -\frac{19}{7} \\ 0 & -11 & 9 & \vdots & 31 \end{bmatrix}$$

$$\implies \begin{bmatrix} 1 & 3 & -2 & \vdots & -7 \\ 0 & 1 & -\frac{5}{7} & \vdots & -\frac{19}{7} \\ 0 & 0 & \frac{8}{7} & \vdots & \frac{8}{7} \end{bmatrix}$$

$$\implies \begin{bmatrix} 1 & 0 & 0 & \vdots & 1 \\ 0 & 1 & 0 & \vdots & -2 \\ 0 & 0 & 1 & \vdots & 1 \end{bmatrix} \implies (x, y, z) = (1, -2, 1)$$

3. $AB = \begin{bmatrix} 4 & -3 \\ 2 & 1 \\ 5 & 0 \end{bmatrix} \begin{bmatrix} 3 & -2 \\ 1 & 3 \end{bmatrix} = \begin{bmatrix} 9 & 1 \\ 7 & -7 \\ 15 & -10 \end{bmatrix}$

4. $\det(A) = \begin{vmatrix} 1 & 2 & -1 \\ 3 & 7 & -10 \\ -5 & -7 & -15 \end{vmatrix} = 1(-105 - 70) - 2(-45 - 50) - 1(-21 + 35)$

$$= -175 + 190 - 14 = 1$$

$$\begin{bmatrix} 1 & 2 & -1 \\ 3 & 7 & -10 \\ -5 & -7 & -15 \end{bmatrix}^{-1} = \begin{bmatrix} -175 & 37 & -13 \\ 95 & -20 & 7 \\ 14 & -3 & 1 \end{bmatrix}$$

5. $a_1 = 8, d = 4, c = a_1 - d = 4$ and $a_n = 4n + 4$

$a_{20} = 4(20) + 4 = 84$. Hence, $S = \frac{n}{2}(a_1 + a_n) = \frac{20}{2}(8 + 84) = 920$.

6. $\sum_{i=0}^{\infty} 3\left(\frac{1}{2}\right)^i = \frac{3}{1 - (1/2)} = 6$ 		**7.** $(z - 3)^4 = z^4 - 12z^3 + 54z^2 - 108z + 81$

8. There are 2 ways to select the first digit (4 or 5), and 2 ways for the second digit. Hence, $p = \frac{1}{4}$.

9. $y^2 = 4x - 4 = 4(x - 1)$

Vertex: $(1, 0)$

Focus: $(2, 0)$

Graph as: $y_1 = 2\sqrt{x - 1}$

$\qquad\qquad\quad y_2 = -2\sqrt{x - 1}$

10. Ellipse

Center: $(2, 0)$

Vertices: $(2, \pm 3)$

$a = 3, b = 2, c = \sqrt{9 - 4} = \sqrt{5}$

Foci: $(2, \pm\sqrt{5})$

11. $x^2 - 4x + 4 + y^2 = 4$

$\qquad (x - 2)^2 + y^2 = 4$

$\qquad \dfrac{(x - 2)^2}{4} + \dfrac{y^2}{4} = 1$

Hyperbola

Vertices: $(0, 0), (4, 0)$

Foci: $(-\sqrt{5}, 0), (2 + \sqrt{5}, 0)$

12. Center: $(0, 2)$,

Vertical axis

$\dfrac{a}{b} = \dfrac{1}{2}$

$c = 2, b^2 = c^2 - a^2 = c^2 - \left(\dfrac{b}{2}\right)^2 \implies \dfrac{5}{4}b^2 = 4 \implies b^2 = \dfrac{16}{5}$

$a^2 = \dfrac{b^2}{4} = \dfrac{4}{5}$

Thus, $\dfrac{(y - 2)^2}{4/5} - \dfrac{x^2}{16/5} = 1.$

13. $x - 2 = 3\cos\theta \implies \dfrac{x - 2}{3} = \cos\theta$

$\qquad y = 2\sin\theta \implies \dfrac{y}{2} = \sin\theta$

Ellipse: $\dfrac{(x - 2)^2}{9} + \dfrac{y^2}{4} = 1$

14. $x^2 + y^2 - 6y = 0$

$\qquad r^2 - 6r\sin\theta = 0$

$\qquad\qquad r = 6\sin\theta$

15. (a)

(b)

❏ Practice Test for Chapter 11

1. Find the vertex, focus, and directrix of the parabola $x^2 = 20y$.

2. Find the equation of the parabola with vertex $(0, 0)$ and focus $(7, 0)$.

3. Find the center, foci, and vertices of the ellipse $\dfrac{x^2}{144} + \dfrac{y^2}{25} = 1$.

4. Find the equation of the ellipse with foci $(\pm 4, 0)$ and minor axis of length 6.

5. Find the center, vertices, foci, and asymptotes of the hyperbola $\dfrac{y^2}{144} - \dfrac{x^2}{169} = 1$.

6. Find the equation of the hyperbola with vertices $(\pm 4, 0)$ and asymptotes $y = \pm\frac{1}{2}x$.

7. Find the equation of the parabola with vertex $(6, -1)$ and focus $(6, 3)$.

8. Find the center, foci, and vertices of the ellipse $16x^2 + 9y^2 - 96x + 36y + 36 = 0$.

9. Find the equation of the ellipse with vertices $(-1, 1)$ and $(7, 1)$ and minor axis of length 2.

10. Find the center, vertices, foci, and asymptotes of the hyperbola $4(x + 3)^2 - 9(y - 1)^2 = 1$.

11. Find the equation of the hyperbola with vertices $(3, 4)$ and $(3, -4)$ and foci $(3, 7)$ and $(3, -7)$.

12. Use a graphing utility to sketch the curve represented by the parametric equation.

    $x = 2t + 1$

    $y = -1 - 3t$

    Then eliminate the parameter and write the corresponding rectangular equation.

13. Use a graphing utility to sketch the curve represented by the parametric equation

    $x = 2 \ln t$

    $y = t^3$.

14. Describe how the plane curves $x = t$, $y = t^2$ and $x = t^2$, $y = t^4$ differ from each other.

15. Find the rectangular coordinates for the point $(r, \theta) = \left(-1, \dfrac{\pi}{2}\right)$.

16. Find the polar coordinates for the point $(x, y) = (-2, -2)$.

17. Convert the equation $x^2 + y^2 = 4x$ to polar form. What is the curve?

18. Sketch the graph of the polar equation $r = \cos 5\theta$ with a graphing utility. Identify the curve.

19. Sketch the graph of the polar equation $r = 2 - 3 \sin \theta$. Identify the curve.

20. Use a graphing utility to graph the polar equation

    $r = \dfrac{1}{1 + \cos \theta}$.

    Identify the conic.

❏ Chapter 1 Practice Test Solutions

1.

x-intercepts: ± 0.894

2.

No x-intercepts

3. $3x - 5y = 15$

Line

x-intercept: $(5, 0)$

y-intercept: $(0, -3)$

4. $y = \sqrt{9 - x}$

Domain: $(-\infty, 9]$

x-intercept: $(9, 0)$

y-intercept: $(0, 3)$

5. $5x + 4 = 7x - 8$

$\quad 4 + 8 = 7x - 5x$

$\quad\quad 12 = 2x$

$\quad\quad\; x = 6$

6. $\dfrac{x}{3} - 5 = \dfrac{x}{5} + 1$

$15\left(\dfrac{x}{3} - 5\right) = 15\left(\dfrac{x}{5} + 1\right)$

$\quad 5x - 75 = 3x + 15$

$\quad\quad\; 2x = 90$

$\quad\quad\;\; x = 45$

7. $\dfrac{3x + 1}{6x - 7} = \dfrac{2}{5}$

$5(3x + 1) = 2(6x - 7)$

$15x + 5 = 12x - 14$

$\quad\; 3x = -19$

$\quad\;\; x = -\dfrac{19}{3}$

8. $(x - 3)^2 + 4 = (x + 1)^2$

$x^2 - 6x + 9 + 4 = x^2 + 2x + 1$

$\quad\quad\quad\quad -8x = -12$

$\quad\quad\quad\quad\quad x = \dfrac{-12}{-8}$

$\quad\quad\quad\quad\quad x = \dfrac{3}{2}$

9. Slope $= \dfrac{-2 - (-5)}{3 - 4} = \dfrac{3}{-1} = -3$

$y + 2 = -3(x - 3)$

$y + 2 = -3x - 9$

$y + 3x = 7$ or $y = -3x + 7$

10. $y - 5 = -3(x + 1)$

$y - 5 = -3x - 3$

$y + 3x = 2$ or $y = -3x + 2$

11. No, y is not a function of x. For example, $(0, 2)$ and $(0, -2)$ both satisfy the equation.

12. $f(0) = \dfrac{|0 - 2|}{(0 - 2)} = \dfrac{2}{-2} = -1$

$f(2)$ is not defined.

$f(4) = \dfrac{|4 - 2|}{(4 - 2)} = \dfrac{2}{2} = 1$

13. The domain of

$f(x) = \dfrac{5}{x^2 - 16}$

is all $x \neq \pm 4$.

14. The domain of $g(t) = \sqrt{4 - t}$ consists of all t satisfying

$4 - t \geq 0$ or $t \leq 4$.

15.

$f(x) = 3 - x^6$
is even.

16.

Relative minimum:
$(0.577, 3.615)$

Relative maximum:
$(-0.577, 4.385)$

17. $f(x) = x^3 - 3$ is a vertical shift of 3 units downward of $y = x^3$.

18. $f(x) = \sqrt{x - 6}$ is a horizontal shift 6 units to the right of $y = \sqrt{x}$.

19. $(g \circ f)(x) = g(f(x)) = g(\sqrt{x}) = (\sqrt{x})^2 - 2 = x - 2$

Domain: $x \geq 0$

20. $\left(\dfrac{f}{g}\right)(x) = \dfrac{f(x)}{g(x)} = \dfrac{3x^2}{16 - x^4}$

The domain is all $x \neq \pm 2$.

21. $(f \circ g)(x) = f\left(\dfrac{x - 1}{3}\right) = 3\left(\dfrac{x - 1}{3}\right) + 1 = (x - 1) + 1 = x$

$(g \circ f)(x) = g(3x + 1) = \dfrac{(3x + 1) - 1}{3} = \dfrac{3x}{3} = x$

22. $y = \sqrt{9 - x^2}, \ 0 \leq x \leq 3$

$x = \sqrt{9 - y^2}$

$x^2 = 9 - y^2$

$y^2 = 9 - x^2$

$y = \sqrt{9 - x^2}$

❑ Chapter 2 Practice Test Solutions

1. $\frac{1}{2}x - \frac{1}{3}(x - 1) = 10$

$3x - 2(x - 1) = 60$

$3x - 2x + 2 = 60$

$x = 58$

2. $(x + 1)^2 - 6 = x^2 + 3x$

$x^2 + 2x + 1 - 6 = x^2 + 3x$

$2x - 5 = 3x$

$x = -5$

3. $A = \frac{1}{2}(a + b)h$

$2A = ah + bh$

$2A - bh = ah$

$\dfrac{2A - bh}{h} = a$

4. Percent $= \dfrac{301}{4300} = 0.07 = 7\%$

5. Let x = number of quarters.

Then $53 - x$ = number of nickels.

$25x + 5(53 - x) = 605$

$20x + 265 = 605$

$20x = 340$

$x = 17$ quarters

$53 - x = 36$ nickels

6. Let x = amount in $9\frac{1}{2}\%$ fund.

Then $15{,}000 - x$ = amount in 11% fund.

$0.095x + 0.11(15{,}000 - x) = 1582.50$

$-0.015x + 1650 = 1582.50$

$-0.015x = -67.5$

$x = \$4500$ at $9\frac{1}{2}\%$

$15{,}000 - x = \$10{,}500$ at 11%

7.

$(1.257,\ 0.743)$

$(-1.591,\ 3.591)$

8.

$(1.248,\ 6.117)$

9. $\dfrac{2}{1 + i} = \dfrac{2}{1 + i} \cdot \dfrac{1 - i}{1 - i} = \dfrac{2 - 2i}{1 + 1} = 1 - i$

10. $\dfrac{3 + i}{2} - \dfrac{i + 1}{4} = \dfrac{6 + 2i - i - 1}{4} = \dfrac{5}{4} + \dfrac{i}{4}$

11. $28 + 5x - 3x^2 = 0$

$(4 - x)(7 + 3x) = 0$

$4 - x = 0 \Rightarrow x = 4$

$7 + 3x = 0 \Rightarrow x = -\frac{7}{3}$

12. $(x - 2)^2 = 24$

$x - 2 = \pm\sqrt{24}$

$x - 2 = \pm 2\sqrt{6}$

$x = 2 \pm 2\sqrt{6}$

13. $x^2 - 4x - 9 = 0$

$x^2 - 4x + 2^2 = 9 + 2^2$

$(x - 2)^2 = 13$

$x - 2 = \pm\sqrt{13}$

$x = 2 \pm \sqrt{13}$

14. $x^2 + 5x - 1 = 0$

$a = 1,\ b = 5,\ c = -1$

$x = \dfrac{-5 \pm \sqrt{(5)^2 - 4(1)(-1)}}{2(1)}$

$= \dfrac{-5 \pm \sqrt{25 + 4}}{2} = \dfrac{-5 \pm \sqrt{29}}{2}$

15. $3x^2 - 2x + 4 = 0$

$a = 3, \ b = -2, \ c = 4$

$x = \dfrac{-(-2) \pm \sqrt{(-2)^2 - 4(3)(4)}}{2(3)}$

$= \dfrac{2 \pm \sqrt{4 - 48}}{6}$

$= \dfrac{2 \pm \sqrt{-44}}{6}$

$= \dfrac{2 \pm 2i\sqrt{11}}{6}$

$= \dfrac{1 \pm i\sqrt{11}}{3} = \dfrac{1}{3} \pm \dfrac{\sqrt{11}}{3}i$

16. $60{,}000 = xy$

$y = \dfrac{60{,}000}{x}$

$2x + 2y = 1100$

$2x + 2\left(\dfrac{60{,}000}{x}\right) = 1100$

$x + \dfrac{60{,}000}{x} = 550$

$x^2 + 60{,}000 = 550x$

$x^2 - 550x + 60{,}000 = 0$

$(x - 150)(x - 400) = 0$

$x = 150 \quad \text{or} \quad x = 400$

$y = 400 \qquad y = 150$

Length: 400 feet
Width: 150 feet

17. $x(x + 2) = 624$

$x^2 + 2x - 624 = 0$

$(x - 24)(x + 26) = 0$

$x = 24 \quad \text{or} \quad x = -26, \text{ (extraneous solution)}$

$x + 2 = 26$

18. $x^3 - 10x^2 + 24x = 0$

$x(x^2 - 10x + 24) = 0$

$x(x - 4)(x - 6) = 0$

$x = 0, \ x = 4, \ x = 6$

19. $\sqrt[3]{6 - x} = 4$

$6 - x = 64$

$-x = 58$

$x = -58$

20. $(x^2 - 8)^{2/5} = 4$

$x^2 - 8 = \pm 4^{5/2}$

$x^2 - 8 = 32 \quad \text{or} \quad x^2 - 8 = -32$

$x^2 = 40 \qquad\qquad x^2 = -24$

$x = \pm\sqrt{40} \qquad\quad x = \pm\sqrt{-24}$

$x = \pm 2\sqrt{10} \qquad\quad x = \pm 2\sqrt{6}\,i$

21. $x^4 - x^2 - 12 = 0$

$(x^2 - 4)(x^2 + 3) = 0$

$x^2 = 4 \quad \text{or} \quad x^2 = -3$

$x^2 = \pm 2 \qquad x = \pm\sqrt{3}\,i$

22. $4 - 3x > 16$

$-3x > 12$

$x < -4$

23. $\left|\dfrac{x - 3}{2}\right| < 5$

$-5 < \dfrac{x - 3}{2} < 5$

$-10 < x - 3 < 10$

$-7 < x < 13$

24.
$$\frac{x+1}{x-3} < 2$$

$$\frac{x+1}{x-3} - 2 < 0$$

$$\frac{x+1-2(x-3)}{x-3} < 0$$

$$\frac{7-x}{x-3} < 0$$

Critical numbers: $x = 7$ and $x = 3$
Test intervals: $(-\infty, 3), (3, 7), (7, \infty)$
Solution intervals: $(-\infty, 3) \cup (7, \infty)$

26. $y = 0.882 + 0.912x$

25. $|3x - 4| \geq 9$

$$3x - 4 \leq -9 \quad \text{or} \quad 3x - 4 \geq 9$$

$$3x \leq -5 \qquad\qquad 3x \geq 13$$

$$x \leq -\frac{5}{3} \qquad\qquad x \geq \frac{13}{3}$$

❑ Chapter 3 Practice Test Solutions

1. x-intercepts: $(1, 0), (5, 0)$
y-intercept: $(0, 5)$
Vertex: $(3, -4)$

2. $a = 0.01, b = -90$

$$\frac{-b}{2a} = \frac{90}{2(.01)} = 4500 \text{ units}$$

3. Vertex: $(1, 7)$
Opening downward through $(2, 5)$

$$y = a(x - 1)^2 + 7 \quad \text{Standard form}$$

$$5 = a(2 - 1)^2 + 7$$

$$5 = a + 7$$

$$a = -2$$

$$y = -2(x - 1)^2 + 7$$

$$= -2(x^2 - 2x + 1) + 7$$

$$= -2x^2 + 4x + 5$$

4. $y = \pm a(x - 2)(3x - 4)$ where a is any real
number

$$y = \pm(3x^2 - 10x + 8)$$

5. Leading coefficient: -3
Degree: 5
Moves down to the right and up to the left.

6. $0 = x^5 - 5x^3 + 4x$

$\quad = x(x^4 - 5x^2 + 4)$

$\quad = x(x^2 - 1)(x^2 - 4)$

$\quad = x(x + 1)(x - 1)(x + 2)(x - 2)$

$x = 0, x = \pm 1, x = \pm 2$

7. $f(x) = x(x - 3)(x + 2)$

$\quad = x(x^2 - x - 6)$

$\quad = x^3 - x^2 - 6x$

8. Intercepts: $(0, 0), \left(\pm 2\sqrt{3}, 0\right)$

Moves up to the right.

Moves down to the left.

x	-2	-1	0	1	2
y	16	11	0	-11	-16

9.

$$3x^3 + 9x^2 + 20x + 62 + \frac{176}{x - 3}$$

$$x - 3 \overline{)3x^4 + 0x^3 - 7x^2 + 2x - 10}$$

$$\underline{3x^4 - 9x^3}$$

$$9x^3 - 7x^2$$

$$\underline{9x^3 - 27x^2}$$

$$20x^2 + 2x$$

$$\underline{20x^2 - 60x}$$

$$62x - 10$$

$$\underline{62x - 186}$$

$$176$$

10.

$$x - 2 + \frac{5x - 13}{x^2 + 2x - 1}$$

$$x^2 + 2x - 1 \overline{)x^3 + 0x^2 + 0x - 11}$$

$$\underline{x^3 + 2x^2 - x}$$

$$-2x^2 + x - 11$$

$$\underline{-2x^2 - 4x + 2}$$

$$5x - 13$$

11.

$$-5 \enspace | \quad 3 \quad 13 \quad 0 \quad 0 \quad 12 \quad -1$$

$$\underline{\quad\quad -15 \quad 10 \quad -50 \quad 250 \quad -1310}$$

$$\quad\quad 3 \quad -2 \quad 10 \quad -50 \quad 262 \quad -1311$$

$$\frac{3x^5 + 13x^4 + 12x - 1}{x + 5} = 3x^4 - 2x^3 + 10x^2 - 50x + 262 - \frac{1311}{x + 5}$$

12.

$$-6 \enspace | \quad 7 \quad 40 \quad -12 \quad 15$$

$$\underline{\quad\quad -42 \quad 12 \quad 0}$$

$$\quad\quad 7 \quad -2 \quad 0 \quad 15$$

$f(-6) = 15$

13. $0 = x^3 - 19x - 30$

Possible rational roots:

$\pm 1, \pm 2, \pm 3, \pm 5, \pm 6, \pm 10, \pm 15, \pm 30$

$$-2 \enspace | \quad 1 \quad 0 \quad -19 \quad -30$$

$$\underline{\quad\quad\quad -2 \quad 4 \quad 30}$$

$$\quad\quad 1 \quad -2 \quad -15 \quad 0 \qquad -2 \text{ is a zero.}$$

$0 = (x + 2)(x^2 - 2x - 15)$

$0 = (x + 2)(x + 3)(x - 5)$

Zeros: $x = -2, x = -3, x = 5$

14. $0 = x^4 + x^3 - 8x^2 - 9x - 9$

Possible rational roots: $\pm 1,\ \pm 3,\ \pm 9$

$$
\begin{array}{r|rrrrr}
3 & 1 & 1 & -8 & -9 & -9 \\
  &   & 3 & 12 & 12 & 9 \\
\hline
  & 1 & 4 & 4 & 3 & 0
\end{array}
\qquad x = 3 \text{ is a zero.}
$$

$0 = (x - 3)(x^3 + 4x^2 + 4x + 3)$

Possible rational roots of $x^3 + 4x^2 + 4x + 3$: $\pm 1, \pm 3$

$$
\begin{array}{r|rrrr}
-3 & 1 & 4 & 4 & 3 \\
   &   & -3 & -3 & -3 \\
\hline
   & 1 & 1 & 1 & 0
\end{array}
\qquad x = -3 \text{ is a zero.}
$$

$0 = (x - 3)(x + 3)(x^2 + x + 1)$

The zeros of $x^2 + x + 1$ are $x = \dfrac{-1 \pm \sqrt{3}\,i}{2}$.

Zeros: $x = 3, x = -3, x = -\dfrac{1}{2} + \dfrac{\sqrt{3}}{2}i, x = -\dfrac{1}{2} - \dfrac{\sqrt{3}}{2}i$

15. $0 = 6x^3 - 5x^2 + 4x - 15$

Possible rational roots: $\pm 1,\ \pm 3,\ \pm 5,\ \pm 15,\ \pm \frac{1}{2},\ \pm \frac{3}{2},\ \pm \frac{5}{2},\ \pm \frac{15}{2},\ \pm \frac{1}{3},\ \pm \frac{5}{3},\ \pm \frac{1}{6},\ \pm \frac{5}{6}$

16. $0 = x^3 - \frac{20}{3}x^2 + 9x - \frac{10}{3}$

$0 = 3x^3 - 20x^2 + 27x - 10$

Possible rational roots: $\pm 1,\ \pm 2,\ \pm 5,\ \pm 10,\ \pm \frac{1}{3},\ \pm \frac{2}{3},\ \pm \frac{5}{3},\ \pm \frac{10}{3}$

$$
\begin{array}{r|rrrr}
1 & 3 & -20 & 27 & -10 \\
  &   & 3 & -17 & 10 \\
\hline
  & 3 & -17 & 10 & 0
\end{array}
$$

$0 = (x - 1)(3x^2 - 17x + 10)$

$0 = (x - 1)(3x - 2)(x - 5)$

Zeros: $x = 1, x = \frac{2}{3}, x = 5$

17. Possible Rational Roots: $\pm 1,\ \pm 2,\ \pm 5,\ \pm 10$

$$
\begin{array}{r|rrrrr}
1 & 1 & 1 & 3 & 5 & -10 \\
  &   & 1 & 2 & 5 & 10 \\
\hline
  & 1 & 2 & 5 & 10 & 0
\end{array}
\qquad x = 1 \text{ is a zero.}
$$

$$
\begin{array}{r|rrrr}
-2 & 1 & 2 & 5 & 10 \\
   &   & -2 & 0 & -10 \\
\hline
   & 1 & 0 & 5 & 0
\end{array}
\qquad x = -2 \text{ is a zero.}
$$

$f(x) = (x - 1)(x + 2)(x^2 + 5)$

$\quad = (x - 1)(x + 2)(x + 5i)(x - 5i)$

18. $f(x) = (x - 2)[x - (3 + i)][x - (3 - i)]$

$\qquad = (x - 2)[x^2 - x(3 - i) - x(3 + i) + (3 + i)(3 - i)]$

$\qquad = (x - 2)[x^2 - 6x + 10]$

$\qquad = x^3 - 8x^2 + 22x - 20$

19. 3i

$$\begin{array}{r|rrrr} 3i & 1 & 4 & 9 & 36 \\ & & 3i & 12i - 9 & -36 \\ \hline & 1 & 4 + 3i & 12i & 0 \end{array}$$

20. $z = \dfrac{kx^2}{\sqrt{y}}$

21. Vertical asymptote: $x = 0$

Horizontal asymptote: $y = \frac{1}{2}$

x-intercept: $(1, 0)$

22. Vertical asymptote: $x = 0$

Horizontal asymptote: $y = 3x$

x-intercept: $\left(\pm\dfrac{2}{\sqrt{3}}, 0\right)$

23. $y = 8$ is a horizontal asymptote since the degree on the numerator equals the degree of the denominator. There are no vertical asymptotes.

24. $x = 1$ is a vertical asymptote.

$$\frac{4x^2 - 2x + 7}{x - 1} = 4x + 2 + \frac{9}{x - 1}$$

so $y = 4x + 2$ is a slant asymptote.

25. $f(x) = \dfrac{x - 5}{(x - 5)^2} = \dfrac{1}{x - 5}$

Vertical asymptote: $x = 5$

Horizontal asymptote: $y = 0$

y-intercept: $\left(0, -\dfrac{1}{5}\right)$

❏ Chapter 4 Practice Test Solutions

1. $x^{3/5} = 8$

$\qquad x = 8^{5/3} = \left(\sqrt[3]{8}\right)^5 = 2^5 = 32$

2. $3^{x-1} = \frac{1}{81}$

$\qquad 3^{x-1} = 3^{-4}$

$\qquad x - 1 = -4$

$\qquad x = -3$

3. $f(x) = 2^{-x} = \left(\frac{1}{2}\right)^x$

x	-2	-1	0	1	2
$f(x)$	4	2	1	$\frac{1}{2}$	$\frac{1}{4}$

4. $g(x) = e^x + 1$

x	-2	-1	0	1	2
$g(x)$	1.14	1.37	2	3.72	8.39

5. $A = P\left(1 + \dfrac{r}{n}\right)^{nt}$

(a) $A = 5000\left(1 + \dfrac{0.09}{12}\right)^{12(3)} \approx \$6543.23$

(b) $A = 5000\left(1 + \dfrac{0.09}{4}\right)^{4(3)} \approx \$6530.25$

(c) $A = 5000e^{(0.09)(3)} \approx \$6549.82$

6. $7^{-2} = \dfrac{1}{49}$

$\log_7 \dfrac{1}{49} = -2$

7. $x = 4 = \log_2 \frac{1}{64}$

$\quad 2^{x-4} = \frac{1}{64}$

$\quad 2^{x-4} = 2^{-6}$

$\quad x - 4 = -6$

$\qquad x = -2$

8. $\log \sqrt[4]{\frac{8}{25}} = \frac{1}{4} \log_b \frac{8}{25}$

$\qquad = \frac{1}{4}[\log_b 8 - \log_b 25]$

$\qquad = \frac{1}{4}[\log_b 2^3 - \log_b 5^2]$

$\qquad = \frac{1}{4}[3 \log_b 2 - 2 \log_b 5]$

$\qquad = \frac{1}{4}[3(0.3562) - 2(0.8271)]$

$\qquad = -0.1464$

9. $5 \ln x - \dfrac{1}{2} \ln y + 6 \ln z = \ln x^5 - \ln \sqrt{y} + \ln z^6 = \ln\left(\dfrac{x^5 z^6}{\sqrt{y}}\right)$

10. $\log_9 28 = \dfrac{\log 28}{\log 9} \approx 1.5166$

11. $\log N = 0.6646$

$\quad N = 10^{0.6646} \approx 4.62$

12.

13. Domain:

$$x^2 - 9 > 0$$

$$(x + 3)(x - 3) > 0$$

$$x < -3 \text{ or } x > 3$$

14.

15. $\dfrac{\ln x}{\ln y} \neq \ln(x - y)$ since $\dfrac{\ln x}{\ln y} = \log_y x$.

16. $5^3 = 41$

$$x = \log_5 41 = \frac{\ln 41}{\ln 5} \approx 2.3074$$

17. $x - x^2 = \log_5 \frac{1}{25}$

$\quad 5^{x-x^2} = \frac{1}{25}$

$\quad 5^{x-x^2} = 5^{-2}$

$\quad x - x^2 = -2$

$\qquad 0 = x^2 - x - 2$

$\qquad 0 = (x + 1)(x - 2)$

$\qquad x = -1 \text{ or } x = 2$

18. $\log_2 x + \log_2(x - 3) = 2$

$\quad \log_2[x(x - 3)] = 2$

$\qquad x(x - 3) = 2^2$

$\qquad x^2 - 3x = 4$

$\qquad x^2 - 3x - 4 = 0$

$\quad (x + 1)(x - 4) = 0$

$\qquad\qquad x = 4$

$\qquad\qquad x = -1$

No solution (extraneous solution)

19. $\qquad \dfrac{e^x + e^{-x}}{3} = 4$

$\quad e^x(e^x + e^{-x}) = 12e^x$

$\qquad e^{2x} + 1 = 12e^x$

$\quad e^{2x} - 12e^x + 1 = 0$

$$e^x = \frac{12 \pm \sqrt{144 - 4}}{2}$$

$e^x = 11.9161 \qquad$ or $\qquad e^x = 0.0839$

$x = \ln 11.9161 \qquad\qquad\quad x = \ln 0.0839$

$x \approx 2.4779 \qquad\qquad\qquad x \approx -2.4779$

20. $\qquad A = Pe^{et}$

$\quad 12{,}000 = 6000e^{0.13t}$

$\qquad\quad 2 = e^{0.13t}$

$\quad 0.13t = \ln 2$

$\qquad\quad t = \dfrac{\ln 2}{0.13}$

$\qquad\quad t \approx 5.3319 \text{ yr or 5 yr 4 mo}$

21. There are 2 points of intersection:

(0.0169, −2.983),

(1.731, 1.647)

22. $y = 1.0597x^{1.9792}$

❑ Chapter 5 Practice Test Solutions

1. $350° = 350\left(\dfrac{\pi}{180}\right) = \dfrac{35\pi}{18}$

2. $\dfrac{5\pi}{9} = \dfrac{5\pi}{9} \cdot \dfrac{180}{\pi} = 100°$

3. $135° \, 14' \, 12'' = \left(135 + \dfrac{14}{60} + \dfrac{12}{3600}\right)°$

$\qquad\qquad \approx 135.2367°$

4. $-22.569° = -(22° + 0.569(60)')$

$\qquad\qquad = -22° \, 34.14'$

$\qquad\qquad = -(22° \, 34' + 0.14(60)'')$

$\qquad\qquad \approx -22° \, 34' \, 8''$

5. $\cos\theta = \dfrac{2}{3}$

$x = 2, \ r = 3, \ y = \pm\sqrt{9 - 4} = \pm\sqrt{5}$

$\tan\theta = \dfrac{y}{x} = \pm\dfrac{\sqrt{5}}{2}$

6. $\sin\theta = 0.9063$

$\theta = \arcsin(0.9063)$

$\theta = 65° \text{ or } \dfrac{13\pi}{36}$

7. $\tan 20° = \dfrac{35}{x}$

$x = \dfrac{35}{\tan 20°} \approx 96.1617$

8. $\theta = \dfrac{6\pi}{5}$, θ is in Quadrant III.

Reference angle: $\dfrac{6\pi}{5} - \pi = \dfrac{\pi}{5}$ or $36°$

9. $\csc 3.92 = \dfrac{1}{\sin 3.92} \approx -1.4242$

10. $\tan\theta = 6 = \dfrac{6}{1}$, θ lies in Quadrant III.

$y = -6, \ x = -1, \ r = \sqrt{36 + 1} = \sqrt{37}$,

so $\sec\theta = \dfrac{\sqrt{37}}{-1} \approx -6.0828.$

11. Period: 4π

Amplitude: 3

12. Period: 2π

Amplitude: 2

13. Period: $\dfrac{\pi}{2}$

14. Period: 2π

15.

16.

17. $\theta = \arcsin 1$

$\sin\theta = 1$

$\theta = \dfrac{\pi}{2}$

18. $\theta = \arctan(-3)$

$\tan\theta = -3$

$\theta \approx -1.249 \text{ or } -71.565°$

19. $\sin\left(\arccos\dfrac{4}{\sqrt{35}}\right)$

$\sin\theta = \dfrac{\sqrt{19}}{\sqrt{35}} \approx 0.7368$

$\sqrt{35}$ $x = \sqrt{35 - 16}$
$= \sqrt{19}$

θ

4

20. $\cos\left(\arcsin\dfrac{x}{4}\right)$

$\cos\theta = \dfrac{\sqrt{16 - x^2}}{4}$

4 x

θ

$\sqrt{16 - x^2}$

21. Given $A = 40°$, $c = 12$

$B = 90° - 40° = 50°$

$\sin 40° = \dfrac{a}{12}$

$a = 12\sin 40° \approx 7.713$

$\cos 40° = \dfrac{b}{12}$

$b = 12\cos 40° \approx 9.193$

22. Given $B = 6.84°$, $a = 21.3$

$A = 90° - 6.84° = 83.16°$

$\sin 83.16° = \dfrac{21.3}{c}$

$c = \dfrac{21.3}{\sin 83.16°} \approx 21.453$

$\tan 83.16° = \dfrac{21.3}{b}$

$b = \dfrac{21.3}{\tan 83.16°} \approx 2.555$

23. Given $a = 5$, $b = 9$

$c = \sqrt{25 + 81} = \sqrt{106}$

≈ 10.296

$\tan A = \dfrac{5}{9}$

$A = \arctan\dfrac{5}{9} \approx 29.055°$

$B = 90° - 29.055° = 60.945°$

24. $\sin 67° = \dfrac{x}{20}$

$x = 20\sin 67° \approx 18.41$ feet

x 20

$67°$

25. $\tan 5° = \dfrac{250}{x}$

$x = \dfrac{250}{\tan 5°}$

≈ 2857.513 feet

≈ 0.541 mi

250 ft $5°$ x $5°$

❑ Chapter 6 Practice Test Solutions

1. $\tan x = \dfrac{4}{11}$, $\sec x < 0 \implies x$ is in Quadrant III.

$y = -4$, $x = -11$, $r = \sqrt{16 + 121} = \sqrt{137}$

$\sin x = -\dfrac{4}{\sqrt{137}} = -\dfrac{4\sqrt{137}}{137}$ $\qquad$ $\csc x = -\dfrac{\sqrt{137}}{4}$

$\cos x = -\dfrac{11}{\sqrt{137}} = -\dfrac{11\sqrt{137}}{137}$ $\qquad$ $\sec x = -\dfrac{\sqrt{137}}{11}$

$\tan x = \dfrac{4}{11}$ $\qquad$ $\cot x = \dfrac{11}{4}$

2. $\dfrac{\sec^2 x + \csc^2 x}{\csc^2 x(1 + \tan^2 x)} = \dfrac{\sec^2 x + \csc^2 x}{\csc^2 x + (\csc^2 x)\tan^2 x} = \dfrac{\sec^2 x + \csc^2 x}{\csc^2 x + \dfrac{1}{\sin^2 x} \cdot \dfrac{\sin^2 x}{\cos^2 x}}$

$$= \dfrac{\sec^2 x + \csc^2 x}{\csc^2 x + \dfrac{1}{\cos^2 x}} = \dfrac{\sec^2 x + \csc^2 x}{\csc^2 x + \sec^2 x} = 1$$

3. $\ln|\tan \theta| - \ln|\cot \theta| = \ln\left|\dfrac{\tan \theta}{\cot \theta}\right| = \ln\left|\dfrac{\sin \theta/\cos \theta}{\cos \theta/\sin \theta}\right| = \ln\left|\dfrac{\sin^2 \theta}{\cos^2 \theta}\right| = \ln|\tan^2 \theta| = 2 \ln|\tan \theta|$

4. $\cos\left(\dfrac{\pi}{2} - x\right) = \dfrac{1}{\csc x}$ is true since $\cos\left(\dfrac{\pi}{2} - x\right) = \sin x = \dfrac{1}{\csc x}$.

5. $\sin^4 x + (\sin^2 x) \cos^2 x = \sin^2 x(\sin^2 x + \cos^2 x) = \sin^2 x(1) = \sin^2 x$

6. $(\csc x + 1)(\csc x - 1) = \csc^2 x - 1 = \cot^2 x$

7. $\dfrac{\cos^2 x}{1 - \sin x} \cdot \dfrac{1 + \sin x}{1 + \sin x} = \dfrac{\cos^2 x(1 + \sin x)}{1 - \sin^2 x} = \dfrac{\cos^2 x(1 + \sin x)}{\cos^2 x} = 1 + \sin x$

8. $\dfrac{1 + \cos \theta}{\sin \theta} + \dfrac{\sin \theta}{1 + \cos \theta} = \dfrac{(1 + \cos \theta)^2 + \sin^2 \theta}{\sin \theta(1 + \cos \theta)}$

$$= \dfrac{1 + 2 \cos \theta + \cos^2 \theta + \sin^2 \theta}{\sin \theta(1 + \cos \theta)} = \dfrac{2 + 2 \cos \theta}{\sin \theta(1 + \cos \theta)} = \dfrac{2}{\sin \theta} = 2 \csc \theta$$

9. $\tan^4 x + 2 \tan^2 x + 1 = (\tan^2 x + 1)^2 = (\sec^2 x)^2 = \sec^2 x) = \sec^4 x$

10. (a) $\sin 105° = \sin(60° + 45°) = \sin 60° \cos 45° + \cos 60° \sin 45°$

$$= \dfrac{\sqrt{3}}{2} \cdot \dfrac{\sqrt{2}}{2} + \dfrac{1}{2} \cdot \dfrac{\sqrt{2}}{2} = \dfrac{\sqrt{2}}{4}\left(\sqrt{3} + 1\right)$$

   (b) $\tan 15° = \tan(60° - 45°) = \dfrac{\tan 60° - \tan 45°}{1 + \tan 60° \tan 45°}$

$$= \dfrac{\sqrt{3} - 1}{1 + \sqrt{3}} \cdot \dfrac{1 - \sqrt{3}}{1 - \sqrt{3}} = \dfrac{2\sqrt{3} - 1 - 3}{1 - 3} = \dfrac{2\sqrt{3} - 4}{-2} = 2 - \sqrt{3}$$

11. $(\sin 42°) \cos 38° - (\cos 42°) \sin 38° = \sin(42° - 38°) = \sin 4°$

12. $\tan\left(\theta + \dfrac{\pi}{4}\right) = \dfrac{\tan \theta + \tan(\pi/4)}{1 - (\tan \theta) \tan(\pi/4)} = \dfrac{\tan \theta + 1}{1 - \tan \theta(1)} = \dfrac{1 + \tan \theta}{1 - \tan \theta}$

13. $\sin(\arcsin x - \arccos x) = \sin(\arcsin x) \cos(\arccos x) - \cos(\arcsin x) \sin(\arccos x)$

$$= (x)(x) - \left(\sqrt{1 - x^2}\right)\left(\sqrt{1 - x^2}\right) = x^2 - (1 - x^2) = 2x^2 - 1$$

14. (a) $\cos(120°) = \cos[2(60°)] = 2 \cos^2 60° - 1 = 2\left(\dfrac{1}{2}\right)^2 - 1 = -\dfrac{1}{2}$

   (b) $\tan(300°) = \tan[2(150°)] = \dfrac{2 \tan 150°}{1 - \tan^2 150°} = \dfrac{-2\sqrt{3}/3}{1 - (1/3)} = -\sqrt{3}$

15. (a) $\sin 22.5° = \sin \dfrac{45°}{2} = \sqrt{\dfrac{1 - \cos 45°}{2}} = \sqrt{\dfrac{1 - \sqrt{2}/2}{2}} = \dfrac{\sqrt{2 - \sqrt{2}}}{2}$

(b) $\tan \dfrac{\pi}{12} = \tan \dfrac{\pi/6}{2} = \dfrac{\sin(\pi/6)}{1 + \cos(\pi/6)} = \dfrac{1/2}{1 + \sqrt{3}/2} = \dfrac{1}{2 + \sqrt{3}} = 2 - \sqrt{3}$

16. $\sin \theta = \dfrac{4}{5}$, θ lies in Quadrant II $\Rightarrow$ $\cos \theta = -\dfrac{3}{5}$.

$$\cos \dfrac{\theta}{2} = \sqrt{\dfrac{1 + \cos \theta}{2}} = \sqrt{\dfrac{1 - 3/5}{2}} = \sqrt{\dfrac{2}{10}} = \dfrac{1}{\sqrt{5}} = \dfrac{\sqrt{5}}{5}$$

17. $(\sin^2 x) \cos^2 x = \dfrac{1 - \cos^2 x}{2} \cdot \dfrac{1 + \cos^2 x}{2} = \dfrac{1}{4}[1 - \cos^2 2x] = \dfrac{1}{4}\left[1 - \dfrac{1 + \cos 4x}{2}\right]$

$$= \dfrac{1}{8}[2 - (1 + \cos 4x)] = \dfrac{1}{8}[1 - \cos 4x]$$

18. $6(\sin 5\theta) \cos 2\theta = 6\{\tfrac{1}{2}[\sin(5\theta + 2\theta) + \sin(5\theta - 2\theta)]\} = 3[\sin 7\theta + \sin 3\theta]$

19. $\sin(x + \pi) + \sin(x - \pi) = 2\left(\sin \dfrac{[(x + \pi) + (x - \pi)]}{2}\right) \cos \dfrac{[(x + \pi) - (x - \pi)]}{2}$

20. $\dfrac{\sin 9x + \sin 5x}{\cos 9x - \cos 5x} = \dfrac{2 \sin 7x \cos 2x}{-2 \sin 7x \sin 2x} = -\dfrac{\cos 2x}{\sin 2x} = -\cot 2x$

21. $\tfrac{1}{2}[\sin(u + v) - \sin(u - v)] = \tfrac{1}{2}\{(\sin u) \cos v + (\cos u) \sin v - [(\sin u) \cos v - (\cos u) \sin v]\}$

$$= \tfrac{1}{2}[2(\cos u) \sin v] = (\cos u) \sin v$$

22. $4 \sin^2 x = 1$

$\sin^2 x = \dfrac{1}{4}$

$\sin x = \pm \dfrac{1}{2}$

$\sin x = \dfrac{1}{2}$ or $\sin x = -\dfrac{1}{2}$

$x = \dfrac{\pi}{6}$ or $\dfrac{5\pi}{6}$ $x = \dfrac{7\pi}{6}$ or $\dfrac{11\pi}{6}$

23. $\tan^2 \theta + (\sqrt{3} - 1) \tan \theta - \sqrt{3} = 0$

$(\tan \theta - 1)(\tan \theta + \sqrt{3}) = 0$

$\tan \theta = 1$ or $\tan \theta = -\sqrt{3}$

$\theta = \dfrac{\pi}{4}$ or $\dfrac{5\pi}{4}$ $\theta = \dfrac{2\pi}{3}$ or $\dfrac{5\pi}{3}$

24. $\sin 2x = \cos x$

$2(\sin x) \cos x - \cos x = 0$

$\cos x(2 \sin x - 1) = 0$

$\cos x = 0$ or $\sin x = \dfrac{1}{2}$

$x = \dfrac{\pi}{2}$ or $\dfrac{3\pi}{2}$ $x = \dfrac{\pi}{6}$ or $\dfrac{5\pi}{6}$

25. $\tan^2 x - 6 \tan x + 4 = 0$

$$\tan x = \frac{-(-6) \pm \sqrt{(-6)^2 - 4(1)(4)}}{2(1)}$$

$$\tan x = \frac{6 \pm \sqrt{20}}{2} = 3 \pm \sqrt{5}$$

$$\tan x = 3 + \sqrt{5} \qquad \text{or} \quad \tan x = 3 - \sqrt{5}$$

$$x \approx 1.3821 \text{ or } 4.5237 \qquad x = 0.6524 \text{ or } 3.7940$$

❑ Chapter 7 Practice Test Solutions

1. $C = 180° - (40° + 12°) = 128°$

$$a = \sin 40°\left(\frac{100}{\sin 12°}\right) \approx 309.164$$

$$c = \sin 128°\left(\frac{100}{\sin 12°}\right) \approx 379.012$$

2. $\sin A = 5\left(\dfrac{\sin 150°}{20}\right) = 0.125$

$$A \approx 7.181°$$

$$B \approx 180° - (150° + 7.181°) = 22.819°$$

$$b = \sin 22.819°\left(\frac{20}{\sin 150°}\right) \approx 15.513$$

3. Area $= \frac{1}{2}ab \sin C$

$$= \frac{1}{2}(3)(5) \sin 130°$$

$$\approx 5.745 \text{ square units}$$

4. $h = b \sin A$

$$= 35 \sin 22.5°$$

$$\approx 13.394$$

$$a = 10$$

Since $a < h$ and A is acute, the triangle has no solution.

5. $\cos A = \dfrac{(53)^2 + (38)^2 - (49)^2}{2(53)(38)} \approx 0.4598$

$$A \approx 62.627°$$

$$\cos B = \frac{(49)^2 + (38)^2 - (53)^2}{2(49)(38)} \approx 0.2782$$

$$B \approx 73.847°$$

$$C \approx 180° - (42.627° + 73.847°)$$

$$= 43.526°$$

6. $c^2 = (100)^2 + (300)^2 - 2(100)(300) \cos 29°$

$$\approx 47,522.8176$$

$$c \approx 218$$

$$\cos A = \frac{(300)^2 + (218)^2 - (100)^2}{2(300)(218)} \approx 0.97495$$

$$A \approx 12.85°$$

$$B \approx 180° - (12.85° + 29°) = 138.15°$$

7. $s = \dfrac{a + b + c}{2} = \dfrac{4.1 + 6.8 + 5.5}{2} = 8.2$

Area $= \sqrt{s(s - a)(s - b)(s - c)}$

$$= \sqrt{8.2(8.2 - 4.1)(8.2 - 6.8)(8.2 - 5.5)}$$

$$= 11.273 \text{ square units}$$

8. $x^2 = (40)^2 + (70)^2 - 2(40)(70) \cos 168°$

$$\approx 11,977.6266$$

$$x \approx 190.442 \text{ miles}$$

9. $\mathbf{w} = 4(3\mathbf{i} + \mathbf{j}) - 7(-\mathbf{i} + 2\mathbf{j})$

$$= 19\mathbf{i} - 10\mathbf{j}$$

10. $\dfrac{\mathbf{v}}{\|\mathbf{v}\|} = \dfrac{5\mathbf{i} + 3\mathbf{j}}{\sqrt{25 + 9}} = \dfrac{5}{\sqrt{34}}\mathbf{i} - \dfrac{3}{\sqrt{34}}\mathbf{j}$

$$= \frac{5\sqrt{34}}{34}\mathbf{i} - \frac{3\sqrt{34}}{34}\mathbf{j}$$

11. $\quad \mathbf{u} = 6\mathbf{i} + 5\mathbf{j} \qquad \mathbf{v} = 2\mathbf{i} - 3\mathbf{j}$

$\quad \mathbf{u} \cdot \mathbf{v} = 6(2) + 5(-3) = -3$

$\quad \|\mathbf{u}\| = \sqrt{61} \qquad \|\mathbf{v}\| = \sqrt{13}$

$\quad \cos \theta = \dfrac{-3}{\sqrt{61}\sqrt{13}}$

$\quad \theta \approx 96.116°$

12. $4(\mathbf{i} \cos 30° + \mathbf{j} \sin 30°) = 4\left(\dfrac{\sqrt{3}}{2}\mathbf{i} + \dfrac{1}{2}\mathbf{j}\right)$

$\qquad\qquad\qquad\qquad\qquad = \langle 4\sqrt{3}, 2\rangle$

13. $\operatorname{proj}_{\mathbf{v}}\mathbf{u} = \left(\dfrac{\mathbf{u} \cdot \mathbf{v}}{\|\mathbf{v}\|^2}\right)\mathbf{v} = \dfrac{-10}{20}\langle -2, 4\rangle = \langle 1, -2\rangle$

14. $\quad r = \sqrt{25 + 25} = \sqrt{50} = 5\sqrt{2}$

$\quad \tan \theta = \dfrac{-5}{5} = -1$

Since z is in Quadrant IV,

$\theta = 315°$

$z = 5\sqrt{2}(\cos 315° + i \sin 315°).$

15. $\cos 225° = -\dfrac{\sqrt{2}}{2} \quad \sin 225° = -\dfrac{\sqrt{2}}{2}$

$\qquad z = 6\left(-\dfrac{\sqrt{2}}{2} - i\dfrac{\sqrt{2}}{2}\right)$

$\qquad\quad = -3\sqrt{2} - 3\sqrt{2}i$

16. $[7(\cos 23° + i \sin 23°)][4(\cos 7° + i \sin 7°)] = 7(4)[\cos(23° + 7°) + i \sin(23° + 7°)]$

$\qquad\qquad\qquad\qquad\qquad\qquad\qquad\qquad\qquad = 28(\cos 30° + i \sin 30°)$

17. $\dfrac{9\left(\cos \dfrac{5\pi}{4} + i \sin \dfrac{5\pi}{4}\right)}{3(\cos \pi + i \sin \pi)} = \dfrac{9}{3}\left[\cos\left(\dfrac{5\pi}{4} - \pi\right) + i \sin\left(\dfrac{5\pi}{4} - \pi\right)\right] = 3\left(\cos \dfrac{\pi}{4} + i \sin \dfrac{\pi}{4}\right)$

18. $(2 + 2i)^8 = [2\sqrt{2}(\cos 45° + i \sin 45°)]^8 = \left(2\sqrt{2}\right)^8[\cos(8)(45°) + i \sin (8)(45°)]$

$\qquad\qquad\quad = 4096[\cos 360° + i \sin 360°] = 4096$

19. $z = 8\left(\cos \dfrac{\pi}{3} + i \sin \dfrac{\pi}{3}\right), \; n = 3$

The cube roots of z are:

For $k = 0$, $\sqrt[3]{8}\left[\cos \dfrac{\pi/3}{3} + i \sin \dfrac{\pi/3}{3}\right] = 2\left(\cos \dfrac{\pi}{9} + i \sin \dfrac{\pi}{9}\right).$

For $k = 1$, $\sqrt[3]{8}\left[\cos \dfrac{\pi/3 + 2\pi}{3} + i \sin \dfrac{\pi/3 + 2\pi}{3}\right] = 2\left(\cos \dfrac{7\pi}{9} + i \sin \dfrac{7\pi}{9}\right).$

For $k = 2$, $\sqrt[3]{8}\left[\cos \dfrac{\pi/3 + 4\pi}{3} + i \sin \dfrac{\pi/3 + 4\pi}{3}\right] = 2\left(\cos \dfrac{13\pi}{9} + i \sin \dfrac{13\pi}{9}\right).$

20. $x^4 = -i = 1\left(\cos\dfrac{3\pi}{2} + i \sin\dfrac{3\pi}{2}\right)$

For $k = 0$, $\cos\dfrac{3\pi/2}{4} + i \sin\dfrac{3\pi/2}{4} = \cos\dfrac{3\pi}{8} + i \sin\dfrac{3\pi}{8}$.

For $k = 1$, $\cos\dfrac{3\pi/2 + 2\pi}{4} + i \sin\dfrac{3\pi/2 + 2\pi}{4} = \cos\dfrac{7\pi}{8} + i \sin\dfrac{7\pi}{8}$.

For $k = 2$, $\cos\dfrac{3\pi/2 + 4\pi}{4} + i \sin\dfrac{3\pi/2 + 4\pi}{4} = \cos\dfrac{11\pi}{8} + i \sin\dfrac{11\pi}{8}$.

For $k = 3$, $\cos\dfrac{3\pi/2 + 6\pi}{4} + i \sin\dfrac{3\pi/2 + 6\pi}{4} = \cos\dfrac{15\pi}{8} + i \sin\dfrac{15\pi}{8}$.

❏ Chapter 8 Practice Test Solutions

1.
$$x + y = 1$$
$$3x - y = 15 \implies y = 3x - 15$$
$$x + (3x - 15) = 1$$
$$4x = 16$$
$$x = 4$$
$$y = -3$$

2.
$$x - 3y = -3 \implies x = 3y - 3$$
$$x^2 + 5y = 5$$
$$(3y - 3)^2 + 6y = 5$$
$$9y^2 - 18y + 9 + 6y = 5$$
$$9y^2 - 12y + 4 = 0$$
$$(3y - 2)^2 = 0$$
$$y = \tfrac{2}{3}$$
$$x = -1$$

3.
$$x + y + z = 6 \implies z = 6 - x - y$$
$$2x - y + 3z = 0 \qquad 2x - y + 3(6 - x - y) = 0 \implies -x - 4y = -18$$
$$5x + 2y - z = -3 \qquad 5x + 2y - (6 - x - y) = -3 \implies 6x + 3y = 3$$
$$x = 18 - 4y$$
$$6(18 - 4y) + 3y = 3$$
$$-21y = -105$$
$$y = 5$$
$$x = 18 - 4y = -2$$
$$z = 6 - x - y = 3$$

4.
$$x + y = 110 \implies y = 110 - x$$
$$xy = 2800$$
$$x(110 - x) = 2800$$
$$0 = x^2 - 110x + 2800$$
$$0 = (x - 40)(x - 70)$$
$$x = 40 \quad \text{or} \quad x = 70$$
$$y = 70 \qquad y = 40$$

5.
$$2x + 2y = 170 \implies y = \frac{170 - 2x}{2} = 85 - x$$
$$xy = 2800$$
$$x(85 - x) = 2800$$
$$0 = x^2 - 85x + 2800$$
$$0 = (x - 25)(x - 60)$$
$$x = 25 \quad \text{or} \quad x = 60$$
$$y = 60 \qquad y = 25$$
Dimensions: 60' × 25'

6.
$$2x + 15y = 4 \implies 2x + 15y = 4$$
$$x - 3y = 23 \implies \underline{5x - 15y = 115}$$
$$7x = 119$$
$$x = 17$$
$$y = \frac{x - 23}{3} = -2$$

7.
$$x + y = 2 \implies 19x + 19y = 38$$
$$38x - 19y = 7 \implies \underline{38x - 19y = 7}$$
$$57x = 45$$
$$x = \frac{45}{57} = \frac{15}{19}$$
$$y = 2 - x = \frac{38}{19} - \frac{15}{19} = \frac{23}{19}$$

8. $y_1 = 2(0.112 - 0.4x)$

$y_2 = \dfrac{(0.13 + 0.3x)}{0.7}$

$\begin{array}{rcl} 0.4x + 0.5y = & 0.112 & \Rightarrow \quad 0.28x + 0.35y = \quad 0.0784 \\ 0.3x - 0.7y = & -0.131 & \Rightarrow \quad \underline{0.15x - 0.35y = -0.0655} \\ & & \qquad\quad 0.43x \qquad\qquad = \quad 0.0129 \end{array}$

$$x = \frac{0.0129}{0.43} = 0.03$$

$$y = \frac{0.112 - 0.4x}{0.5} = 0.20$$

9. Let x = amount in 11% fund and
y = amount in 13% fund.

$$x + y = 17000 \implies y = 17000 - x$$
$$0.11x + 0.13y = 2080$$
$$0.11x + 0.13(17000 - x) = 2080$$
$$-0.02x = -130$$
$$x = \$6500$$
$$y = \$10500$$

10. Using a graphing utility, you obtain

$y = 0.7857x - 0.1429$. Analytically, $(4, 3), (1, 1), (-1, -2), (-2, -1)$.

$$n = 4, \sum_{i=1}^{4} x_i = 2, \sum_{i=1}^{4} y_i = 1, \sum_{i=1}^{4} x_i^2 = 22, \sum_{i=1}^{4} x_i y_i = 17$$

$\begin{array}{rcl} 4b + 2a = & 1 & \Rightarrow \quad 4b + 2a = \quad 1 \\ 2b + 22a = & 17 & \Rightarrow \quad \underline{-4b - 44a = -34} \\ & & \qquad\quad -42a = -33 \end{array}$

$a = \dfrac{33}{42} = \dfrac{11}{14}$

$b = \dfrac{1}{4}\left(1 - 2\left(\dfrac{33}{42}\right)\right) = -\dfrac{1}{7}$

$y = ax + b = \dfrac{11}{14}x - \dfrac{1}{7}$

11.

$\begin{array}{l} x + y \qquad = -2 \\ 2x - y + z = 11 \\ \quad 4y - 3z = -20 \end{array}$ $\implies$ $\begin{array}{l} -2x - 2y \qquad = 4 \\ 2x - \underline{\quad y + z = 11} \\ \quad -3y + z = 15 \end{array}$

$\begin{array}{l} -9y + 3z = 45 \\ \underline{4y - 3z = -20} \\ -5y \qquad = 25 \end{array}$

$$y = -5$$
$$x = 3$$
$$z = 0$$

12.

$$
\begin{array}{rcl}
4x - y + 5z = 4 & \Rightarrow & 4x - y + 5z = 4 \\
2x + y - z = 0 & \Rightarrow & -4x - 2y + 2z = 0 \\
\hline
2x + 4y + 8z = 0 & & -3y + 7z = 4
\end{array}
$$

$$
\begin{array}{r}
2x + 4y + 8z = 0 \\
-2x - y + z = 0 \\
\hline
3y + 9z = 0 \\
-3y + 7z = 4 \\
\hline
16z = 4
\end{array}
$$

$$z = \tfrac{1}{4}$$
$$y = -\tfrac{3}{4}$$
$$x = \tfrac{1}{2}$$

13.

$$
\begin{array}{rcl}
3x + 2y - z = 5 & \Rightarrow & 6x + 4y - 2z = 10 \\
6x - y + 5z = 2 & \Rightarrow & -6x + y - 5z = -2 \\
\hline
& & 5y - 7z = 8
\end{array}
$$

$$y = \frac{8 + 7z}{5}$$

$$
\begin{array}{r}
3x + 2y - z = 5 \\
12x - 2y + 10z = 4 \\
\hline
15x + 9z = 9
\end{array}
$$

$$x = \frac{9 - 9z}{15} = \frac{3 - 3z}{5}$$

Let $z = a$, then $x = \dfrac{3 - 3a}{5}$ and $y = \dfrac{8 + 7a}{5}$.

14. $y = ax^2 + bx + c$ passes through $(0, -1)$, $(1, 4)$, and $(2, 13)$.

At $(0, -1)$: $-1 = a(0)^2 + b(0) + c \Rightarrow c = -1$

At $(1, 4)$: $4 = a(1)^2 + b(1) - 1 \Rightarrow 5 = a + b \Rightarrow 5 = a + b$

At $(2, 13)$: $13 = a(2)^2 + b(2) - 1 \Rightarrow 14a + 2b \Rightarrow$

$$
\begin{array}{r}
5 = a + b \\
-7 = -2a - b \\
\hline
-2 = -a
\end{array}
$$

$$a = 2$$
$$b = 3$$

Thus, $y = 2x^2 + 3x - 1$.

15. $s = \frac{1}{2}at^2 + v_0 t + s_0$ passes through $(1, 12)$, $(2, 5)$, and $(3, 4)$.

At $(1, 12)$: $12 = \frac{1}{2}a + v_0 + s_0 \implies 24 = a + 2v_0 + 2s_0$

At $(2, 5)$: $5 = 2a + 2v_0 + s_0 \implies -5 = -2a - 2v_0 - s_0$

At $(3, 4)$: $4 = \frac{9}{2}a + 3v_0 + s_0 \implies \overline{19 = -a \qquad + s_0}$

$$15 = 6a + 6v_0 + 3s_0$$
$$-8 = -9a - 6v_0 - 2s_0$$
$$\overline{7 = -3a \qquad + s_0}$$
$$-19 = a \qquad - s_0$$
$$\overline{-12 = -2a}$$
$$a = 6$$
$$s_0 = 25$$
$$v_0 = -16$$

Thus, $s = \frac{1}{2}(6)t^2 - 16t + 25 = 3t^2 - 16t + 25$.

16. $x^2 + y^2 \geq 9$

17. $x + y \leq 6$

$\qquad x \geq 2$

$\qquad y \geq 0$

18. Line through $(0, 0)$ and $(0, 7)$: $x = 0$

Line through $(0, 0)$ and $(2, 3)$: $y = \frac{3}{2}x$ or $3x - 2y = 0$

Line through $(0, 7)$ and $(2, 3)$: $y = -2x + 7$ or $2x + y = 7$

Inequalities: $\qquad x \geq 0$

$\qquad\qquad 3x - 2y \leq 0$

$\qquad\qquad 2x + y \leq 7$

19. Vertices: $(0, 0)$, $(0, 7)$, $(6, 0)$, $(3, 5)$

$z = 30x + 26y$

At $(0, 0)$: $z = 0$

At $(0, 7)$: $z = 182$

At $(6, 0)$: $z = 180$

At $(3, 5)$: $z = 220$

The maximum value is z is 220.

20. $x^2 + y^2 \leq 4$

$(x - 2)^2 + y^2 \geq 4$

❏ Chapter 9 Practice Test Solutions

1.
$$\begin{bmatrix} 1 & -2 & 4 \\ 3 & -5 & 9 \end{bmatrix}$$

$-3R_1 + R_2 \rightarrow \begin{bmatrix} 1 & -2 & 4 \\ 0 & 1 & -3 \end{bmatrix}$

$2R_2 + R_1 \rightarrow \begin{bmatrix} 1 & 0 & -2 \\ 0 & 1 & -3 \end{bmatrix}$

2. $3x + 5y = 3$

$2x - y = -11$

$$\begin{bmatrix} 3 & 5 & \vdots & 3 \\ 2 & -1 & \vdots & -11 \end{bmatrix}$$

$-R_2 + R_1 \rightarrow \begin{bmatrix} 1 & 6 & \vdots & 14 \\ 2 & -1 & \vdots & -11 \end{bmatrix}$

$-2R_1 + R_2 \rightarrow \begin{bmatrix} 1 & 6 & \vdots & 14 \\ 0 & -13 & \vdots & -39 \end{bmatrix}$

$-\frac{1}{13}R_2 \rightarrow \begin{bmatrix} 1 & 6 & \vdots & 14 \\ 0 & 1 & \vdots & 3 \end{bmatrix}$

$-6R_2 + R_1 \rightarrow \begin{bmatrix} 1 & 0 & \vdots & -4 \\ 0 & 1 & \vdots & 3 \end{bmatrix}$

Answer: $x = -4, y = 3$

3. $2x + 3y = -3$

$3x - 2y = 8$

$x + y = 1$

$$\begin{bmatrix} 2 & 3 & \vdots & -3 \\ 3 & 2 & \vdots & 8 \\ 1 & 1 & \vdots & 1 \end{bmatrix}$$

$\begin{matrix} R_1 \rightarrow \\ \\ R_3 \rightarrow \end{matrix} \begin{bmatrix} 1 & 1 & \vdots & 1 \\ 3 & 2 & \vdots & 8 \\ 2 & 3 & \vdots & -3 \end{bmatrix}$

$\begin{matrix} -3R_1 + R_2 \rightarrow \\ -2R_1 + R_3 \rightarrow \end{matrix} \begin{bmatrix} 1 & 1 & \vdots & 1 \\ 0 & -1 & \vdots & 5 \\ 0 & 1 & \vdots & -5 \end{bmatrix}$

$\begin{matrix} R_2 + R_1 \rightarrow \\ -R_2 \rightarrow \\ -R_2 + R_3 \rightarrow \end{matrix} \begin{bmatrix} 1 & 0 & \vdots & 6 \\ 0 & 1 & \vdots & -5 \\ 0 & 0 & \vdots & 0 \end{bmatrix}$

Answer: $x = 6, y = -5$

4. $x \quad + 3z = -5$
$2x + y \quad = \quad 0$
$3x + y - \ z = -3$

$$\begin{bmatrix} 1 & 0 & 3 & \vdots & -5 \\ 2 & 1 & 0 & \vdots & 0 \\ 3 & 1 & -1 & \vdots & 3 \end{bmatrix}$$

$$\begin{matrix} \\ -2R_1 + R_2 \rightarrow \\ -3R_1 + R_3 \rightarrow \end{matrix} \begin{bmatrix} 1 & 0 & 3 & \vdots & -5 \\ 0 & 1 & -6 & \vdots & 10 \\ 0 & 1 & -10 & \vdots & 18 \end{bmatrix}$$

$$\begin{matrix} \\ \\ -R_2 + R_3 \rightarrow \end{matrix} \begin{bmatrix} 1 & 0 & 3 & \vdots & -5 \\ 0 & 1 & -6 & \vdots & 10 \\ 0 & 0 & -4 & \vdots & 8 \end{bmatrix}$$

$$\begin{matrix} -3R_3 + R_1 \rightarrow \\ 6R_3 + R_2 \rightarrow \\ -\frac{1}{4}R_4 \rightarrow \end{matrix} \begin{bmatrix} 1 & 0 & 0 & \vdots & 1 \\ 0 & 1 & 0 & \vdots & -2 \\ 0 & 0 & 1 & \vdots & -2 \end{bmatrix}$$

Answer: $x = 1, y = -2, z = -2$

5. $\begin{bmatrix} 1 & 4 & 5 \\ 2 & 0 & -3 \end{bmatrix} \begin{bmatrix} 1 & 6 \\ 0 & -7 \\ -1 & 2 \end{bmatrix} = \begin{bmatrix} -4 & -12 \\ 5 & 6 \end{bmatrix}$

6. $3A - 5B = 3\begin{bmatrix} 9 & 1 \\ -4 & 8 \end{bmatrix} - 5\begin{bmatrix} 6 & -2 \\ 3 & 5 \end{bmatrix}$

$$= \begin{bmatrix} 27 & 3 \\ -12 & 24 \end{bmatrix} - \begin{bmatrix} 30 & -10 \\ 15 & 25 \end{bmatrix}$$

$$= \begin{bmatrix} -3 & 13 \\ -27 & -1 \end{bmatrix}$$

7. $f(A) = \begin{bmatrix} 3 & 0 \\ 7 & 1 \end{bmatrix}^2 - 7\begin{bmatrix} 3 & 0 \\ 7 & 1 \end{bmatrix} + 8\begin{bmatrix} 1 & 0 \\ 0 & 1 \end{bmatrix}$

$$= \begin{bmatrix} 3 & 0 \\ 7 & 1 \end{bmatrix}\begin{bmatrix} 3 & 0 \\ 7 & 1 \end{bmatrix} - \begin{bmatrix} 21 & 0 \\ 49 & 7 \end{bmatrix} + \begin{bmatrix} 8 & 0 \\ 0 & 8 \end{bmatrix}$$

$$= \begin{bmatrix} 9 & 0 \\ 28 & 1 \end{bmatrix} - \begin{bmatrix} 21 & 0 \\ 49 & 7 \end{bmatrix} + \begin{bmatrix} 8 & 0 \\ 0 & 8 \end{bmatrix}$$

$$= \begin{bmatrix} -4 & 0 \\ -21 & 2 \end{bmatrix}$$

8. False since

$(A + B)(A + 3B) = A(A + 3B) + B(A + 3B)$
$\qquad\qquad\qquad = A^2 + 3AB + BA + 3B^2.$

9.

$$\begin{bmatrix} 1 & 2 & \vdots & 1 & 0 \\ 3 & 5 & \vdots & 0 & 1 \end{bmatrix}$$

$$-3R_1 + R_2 \rightarrow \begin{bmatrix} 1 & 2 & \vdots & 1 & 0 \\ 0 & -1 & \vdots & -3 & 1 \end{bmatrix}$$

$$\begin{aligned} 2R_2 + R_1 \rightarrow \\ -R_2 \rightarrow \end{aligned} \begin{bmatrix} 1 & 0 & \vdots & -5 & 2 \\ 0 & 1 & \vdots & 3 & -1 \end{bmatrix}$$

$$A^{-1} = \begin{bmatrix} -5 & 2 \\ 3 & -1 \end{bmatrix}$$

10.

$$\begin{bmatrix} 1 & 1 & 1 & \vdots & 1 & 0 & 0 \\ 3 & 6 & 5 & \vdots & 0 & 1 & 0 \\ 6 & 10 & 8 & \vdots & 0 & 0 & 1 \end{bmatrix}$$

$$\begin{aligned} -3R_1 + R_2 \rightarrow \\ -6R_1 + R_3 \rightarrow \end{aligned} \begin{bmatrix} 1 & 1 & 1 & \vdots & 1 & 0 & 0 \\ 0 & 3 & 2 & \vdots & -3 & 1 & 0 \\ 0 & 4 & 2 & \vdots & -6 & 0 & 1 \end{bmatrix}$$

$$\begin{aligned} -R_2 + R_1 \rightarrow \\ \tfrac{1}{3}R_2 \rightarrow \\ -4R_2 + R_3 \rightarrow \end{aligned} \begin{bmatrix} 1 & 0 & \tfrac{1}{3} & \vdots & 2 & -\tfrac{1}{3} & 0 \\ 0 & 1 & \tfrac{2}{3} & \vdots & -1 & \tfrac{1}{3} & 0 \\ 0 & 0 & -\tfrac{2}{3} & \vdots & -2 & -\tfrac{4}{3} & 1 \end{bmatrix}$$

$$\begin{aligned} \tfrac{1}{2}R_3 + R_1 \rightarrow \\ R_3 + R_2 \rightarrow \\ -\tfrac{3}{2}R_3 \rightarrow \end{aligned} \begin{bmatrix} 1 & 0 & 0 & \vdots & 1 & -1 & \tfrac{1}{2} \\ 0 & 1 & 0 & \vdots & -3 & -1 & 1 \\ 0 & 0 & 1 & \vdots & 3 & 2 & -\tfrac{3}{2} \end{bmatrix}$$

$$A^{-1} = \begin{bmatrix} 1 & -1 & \tfrac{1}{2} \\ -3 & -1 & 1 \\ 3 & 2 & -\tfrac{3}{2} \end{bmatrix}$$

11. (a) $x + 2y = 4$
$3x + 5y = 1$

$$\begin{bmatrix} 1 & 2 & \vdots & 1 & 0 \\ 3 & 5 & \vdots & 0 & 1 \end{bmatrix}$$

$$-3R_1 + R_2 \rightarrow \begin{bmatrix} 1 & 2 & \vdots & 1 & 0 \\ 0 & -1 & \vdots & -3 & 1 \end{bmatrix}$$

$$\begin{aligned} -2R_2 + R_1 \rightarrow \\ -R_2 \rightarrow \end{aligned} \begin{bmatrix} 1 & 0 & \vdots & -5 & 2 \\ 0 & 1 & \vdots & 3 & -1 \end{bmatrix}$$

$$X = A^{-1}B = \begin{bmatrix} -5 & 2 \\ 3 & -1 \end{bmatrix} \begin{bmatrix} 4 \\ 1 \end{bmatrix} = \begin{bmatrix} -18 \\ 11 \end{bmatrix}$$

$x = -18, y = 11$

(b) $x + 2y = 3$
$3x + 5y = -2$

$$X = A^{-1}B - \begin{bmatrix} -5 & 2 \\ 3 & -1 \end{bmatrix} \begin{bmatrix} 3 \\ -2 \end{bmatrix} = \begin{bmatrix} -19 \\ 11 \end{bmatrix}$$

$x = -19, y = 11$

12. $\begin{vmatrix} 6 & -1 \\ 3 & 4 \end{vmatrix} = 24 - (-3) = 27$

13. $\begin{vmatrix} 1 & 3 & -1 \\ 5 & 9 & 0 \\ 6 & 2 & -5 \end{vmatrix} = 1(-45) + 3(25) + (-1)(-44) = 74$

14. $\begin{vmatrix} 1 & 4 & 2 & 3 \\ 0 & 1 & -2 & 0 \\ 3 & 5 & -2 & 1 \\ 2 & 0 & 6 & 1 \end{vmatrix} = -7$

15. $\begin{vmatrix} 6 & 4 & 3 & 0 & 6 \\ 0 & 5 & 1 & 4 & 8 \\ 0 & 0 & 2 & 7 & 3 \\ 0 & 0 & 0 & 9 & 2 \\ 0 & 0 & 0 & 0 & 1 \end{vmatrix} = 6(5)(2)(9)(1) = 540$

16. Area $= \dfrac{1}{2}\begin{vmatrix} 0 & 7 & 1 \\ 5 & 0 & 1 \\ 3 & 9 & 1 \end{vmatrix} = \dfrac{1}{2}(31)$

$= 15.5$ square units

17. $\begin{vmatrix} x & y & 1 \\ 2 & 7 & 1 \\ -1 & 4 & 1 \end{vmatrix} = 3x - 3y + 15 = 0$

OR $= x - y + 5 = 0$

18. $x = \dfrac{\begin{vmatrix} 4 & -7 \\ 11 & 5 \end{vmatrix}}{\begin{vmatrix} 6 & -7 \\ 2 & 5 \end{vmatrix}} = \dfrac{97}{44}$

19. $z = \dfrac{\begin{vmatrix} 3 & 0 & 1 \\ 0 & 1 & 3 \\ 1 & -1 & 2 \end{vmatrix}}{\begin{vmatrix} 3 & 0 & 1 \\ 0 & 1 & 4 \\ 1 & -1 & 0 \end{vmatrix}} = \dfrac{14}{11}$

20. $y = \dfrac{\begin{vmatrix} 721.4 & 33.77 \\ 45.9 & 19.85 \end{vmatrix}}{\begin{vmatrix} 721.4 & -29.1 \\ 45.9 & 105.6 \end{vmatrix}} = \dfrac{12{,}769.747}{77{,}515.530} \approx 0.1647$

❏ Chapter 10 Practice Test Solutions

1. $a_n = \dfrac{2n}{(n+1)!}$

$a_1 = \dfrac{2(1)}{3!} = \dfrac{2}{6} = \dfrac{1}{3}$

$a_2 = \dfrac{2(2)}{4!} = \dfrac{4}{24} = \dfrac{1}{6}$

$a_3 = \dfrac{2(3)}{5!} = \dfrac{6}{120} = \dfrac{1}{20}$

$a_4 = \dfrac{2(4)}{6!} = \dfrac{8}{720} = \dfrac{1}{90}$

$a_5 = \dfrac{2(5)}{7!} = \dfrac{10}{5040} = \dfrac{1}{504}$

Terms: $\dfrac{1}{3}, \dfrac{1}{6}, \dfrac{1}{20}, \dfrac{1}{90}, \dfrac{1}{504}$

2. $a_n = \dfrac{n+3}{3^n}$

3. $\displaystyle\sum_{i=1}^{6}(2i-1) = 1 + 3 + 5 + 7 + 9 + 11 = 36$

4. $a_1 = 23,\ d = -2$

$a_2 = a_1 + d = 21$

$a_3 = a_2 + d = 19$

$a_4 = a_3 + d = 17$

$a_5 = a_4 + d = 15$

Terms: 23, 21, 19, 17, 15

5. $a_1 = 12,\ d = 3,\ n = 50$

$a_n = a_1 + (n-1)d$

$a_{50} = 12 + (50-1)3 = 159$

6. $a_1 = 1$

$a_{200} = 200$

$S_n = \dfrac{n}{2}(a_1 + a_n)$

$S_{200} = \dfrac{200}{2}(1 + 200) = 20{,}100$

7. $a_1 = 7,\ r = 2$

$a_2 = a_1 r = 14$

$a_3 = a_1 r^3 = 56$

$a_4 = a_1 r^3 = 56$

$a_5 = a_1 r^4 = 112$

Terms: 7, 14, 28, 56, 112

8. $\displaystyle\sum_{n=0}^{9} 6\left(\dfrac{2}{3}\right)^n,\ a_1 = 6,\ r = \dfrac{2}{3},\ n = 10$

$S_n = \dfrac{a_1(1 - r^n)}{1 - r} = \dfrac{6\left(1 - (2/3)^{10}\right)}{1 - (2/3)} \approx 17.6879$

9. $\displaystyle\sum_{n=0}^{\infty}(0.03)^n,\ a_1 = 1,\ r = 0.03$

$S = \dfrac{a_1}{1 - r} = \dfrac{1}{1 - 0.03} = \dfrac{1}{0.97} = \dfrac{100}{97} \approx 1.0309$

10. For $n = 1$, $1 = \dfrac{1(1+1)}{2}$.

Assume that $1 + 2 + 3 = 4 + \cdots + k = \dfrac{k(k+1)}{2}$.

Now for $n = k + 1$,

$1 + 2 + 3 + 4 + \cdots + k + (k+1) = \dfrac{k(k+1)}{2} + k + 1$

$\qquad\qquad = \dfrac{k(k+1)}{2} + \dfrac{2(k+1)}{2}$

$\qquad\qquad = \dfrac{(k+1)(k+2)}{2}.$

Thus, $1 + 2 + 3 + 4 + \cdots + n = \dfrac{n(n+1)}{2}$ for all integers $n \geq 1$.

11. For $n = 4$, $4! > 2^4$. Assume that $k! > 2^k$. Then

$(k+1)! = (k+1)(k!) > (k+1)2^k > 2 \cdot 2^k = 2^{k+1}.$

Thus, $n! > 2^n$ for all integers $n \geq 4$.

12. $_{13}C_4 = \dfrac{13!}{(13-4)!4!} = 715$

13. $(x+3)^5 = x^5 + 5x^4(3) + 10x^3(3)^2 + 10x^2(3)^3 + 5x(3)^4 + (3)^5$

$\qquad\qquad = x^5 + 15x^4 + 90x^3 + 270x^2 + 405x + 243$

14. $_{12}C_5x^7(-2)^5 = -25,344x^7$

15. $_{30}P_4 = \dfrac{30!}{(30-4)!} = 657,720$

16. $6! = 720$ ways

17. $_{12}P_3 = 1320$

18. $P(2) + P(3) + P(4) = \dfrac{1}{36} + \dfrac{2}{36} + \dfrac{3}{36}$

$\qquad\qquad\qquad\qquad = \dfrac{6}{36} = \dfrac{1}{6}$

19. $P(K, B10) = \dfrac{4}{52} \cdot \dfrac{2}{51} = \dfrac{2}{663}$

20. Let A = probability of no faulty units.

$P(A) = \left(\dfrac{997}{1000}\right)^{50} \approx 0.8605$

$P(A') = 1 - P(A) \approx 0.1395$

❑ Chapter 11 Practice Test Solutions

1. $(x - 0)^2 = 4(5)(y - 0)$

Vertex: $(0, 0)$

Focus: $(0, 5)$

Directrix: $y = -5$

2. $(y - 0)^2 = 4(7)(x - 0)$

$$y^2 = 28x$$

3. $a = 12, b = 5, h = k = 0,$

$c = \sqrt{144 - 25} = \sqrt{119}$

Center: $(0, 0)$

Foci: $\left(\pm\sqrt{119}, 0\right)$

Vertices: $(\pm 12, 0)$

4. Center: $(0, 0)$

$c = 4, 2b = 6 \implies b = 3,$

$a = \sqrt{16 + 9} = 5$

$$\frac{x^2}{25} + \frac{y^2}{9} = 1$$

5. $a = 12, b = 13, c = \sqrt{144 + 169} = \sqrt{313}$

Center: $(0, 0)$

Foci: $\left(0, \pm\sqrt{313}\right)$

Vertices: $(0, \pm 12)$

Asymptotes: $y = \pm\dfrac{12}{13}x$

6. Center: $(0, 0)$

$a = 4, \pm\dfrac{1}{2} = \pm\dfrac{b}{4} \implies b = 2$

$$\frac{x^2}{16} - \frac{y^2}{4} = 1$$

7. $p = 4$

$(x - 6)^2 = 4(4)(y + 1)$

$(x - 6)^2 = 16(y + 1)$

8.

$$16x^2 - 96x + 9y^2 + 36y = -36$$

$$16(x^2 - 6x + 9) + 9(y^2 + 4y + 4) = -36 + 144 + 36$$

$$16(x - 3)^2 + 9(y + 2)^2 = 144$$

$$\frac{(x - 3)^2}{9} + \frac{(y + 2)^2}{16} = 1$$

$a = 4, b = 3, c = \sqrt{16 - 9} = \sqrt{7}$

Center: $(3, -2)$

Foci: $\left(3, -2 \pm \sqrt{7}\right)$

Vertices: $(3, -2 \pm 4)$ OR $(3, 2)$ and $(3, -6)$

9. Center: $(3, 1)$

$a = 4, 2b = 2 \implies b = 1$

$$\frac{(x - 3)^2}{16} + \frac{(y - 1)^2}{1} = 1$$

10. $a = \dfrac{1}{2}, b = \dfrac{1}{3}, c = \sqrt{\dfrac{1}{4} + \dfrac{1}{9}} = \dfrac{\sqrt{13}}{6}$

$$\frac{(x + 3)^2}{1/4} - \frac{(y - 1)^2}{1/9} = 1$$

Center: $(-3, 1)$

Vertices: $\left(-3 \pm \dfrac{1}{2}, 1\right)$ OR $\left(-\dfrac{5}{2}, 1\right)$ and $\left(-\dfrac{7}{2}, 1\right)$

Foci: $\left(-3 \pm \dfrac{\sqrt{13}}{6}, 1\right)$

Asymptotes: $y = \pm\dfrac{1/3}{1/2}(x + 3) + 1 = \pm\dfrac{2}{3}(x + 3) + 1$

11. Center: $(3, 0)$

$a = 4, c = 7, b = \sqrt{49 - 16} = \sqrt{33}$

$$\frac{y^2}{16} - \frac{(x - 3)^2}{33} = 1$$

12. $_{13}C_4 = \dfrac{13!}{(13 - 4)!4!} = 715$

13. $(x + 3)^5 = x^5 + 5x^4(3) + 10x^3(3)^2 + 10x^2(3)^3 + 5x(3)^4 + (3)^5$

$= x^5 + 15x^4 + 90x^3 + 270x^2 + 405x + 243$

14. $_{12}C_5 x^7(-2)^5 = -25{,}344x^7$

15. $(r, \theta) = \left(-1, \dfrac{\pi}{2}\right) \implies (x, y) = (0, -1)$

16. $(x, y) = (-2, -2) \implies (r, \theta) = \left(2\sqrt{2}, \dfrac{5\pi}{4}\right)$

(Answer is not unique.)

17. $x^2 + y^2 = 4x$

$r^2 = 4r \cos \theta$

$r = 4 \cos \theta$

Circle

18. Rose curve

19. Limaçon

20. Parabola